WASPS

THE SPLENDORS AND MISERIES
OF AN AMERICAN ARISTOCRACY

MICHAEL KNOX BERAN

PEGASUS BOOKS
NEW YORK LONDON

WASPS

Pegasus Books, Ltd.
148 West 37th Street, 13th Floor
New York, NY 10018

Copyright © 2021 by Michael Knox Beran

First Pegasus Books edition August 2021

Interior design by Maria Fernandez

Library of Congress Cataloging-in-Publication Data is available.

ISBN: 978-1-64313-706-3

10 9 8 7 6 5 4 3 2 1

Printed in the United States of America
Distributed by Simon & Schuster
www.pegasusbooks.com

To my wife and my daughters,
and in memory of Barbara Ward and L. Hugh Sackett

CONTENTS

Se tu segue tua stella,
non puoi fallire a gloriosa porto . . .

If you follow your star,
you will not fail to find a glorious harbor . . .
—Dante, *Inferno*

❧

del bello ovile ov' io dormi' agnello . . .

the fair sheepfold, where a lamb I slumbered . . .
—Dante, *Paradiso*

A WASP Genealogy

This is an incomplete genealogy, and is intended merely to show interconnections among the people who figure in this book, whose names are printed in boldface.

Francis Peabody = Martha Endicott
(1801–1867)   (1799–1891)

John Clarke Lee = Harriet Rose
(1804–1877)   (1804–1885)

Catherine Peabody = John Lowell Gardner
(1808–1883)   (1804–1884)

J. P. Gardner
(1828–1875)
=
Harriet Amory
(1835–1865)

Helen Bloodgood = Francis Peabody
(1834–1911)   (1831–1910)

S. E. Peabody = Marianne Lee
(1825–1909)   (1828–1911)

George Lee = Caroline Haskell
(1830–1910)   (1835–1914)

Isabella Stewart = J. L. Gardner
(1840–1924)   (1837–1898)

Florence Wheatland = Jacob Peabody
(1870–?)

Fannie Peabody = Endicott "Cotty" Peabody
(1860–1946)   (1857–1944)

Alice Hathaway Lee = Theodore Roosevelt
(1861–1884)   (1858–1919)

William Amory Gardner
(1863–1930)

Richard Peabody = Mary Jacob = Harry Crosby
(1892–1936)   (1892–1970)   (1898–1929)

Malcolm Peabody = Mary Parkman
(1888–1974)   (1891–1981)

Alice Roosevelt = Nicholas Longworth
(1884–1980)

Henry Dwight Sedgwick = Sarah Minturn
(1861–1957)   (1865–1919)

Endicott Peabody
(1920–1997)

Desmond Fitzgerald = Marietta Peabody
(1910–1967)   (1917–1991)

Helen Peabody = Minturn Sedgwick
(1897–1976)   (1890–1948)

Ronald Tree

"Fuzzy" Sedgwick = Alice deForest
(1904–1967)   (1899–1976)

(1908–1988)

Michael Post = Edith Minturn "Edie" Sedgwick
(1943–1971)

John Hay = **Clara Stone**
(1838-1905) | (1849-1914)

Harvey Cushing
(1869-1939)
=
Katharine Crowell
(1870-1949)

Edith May Randolph = **William Collins Whitney** = **Flora Payne**
(1854-1899) | (1841-1904) | (1842-1893)

William Payne Whitney = *Helen Hay*
(1876-1927) | (1875-1944)

Harry Payne Whitney = **Gertrude Vanderbilt**
(1872-1930) | (1875-1942)

engaged

Flora Payne "Fouf" Whitney to **Quentin Roosevelt**
(1897-1986) | (1897-1918)

Willard Straight = **Dorothy Whitney**
(1880-1918) | (1887-1968)

Michael Straight = *Nina Gore Auchincloss Steers*
(1916-2004) | (1937-)

Vincent Astor = *"Minnie" Cushing*
(1891-1959) | (1906-1978)
=
J. W. Fosburgh
(1919-1978)

Bill Paley = **"Babe" Cushing** = *Stanley Mortimer*
(1901-1990) | (1915-1978) | (1913-1999)

J.H. "Jock" Whitney = *Betsey Cushing* = **James Roosevelt**
(1904-1982) | (1908-1998) | (1907-1991)

Carter Burden = *Amanda Jay Mortimer*
(1941-1996) | (1944-)

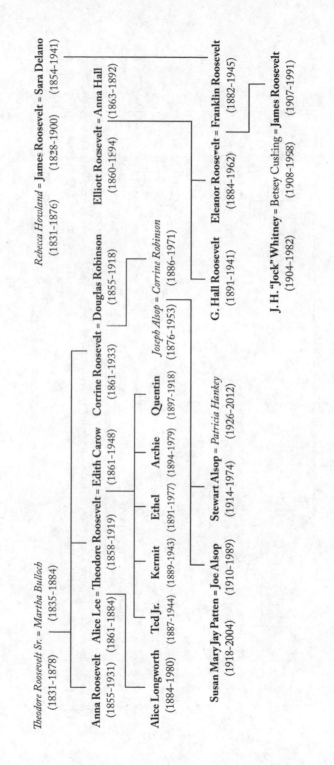

Theodore Roosevelt Sr. = Martha Bulloch
(1831–1878)   (1835–1884)

Rebecca Howland = James Roosevelt = Sara Delano
(1831–1876)   (1828–1900)   (1854–1941)

Anna Roosevelt   Alice Lee = Theodore Roosevelt = Edith Carow   Corrine Roosevelt = Douglas Robinson   Elliott Roosevelt = Anna Hall   Eleanor Roosevelt = Franklin Roosevelt
(1855–1931)   (1861–1884)   (1858–1919)   (1861–1948)   (1861–1933)   (1855–1918)   (1860–1894)   (1863–1892)   (1884–1962)   (1882–1945)

Alice Longworth   Ted Jr.   Kermit   Ethel   Archie   Quentin   Joseph Alsop = Corrine Robinson   G. Hall Roosevelt   J. H. "Jock" Whitney = Betsey Cushing = James Roosevelt
(1884–1980)   (1887–1944)   (1889–1943)   (1891–1977)   (1894–1979)   (1897–1918)   (1876–1953)   (1886–1971)   (1891–1941)   (1904–1982)   (1908–1958)   (1907–1991)

Susan Mary Jay Patten = Joe Alsop   Stewart Alsop = Patricia Hankey
(1918–2004)   (1910–1989)   (1914–1974)   (1926–2012)

John Jay = Sarah Livingston
(1745-1829)   (1756-1802)

William Jay = Hannah McVickar
(1789-1858)   (1790-1857)

John Jay = Eleanor Field
(1817-1894)   (1819-1909)

Henry Grafton Chapman = Eleanor Jay
(1833-1883)   (1839-1921)

Eleanor Chapman = Richard Mortimer
(1864-1929)   (1852-1918)

Elizabeth Chanler = **John Jay Chapman**
(1866-1937)   (1862-1933)

Averell Harriman = Kitty Lawrance
(1891-1986)   (1893-1936)

Stanley Grafton Mortimer = Katherine Tilford
(1889-1947)   (1890-1970)

Bill Paley = "Babe" Cushing = Stanley Grafton Mortimer = Katherine Harriman
(1901-1990)   (1915-1978)   (1913-1999)   (1917-2011)

Amanda Jay Mortimer = Carter Burden
(1944-)   (1941-1996)

Mary Rutherford Clarkson = Peter Augustus Jay
(1786-1838)   (1776-1843)

Peter Augustus Jay = Josephine Pearson
(1821-1855)   (1829-1852)

Augustus Jay = Emily Astor Kane
(1850-1919)   (1854-1932)

Peter Augustus Jay = Susan McCook
(1877-1933)   (1879-1977)

Chanler Chapman
(1901-1982)

Laura Prime = John Clarkson Jay
(1812-1888)   (1808-1891)

Peter Augustus Jay = Julia Post
(1841-1875)   (1847-1949)

Louisa Shaw Barlow = **Pierre Jay**
(1873-1965)   (1870-1949)

Bill Patten = **Susan Mary Jay** = Joe Alsop
(1909-1960)   (1918-2004)   (1910-1989)

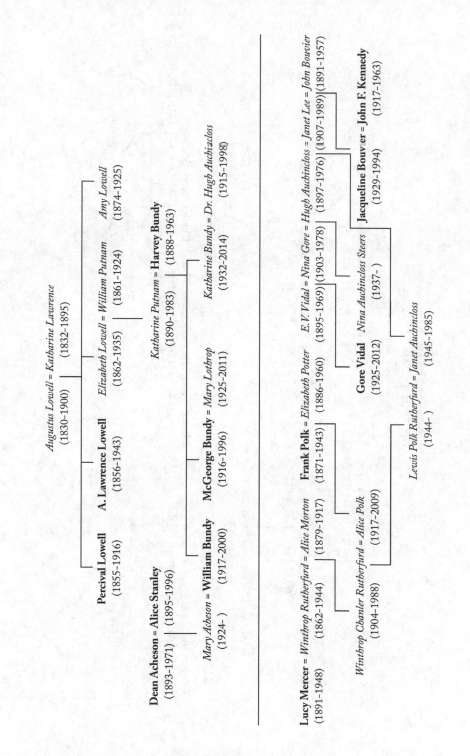

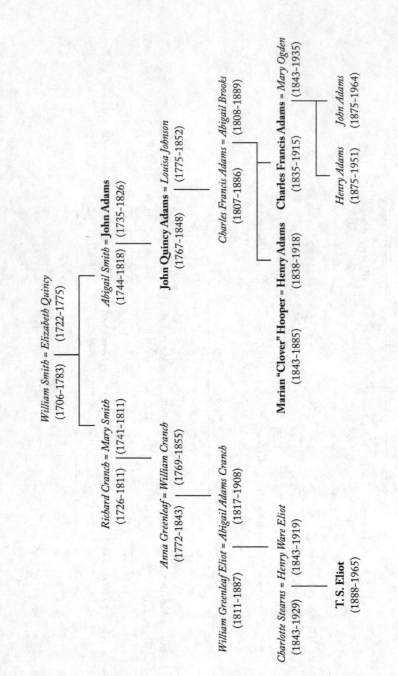

Eleanor Roosevelt, Sara Delano Roosevelt, Franklin Roosevelt, and Fannie Peabody before morning prayer at St. John's Church, Washington.

Preface

How do you write about flawed people in a scrupulous age? Most accounts of elite establishments are ponderously genealogical (*Debrett's Peerage*, the *Golden Book* of Venice), narrowly sociological (Marx, Veblen, Pareto, C. Wright Mills), or romantically embellished (Livy's narrative of the early Roman ruling class, and the not less imaginative accounts of aristocracy in Proust, Lampedusa, Faulkner, and Waugh). What is wanted is a history, like that of the elites of old Israel in the *Nevi'im* or books of the prophets, which illuminates both the acts of the ruling personalities and their inspirations—the ends and purposes that incited them, and made them a little mad. The modern historian of a patrician class cannot, of course, know the imaginations of his subjects quite so intimately as that; he must be content if, in sifting a mass of gossip and innuendo, he can find here and there the fragment of a higher motive. As for baser inducements, vanity, power, opportunity for sexual malfeasance, and the like, there is never any shortage of that sort of evidence where human beings are concerned.

The men and women at the heart of this book did much to shape the America in which we live: so much, indeed, that it is not easy to understand our problems without some knowledge of their mistakes. Yet they present those who would understand them with special challenges, beginning with their name. They were, by and large, descended from the well-to-do classes of colonial and early republican America, from New England merchants and divines, from Boston Brahmins and Anglo-Dutch Patroons. But the Civil War and its attendant changes altered their place in life, and they emerged from the crisis as something different from what their forebears had been: as both a class and a movement, self-consciously devoted to power and reform. What to call them? The term WASP—White (or Wealthy, if redundancy is to be avoided) Anglo-Saxon Protestant—fumbles their background, betraying the sociologist's inclination to use a term like Anglo-Saxon when the plainer, more obvious English one would do. (In this case, English.) For there is nothing especially Saxon or Angle about America's WASPs. Insofar as they embody any English strain, it would be the Norman. Like the Normans, the WASP oligarchs possessed a corrosive blood-pride, one that they could only with difficulty reconcile with their sense of themselves as suffering idealists, groping their way through dark places in the hope of glimpsing the stars.

But in fact WASPs were not an English but an American phenomenon, and it was not their English blood that particularly distinguished them or, for that matter, their Protestant religion. A large number of Americans who were of English descent, who were communicants in a Protestant church, and who might even have been rich, were nevertheless not WASPs. On the other hand, people who were not of English extraction or were only partially so (the Roosevelts, for example, and the Jameses) figure largely in the WASP story. For it was not blood or heredity, but a longing for completeness that distinguished the WASPs in their prime.* Yet the acronym we have fixed upon them is, in its absurdity, faithful to the tragicomedy of this once formidable tribe, so nearly visionary and so decisively blind, now that it has been reduced in stature and its most significant contribution—the myth of regeneration it evolved, the fair sheepfold of which it dreamt—lost in a haze of dry martinis.

---

* The WASPs' idea that we are, many of us, suffering under the burden of our unused potential—drowning in our own dammed-up powers—does not make up for the evils of their ascendancy. But it may perhaps repay study.

Dean Acheson with Jack Kennedy, on whose vitality WASPs preyed on in the era of their decline and fall.

ONE

Twilight of the WASPs

demon duri . . .

durable demons . . .
—Dante, *Inferno*

In 1950 photographers from *Life* magazine descended on the ranch outside Santa Barbara to shoot pictures of the golden family. Francis Minturn "Duke" Sedgwick, heir to the Sedgwicks of Stockbridge, Massachusetts, had come to California from the East for the sake of his health, and on three or four thousand acres of tableland at Corral de Quati and, later, at Rancho La Laguna he created a kingdom of his own, one in which he could raise his family in seclusion from the world. "It was just paradise," his oldest child, Alice, who was known as Saucie, said. "My parents owned the land from horizon to horizon in every direction. . . . Imagine a situation like that where nobody entered who wasn't invited or hired!"

Her father was a figure of enchantment. He rode out each morning on Gazette, a dappled gray mare, or Flying Cloud, a pale strawberry roan, and was four hours in the saddle, herding his cattle. The thick, close-cropped hair, the strong, smooth-shaven jaw, the brilliant smile that blazed out of the dark tan—Francis Sedgwick was an extraordinary physical specimen. Yet the eyes, surprisingly in one so fair, were brown, and shone with an odd light—a glint of genius or mania. For Francis was no mere ranchero. "Fuzzy," as his children called him, was in aspiration a Renaissance man. He painted, he sculpted, he even wrote fiction, and his little city-state on the Pacific seemed almost Greek in its beauty, suffused, Saucie said, with the light and feeling of the gods.

Yet for all that Fuzzy was cracked, a living exhibition of the corruption and decay of the WASP ideal. "After breakfast," Saucie remembered, he would do "his exercises by the pool in this little loincloth he wore. It wasn't a real jockstrap, but a neat little thing which looked more like a cotton bikini. He also did his writing there, sitting in the sun in this cotton bikini with a great big sombrero on his head. He was always nearly naked." Fuzzy was neither the first nor the last WASP to think himself a Sun God, but he carried the fantasy beyond the bounds of propriety. He sent Saucie to the Branson School in Marin County, and when he came to visit her, the girls "stood at the windows and stared at him. He was so beautiful . . ." But they were soon disillusioned. Life might have been, as Saucie said, a cup her father was determined to drink to the dregs, but the life he desired was "raffish and violent." He swaggered through it in oversized cowboy boots, and with his "enormous thorax" and the "muscles of his arms and chest and abdomen" he seemed, his daughter thought, a "priapic, almost strutting" figure. A bridesmaid in the wedding of another of his daughters, Pamela, was, on arriving at La Laguna, "immediately ushered into the presence of this 'man,' this father with his exaggerated views about human beauty. Nobody who wasn't beautiful was allowed to be around. He began by making comments about each of the bridesmaids, the length of our legs, the size of our bosoms. . . . It was a stud farm, that house, with this great stallion parading around in as little as he could. We were the mares."

He would choose a girl and invite her to his studio. "It was sort of like the emperor selecting a vestal virgin," the bridesmaid shuddered as though at the recollection of a close escape from the Borgias. "We all knew we'd better not go. We all thought that this was against the rules . . . an eighteen-year-old and a fifty-year-old . . . no, no, no. . . ." The man was "a fauve, a wild beast." There "was something *malsain*"—unhealthy—about him, a "Marquis de Sade undercurrent that thirty years later I can feel in my flesh right now. The way he *looked* at people. He undressed every woman he saw. His eyes, they would just become cold."

Francis Sedgwick's seventh child, Edith Minturn, who was known as Weasel, Miss Weedles, or simply Edie, was appalled by her father's predations. He would come "strutting out in a little blue bikini like a peacock," Pamela's bridesmaid remembered, to flirt with the schoolgirls. Edie was "wearing very short shorts, those long legs, and a man's white shirt, a very thin girl with brown cropped hair, and she said something like, 'Oh, for God's sake, Fuzzy!'"

She was eleven or twelve at the time, "so thin, and suddenly she zipped off, just *phftt*, like that. It certainly didn't deter him. . . ." Another time she found her father "just humping away" in the blue room at La Laguna. It "blew her mind."

Insulated from the noise and chaos of America—the vulgarity WASPs dreaded—Fuzzy waved his wand and created in the California hills an oasis instinct "with laughter and conversation," the "life of Greek gods." WASPs were always to chase a dream of rebirth, some improbable garden of Apollo; but in their decadence the dream became rancid. Once they had known how to make their desires productive, and bred leaders like Theodore and Franklin Roosevelt. Now, in characters like Francis Sedgwick, they were becoming mere headcases, *Mayflower* screwballs, the poet Robert Lowell called them, fit only for the asylum.

BABE PALEY KNEW WHICH WAY the wind was blowing. Her mother, Katharine Cushing, who was called "Gogsie," had been ambitious of social distinction, and she had taken pains to ensure that her three daughters made brilliant marriages. The eldest, Mary, who was known as Minnie, married Vincent Astor. Betsey, the middle girl, married, first, Franklin Roosevelt's son James and later John Hay "Jock" Whitney, who was senior prefect of Fuzzy Sedgwick's form at Groton, the Massachusetts prep school, and afterward ambassador to the Court of St. James's: one of the richest men in the United States, an American Duke of Omnium. Babe duly honored her family's household gods and married Stanley Grafton Mortimer Jr., a Standard Oil heir. But she had the wit to perceive, as early as the 1940s, that the WASP ascendancy was rapidly declining toward the grave. WASP men were becoming so—dull; a woman wanted not a dud from the *Social Register* (somewhat oxymoronically known as the "stud book") but energy, dynamism, the hairy back of the satyr. Babe readily divorced Mortimer and married a stallion, Bill Paley of C.B.S. She knew her horseflesh.

Paley, too, stood something to gain from the marriage. Few pleasures are more alluring to the founder of a new family than the caresses of a daughter of an old one, and even as Paley's own career presaged the demise of the WASP establishment, he was enchanted by its style. Old blood, it is true, found his emulation of patrician manners a little forced. He attempted to recreate, at Kiluna Farm on Long Island, the elegant negligence of a Whig country house. But Lady Diana Cooper, who though descended from an English Tory family knew her Whig country houses, thought he tried too hard. Bill was, she said, "very attractive," if "a little oriental," as she delicately put it: it was his "luxury taste" that appalled her. She pretended that this was only because it embodied a standard "unattainable to us tradition-ridden tired Europeans," who were used to things being shopworn (as if she envied Bill his tackiness). She made short work of the room in which she slept at Kiluna, with its little table "laid, as for a nuptial night, with fine lawn, plates, forks and a pyramid of choice-bloomed peaches, figs, grapes," and its bathroom in which were to be found "all the aids to sleep, masks for open eyes, soothing unguents and potions." (It was not done thus at Haddon Hall or Belvoir Castle.) But Lady Diana visited Kiluna Farm during the reign of Bill's first wife, Dorothy; one of Bill's motives in putting Dorothy away and installing Babe in her place was to have a consort whose taste was well-nigh faultless, for as Truman Capote observed, Babe had "only one fault; she was perfect; otherwise, she was perfect."

She had been born, in 1915, in Boston, the youngest child of Harvey Cushing, the brilliant brain surgeon. Admired for her "willowy" figure, her "raven" hair, and the "classically perfect features" of her face (which had been carefully reconstructed after a 1934 car accident), she had endured a cynical upbringing. Her father was a good WASP, devoted to the care of others and the pursuit of knowledge, while earning a sensible income and achieving a notable professional reputation. But her mother, with a certain justness of perception, saw that good works by themselves never really cut it in WASPdom. One needed a fortune and a name.

Nothing short of tycoons would do for the girls, and Gogsie was not entirely pleased with Betsey's marriage, in 1930, to Jimmy Roosevelt. For though the Roosevelts were socially at the top of the heap, their fortune was much smaller than those of their Hudson River neighbors, and the cash was entirely controlled by the family matriarch, Franklin's mother Sara, a tightfisted old witch. Franklin himself was a charming man, but he was married to the eccentric Eleanor, who omitted to shave her armpits. On the other hand, when Minnie caught the eye of the disagreeable Vincent Astor, Gogsie was delighted at the prospect of a union with the Astor millions; and she all but dragged her daughter (who preferred artists to millionaires) to the drawing room of Heather Dune, her summer house in East Hampton, where the marriage took place in September 1940.

Babe, for her part, managed to be not wholly corrupted by Gogsie's meretricious philosophy. After finishing school at Westover she became a respected editor at *Vogue* and was tempted to make a career of it. What was no less strange, she had, in spite of her success in the high-bitch world of fashion, a natural, unfeigned kindness. "Babe was a wonderfully warm human being," Millicent Fenwick, one of her colleagues at *Vogue* and a future congresswoman, remembered: she would give you the coat off her back—in Millicent's case a handsome gray squirrel that proved useful on a winter trip to London. Even such a potential rival as Gloria Vanderbilt conceded that Babe was "beautiful, kind, loyal." For there was "nothing mean or hard" in her: she was "lovely, and slim, and gracious," a creature "without envy or guile."

WHAT BABE HAD, BESIDES DECENCY, was the WASP desire to rise above the Yankee passion for utility, to overcome the antipathy to graces that make life bearable. In this Bill Paley, with his plutocrat-gangster manners, could not help her, and at all events he soon lost interest in her and "abandoned her sexually," though she was scarcely forty. He went back to his first love, C.B.S., and to flings with sundry women; she was left to manage the houses and head the best-dressed list. Yet even as she was consigned to this ornamental role, she was conscious of its vapidity. The fatuities of *Women's Wear Daily* might suffice for Gogsie or the Duchess of Windsor, but Babe burned with a brighter flame, and lived her life in a way that suggested that opulence, when governed by taste, could raise life to a higher and nobler plane, as it had done in the courts of the Renaissance in an age that knew nothing of *Women's Wear Daily*.

She never quite lived up to it; her houses lacked the ease of their Old World models. Too much facile elegance, they said, too many ambitious pains: Babe fretted not only over the taste of the food served on her plates, but the colors, as though she were Poussin at work upon a canvas. She wanted to be her own "living work of art," yet even before lung cancer got the better of her she knew all the fatigues of her class in its last decay.

It was Truman Capote who supplied the fresh infusion of plasma. A "not unpleasant little monster," the man of letters Edmund Wilson said, "like a fetus with a big head," Capote acted the witty Shakespearian fool in the courts of those whom he styled, not altogether in irony, the Beautiful People. From the moment he met Babe, on Bill Paley's airplane as it was about to take off for Jamaica, he was beguiled by her, and she, for her part, was liberated by his conversation, a stream of insinuating talk.

But it was not simply the venom of his gossip or even the patience with which he helped her to read Proust that drew her to him. The strange, androgynous creature with the "campy high-pitched Southern whine," punctuated by shrieks and giggles, renewed her faith in herself. For something had gone out of the WASPs; they had lost the tranquil confidence of their forebears, the easy mastery that characterized the Roosevelts in statecraft and Edith Wharton and Nannie Cabot Lodge in style. The Depression and two World Wars leveled the playing fields, and in their decline WASPs found themselves drawn to outsiders on whose vitality they could feed. In the vampiric phase of WASPdom, white-shoe institutions that once shunned strangers (anyone not of the old tribal connection) turned to them for the lifeblood that might reanimate their order. In the same way Babe Paley turned to Truman Capote: here was an impresario who could do for her something akin to what Proust did for Countess Greffulhe, the forgettable airhead who attained immortality as the Duchesse de Guermantes in *Remembrance of Things Past*: make her interesting to herself.

The predator in Truman saw in Babe what others failed to see, that living a life so effortlessly perfect was, in fact, hard work, and bred its own unhappiness. Wherever Babe appeared flashbulbs popped and admirers fawned. Her clothing, her jewels, her flat in the St. Regis, her gardens at Kiluna, her tropical pavilion at Round Hill, provoked astonishment and envy. Her royal progresses, undertaken with her fellow Beautiful Persons, were lavishly reported in the press; now she lay, in luxurious indolence, amid the beaten gold of Gloria Guinness's yacht as it sailed in the Aegean, now she steamed up the Dalmatian coast with Marella Agnelli, the countess of Fiat. Yet of all the jeweled beauties who constituted her set, it was she who obtained a peculiar eminence, unrivaled until the appearance of Jacqueline Kennedy. "She might have been painted by Boldoni or by Picasso during his Rose Period," gushed Billy Baldwin, who helped her to furnish her houses. "So great is her beauty that no matter how often I see her, each time is the first time."

But the goddess was unable to believe in her cult. What she needed, Truman saw, was a priest, one who would tend the altars, maintain the mysteries, furnish the texts. It was an office he was himself only too happy to fill. (It is believed that he supplied Babe with that beatitude of her class, "You can never be too rich or too thin.") Amid the clouds of incense that wafted from his thurible, she could momentarily forget that she was merely another creature of WASP decadence, sunk in the vanities of café society. She could see herself as he saw her, a palm-nymph cast out of an Assyrian garden, a blithe spirit who could "fly where others walk." Once this sense of superiority came easily to WASPs; now they needed help.

"MY GOD, THE FATHER WAS something! A cross between Mr. America and General Patton." But Fuzzy Sedgwick's machismo was deceptive; so exaggerated a masculinity had its origin not in strength but in a dread of weakness and effeminacy. He had been born, in New York City, in 1904, and had grown up a sickly, delicate child; he passed much of his life in the shadow of men much stronger than he himself was. His older brother Minturn was a natural athlete who played for the only Harvard team to win a Rose Bowl. "This boy doesn't need a nanny," the family doctor said at Minturn's birth. "He needs a trainer." Francis was a much slighter figure—"he just didn't have the physique"—and though avid of athletic distinction, he "never won a single H"—a single varsity letter—at Harvard. It was Minturn who was given the nickname "Duke" by his schoolmates; Francis, five years younger, acquired it as a hand-me-down, a courtesy title. Yet he "clung to 'Duke' for the rest of his life," even after Minturn told him bluntly that it was he who was "the *real* Duke." "You," he said, "will always be 'Little Duke.'"

At Groton, a tiny school in Massachusetts, Francis encountered, in the headmaster, Endicott Peabody, a still more formidable figure of masculine strength. Cotty Peabody stood six feet tall and was hard as nails. "If you put your hand on his upper arm," one of his old boys said, "it felt like the branch of an oak tree." Theodore Roosevelt thought Cotty the "most powerful personality he had ever encountered." "I don't think I ever met a man," the novelist Louis Auchincloss said, "who radiated such absolute authority." Franklin Roosevelt, too, fell under Peabody's sway and cited his old schoolmaster as the greatest influence in his life after his parents. When, long after Roosevelt's schooldays were ended, Peabody came to the Oval Office to bid goodbye after a stay in the White House, the president, watching him go out the door, was heard to say, "You know, I'm still scared of him."

Confronted with a figure so supercharged with manliness, Francis wilted. It was at Groton that he suffered the first of those nervous collapses that were to vex him throughout his life, and upon withdrawing from the school he was sent to California to recover. The pattern repeated itself after Harvard and its most exclusive WASP habitat, the Porcellian Club. He had, before graduating, procured an introduction to the financier Clarence Dillon, who invited him to travel with him in Europe as part of an extended job interview. The prospect of a magnificent career opened up, and Dillon obtained for him a position in the London office of Lazard Frères, the banking house. But Francis broke down under the strain, and the spell of nervous prostration was the end, Minturn said, "as far as his financial possibilities with the Dillon Empire were concerned."

A Groton schoolmate, Charlie deForest, came to the rescue, offering the neurotic sufferer the sanctuary of Tylney Hall in the English countryside. There Francis renewed an acquaintance with Charlie's sister Alice, and he and Alice were soon engaged to be married. Once again Francis found himself in the shadow of a more competent man, this time Alice's father, the railroad bigwig Henry Wheeler deForest. Francis took courses at Harvard Business School and tried to fit himself into the mold of a businessman like his future father-in-law, but again he fell to pieces. He retired to the Austen Riggs Center in Stockbridge, where he languished in a private room and was diagnosed with manic-depressive psychosis.

Advised by his doctors "to develop his artistic side," Francis, after his marriage to Alice freed him from money cares, chucked business to become a sculptor in New York. But his new vocation only heightened his fear that he was not a real man; in the world he knew the arts were suspect, a vocation for weaklings and "fairies." "I think he was ashamed not to be a banker like everyone else who took the Long Island Rail Road into town," Saucie said, "so he commuted into New York wearing a bowler hat and carrying an umbrella." When the butler drove him to the station each morning, he looked as though his destination were an office on Wall Street rather than an atelier on East Fifty-seventh.

CALIFORNIA OFFERED ESCAPE, A REFUGE from the WASP competitions of the East, and on land purchased with his father-in-law's money Francis found the mastery that eluded him at Groton and Harvard and Lazard Frères. Here, with his gift for make-believe, he could build up his body and create the pleasure dome that haunted his imagination, an "ideal world," Saucie called it, an Arcadia of sunlight, presided over by a golden figure clothed in white.

The "surface looked so good," she said, that it was only with difficulty that you saw the unseemliness that lurked beneath. Yet the Greek or Renaissance fantasy of Corral de Quati and Rancho La Laguna, warped though it was, had its origin in ideas that had long animated the class to which Francis Sedgwick belonged. After the Civil War, WASPs reinvented themselves, overcoming a tendency to weakness and breakdown in order to try to raise up a nation sunk in the corruption and crassness of the Gilded Age. They went in for political reform, as championed by the Roosevelts, and founded institutions intended to produce a patrician class that would regenerate America.

But the civic humanism that inspired this earlier WASP renaissance had little currency in the America in which Francis Sedgwick found himself in the 1940s and '50s. The old patrician passions, finding no constructive outlet, assumed in him a morbid form. Visitors to his dukedom on the Pacific noted how much of the old WASP idea he had incorporated in its design. He "brought his children up on this huge ranch," the writer John P. Marquand Jr. said, "in the Groton-Harvard-Porcellian Club myth that he lived in." But the ranch was Groton and Harvard as reflected in a circus mirror, with all the proportions distorted. Liberated from the real competition of his contemporaries, Francis entered into imaginary contests with his surrogate fathers, his aged headmaster and his dead father-in-law, striving to outdo them precisely by smashing their idols and breaking their taboos. (Endicott Peabody was hardly a match for him in the seduction of young girls.) The true aristocrat, Fuzzy believed, must liberate himself from New England prudishness and constraint: only then could he bring about a more vital humanism in the sunshine of the West, amid the sagebrush and chaparral of the Santa Ynez. His children were to be his guinea pigs, and his prodigies. "I was Miss Mozart," Sukie Sedgwick remembered. "Edie was Miss Rembrandt. Minty was Mr. Leonardo. Christ, we were all supposed to be God knows what—geniuses to add to Fuzzy's pyramid."

The problem, for more normal WASPs who clung to the ideals of patrician humanism, was that Fuzzy, in his madness—his fetish of blond sleekness, his insistence on the beauty and genius of the aristocrat—laid bare a contradiction at the heart of their ascendancy. Either aristocracy was, as Fuzzy maintained, right, and blood-pride legitimate, or the WASPs themselves, in attempting to erect a patrician order in America while pretending to be adherents of equalitarian democracy, were hypocrites. In their prime the WASPs could paper over the problem with a rhetoric of service and humility. But now they were too tired.

JOSEPH WRIGHT ALSOP V WAS beside himself. His great friend John Fitzgerald Kennedy had been inaugurated as president of the United States earlier that day, and although Joe himself would later be coy about the matter, he had reason to believe that the young leader would call on him in his house at 2720 Dumbarton Avenue in Georgetown after the night's official revels were ended. He was in high spirits as he dined that evening with his friends Phil and Kay Graham of the *Washington Post* and Cold War diplomat Chip Bohlen and his wife, Avis. Afterward they all got into a big car and rode through the snow to one of the inaugural balls, drinking "several more bottles of champagne," Joe said, "during the course of our journey." The ball proved a bore, but when Joe went out into the street, he found a foot of snow on the ground and all the cabs taken. "He was close to hysterical," the *Wall Street Journal*'s Phil Geyelin recalled. "He was desperate to get a taxi."

Like Fuzzy Sedgwick, Joe Alsop, who had been born in 1910, was of the old WASP connection—his grandmother was Theodore Roosevelt's sister—and like Fuzzy, he had come up through Groton, Harvard, and the Porcellian Club. But unlike Fuzzy, Joe found a way to trade on his eccentricities. As a boy and young man he had been fat, and at Groton he had been the "butt of teasing" on account of his bookish disposition and his "almost ladylike interest in people's clothes and things of that nature," or so his friend and classmate Dickie Bissell (the future C.I.A. grandmaster who persuaded Kennedy to invade the Bay of Pigs) remembered. But at Harvard he turned his weaknesses into strengths; he invented for himself a semi-comic persona, that of the foppish, epicene toff practicing the dark arts of aristocracy in a demotic age. He addressed cabmen as "my good sir" and women as "*dahling*." He spoke not of his bath but his *bahth*, and he pronounced his surname in English fashion, *Awlsup*. With a martini in one hand and a Benson & Hedges cigarette (sheathed in ivory) in the other, he would eviscerate, with wit and learning, whatever popular delusion or instance of the corruption of taste had most recently appalled him. Should anyone venture to disagree with him, he would beat him down with all the arts of derision of which he was a master.

So rococo and bouffe were Joe's performances that they beguiled even as they exasperated, but the persona hardened with age. The aggrieved patrician condemned everything from the ascendancy of the social sciences to the custom of holding hands while praying. (As with Evelyn Waugh's Gilbert Pinfold, it was never later than Joe Alsop thought.) In England he pronounced the pub food inedible and growled at the publican. (What did he expect, his stepson wondered? It was pub food.) In his rare plunges into middle America he was apt to be disconcerted by the coarseness of the native customs. Scarcely had he arrived in Waco, Texas, to attend the wedding of a nephew than he was agitated by the sight of a large sign outside the Ramada Inn in which he was staying, WELCOME TO JOE AND CANDY'S WEDDING. The suburban ranch house of the bride's family seemed to him a "nightmare," and the wine ("American, since no other was available") was an ordeal for his palate.

Yet the exercise in self-caricature, or as Joe might have said, in the art of giving style to one's character, worked: he made himself into a personage, and assisted by tribal connections, he rose fast. At the height of the Great Depression, his grandmother (Uncle Teddy's sister) obtained for him, through the good offices of Mrs. Ogden Reid, a job as a reporter on the *New York Herald Tribune*, an oracle of the WASP establishment then in the possession of the Reids. In this first employment Joe did nothing to relax his WASP hauteur. "Boy, get me a pencil," he snapped at a copyboy, the *Tribune's* future foreign correspondent Barrett McGurn. But Joe proved a talented writer, and he was soon dispatched to Washington to cover the Senate. Here his fellow Roosevelts could help him. He dined in the White House with Cousin Eleanor and Cousin Franklin and spent Christmas Day with them; he was impressed by their WASP good taste, a "style of life" that seemed to him "pretty close to the perfect style of an American President." For there was no plutocratic gaucherie about the Roosevelts; they lived, Joe thought, "like a rather old-fashioned American gentleman's family in 'comfortable circumstances,'" and there was nothing in their manner of life "that could be said in the smallest degree to be glossy, or particularly conspicuous, or likely to meet with the approval of the new group known as the 'beautiful people.'"

The food in the Roosevelt White House was, Joe admitted, execrable, for Cousin Eleanor, in her "extreme puritanism," thought it virtuous to eat badly. The drinks, however, "being the President's department," were not "actively repellent." F.D.R. made "a good old fashioned" though only "a fair martini," about "the color of spar varnish." Yet the president did more than mix cocktails for Joe: he helped him discover his vocation as a prophet of what *Time* publisher Henry Luce had begun to call the American Century. As Roosevelt attempted to persuade a reluctant nation to intervene in the Second World War, he gave Joe and his colleague Robert Kintner extraordinary access to the administration's decision-making. The result was an instant book, *American White Paper*, which gave the public a glimpse into the drama behind the scenes, the secrets of the palace. But if the book was an exercise in reportorial flair that admitted the reader to the corridors of power, it was also an urgent polemic. If America was to preserve its way of life, Joe argued, it could not allow Hitler to dominate Europe and Asia and through them the rest of the planet: on the contrary, America must use its "power and resources to make the world a decent place to live in" by standing up to aggression as Cousin Franklin was doing.

It was heady stuff. There were in those days half a dozen great houses in the capital presided over by highbred hostesses—Mrs. Robert Bliss, Mrs. William Eustis, Mrs. Truxton Beale, Mrs. Robert Bacon, Mrs. Dwight Davis. In them Joe encountered people much like himself, united by tribal memories, inside jokes and esoteric nicknames, and a desire to direct the destinies of a nation. Some of these diners, among them Dean Acheson and Averell Harriman, were to become proconsuls of the American Century. Conversations over cocktails or, after dinner, brandy, led to public action: committees like the WASP-dominated Century Group, to which Alsop and Acheson belonged, worked to defeat Hitler, and after Hitler put the revolver to his head in the bunker in the Wilhelmstrasse, they turned their attention to Stalin.

Joe, who spent the Second World War in China helping General Claire Chennault use American air power against the Imperial Japanese Army, returned to Washington in 1945 to embark, with his younger brother Stewart, on a newspaper column, "Matter of Fact." Seeking both to break news and shape opinion, the Alsop brothers warned of the dangers of Soviet imperialism and made the case for initiatives (among them the Truman Doctrine and the Marshall Plan) intended to counter Soviet aggression. At its height "Matter of Fact" appeared in dozens of newspapers and reached some 25 million readers; in foreign capitals it was read as a semiofficial voice of the American imperium.

No journalist was more severe in his enmity toward Moscow than Joe. The struggle between East and West, he told the Nieman Fellows at Harvard in 1947, was a clash of visions fully as momentous as that between the Persians and the

Greeks in the dawn of the West. Yet the aesthete in Joe was never eclipsed by the Cold Warrior—rather as though Oscar Wilde, at the height of the *Yellow Book* decadence, had been a staunch British Empire man, ready to throw some kindling into the bonfire after the relief of Mafeking. Alsop would emerge from his bedroom in the morning in a purple dressing gown piped with lilac, and his house at 2720 Dumbarton Avenue was an epicure's delight, rich with Louis Quinze gilt, curious folios, jade and lacquer from Asia. The place was seductive; all the great figures of Washington went there. The men of high place in the state came, McGeorge Bundy, George Kennan, Robert McNamara, Paul Nitze; the spies came, Allen Dulles, Frank Wisner, Dickie Bissell; the wits, or those who passed for such, came, Isaiah Berlin, Arthur Schlesinger, Phil Graham; the *grandes dames* came, Bunny Mellon, Kay Graham, Alice Roosevelt Longworth, who was Joe's cousin. Even the traitors came, among them Guy Burgess, the once charming madcap, a sort of Etonian dervish, now bloated and filthy, his powers of mind lost in a drunken ruin. Joe asked him to leave when he began to traduce the American Republic.

The wine was first rate. Joe preferred Bordeaux vintages, and he was partial to his friend Alain de Rothschild's Château Lafite. The caviar *aux blinis* and the terrapin soup were as good; and the exotic garden and the belligerent toucan (it once spat its food out on Bob McNamara's bald spot) were complimented by a comical butler, José, whose services became, during the course of an evening, entertaining in their own right as he consumed the heeltaps left in discarded glasses.

But Joe himself supplied the higher entertainment. His mind was baroque, a thing of devious curves and deceptive concavities, of trompe l'oeil artifices and unnerving chiaroscuros. With odd pauses and interjections—an assortment of "ehs," "ahums," and other "learned catarrhal noises"*—he would lead his guests through the gossip and innuendo of the day ("gencon," he called it: general conversation) to the great questions of war and peace. But the luxury and frivolity of 2720 Dumbarton Avenue—the high learning and Bacchic revelry strangely interfused with civic purpose—reflected something more than the whims of an idiosyncratic personality. Joe's was a late attempt to realize an old WASP dream

---

* Reporting on the 1960 Wisconsin primary, Joe interviewed, in a Milwaukee suburb, a woman who had emigrated from Poland. "Mister," she said at the conclusion of their talk, "you mind if I ask you why do you speak so broken?"

of human completeness, a developing of all sides of one's nature to satisfy some longing in the soul.

ONLY JOE NEEDED MASKS. THE lacquered mandarin knew what he was about when, forsaking his calligraphy, he acted the bully, browbeating anyone who seemed to be going soft on the Commies. The pugnacious manner was self-protective; the arrogance of the façade—the large round spectacles, the "high Oxonian" speech—concealed a good deal of tenderness. Kay Graham, who as empress of the *Washington Post* did not want for pals, said that Joe was one of the "two or three best" friends she made in life. But there were other tendernesses that Joe found more difficult to acknowledge. Once, gossiping into the night with his friend Isaiah Berlin, he became uncharacteristically solemn.

"Isaiah," he said, "there's . . . uh . . . something . . . I . . . uh . . . something I'm about to tell you."

"What's that, Joe?"

"I . . . uh . . . I . . . uh . . . I am . . . uh . . . uh . . . I am a homosexual."

"Oh, Joe, everybody knows that. Nobody cares."

In fact everybody did not know. Joe routinely mocked "pansies" and "fairies." "Oh, he's one of *those*, isn't he?" he would ask contemptuously. Many of those closest to him thought him asexual, but he had had an affair, in the 1940s, with a handsome sailor called Frank Merlo, who afterward became the lover of Tennessee Williams, and in San Francisco he had been picked up by the police during a "sweep of a popular gay rendezvous spot."

Another assignation had graver consequences. In February 1957 Joe was in Moscow, fighting the Cold War over drinks in the Grand Hotel, when he was approached by a reporter for TASS, the Soviet propaganda service, and a young man who called himself Boris, an "athletic blond" whom Joe remembered as a "pleasant-faced, pleasant-mannered fellow" oddly eager to discuss French literature with him. Boris suggested that they meet the next day in his room in the hotel. Perhaps they might read a little Nerval? The room was equipped with hidden cameras, and soon Soviet intelligence agents appeared brandishing inculpatory pictures and pressing Joe to spy for them or, as they phrased it, to furnish them with "advice" in the "cause of peace."

Joe sent a note of alarm to his friend Chip Bohlen, the American ambassador in Moscow, and after vicissitudes he made his way back to the West. Bohlen, in turn, alerted Frank Wisner, the C.I.A.'s director of covert operations, who urged Joe to write an account of the attempt at entrapment for the American authorities. "This is the history of an act of very great folly," Joe began in his best Edward Gibbon manner, "unpleasant in itself," but "not without interest" for the light it cast "upon our adversaries in the struggle for the world . . ."

The incident would haunt him, for although it was not publicly revealed until after his death in 1989, the scent of carrion could not long remain undetected in the vulturedom of Washington; and at all events the F.B.I. director, J. Edgar Hoover, gave the compromising materials a wide circulation. But the effect of the episode on Joe's private morale went deeper; he clung the more fiercely to his masks because what lay beneath them was (to him) intolerable. Not for him the (real or affected) nonchalance of Walt Whitman, Americano, "one of the roughs": Joe looked upon his longings as a weakness, one more evidence of a thinning of the WASP blood, a slowing of the metabolism. What would Uncle Teddy say?

Everywhere he looked Joe now saw presages of decay. He was not yet fifty, but he felt flabby and goutish. Once he and his Harvard chums, in their reunions in Cambridge, could drink martinis for four days straight; now a single day of gin and vermouth undid them. The American Century grew out of the tough, realistic statesmanship of WASPs like Uncle Teddy and Cousin Franklin, with their effortless superiority. Dean Acheson, Averell Harriman, George Kennan, Robert Lovett, and Chip Bohlen had carried the work forward, developing the containment strategy that countered Stalin on behalf of peoples who might otherwise have been lost in despotism.

But who were their successors? In 1956 the most prominent WASP statesman was Adlai Stevenson, the image, Alsop thought, of preppy lassitude and impotent liberalism, "Mr. Eleanor Roosevelt." Was it any wonder, amid so much weakness and effeminacy (like Fuzzy Sedgwick, Joe mocked Adlai as womanish) that America was losing the Cold War? Only a leadership class deficient in virility would permit the Soviets to outstrip America in the race for warheads. (Joe believed, erroneously, that a "missile gap" had opened up, giving the Soviets a decisive advantage in the arts of thermonuclear destruction.) At Harvard he spoke to the younger generation of a "sickness of the soul—a loss of certainty—a failure of assurance" that was crippling the West. The degeneration was nowhere more evident than in the class to which he himself belonged, the WASPs, whom he believed bore a special responsibility, by reason of their training, their knowledge of history, and their intimacy with the state, for the future of the planet.

JOE, FORLORN IN THE SNOW on that inaugural night in January 1961, was rescued by Peter Duchin, the pianist and bandmaster who, as an orphan, had been raised by Marie and Averell Harriman. Peter gave Joe a lift, and though the trip through the snow was by no means easy, they at last reached 2720 Dumbarton Avenue, where Joe had put a quantity of champagne on ice. He now dispensed it to "what seemed an endless stream of guests."

Shortly before two o'clock in the morning there was knocking at the door. "I can still summon," Joe wrote many years later, "the picture of the new President standing on my doorstep. He looked as though he were still in his thirties, with snowflakes scattered about his thick, reddish hair."

In the ghoulish demise of WASPdom, Joe was only too happy to feed on the vitality of Jack.[*] Here, he believed, was a statesman with "real Rooseveltian possibilities," a "Stevenson with balls." The Kennedys made him feel twenty years younger. "Jackie and the President," he said, "gave occasional small dances at the White House that were as good as any parties I have been to." Doubtless it *was* amusing to go through "bottle after bottle of Dom Pérignon" in the company of the new president, and to feed at "an enormous gold bucket" of fresh caviar, all the while laughing at the tastelessness of the Eisenhowers, whose attempts at interior decoration were sadly on display. "I can only recall," Alsop wrote, "the peculiar combination of vomit-green and rose-pink that Mrs. Eisenhower had chosen for her bedroom and bathroom," a faux pas he found almost as appalling as the fact that he had to tell his "cousin Franklin Roosevelt Jr. that he could not go on calling the President 'Jack,' however close they had been in the past—a point he ought have known."

Joe, feeling his bachelorhood to be a liability in one so close to the new president, sought a beard, and he enlisted Arthur Schlesinger, the Kennedy courtier and historian, to help him woo Susan Mary Patten, the widow of his old Groton and Harvard classmate Bill Patten, who had died not long before of a lung ailment.[†]

---

[*]   Henry James's novel *The Sacred Fount*, in which the worn-out characters seek to obtain a fresh infusion of vitality by tapping the hidden springs of others' dynamism, may be read as parable of the plight of the WASPs.

[†]   Schlesinger, in his appeal to Susan Mary, invoked Henry James's novel *The Ambassadors* and quoted the words uttered by Lambert Strether in Gloriani's garden in the Rue du Bac: "Live all you can; it's a mistake not to." It was shrewd of Arthur: WASPs were always missing things in life, and reproaching themselves for having missed them.

Susan Mary, or Soozle, as she was called, was a woman of considerable elegance who had accomplished the not easy feat of charming Evelyn Waugh when she endured his hospitality at Piers Court. (Waugh appeared at a "family" dinner in white tie and decorations and called upon Soozle to make a speech describing the Queen's coronation, which she had recently witnessed.)* Joe, in courting Soozle, frankly confessed to her his homosexuality; she, for her part, believed that she could "cure" him of it. He was, she told her friend Marietta Tree, the society doyenne and granddaughter of Endicott Peabody, a "very shy, complicated, brave and fine man. . . . the extraordinary thing is that I've fallen in love with him." But the woman who during a long affair had gratified Winston Churchill's protégé Duff Cooper, the British statesman, was sexually so much cold mutton for Joe, and theirs would be a *mariage blanc*.

Joe resented Soozle's competences. (He couldn't, among other things, drive a car.) He avenged himself by bullying her. "Oh, that's petty nonsense," he would say when he cut her short in front of guests. "You know better than that." Susan Mary's son by Duff Cooper, Bill Patten Jr., described the marriage as an exercise in mutual frustration tempered by platonic affection. Yet they presided over a great house, the most amusing in the capital; President Kennedy dined there more often than he did in any other private residence in Washington. There was always gossip; the young Bill Patten remembered a lunch to which Truman Capote and Alice Roosevelt Longworth came, and how everyone laughed about the way President Kennedy had persuaded Marella Agnelli to swim naked in the White House swimming pool.

Joe and his fellow WASPs were only too delighted to have Jack and Jacqueline (exotically blooded and nominally papist though they were) reanimate them; Averell Harriman himself, who in his stiffly magnificent condescension might have been a Whig duke, was persuaded to dance the "Twist" with Mrs. Kennedy in the family quarters of the White House. The champagne, the sex, the feeling that they were once again a power in the state—all of this invigorated the fainéant WASPs. But it was the lurid ebullience of a narcotic. WASP Washington in the age of Kennedy was morbid; there was a whiff about it of Parisian

---

* "Your torturing of Susan Mary," Nancy Mitford wrote Waugh, "is all over Paris—poor little thing looks more like a Nazi victim than ever." Waugh, who praised Soozle as a "tough & appreciative little guest," said that he counted on "large bumpers of goodish wine dulling my guests' consciousness of their discomforts" at Piers Court.

society in the days before the Revolution of 1789, of dancing in the shadow of the guillotine.

EARLY IN 1965 FUZZY SEDGWICK's daughter Edie encountered Andy Warhol at a party in the penthouse apartment of Lester Persky, the producer, on East Fifty-ninth Street. Warhol asked Edie to come down the next day to the Factory, his studio on East Forty-seventh. "Why don't we do some things together?" he said.

She soon appeared in Warhol film's *Vinyl*, smoking a cigarette and flicking the ashes on a young man who was being tortured. People were intrigued. "Who's the blonde?" Then came *Beauty #2*. The camera "was focused on a bed throughout," Edie's friend George Plimpton remembered. It was "of the hospital variety, with a white sheet on it, upon which lay Edie Sedgwick and a character from Warhol's Factory named Gino Piserchio." He looked like the Spanish bullfighter El Cordobés, Plimpton said, "a dark, small, but muscular figure . . . . Edie was almost naked as well . . ."

"Oh, she's so *bee-you-ti-ful*," Warhol would exclaim. If, as he maintained, art is what you can get away with, Edie was an artist. The mad girl seemed to subsist on caviar and Bloody Marys, and to live much of her life in limousines; once she appeared at a party clothed only in a leopard-skin coat. But she had the assurance of her class and the authority of her voice, the breathy, perfectly enunciated syllables in which she had been bred up. It was "straight Grotonian all the way through," an acquaintance remembered, a way of speaking she had learned from her father, who had impressed it upon all his children "that they were Sedgwicks." The "way you pronounced words implied a certain attitude that you took toward life . . ." "We learned English the way the English do," Edie's brother Jonathan said. This was not quite right; anyone who listens to Edie's talk, as it is preserved in her film and television appearances, will find that is not that of an Englishwoman. It is a Mid-Atlantic voice with ancestral echoes, memories of an age long since vanished, its tone that of forebears like her grandmother Sedgwick (née Minturn), whose sister Edith (for whom Edie was named) had been famously painted by John Singer Sargent (*Mr. and Mrs. I. N. Phelps Stokes*) and whose sister Mildred had excited the lust of the philosopher Bertrand Russell.

On the ranch at La Luguna, Edie always rode the best-looking horse, and wherever she went she made an impression. When, arriving in deep fog at New

London, she was told there was no going to Fishers Island that day, she commandeered Jock Whitney's yacht. A young man remembered the boat arriving out of the mists, first the "bow and all these men in white running up and down with ropes, and then the bridge with the captain, the radar going dot, dot, dot, dot, and the lighted portholes, and then the brass, polished teak, highly formal living room with Edie in the middle of it surrounded by people in director's chairs," the center of attention, a WASP "It" girl.*

Yet for all that Edie was scarred, maimed by her experience of Fuzzy's eccentric academy in the hills. As a girl she had what she called "icky feelings," and as a teenager she developed an eating disorder. She was taken out of the Branson School in California and sent to St. Timothy's, a finishing school in Maryland, which she left before graduating; she was later treated at Silver Hill, the sanitarium in New Canaan, Connecticut. As much as Babe Paley and Joe Alsop, Edie was a WASP in need of a reanimator, and in Andy Warhol she seemed to find a Svengali who could draw out her secret. He, for his part, was taken by a poise quite out of his star. He had grown up in Pennsylvania steel country, where the rivers ran orange and furnaces lit up the night; Edie, who had been bred in a WASP seminary modeled on a Renaissance court, was for him something new under the sun, a person who knew nothing of the acrid world from which he had sprung. She had grown up apart from the mass-produced culture of middle- and working-class America, that factory-made world of mechanical reproduction that made such a deep impression on Warhol's own imagination, and to which he paid an ambiguous homage with his Campbell's soup cans and Brillo boxes.

She "was always brilliantly late," a Factory groupie remembered. But Warhol never complained. "She knows what she's doing," he would say. He "trusted her aristocratic instincts." "He was an arriviste," his friend the poet Rene Ricard said. "And Edie legitimized him, didn't she? He never went to those parties before she took him. He'd be the first to admit it." She knew the art of coming to a place at the moment "when the tension was at its greatest," and when they swept into Lincoln Center, the photographers were "as hysterical as if Mrs. Kennedy was making an entrance." It was the same in Philadelphia, where Warhol's art was being exhibited and where they were mobbed by enthusiasts deliriously chanting, *Edie and Andy, Edie and Andy.*

---

* As Rudyard Kipling defined "It-ness": "It isn't beauty, so to speak, nor good talk necessarily," says a character in Kipling's story "Mrs. Bathurst." "It's just 'It.'"

But if Warhol admired Edie's elegance, he resented a grace that he (in self-imagination the churlish commoner, the plebeian roturier) could never possess. The gloomy passions of his artist's soul were excited by the possibilities of her degradation—the descent of the WASP thoroughbred to the lower depths of the Factory, the abasements of its couch, its black-painted toilet, its innumerable nauseas. Where Babe Paley met Truman Capote on her own terms, as a woman of fashion condescending to a courtier, Edie approached her revivifier as a suppliant, and almost as a vassal. In the Factory it was Warhol who wielded the scepter; it was he who anointed Edie a "superstar," and he who turned up the klieg lights to strip her of her mystique. For by 1965 the deferences that had long sustained WASPdom were breaking down, and it was becoming commonplace to compare the faltering WASP establishment to the dying nobility of eighteenth-century France. But the revolution by which the WASPs were laid low was an opera buffa one, with Warhol himself burlesquing the parts of both Sade and Robespierre.* The actor Robert Olivo, who called himself Ondine, remembered how he stared. He "was just *watching* with this watching eye . . ." Like Balzac's Vautrin, he derived pleasure from the young flesh at which he stared, even as he consigned it to hell.

The emblem of her burnt-out class, Edie Sedgwick submitted to the stares. (It is characteristic of a decadent aristocracy that it embraces its predators; thus in the French Revolution the Duc d'Orléans, the cousin of Louis XVI, rechristened himself Philippe Égalité and dallied with the Jacobins—they guillotined him anyway.) Edie complied even as she foresaw and perhaps desired her doom. "I would like to go down into the depths of the underworld," she once said, "the depths of darkest experience, and come back and tell about it." It was a wish that was to be only partially granted. She descended to the inferno, but never returned to give a true accounting of the horror.

IN MARCH 1965, ABOUT THE time Edie was filming *Vinyl* in New York, Brigadier General Frederick Karch led the 9th Marine Expeditionary Brigade ashore at Da Nang Bay in Vietnam. President Lyndon Baines Johnson was steadying

---

*   Yet the revolutionist who smashed the pillars was at the same time a Byzantine Catholic who went piously to Mass, and who in his silk-screened images of Marilyn Monroe and Jacqueline Kennedy revived the icon as an artistic form. Did the impulse to atone amount to genuine contrition, or was it only another kind of playacting? It is not easy to say, but at all events Mephisto always returned to the diableries of his Factory.

himself to lead a ground war in Southeast Asia, but even as he believed that he had little choice but to send Americans into combat, he wanted assurances that he was doing the right thing, the good thing. And so he assembled the aging knights of the WASP ascendancy, which even in its decrepitude seemed to him a power in the state.

At Johnson's directive, a group of WASP magnificos that included Dean Acheson, the former secretary of state, and Robert Lovett, the former secretary of defense, were summoned to the eighth floor of the State Department, where amid the eighteenth-century Chippendale of the Diplomatic Reception Rooms they were copiously briefed as to the desperate nature of the situation. There was nothing for it, the experts told them, but to dispatch 200,000 more combat troops to the jungles and rice fields of Indochina.

Afterward a smaller group went to the White House for a drink with the president. They found him in a maudlin mood. Over cocktails in the Cabinet Room, he complained of the misery of office. Everything conspired against him, "Fate, the Press, the Congress, the Intellectuals . . ." Acheson, who with his guards' moustache and patrician bearing might have been a grandee painted by Velásquez, grew impatient. The dominant WASP in the room, he had run the tribe's cursus honorum—Groton, Yale, Harvard Law, a Supreme Court clerkship, a successful Washington law practice leavened with stints of public service—before taking command of Harry Truman's State Department in 1949 to lay the foundation for a postwar Pax Americana. "I blew my top," Acheson remembered, and cutting short the president's self-pitying monologue he told him "he was wholly right on Vietnam, that he had no choice except to press on, that explanations were not as important as successful action."

It was the green light Johnson wanted. Whatever their private misgivings, Acheson and his fellow WASPs assured him that there must be "no question of making whatever combat force increases were required" in Vietnam. A fatal moment, or so Acheson's son-in-law William "Bill" Bundy, assistant secretary of state for East Asian and Pacific affairs, recalled: the instant when Lyndon Johnson committed the United States "to land war on the mainland of Asia."

It was a moment, too, that revealed how feeble the WASP establishment had become. The briefings Acheson and his fellow Wise Men received were, Bundy later admitted, "quickie consultations" intended to elicit the response the administration sought. What (in theory) distinguishes the patrician forti-fied by a humane education and a large experience of affairs is the confidence to question and to probe, to see through sham data and spurious analogies, to view the technical arguments of experts in the higher light of history and the human capacity for self-delusion. But in the twilight of the WASPs, the leading figures could only nod their heads as men like Robert McNamara, Johnson's technocratic secretary of defense, marshalled their metrics. "You've got to do it," one of the Wise Men was heard to say. "You've got to go in."

Bill Bundy and his younger brother, McGeorge "Mac" Bundy, Johnson's national security advisor, helped to orchestrate the briefings that bedazzled the aging WASPs. It was Mac, in fact, who gave them the name Wise Men, urging Johnson to consider their usefulness in his effort to pursue a hawkish course in Vietnam. Yet even as he manipulated the WASP magi, Mac Bundy admired them and saw himself as in their line, the apostolic succession that descended from Henry L. Stimson, the Andover, Yale, and Harvard–trained lawyer whom Franklin Roosevelt chose to head the War Department in the fight against Germany and Japan. Mac's father, Harvey Bundy, had been brought into the public service by Stimson, and Mac himself had helped Stimson to compose his memoirs. The cleverest boy Groton had ever seen, the prodigy of Yale and Skull and Bones, the youngest dean in the history of Harvard, Mac seemed foredestined to carry on the traditions of his class.

But in Mac, too, there was the soft place, the place tender with decay. A late-born figure, coming to power when the WASP ascendancy was running to seed, he made up for it with an extravagant self-confidence. He was the guy so smart Jack Kennedy wanted to make him secretary of state,* the polymath so worldly Charles de Gaulle, having addressed him in the slow and stupid French he reserved for Americans, was surprised to find himself conversing with a young man whose talk might have been that of an intellectual in the Latin Quarter. But beneath what a friend called Mac's "arrogance and hubris"—beneath the masterly state papers and the surgically precise NSAMs (National Security Action Memoranda)—Mac had doubts. Many years later he confessed that he had had "reservations" about Johnson's Vietnam policy, and said that it "can be argued" that he had not pressed those reservations "hard enough." But he had been bound, he said, by a code of loyalty to his chief, "to help the President do

---

* Kennedy concluded that Bundy's comparative youth (he was forty-one in 1960) would be held against him: "Two baby faces like mine and his are just too much." He eventually chose the intellectually undistinguished Dean Rusk. When someone complained to Dean Acheson that it was hard to tell what Rusk was thinking, he replied, "Did it ever occur to you that he *wasn't* thinking?"

it his way." Such loyalty was, however, strangely congruent with self-interest, for Bundy still aspired to be secretary of state, an office in the gift of Lyndon Johnson. It can be argued that it was not from virtue alone that he suppressed his doubts.

JOE ALSOP DID HIS BEST to persuade both Mac Bundy and Lyndon Johnson to overcome whatever dovish scruples constrained them from calling up the reserves and making a stand in Vietnam. He was still recovering from the death of his hero Jack Kennedy; he had been in the garden room of 2720 Dumbarton Avenue when Susan Mary burst in with the news from Dallas. "I didn't think that he had that much emotion in him," Joe's secretary, Evelyn Puffenberger, thought as she watched her sobbing boss. But even as he "howled like a dog" for the dead president, Joe rallied to the standard of the living one, and he praised Lyndon's efforts to unite the country in the midst of grief. "You haven't put a damned foot one-quarter of an inch wrong," he told the president over the telephone. "I've never seen anything like it. You've been simply marvelous in the most painful circumstances." As with royalty, so with presidents, one must lay it on with a trowel; yet even as Joe stroked the presidential ego, he reminded Johnson that, just as Kennedy hadn't blinked during the Cuban Missile Crisis, he must not "duck" his own test of manliness in Southeast Asia.

Joe was the most hawkish of the WASP mandarins, penning columns so fierce that rival pundit Walter Lippmann said that if Johnson did go to war, Alsop would bear much of the blame. Setting out for yet another tour of Vietnam, Joe felt, he told his friend Philippe de Rothschild, "like a very old dog returning to his vomit." But he was enchanted by the tropical squalor and imperial ambience of the place; Saigon in the sixties was the capital of the sort of louche colonial raj that appeals to the traveler of a romantic or depraved cast of mind. The shimmer of the East was bewitching, and much as Venice did Thomas Mann's Gustav von Aschenbach, Vietnam deceived Joe Alsop into thinking that an old man could be young again. In Saigon he stayed with the American ambassador, his old friend Henry Cabot Lodge; after Lodge's exit, he could often be found in the Hôtel Majestic, made memorable by Graham Greene in his novel *The Quiet American*. Military helicopters took him farther afield, and once, when the gunners strafed the Viet Cong, he was "like a kid at an amusement park." "Oh, my word," he exclaimed, "I do believe we're receiving fire." It was like Uncle Teddy going up Kettle Hill.

Joe was exhilarated by all that he saw and felt; he rather liked the idea, Mac Bundy thought, of having "a little old war" in Indochina on his hands. But Joe saw only what he wanted to see, and he had lost the ability to digest new information. He "didn't ask questions," Frank Wisner, Jr., a young foreign service officer, recalled: "his mind was made up." A heavy drinker from his Porcellian days, Joe on his excursions in Southeast Asia went over the top, routinely getting drunk at both lunch and dinner, and picking fights with anyone who disagreed with him. After one drunken bout in Saigon, his old friend Charles Murray, the veteran Time-Life correspondent, was blunt: "You're the epitome," he told Joe, "of the failed establishment."

He was hardly the only aging mandarin whose judgment failed him. After another sham briefing of the Wise Men in November 1967, Dean Acheson overcame twinges of doubt to tell President Johnson that the war was one "we can and will win." It was not until the Tet Offensive in January 1968, when seventy or eighty thousand disciples of Ho Chi Minh carried the fight to the cities of South Vietnam and the precincts of the American embassy itself, that Acheson began to ask the questions he should have asked before. But by then it was too late.

As MUCH AS THE EMBASSY in Saigon, the WASPs themselves were under siege. Their reanimators had failed them. Jack Kennedy was dead, and Andy Warhol washed his hands of Edie Sedgwick. (She died of a drug overdose at twenty-eight.) The Bundy brothers, Mac and Bill, were branded war criminals, and Joe Alsop was satirized in a Broadway play as Joe Mayflower, a flamboyant toff spoiling for blood in the Far East.

Truman Capote joined the jacquerie, publishing an excerpt from his novel-in-progress, *Answered Prayers*, in which he avenged himself on the high mondaine bitches who had toyed with the court dwarf, offering up a thinly disguised account of the night Bill Paley cheated on Mrs. Paley with the "governor's wife," either Happy Rockefeller (the second wife of Nelson Rockefeller) or Marie Harriman (the second wife of Averell Harriman), depending on which calumnist you credit. Why, Capote asked, "would an educated, dynamic, very rich and well-hung Jew" like Paley "go bonkers" for a "cretinous Protestant sized forty who wears low-heeled shoes and lavender water?" Yet go bonkers Bill did; one of the "most attractive guys who ever filled a pair of trousers used to get a hard-on every time he looked at that bull dyke . . ." Paley, Capote averred, could "have any woman he wants, yet for years he yearned after yonder porco . . ."

Why? Because, Capote argued, Paley suffered from the most virulent kind of WASP envy. And the "governor's wife" was, even more than Babe herself (who was something of a rebel: after all, she married Bill), the feminine embodiment of the WASP ascendancy. The "governor's wife" was the living symbol of everything forbidden to Bill "as a Jew, no matter how beguiling and rich he might be: the Racquet Club, Le Jockey, the Links, White's—all those places where he would never sit down to a table of backgammon, all those golf courses where he would never sink a putt—the Everglades and the Seminole, the Maidstone, and St. Paul's and St. Mark's et al., the saintly little New England schools his sons would never attend.* Whether he confesses to it or not, that's why he wanted to fuck the governor's wife, revenge himself on that smug hog-bottom, make her sweat and squeal and call him daddy . . ." Only the longed-for assignation was sullied, Truman wrote, by Mrs. Rockefeller's (or Mrs. Harriman's) bloody effluvia.

Capote was even crueler to Ann Woodward, who after a dinner party in Oyster Bay for the Duchess of Windsor killed her husband, William Woodward Jr., the Groton and Harvard banking heir, with a twelve-gauge shotgun. (Her marksmanship was afterward signalized in the nickname "Bang-Bang.") "Of course it wasn't an accident," Capote wrote. She killed Billy Woodward "with malice aforethought. She's a murderess." Even before her husband's death, Ann had led a loose life, and Capote was not one to overlook her "whirl on the continental carousel." From "Nice to Monte she was known by every male past puberty as Madame Marmalade—her favorite *petit déjeuner* being hot cock buttered with Dundee's best. Although I'm told it's actually strawberry jam she prefers . . ."

Ann Woodward died by suicide shortly before "La Côte Basque 1965," one of the chapters in *Answered Prayers*, was printed in *Esquire* in 1975. (It is said that she had been given an advance copy of the magazine.) "Well, that's that," her mother-in-law, Elsie Woodward, was heard to say. "She shot my son, and Truman murdered her . . ." What remained of the WASP beau monde was appalled by Capote's assault on their kind. "I read it, and I was absolutely horrified," Babe's friend Slim Keith told George Plimpton. "The story about the sheets, the story about Ann Woodward . . ." Babe herself, dying of cancer, spoke of "Truman with total loathing as this 'snake' who had betrayed her." In publishing his roman à

---

* In fact Paley's adopted son, Jeffrey, went to Taft and Harvard, and afterward wrote for the *International Herald Tribune*, a paper controlled by his stepmother's brother-in-law Jock Whitney.

clef, Capote signed his own death warrant so far as WASP society was concerned: but he also showed how vacuous that society had become.

WASPs LIKE EDIE SEDGWICK AND Babe Paley could still inspire envy and resentment, the love-hatred Warhol and Capote each felt for his *gloriosa donna*. But the ground was shifting; in the autumn of 1964 the first episode of *Gilligan's Island* aired on Bill Paley's C.B.S. network, and in the character of Thurston Howell III the WASPs began their descent from the sublime to the ridiculous. (Touché, Bill!) The non-rhotic, Mid-Atlantic English that had stirred the country when Franklin Roosevelt spoke it—dropping the *r*'s in words like *fear* and *Harvard*—became the dialect of a lock-jawed clown.*

As they lost caste in America, WASPs drew closer to another defunct class, the superseded European aristoi and their not always attractive hangers-on, characters like Claus von Bulow, Mona von Bismarck (an American who married Otto von Bismarck's grandson), and the actor-playboy Prince Ruspoli, better known as Dado—the incubi and succubi of the Old World at its most debased. The *Almanach de Gotha* was assimilated to the *Social Register*; and while such WASPs as Kingman Brewster, Elliot Richardson, Potter Stewart, and Bill Weld continued to toil in the public service, the scene inexorably shifted from the political capitals to the jet-set watering holes, to the carnival (or inferno) of Fellini's *La Dolce Vita*.

Like Edward Gibbon's decadent Romans, the degraded WASPs enjoyed and abused the advantages of wealth and luxury; we are very far, here, from the morality of Endicott Peabody, with his code of self-discipline, patriotic obligation, and modesty in the gratification of the passions. But demoralization was inevitable, when all the deeper purposes of WASPdom were breaking down. Patrician privilege was at the core of the WASPs' being: but the WASP belief that such privilege could be justified through meritorious public service didn't wash with the kids in the streets, protesting an

---

* Americans "known for being lifelong speakers of the Mid-Atlantic accent," says one writer, "include William F. Buckley, Jr., Gore Vidal, H. P. Lovecraft, Franklin D. and Eleanor Roosevelt, Alice Roosevelt Longworth, Averell Harriman, Dean Acheson, George Plimpton, Jacqueline Kennedy Onassis (who began affecting it while at Miss Porter's School), Louis Auchincloss, C. Z. Guest, Joseph Alsop, Julia Child, and Cornelius Vanderbilt IV. Except for Child, all of these speakers were raised, educated, or both in the Northeastern United States. This includes just over half who were raised in New York (most of them in New York City) and five who were educated at the private boarding school Groton in Massachusetts: Franklin Roosevelt, Harriman, Acheson, Alsop, and Auchincloss."

establishment with blood and napalm on its hands. Then again the WASPs sought to do justice to all sides of their nature, to live up to an ideal of human potential ordained by God or, failing that, discernible through human reason. But if human beings were, in fact, a freak of evolution, an accident of natural selection—if man, far from being the paragon of animals, was one more quintessence of genetic dust—were they not chasing a mirage? WASPs made a specialty of institutions like the prep school, which used myth, ritual, and a hygienic athleticism to mold character. But those techniques grew out of the belief that there are objectively better and worse ways of *being* molded; in a postwar Age of Aquarius that had gotten beyond conventional morality, such formative enterprises were suspect, a threat to the authentic, untutored self. In a world of noble savages, what was the point in being a WASP, with all the painful corrective training the breed required?

As the WASPs lost faith in their verities, much of what remained of their order was ingested in the gaudy, cosmopolite society chronicled in the pages of magazines like *Vanity Fair* and the *Tatler*. Brooke Astor directed the New York field office of this insipid, gala-ridden monde; her great chance in life came when Vincent Astor, in search of a third wife, found that none of the obvious candidates would have him. "He was a very disagreeable man," Louis Auchincloss recalled, and his previous marriages, to Helen Huntington and Babe Paley's sister Minnie, ended in divorce. He tried to persuade Janet Newbold Bush (George H. W. Bush's aunt) to take him on, but she turned him down flat. "I don't even like you," she is supposed to have said. He pointed out that he was old and likely to die soon. "But what if you don't?" she shot back.

Eventually Vincent married Brooke, and at his death in 1959 she inherited his fortune. A year later the WASP writer Cleveland Amory published *Who Killed Society?* and proclaimed the death of the old patrician order. Amory, however, did not reckon on the force of will that lay concealed beneath Mrs. Astor's silken flounces. She infused new life into her moribund class, although she did it in ways that would have made Edith Wharton, with her old New York Knickerbocker breeding, raise her eyebrows. "Don't tell me all this modern newspaper rubbish about a New York aristocracy," Mrs. Wharton makes Newland Archer's mother say in *The Age of Innocence*. "Our grandfathers and great-grandfathers were just respectable English or Dutch merchants." Anyone who put stock in the notion of an "American aristocrat," Joe Alsop said, would "have been dismissed as 'common'" by the upper-crust tribe to which he and Mrs. Wharton belonged.

Yet Mrs. Astor, far from shrinking from her newspaper image as a New York princess of the blood, acted the part of Astor sultana with skill, cunning, and an almost indecent joie de vivre.

Mrs. Astor supposed her tactics justified by the threat to her class. Her tribe confronted not the guillotine, but something almost more painful: indifference. To overcome it she engaged a public-relations agent and wrote advice on how to conduct oneself at dinner parties for *Vanity Fair*. She flirted with the press and affected a romantic interest in the journalist Charlie Rose. By playing the coquette with the media she ensured its complaisance; and when, as New York's most celebrated almsgiver, she went slumming in Harlem and the South Bronx, the camera shutters clicked.

This *grande doyenne* style, which in a less adroit performer would have brought ridicule, secured Mrs. Astor's triumph. The gorgeous costumes, the glittering dinners, the flashing jewels worked their magic. She "never went out at night," Louis Auchincloss said, "with less than a million dollars around her neck." Her households were run on a ducal model, with a retinue of chambermaids, a butler (trained at Buckingham Palace), and a chauffeur; her son, Anthony "Tony" Marshall, was thought to have used her poorly when, after she had fallen into a cruel dotage, he pressed her to fill her rooms with Korean deli flowers instead of better cut ones. It scarcely mattered that the splendor was false, that behind the façade lay a wizened old woman who referred to her daughter-in-law as "that bitch." The illusion, Mrs. Astor knew, was enough.

Yet for all her astuteness in keeping WASPland in the public eye, Mrs. Astor cheapened the coin. The old preppy nobility had been composed of people who, like Dean Acheson and the Roosevelts, had done the state some service. But there was always an airhead faction within WASPdom that aspired to tinsel aristocracy: thus in the late nineteenth century Mrs. William B. Astor hallowed her Four Hundred, supposedly the crème de la crème of the Republic, and Cornelia Bradley-Martin threw her egregious ball—at a time when much of the country was suffering on account of the Panic of 1897. It was poor stuff, derivative in its culture, mock-European in its style; the wine was insufficiently mellowed, and age did nothing to improve the vintage. Yet Mrs. Astor nevertheless guzzled it down in her effort to retrieve the fallen fortunes of the WASPs.

SHE DID NOT SUCCEED. THE WASPs fell hard, and they fell fast. Yet when, in 2018, George H. W. Bush died, there was a moment of confused sorrow and muddled regret for an age which had passed. Commentators spoke of the virtues of the WASPs, their good manners, their devotion to the public service, their humility. But it was not the whole story. The WASPs were in fact a rather hard-nosed group, with a keen sense of their own interests and a love-sickness for power. Overlooked by the commentariat were all the deeper impulses that animated them and made their fall something more than the tragicomedy of a class. With the extinction of the WASPs, a chapter closed, the dissipation of a complex of hopes and desires that came into being when, more than a century before, a group of young people vowed to regenerate their country. To understand what the WASPs were really about, we must go back to the beginning.

Nathaniel Hawthorne exposed the morbidities of a dying Puritanism, the "perfectionist enterprise" that inspired and blighted the WASP mind.

TWO

A Dying Race

la valle d'abisso dolorosa . . .

the valle of the sad abyss . . .
—Dante, *Inferno*

You find comparatively few murderers among WASPs. Harry Kendall Thaw (the Pittsburgh coal heir who shot Stanford White, the beaux arts architect, on the rooftop of Madison Square Garden in 1906), Jean Harris (the Smith College alumna and Madeira School headmistress who murdered the diet guru Dr. Herman Tarnower in 1980), and William Bradford Bishop (the Yale-educated diplomat who bludgeoned his family to death with a sledgehammer in Bethesda, Maryland, in 1976) very nearly exhaust the list of WASPs who killed *other* than in the service of the state and the intelligence agencies. As for Lizzie Borden (she of the forty whacks), Henry Judd Gray (the double-indemnity murderer), and Theodore "Ted" Bundy, they were not the sort of people with whom WASPs were on visiting terms, however many genetic haplogroup markers they might have had in common.

WASPs are creatures of guilt and self-questioning, more likely to kill themselves than kill others. Suicide blighted whole families. There were the Sturgises, an old Boston family with a "tendency to suicidal mania." Ralph Waldo Emerson spoke of his horror when, in June 1853, he heard the "dismal tidings" that young Susan Sturgis Bigelow had swallowed arsenic: three of Susan's sister Ellen's children (one of whom was to marry Henry Adams) would also go on to kill themselves. The Gardners too: Joseph Peabody Gardner, in whom was concentrated the blood of a dozen old Massachusetts families, blew his brains out in 1875. His son, Joseph Peabody Gardner Jr., died by suicide eleven years later. Theodore Roosevelt's son Kermit, his grandson Dirck, and his granddaughter Paulina all killed themselves; Eleanor Roosevelt's father, Elliott (Theodore's brother), and her brother Hall both drank themselves to death. Medill McCormick, of Groton, Yale, and the *Chicago Tribune*, sought relief, by turns, in newspaper work, drink, Jungian psychotherapy, and the Senate before he swallowed a fatal dose of pills in a Washington hotel room in 1925; John Gilbert Winant, whose career took him from St. Paul's School and Princeton to the governor's mansion in New Hampshire and the embassy in London, shot himself in the head in 1947. Edie Sedgwick was preceded to the grave by her two older brothers, Francis, who killed himself at Silver Hill in New Canaan in 1964, and Robert, who crashed his motorcycle into a New York City bus in 1965. As for the two boys of William Woodward (shot dead by Ann), James leapt to his death from the ninth floor of the Mayfair House Hotel on Park Avenue in 1978; William jumped from his fourteenth-floor apartment on East Seventy-second Street in 1999.

The suicides were only the most overt sign of trouble in the culture or the blood; WASPs have long been haunted by the despairs, lunacies, and hysterias in their domestic histories. The Sedgwicks called it "the family disease," a malady that oppressed their house ever since Theodore Sedgwick made his fortune in western Massachusetts in the late eighteenth century, more than a century and half before his descendant Edie stripped off her clothes for Andy Warhol. Emily Dickinson spoke of "the Hour of Lead," of a funeral "in my Brain," Henry Adams complained of ennui, John Jay Chapman lamented his "queerness," which as a boy led him to make "mysterious gestures before imaginary shrines" and as an adult got him the nickname "mad Jack." Louisa May Alcott, a golden child of Emerson's Concord who would go on to write *Little Women*, contemplated suicide, and "thought seriously" of jumping into the water of the Mill Dam in Boston.

Were WASPs more troubled than other people? Probably not. But they were more articulate. Their miseries got into the record, and did something to shape the destinies of the United States. Reticent though they were in person, they were voluble on paper. At some level they want us to pay attention.

WASP FAMILIES LIKE THE STURGISES, the Sedgwicks, the Gardners, and the Roosevelts were all, even at their lowest ebbs, doing quite well out of life. What went wrong? The New England heritage had something to do with it. (Even those WASPs who, like the Roosevelts, identified themselves with other regions were connected by a hundred ties to the land of the Puritans.) The New England soil was rich in neurotic possibility; the early New Englanders had not only, in Henry Adams's words, to "wrestle with nature for a bare existence," they had to do it under the burdens of their perfectionist enterprise. The Puritan effort to build a new Jerusalem in the American wilderness was not a formula for sanity; it was abandoned precisely because it *did* induce lunacy, not least in (the somewhat optimistically named) Salem itself, the center of witch hysteria. Puritanism was supplanted, in the eighteenth century, by a less demanding (and less fulfilling) Yankeeism, with its easier idolatry of moneymaking. But by then it was too late: the older vision had inflicted enduring wounds.

The Puritan guilts and manias (it is not easy to live in a city on a hill) lingered in New England long after the demise of Puritanism. You sensed them in the dying villages, with their mouldering houses and sapless apple trees, bereft of youth and vitality, for the enterprising children have escaped to seek their fortune in the cities or the West. In the old greens and on the moribund farms, the memory of primeval Puritanism survived, "shrouded in a blackness ten times black," in tales of wizards and witch-meetings, malignant groves, a shadowed Satanism, the sort of morbidity Nathaniel Hawthorne and (more recently) Stephen King retail in their books. WASPs in the late nineteenth century were drawn to the haunted countryside, and not only on account of its quaintness or its closeness to nature: they found, in the cranks and recluses, the eccentric spinsters and cracked seers, a reflection of their own uneasy souls.

New England was a tragedy. The ancestors, dreaming first of a puritanical Jerusalem and later (after that project failed) of a Republic of Virtue (or "Christian

Sparta," in the words of Samuel Adams), had sailed too close to the sun, and the descendants suffered for their hubris. The lesson of the degenerate villages was reinforced by the literature the WASPs read. Hawthorne taught them that they labored under a curse, some grievance in the granite, and they had only to look to the asylum in Somerville north of Boston (McLean Hospital), its wards filled with deranged descendants of old New England families, to know that it was so. Behind the black veil of the New England conscience something sinister was at work, corrupting the bloodstock and producing mad or feckless heirs. Henry Adams, looking back on the New England colonists in their prime, saw a long line of Puritans and Patriots who had done much to create America's culture and institutions. But nearer his own time he found the characteristic specimens weak and dilettantish, "ornamental" gentlefolk subsidized by their forebears' spadework, spoilt children who could "scarcely have earned five dollars a day in any modern industry."

Such energy and purpose as the WASPs possessed found few outlets in a modern economy. They were drawn to the old public virtues, to the statecraft their ancestors had practiced as well as to the sort of "soft" civic work that adorns a place with art and poetry. But politics, as the nineteenth century wore on, came to be controlled by political bosses who were not (in the eyes of WASPs) gentlemen, and art in America was a profession only a shade more respectable than harlotry. Boston was, in its own conceit, the American Athens, yet we have Professor George Santayana's word for it that in "good Boston society" artists, if they were tolerated, were looked upon as "parasites" and not as "persons with whom the bulwarks of society" could have "any real sympathy." The Calvinist austerity remained after the Calvinist consolations faded; Yankees, with their zeal for compound interest, were as suspicious of the creative impulse as the Puritans, with their zeal for divine election, had been before them.

BUT IT WAS ONLY WHEN the children of the Puritans and the Patriots confronted, after the Civil War, a class that not only mocked their pretensions but also threatened to usurp their place in the hierarchies that the real crisis came. "In the reaction after the colossal struggle of the Civil War," Theodore Roosevelt wrote, "our strongest and most capable men" threw their "whole energy into business, into moneymaking, into the development, and above all the exploitation and exhaustion at the most rapid rate possible, of our natural resources . . ." These industrialists and plutocrats were, Roosevelt said, "shortsighted and selfish," but they were also masterful. Under their alien regime the descendants of the Brahmins—the New England statesmen and sages who had done so much to build the Republic—found themselves reduced in stature, *smaller* than their ancestors had been. They could no longer play the part, Edmund Wilson said, of a "trained and public-spirited caste," for not only did the new society not "recognize them," it forced them to make their way in "a world that broke" many of them.

The fall was the more bitter when they reflected that the North, in vanquishing the Southern planters in the war, had destroyed the only group in America that could rival the Brahmins as a patrician leadership caste. With the destruction of the children of the Cavaliers—now reduced to so much "grey debris"—the children of the Puritans expected to come into their own, only to find that the war itself, and the new industrial power it had called into being, had created an elite more formidable than the defunct Southern aristocracy.

They stare out at us from the canvases of Sargent, well-to-do but uncertain young people, the splendor of whose poses is diminished by a certain vacuousness in their expressions, an emptiness in their eyes. Some committed suicide; others were sent to lunatic asylums or languished in self-doubt and nervous debility, an affliction they knew as neurasthenia, for which reading Dante was the only cure. Oppressed by the gloom of what the critic Lewis Mumford called the Brown Decades, in which coal smoke and perverse fashions combined to color the world with "mediocre drabs, dingy chocolate browns, sooty browns that merged into black," they suffered, in lugubrious rooms furnished somberly in walnut, from obscure hurts and identified with the *roi mehaignié*—the wounded king—of the Grail legend. They were conscious of desolation, a barrenness in things, of belonging, in the poet George Cabot Lodge's words, to "a dying race,"* one that had ever fewer means of distinguishing itself from the plutocracy that had outstripped it and the middle classes rising up to challenge it.

There was John Jay Chapman, who in 1887 was studying law at Harvard and already sensing in himself the misfit who, in Edmund Wilson's words, was to spend his life "beating his head against the gilt of the Gilded Age." Reading Dante in his spare time, he found himself, like the poet, in hell. He refused to accept the word of the girl whom he loved, Minna Timmins, that she loved him

---

*   The word "race" was, when Lodge wrote, used to describe not only what observers took to be each of several large phenotypical divisions among human beings, but smaller groups descended from common ancestors. When Lodge called America's "well-to-do classes" of primarily New England stock a "dying race," he was describing what today would be called a social group.

in return, and in a fit of rage he thrashed a man whom he (wrongly) suspected of having designs upon her virtue. When his friend Wendell Holmes tried to convince him that the girl *did* love him and that he was mad to think otherwise, he accused the future Supreme Court justice of being a spiritual "detective" and dreamt of bloody vengeance. In the climax of his ravaged state Chapman retired to his rooming house in Cambridge and put his hand to the coal fire. When he took it out, the charred knuckles and finger bones were exposed, a prefiguration of the ordeals he was to undergo as a living anachronism, upholding (as Edmund Wilson believed) the ideals of the early Republic in a different world.

George Cabot Lodge was another crippled soul. The oldest son of Henry Cabot Lodge, the Massachusetts politician, he was descended from New England's political and cultural elite, and both his inheritance and his education led him to aspire to the old New England "effort at the Perfect." "Bay," as he was called, wanted to be a poet, and after Harvard he went to Europe in the hope that he might there get his music out and become a light bearer, a cultural leader. (The poet as liberator.) But in Paris he broke down; there were "hideous weeks of madness" in which he felt himself "losing my grip, my aggressiveness, my force of mind . . ." He wanted to "work with the tide and not against it," to "adapt myself to my time and to become a moneymaker." But he could not, he said, "stifle my own self," the ideals that his education and traditions had prepared him to uphold. His Brahmin family was only too happy to subsidize his vocation; Edith Wharton, who thought him one of "the most brilliant and versatile" young men she had ever known, testified that his father, the senator, *wanted* to see young George a poet. He had been raised in "a hot-house of intensive culture," and it "never occurred to his family that he was not meant for an active task in letters." Caught between two worlds, divided against himself, George Cabot Lodge found himself "turning sick and cold and saying to myself, 'See, your life goes, goes, goes . . .'" And indeed it did go—fast. He died young, having failed to make a mark.[*]

The case of Richard Henry Dana III was similar. Like George Cabot Lodge and John Jay Chapman, Dana came from a line of statesmen and poets, of doers and thinkers. His father had sailed before the mast and helped to found, in the 1840s, the antislavery Free Soil Party; his eighteenth-century

---

[*]   His son Henry Cabot Lodge, a product of the WASP revival, did make a mark. He was senator from Massachusetts before he lost the seat to John F. Kennedy in 1952; he went on to be Richard Nixon's running mate in 1960 and Kennedy's ambassador to Saigon, where he played a part in the debacle that contributed to the demise of his revivified class.

great-grandfather had been delegate to the Continental Congress, envoy to Russia, and chief justice of the Supreme Judicial Court of Massachusetts. More distantly Dana was related to the poet Anne Bradstreet, the "Tenth Muse" of Puritan New England. But no more than George Cabot Lodge or John Jay Chapman was he was able to make a place for himself in the gilded, gold-leaf America of his time. Like other WASPs who tried to live up to the traditions of their ancestors, he passed his life in "bewildered efforts to find some way of being useful." The civic ideals he had inherited were outmoded; he had, the writer Van Wyck Brooks said, "the patrician's pattern of mind in a world that had ceased to afford scope to patricians."

THE CHILDREN OF THE BRAHMINS blamed their weaknesses, their fatigues, their failures—the scruples that prevented them from getting on in the world—on neurasthenia. They actually believed it to be a medical condition. In his 1881 book *American Nervousness: Its Causes and Consequences*, the WASP physician Dr. George Miller Beard described neurasthenia as a disease caused by "lack of nerve-force" and productive of such symptoms as, but not limited to, insomnia, bad dreams, mental irritability, nervous dyspepsia, fear of society, fear of responsibility, lack of decision in trifling matters, profound exhaustion, and excessive yawning.

In fact neurasthenia was a state of mind, one that had a good deal in common with other kinds of soul-sickness that have troubled human beings since the beginning of time. The "black bile" (*melancholia*) of the Greeks, the *acedia* or muddy listlessness of the medieval souls who, in Dante's words, are "sad in sweet air brightened by the sun," the "spleen" of the eighteenth-century English Augustans, with its attendant "Vapours, Lowness of Spirits, Hypochondriacal and Hysterical Distempers, &c.," the *ennui* of Pascal and the *noia* of Leopardi, the *nausée* of Sartre—neurasthenia was another version of the immemorial despondencies.

What distinguished the WASP neurasthenic was his (or her) consciousness of unused powers in the soul that he (or she) sought to discharge in civic and creative activity. You see it most clearly in Henry Adams, who adopted the pose of a neurasthenic weakling oppressed by his New England heritage, looking on life rather than living it, and doomed to fail in an America that had little use for the patrician's theory of virtue. The pose was ironic—the man who wrote *The Education of Henry Adams* was not in any ordinary sense a failure: but it enabled Adams to explain why the best and brightest of his generation so often fell into neurotic despair. Neurasthenia, he maintained, was the natural response of gifted natures to an environment unsympathetic to their gifts. It was the inevitable reaction of those who, resisting the fragmentary part-lives on offer in the Gilded Age marketplace, sought to do justice to the whole of their nature in a land where the two great perfectionist experiments (New England Puritanism and Yankee commercial democracy) were culturally inadequate precisely because they were founded on too narrow a conception of human flourishing.

Neurasthenia was hell. But Adams learned from Dante that hell was good, a thing, indeed, instituted by divine love, *'l primo amore*. For in deserving cases the path through *la città dolente*, the suffering underworld city, led, if not to sanity and salvation, at any rate to small victories over hellishness. This was the tradition of productive lunacy, the belief that you can't attain the Jerusalem of your heart's desire without first submitting to a Babylonian captivity. In writing the life of his dead friend George Cabot Lodge, Adams spoke of the young man's "philosophic depression," the dejection one feels when one's powers find no release in joyful activity and one's soul is condemned to feed upon itself. But the lassitudes of neurasthenia, exempting the sufferer from the demands of the marketplace, could also, Adams suggested, buy one time—to plot a comeback, and obtain one's revenge on those who doubted one's virtue.

FOR OUT OF THE NEUROTIC ruins emerged a patrician caste devoted to civic reform and the renewal of society. Caught, as they supposed, between barbarians above and barbarians below—between gilded tycoons and a mass-produced middle class—the children of the Brahmins overcame their debilities and reinvented themselves as WASPs.

The counterrevolution was bold. Like Dante before them, they wanted to reform the corrupt city and at the same time create a stable world order (the American Century). And like Dante, they rebelled against the idea of living an empty life and dying a meaningless (hellish) death. They were driven by a notion of human completeness, one that distinguishes them from the parochialism and self-complacency of more recent power establishments narrowly founded on money and technical expertise. They absorbed Dante's faith in the humanities and attempted to revitalize liberal education, which was not for them, as it is for us, an antiquated heirloom, practically useless: they believed that it could both unlock human potential and promote the civic virtues, which they looked on as a salve for a variety of psychic wounds.

One must not exaggerate their virtues or overlook their vices. There was a certain amount of simple arrogance in them, and too little of the magnificence that sometimes excuses it. The WASP never possessed the *grandezza* of the Venetian magnifico or the Roman patrician, nor has any artist succeeded in turning the hierarchic vanities of the preppies into elegiac poetry as Waugh and Lampedusa do the pretensions of the sinking toffs who figure in their own works of aristocratic devotion.

Yet for all that they had an instinct for good form, no mean gift in a country which, Emerson said, "is formless, has no terrible & no beautiful condensation." You see it in their houses, in the understated charm that never sacrifices comfort to pretension; you are always coming on odd little rooms of flowered chintz and cozy untidiness, devoted to conversation, leisure, books. The manners are as comfortable as the armchairs, are such as put a guest at ease; the tones of voice are pleasing, modulated with a tact that unfailingly avoids the awkward question. Still more do you see it in their institutions, in the ancient though nowadays little-studied arts by which they created places that commanded the heart and molded a type alive to possibilities we seem to have lost. Many have admired the WASPs for their effort to shape character in accordance with an ideal: but few have studied *how* they did it, or examined the techniques, the institutional artistry, by which they wrought upon the soul.

There is, to be sure, great difficulty in writing about people whose time has passed, who were bathed in the lukewarm bath of snobbery, who, with flashes of insight, were largely mediocre, and who were as narrowly European in their culture as they were complacently white in their pedigree arrogance. As for their other defects—where does one begin? And yet they were pretty nearly alone, among Americans, in pursuing the purposes they did. For all their arrogance and resentment, they sought a path to a new life.

Isabella Stewart Gardner felt her powers rotting within her, but unlike the diffident characters in Henry James's stories, she broke out of her cage.

THREE

Mrs. Jack Gardner and Her Unlikely Swan

Quando leggemmo il disïato riso
esser basciato da cotanto amante,
questi, che mai da me non fia diviso,
la bocca mi basciò tutto tremante. . . .
quel giorno più non vi leggemmo avante . . .

When we read how the longed-for smile
was kissed by such a lover,
he, who will never be divided from me,
kissed my mouth all trembling . . .
that day we read no more . . .
—Dante, *Inferno*

S he was by nature theatrical, a creature made for spectacles, masquerades, the *fêtes champêtres* of Watteau. But in Boston, the city of the Puritans, Isabella Stewart Gardner found no better scope for her exhibitionist temperament than the melodrama of a sickroom. Scarcely more than twenty years old, she grew painfully thin and languished in bed.

She was not a Bostonian by birth. Her father, David Stewart, a linen merchant in New York who had invested profitably in iron, took her as a girl to Paris, where she and her family fell in with the John Lowell Gardners of Beacon Hill, Boston. Little Belle Stewart was short of stature and plain of face, but she had a spark. She succeeded in making the John Lowell Gardners' ponderous son Jack laugh, and in the spring of 1860 the couple were married in Grace Church in New York City.

Jack Lowell took Isabella back to Boston, but she found the city cold, and not simply on account of the climate. There was (still is) something forbidding in Beacon Hill's top-drawer Brahmin society. Puritanism had given way to Unitarianism, but the old spirit lingered in ideals of parsimonious respectability. Each day her husband, who was known as Mr. Jack, went, as so many other Proper Bostonian males did, to a counting house in State Street, where he steadily built up his capital. The women were as joylessly industrious. While the husbands banked, the wives knitted, in little sewing circles founded on the pleasures of exclusion. Belle Gardner, the arriviste from New York, was among the excluded.

She found such refuge as she could in the semi-invalidism of neurasthenia, and she was at times so weak that when she and Mr. Jack visited Mr. Jack's cousins, the Peabodys, she had to be lifted from the carriage. There was a ray of light. In 1863 she gave birth to a boy, another John Lowell Gardner whom she and her husband called Jackie. But the child sickened and died. The doctor prescribed the requisite cure for well-to-do patients—foreign travel, and as soon as practicable the Gardners embarked on the first of a series of grand tours. The sunshine of Egypt and the glamour of Paris revived Belle's spirit, but they also deepened her dread of the Massachusetts winter. Stopping in London after one of her voyages, she told Henry James of her reluctance to go back to a city where she had "neither friends, nor lovers, nor resources of any kind left."

WASPs ARE BORN IN THE consciousness of a void in their lives, a sense that their shrunken existences are a mockery of life's promise. In this they differ from those of their own kind who are content, indeed determined, to live in an unchanging tradition—who, like the Apleys, the Beacon Street Brahmins in John Marquand's novel *The Late George Apley*, are pleased that their environment has prevented them from becoming anything other than what everyone else in their class is. WASPs, by contrast, are drawn to an old Greek maxim: become what *you* are. Like Lambert Strether in Henry James's novel *The Ambassadors*, they feel their unused powers rotting within them, but unlike the diffident Strether, they resolve to fight back, to break out of their cages.

Isabella Stewart Gardner was one of these WASPs, struggling to impose her inner romance on an alien environment. Her tactics were outrageous, even vulgar, but in a city whose leading citizens had been bled dry by Puritanism and frugality, ostentation was poetry. Casting off her neurasthenic shell, Isabella established, in her house in Beacon Street, a court of her own, one that outshone those of the women who snubbed her, and she went about imperially gowned in the latest masterpieces of Worth, the Parisian couturier who dressed the Empress Eugénie. Brahmin matrons raised their eyebrows when Isabella dared to drop the hooped crinoline in favor of dresses that revealed her pretty figure. But such was her violent elegance that no sooner did she enter a room than it seemed to make obeisance to her person as though to royalty. Brahmin matrons were soon instructing their own modistes to copy Mrs. Jack.

A rare flower indeed, filched from a hothouse in hell, or so one of her detractors whispered. Tales of her extravagance multiplied. It was said that she employed not only a butler in her house in Beacon Street but *two* footmen, an affront to the simplicity of the Puritan city. She arranged for pugilists to box in her salon for the delectation of her girlfriends—it lasted seventeen rounds; and she was seen carrying away two lion cubs from the zoo. Yet she swept all before her. "*C'est mon plaisir*," she would say. "It is my pleasure." It was the note of a great queen. Henry James was impressed by the authority of her gestures, the audacity of her display, although he regretted the "eccentric ways" in which this queenliness was expressed. She was "not a woman," he exclaimed, she was "a locomotive—with a Pullman car attached."

Still something was missing.

EARLY IN 1882 A YOUNG WASP called Frank Crawford appeared on Mrs. Gardner's doorstep in Beacon Street. He was a magnificent physical specimen, "one of the handsomest men I have ever seen," one of his cousins said. He "would pose before the mirror quite openly, rejoicing in his strength and beauty like any vigorous young animal." Nor was Frank's mind less supple than his body. He had been born in Tuscany to American parents—his mother was the sister of Julia Ward Howe, the author of "The Battle Hymn of the Republic"—and he knew Italy better perhaps than he did America. Sent, as a boy, to St. Paul's School in Concord, New Hampshire, he had gone on to England to take first-class honors at Cambridge. He was at home in Latin and Greek as well as Sanskrit, and for the sake of privacy he composed his diary in Urdu.

In the meantime Mr. Jack Gardner, sitting in the Somerset Club over his Burgundy, was growing each day a little stouter, a little balder, a little duller, if that were possible. Was it any wonder that Isabella should have rested her eyes complacently on Frank? Yet it was a delicate business for them both. An ill-judged liaison could destroy a woman's reputation even in New York: Boston was that much more prim. But Isabella was ready to run risks.* The respectable Bostonian met the challenge of life and the inevitability of death by acting as though he were dead already; Isabella, like many emergent WASPs, embraced the new, though possibly no less dubious, philosophy of saying "yes" to life. She went so far as to ask young Frank to . . . read Dante with her.

He seemed to know everyone in the great world beyond Boston, and casting a vivid light, false, perhaps, but alluring, on the latest scandals in London and New York, he gave Isabella a new idea of style and possibility. Sturgis Bigelow (a scholar of Japan and son of the unfortunate Susan Sturgis Bigelow who swallowed arsenic) thought Isabella a magnificent "gloom-dispeller" and "corpse-reviver," but Frank was at least her equal as a child of the sun. Like Paolo and Francesca in the poem they were reading, they fell in love. It was an affair of the heart and possibly of the flesh: still more of the spirit. Isabella, conscious of a vacancy in Boston, wanted to understand the richer poetry her lover had mastered, and she was pleased that the stepchild of Tuscany could help her with her Dante, the poet to whom Boston's enlightened souls looked as a medium of regeneration.

She had another motive for deepening her perception. She and Mr. Jack were at Constantinople when word reached them that Mr. Jack's brother Joseph

---

* In the England of the 1860s, Algernon Swinburne was compelled to leave Wallington Hall, the country house of Sir Walter and Lady Trevelyan, after the host discovered that the poet had lent his wife a French novel. "It was nothing worse, I believe, than a volume of the *Comédie Humaine*," Edmund Gosse wrote in his *Life of Swinburne*, "but he was a rash man who in those days recommended a French book to an English lady." The manners of Boston in the 1880s were certainly not *less* severe.

Peabody Gardner, a widower whose wife had died in childbirth ten years before, had blown his brains out. He left three orphaned boys—Joe Jr., fourteen, William Amory, twelve, and Augustus, ten. Mr. and Mrs. Jack, childless themselves after little Jackie's death, adopted the boys and took them into their hearts. Determined to be a good foster-mother, Isabella set out to remedy the deficiencies of her own limited schooling. Henry James himself had pronounced the boys brilliant, and in order to keep up with them Isabella was soon haunting the lecture room of Charles Eliot Norton at Harvard.

Norton, a scholar of Dante, was an impresario of the culture that would shape the emerging WASPs. Wits jested that it was characteristic of Boston that it should have chosen for its high priest of taste a connoisseur of painting who was half blind and a lover of music who was largely deaf. But Norton's weaknesses were counterbalanced by a personal charm which must have been very great. His friend John Ruskin, the Victorian prophet of art, spoke of the "bright eyes, the melodious voice, the perfect manner" that enchanted even the most fastidious, and he credited him with possessing "the sweetest quiet smile I ever saw on any face (unless, perhaps, a nun's, when she has some grave kindness to do) . . ."

Norton had read Ruskin's *Modern Painters*, and both men were drawn to the Italian Middle Ages and more especially to its artistry of place and community. They were certain that the medieval city of Dante, for all its murderous passions, offered "an example of integrity and civic pride and beauty" from which a modern commercial age had much to learn. Isabella's nephew and adopted son William Amory (pronounced *Emory*) early succumbed to the last enchantment of the Middle Age. He was an odd and gifted child, with red hair and eyes ingenuously, protuberantly blue. Isabella gave him such training, Amory's friend John Jay Chapman remembered, "as one connects with the idea of a British nation," a "mixture of devotion and rigor." At fifteen Amory passed his Harvard entrance examinations, but Isabella thought him too young for college and took him instead to Europe, where touring the cathedral towns he showed himself master of such a stock of learning as would have done credit to a much older scholar. Entering Harvard College in 1880, he was soon recognized, Chapman said, as "the best educated man in the class of '84," possessed of a "super-normal sensitiveness of nervous structure" and a prodigious memory. Professor Goodwin, the Eliot Professor of Greek Literature, thought him "the best scholar he had ever taught," and the young man who was intimately familiar with the Gothic art of Chartres and Beauvais was soon as steeped in the Athens of Sophocles and Plato.

Otherworldly, eccentric, free from conventional ambition, Amory's gift was less for scholarship than romance. He wove "fairy tales in a prosaic world," Ellery Sedgwick (great-uncle of Edie) remembered: "there was about him a fantastic quality which seemed in common touch with all the creatures of fancy from leprechauns to giant killers." Amory was, indeed, reluctant to forsake the imaginative playfulness of childhood, and like such other Victorians as Lewis Carroll and Ruskin himself, he was preoccupied with childish innocence. Understandably: his own had been shattered by the death of his mother and still more by the suicide of his father. At Harvard he saw others whose innocence had been corrupted in no less disturbing ways, young men poorly prepared for independence and already old in the vices of ostentation, cynicism, drink, and sycophancy. Gilded Age corruption, Amory believed, had its root in a defective system of education.

But what could he do about it? The way was open to a career at Harvard, where he might serve as a mentor to youth. But by the time a boy reached Harvard, it was often too late. The question became more pressing in 1883, the year in which his foster-mother's dalliance with Frank Crawford was abruptly broken off. No one now knows what brought about the end of the affair, but something seems to have scared the lovers; perhaps Mr. Jack, rousing himself from the apathies of the Somerset Club, grew suspicious. (Paolo and Francesca were all very well as poetry, but before their reunion in hell, where Dante encountered them, they had been slaughtered in bed by Francesca's husband, Mr. Jack Malatesta.) When Frank left a despondent Isabella to take ship for Europe that spring to write novels, Amory was approaching his final year at Harvard and had as yet no idea of what to do with himself. He was rich and had no need to earn his living; he might freely indulge his taste for travel, yachting, and curious scholarship. But dilettantism did not appeal to him. Then he learned that a cousin of his, a young man called Cotty Peabody, was intent on founding a school that was to be unlike any other in America or England.

The unlikely swan knew what he would do.

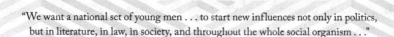

FOUR

Henry Adams Fails to Reform America

La gente nuova e i sùbiti guadagni
orgoglio e dismisura han generata,
Fiorenza, in te, sì che tu già ten piagni . . .

The new people and the quick riches
have begot pride and excess in you,
Florence, and already you weep for it . . .
—Dante, *Inferno*

Y̶ou'll be thinkin' you'll be president too!"
So the Irish gardener said to the boy Henry Adams at Quincy, the homestead south of Boston that served Adams's president grandfather, John Quincy

Adams, and president great-grandfather, John Adams, as a refuge from public employments. The remark so impressed Henry Adams that he never forgot it. That there should be a doubt of his being president was to him a new idea. As "influences that warped a mind," none compared, he said, to the sight of John Quincy Adams's bald head as it bobbed in its pew each Sunday in the Unitarian church in Quincy. Sitting behind his president grandfather, looking above the bald head to the tablet commemorating his president great-grandfather, the boy Henry assumed that "what had been would continue to be." The Irish gardener was more perceptive.

In Henry Adams you find certain qualities of the WASPs expressed in their purest or, depending on your point of view, their most corrupt form. There was, first of all, the proximity to power, to people in whom the habit of giving orders had become second nature. Henry Adams did not, in fact, like his grandfather John Quincy Adams: rather the reverse. But as a boy he was on familiar terms with him. He hung about the old man's library, deranged his papers, ransacked his drawers; a president, he said, "was a matter of course in every respectable family." Henry Adams felt no special reverence for his grandfather, but he vividly remembered the ease with which the old man dominated his environment. The boy Henry was six or seven years old and in a "passionate outburst of rebellion against going to school" one morning when the door at the top of the staircase in Quincy opened and the old president came slowly down the stairs. Putting on his hat, he took the boy's hand without a word and brought him up the hot road to school. In the grip of his grandfather's authority, the boy was "paralyzed by awe," yet at the same time he found himself admiring the mysterious faculty that *could* paralyze another human being with awe. To generalize (though not extravagantly), a true WASP not only grows up in proximity to power, he grows up wanting the same kind of power for himself. His rhetoric of service, humility, and civic conscience is rarely altogether false. But neither is it ever wholly true. WASPs *like* to give orders.

Both their proximity to power and their longing for it stimulate in young WASPs a conviction that they are destined to possess it themselves. When, at the age of twelve, Henry Adams was taken to Washington by his father, Charles Francis Adams, for the first time to meet the president—a WASP initiation rite that little Franklin Roosevelt's father would be careful to observe—he took to it instinctively, enchanted by the fragrance of the catalpa trees and the mock splendor of the half-finished buildings, "like white Greek temples in the abandoned gravel-pits of a deserted Syrian city." The White House itself seemed almost a personal possession, for all "his family had lived there, and, barring the eight years of Andrew Jackson's reign, had been more or less at home there ever since it was built." He "half thought he owned it, and took for granted that he should some day live in it" himself.

The next step in the WASP cursus honorum (for the WASP as for the Roman, honor and power amounted to very nearly the same thing) was a properly "exclusive" school, one that had bred a succession of leaders and would strengthen in the young person the conviction that he (mostly *he*'s in those days, though *she*'s would soon gain ground) was a WASP of destiny, intended for the service of the state. For Henry Adams, the school was Harvard College, and four years in that seminary in Cambridge, which culminated in his election as class orator, did nothing to disabuse him of his sense of future grandeur. At the same time Harvard enabled him to measure his abilities against those of rival contenders for power, and he fixed a wary eye on William Henry Fitzhugh "Rooney" Lee, the son of Colonel Robert E. Lee of the Second United States Cavalry. "Tall, largely built, handsome, genial, with liberal Virginian openness toward all he liked," Rooney Lee had the "Virginian habit of command and took leadership as his natural habit." He embodied the spirit of the Southern planters, the only group that could challenge the New England Brahmins' conception of themselves as the Republic's preeminent leadership caste. For a year or more, Adams remembered, Lee led their class at Harvard, but the descendants of the Puritans gradually overmastered the sons of the Cavaliers, and Lee "seemed slowly to drop into the background." The habit of command was not enough; one needed brains, Adams saw, as well as sanity in one's vices. When a Virginian "brooded a few days over an imaginary grief and substantial whiskey," he wrote, "none of his Northern friends could be sure that he might not be waiting, round the corner, with a knife or pistol, to revenge insult by the dry light of delirium tremens."

But although the Adamses were an antislavery family and the Lees lived on the labor of their bondspeople, Henry Adams's friendship with Rooney Lee was "unbroken and even warm," and when the Virginian was offered a commission in the United States Sixth Infantry, he asked the son of Massachusetts to "write his letter of acceptance, which flattered Adams's vanity more than any Northern compliment could do." That the child of the Cavaliers should acknowledge the abilities of the child of the Puritans was, for Adams, yet another whisper of destiny.

⚯

THREE YEARS AFTER HE GRADUATED from Harvard College, in the fateful winter of 1860–61, Henry Adams again went with his father to Washington, this time to watch the United States collapse. As, one by one, the Southern states seceded and his friend Rooney Lee was commissioned a captain in the Confederate cavalry, Adams doubted Abraham Lincoln's ability to save the Republic. Had he bet his life "on the correctness of his estimate of the new President," he afterward said, "he would have lost." Studying Lincoln at the "melancholy function called an Inaugural Ball," he looked for a sign of greatness, but saw only a "long, awkward figure; a plain, ploughed face; a mind, absent in part, and in part evidently worried by white kid gloves."

Yet Adams soon obtained through Lincoln a coveted if unofficial diplomatic post. The new president was in the midst of settling the vexatious question of which office-seeker should have the Chicago Post Office (a patronage plum) when, almost as an afterthought, he dispatched Charles Francis Adams as envoy to Great Britain. Henry Adams would serve as his father's private secretary, and in London he neatly combined two experiences that went into the making of so many WASPs, a political or diplomatic apprenticeship and an encounter with the society of the Old World. There were dinner parties in Belgravia, house parties in the country, breakfasts in Upper Brook Street with Monckton Milnes, a dilettante poet who was at the same time a consummate man of the world.* Adams saw the great figures of the age, from Garibaldi, the liberator of Italy, to Gladstone, the leading liberal statesman, bowed "to half the dukes and duchesses in England," brushed against royalty. It was not every young American who found himself sitting over the Duke of Argyll's claret in Argyll Lodge instructing the philosopher John Stuart Mill in the merit of tariffs on manufactured goods.

Not that he could ever believe that the London dinner party and the English country house represented "the perfection of human society," as more naïve Americans did. The food, for one thing, was bad (and mostly catered from Gunter's in Berkeley Square), and he detested the anti-Lincoln prejudices of the British

---

* Milnes, who opened many doors for Adams, has been described as a "villainous tempter," a "feline" creature of "Mephistophelean malice" who corrupted the young by taking them "through the Inferno of his library" of erotica at Fryston in Yorkshire. This is the melodrama of scholars; Adams's encounter with Milnes and the society of the Old World, though it certainly affected him, was not an initiation in deviltries.

establishment, which was largely rebel in its sympathies in the American Civil War. The upper-crust society of Mayfair was little more than a "polite mob" in whose manners the crudeness of Hogarth's and Rowlandson's London still lingered, yet he found in it, too, a social charm, an aristocratic ease and complexity of manner, unknown in Boston.* He only wished that he could combine his political education with a sentimental one, and in his imagination he pictured an attachment to a highbred woman, bored by her husband, who might polish his manners and soften his barbarism, as in a French novel. But such a liaison was not seriously to be contemplated by a young Bostonian who, like Adams, had not yet emancipated himself from Boston's "sacred rage" against pleasure. Besides, it "would have scandalized his parents."

The real romance, for Adams, was power, and he was struck by the way British patricians reconciled immense ambition with a civic conscience and a high literary culture. An aspiring young Briton who took up his pen to advance a program of reform might soon find himself with a seat in Parliament and even playing a part in the direction of affairs. Thomas Babington Macaulay's Whiggish historical essays prepared the way for the first Reform Bill, which expanded voting rights, while Benjamin Disraeli's novels were the inspiration of Young England, a conservative reform movement. Adams saw in these writers models to be emulated, and he dreamt of founding, in America, a movement of his own. What "we want," he confided to his brother Charles in 1862, "is a *school*. We want a national set of young men like ourselves or better, to start new influences not only in politics, but in literature, in law, in society, and throughout the whole social organism of the country. A national school of our own generation. . ."

Such a school was, he knew, precisely the sort of thing America had "no power to create," for America had no power to "centralize ability." There was no "means, power or hope of combined action for any unselfish end." But he proposed to find a means.

HE RETURNED TO AMERICA IN 1868 determined to make his program of reform real. And who could doubt that such a program was needed? For plainly the Republic was in a bad way. A machinery of "capital, banks, mines, furnaces,

---

* Milnes himself spoke contemptuously of that "grove of barren fig-trees called London Society." Yet if he thought this true, it is not easy to see why he should have passed so much of his life in Upper Brook Street, entertaining that very society. At all events, such was the barrenness of which he complained, that in a few months in 1863 he numbered among his guests at breakfast or dinner Thackeray, Ruskin, Gladstone, Matthew Arnold, and Benjamin Jowett.

shops, power-houses, technical knowledge" had grown up to make an untamed continent habitable for civilized people. But the machinery that so efficiently mined coal and built railroads was overwhelming the country's fragile political institutions. A quaint eighteenth-century Constitution could never do the work, Adams believed, of a "twenty-million horse-power" nation, nor could it contain the new forms of plutocratic power that were coming into being with the explosion of industrial force. Predatory financiers like Jay Gould, whose net stretched from New York's Tammany Hall to the Washington of President Ulysses S. Grant, foreshadowed, Adams was convinced, a new Caesarism,* in which "mere private citizens" would "ultimately succeed in directing government itself."† But it was not idealism alone that motivated the emergent WASP in Adams. His program, if implemented, would get the better precisely of those new men who were usurping the place of families like the Adamses in the nation's hierarchies. (Reform as a way of getting even.) It was with these mixed motives that he went down to Washington to expose the villains whose evildoing "smirched executive, judiciary, banks, corporate systems, professions, and people, all the great active forces of society, in one dirty cesspool of vulgar corruption."

Only the obstacles in his path were greater than he had imagined. He looked, for an ally, to the newly elected President Grant, for no one doubted that the intention of Lincoln's favorite general was "one of reform." But a brief exchange with the chief executive satisfied Adams that there was no hope to be looked for in the White House. The evolution of American statesmen from President Washington to President Grant was, he jested, "evidence enough to upset Darwin." Yet he found the city on the Potomac, so stupid politically and so morally vicious, to be socially charming. (The WASP has, in all generations, had a soft spot for Washington.) The town itself was primitive, a mere "political camp" in the eyes of one who, like Adams, had gazed on Regent Street and the rue de Rivoli. There "were no theatres, no restaurants, no *monde*, no *demi-monde*, no drives,

---

* Adams drew on his brother Charles's belief that Commodore Vanderbilt had unconsciously "introduced Cæsarism into corporate life," and was "the precursor of a class of men who will wield within the State a power created by the State, but too great for its control."

† Tocqueville had long before warned of the inadequacy of the elites that were coming into being with the growth of freedom and democracy—elites that exhibited all the corruption of the ancient aristocracies and possessed none of their higher feelings. When barbarians encounter a higher civilization, they first embrace its vices, and next enlarge upon them. Even so the Gilded Age magnificos aped all that was least attractive in the aristocratic tinsel of the Old World—and made it yet more tawdry.

no splendor, and, as Mme. de Struve used to say, no *grandezza*." It hardly mattered. In Washington Adams found himself looked on as a young duke, much in demand in that genial if limited society. He delighted in the simple manners of the place and rejoiced in the softness of the climate, the "overpowering beauty and sweetness" of the Maryland autumn and the still more potent allure of the Washington spring; Mme. de Struve herself—she was the wife of the Russian envoy—could not deny it. Adams "loved it too much, as though it were Greek and half human."

He began at once to write for the press. With his social connections and confidential sources he could hardly help, he believed, "saying something that would command attention." Together with a little knot of conspirators he wrote articles, exposed stockjobbers, and made the case for a reformed civil service on British and Imperial Chinese models, purged of party hacks by means of competitive examination. At the same time, wound up "in a coil of political intrigue," he laid plans for an independent "party of the centre" to be led by good men who disdained both the bosses who controlled the dominant parties and the industrialists who bribed the bosses to corner the markets.

HENRY ADAMS WAS BUSY, BUT behind the incessant energy lay the dread, not merely of failure, but of breakdown. The possibility of ending as another *Mayflower* screwball in the Somerville Asylum was real to him. Like other emerging WASPs, he was forming his life in reaction to familial ghosts. Of his two uncles on his father's side, the eldest, George Washington Adams, was a melancholic drunkard who killed himself at twenty-eight. George's brother—Henry's Uncle John—was another failure whom drink brought to an early grave. George and John were themselves following in the footsteps of two of their own uncles. Charles Adams, the second son of Henry's great-grandfather John Adams, died at thirty of cirrhosis of the liver, having been disowned by his president father, who denounced him as a "madman possessed by the devil. . . . David's Absalom had some ambition and some enterprise. Mine is a mere rake, buck, blood and beast." Charles's brother Thomas, the third and youngest son of John Adams, was another ne'er-do-well sodden with drink and underachievement.

When his own articles made a stir, Henry seemed safely out of the wood of neurasthenic failure, and he looked forward to a rapid ascension into a position of leadership. But nothing happened. America was not England; a splendid literary effort was not likely to launch a young man on a career like that of

Macaulay or Disraeli. Party leaders brushed aside Adams's criticisms of the patronage machine, and insider trading on the stock exchanges was as rife as ever. The "legitimate politics" of public virtue that he foresaw overcoming the "tendency of our political system to corruption" failed to materialize, and his own ambitions were mocked in the newspapers. He had "altogether too much of the English and diplomatic and supercilious character," it was said, to become "a useful public man."

Evidently he was not so safe as he thought. The political prizes he sought eluded him, and he was conscious of alarming symptoms in his own psychological makeup. "My disease," he would later say, "is *ennui*." It would steal upon him unexpectedly, the state of mind William James knew as anhedonia, the inability to experience pleasure, a weariness that Tolstoy described as the desire for desire and Baudelaire called *le cafard*, the big fat cockroach of life, sinking its hairy mandibles into the unwitting soul. But having been beaten, in the game of power, by the new people—the party bosses and stockjobbing tycoons—Adams had, at last, found what the WASP needs if he or she is to overcome weak nerves and accomplish anything significant.

He had found something to hate.

STILL SMARTING FROM HIS EXPERIENCE in Washington, Adams returned like a kicked puppy to Massachusetts to take up a professorship in medieval history at Harvard. Two years later, in June 1872, he married Marian Hooper. Known as Clover or Clo, she had a mind that was a match for his own—Henry James compared her to Voltaire—and she was soon to become accomplished in the new art of photography or "drawing with the sun," as Ruskin called it. Even so Henry's brother Charles remembered having doubts about the marriage. "Heavens!—no!" he recalled saying at the prospect of his brother uniting himself to a girl who, he suspected, had inherited suicidal tendencies from her Sturgis relations. The Sturgises were "all as crazy as coots. She'll kill herself just like her aunt" (the unfortunate Susan Sturgis Bigelow who swallowed arsenic). If Charles is to be believed, Clover was prone to fits of depression: she was also perhaps overly dependent on her father, the kindly Dr. Hooper of Boston.

She and Henry had no children, but the marriage seemed happy, and Henry would remember the decade in which they wed fondly. The "seventies . . . we were really happy then," he said, discreetly passing over the eighties in silence. Although he was loath to admit it, he made a good professor, sipping sherry in the seminar room as he introduced young Harvard scholars to the latest techniques in historical inquiry. But the dream of statesmanship died hard. He edited an influential quarterly, the *North American Review*, in which he promoted the cause of reform, and he went down, whenever he could, to New York and Washington to build up his independent "party of the centre." Yet very little came of it, and as the cinders of his charred ambitions cooled, he gave up his desire to make history and began instead to write it, the last refuge of the aborted statesman.

Other WASPs, most notably the Roosevelts, would succeed as political reformers; Henry Adams was among the first of the breed to experience an early and mortifying failure. The collapse of his reform endeavors and his "party of the centre" forced him to find another way to account for himself. In turning from the politics of reform to the study and writing of history, he sought a way to justify his existence after it seemed to go all wrong, and a means of understanding his failure in the light of his country's larger experience. Giving up his professorship at Harvard, he went back to Washington, drawn to it not only on account of its archives but because it was the only place in America "where society amuses me, or where life offers variety." In Washington he and Clo lived in style, kept as many as half a dozen servants, and established a choice salon. She occupied herself with her wet-plate photography; he investigated the records of the State Department.

In writing his various histories, not least his history of himself, Henry Adams was to find a way to dish the plutocrats and party hacks who, he said, had done the "most to block his intended path in life." But his work would be little more than a forgettable act of literary revenge had not a deeper impulse been at work. In trying to figure out where the Republic his ancestors founded went wrong, Adams, the spoiled child of those nation-builders, was to articulate a grievance that was in some respects the making of the WASPs.

Amory Gardner, Endicott Peabody, and Sherrard Billings, intent on creating
a school that would "differ . . . from any in England or America."

FIVE

Cotty Peabody Leaves the Bank

Là sù di sopra, in la vita serena,
rispuos' io lui, mi smarri' in una valle . . .

There, in the bright air above,
I told him, I went astray in a valley . . .
—Dante, *Inferno*

They called him the Sun God. The young Endicott Peabody, or Cotty, as
he was called, was a "wonderful specimen," a cousin remembered, "of
stalwart youth . . . broad shouldered, fair-haired, blue-eyed, with an irresistible
capacity for laughter . . . . There wasn't a young man far or near as good looking
as he was, but he seemed quite unconscious of the effect he was producing, and
that added to his charm."

He had been born in Salem, Massachusetts, in 1857, the great-grandson of a merchant grown rich in the East India and China trades, indigo, silks, sugar, spice, and opium. But the China and East India trades died away, and Cotty's father, Samuel Endicott Peabody, did the prudent thing by going into private equity. The old shipping aristocracy, nabobs of the "poetic blue-water phase of commercial development," was no more; a young Brahmin must make his peace with the new princes of industrial capital. Samuel Endicott Peabody married the daughter of the founder of Lee, Higginson & Co., a Boston investment firm, and in 1871 he was offered a partnership in the London bank of Junius Spencer Morgan, the father of J. P. Morgan, the American Midas. He took his family to England and sent thirteen-year-old Cotty to school at Cheltenham, where we find him, a handsome lad, playing cricket, arguing with the headmaster (who, he conceived, had been unjust), and being altogether what one of his mates called "a most audacious fellow."

Three years at Trinity College, Cambridge, followed, and after taking a degree in law, Cotty returned to America to accept a position at Lee, Higginson & Co. He was, to all appearances, a forthright soul not given to doubts, and everything seemed to mark him out for a splendid career in business.

But appearances may be deceptive. Alluding to Matthew Arnold's poem "The Buried Life," Cotty confessed that there were times when he felt "a nameless sadness over me steal." He saw evil in the world, and vaguely sensed in himself gifts that had not their scope in the computation of interest in a bank. Some of his frustration was no doubt sexual; he was courting, not very successfully, a pretty cousin of his called Fannie Peabody. But the problem went deeper. He was perplexed, he said, by "social problems" to which he saw no obvious solution, and he complained that his work in State Street "doesn't lead to anything and has little in it except a fortune, if that." Then again the crudeness of America in the Gilded Age depressed him. His friend John Jay Chapman described how, coming home after a sojourn in Europe, "the ugliness of everything appalled me." Peabody knew what he meant; there was very little, in America, of the glow of poetry and order he had found in certain English communities, where what Wordsworth called "old usages" and the "colouring of other times" softened the "vulgar light" of "present, actual, superficial life." America, in Henry James's words, seemed "barren of romance and grace." "What a horrible day it is has been!" Peabody exclaimed as he looked out on the desolate New England scene. "It is in a great part subjective on my part, however, for instead of jumping at the sight of the pure soft snow my heart seems to sink each time that I look at it. It is only for a time, I suppose, but it makes a great difference in the way that we look at the world—whether we are ourselves happy or despondent . . ."

YOUNG COTTY FOUND NO COMFORT, in his despondency, in his family's religious tradition, the "corpse-cold" creed, as Emerson called it, of New England Unitarianism. But in England he had felt the appeal, at Cheltenham and in Cambridge, of Anglicanism, and one day, despairing of State Street, he went over to Trinity Church in Copley Square to seek the counsel of the Right Reverend Phillips Brooks. A physical giant of a man, Brooks was one of the foremost preachers of the day, and the pews of Trinity Church, recently rebuilt in the Romanesque style by Henry Hobson Richardson, were crowded with well-to-do Unitarians and Congregationalists seeking a richer liturgical experience than their own creeds supplied. WASPs were born, in part, in a rebellion against New England prose, and many Proper Bostonians were persuaded by Brooks's pulpit eloquence—it was at least as garish as Richardson's arches—to embrace the Protestant Episcopal Church, the American goddaughter of the Church of England.* Cotty Peabody was one of the converts. "I turned to Phillips Brooks," he wrote, "as many a young man had done before in his attempt to find out what God intended for his life. He decided me to give up business and enlist for the work to which I believed I had been called."

And so Cotty left Lee, Higginson to enter the Episcopal Theological School in Cambridge and to be ordained a priest in the Protestant Episcopal Church. Yet he had little interest in dogma or doctrine. Christ for him was an agent of the regeneration of souls. By serving Christ one could hope, he said, "to do some good in the world." But *could* one do good in the world? All his life Peabody seemed the most confident of men, a stranger to anguish, "a dominant and dominating personality." But the habit of the stiff upper lip, inculcated both in his Salem boyhood and his English youth, was strong, and beneath the commanding exterior there was a good deal of uncertainty and self-reproach. At times he was sure that he could bring the light of Christ to others, "then at other times there seems to be an impenetrable cloud with no light behind it. It

---

* In his novel *Esther*, Henry Adams portrayed Brooks, who was his second cousin, as Stephen Hazard, an archaic and spiritually unsatisfactory dogmatist. Yet Santayana maintained that Brooks's Anglicanism "was not really backsliding towards superstition, as Old Boston might think; everybody knew that Bishop Brooks was as liberal as any Unitarian, only nicer . . ."

is good for one, I suppose, if one can only look at it in the right way. I fear I do not at times. Indifferent at other times, almost without faith, I seem to be as far away from a Christian patience and true love for the Master as ever. . . . But I must not go on in this way."

It came to his attention that in Tombstone, Arizona Territory, the little Episcopal parish was in need of a pastor. The gunfight at the O.K. Corral had taken place not long before, and the town was said to be "the rottenest place you ever saw." Peabody accepted the call. Although he spent less than a year in Tombstone, his pastorate was a success. The son of Salem and Cheltenham and Trinity College won over the rough town, with its cowboys and desperados. It was said that a gang of "hoodlums, thinking to cow the eastern tenderfoot," threatened to "ride him out of town on a rail." But something in "Peabody's steady gaze, his huge hands and massive frame," made them think better of it. The *Tombstone Epitaph* was impressed: "Well, we've got a parson who doesn't flirt with the girls, who doesn't drink beer behind the door, and when it comes to baseball, he's a daisy."

Peabody himself would later dismiss tales of his vanquishing bandits as "largely legendary." But his actual achievement was creditable. He oversaw the construction of a church, the first Episcopalian one in Arizona, and he organized a baseball team as an alternative to more vicious recreations. And he ministered to the downcast and the outcast, to all who were poor in spirit. Yet he felt himself a failure. "I am feeling somewhat blue and depressed to-night and am going to vent it upon you," he wrote to a friend in the East. At the Lenten service "I did very poorly indeed. . . . I tried to lecture on St. Paul. I had intended to speak without my notes as much as possible, but I saw one or two of the people closing their eyes, evidently on slumber bent. . . . I may be, in fact I think I am, over-sensitive in such matters, but little things—such as a person smiling or going off for a snooze—put a complete damper on me . . . I do not accomplish anything like as much as I ought. At 1:30 I feel blue and homesick generally . . ."

He went back to Massachusetts in doubt as to whether he had any gift for pastoral work. "It is a grand gift," he said, "that of being able to bring people out and inspiring them with confidence in one's sympathy." But did he possess it? In the midst of these doubts he was called to St. Mark's School, an Episcopal boys' school in Southborough, Massachusetts, to preach during Holy Week. He loved being back in a school and had some hope that he might be appointed headmaster. But the headmastership went to a Mr. Peck, who was not even a man of the cloth.

Cotty Peabody would have to make a school of his own.

IT WOULD NOT BE JUST any school. It is sometimes said that Peabody sought to create, in Massachusetts, an American version of Eton or Harrow, schools that had for centuries educated the English upper classes. But although Peabody had been happy at Cheltenham and admired Dr. Thomas Arnold's work as a reformer at Rugby, he later said that the English schools taught him mostly what *not* to do.

To do any real good, he believed, a school had to get at the soul of a boy, and to do this it must be much smaller than Rugby or Eton, not more than fifty or a hundred boys. There must, too, be fewer barriers between masters and pupils than was the case in the English public schools. In the school he intended to found, teachers and students would "live together, work together, and play together in friendly fashion with friction rare."

It was a novel, even a revolutionary idea. Arnold of Rugby had, indeed, tried to merge the master in the friend, for it was only as a friend that a master could look into the "inner heart" of a boy and find out what he really needed. But in practice, the English iconoclast Lytton Strachey observed, Arnold "ruled remotely." His appearances in the lower forms "were rare and transitory." The older boys saw "more of him, but they did not see much," and "it would often happen that a boy would leave Rugby without having had any personal communication with him at all." It was much the same at Cheltenham. Peabody remembered how his house master kept his charges at arm's length with "sarcasm" and "satirical remarks."

It would be different in Cotty's school. He would not simply teach boys but *reach* them. He would draw out their hidden potential and send them into the world as a force for good.

WHATEVER HIS INWARD UNCERTAINTIES, PEABODY had the knack of inspiring confidence. He was fair, extraordinarily so, with the kind of looks which that age instinctively trusted. And then he was so earnest; hardly had he resolved to found a school than gifts from fellow WASPs came pouring in. Some gave cash. The Lawrence family, into which three of his siblings married, offered land. Not far from the Lawrence homestead in the town of Groton, thirty-five miles northwest of Boston, was a farm of ninety acres. Cotty went out to see it one day in June 1883. He was in one of his funks, confessing to a friend that he was "far from God" and utterly alone. But his mood soon brightened. "Mrs. Lawrence drove me to a spot which has been selected for 'the School' and surely a fairer place one seldom sees. It is a large plateau overlooking a glorious valley with great hills and mountains beyond. It would do good to live there and it would surely be a fine thing for boys to grow up amid such scenery." Frederick Law Olmsted, the landscape architect, was induced to go out and see the site: he pronounced it good.

A board of trustees was rapidly formed. Phillips Brooks consented to be its president, and J. P. Morgan lent it the prestige of his name. It is not easy to know what motives induced Morgan and the other millionaire trustees, all of whom were doing quite well out of the Gilded Age, to back a reformist school, but back it they did, and early in 1884 the announcement went out over their names.

"It is our purpose to open a School for Boys next autumn at Groton, Massachusetts . . ."

Venice strengthened Isabella Stewart Gardner's desire "to show Boston what it was missing."

SIX

Mrs. Jack Seeks
a Humanized Society

speranza cionca . . .

crippled hope . . .
—Dante, *Inferno*

The "secret of her perpetual youth," Bernard Berenson said of Isabella Stewart Gardner, "is that she is a vampire and feeds on one young person after another." He first encountered this "wily old Circe" as a student at Harvard, probably after one of Charles Eliot Norton's lectures. She, for her part, was intrigued by the exotic creature Harvard nobs looked down upon as a "Polish

Jew" with "brash and pushy" manners. (Berenson had been born in Lithuania.) Here, she thought, was a young genius whom she might take up, encourage, and in due course suck dry.

She subscribed to a fund to send Berenson to Europe, but was disappointed by his want of application. The young man seemed to do little in his travels but compose letters and loiter in museums. She would not subsidize dilettantism, and writing him down as a bad debt she broke off communication. He, for his part, deplored her want of sympathy; her "egotism" and "monstrous vanity" made her impatient of anyone who was not immediately serviceable to her. Did she not see what he was up to? And yet it was not easy for him to say just what he *was* up to. He hardly dared confess even to himself the extent of his ambitions at this period in his life. He wanted to be a universal man after the fashion of the Renaissance, a second Goethe, the reviver of the humane traditions of Weimar and Florence. He resented the brusqueness of his patroness, who in her American hurry would have cracked the whip on Leonardo himself. Yet for all that, Mrs. Jack's was "the biggest and deepest and most fascinating nature" he had yet encountered. Her aspirations were in their own way lofty; as much as John Jay Chapman and the young Henry Adams, she was a WASP patriot who wanted to perfect America, or at any rate so much of it as came within her ken.

"I am not as stupid as you think I am," she told Berenson. She had been educating herself. She had learned, from Professor Norton, that other civilizations might in certain respects have surpassed that of Boston, and in Venice she had discovered that the last enchantment of the Middle Age was real. Her heart, she confided to Berenson, ached for the island city, and she and Mr. Jack went there regularly, taking rooms of "gloomy opulence" in the Palazzo Barbaro, "upholstered with every comfort."* The marble, the velvet, the gilt gesso, the hot light of the balconies, delicately suspended above the canal—the palazzo was nothing to be sneezed at. But it was not the grandeur of the Venetian palace alone that spoke to Mrs. Jack: so also did the artistry of the Venetian squares and the gospel preached in the Venetian churches. Mrs. Gardner was herself a churchgoing Episcopalian, one who washed the steps of Boston's Church of the Advent with palm fronds on Maundy Thursday. But what was still medieval in Venice exceeded, in spiritual depth and powers of social

---

* It figures, in Henry James's novel *The Wings of the Dove*, as the Palazzo Leporelli, the "great gilded shell" in which Milly Theale dies.

cohesion, anything conceived of in Anglo-Catholic Boston. The beauty of the city strengthened her vocation, in her friend Professor Santayana's words, "to show Boston what it was missing."

Much like the tycoon Adam Verver in James's *The Wings of the Dove*, Mrs. Gardner wanted to bring to the New World the artistic and spiritual fruits of the Old. (Art and spirit were for late nineteenth-century minds closely related: in the philosophy of Mr. Ruskin, art proceeded from faith, while in the theory of Professor Santayana, faith was an illusion contrived by art, "literally false but poetically true.") Mrs. Jack was not a philosopher, but she had recently inherited more than a million dollars from her father, and she and Mr. Jack had begun to acquire paintings with the idea of eventually creating a museum in Boston, rather as James's Verver seeks to establish a "collection" for the edification of his own hometown. The idea of museum building was in the air, a potential cure, WASPs believed, for America's cultural maladies. (Art as a means of regeneration.) New York's Metropolitan Museum of Art had been founded in 1870 with the help of WASPs like Howard Potter, the Brown Brothers banker; Martin Brimmer, the uncle of John Jay Chapman's girlfriend Minna Timmins, was busy building up Boston's newly established Museum of Fine Arts.

Mrs. Gardner was as yet a beginner, just starting on her quest to bring artistic and spiritual enlightenment to her native country. She was working to master the principles of acquisition when she received from Berenson a book he had recently published called *The Venetian Painters of the Renaissance*. Her protégé had been busier than he seemed. He had gone to school to Walter Pater, the oracle of Victorian aestheticism, and he knew Pater's book *The Renaissance*, he told Mrs. Gardner, "almost by heart." Many a midnight he would on coming home take up the book, "and meaning to glance only at a passage here or there, would read it cover to cover." Pater urged young aesthetes to pursue beauty "not in the most abstract, but in the most concrete" way, to find not a universal formula for it, but the formula that expresses "most adequately this or that special manifestation of it." In studying the Venetian masters, Berenson followed Pater's advice. He sought to isolate the "special manifestation" of beauty unique to each painter, the qualities which distinguished it from that of all others.

Berenson learned something, too, from the Italian connoisseur Giovanni Morelli, who taught him to pay attention to the most apparently mundane details when studying a painting, a method that led Charles Eliot Norton to denounce the "ear and toe-nail school" of art criticism. But if Berenson's techniques showed a healthy respect for the quotidian, they also grew out of ideas concerning the power of painting over the imagination that owed something to Goethe, Nietzsche, and his own libido. A great master, Berenson believed, created the illusion that his two-dimensional surface was in fact three-dimensional by making the beholder feel as though he could actually touch and grasp the things portrayed. When we behold an image of Giotto's, he wrote, "our palms and fingers accompany our eyes . . ." In the same way the flesh of Botticelli's goddess in *The Birth of Venus* seems to us really caressible: "the tactile imagination is roused to a keen activity, by itself almost as life-heightening as music," for the nude figure is "the best vehicle for all that in art which is directly life-confirming and life-enhancing."

Berenson knew another moment of illumination when, sitting in a café at Bergamo in northern Italy, he vowed to authenticate the work of the sixteenth-century painter Lorenzo Lotto. Going about Lombardy with the fervor, he said, of a "medieval pilgrim," he made his way to remote villages where "there was often nothing to eat but hard bread, onions and anchovies," and refused to stop until he was "sure that every Lotto *is* a Lotto." He had "no thought of reward," but the work undertaken as a labor of love proved immensely lucrative. The slum child who had once to sing for his supper was soon the master of techniques which, by exposing the doubtful attributions of earlier connoisseurs, made him valuable to the new plutocracy. Bankers and industrialists turned to him for assurance that the Old Master for which they were to pay a king's ransom really *was* an Old Master, not the work of some less vendible name. (No one wanted to make the mistake of poor Louisine Havemeyer, of American Sugar Refining Company money, who came back from Europe with a boatful of bogus Titians.) Naturally the tycoons paid Berenson handsomely for his trouble: and the votary of art condescended to take his place among the brokers of paintings. It was, at least, a not uncomfortable place, as the Villa I Tatti, Berenson's headquarters in Fiesole, sufficiently proves.

"HOW MUCH," BERENSON WROTE TO Mrs. Jack in August 1894, "do you want a Botticelli? Lord Ashburnham has a great one—one of the greatest: a death of Lucretia. . . . I understand that although the noble lord is not keen about selling it a handsome offer would not insult him. I should think it would have to be about three thousand pounds . . ." Berenson would later call the encounter that led to his collaboration with Mrs. Jack a "fatal moment" of mutual temptation. She would help to make him one of the richest art authenticators of his time; he would minister to her desire for cultural influence and aesthetic supremacy. One after another the canvases came to Beacon Street, a Rembrandt, a Guardi, a Titian, a Giorgione, a Velasquez, a Van Dyck, a Rubens, a Raphael, a Giotto—the "picture-habit," Mrs. Gardner remarked, "is as bad as the morphine or whiskey one . . ."

The relationship between the collector and her mystagogue was not without difficulties. Mr. Jack suspected that Berenson was not entirely scrupulous in money dealings with his wife, and when she wrote to Fiesole to tell her friend that there "is a terrible row about you. . . . vile things have been said to Mr. Gardner," Berenson was reported to have been "almost suicidal" with remorse, and perhaps also with fear of the loss of future commissions. But Mr. Jack expired of a stroke of apoplexy soon after the alleged improprieties came to light, and although Mrs. Jack was herself sufficiently annoyed with her friend to threaten a lawsuit—Berenson's "mendacity," Santayana said, "is too abundant to deceive"—they patched things up and continued their collaboration. "We may between us have made one or two mistakes," Berenson wrote to her in 1907, "but we have brought together masterpieces of a beauty, of a splendor, and of a harmony, that nothing in the last twenty years can touch."

Mrs. Gardner and "B. B.," as Berenson's friends called him, were pioneers in the WASP effort to realize humane ideals through art and the building up of museums, institutions which, in an age when conventional religion was losing its mystique, came to resemble holy shrines. But Mrs. Gardner's collecting would leave a number of WASP reformers unsatisfied. Not so much because it was intimately connected to her love of luxury. An opulence such as hers will, no doubt, always appear tawdry beside true purity of spirit. But those who know their own souls to be sufficiently vile will cheerfully acquiesce in any expedient that might give our days a dignity they do not naturally possess. No, Mrs. Gardner's detractors did not grudge her those harmless elegances—fabrics, cuisines, purloined paintings—which might disguise, if they could not abolish, whatever was unsatisfactory in herself. The problem, for a new generation of reformers, was that she did not carry her passion for form far enough, that she stopped at the dress shop, the dinner party, and the picture gallery: hardly the program of a true regenerator. Her work fell short of her own Venetian ideal, and of Berenson's desire, hardly less quixotic than Henry Adams's, to revive humane forums in which "poetry, music, ritual, the visual arts, the theatre" might cooperate "to create the most comprehensive art of all, a humanized society . . ."

"There was fire in everything I touched, the fire of the activity of
that part of me which was meant to be used . . ."

SEVEN

The Lost Hand of
John Jay Chapman

Non è sanza cagion l'andare al cupo . . .

His going into darkness is not without reason . . .
—Dante, *Inferno*

They were searching for something.

Twenty-three-year-old Vida Scudder, born in India to Congregation-
alist missionaries from New England, went to Oxford in her quest for purpose,
and to the lectures of Mr. Ruskin, who was then the Slade Professor of Art.
Her eyes were opened to what Mr. Ruskin conceived to be the ugliness and

selfishness of the age, and she came away believing that if one were to obtain one's Grail, one must be willing to make sacrifices for it. One might even have to suffer.

To more commonsensical minds, such thinking was morbid, but to WASPs like Vida Scudder and John Jay Chapman, it was necessary wisdom. Chapman was at this time a student at Harvard, absorbing Dante's idea that if you want to see the stars you must first go through hell. He would cross the river from Cambridge and meet his girlfriend, Minna Timmins, in a little-used room at the top of the Athenæum, the private library in Beacon Street, where they would read the *Divine Comedy* together.

His mental state was troubled. No sooner would he enter a room than he would find the air "full of voices, demons." It seemed to him that he could hear "angels speak and struggle in people's hearts." As he went through Dante with Minna, he sensed that she, too, was suffering. The daughter of an American father and an Italian mother, she "was tall, dark, athletic with a freedom of limb and motion that is not found north of the Alps—a spiritual vigor that seemed allied to Michael Angelo's Sibyls." He concluded, wrongly, that a mutual acquaintance of theirs, Percival Lowell,* was trifling with her affections. When he encountered Lowell at a party in Brookline, he asked him "to step on the lawn, and there I beat him with a stick—whence procured I don't know—about the head and shoulders."

His next memory was of going back alone to his "small, dark, horrid little room" in Cambridge. A coal fire was burning. "I took off my coat and waistcoat, wrapped a pair of suspenders tightly on my left forearm above the wrist, plunged the left hand deep in the blaze and held it down with my right hand for some minutes. . . ." When, afterward, he examined the result, he said to himself, "This will never do."

He wrapped his hand up in a coat and started for Boston in one of the horse-drawn streetcars. "On arriving at the Massachusetts General Hospital I showed the trouble to a surgeon, was put under ether, and the next morning waked up

---

* He was the brother of the Imagist poet Amy Lowell and of A. Lawrence Lowell, the future president of Harvard. A student of Japan and the Far East, Lowell was also an astronomer who was later known for his theory of intelligent life on Mars, a conceit that inspired H. G. Wells's 1898 novel *The War of the Worlds*. What Lowell took to be irregularities in the orbits of Uranus and Neptune led him to propose another mistaken theory, that the supposed discrepancies were caused by an as yet unperceived Planet X.

without the hand and very calm in spirits." He told himself there was "nothing diabolical or insane or inhuman" in what he had done. There was rather "something Promethean in it." The fire he stole from the gods had burnt him, but now it lived in him. "There was fire in everything I touched, the fire of the activity of that part of me which was meant to be used . . ."

BUT USED FOR WHAT? CHAPMAN was conscious of his descent from John Jay, the revolutionary patriot and first chief justice of the United States, and in searching for purpose he thought to emulate his ancestor's life of public virtue. He had before him, too, the example of the Roman hero Mucius Scaevola, who had thrust his own hand into the fire to demonstrate his devotion to the Roman Republic. Such a sacrifice, Scaevola showed, could be an act of patriotic consecration.

But was it not also a crippling wound? A highly developed civic conscience, in the Gilded Age, was more often than not an impediment to success. Chapman had had, at Harvard, the old liberal education that equips one to contribute to one's city or country. But in the America of Chapman's youth, such an education, Edmund Wilson observed, was likely to be a "troublesome handicap." The "all-around humanism" and civic commitment it inculcated had played a part in the founding of the American Republic, but in Chapman's time its value was at best equivocal. The "period after the Civil War—both banal in a bourgeois way and fantastic with gigantic fortunes—was a difficult one for Americans brought up in the old tradition," Wilson wrote. The classical education they had been given and the "kind of ideals it served no longer really counted for much." Those who "had taken it seriously were launched on careers of tragic misunderstanding," and the "rate of failure and insanity and suicide in some of the colleges classes of the 'eighties shows an appalling demoralization."

Yet Chapman insisted, with the same obstinacy with which he had held his hand to the flame, that this humane education was the best remedy for what was unsatisfactory in American life. He questioned the wisdom of Harvard's president, Charles W. Eliot, who, he believed, was sacrificing the liberal arts tradition of Harvard College on the altar of the research and professional school university he was building. Eliot, Chapman said, had "a Puritan dread of the humanities." There was "about as much love of learning" in him "as there was in Jay Gould." His policy was "to make Harvard large and well known," a "place where everything was taught," and under his regime the "little sprouts and spears of true university life that had slowly and painfully taken root about Harvard Square during two hundred years" were one by one being pulled up.*

Chapman disliked especially Eliot's habit of dismissing professors with a gift for teaching in order to promote specialists. Instructors were "being picked out *because* of their unenthusiasm" as teachers. Eliot's ideal was the research specialist for whom teaching was a chore; Chapman's ideal was William James, a giant in several fields who was at the same time a true teacher, one whom you could talk to as you would a friend. "I confess to having always trespassed upon him and treated him with impertinence, without gloves, without reserve," Chapman said. Yet James not only bore it but loved it, his replies suffused with "the most spontaneous and celestial gayety," for "his humor was as penetrating as his seriousness."† "Come, let us gossip about the universe," he would say, as though the world were a Beacon Hill lady caught in assignations or a Harvard don fallen into drink. Still for all his playfulness there was, Chapman saw, "a deep sadness about James," and this, too, was instructive for young WASPs who knew themselves to be neurotic basket cases. As he strode about the Harvard Yard, James, the chronically sick soul who had felt "a horrible fear" of his own existence, showed that one could be a productive neurasthenic.

Chapman was convinced that President Eliot's reforms were undermining the informal, out-of-the-lecture-hall teaching that James, like Socrates before him, practiced. There was growing up "a tacit understanding at Harvard that social intercourse between the faculty and the students was bad form," and when Louis Dyer, a professor of Greek who had been influenced by his experience of Oxford, ventured to give smoking parties in his rooms, "they soon stamped him out." Yet an older tradition lingered, and a few teachers remained who were, like James, "domestic and approachable." Chapman parodied the plummy, over-cultivated speech of Charles Eliot Norton ("I purpose this afternoon to make a few remarks on the hor-ri-ble vul-gar-ity of EVERYTHING . . ."). Yet Norton was, Chapman said, "a man of remarkable force, of remarkable goodness, of

---

* Professor Santayana agreed with Chapman's assessment: universities reformed on the Harvard model, he wrote, had little "to do with *education*, with the transmission of a particular moral and intellectual tradition." The teacher was no longer a mentor "with his hand on a lad's shoulder," and was instead "an expert in some science, delivering lectures for public instruction . . ."

† Chapman did not exaggerate, if the testimony of another of James's students may be credited. To Learned Hand, James was "a living angel. . . . descended from whatever powers there are that make this planet a decent place."

untiring public spirit." He had the old pastoral instincts; he cared about his students. So, too, did George Herbert Palmer, a kindly, holy, gloomy man. When someone observed that he taught Greek, he shook his head. "You are mistaken. I do not teach Greek. I teach boys. Greek is what I start with." Palmer "used to give readings from his translations of the *Odyssey*," Chapman said, "in a lyrical falsetto monotone that suggested the peculiar limbo of moral feeling which foreshadows suicide." But he knew his scholars in the college and kept them in sight after they left it.

WHILE STILL IN THE HOSPITAL, Chapman was visited by Dr. Reginald Heber Fitz, the well-known physician, who asked him whether he was sane. "That is for you to find out," Chapman replied. The doctor reported him as sane, and after he was discharged he was taken in by Judge Oliver Wendell Holmes and his wife Fanny, in whose house he convalesced and began his "struggle toward something like reality."

Minna herself loved him as much as she had ever done. "Oh, you, most beloved," she exclaimed as though she had emerged from a page of Swinburne. "*Yours*, yours, I am. You bought me with the soul of fire, the blood of your flesh—I am your wife now." He went to old Mr. Brimmer, Minna's uncle and guardian, to ask for her hand. With a good deal of reluctance Mr. Brimmer consented to an engagement, but he insisted that no marriage take place for at least a year. He hoped that in the interval his niece would forget this most "unfortunate young man."

Who could blame him? Dr. Heber Fitz had reported Chapman as sane, but his sanity was of the sort that comes near to madness, and even sympathetic observers thought his condition "hardly other than pathological." His visions, so far as he was concerned, were true, and he refused to give them up even though the world thought them strange and morbid. He was still very much under the influence of Dante, and to take Dante as a guide to life in the America of railways and petroleum trusts was to invite suspicions of lunacy.

Chapman was drawn to Dante not simply because his was a poetic reworking of a despair he felt in himself, but because his work was full of practical hints for the better ordering of life. Dante described the Florence of his youth as humane in scale, a "fair sheepfold" where as a young lamb he had been mentored by teachers like Brunetto Latini, who helped him to become not only a poet but also a citizen. Such humane centers fostered a range of interconnection among citizens that was impossible in larger units. It was, Chapman saw, the key to their educative power, their ability, as a scholar of humane education has written, to release the powers of a "young soul, breaking down the restraints which hampered it, and leading it into a glad activity . . ."

As institutions like Harvard ceased to be communities devoted to the pastoral care of their charges, as they became immense machinelike institutions with little human warmth, they would, Chapman believed, cease to develop the powers of their students. They would be unable to produce leaders who might make American civilization something more than the gigantic railway station he thought it threatened to become.

No doubt it was foolhardy for a young man to go out into the world intent, as "mad Jack" was, on doing battle for a handful of notions derived from Dante. But he had the strength of his mutilation. The stump that remained preserved the memory of a defiance that would carry him through the trials he was to endure.

Cotty and Fannie Peabody. The "principle which underlies the whole system of the school is the principle of love."

EIGHT

A Glorious and Most Intensely Interesting Life

Incipit vita nova . . .

Here begins a new life . . .
—Dante, *La Vita Nuova*

Why they came to Cotty Peabody's school is a bit of a mystery.

There was little Harry Payne Whitney, the son of Williams Collins Whitney, one of the more ambiguous figures of the Gilded Age, a man who had chucked reform to become a "traction" magnate, making a pile through dubious dealings in streetcars. Not that he needed the money; his wife, Flora

Payne, the daughter of one of the richest families in Ohio, was rolling in it. But Whitney had been seduced by the very culture he sought to redeem, and was now devoting himself to the acquisition of palatial houses, vast estates, stables full of thoroughbred horses. Throwing away "the usual objects of political ambition like the ashes of smoked cigarettes," he was bent, Henry Adams said, on satiating every taste, gorging every appetite, "until New York no longer knew what most to envy, his horses or his houses."

There was Pierre "Pete" Jay, the great-great-grandson of John Jay and cousin of "mad Jack" Chapman, a future Federal Reserve official whom Peabody was to pronounce the "most perfect gentleman" he ever knew, and there were Henry Adams's nephews, Henry and John, sons of his brother Charles, the Civil War soldier and Union Pacific executive. There was Ellery Sedgwick, a scion of the Sedgwicks of Stockbridge, the family that produced Edie, and there was Warwick Potter, a young scholar of "a very attractive and winning personality" who was to win the heart of the philosopher George Santayana.

The parents of these boys were taking a risk in sending them to Groton. The school was new and its three young masters untried. Endicott Peabody was twenty-seven; Sherrard Billings, a friend of Peabody's from the seminary, was twenty-six; and William Amory Gardner, Peabody's cousin, was just twenty-one. None had done much teaching. But the trustees had been astute in the announcement they sent to prospective parents. "Every endeavor," they wrote, "will be made to cultivate manly, Christian character, having regard to moral and physical as well as intellectual development." The idea of muscular Christianity was in the air; parents fretted that their boys were growing up to be spoiled, neurasthenic weaklings, without what Thomas Hughes, the Rugby graduate and author of *Tom Brown's School Days*, called "vigor and manliness of character." "The whole generation is womanized," says Basil Ransom in Henry James's novel *The Bostonians*, "the masculine tone is passing out of the world; it's a feminine, a nervous, hysterical, chattering, canting age, an age of hollow phrases and false delicacy and exaggerated solicitudes and coddled sensibilities."

Henry's brother William would later explain the psychological rationale for muscular Christianity and institutions which, like Groton, embraced it. They grew, he said, out of a nineteenth-century cult of healthy-mindedness, one that sought to "cure" the soul of weakness and purify it of "doubt, fear, worry, and all nervously precautionary states of mind" by altering a person's way of thinking. Thus football was not, for Endicott Peabody, merely a game: it was a means of effacing, in the mind of a boy, neurotic fearfulness, that "mark of the beast," and cultivating in its place courage, physical and mental toughness, an over-richness of will. A spartan way of life supplemented the rigors of athletic discipline: at Groton the boys took cold showers and slept in bare cubicles that inured them to discomfort.

Peabody believed in his program because he had lived it. Although he prudently refrained from advertising his own neurasthenic struggles—to all but a few confidants he seemed the embodiment of sanity and masculine strength—he had found from personal experience that the best cure for soul-sickness was a regimen of strenuous living. To parents who dreaded the appearance, in their boys, of any sign of neurasthenic "effeminacy," Peabody's methods of cultivating manly character were reassuring, and persuaded at least a few of them to take a chance on an institution that was to play a part in the evolution of the nineteenth-century Brahmin into the twentieth-century WASP.

Yet it is easy to make too much of muscular Christianity at Groton. Peabody did, indeed, think exertion good for boys, an antidote to a civilization that was breeding too many soft, self-indulgent little men. But it was not an austere and athletic hygiene alone that made his school different from other schools.

GROTON SCHOOL OPENED IN OCTOBER 1884 with two dozen boys. Brooks House, the original building, was designed by the Boston architects Peabody & Stearns in what has been described as a Kentish Manor style, though it seems to have owed more to the Red House of William Morris and Philip Webb. It stood in a high meadow with apple trees to the south; to the west lay the valley of the Nashua and beyond it, the peaks of Wachusett and Monadnock, with their scenery of high clouds and fiery sunsets.

The "family idea," as it was called at Groton, was paramount. The whole school slept under one roof, worshipped together, studied together, and took meals together at three tables in the dining hall. The intimacy between students and teachers was strengthened both by the closeness of their ages and their quarters. Photographs show the whole lot of them, a rather ragamuffin bunch, sitting on the front steps or playing scrub in rolled shirtsleeves on a sunlit field waving with tall grasses.

They became friends. Walter Hinchman, an early Groton master, said that Peabody "was the first to make friendship between masters and boys a natural, accepted fact—a condition now taken for granted in most schools, but almost unknown" in the nineteenth century. "There was an intimacy at the heart of things that was peculiar to the genius of the place," one graduate wrote. George Santayana sensed it in Warwick Potter, whom he taught at Harvard. "Warwick and his brothers," he wrote, were "among the very first pupils of Mr. Peabody, so that they received the fresh imprint of all those high and amiable intentions, and all that personal paternal care and spiritual guidance which it was Mr. Peabody's ideal to supply."

The young George Rublee, in later life a Progressive-era reforming lawyer, would be grateful for that care and guidance. A Wisconsin native who had spent much of his boyhood abroad, he went first to Exeter, where he "became discouraged" and "stopped studying." His alarmed father consulted Harvard's Charles Eliot, who advised him to send the boy to the new school at Groton as a "sort of last chance." At Groton Rublee found something entirely different from anything he had known before, "truly a common life, like that of a large family each member of which seeks to help the other." The "controlling principle which underlies the whole system of the school," he afterward wrote, "is the principle of love." When, in Rublee's second year, Peabody brought his bride, Fannie, to Groton, the family idea was complete. The young headmaster rejoiced in the life of his school, "a glorious and most intensely interesting life, and one for which we may feel thankful that God has allowed us to take part in."

THERE WAS NO RIGID DISCIPLINE in those days. Amory Gardner, whose gentleness was apt to be taken advantage of, was forced, indeed, to devise a punishment called the "black mark" to keep order in study hall, but the presence of Mr. Peabody, or the Rector, as he was soon called, was generally enough to keep the boys in line. Out of doors you could do anything to him, Ellery Sedgwick remembered, short of pelting him with snowballs. But in his study it was a different matter. "To be alone there, on instant summons, with your heart open and no desires hid, was like cramming for the Last Day." The Rector put the fear of God in the boys, but as one of them said, "I have never known a more tender-hearted man or one with a greater fund of natural sympathy. . . . I loved him as I have loved few men, but I was always a little afraid of him."

The life of those early days is mostly irrecoverable now. Memories were handed down of Sunday walks, study fires, football scrimmages, of the first warm days of the spring and of Mr. Gardner lounging in his canoe on the river, a cigarette dangling from his mouth and a volume of Sophocles in his hand. Others remembered the winters, the snowshoe walks over the hills, the skating and "coasting" over the snow. "I remember walking with the Rector over the hills beyond Groton," one boy recalled, and coming back from coasting on Joy's Hill with the "whole top of Wachusett . . . a flame of gold." Still another remembered Sunday afternoons in the chapel, the sun streaming through the painted windows, and the Rector's pleading voice. "Keep innocency, for that will give a man peace at the last . . ."

IT WAS INTENSELY A COMMUNITY. The school was soon to have the reputation of being exclusive, but its atmosphere was not snobbish. Whatever splendor individual boys knew at home, at Groton they all lived the same spartan life, and during a Massachusetts winter personality and a sense of humor counted for a good deal more than phantom riches. Nor were all the boys rich. "Pierpont Morgan was President of the Board of Trustees," Ellery Sedgwick wrote, "and there were a number of boys whose mothers' names appeared regularly in the social column of the *New York Herald*, but I am mistaken if term bills were not of major concern to at least half the parents."

The older boys assisted in keeping up this diminutive Sparta. They were at first known as Paddocks, superior beings whose summons could not safely be ignored. (The school had been reading *Macbeth* and had been struck by the line, "Paddock calls . . .") In time the Paddocks evolved into prefects on the English model. Lytton Strachey mocked the prefectorial system as promoting the "oligarchy of a dozen youths of seventeen." But Cotty Peabody saw its educational value. When the "older and more positive leaders are given the responsibility and the authority of masters," he wrote, they "generally play up to it satisfactorily." If, as Richard Hofstadter remarked, Groton became a "little Greek democracy of the elite," it was so in part because the students had a chance to play at Solon or Pericles.

THE TROUBLE BEGAN WHEN ONE of the boys, forsaking Pericles, took up the part of Alcibiades. The school had found strong leaders in its first senior prefects. The slacker George Rublee had become a success, the star of the school, and Howard Cushing, who would go on to be a noted painter, ruled with tact and good humor. Their loss was much felt when school resumed in September 1887. After Christmas everyone settled down to a contented and prosperous condition, but in the spring there was a falling off. Edward Perkins Carter, who had succeeded Cushing as senior prefect, returned from the spring break considerably after its scheduled date, having been, it was said, "to see a girl." The Rector demoted him, making Pierre Jay senior prefect. Carter, embittered, persuaded a number of his mates to form secret clubs in opposition to the school, and together they went off surreptitiously to build huts in the woods.

The Rector expelled Ed Carter, reporting to the trustees that the boy had "become opposed to the school" and done "much to thwart its purpose." But it was likely only in the summer, when he was told of the secret clubs, that Peabody learned of the attempt to introduce the English practice of "fagging" at Groton, with Warwick Potter being made a "fag" or body servant, charged with waiting on older boys as was done in schools like Eton and Harrow. (Warwick's nicknames at Groton were "the Biddy," a word for a female servant, and "Miss Ryan," a name the boys would have associated with young serving women.)* Peabody was incensed that his fellow masters, Amory Gardner and Sherrard Billings, had not told him the extent of the misbehavior as soon as they learned of it. "I daresay you kept it back through kindness," he wrote to Gardner from Kernwood, his boyhood home in Salem, but "fact is the only basis on which we can work, and it is better that I should suffer if I can do good to the school than that I should be living in a fool's paradise."

On long walks that summer or sailing the stretch of sea from Beverly Harbor, north of Boston, to Marblehead, Peabody reflected on the prefect revolt of the spring. Why had the masters "received opposition rather than assistance from those whom we looked upon as our natural allies"? Evidently the "influence of boys upon one another was even greater than I expected," he told the trustees: "even a very weak boy can do much harm if he is started in the wrong direction." Yet it was not enough, he believed, simply to give a boy like Ed Carter the chuck. What was needed was a greater spirit of discipline. The family idea, valuable as it was, was in some respects naïve. A tiny school—as late as 1888 Groton enrolled fewer than fifty WASPs—could never have the kind of order that was possible in a larger, more regimented institution, or so Cotty Peabody came to believe. We "have to keep up the same spirit of friendship and love," he told Amory Gardner, but "a certain amount of formality must exist in order that there may be good discipline."

---

* "The Biddy's been seen to my own certain knowledge/With a beaver, rigged up like a dude at a College . . ." "'Oh, what are the wild waves saying to thee,/Miss Ryan?' I said aloud;/The answer was drowned by a gurgling sound,/As she clung to the quivering shroud. . ." See Mr. Gardner's poems for the school's birthdays in October 1887 and October 1888 in *Groton School Verses*.

His cousin's laxity was, in Peabody's eyes, part of the problem. "I do not wish to convey the idea," he wrote to Gardner, "that I think you skirt your duty to be popular. You are too good a man to do that—but I do think you want to manage boys in your way and not in the school way. . . . This makes it especially hard on the other masters. When they censure boys or punish them a very common remark is, 'Mr. Gardner wouldn't do that.'" The difficulty, Peabody said, was that his brilliant young colleague did not, in spite of his summa cum laude degree from Harvard, "appreciate sufficiently the existence of sinfulness in boys. . . . They are very imitative and will do everything they see you do . . . and will always go a good bit further than you. I have noticed this in the parlor where I have seen the boys lying at almost full length by the side of you on the sofa. And I am sure that it must stand in the way of your keeping order in class."

Of course the "boys are better for your presence as is every one of us at Groton," Cotty reassured his cousin. But he left little doubt that the school would have to change. "We began this work together and are going on with the same spirit, but there must be different manifestations of that spirit as the changes come. To learn how to accommodate ourselves to the new growth and to meet the many different questions which come before us in the right way is the ever present problem of those who are trying to do what they can to make the world in any way better."

AMORY GARDNER WAS UNCONVINCED. STILL recovering from the shock, a short time before, of his older brother Joe Jr.'s suicide, he told Cotty that he would of course "try to do better" in matters of discipline, though he did not think he had "done much harm so far, except in matters of tidiness and sitting up straight." But it would be a mistake, he said, "to enlarge the school if *anything* is to damage in the *smallest* degree the most *perfect mutual* confidence and intimacy between masters and boys." How, he asked, could he "conscientiously back up, or *honestly* appear to back up" a policy of expansion "which in my heart I believe to be wrong and fatal?"*

If the Rector was newly consumed by the sinfulness of young WASPs, Amory Gardner continued to dwell on their precarious innocence. They needed mentors, not martinets. He had seen, at Harvard, every variety "of profligate, hypocrite, toady, or egotist that college or the world" could produce, and he was

---

* Gardner subscribed to William James's belief that the "bigger the unit you deal with, the hollower, the more brutal, the more mendacious is the life displayed."

determined to save Groton boys from such fates. "I do so long to keep unspotted the boys," he wrote, "that I am tempted to sacrifice almost every consideration of order, soberness, and discipline to gain my end." A too-severe emphasis on order in a larger school would estrange the boys from their teachers, and already he trembled when he heard one of the new masters, Guy Ayrault, discipline a boy called Cochrane.

"It is because I care so terribly," he told Cotty, "that I say it over and over again. If they learn to hate the school, it will go the way of all other schools and that is far worse than useless. They didn't use to hate. Why should they ever do so? Suppose it is their fault. Is their young soul's tragedy any less tragic? God forgive us if by anything we have done or left undone any boy goes away from this school worse than if he had never come. And yet there will be such boys. I fear they will form the majority when the school is large. They do at most schools. Why not at Groton unless we differ as we do now from any in England or America?"

COTTY PEABODY PREVAILED, AND IN December the trustees announced their intention to enlarge the school "by the addition of a New Dormitory and a School-house, making thereby accommodations for one hundred and fifty boys in all . . ." But his cousin was unreconciled. If masters were to know "a boy's real self," they had to know, not "only the boy, but all his near associates in work time, play time, dinner time, and go-to-bed time," a knowledge that would be difficult if not impossible to acquire in a larger school. The experiment to which he had pledged himself was as radical, in its way, as older New England efforts at the perfect, as Brook Farm or Walden or the Shaker villages. Groton was to be a school that would reach the souls of its students and produce leaders who would change the world. But it now threatened to become only another machinery of corruption.

Lizzie Cameron as a young woman.
Henry Adams felt the Madonna in her.

NINE

The Madonnas of Henry Adams

ché dentro a li occhi suoi ardeva un riso
tal, ch'io pensai co' miei toccar lo fondo
de la mia gloria e del mio paradiso . . .

in the smile that glowed within her eyes
I thought I touched with my own
the depth of my glory and my paradise . . .
—Dante, *Paradiso*

Henry Adams's inquiries into where the American Republic went wrong were interrupted when, on a Sunday morning in December 1885, he went upstairs to find that his wife, Clover, had swallowed potassium cyanide, a compound she used in her wet-plate photography. Clover's name is nowhere to be found in the pages of her husband's memoir, *The Education of Henry Adams*, a silence that gives the impression that her death was the gaping hole in his life, a loss so great he could not speak its name. "Better to have loved and lost than never to have loved at all," Tennyson says. Better still, Adams suggests, never to have uttered the loved one's name again, that her memory might languish undisturbed in some cobwebbed Gothic chamber of the soul like Miss Havisham and her wedding cake, sealed against profane intrusion.

Yet if Adams was in some respects even more zealous than Victoria herself (after the death of Albert) in upholding Victorian conventions of mourning a deceased spouse, he was far from conforming to that staple of Victorian sentiment, the widower who so laments the loss of his first love that he can never love again.[*] For he did love again, and a good deal more intensely the second time. The woman who aroused him most deeply seems to have been not Clover but Lizzie Cameron, the "very dangerously fascinating" niece of the warrior William Tecumseh Sherman. It is only with her that he drops, for a moment, the ironic mask he condemned himself to wear, as a monk might, in a moment of ecstasy, strip off his hair shirt. They first met in January 1881, half a decade before Clover's death, in the Washington drawing room of Adams's best friend John Hay. (Hay had been Lincoln's private secretary and was to be McKinley's and Theodore Roosevelt's secretary of state.) She was twenty to his forty-two—much younger, but just as married, in her case to Senator J. Donald Cameron of Pennsylvania, a hard-faced, hard-drinking public man and railroad tycoon, the son of former secretary of war Simon Cameron, sacked by Lincoln for corruption. Adams fell at Lizzie's feet, and by May 1883 he was writing to tell her how desperately unhappy he was that she was going away to Europe. A year later, following a summer in which he and Clo were "bored to death with ourselves," he wrote brightly to Lizzie that he would dedicate a poem to her and that he would have her "carved over the arch of my stone door-way." But nothing he did or said, he told her, could "fully express the extent to which I am yours." The language was safely ironic, phrased in the accents of medieval courtly love, the idiom of Petrarch and Dante; but the passion was real.

After Clover's death, the question became more pressing. "I want," Adams told her, "more than I can have." Of course she must refuse him: "your position,"

---

[*]   Adams's friend Theodore Roosevelt felt the pull of the ideal. His daughter Alice said that he "obviously felt tremendously guilty about remarrying" after the death of his first wife (Alice's mother) "because of the concept that you only loved once and you never loved again."

he said, "is right enough, and easily held; mine is all wrong and impossible; you are Beauty; I am the Beast . . ." Yet for all that he was not "old enough to be a tame cat," and since she could accept him in no other character, he had little choice but to go away for intervals of monkish penance.

Whenever he drew too close, she held him to his promise. He dutifully took to the road, but found it agony. "I have passed a bad *quart d'heure*," he wrote after one of their partings, "since bidding you good-bye in your Hansom cab across the darkness of Half Moon Street." After another of his dismissals he set off for Polynesia, but no sooner did he reach San Francisco than a "sudden spasm came over me just at the foot of the hotel stairs. . . . I would desperately like to be with you." Again it was hell, but he managed to get "over it with the help of a bottle of champagne and a marvelous dinner . . ."

And so the man who dreamt of reforming his country, of becoming a power in the Republic through revolutions "not only in politics, but in literature, in law, in society," became a wanderer, drifting now in the waters of the Caribbean, now in those of the Pacific and the Indian Ocean. He was sighted at Havana and Tahiti, in Mexico and Ceylon, at Bali and Tokyo, a well-accoutered nomad who wanted "only to sleep forever in the trade-winds under the southern stars."

THE TRANSFORMATION OF HENRY ADAMS from political reformer in the emerging WASP mold into intellectual drifter was accomplished by degrees. Pride and conceit contributed to his failure as a public man. John Jay Chapman thought him one of the Republic's choicer egotists, "combing his golden hair with a gold toothpick in the sunset." (The language was figurative; Adams began to lose his hair early.) Oliver Wendell Holmes concurred. "If the country had put him on a pedestal," he told the novelist Owen Wister, "I think that Henry Adams with his gifts could have rendered distinguished public service. . . . He wanted it handed to him on a silver plate."

Shut out of power himself, he fell to making fun of those who possessed it, and when he was not traveling, he gathered around him, in his house in Washington, at 1603 H Street on Lafayette Square, friends who could share in the joke. His breakfasts, served at half past noon, were modeled on those of his English friend Monckton Milnes. "A word from him went far," he said of Milnes. "An invitation to his breakfast-table went farther." Adams did not issue invitations to his breakfast table: those who knew came, and were encouraged to bring others who could contribute to the fun. Cecil Spring Rice, a young British diplomat who was often in 1603 H Street, delighted in the atmosphere of WASP mischief, describing the Adamses as a family "as odd as can be" who made "a sort of profession of eccentricity."

But more even than laughter, Adams required that closely related thing, friendship, and for this he depended greatly on two of his neighbors in Lafayette Square, John Hay, whose house was next to his own, and Lizzie herself, who lived with her husband, the senator, at 21 Madison Place. The career of Hay had been one of almost unbroken good fortune. Aside from the usual neurasthenic complaints, which he sought to relieve by consulting S. Weir Mitchell, the Philadelphia neurologist, Hay had gone happily from success to success. He was barely out of Brown when he attached himself to the rising star of Abraham Lincoln, and in the White House he and John Nicolay, Lincoln's other secretary, had their desks in what is now the Queen's Sitting Room and their beds in what is now the Queen's Bedroom; Lincoln himself is said to have loved Hay "as a son." (An ambiguous distinction; Lincoln's relations with his own oldest boy, Robert Todd Lincoln, were cool.) Hay was drinking whiskey with Robert Todd when he learned that Lincoln had been shot, and he was among those who watched the president die. Afterward he served in various diplomatic posts and as a writer on the *New-York Tribune* under Horace Greeley and Whitelaw Reid. At thirty-five he married Clara Stone, the daughter of one of the richest men in Ohio; a decade later his *Abraham Lincoln: A History*, a massive literary tombstone written jointly with John Nicolay, made him a celebrity in the world of letters. Yet curiously enough Hay was unspoiled by his good fortune. He had an endearing way about him, and though he was in theory a Social Darwinist who believed that failure was "a judgment on your laziness and vices, or on your improvidence," he went to great pains to help friends who, having courted the "bitch-goddess" of success less effectually than he, had need of his kindness.

Lizzie was for Adams a still fonder attachment. She came often to 1603 H Street with her daughter, little Martha Cameron; sometimes she would send the child alone, and Adams would be the nanny. Through "incessant bribery and attentions"—so many chocolate drops and ginger-snaps—the sage won her over; his study became a nursery, and his desk was transformed into a shop adorned with a sign advertising the services of Mme. Marthe, Modiste. On warm evenings Adams would join Senator and Mrs. Cameron for juleps on their veranda as the music of the old sorrow songs, sung by former slaves, came over Lafayette Square with an "echo of haunting melody."

Altogether it was what Hay called a "pleasant gang," one "which made all the joy of life in easy, irresponsible Washington." The Adams gang—for it was Adams, Hay said, who formed "the only principle of cohesion in it"—grew larger when Henry Cabot Lodge and his wife, Anna, who was called Nannie, joined it. Nannie's sister Evelyn would marry Henry's brother Brooks, and Cabot had once been Henry's Harvard pupil and almost a younger brother to him. He was now a man of consequence in Washington, having served first as a congressman representing the Massachusetts Sixth District and afterward as senator. Nannie called him "Pinky" when he was being pompous, and Henry came to dislike his senatorial dogmatism. But as with everyone else he found Nannie entirely charming, one of the "dispensers of sunshine over Washington." Her eyes, John Singer Sargent said, were of a peculiar blue that he could not get out of his head, and he regretted that he had never painted her; Theodore Roosevelt, who would also join the Adams circle, thought Nannie looked "as queens ought to look, but as no queen I have ever seen does look."

There were circles within the circle; Hay's wife, Clara, the Ohio heiress, and Lizzie's husband, Don, the Pennsylvania senator, were admitted to the club only by spousal courtesy, for they were dull; and Cabot Lodge himself, though above what Adams called the "waste places of average humanity," was suffered only because he was married to Nannie and was through her the father of George Cabot Lodge, the poet. In time Nannie and John fell in love. It was a romance constrained, however, by the taboos of the age. They might occasionally have what Lizzie called "a little walk together," but as a rule they could not be seen together in public by themselves without risk of scandal. Lizzie and Henry gave them such cover as they could, and when Clara was in Ohio and Cabot was detained in the Capitol, the four of them formed an ostensibly innocent quartet. But when Henry was away, drifting, there were difficulties. Who was to be the fourth string in the quartet? A solution was found. "Cabot has to be the fourth man in all these parties," Lizzie said, even as she found the effort to connive at adultery in the company of the cuckold "a little fatiguing."

Lizzie's and Henry's own "partnership," as Lizzie called it, was hardly less fatiguing. In 1898, when Senator Cameron (by this time out of office) took the lease of Surrenden Dering, a vast manor in Kent, Henry James saw a good deal of the pair. A longtime student of WASP vampirism, he was struck by the way Lizzie "sucked the lifeblood of poor Henry." Theirs was, he said, "one of the longest and oddest American *liaisons* I've ever known," a case study he made use of in his own investigation of human bondage, *The Sacred Fount*, which was published in 1901. Adams was only too pleased to have Lizzie prey upon his brain—he had mind to spare; it is less easy to say how he felt when she began to feed on the body of his friend and honorary nephew, a handsome young poet called Joseph Trumbull Stickney, recently graduated from Harvard. "I do not know how he would wear," Lizzie said after dining with the youth in Paris, "but I am willing to try." Soon their "excursions," as she called them, took them as far afield as Florence, where Stickney's friend George Cabot Lodge reported that "Mrs. Cam and Joe flirted together daily for about six weeks—very busy."

Joe Stickney soothed Lizzie's raveled nerves, but she needed something from Adams that he alone could give, and she was sometimes cruel in the way she enforced his allegiance. George Cabot Lodge was appalled by the way she exhibited her dalliance with Stickney in front of the older man, and there had been venom, a decade earlier, in her apparently lighthearted account of the "real Parisian spree" she had enjoyed with John Hay. "I hope that you are jealous?" she wrote to Adams at the time. (The question mark was a nice touch.) "Please don't tell him I told you, but we dined in *cabinet particulier*, and went in a lower loge to a ballet. I actually felt wicked and improper. He did too, for he felt obliged to follow up the precedent and to tell me how much he loved me. I feel as if we'll always have this delicious little secret between us—only I have to take you in." When, later in the same year, Adams himself appeared in Paris after a long voyage in the Pacific with the artist John La Farge, Lizzie received him with distinct coolness. There would be no *cabinet particulier*, no lower loge, for him.

Stinging under the thwack of Lizzie's lash, Adams retreated to Wenlock Abbey, a Cluniac priory in Shropshire which, having fallen into ruin at the Reformation, had been made into a county seat by his friends the Milnes Gaskells. But he did not break with Lizzie. In a dark letter he told her he would come back to her "gaily, with a heart as sick as ever a man had who knew that he should lose the only object he loved because he loved too much." At the same time he intimated that he had found in monasticism and the Middle Ages a way of sublimating or divinizing his unrequited love. "Progress has much to answer for," he wrote, "in depriving weary and broken men and women of their natural end and happiness." He pictured himself a monk "contented in the cloister," and he spoke of the consolatory power of the Virgin and her miraculous Child, in whom were to be found "all the human interest and power that religion ever had."

BUT THE "SECLUSION AND PEACE" Adams found at Wenlock could not wholly assuage the sting of his defeats in politics and love, and he fell into fits of temper that neither his good breeding nor his ironic façade could entirely conceal. "I am myself more than ever at odds with my time," he wrote in an unguarded moment. "I detest it, and everything that belongs to it, and live only in the wish to see the end of it, with all its infernal Jewry. I want to put every money-lender to death, and sink Lombard Street and Wall Street under the ocean." Wounded in his aspirations, he spoke contemptuously of "the Jew banker," the image, for him, of a new plutocracy of émigré Europeans and swamp Yankees whose usurious money-grubbing (as he conceived it) was replacing the "old Ciceronian idea of government by *the best*" to which his own family had long subscribed.*

Adams had the vice of the intellectual who strives always to be original, yet the resentments that festered in him were common enough in the class to which he belonged. Richard Hofstadter called them Mugwumps, the remnant of a mostly superseded elite made up of "the old gentry, the merchants of long standing, the small manufacturers, the established professional men, the civic leaders of an earlier era." As an "old-family, college-educated" class, the Mugwumps were imbued, Hofstadter said, with the New England idealism; they looked to Boston Brahmins and Concord sages for cultural models. Accustomed to lead, they now found themselves shunted aside. In their "personal careers, as in their commu-nity activities," they were "checked, hampered, and overridden by the agents of the new corporations, the corrupters of legislatures, the buyers of franchises, the allies of political bosses. . . . They were less important, and they knew it."

Lamed in will and power of action, Adams wallowed in the same uneasinesses, and fell to insisting the more vehemently on the two things that distinguished him from the moneyed barbarians who had beaten him in the game of power, his superior culture and the purity of his descent from so many New England worthies. Pride and anger brought him to perhaps the lowest point in his writ-ings, the howl with which the defunct Brahmin lamented that his "world was dead. Not a Polish Jew fresh from Warsaw or Cracow—not a furtive Yacoob or Ysaac still reeking of the Ghetto, snarling a weird Yiddish to the officers of the customs—but had a keener instinct, an intenser energy, and a freer hand

---

* Dante had abused the plutocrats of his own time in a manner hardly less unseemly, and he rejoiced in the thought of Filippo Argenti—Silver Philip, who shod his horse in precious metals—wallowing in the filth of the Fifth Circle of Hell.

than he—American of Americans, with Heaven knew how many Puritans and Patriots behind him, and an education that had cost a civil war . . ."

It was a howl of impotence, of frustration in what Henry James called a "disappointed and ineffectual personal career." But it was also a kind of odious catharsis, an effort, in one bred to preserve a façade of good form, to relieve an accumulation of pent-up anger: Adams's rant was the sort of thing one might, in the old days, hear an embittered WASP say after the second or third, or even the first martini. Yet the howl served another purpose. It was a means by which the patrician in a democracy (whose status must always be insecure) could define himself by what he was not. Adams was, he said, "different from all my contemporaries. . . . I detest them and everything connected with them, and I live only and solely with the hope of seeing their demise, with all their accursed Judaism." In fact Adams did not differ from the greater number of his WASP contemporaries in his prejudice against Jews. Lizzie Cameron shared his anti-Semitism, as did, in one degree or another, Theodore Roosevelt, Theodore's niece Eleanor, their cousin Franklin, and a good number of the other characters who figure in this book. Contempt for Jews flourished at Harvard and Yale and in the schools that prepared students to enter them: it formed a part of the ethos of banks, law firms, clubs, and other WASP cartels.

The anti-Semitism of WASPs like Adams betrayed their self-doubt. There is a scene in Santayana's novel *The Last Puritan* in which the narrator contrasts the young Oliver Alden, bred to America's WASP forms, with the young Mario Van de Weyer, bred to English ones. Oliver is "tongue-tied, stolid, and correct." Mario, on the contrary, resembles a prince in the Arabian Nights. He is like Mozart's Cherubino—a creature "so exquisitely dressed, so merry, so unconcerned about everything, so innocently sparkling," that to Oliver "he hardly seemed human at all: more like some Chinese figurine, all ivory and silk, that should suddenly have come to life, begun to dance, to quote the poets, and to laugh at everything . . ." Mario has been trained in the old aristocratic school. Eton Colleges and Brigades of Guards, Brooks's Clubs and White's, Blenheim Palaces and Castle Howards, Oxfords and Cambridges—sanctuaries of snobbery and knavery to be sure, but ones that contrived, Santayana says, to produce a type that believed in itself, and compelled others to believe. Such a training brands the soul as distinctly as the tonsured head distinguishes the apprentice monk or the jeweled button the promoted mandarin. If the Old World patrician was not, like a Byzantine court eunuch, physically disfigured by his initiation into the mysteries of his caste, he was hardly less psychically maimed. In later life English statesmen and guardsmen, jurists and bishops, blanched at the recollection of the Long Chamber at Eton and the indignities inflicted upon the "fag." But having been broken they became strong; their weird confidence, their remarkable poise, betokened an inner self-trust, akin to that of the Jesuit missionary or the captain of Marines. It does not occur to Santayana's Mario to *doubt* his playing-fields-of-Eton superiority; he has died to its myth, and been born again in its illusion.

Adams and his fellow WASPs had nothing like this to sustain their amour propre; nor did they have the memory, as European elites did, of a feudal over-lordship or a gentry tradition to buck them up and distinguish them from what Emerson called the "acrid mass" of their fellow citizens. The anti-Semitism of European patricians was a byproduct of their strength, that of their American counterparts of their weakness: the descent of jittery toffs into a dismal sort of scapegoating.

IN HIS NOVEL *PANDORA*, HENRY James portrayed Adams as Alfred Bonnycastle, a patrician so estranged from his country that he thinks it "vulgar" to invite the president of the United States to his house. (Count Otto, the young German diplomat in the story, is "bewildered" to find that in the "national capital, in the houses he supposed to be the best, the head of the State was not a coveted guest . . .") But James does not pursue the question of Adams's estrangement except to attribute it to the disappointment of a man who "was not in politics, though politics were much in him." There was, however, another, deeper reason for Adams's disaffection. He mocked his education, his Mr. Dixwell's School in Boylston Place, Boston, and his Harvard College across the river in Cambridge. It was all a swindle. Yet his schooling, however inept, had done what it was meant to do. It had prepared him to be a civic generalist. Only his schoolmasters had neglected to tell him that Athens was dead. With wit and irony he mocked them in *The Education of Henry Adams*. Yet all his days he strove to live the spacious, many-sided life of a citizen of Athens or Florence in their prime.

His idea of himself was fixed beyond revision when, too late, he learned that the modern American must specialize. The American's education (if he had had, as Adams did, a training in the liberal arts) taught him to live all he could, to make a full use of his powers along Aristotle's lines of excellence. But in America there was no obvious forum for human completion. The whole-souled ideal had given way to a narrow technical competence that left the heart unsatisfied. All the Americans' nervous energy, Adams wrote, was "oriented in one direction."* The Athenian moved easily and unselfconsciously from practical affairs to artistic and philosophic ones, from the cultivation of his private garden to public and poetical labors on behalf of the polis. But for the American, "work, whiskey, and cards were life."

WANDER THOUGH HE MIGHT AFTER Clover's death, Adams always returned to his house on Lafayette Square "as a horse goes back to its stables." The heavy Romanesque masonry, the work of his old Harvard schoolfellow H. H. Richardson, afforded a refuge from the curious and the vulgar. It was here, amid his Blake prints and Japanese vases, before a chimneypiece fashioned of Mexican onyx "of a sea-green translucency so exquisite as to make my soul yearn," that the small, balding, bearded man, tiring of the effort to embalm some fragment of truth or falsity in lucid prose, could assemble about him amusing souls for a good gossip, the more malicious the better. The talk was not infrequently at the expense of the current occupant, whoever it happened to be, of the large house across the square—the "slaughter-house," as Adams called the White House now that it was safely out of reach. It was "bloody and dreary" with associations for him that went back to the time of his great-grandmother, Abigail Adams, or so he told Lizzie Cameron.

Lizzie, with all her absurdity, changed him, and deepened his sense that he could not do justice to his nature under purely American conditions. If his education had led him to Athens, Lizzie pointed the way to Chartres. He claimed, and perhaps even believed, that through her he experienced that power in woman out of which religions of mother-goddesses and love-goddesses are made, the line of Cybele and Astarte. He discovered that life has a sensuous side, and that one need not shun it; and he tasted, in his travels, the different phases of the human encounter with Eros, from the Edenic nudity of Polynesia to its ideal denial in the Buddhism of Anuradhapura. Yet none of it expressed all that he felt in Lizzie herself, as a woman and as the mother of a child, little Martha Cameron. He felt the Madonna in her.

He was in Europe "collecting spires"—studying cathedrals—when he found, in the roses and apses of Chartres, the cultural equivalent of her womanhood. His medievalism was a reworking of his passion for Lizzie, which he knew now

---

* Henry James deplored the same human shrinkage in his portrait of the financier Abel Gaw in *The Ivory Tower*. To say that Mr. Gaw was surrounded by a desert, James wrote, "was almost to flatter the void into which he invited one to step. He conformed in short to his necessity of absolute interest—interest, that is, in his own private facts, which were facts of numerical calculation altogether: how could it not be so when he had dispossessed himself . . . of every faculty except the calculating? If he hadn't thought in figures how could he possibly have thought at all?"

to be hopeless, but it was also an admission that his faith in political reform had been an unsatisfactory one. No effort of politics, he came to believe, could redeem what was wrong in the civilization for which America was preparing the way, a chaotic "multiplicity," as he called it, that bred hysteria and neurosis and thwarted the need for unity and community. America "contained scores of men worth five millions or upwards," he said, "whose lives were no more worth living than those of their cooks." (Accustomed to look down on house servants, he seems to have taken it for granted that a cook's life is not worth living.) The country, he maintained, was "a banker's Olympus," and even as he cut his coupons and collected his dividends, he "hugged his antiquated dislike of Bankers and Capitalistic Society" until he became "little better than a crank." Like Carlyle and Ruskin before him, he looked to the Middle Ages for an antidote to what his friend Matthew Arnold, in his poem "The Scholar-Gypsy," called

> *this strange disease of modern life,*
> *With its sick hurry, its divided aims . . .*

Only Adams differed from these thinkers in making the Virgin Mary the focus of his medievalism. He claimed to have encountered her at Chartres, where indicating her child she confided her secret: "We are Love!" It was this element of feminine, of maternal grace, expanded into a social ideal, that made the older civilization superior, in Adams's eyes, to America's modern and mercenary one. The twelfth century, he liked to say, "never knew *ennui*," while his own, which shrank "from the touch of a vision or a spirit," was swamped in it. He was certain that the Queen of Heaven's antidotes to dejection—compassion and creative idiosyncrasy in the service of community—were yielding, under a psychologically unbalanced system, to a standardized anarchy.* "All the steam in the world," he said, "could not, like the Virgin, build Chartres," or the common life that throve about it. For as much as Ruskin or Arnold, Adams was what the historian T. J. Jackson Lears has called an "antimodern vitalist," one who shuddered at the devitalizing shallowness of soul he saw around him.

The fruit of Adams's pilgrimages—from reform politics to Lizzie Cameron, from the worship of a woman's flesh to the poetry of Dante and the Virgin

---

* Time itself was standardized when, on November 18, 1883, American railroad engineers imple-mented a system of standard time that synchronized clocks within four newly differentiated time zones on the continent.

Mary—was his book *Mont-Saint-Michel and Chartres*, a study of medieval unity. Its mystical thesis is that the Virgin and her child, having redeemed through Love all that is redeemable in man, make it possible for man to find form and unity (as opposed to standardization) amid the chaos of life. Yet Adams did not even attempt to show that the unifying vision could be of any mortal use in the fragmented America of his time, shivered as it was into sixty or seventy million pieces. Like his adoration of the Virgin, Adams's apprehension of ideal community was otherworldly and utopian, the private amusement of a man who felt himself unspeakably old, a "long-established ghost," resigned to earthly impotence.

Adams, the sage who figures so largely in the drama by which the WASPs attempted to rise phoenixlike from the ashes of the Brahmins, had reached a dead end. He was the first of the WASPs, and the last of the Brahmins. Like the WASPs, he resented his age and wanted to reform it. But unlike them he would not compromise with his century: he was as inflexible as any Brahmin in adhering to his revelation, his faith that in an age of railroads and technicians one might know a different sort of life.

Hollis Hall at Harvard, where George Santayana roomed. He deplored a
university growing ever "more multifarious and more chaotic."

TEN

A Constancy in the Stars: The
Harvards of George Santayana

maestro di color che sanno . . .

the master of those who know . . .
—Dante, *Inferno*

Draped in a longish military cape—a wizard's mantle, one of his students
thought—George Santayana made his way through the Harvard Yard.
The leaves of the elms were falling and his aspect was melancholy. He had just
learned of the death of Warwick Potter. The young man had fallen ill on the
steam yacht *Sagamore*, on which he was embarked on a round-the-world cruise

with his old Groton classmate Edgar Scott and his old Groton master Sherrard Billings. He was twenty-two at the time of his death.

Santayana remembered how "full of laughter" the young man had been, a laughter nonetheless tinged with sadness, the "innocent youthful side of repentance, of disillusion, of understanding." So constant a companion had Warwick been "at the club, during our poetry-readings in my room, and our walks that I insensibly came to think of him as a younger brother and as a part of myself." Warwick was (by Santayana's standards) not clever, but he had been educated "after the Groton manner," he "had heard of everything, knew the points of the compass in morals and history, and had good taste in English literature. He also had good taste in choosing his friends and in judging them: and his intimates were not of his own type: they were not good pious boys, but captains of crews and owners of yachts: young men who had experience far beyond his own innocence. He was not out of place in their society, as he was not in that of his masters at Groton or in mine." One could sit with him "by the fire over a mild whiskey and soda, until the early hours," Santayana said, "discussing Falstaff and Prince Henry, or the divinity and humanity in Christ, or the need of arms to give strength to letters." But it was difficult to know what Warwick "would have turned into if he had lived." The dominant trait in him "was clear goodness, the absence of all contaminations, such as the very young are sometimes proud of. He was sure, in great things as in little, to prefer the better to the worse . . . . He felt at home in England and in the Church. He was civilized." Santayana admitted that Warwick was too young to "have been tried in the furnace and proved to be pure gold." But for all that he had no doubt but that the young man was "pure gold."

In his sonnet sequence "To W. P." he expressed his grief: "With you a part of me hath passed away . . ." The part of Santayana that sought fulfilment in the world withered and died with Warwick, or so he claimed. Warwick was, he said, "my *last* real friend," and after his death he underwent what he called a "philosophic metanoia," a change of heart that led him to disinfect himself of the taint of worldly things. Possession, Dante teaches, is one with loss. Henceforth, Santayana vowed, he would live philosophically, in the mind and the imagination, a "disillusioned spirit" who had apprehended the secret of wisdom—that to "possess things and persons in idea is the only pure good to be got out of them; to possess them physically or legally is a burden and a snare."

Santayana turned thirty that December, but he felt himself much older. His "joy in youth" had failed with Warwick's death. Not entirely, to be sure: there was a wistful affair of the heart with a young British guardsman (he commanded the guard at the Bank of England), and a more substantial intimacy with Bertrand Russell's brother, Lord Russell, the so-called "wicked earl," an Edwardian voluptuary whom Santayana likened to "a tiger well fed, with a broad margin of leisure for choosing his prey." These were human lapses from his official philosophy, as perhaps also was his teaching at Harvard itself. He disliked being a professor (no job for a philosopher!) and was apt to be contemptuous of Harvard, with its "muddy paths and shabby grass, the elms standing scattered at intervals, the ugly factory-like buildings, the loud-voiced youths passing by, dressed like shop-assistants . . ." Yet he became one of the college's most remarkable teachers. And not simply in the lecture hall; probably more real education took place in his rooms in Stoughton Hall, where over beer and Scotch whisky he and his students read poetry together, "most often Keats, but often also Shelley, or Shakespeare's sonnets and songs." He exerted an influence, greater perhaps than he might have liked, on the young WASPs who came under his spell, and he did much to shape their nascent culture.

HE WAS NOT A WASP himself, and would no doubt have resented being lumped in with them. He had been born, in 1863, in Madrid. His father was an administrator in the Spanish colonial service, by then retired; his mother, who had been born in Glasgow of Spanish parents, had before her marriage to Santayana's father been the wife of George Sturgis of Boston—an enterprising young Brahmin who had sought his fortune in the South Seas and died young. Santayana was a boy of eight when, in 1872, his father took him to America to live with his mother in Boston. His parents were by this time separated, and it was thought best that the boy should live in America, both for the sake of his education and in acknowledgement of the utility of the Sturgis connection, for the family had (in addition to a propensity to lunacy) money and influence. The elder Santayana returned to Spain; young Jorge, or George, as he was now called, was sent first to the Brimmer School and then to the Boston Latin School, where he rose to be the leading boy; afterward he entered Harvard College.

Santayana had mixed feelings about the institution that was to be his home for thirty years. He found much to approve in the compact society of the college itself, a little city-state off Harvard Square where "an exact but familiar and humanistic learning" spasmodically flourished. On the other hand, he had nothing but contempt for the university President Eliot was building as it grew every day "more multifarious and more chaotic." He was sure that Eliot was killing the genius of the place. But the firebrand never burns brighter than in the instant before it is extinguished, and Harvard in Santayana's time glowed with a faith in liberal education at odds with the avowedly practical policy of the university—a radiance associated with such names as William James, Josiah Royce, Bernard Berenson, Learned Hand, Van Wyck Brooks, and Walter Lippmann. Yet in the annals of Harvard humanism Santayana himself was as influential a figure as any of these, and the young WASPs who studied under him—even the gentleman's C scholars who could make but little of his philosophy—looked up to the sage with the "fine domed forehead" and "brilliant myopic brown eyes." "Just why Santayana was in Cambridge nobody knew," Lippmann said. But "somehow the gorgeous bird had been caged, and had been trained to soliloquize loudly enough so that the students could overhear him." They might not have understood the song, but they listened to it. For WASPs were always to put great stock in liberal education; and at Harvard no one was more closely identified with the quasi-mystical power of the humanities than Professor Santayana.

WHAT MADE SANTAYANA'S HUMANISM COMPELLING was the candor with which he denounced all that was weak and ineffectual in America's humanities. The country's leading colleges had begun as Puritan seminaries: what was liberal and humane in the curriculum was at the mercy of the orthodox and intolerant. Puritanism faded, but it was not supplanted by a vigorous humanism. All that was vital in America was concentrated not in its artistic and literary culture but in its practical life, in "invention and industry and social organization." Its humanities, Santayana said, were merely decorative and ornamental—so much "genteel tradition."

Santayana's criticism was the more penetrating for having been informed by his own experience of Spain and more especially of Ávila, the town in which he passed the most impressionable years of his boyhood. In his memoirs he described Ávila as "an *oppidum*, a walled city, a cathedral town, all granite and grandeur" on a plateau overborne by the rocky heights of the Sierra de Ávila. The "austere inspiration of these mountains, these battlemented city walls and these dark churches could not have been more chivalrous or grander," Santayana said, for old and shrunken though it was, Ávila had its living humanities, a poetry that grew out of its history, its tradition, its religion—an idea of order that brought art into the midst of life and made the place a *place* in the way no American town ever is.*

For America, Santayana believed, had very little of this living poetry. Its aboriginal Calvinism was hostile to art on graven-image theological grounds, and the Yankee materialism that succeeded it opposed it for practical and parsimonious reasons. The result, Santayana said, was a "spiritual penury" and cultural drabness that made an "exile and a foreigner" of everyone who had a "temperament at all like mine." The American "scene was filled with arts and virtues which were merely useful or remedial," never beautiful and ideal. Every "door was open in the one direction and shut in the other," so that a certain kind of soul was driven to despair. He "either folds up his heart and withers in a corner—in remote places you sometimes find such a solitary gaunt idealist—or else he flies to Oxford or Florence or Montmartre to save his soul—or perhaps not to save it."

Santayana knew some of these gaunt idealists at Harvard. They formed a school known as the Harvard Pessimists on account of the morbidity of their verse, suffused as it was with autumnal gloom. George Cabot Lodge and Lizzie Cameron's lover Joe Stickney were its leading lights; Santayana was particularly close to Stickney, an "exceptionally cultivated" young man who had been "educated by his father (an unemployed teacher) to perfection." (Santayana thought Stickney one of the three best-educated men he ever encountered, the others being Bertrand Russell and Baron von Westenholz, the last an unstable Hamburg aristocrat who died by suicide in 1939.) Stickney had a number of claims to distinction beyond that of having succeeded where Henry Adams failed in bedding Lizzie Cameron. An accomplished student of Greek, he was the first WASP to take a *doctorat ès lettres* in the University of Paris, where his defense of his thesis in the Sorbonne, beneath a portrait of a scarlet-robed Cardinal Richelieu, impressed judges not disposed to be sympathetic. But as for Stickney's verse, it seemed to Santayana as feeble as that of the other Pessimists: "in spite of flashes of gun-powder—for I will not call it lightning or genius," it was "turbid and turgid beyond endurance."

If Santayana cared little for the poetry of these young men, he sympathized with their plight. They were, "Stickney especially, of whom I was very fond . . . visibly killed by the lack of air to breathe" in America. People "individually were

---

* "Poetry is called religion," Santayana maintained, "when it intervenes in life."

kind and appreciative to them, as they were to me, but the system was deadly, and they hadn't any alternative tradition (as I had) to fall back upon." They embodied a strain of WASP estrangement that in the twentieth century would find expression in such expatriated exiles as T. S. Eliot, another of Santayana's students who was in some ways the last and greatest poet in the Pessimist school.

YET THERE WAS, AT HARVARD, another group of apprentice WASPs who, if they absorbed Santayana's pessimistic appraisal of American culture, were as impressed by what was optimistic in his philosophy. Rather than despair in the face of the city's defects, they wanted to fix them.

One of these young men was Learned Hand, who entered Harvard College two years before Stickney. His background was typical of the emerging WASPs. Born to a family of lawyers of old New England descent, he grew up in Albany, New York, in an atmosphere of decaying Brahminism. "I was, of course, like my father and the whole damn crew, a neurasthenic, a neurotic." His father, he said, was "a very, very nervous, apprehensive kind of man, always imagining he was sick or something. . . . He was too sensitive." His mother, for her part, was "a very fearful woman. That was the bad thing about the whole Puritan tradition. It was apt to leave a constant anxiety complex . . ."

Hand inherited his parents' nervous infirmity; he was, he said, "a very insecure person, very fearful; morbidly fearful." At Harvard he felt himself an "outsider," excluded from final clubs dominated by the "swells" and "grandees" of the boarding schools, and his failure to make the Porcellian—"*the* undergraduate citadel," in Joe Alsop's words, "of the WASP Ascendancy at Harvard"—rankled to the end of his life.* He grew a beard and worked hard at his studies; his classmates called him the "Mongolian Grind." His mind ripened; Harvard, he said, "was to me the awakening of all those things that since then have been dearest."

"Even in his eighties," his law clerk Gerald Gunther remembered, Judge Hand's "face would glow as he recalled the young Santayana." "We thought him," Hand said, "really the most wonderful thing that ever was made." What

---

* In addition to gratifying the more snobbish passions of WASPs, Porcellian had the distinction of giving those of its members who in later life were bored by their more pedestrian duties a field for useful activity. In February 1942 Leverett Saltonstall "was offered the position of Grand Marshal of Porcellian and, though occupied as Governor of Massachusetts and warned by more than one of his advisers that the club Grand Marshalship was of extremely doubtful political value, he eagerly embraced the post."

he got from Santayana was not a civics lesson but a habit of large-mindedness, a contempt for narrowness, the sort of meanness that interferes with the full development of one's powers—a habit of mind that has often made possible the bold original contribution. If some of Santayana's Harvard protégés became, like Wallace Stevens, Robert Frost, and T. S. Eliot, artists and poets, others, like George Rublee, Felix Frankfurter, Julian Codman, and the Cutting brothers (William Bayard and Bronson) developed civic consciences, as did Hand himself.

Standing at the lectern, dressed almost dandyishly in a "piqué vest, spats, and suede gloves,"* Santayana took pleasure in startling ingenuous youth. The intellectual gadfly Max Eastman compared his eyes to those of Milton's Satan; Walter Lippmann thought that he resembled "Leonardo's Mona Lisa with a little pointed beard." His godless naturalism, which he reconciled with an intensely felt spiritual life, absorbed in the "pure intuition of essence,"† appalled even so urbane an intelligence as Stickney's. Life, for Santayana, was "something confused, hideous, and useless," yet the typical thinking person could not accept this and went on "madly filling the universe with images of his own reason and his own hopes," a tissue of "metaphysical illusion."‡ Santayana's calm and philosophic acceptance of the abyss was too much for Stickney. "He feared me," Santayana said. To him "I was a Mephistopheles . . ."

He unnerved his students, and brought them to know those powers in themselves that came from what he called a "constancy in the stars": a reluctant teacher who nevertheless stood intellectual godfather to a couple of generations of fledgling WASPs. For in his own detached way he cared about them, knew their faults, foresuffered their dooms. This was in keeping with his philosophy, which held that "charity will always judge a soul, not by what it has succeeded in fashioning externally, not by the body or the words or the works that are the wreckage of its voyage, but by the elements of light and love that this soul infused into that inevitable tragedy."

---

* Lippmann remembers Santayana's appearance of "perfect style, with his pearl gray beard and pearl gray tie and pearl gray spats and pearl gray gloves." He omitted only the pearl gray prose.

† "Nature is well-ordered enough to have produced spirit, yet chaotic enough to have left it free. . . . Before producing spirit, however, a very great constancy had to be established first in the stars, so that an earth might exist" where spirit could flower.

‡ "Why shouldn't things be largely absurd, futile, and transitory? They are so, and we are so, and they and we go very well together."

Theodore Roosevelt dreamt of a restoration of "pure government."
He also believed it would not do to be *too* pure.

ELEVEN

Teddy

Non impedir lo suo fatale andare . . .

Do not block his fatal path . . .
—Dante, *Inferno*

J ack Chapman and Minna Timmins were married in the summer of 1889 in the Brimmers' summer house at Prides Crossing on the sea north of Boston. Jack's friend Amory Gardner was best man; Cotty Peabody performed the marriage rite. Afterward the newlyweds took up residence in New York City, where Jack practiced law and interested himself in reform politics. Like many WASP males, he worried that he was insufficiently manly. His soul, he lamented, was "like a woman's in many ways." Was he not drawn to literature, a "woman's business," and to the violin? But in the rough and tumble of politics he hoped to recover the masculine virtues.

He joined the City Reform Club, which, remodeled as the City Club, became a force in the Good Government or Goo Goo movement, devoted to cleaning up corruption in the Democrats' Tammany Hall and in the Republican party machine. He was soon recognized, together with Warwick Potter's uncle, Henry Codman Potter, the Episcopal bishop of New York, as the most uncompromising of the Goo Goos.* "My line of politics is war—war—war," Chapman wrote. There is "nothing one may not do. I almost throw some men out of the window—I get so violent, and I suddenly turn as heavy and icy as cold lemon-pie. Some men are to be taken by the throat, some jollied, some taken aside into an alcove—and, by Jove, all men are nothing but dough so far as I can see."

Chapman, certainly, did not make Henry Adams's mistake. Far from holding himself aloof from the grittiness of politics, he found satisfaction in it. He became a poll watcher, testified before committees, spoke on street corners. With his large physique and ghoulish stump, he was an imposing figure, and he once collared "a ruffian in the crowd who was interrupting" him. (Afterward he invited the man to have a drink with him.) But if his style differed from Adams's, his object was much the same: the creation of a viable independent party. He knew that third-party movements seldom succeeded, but he believed that his Independent Party would prove an exception—if he could persuade his fellow Porcellian Theodore Roosevelt to run on its ticket.

IN FEBRUARY 1884 ROOSEVELT WAS a still boyish twenty-five-year-old delegate in the New York State Assembly. He was at work in Albany when he received a telegram informing him that his blond, Boston-Brahmin wife Alice had given birth to a baby girl. By the time he reached the Roosevelt house on West Fifty-seventh Street in Manhattan, both his wife and his mother were dying.

His friend Cotty Peabody, a cousin of Alice's, went at once to see him and "found him wonderfully calm. I never saw such strength in my life . . ." Beneath the calmness was a reluctance to grieve. Grief was allied to neurasthenia, and the only cure for both was frenetic activity. "Get action," Roosevelt said. "Do things; be sane; don't fritter away your time; create, act, take a

---

*   Bishop Potter's father, Alonzo Potter, the Episcopal bishop of Pennsylvania, had ordained Phillips Brooks a priest.

place wherever you are and be somebody; get action." Life had to be lived in the "fellowship of the doers," in an unrelenting round of different pursuits. "Black care," he said with a nod to Horace, "rarely sits behind a rider whose pace is fast enough."

As much as Henry Adams, Roosevelt sought to defy the narrowness of the age, which he, like Adams, blamed on its overabsorption in getting and spending. (His family had left him a considerable fortune, so he had less to worry about on the score of getting than most people.) But unlike Adams, who was a functioning neurasthenic, Roosevelt dreaded any compromise with the hysterias of the Brown Decades. As a boy he had been sickly, myopic, fearful, and eccentric, with the makings of a full-fledged neurotic. "There were all kinds of things I was afraid of," he confessed. How he overcame his fears through strenuous exertions with barbells and dumbbells, in confrontations with prize fighters, grizzly bears, gunfighters, and "mean" horses, has since passed into fable. But the dread of neurasthenia remained; and he had only to look at his brother Elliott, drinking as many as half a dozen bottles of champagne a day, followed by brandy and anisette, to know that he could never relax his vigilance.

Narrowness and neurasthenia were for Roosevelt closely connected: they were products, he believed, of a civilization that simultaneously dulled the spirit and enervated the body. "The wealthier, or as they would prefer to style themselves, the 'upper' classes," he wrote, "tend distinctly toward the bourgeois type," a "miracle of timid and short-sighted selfishness." The riches that impoverished their imaginations made them soft and flabby of flesh, and estranged them from the "rougher and manlier virtues" of the healthy-minded.

Roosevelt's life was an effort to resist such desiccation. The good bourgeois labored over his desk or lounged in his club chair; Roosevelt was out of doors whenever practicable, living the strenuous life. Yet the boxing, the rowing, and the mountain climbing did not entirely eliminate the stigma of sissiness, and when he made his debut in the New York State Assembly, dressed foppishly after the fashion of Harvard, there were taunts of "Jane Dandy" and "Oscar Wilde." Further strenuousities were evidently needed, and Teddy went West, to the Badlands of the Dakota Territory, where he became a cowboy and a ranchero.

Roosevelt was always to have more in common with bourgeois haters on the Right, such as the Adams brothers, Henry and Brooks, than with those on the Left, who were after all not gentlemen. His objection to a getting-and-spending civilization was less economic than cultural and hygienic.* He deplored the sort of personality commercial America fostered—that of the "glorified huckster or pawnbroker." But he could hardly quarrel with the abundance it made possible: it was because his own bourgeois forebears had toiled so assiduously that he was able to live as largely as he did. He wanted not to scrap America's commercial civilization but to save it from the "dull, purblind folly of the very rich men" who dominated it, and to counter their meanness with a nobler conception of human flourishing.

WITH HIS HISTRIONIC STRUTTING, HIS perpetual bursting forth into falsetto arias of muscular-jingo rhetoric, and his commedia dell'arte flamboyance—Il Capitano come to life—Roosevelt was too rococo, and in some ways too great, a character to be a true WASP. He had the WASP breeding, and when he was not on stage could revert to type, a miracle of gentlemanlike tact and courtesy. But as a rule he left the WASP taste and the WASP reticences to his childhood playmate and second wife Edith Carow Roosevelt. She was a true WASP, one who divided the world into two classes, those of her kind, who understood, and those "not *de nôtre monde*; they don't understand." The incomprehension of the vulgar was painful to her, but she made it a rule never to show it. Instead she would smile. "*On sourit. La gaieté c'est une politesse*," she would say. One smiles—a (feigned) cheerfulness is true politeness.

As a student at Harvard Teddy boasted that he stood "nineteenth in the class. . . . Only one gentleman stands ahead of me." But in later life he tried to overcome the snobbery of the WASP within, and by inspiring club lizards and polo zealots to interest themselves in politics he did much to shape emerging WASP culture. In the New York of his youth, a gentleman, in Edith Wharton's words, did not "stoop to meddle with politics." Roosevelt did away with that taboo; he showed that a gentleman could be a public man, and that a public man could be a well-rounded man, one who combined service with sport, and who was not afraid to use his brain. He was, throughout his life, a rapacious reader: as a writer he was prodigious to the point of being tiresome. At the same time, he warned young WASPs not to become intellectuals. To make

---

* He was drawn to Brooks Adams's *The Law of Civilization and Decay*, in which Adams argued that modern economic civilization was destroying the heroic, imaginative, and artistic virtues of earlier phases in human development. The warrior, the priest, and the artist were giving way to the banker.

oneself cultivated was to make oneself weak. Roosevelt himself had, Richard Hofstadter said, a degree of cultivation rare in a politician. But it was broad rather than deep: there was much in the old humane ideal that hardly existed for him. The tragic poetry handed down from Athens, the city's free play of mind, its speculative philosophy, the erotic element in its worship of the body—well, all of that was more in the line of Henry Adams or Henry James; it dulled the habits of dogmatism one needed if one was to be a leader of men.*

Roosevelt taught young WASPs another lesson. As much as Jack Chapman, he dreamt of the restoration of "pure government" in America. But it would not do to be *too* pure. His realism or cynicism was evident when, in 1884, he and his fellow Mugwumps opposed the nomination of James G. Blaine as Republican candidate for president. (The man reeked of corruption.) But when Blaine, in fact, did win the nomination, Roosevelt discovered unsuspected virtues in the "plumed knight" from Maine, and went on to campaign vigorously for him in the general election.

JACK CHAPMAN, IN THE MEANWHILE, had his eye not only on Theodore Roosevelt but also on a young woman called Elizabeth Astor Winthrop Chanler. She was a daughter of old New York, beautiful in a slender brunette way; she had been orphaned young and been left a great deal of money. (Her great-grandfather, William Backhouse Astor, was said to have been the richest American of his day.) Miss Chanler grew up in a manor on the Hudson called Rokeby, among a wild brood of brothers and sisters to whom, in the absence of parents, she was little mother, a role in which she was assisted by Black Jane, a former slave who did much to keep the household in order. At least one of the Chanler siblings, John Armstrong "Archie" Chanler, would go demonstrably crazy. He was transfixed by Napoleon, whom he believed that he resembled, and he would later be committed to New York's Bloomingdale Asylum; he carried with him a silver-capped cane on which were engraved the words LEAVE ME ALONE. Elizabeth's own health was delicate, and she was sent to school in England on the Isle of Wight on the theory that the soft, seaborne

---

* Roosevelt did, however, have the characteristic WASP admiration for Dante, and in 1911 he composed an essay, "Dante and the Bowery," in which he argued that no modern poet could do justice, as Dante did, to "what is elemental in the human soul" using the everyday language of his time. He judged Whitman's attempt to do so "self-conscious," "defiant," and "not quite natural," and he overlooked the French Symbolists. T. S. Eliot's poetry had not yet been published.

climate would do her good. Miss Sewell, the schoolmistress, thought her "one of the most winning little creatures imaginable," and she pitied the girl when she developed a limp and was for two years strapped to a board to prevent curvature of the spine.

Yet Bessie Chanler endured, made her debut before Queen Victoria, and sat to John Singer Sargent in his studio in Chelsea. "I have painted you," he told her in Tite Street, "*la penserosa*." For her face was thoughtful—really it was (so he said) that of a Madonna; and then, too, there was that touch of *morbidezza* in it, a softness not untinged with sadness. Her family thought Bessie fragile, and set her down for a saint or a spinster, but in New York she discovered another aspect of her nature when she fell madly in love with Jack Chapman. He was, to be sure, married; but the attraction was great, and Miss Chanler was persuaded by her sister Margaret to go away on a long voyage in order that scandal might be averted. She was in Calcutta when, in March 1897, she learned that Jack's wife, Minna, had suddenly died. She returned by rapid stages to New York, where she and Jack were quietly married in April 1898.

TEN WEEKS LATER JACK CHAPMAN's friend Theodore Roosevelt burst into fame. He had been a force in politics before he was twenty-five, but it was only in the summer of 1898, with the expedition of his Rough Riders to Cuba, that the thirty-nine-year-old entered upon American immortality and became useful to WASP idealists.

Roosevelt had for some time been looking for an opportunity to prove just how truly un-middle-class he was, and in 1895 he had spoiled for a fight with England over a boundary dispute in Venezuela, telling Henry Cabot Lodge that the "country needs a war." If the typical bourgeois dreaded violent death, he went out of his way to stare it in the face, and the sinking of the *Maine* in Havana harbor and the war that followed gave him the test that he craved. Leading his men, on the first of July 1898, up Kettle Hill at Santiago de Cuba to confront the Spanish army, he experienced at last that "joy in battle" that every real man knows, the joy that comes when "the wolf begins to rise in his heart . . ." It was, he said, "the great day in my life."

He came back from Cuba a hero, the most famous man in the United States. Scarcely had he disembarked near Montauk Point, at the eastern end of Long Island, when Jack Chapman called upon him at Camp Wikoff. "I shall never forget the lustre that shown about him," Chapman remembered. Never before had he encountered such "genius," such "personal power." Someone accused him of being in love with Roosevelt, and the newlywed Chapman did not deny it. "I never before nor since have felt that glorious touch of hero-worship which solves life's problems by showing you a *man*."

Chapman wanted Roosevelt to run as the Independent Party's candidate for governor of New York in the coming election. At the head of an Independent ticket with "decent men from both parties behind him," he would be the "instrument of the citizen destroying the Boss." Roosevelt replied that he would be delighted to accept the Independent nomination, but only on the condition that he received the Republican nomination as well. Should he *not* receive the Republican nomination, he must decline to run as an Independent, for the Republicans would never forgive him for running against the party. All this was satisfactory to Chapman; he had no objection to Roosevelt's taking office with the support of both Republicans and Independents.

But it was not satisfactory to Senator Thomas Collier Platt, the boss who controlled New York's Republican patronage machine and who with some misgivings was preparing to offer Roosevelt the Republican nomination for governor. Platt loathed the Independents, whose very program, indeed, contemplated the extinction of his kind. He made it clear that if Roosevelt wanted the Republican nomination, he must throw over the Independents.

Roosevelt, who had once described Platt's influence as "simply poisonous," was in an awkward position. He had publicly affirmed that the Independent nomination would be "most flattering and gratifying" to him. What was no less serious, he had given his word to Chapman, one Porcellian to another, that he would not agree to take the Independent nomination and "then later throw us down by withdrawing from the ticket" under Republican pressure. Senator Platt was now insisting that he do just that and publicly disavow the reformers. Chapman wrote to Roosevelt to remind him of their agreement:

> Dear Teddy . . . You will remember that you told Klein and myself that you would, if nominated by the Republicans, be glad of our nomination, as it would strengthen your hands; and Tucker tells me you said the same thing to him, and that simultaneous nominations would be satisfactory. . . .

Chapman was reluctant to believe that ambition could have so "addled the brains and rotted the moral sense" of his friend and fellow Porc as to allow him to stiff the Independents. It would, after all, be "such a terrible example of the powers of the boss . . ." But stiff the Independents Roosevelt did.

There was a final scene at Sagamore Hill, Roosevelt's estate at Oyster Bay on Long Island. Chapman, in his own words, "unloaded" on Roosevelt, and accused him of being a "broken backed half good man," a "trimmer who wouldn't break with his party" but who would allow himself to be broken by it. Roosevelt "received all this," Chapman said, "with a courtesy, deference, and self-control that were absolutely marvelous. I never expect to see such an exhibition of good breeding as Roosevelt gave that night. We shook hands the next morning at parting, and avoided each other for twenty years."

Roosevelt could afford to be courteous. When you cast a man aside, it costs nothing to be polite. The third-party dreams of men like Chapman and Henry Adams were, he concluded, whimsical; the Mugwumps and the Goo Goos were fools, without any "knowledge whatever of practical affairs," the sort of men who constitute "the lunatic fringe in all reform movements." It was a lesson that would imprint itself on the minds of several generations of WASPs.

It would not do to be *too* pure.

Going among the textile workers, Vida Scudder preached
a double gospel of Christ and Karl Marx.

TWELVE

Vida Scudder Emulates St. Francis

ti si farà, per tuo ben far, nimico . . .

your good deeds will be your enemy . . .
—Dante, *Inferno*

For WASPs like Vida Scudder, a humanism that ended, as Mrs. Jack Gardner's did, in museums and concert halls was wholly inadequate. She had been born in 1861 at Madurai in southern India; her father, Dr. David Coit Scudder, had been called to British India to preach the Gospel to the Tamils. One day in 1862 he attempted to swim the Vaigai River and was drowned. Little Vida was taken by her mother, Harriet Louisa, home to Massachusetts, where they lived on the outskirts of Boston in an atmosphere of decaying gentility. "We were well-to-do," Vida remembered, "then we were poor, and for the most part, like many New England families of those days, we were not specially concerned as to whether we were poor or rich, but greatly concerned over our vowels, discriminating among our neighbors on grounds not of their possessions but of their enunciation."

She was an odd little girl, touched by the feeling that the world around her was unreal, and she would disconcert her mother by thrusting her hands into the nettles to prove that they existed. "I *like* it so!" she would cry, as the "delicious" stings convinced her of an "existence outside" herself. The feeling that she was not of the world, that she was somehow set apart from it, would develop, over time, into a dread that she was living life at second hand, making language do duty for things, "using words" to make up for what "you have not lived." For she was unable "to find reality anywhere." The "most solid phenomena disappeared" as soon as she came near them. "This sounds absurd," she wrote, "and people may think I am talking nonsense. Yet I am trying to present a central and persistent agony," the "truly awful" feeling that one "was not a real person, but only a sort of phantom, a hollow imitation of a person, created in mockery, an image on a screen . . ." From childhood on "the evasiveness of all I loved and touched and saw tormented me."

T. S. Eliot would dismiss Vida Scudder as "a sentimental old lay preacher in the guise of a Professor of English Literature," and there is some truth in the characterization. But the state of mind she described, the feeling that she was living in an unreal city, would play a part in the psychological makeup of a number of WASPs, not least Eliot himself.

MOTHER AND DAUGHTER SOON WENT abroad again, this time to Rome, perhaps because they could live more cheaply there. The city, not "yet scraped and fenced" for tourists, made a deep impression on Vida. Her mother took a house on the Pincian Hill with a garden of roses and violets over which a naked, armless nymph presided. Uncleaned, unexcavated, and unrestored, Rome was still medieval in its colors and its forms, and Vida delighted in the flowers that grew wild in the Colosseum, a "playground for botanists." When she and Harriet returned, four years later, to Boston, the Puritan city seemed "prosaic, empty, unworthy of chronicle."

In Boston Vida was sent to Miss Sanger's Private School for Girls, where she made the acquaintance of the beautiful Gibbens sisters. (Alice was to marry William James.) Later, in the Girls' Latin School, she came to know the "wholesome mortifications" that beset the young learner of dead languages. Like so many WASPs, she was converted by her galley-slavery in Latin and Greek to the virtues of liberal education, and progressive though she later became, she would be skeptical of John Dewey's educational hedonism. "When I hear casual talk about Progressive Education," she wrote, "and the need to indulge the aptitudes" of children and "to encourage their 'self-expression'—sacred phrase!—by letting them follow the line of least resistance and do what they enjoy, I wonder what would have happened to me if my young nose at the critical point of adolescence had not been rubbed in the Latin subjunctive." Here, for better or for worse, was the voice of the true WASP.

A classical education had long been the approved thing in Boston, but Vida's next step, conversion from the Congregational Church of the Puritans to Anglicanism, represented a break with the old ways. Her embrace of the Episcopal Church was one instance of a larger alteration in manners that took place in Boston after the Civil War, a revolution in sentiment that opened a new chapter in what Emerson called the "interior & spiritual history of New England." Forsaking the old Puritan churches, with their shrinking congregations, Vida and her mother worshipped in Boston's Trinity Church, and Vida long remembered the "massive inspired figure of the young preacher" who persuaded them to remain in his sheepfold, Phillips Brooks.* But Vida's grandmother, who lived in the memory of her son's missionary death in India, was shattered. This aging Puritan gentlewoman, as Vida called her, had no sympathy for the "fresh influx of spiritual force" Brooks represented. "I am glad your father did not live to see this day," she said to her granddaughter after she was presented by Brooks to the Bishop of Massachusetts for confirmation.

The aging Puritan gentlewoman would have been even more appalled could she have foreseen the changes Vida was to undergo during another spell of the Old World. In Paris, where she studied art with Louisa May Alcott's sister,

---

* As Puritanism faded, Dr. John Gorham Palfrey, a friend and political ally of the Adamses, felt bound in conscience to defend it, and in his *History of New England* he composed what Henry Adams called an apologia justifying the "ways of God to Man, or, what was much the same thing, of Puritans to other men." A duty rather than a pleasure, for Palfrey was an urbane man who delighted in the unpuritanical amenities of higher English life. He yearned, Adams said, "for the ease of the Athenæum Club in Pall Mall or the Combination Room at Trinity" in Cambridge. His descendants have carried on his ideals both of learning and self-flagellating duty, the most recent, John Gorham Palfrey VII, having been successively a professor in Harvard Law School, headmaster of Phillips Academy Andover, and president of the MacArthur Foundation.

the "gay, svelte, charming" Abigail,* she felt the tug of Catholicism itself, and under the influence of such Catholic thinkers as Hugues-Félicité Robert de Lamennais, Charles Forbes René de Montalembert, and Maurice de Guérin she for the first time saw "the revolutionary social implications" of the Christian faith. Her grandmother, with her Calvinist abhorrence of Rome, looked upon Catholicism's ritual poetry as so much diabolic harlotry, but Vida herself saw in it a means of drawing people out of themselves and promoting fellowship and community. The radical Protestantism of New England had led, or so it seemed to her, to sectarian anarchy, as individuals spun off into ever more eccentric units, ending, finally, in an aloneness that negated the possibility of common life. In the French Catholicism of Lamennais and the Anglo-Catholicism of John Henry Newman and England's Oxford Movement, Vida discovered spiritual disciplines that mediated between the fragment and the whole, the individual and the community. Here was a more potent humanism than that of Mrs. Jack Gardner and her museum, one that brought art and poetry into the midst of life.

As a GIRL VIDA TOYED with a "private fairy tale" in which, "disguised as a boy, she crept into Harvard." But in 1880 she entered Smith College as one of the first generation of American women to go, not to finishing school, but to college.† It was at Smith that she met the friend for whom she was to feel a "passionate tenderness." The daughter of an itinerant schoolteacher and his wife, Clara French had lived, by turns, in New York, Vermont, and Pennsylvania; her childhood was happy. No girl "played with heartier enjoyment than Clara," an acquaintance remembered, though she "did not care so much for the society of children of her own age." Like Vida Scudder, Clara French, too, was an Episcopalian, but a strain of Puritan seriousness of purpose early discovered itself in her. Her elders were impressed by her "truthfulness, honesty, conscientiousness, and purity of thought and act." She was, even as a child, "introspective and analytical," and she closely "studied her motives of thought and deed."

At Smith, where Vida and Clara had rooms in Dewey House, they drank beer, played skittles, read poetry—Matthew Arnold, Browning, Swinburne (the last in

---

* She was the model for Amy in *Little Women*.

† Of the Seven Sisters, as the early women's colleges came to be called, six were founded in the three decades between 1860 and 1890: Vassar in 1861, Wellesley in 1870 (it opened in 1875), Smith in 1871 (it opened in 1875), the Harvard Annex (Radcliffe) in 1879, Bryn Mawr in 1885, and Barnard in 1889. Only Mount Holyoke, founded in 1837, is of an earlier date.

secret). In the mornings they fussed over their hair and made their complicated Victorian toilettes, and at night they stayed up to all hours discussing Religious Doubts. But four years of what Vida called "Girls, Girls, Girls" left her yearning for a more various society, and after she and Clara obtained their undergraduate degrees they went to Oxford for graduate study, the first American women to do so. Under those dreaming spires they sat at the feet of Mr. Ruskin, "an ardent graceful sensitive person," as Vida remembered him, and were informed by him that the "social order was gravely diseased."

It was Mr. Ruskin who awakened in Vida what she called her "passionate sense" that "the Middle Ages rather than the nineteenth century were my natural home." And it was Mr. Ruskin, himself the only child of a rich sherry merchant, who made Vida feel, for the first time, guilt over her comfortable position in life. She had, she was appalled to discover, grown up in "a garden enclosed," an "enclosure of gracious manners, regular meals, comfort, security, good taste." But beyond the garden's walls others were going hungry. A "desperate wish" to atone for her comforts, to mortify her flesh, "to do violence" to herself came over her, and she bore more than a passing resemblance to Olive Chancellor in Henry James's novel *The Bostonians*, who cherishes a "secret" and "most sacred hope" that she might be "a martyr and die for something." At all events Vida went out in search of poor neighborhoods and "dirty garrets," much as Olive Chancellor is possessed by an "immense desire to know intimately some *very* poor girl."

A caged bird, beating her wings "against the bars" of her class, Vida yet knew that she was not original. The desire of well-off persons to go among the poor was, in the 1880s, becoming commonplace. The young Beatrice Potter, the daughter of an English venture capitalist, was as stung by conscience as Vida Scudder, and she went as a sort of princess in disguise to live among mill workers in Lancashire. It was the same in France, Germany, and Scandinavia, where the well-meaning rich sought to abase themselves among the poor and to humble in the dust the pride of money and power. Nowhere, perhaps, was the desire to atone more acute than in the eastern extremity of Christendom, in the Russian Empire, where young idealists known as *Narodniki* were going "to the people."* They wanted to know and help and perhaps even enlighten the Russian peasant

---

* In the "mad summer" of 1874, James Billington writes, "more than two thousand students and a number of older people and aristocrats were swept away by a spirit of self-renunciation." In "almost every province of European Russia, young intellectuals dressed as peasants and set out from the cities to live among them, join in their daily life, and bring to them the good news that a new age was dawning."

and the Petersburg worker, in the belief that by doing so they might "redeem their own sin: that of being born into privilege."

THE GUILT THAT YOUNG WOMEN like Vida Scudder and Beatrice Potter felt in the face of the poor amounted to a break both with much contemporary religious opinion (which held that worldly fortune is a sign of divine favor) and much contemporary moral orthodoxy (which ascribed poverty to failure of character).* Instead of pride in wealth and status, the new penitents were oppressed by a "sense of sin," a consciousness of defects in their own souls, or so Samuel Barnett, an Anglican priest who ministered to the poor in London's East End, believed.

But their penance took different forms. Beatrice Potter was drawn to the Fabian Socialism of George Bernard Shaw and of her own future husband, Sidney Webb. Vida Scudder owed more to the Christian Socialism of John Frederick Denison Maurice, an Anglican theologian, and Samuel and Henrietta Barnett, who established Toynbee Hall in Whitechapel, a civic and educational community in which university students sought redemption by mentoring the urban poor, a sort of Oxbridge college translated to an East End slum.† Under the inspiration of Maurice, Vida became "ardently and definitely a socialist," a more ardent socialist, indeed, than Maurice himself, who "never questioned the right of private property so long as the owner realized his social responsibility." Vida went further, and after Lenin and the Bolsheviks established communism in Russia, she would declare that her "delight in the vast Russian experiment never wavers." But the "ultimate source" of her socialist convictions, she maintained, "was and is Christianity."

AFTER OXFORD VIDA AND CLARA returned to America to become instructors in English literature at Wellesley. But scarcely had they taken up their new positions when Clara lay dead of typhoid fever. "From the day that the friend of my

---

* "Godliness," the Episcopalian holy man William Lawrence declared, "is in league with riches." Lawrence, who succeeded Phillips Brooks both as bishop of Massachusetts and as president of the Groton board of trustees, was a WASP potentate who sat on the Harvard Corporation and who, true to his faith in the godliness of riches, was instrumental in establishing the Business School at Harvard. In his spare time he composed hagiographies of Phillips Brooks and Henry Cabot Lodge.

† Toynbee Hall continued to offer the privileged sinner a path to redemption as late as the 1960s, when John Profumo, disgraced in scandalous amour, resigned his seats in the House of Commons, the Cabinet, and the Privy Council to clean its latrines. He was soon promoted to office work and proved useful in soliciting capital for the institution.

youth died," Vida wrote, "the door to what people call passion swung to in my heart." The remainder of her life would be "passed in calmer air," with the door to passion closed. She would afterward have other companions, and would live in a "Boston marriage" with the writer Florence Converse.* But never again would she love anyone in the way she loved Clara French.

Santayana, after Warwick Potter's death, transmuted erotic passion into philosophy: Vida's remodeled desire found expression in teaching and Anglo-Catholic charity. On a visit to Smith she was walking with friends in the meadows overlooking the Connecticut River when they hit upon the idea of establishing, in America, Settlement Houses modeled on London's Toynbee Hall. Soon thereafter she and her Wellesley colleague, the poet Katharine Lee Bates (author of the anthem "America the Beautiful"), formed the College Settlements Association under the patronage of Phillips Brooks. In 1889 a College Settlement was established in Rivington Street in lower Manhattan; in 1892 Denison House in Boston's Tyler Street, in the old South Cove, opened its doors. (Jane Addams independently opened Hull House in Chicago in 1889.) A Boston journalist, shocked by the sight of well-bred college women going among the poor in Tyler Street, compared the "falling of their young unsullied lives" into a "wretched vicious dismal quarter" of the city to the "falling of a lily in the mud." Such remarks exasperated Vida and her fellow workers "past endurance," for they found, Vida said, not sordidness but "poetry in the hearts of the people" in Tyler Street.

In 1901 VIDA TURNED FORTY and promptly broke down. For many weeks she lay "sleepless in a darkened room." It was another of those obscure nervous crises that were once so prominent a feature of WASP life. In this case breakdown preceded a conversion experience, one that led Vida to pledge herself to the ideals of St. Francis. A pilgrimage to Assisi, where the saint's biographer, Paul Sabatier, showed her the shrines and sacred places, sealed her "consecration to the effort to relate the history and teaching of the *Poverello* [the poor little one] to modern needs . . ." Those needs were, she believed, great. The "vast industrial energies" of the new civilization were devoted to "life's mere machine" and had nothing to say to its spirit. America, in particular, with its sweatshops and tenements,

---

* In her memoir *On Journey,* Vida said that she was never in her life in a sexual relationship with anyone. "I want to register my conviction," she wrote, "and I wish I might have a great many masculine readers at this point, that a woman's life which sex interests have never visited, is a life neither dull nor empty nor devoid of romance."

its furnaces and factories, seemed to be becoming a crueler place: "hell with the lid lifted," said a visitor to Pittsburgh. Something had gone wrong, or so more sensitive WASPs believed. The writer William Dean Howells made the genteel heroine of his 1888 novel *Annie Kilburn* uneasy in her privilege as she confronts poverty and despair in a Massachusetts town: "there's something in the air, the atmosphere, that won't allow you to live in the old way if you've got a grain of conscience or humanity."

What was needed, Vida believed, was a dose of the Middle Ages, of Franciscan charity, of love of one's neighbor. In the very years during which Henry Adams, "buried," as he said, "in the twelfth century," was content to contemplate his social ideal of Chartres, the Virgin and her miraculous Child, in some degree of literary retirement from the world, Vida sought to realize her own vision of agape (compassionate love) through charitable work. She promoted her Settlement Houses and preached the Social Gospel, the mantras of a movement that sought to find Christian solutions to social and economic problems. Visiting Denison House whenever she had time to spare, she was also active in the Church of the Carpenter in Tremont Street, a Christian Socialist mission in which the congregants revived the "agape feasts" (communal dinners) of the early Christians.*

She grew more radical. In her private oratory were to be found a crucifix and a red flag, and she made no secret of her aspiration to combine Franciscan Christianity with the revolutionary socialism of Karl Marx. Noting how St. Thomas Aquinas had, seven centuries before, reconciled the philosophy of Aristotle with the theology of Christ, she looked forward to a time when a thinker would "perform a like service by synthesizing the Catholic faith and Karl Marx."

Her fervent piety and charitable zeal were a reproach to those lukewarm Laodicean souls who, in the language of the Book of Revelation, "art neither cold nor hot." In *Annie Kilburn*, Howells makes his WASP clergyman, the Reverend Julius W. Peck, desire to go "teaching among the mill hands," but in reality it was a WASP woman, Vida Scudder, who took the lead in forging connections between the WASPs and the workers. In 1912 she went up to Lawrence, Massachusetts, the site of mills and looms that funded the WASP way of life, to

---

* Howells was another communicant in the Church of the Carpenter, as was Ralph Adams Cram, a leading WASP architect and a master of Revived and Collegiate Gothic. Cram was an advocate of "walled towns," sanctuaries in which richer forms of common life might exist in the midst of modernity's chaotic sprawl.

address striking textile workers. "I speak for thousands beside myself," she told them, "when I say that I would rather never again wear a thread of woolen than know my garments had been woven at cost of such misery as I have seen and known past the shadow of a doubt to have existed in this town." The outraged editors of the *Boston Evening Transcript* denounced her appearance in Lawrence as a "crime" and demanded that she resign her professorship at Wellesley. The Wellesley trustees (of whom Bishop Lawrence was one) did not seek her resignation, but they did persuade her to give up, for a time, the teaching of her course "Social Ideals in English Letters."

LIKE JAMES'S OLIVE CHANCELLOR, VIDA Scudder felt a "strange hunger for fellowship" with those who were not of her own class, yet like Olive Chancellor she shrank from what she found loathsome in those whom she wanted to help. She spoke candidly of her "nauseating distaste for humanity," a revulsion that grew particularly strong whenever she found herself in crowded places, on buses or in trolley cars. (Olive Chancellor, too, loathes public conveyances "in which every sense" is "displeased.") To overcome this nausea, Vida developed the habit, whenever she was in a public place, of pausing on each unsympathetic face and saying to herself, "God loves you. With tender, distinctive, seeking love. He rejoices in His creation."

She was embarked on a "quest for reality," but a certain New England primness continuously intervened between herself and the world. What she called, with so many genuflections to Dante, her journey led, all too often, not to the real but to the precious: the word "lovely" has a large place in her vocabulary. When Beatrice Potter (by this time Mrs. Sidney Webb) depicted her own path from privilege to radicalism, she did so with a humor and irony that brought the pilgrimage to life. Vida's very different style of memoir holds everything at arm's length, so that even her charity is touched with unreality. Mrs. Webb saw how easily benevolence may be corrupted into "pharisaical self-congratulation": to find that one's touch is received by the less fortunate as a cure for so many scrofulas is fatal to modesty, and even to decency. But Vida, with all her protestations of humility, had very little of this self-knowledge. She was inwardly sure (as the WASP is apt to be) that she was, in fact, a very superior person.

She was brave and daring and decent, yet it is not clear how much practical good Vida Scudder did. Marx and Lenin proved false prophets, and the poor whom she sought to help had as little interest in the humanities (the beau idéal of the Settlement House) as most other people do. Santayana, contemplating the labors of another fervidly altruistic Massachusetts woman, Sarah Whitman, remarked sadly but perhaps accurately that our "good works, alas, are often vainer than our vanities."

But Vida's good works were not altogether vain. Together with such reformers as Jane Addams, Ellen Starr, and Helena Dudley, she tended the flame of WASP charity. The light attracted others; in New York a group of well to do WASP women led by Mary Harriman and Dorothy Whitney were inspired to create a Junior League for the Promotion of the Settlement Movement. Miss Harriman, a daughter of railroad tycoon E. H. Harriman, was moved by Vida's call for debutantes to work in the slums, and went so far as to enroll in Barnard College to study economics and sociology. Miss Whitney, the youngest child of William Collins Whitney, was no less stirred by the work of Settlement House reformers. "I had a most wonderful morning with Miss Jane Addams," she wrote her future husband Willard Straight. A daughter of Gilded Age capitalism, she wanted to soften and humanize the world in which her father had made his fortune, "to work, and help, and carry through something which may be useful."

That Vida Scudder's vision of Franciscan compassion and Marxist political economy should have culminated in the Junior League might amuse the ironist: the moralist is more likely to be conscious of the hazards of Dorothy Whitney's and Mary Harriman's slumming. Henry James composed a novel on the theme, *The Princess Casamassima*, in which he portrayed the enlightened pity of his American-born princess—a type and figure of upper-crust benevolence—as growing out of an unconscious desire to lord it over others. The desire for abasement that James satirized in Olive Chancellor in *The Bostonians* ends in the despotic empathy of the woman who gives her name to *The Princess Casamassima*. Absolute pity corrupts, if not absolutely, thoroughly enough to thwart the good intentions of the pitiers.

Vida Scudder foreshadowed many of the weaknesses of WASP philanthropy, but her methods had this virtue—they got WASPs out of themselves. The Viennese ladies who in the same era lay on the couch in the consulting room of Dr. Freud in Berggasse 19 stewed in their own neuroticisms. Their American counterparts found, in the good works and mildly Sapphic companionship of Settlement House charity and Junior League luncheons, a means of resisting neurasthenic invalidism: a feminine version of Theodore Roosevelt's masculine cult of football and homoerotic athleticism.

Vida Scudder, in the end, did find reality.

The figure Augustus Saint-Gaudens sculpted to mark the grave of
Clover Adams, a monument to WASP neurasthenia.

THIRTEEN

The Visionary Neurasthenics

portando dentro accidioso fummo:
or ci attristiam ne la belletta negra . . .

we carried sloth within us
and now we are sad in the blackened mud . . .
—Dante, *Inferno*

Early in 1868, nineteen-year-old Alice James, the younger sister of William and Henry, was sitting with her father in the library of the James house in Quincy Street in Cambridge when she was seized by a desire to knock dad's head off "as he sat with his silver locks, writing at his table." It was, she later recalled, the first time she broke down "acutely," too weak in "moral power" to impose a "muscular sanity" on the wild and murderous passions of her soul. In an instant she knew "all the horrors and suffering of insanity," for her mind, "worn out with its constabulary functions," could no longer, she said, police the "waves of violent inclination" that washed over her.

For the quarter of a century of life that remained to her, Alice James, as brilliant as Henry and William, or so the brothers themselves maintained, would languish in genteel invalidism. The "slightest exertion," her mother said, was apt to bring on one of her "nervous turns." Tasks such as study and thought, so important to a James, were often beyond her, for such a "violent revolt in her head" would take place that she would, she said, have "to 'abandon' my brain, as it were."

Various causes were conjectured. Hers was said to be a case of "nervous hyperesthesia" or "rheumatic gout" of the stomach; "neurasthenia and neuralgia and headache" seemed to play a part in the business, as did "weariness and palpitation and disgust." Her brother Henry had little patience for such fatuities: he put his sister's condition down to an "intense horror of life."

For Alice James, "a clear, strong intelligence, housed in pain," neurasthenia was a curse. But it could also be a blessing. For Theodore Roosevelt it was a thing to be conquered directly, through strenuous exertion: his neuroticism forced him to make a man of himself. But for other WASPs neurasthenia was a process. It afforded them a holiday from practical tasks, giving them time to figure out who they were and what they were about. Jane Addams emerged from neurasthenic invalidism to found Hull House in Chicago: Henry James passed through a phase of "obscure hurt" in his struggle to become an artist.

Neurasthenia, the WASP disease, was not (except in a few trifling and incidental details) a new thing. It was a modern variation on crises that have been undergone since the beginning of time by those who have drunk deep at the dark well of their nature. Buddha retires to his fig tree in search of illumination, Heraclitus shuns the chatter of the Ephesians to "seek for himself," St. Francis strips off his clothes to find God, David Hume agonizes, at La Flèche, over who and what he is, Wordsworth seeks revelation in the lonely places of Cumbria. WASPs, being WASPs, were less extravagant in their own locusts-and-wild-honey phases; a sickroom tended by house servants served them for a fig tree, a veranda on Cape Ann or Nantucket did duty for a Walden cabin. But they, too, were trying to figure out who and what they were—were trying to work out the justification of their life, and its salvation.

They did so in the teeth of a Yankeeism that looked upon such soul-work as unconscionable laziness, hence the need for a medical cover and a Greek nomenclature. (*Neura*, in Greek, means nerves, *asthenes* means weak or sickly.) The Old World supplied introspective WASPs with additional excuses. In England, in the nineteenth century, a spell of visionary listlessness had become almost as obligatory, for the morally or mentally ambitious, as an Oxbridge degree or a tour of the Continent. Wordsworth set the tone, persuading young people uncertain of their path in life that it was better to "stray about voluptuously through fields and rural walks," to "ask no record of the hours," and to give themselves to "vacant musing," "unreproved neglect," and "deliberate holiday," than it was to live laborious days in competition for the prizes of London, for the gold of the City or the high offices of Westminster. John Stuart Mill and Charles Darwin passed through lazy intervals of funk and mental crisis in preparation for their subsequent tasks, as did Florence Nightingale; Thomas Carlyle had his wilderness years, and John Ruskin languished under his plague-cloud, deepening his perception.

WASPs, too, sought to recover through neurasthenia what the Romans called *otium*—the higher idleness, a creative indolence that was rapidly disappearing from the world. The agitation and hurry of life had grown so intense that people no longer knew how to weave the garlands of repose. They were "ashamed of resting," Nietzsche wrote, and "prolonged reflection" gave them a bad conscience. One thought "with a watch in one's hand," even as one ate "one's midday meal while reading the latest news of the stock market."

Nietzsche resembled WASPs in despising neurasthenic weakness and making use of it himself. For all its liabilities, neurasthenia was a way to escape an age that would "rather do *any*thing than nothing." "The man who lies ill in bed," Nietzsche said, temporarily escapes the stupid bustle of the world: he "discovers that what he is ill from is usually his office, his business, or his society, and that through them he has lost all circumspection with regard to himself: he acquires this wisdom from the very leisure to which his illness has compelled him."

THE DANGER WAS THAT NEURASTHENIA could become a way of life, and the malingerer an addict of illness—the fate of Alice James, the fainéant characters in Thomas Mann's novel *The Magic Mountain*, and innumerable "cultured invalidish ladies with private means" in England and America. But Henry Adams bore witness to the virtues of neurasthenia. In his book *The Education of Henry*

Adams he created a character—a caricature of himself—who is too weak to accomplish anything worthwhile. This Henry Adams traces the origin of his nervous debility to a bout of scarlet fever in childhood. At first "the effect was physical." He "fell behind his brothers two or three inches in height, and proportionally in bone and weight." But his mind, too, cooperated in the "fining-down process of scale." He was "not good in a fight, and his nerves were more delicate than boys' nerves ought to be." He "exaggerated these weaknesses as he grew older," and ascribed to them those qualities that unfitted him for conventional action—a habit of doubt, of distrusting one's judgment, a hesitation to act except as a choice of evils, a shirking of responsibility and a horror of *ennui.*

Adams shows himself, in the *Education,* unwilling to pursue a conventional career; he dabbles, by turns, in the law, diplomacy, journalism, political reform, a Harvard professorship, medieval history, novel-writing, travel-writing, history-writing, but he commits himself to none. He poses as a fatigued spectator for whom all is vanity and vexation of spirit. But the reader comes to see that all this dilettantism and apparent weakness have had a purpose: they have prepared Adams to write the *Education* itself, and in it to diagnose the predicament of his class, to account for its historic decay, and to suggest a way forward. The *Education* in some measure invented the WASPs, and the book remains the tribe's foremost primer, vade mecum, and guide for the perplexed.

Neurasthenia nourished the literary imagination that underlay Adams's flawed but illuminating account of the development of the WASP mind. He knew that the writing-room and the sickroom, never far apart, were incestuously close in the nineteenth century: the books that bit deepest were recapitulations of their authors' suffering. The neurasthenic protagonists of the Bildungsromans—Carlyle's Diogenes Teufelsdröckh, Stendhal's Julien Sorel, Charlotte Brontë's Jane Eyre, Tolstoy's Pierre Bezukhov—struggle to find their place in an age that has little use for their aspirations: they must either brutalize their ideals and outrage their natures or live as pariahs and untouchables, separated from the mass of their fellows by an abyss of sympathy.[*] In the *Education*

---

[*]   Haunting the *Bildungsroman* is the ghost of *Hamlet.* Henry Adams must from an early period in his reading life have been drawn to a character whom the nineteenth century understood as a neurasthenic sufferer, unable to act and afraid to live, who yet through play-acting, the experience of tragedy, and a kind of inward regeneration finds his way, at last, to life, to vitality and serenity of being.

Adams, for all his ironical levity, lays claim to the same ground, and portrays the same struggle to enlist neurasthenia in the service of the visionary and reformist faculties of the mind: he shows that WASPs, too, have wrongs to right.

UNLIKE WALT WHITMAN, HENRY ADAMS did not hear America singing. Looking out of a club window on the turmoil of Fifth Avenue, he saw only anarchy and chaos, "the air and movement of hysteria." Prosperity "never before imagined, power never yet wielded by man, speed never reached by anything but a meteor, had made the world irritable, nervous, querulous, unreasonable and afraid." The "vigorous and unscrupulous" energies of the plutocrats had torn "society to pieces and trampled it under foot," while a discontented citizenry perpetually chased a brighter sun that continually eluded it.

But these were only the symptoms, Adams was convinced, of a deeper problem. His historical studies led him to doubt whether his country was capable of rising, as other civilizations had occasionally done, above mere "physical content" to attain a "higher order" of "intelligence or morality." American democracy had created a "vast and uniform" society as well as prosperous one, but it had little power to "ennoble" its citizens or uncover their deeper potential. Remarkably enough, Adams traced this incapacity to an insufficiency of light in the very ancestors whom he and his fellow WASPs professed to venerate. In this he was something of a traitor to his class: demoralized WASPs in the decades after the Civil War were finding a dubious refuge in ancestor worship. They might not be as rich as the Gilded Age tycoons who had surpassed them, but they possessed superior pedigrees, the blood-fetishes on which such WASP cartels as the Daughters of the American Revolution (founded in 1890) and the *Social Register* Association (which dates from the 1880s) rested.* Adams himself, as we have seen, was not above such consolations. "Never in his life," he wrote, "would he have to explain who he was." He was an Adams. But the historian in him was, at times, stronger than the snob, and overcoming the "dominion of blood and sepulcher," he showed that the Puritans and Patriots in his line could not escape blame for the state of the country they had created. The laws and markets they ordained had made possible a freedom and a material abundance

---

* To be sure, a number of WASPs looked on the *Social Register* as demotically lax in its standards. One Proper Bostonian is reported to have described it with contempt as a "damned telephone book."

that were the envy of the world. The problem, Adams believed, was that these institutions engaged only a narrow spectrum of the passions and the virtues. What the ancestors did they did well: but they did not do enough. In raising the fabric of American democracy on so shallow an emotional foundation, the architects of America's civil establishments contented themselves with a system that overstimulated one or two of the citizen's appetites, while whole regions of her moral and instinctual life lay fallow.

Adams's dinner-party acquaintance John Stuart Mill had similarly broken with a patriarchal faith, and for similar reasons. Mill had, as a teenager, adopted his father James Mill's philosophy (utilitarian and boring) as his own, and he had discovered in it "what might truly be called an object in life; to be a reformer of the world." During several years the young Mill's "own happiness was entirely identified" with his father's program. But in time he awakened from his heritage as from a dream, and was plunged into a nightmare:

> It was in the autumn of 1826. I was in a dull state of nerves, such as everybody is occasionally liable to; unsusceptible to enjoyment or pleasurable excitement; one of those moods when what is pleasure at other times, becomes insipid or indifferent; the state, I should think, in which converts to Methodism usually are, when smitten by their first "conviction of sin." In this frame of mind it occurred to me to put the question directly to myself: "Suppose that all your objects in life were realized; that all the changes in institutions and opinions which you are looking forward to, could be completely effected at this very instant: would this be a great joy and happiness to you?" And an irrepressible self-consciousness distinctly answered, "No!" At this my heart sank within me: the whole foundation on which my life was constructed fell down. All my happiness was to have been found in the continual pursuit of this end. The end had ceased to charm, and how could there ever again be any interest in the means? I seemed to have nothing left to live for.

Mill fell into a "dry, heavy dejection" that he carried with him "into all companies, into all occupations." The cloud grew thicker; Coleridge's poem "Dejection: An Ode" exactly described, he said, his state of mind:

A grief without a pang, void, dark and drear,
A drowsy, stifled, unimpassioned grief,
Which finds no natural outlet or relief
In word, or sigh, or tear . . .

Relief came only with Mill's recognition that his father's limited philosophy was itself a cause of his despondency. It did not give a "proper place, among the prime necessities of human well-being, to the internal culture of the individual," nor did effect a proper "balance among the faculties of the mind" or take into account "the importance of poetry and art as instruments of human culture."

Just as the young Mill sought to humanize his father's creed with the higher "culture of the feelings" he found in Wordsworth, so Adams countered the efficient but narrow Yankeeism of his forebears with a more generous notion of possibility, one that owed something to his friend Matthew Arnold's idea of developing "all sides of our humanity." England, Arnold argued, had forsaken the "splendid spiritual effort" of the Elizabethan Age and was now devoting itself to coal and "industrial operations depending on coal." This philistine equation of national greatness with coal led Englishmen to develop one or two sides of their being "at the expense of all others," and made for a nation of "incomplete and mutilated men." America, Adams believed, was in a similar case: it, too, was producing citizens "stunted and enfeebled" in their nature and potential. He himself, he saw, was one of them.

BLAMING THE PARENTS FOR THE failures of the children would become, in the heyday of Freudianism, a WASP pastime. Henry Adams anticipated the trend, urging his wounded contemporaries to rouse themselves from their neurasthenic fatigues and repair the errors of the ancestors.* His discovery of the primal sin of the fathers—their narrowness of vision—illuminates WASP culture and in some

---

* Together with memories of color (sitting "on a yellow kitchen floor in strong sunlight"), illness and taste (coming down with scarlet fever and his aunt "entering the sickroom bearing in her hand a saucer with a baked apple"), and displacement (being "bundled up in blankets" and carried from his family's house in Hancock Avenue to a new, larger one in Mount Vernon Street), some of Adams's most vivid early recollections are of filial resentment: of his grandfather John Quincy Adams for making him go to school, and of his great-grandfather John Adams for being a dull writer whose work he was forced to help his father edit. How mortifying, for Henry, that these forebears, with all their faults, should have had, by any worldly measure, so much greater success than he! It must have been an unconscious satisfaction to him that the Republic they founded was inadequate.

measure explains it. He made articulate the partly formed, half conscious idea of the WASPs that, however much they might venerate their forebears, there was something missing in the civilization they created. Political reform by itself could not fill the void. It must be supplemented by cultural regeneration, and cultural regeneration—this was the crucial insight—was impossible without forums in which the soul, protected from the rapidity and chaos of American life, could ripen. Looking back longingly to the stoas and porticos of the Mediterranean, Adams was never more of a WASP than when he reflected on the virtues of the old civic culture, the "classic and promiscuous turmoil of the forum, the theatre, or the bath," formative institutions "which trained the Greeks and the Romans" in their prime, and brought alive parts of their nature that would otherwise have been neglected, but which were unknown in America.

Yet Adams's most delicate stroke was his suggestion that the cultural revolution he contemplated was unrealizable. The acceleration of mechanical power in America would, he predicted, doom the efforts of the preppy rebels and frondeurs; the WASP coup d'état he advocated would ultimately fail. In effect *The Education of Henry Adams* dared its readers to prove its author wrong.

Amory Gardner, who gave Groton its chapel, believed with the Greeks that a "poet was in the broadest and deepest sense the educator of a people."

FOURTEEN

Billy Wag's *Paideia*

fatti non foste a viver come bruti,
ma per seguir virtute e canoscenza . . .

you were not made to live as brutes,
but to follow virtue and knowledge . . .
—Dante, *Inferno*

One day the boys put Amory Gardner's chair on his desk "to see what he'd do." When Mr. Gardner came in he "simply climbed on the desk into the chair and began the class." He asked whether the boys had their "squibs"—their lessons—in order. No, they hadn't, they said, whereupon he did a "frantic dance on the desk" and pretended to pull his hair out by the roots. When Mr. Gardner's cousin, the Rector, who happened to be passing by, looked in, disapproval was "written in every inch of his large frame."

Later they argued all the way to the Rector's study. "Amory, it's an impossible situation for the other men when you allow the boys to carry on so." "Cottie, I deeply resent your interfering in my teaching. I seriously object to being treated like a little boy. Either my method of teaching is sound or it is not." "No one is interfering with your teaching. The trouble is you're not teaching. You're demoral izing the entire school." "I might as well resign right now, but before I do I insist that you allow me to speak to the school and explain why I am resigning and why I heartily disapprove of Groton." "You know very well, Amory, I will not let you address the school and that furthermore I wouldn't let you resign even if you seriously intended to." Whereupon, it is recorded, Mrs. Peabody came into the room and took them both for a walk.

Amory Gardner was not pleased with the changes at Groton. New buildings were going up. Hundred House, with its bright white porticos, enclosed one side of the Circle, the great oval lawn—a happy inspiration of Frederick Law Olmsted's—around which the school was arranged. The Schoolhouse rose in its gold-capped bell tower to check another. The buildings made possible a larger school: there were now more than eighty young WASPs at Groton and there would soon be almost a hundred. Yet Amory Gardner's cousin insisted that they had retained the "family aspect" of the place, the very essence of the experiment. There has "been quite as homelike a feeling, as close an intimacy of masters and boys as existed in the first year of our history," Cotty Peabody wrote to the trustees. Hundred House, the new residential building, was not simply a dormitory, it was "the house of the Head Master, where live not simply his own immediate family but the Masters, boys, and servants, all uniting to constitute one family. It is not a dormitory where boys room and board: it is a home where they live."

Not less important, in Peabody's eyes, the school had now something of the "*esprit de corps* which comes to a larger body." Standards of conduct "are definitely more established and those who come to the school are probably more quickly impressed by them than they have been before." There would be no more Ed Carters, no more subversive hut-building, no more prefect revolts at Groton.

Mr. Gardner, or Billy Wag, as the boys called him, was skeptical. True, the school was still smaller than most schools. And no doubt the Circle helped: the life of the school revolved around it, drawing everything to one center, and shaping the encounters of the students and teachers who each day ate and played, studied and prayed together, as though in some medieval commune untouched by time.*

But it was not enough. Groton's very "flavor" and "personality," Mr. Gardner believed, hung in the balance. He would have to do something.

THERE WAS A CONTINUOUS TENSION, sometimes playful, sometime serious, between Amory Gardner and the Rector. Billy Wag was, by nature and through continuous smoking, nervous, dyspeptic, and frail, and he shrank from overbearing persons. He had a large house built for himself next to the campus in which he lived with his servants, "the excellent Percy" and "the invaluable Mary," in the fear of "offending whom he spent the balance of his days." The robust Peabody and his no-nonsense lieutenant, Sherrard Billings, were much amused by the nervous sensitivity of their delicate colleague. Once, in "a spirit of mischief," Billings told Billy Wag that an especially formidable mother "would, I felt sure, want to consult him." "Amory. . . . got quite frantic and said if the school did not protect him against weeping mothers he would resign. I explained to him that his very work as a schoolmaster involved relations toward parents the duties of which he might not shirk. He announced that in that case he would resign." "I thought I should die laughing at him," Billings said.

The Rector was an Old Testament patriarch, the ultimate father figure in an age when patriarchy was dying. Mr. Gardner embodied a more indulgent, forgiving, maternal style of teaching and parenting.† The Rector was the straightest of straight arrows; Mr. Gardner, recent scholarship suggests, was gay. In those days gay men could not, of course, hope to have families of their own without

---

* The Circle, Peabody said, was intended to "emphasize the unity as well as the comprehensiveness" of Groton as a place in which one could realize one's nature, a humanity defined not simply by one's commonplace needs but by one's higher aspirations. With Hundred House to the south, the Schoolhouse to the north, the gymnasium and the chapel to the east, and the mountains and the sunset to the west, the Circle represented to the student "the all-round man with learning and physical strength and home life and spiritual truth coming as a matter of course into his expanding nature."

† Mr. Gardner was not alone, among WASPs and honorary WASPs, in moving away from Puritan patriarchy and experimenting with models of maternal nurture inspired, consciously or unconsciously, by pagan and Catholic models. Henry Adams saw in the Madonna and Child the perfection of human society, while Roxana Beecher (the mother of Harriet Beecher Stowe, author of *Uncle Tom's Cabin*) and Henry James, Sr. (the father of William, Henry, Alice, *et alia*) experimented with a more feminine approach to parenting and education.

stooping to dissemble, and many found substitutes by entering the caring professions. Walt Whitman became a nurse, John Henry Newman a priest. Mr. Gardner became a teacher, the school's "resident aesthete," as one scholar has called him. Yet most studies of the Groton experiment, transfixed by Peabody, have overlooked Mr. Gardner's contributions. When the Rector got carried away with football and muscular discipline, Billy Wag, who stood for art and sensitivity, acted as a counterweight. Lounging "in his canoe, smoking endless cigarettes, reading Russian novels and Greek tragedies," he reminded one of his students, Matthew Arnold's grandson, Arnold Whitridge, that "there was a world" beyond the playing field.

E. M. Forster said that the boarding schools of England sent forth boys "with well-developed bodies, fairly developed minds, and undeveloped hearts" into a world of "whose richness and subtlety" they had "no conception." Mr. Gardner wanted Groton to be a place that would develop the heart and give young WASPs some idea of the richness and subtlety of the world: a place that might, moreover, be bearable for odd and gifted boys, who as a rule find the discipline, conformity, and want of sympathy in a boarding school oppressive.

He did not wholly succeed; his cousin, the paterfamilias of the school, was always the dominant figure. Each morning after chapel, Endicott Peabody would come into the great schoolroom in the Schoolhouse, with its oaken rafters and busts of eminent sages,* for roll call and announcements. "He never hurried," one graduate remembered. "He never sauntered. He always looked the school right in the eye as though he was looking for trouble. The quick cadence of his step was always exactly the same. His black shoes were polished. His blue suit, starched collar, white bow tie, also starched, were always exactly and precisely as expected."

George Biddle, who would become an artist, remembered how, one Saturday at roll call, the Rector read off the weekly list of black marks (demerits for misconduct). Biddle had received twenty-two. (The "usual allowance for a healthy-spirited boy" was three or four.) "I was already somewhat nervous," he said, but when the Rector "reached my name on the school list and paused a long minute, scowling, without pronouncing it, I was really jittery." At length Peabody "looked up slowly, searching me out, and said: 'Biddle, go to my study.' As I worked my way forward between the rows of desks, I could not in sheer nervousness take my eyes off his angry stare. What had at first been a smile of

---

* The sages had been selected on the advice of Charles Eliot Norton.

frightened deprecation grew into a yawning rictus of despair." Yet when they were alone together the Rector was gentle. "George," he said, "if I had not known you were such a good boy, I should have sent you home long ago."

Peabody's pastoral concern for his boys—"he loved them all," Walter Hinchman said—was real, but they could never quite bring themselves to trust it. "The way he walked," one of his graduates said, "was incompatible with the way he talked; and the boys believed their eyes rather than their ears." They admired his strength, his toughness, his habit of command, and were reluctant to cultivate qualities that seemed at odds with it. The effect, Biddle said, "was to stifle the creative impulse. . . . In other respects the school was admirable."

Those who did go their own way had a hard time of it. Dean Acheson, who in his words "bucked the Establishment and the system" at Groton, was made to suffer for it by his schoolmates, who danced around the future secretary of state and mocked him as a "fairy." "Oddity," said Oliver La Farge, who would win the Pulitzer Prize for his novel *Laughing Boy*, "was inferiority" at Groton. And yet for all that, the school produced a number of graduates who in later life were odd and original characters, as well as questioners of conventional wisdom: Mr. Gardner's heterodoxy was not in vain. The very act of resisting the school's narrowness seems to have toughened, in a few boys at least, whatever faculties make for boldness in life. "At Groton, I didn't happen to feel like conforming," Acheson later said. "And to my surprise and astonishment, I discovered not only that an independent judgment might be the right one, but that a man was actually alive and breathing once he had made it." Acheson's friend Averell Harriman, of the form of 1909, had something similar in mind when he told Arthur Schlesinger that "the only recipe for success is to be unhappy at Groton."

AMORY GARDNER'S INFLUENCE WAS FELT in other ways. The Rector was a low or, perhaps more accurately, a broad churchman; Mr. Gardner was a high-church Anglo-Catholic who had been moved by the sight of Cardinal Newman, robed in "gorgeous scarlet," celebrating Mass amid clouds of incense. He gave Groton its current chapel. Designed in the Gothic Revival style by the English architect Henry Vaughan, it culminates in a tower that rises (somewhat theatrically, critics have objected) above the campus, its pinnacles directing the eyes of young WASPs heavenward.

Medievalism and Revived Gothic were in vogue in the late nineteenth century. But Groton's chapel owed less to John Ruskin, the Victorian prophet who in his hatred of Palladian and neoclassical architecture was drawn to the sublime "savageness" and "grotesqueness" of Gothic, than it did to Mr. Gardner's belief that at the bottom of every really vital institution there is always a whiff of poetry or mysticism.* The play of light and shadow in the chapel was meant to appeal to the imagination of boys, yet if Gardner was a medievalist in his love of obscurity and half-light, he was in his educational theory drawn to the clarity of the classical Greeks. He was steeped in the Greek conviction that art "has a limitless power of converting the human soul—a power which the Greeks called *psychagogia*," the turning of the psyche. Even more important, for Gardner, than the architecture of his chapel was its music. He subscribed to the idea with which the Greeks changed the world, or, at any rate, opened the mind, the belief, in Plato's words, that music and poetry (the Greeks did not distinguish between the two as we do) are the most important element in education because their rhythms and harmonies sink "furthest into the depths of the soul and take hold of it most firmly by bringing it nobility and grace."

It would be difficult to say whether Amory Gardner was more enamored of the medievalism of his age—the passion for Gothic that Ruskin and Pugin helped to arouse—or its Hellenism, the "sweetness and light" that Matthew Arnold, following a hint from Jonathan Swift, thought the essence of Greek culture. This Hellas of the Victorians has been described as "a shimmering fantasy," quite unfaithful to the historical facts, and it is easy to detect, in Arnold's rhapsodies on the "aërial ease, clearness, and radiancy" of the Greeks and Pater's effusions on their "flawless" beauty, an element of romantic escapism. But Gardner was working in a somewhat different vein, and he insisted that the Greeks knew what they were about when they used literature and poetry to stimulate the mind. The sort of liberating teaching that found its way into the 1989 film *Dead Poets Society* had its origin in teachers who, like Gardner, believed with the Greeks that a certain kind of education can inspire in a young person a higher idea of what a human being might be.

---

* George Biddle saw that Endicott Peabody was also imbued with the curious medievalism that characterized a good deal of early WASP culture. His neo-medievalism, Biddle thought, "was possibly as radical an influence on secondary education in 1890 as the City and Country and Walden Schools of the succeeding generation." Where the progressive educators "had their roots in the thought-mechanism of Freud and Dewey's pragmatic psychology," Peabody "drew from a system stemming from the Middle Ages. Probably Mr. Peabody's most radical innovation was the attempt to break down on various fronts the wall which since the days of Pierre Abelard had separated boys from masters." It was characteristic, both of the man and the age, that on Sunday evenings Peabody should have read Dante aloud to the sixth formers (in Charles Eliot Norton's translation, of course).

It was possibly the most radical aspect of the experiment. The humane education invented by the Greeks, so powerful in intention, was by the nineteenth century almost a dead letter—a thing being carried on mechanically, a rote exercise in learning dead languages with little appreciation for their living power, an often abysmal grind. Amory Gardner wanted to recover its original purposes. He knew that when, as Plato says, the Athenian grammatists "set the works of good poets before the children on their desks to read and make them learn by heart," their object was not, in fact, to torment the young. They believed in their bones that art and literature could change the soul, that a "poet was in the broadest and deepest sense the educator of his people."*

As a result of Mr. Gardner's labors, education went on at Groton, if not quite as it had done in Athens, at any rate in an atmosphere of choirs and poetries. (As much as Henry Adams's *Mont-Sant-Michel and Chartres*, Groton was a WASP exercise in "antimodern vitalism.") The hymns of morning chapel, derived from the Psalms or from medieval canticles done into English, blended, in the brains of the boys, with the poetry they encountered in the Schoolhouse, the music of Homer and Shakespeare. Archaic as such methods appeared in a progressive age, they worked: and in later life Mr. Gardner's boys recalled the awakening power of those poetries. "I remember one December morning, the campus swathed in mist, and going to chapel and hearing *Veni Emmanuel*, of Israel mourning in lonely exile, and thinking, strangely, of the wounded stag in Virgil, stricken by Ascanius—for we were reading the *Aeneid* that year—and it seemed in that moment that I knew all the pity and sorrow in the world . . ." Dean Acheson himself, the rebel of the form of 1911, would go on to praise what he called, in a 1966 address at Groton, the "old Greek" ideal of fulfillment, a notion of human completeness he first encountered in his old school.

※

---

* Dante, with his faith in the liberal arts and his belief that great books are tools that help one to realize one's potential, was another influence on Mr. Gardner, who kept a bust of the poet in his classroom in the Schoolhouse. (It is now the Gardner Library.) Dante makes Virgil—*l'altissimo poeta*, whose work was the foundation of liberal education in the West for more than a millennium—his teacher and guide in the *Divine Comedy*: and the poem is itself intended to be, among other things, an education in humane letters, incorporating and reworking elements of the literary and philosophic canon in its author's pursuit of an ideal of completeness.

It was the *paideia*[*] of Billy Wag, an immersion in the best that has been thought and said in the world, with the object of opening students' minds, and it did something to make up for what was lost in the larger school Groton became. With his practical medievalism and his revived Hellenism, Gardner was, his student Ellery Sedgwick said, a *lusus naturae*, a freak of nature, a benign Harlequin. With "Aeschylus or Homer doubled back in his pocket to keep the place, he would hover about the school he loved beyond all earthly things, kindling the brains of the intelligent to a pure flame . . ."

He "poured his whole soul into his teaching," one of his old boys remembered, "and wore himself out in the classroom," a classroom that bore more than a passing resemblance to the one Wordsworth described in his elegy, "a play-house in a barn/Where Punch and Hamlet play together." "That he was teaching a dead language," Arnold Whitridge said, "never occurred to him or to us." A Greek lesson was never simply an exercise in declining nouns or conjugating verbs. A passage about dogs in the *Iliad* would lead Billy Wag to the architecture of Belgium, the canals of Holland and New York, the burial of the dead, famous epitaphs, the battle of Thermopylae, Aegean steamers, and the unreasonableness of publishers.

Above all, he wanted his boys to think for themselves: only then could they withstand the collision with the world that would come. When the "tempest and dark hour are upon him," he said, the "obedient little boy" who had learned by rote was lost. He held fast to his idea that a different kind of education in a different kind of school would turn out men who would be of some service to the world.

---

[*] *Paideia* is an untranslatable Greek word that encompasses child-rearing, education, culture, literature, and philosophy, indeed the whole effort to mold the soul in accordance with an ideal.

It was through his public service, the neurasthenic Stimson confessed, that he got out of the "dark places" and saw the stars.

FIFTEEN

Henry Stimson Sees the Stars

se mai sarai di fuor da' luoghi bui . . .

if ever you get out of these dark places . . .
—Dante, *Inferno*

The family of Henry Stimson was as neurotic as the most respectable WASP could desire. His grandfather, Henry Clark Stimson, was a successful stockbroker with a seat on the New York Stock Exchange, but he hated the work and its pressures, suffered from nightmares, and felt himself perpetually on the verge of breaking down. After the Panic of 1873, in which he lost most of his money, he retired, and between his wife's trust income and what remained of his own fortune, he was able to live the life of a comfortable neurasthenic rentier in a brownstone on East Thirty-fourth Street.

It was much the same in the next generation. Henry Stimson's uncle, John, became a painter, his father, Lewis, yet another unhappy stockbroker. In 1871, when Henry was four, his father left Wall Street to become a doctor. Four years later his wife died, and Henry was raised by his grandparents and a maiden aunt in the brownstone on the Thirty-fourth Street. He found the city oppressive. His mother's death, he said, was a "crushing blow" not only to him but also to his father, who, although he never remarried, seems to have been often absent from his son's life. Then, too, the boy loved the outdoors, but other than the cobbled streets there was no place to play, not even Mr. Olmsted's Central Park, where the meadows "were strictly fore-closed against trespass."

At thirteen "there came a great change." He entered Phillips Academy Andover, the oldest and most illustrious of American boarding schools. Founded in 1778 by Samuel Phillips as a Puritan academy intended to protect its charges from the "Deformity and Odiousness of VICE," it soon became a proving ground for young Brahmins, for Lowells, Longfellows, Quincys, and Holmeses. When Stimson arrived on Andover Hill in 1880 the school was emerging from a period of stagnation, and under the leadership of Cecil Bancroft it had just begun to recover its old reputation for excellence. Stimson was impressed both by the rigor he found in the classroom and by the lack of constraint outside of it. The culture of Andover, he said, was one of "perfect freedom, tempered by expulsion." In contrast to "the paternalistic and highly supervised life" of Anglican schools like St. Paul's and Groton, Andover, and its familial rival, Phillips Exeter, were, the preppy sociologist Digby Baltzell has written, "more like small colleges," encouraging "self-reliance in a more permissive atmosphere." In this liberating environment Stimson's mental and physical horizons broadened. The school opened up for him a "new world of effort and competition" as well as of natural beauty, for he came to love the "hills and woodlands of northern Massachusetts."

Ever since Andover's Calvinist days, when the pious faculty looked with trepidation on the Unitarian heresies of Harvard, the school sent most of her graduates to Yale, and in 1884 Stimson followed what he called the "deeply rutted route" to New Haven. Yale at that time did not have the academic preeminence it would later attain, and in its intellectual deserts Stimson encountered no minds of the caliber of George Santayana or William James. The only teacher he acknowledged in his account of his college days was

William Graham Sumner, from whom he took a class in economics. But if Yale's classes were dull, its social life was stimulating. Santayana himself, who went down to see the school with Warwick Potter in 1892, found it "a most living, organic, distinctive, fortunate place, a toy Sparta to match our toy Athens at Harvard."

WHAT STIMSON GOT AT YALE was less liberal education than a course in club-bableness. In the masculine and sporting atmosphere of the college he learned to be a good sport, and in his junior year he attained the ultimate proof that he measured up when he was tapped for Skull and Bones. All his life Stimson would have a great and perhaps excessive faith in the WASP institutions to which he belonged, and in their ability to separate the wheat from the chaff. To have made the grade at Andover, Yale, Bones, the Century, and the Down Town, was for him evidence of character. He was never quite sure about a fellow without the right imprimaturs, but as for the properly pedigreed man, well, you could trust him implicitly. You would willingly see your sister marry him, and just as happily offer him a position in your firm. Indeed the story is told that Stimson, having been favorably impressed by one of his law clerks, could only with the difficulty be persuaded that the young man had *not* been at Andover or Yale.

After college in New Haven came law school in Cambridge, where Stimson found a "spirit of independent thinking unlike anything I had met before." The intellectual vitality of Harvard was seductive, and in his enthusiasm for knowledge he allowed himself the luxury taking of courses in the philosophy department. The sirens' song was enchanting, but he kept his head, and in 1890 he dutifully entered a law office at 52 Wall Street in New York. He disliked it so much that his worried father sought the advice of his old friend and Yale classmate William Collins Whitney. Whitney was himself the most important client of Elihu Root, the leading lawyer in New York, and he proposed that the promising young man should go to work for him.

Stimson soon found himself employed in the office of Root & Clark on the fourteenth floor of the Liberty Mutual Building, absorbed in legal work for the Whitney empire. Whitney's "notoriously profitable" street car enterprise was adding a new Broadway line, the cars of which were to be drawn by cables rather than horses. Whitney had, too, an abundance of political interests, closely connected to his business ones.* He seemed, at times, to hold the Democratic Party itself in the palm of his hand, and he was instrumental in Grover Cleveland's two elections as president of the United States. With some reluctance he served as secretary of the navy in Cleveland's first administration, but he declined a place in the second, though both the State Department and the London Embassy were said to have been his for the asking.

Whitney was a smoothly plausible figure, handsome and coolly intelligent; Henry Adams envied him his cynicism, which was real, and not, like Adams's own, the mere scar tissue of wounded idealism. But Whitney's deeper motives are a mystery. His marriage to Flora Payne was, by the early nineties, mostly hollow, and he was in love with a pretty widow, Mrs. Arthur Randolph.† When Flora reproached him for his infidelity, he professed innocence. Edith Randolph was, he said, merely "companionable, and bright spirited. I enjoyed her socially. Why shouldn't I?" Flora raised her eyebrows; it was not the first time her husband had been engrossed in a woman who was not his wife. Madame Reuterskiold and Sally Davis, Fanny Woolsey and Mrs. Hulbert, the list went on. And then there was Ellen Hopkins. When, Flora said, she was herself "broken hearted and really out of my mind, all you and Ellen thought of was to get away with each other and 'gas.'"

Whitney was not a Victorian lecher after the fashion of, say, Queen Victoria's own son, Edward Albert, Prince of Wales. Unlike the future Edward VII, he observed the proprieties, or seemed to. His manners were good. He was generous, very much the Yale and Skull and Bones man, with a winning way about him. Yet his extravagance rivaled that of the most garish figures of the age. His oldest daughter, Pauline, made her debut amid a profusion of orchids in a monstrous house on Fifth Avenue, in a ballroom plundered from a French château. His oldest son, Harry Payne Whitney, married Gertrude Vanderbilt amid ostentation that might have made Trimalchio stare. Whitney's apologists have tried to

---

* Abram Hewitt, a fellow, though a more faithful "Bourbon" Democrat sympathetic to free trade, the gold standard, and laissez-faire economics, thought Whitney one "of the most sinister figures" of the age, a master of Gilded Age graft. His streetcar successes depended on his bribery of the Tammany sachems, and he was said to have been party to the purchase, for his father-in-law, Henry Payne of Ohio, of a seat in the United States Senate, a transaction in which $100,000 was distributed to the more corruptible legislators at Columbus. But it is unlikely that extent of Whitney's malfeasance will ever be fully known, so intricate was the web he wove: one might as well try to untwine the clotted hairs in a drain.

† "Well!" Whitney wrote to Flora. "We have made quite a failure of it, but for the sake of the children and society we will say nothing."

explain this vulgarity as the lavishness of a Medici prince. But Whitney patronized very few artists, and his taste was hideous. The sphinx was, finally, without
a secret; beneath the gaudy display and uncommon abilities there was a hollowness. He was so little afraid of neurotic despair—the bruised and aching inner
life so many WASPs dreaded—that he actually encouraged his sons in vacuous
pursuits that would leave them with time and themselves on their hands. Both
Harry and Payne were at Groton under Mr. Peabody, but neither responded to
his call to service; they instead became sportsmen and club kings.

HENRY STIMSON WAS IN A different mold. He prospered under Elihu Root,
who became his mentor and took him into partnership. But the profession of
law was never, he said, "thoroughly satisfactory to me, simply because the life
of the ordinary New York lawyer is primarily and essentially devoted to making
money—and not always successfully so." There was no relish of salvation in it,
and no room for public spirit. Such sentiments would have been incomprehensible
to Whitney, Stimson's patron and fellow Bonesman, whose sole ambition *was* to
make money and whose work in the public service was undertaken primarily
to advance his private interests. But unlike Whitney, Stimson was a characteristic
WASP, one who needed the inspiration of a higher purpose to make his life at
all bearable. The historian Lewis Namier once said that "men do not go into
politics for their health." This might have been true of the eighteenth-century
English squires whom he was studying, but for WASPs like Stimson it was quite
otherwise. They found the respectable professional work they were expected
to do stifling; it demanded a suppression of natural gifts and energies which,
once obstructed, invariably produced the symptoms of which Stimson himself
was always complaining, insomnia, poor digestion, bad nerves, the whole ships
catalogue of neurotic fatigue.

He found, as Theodore Roosevelt did, a degree of relief in camping, hunting,
the hygienic virtues of the strenuous life. For many years he "spent a portion of
nearly every year in the mountains and forests of the western Rockies or Canada,
exploring, hunting, traveling by horse, foot, or canoe." It made him feel better.
But he yearned, too, as Roosevelt did, for the still more potent psychic satisfactions of public service. He got his chance when, in 1906, he was appointed
United States Attorney for the Southern District of New York. He immediately
set about making the office an instrument of reform. Like Roosevelt, he wanted
to save capitalism from the capitalists, or at any rate from the fraudulent and

monopolistic ones whose stupidity, he believed, was preparing the way for revolution. He was nothing if not righteous; in two of his most significant prosecutions, he brought suit against clients of his own former law firm, the National Bank of North America and the American Sugar Refining Company (which had supplied the cash for poor Louisine Havemeyer's spurious Titians).

Yet what is no less revealing than the trust-busting élan of Stimson's public service is the way it relieved an accumulation of personal despair. Stimson was, in his own way, a WASP humanist, one who believed that man (being neither a beast nor a god) is a *zōon politikon*, a creature of his community, one who fulfills a part of his nature in contributing to the public good. In the eyes of his old Yale professor, William Graham Sumner, this was economic heresy: but it had the merit of relieving dyspepsia. The means by which Stimson sought to serve the public were different from those of Theodore Roosevelt. Roosevelt courted votes in the democratic arena; Stimson ran for office only once, in 1910, when he was the Republican candidate for governor of New York. "His cultured accent," a journalist wrote, "his uneasy platform presence, his cold personality, almost every detail of his manner betrayed his birth and breeding, gave his electorate an impression of a young aristocrat who condescends to rule, and who, though he may be a good ruler, condescends." He lost the election, and during a long career did almost all of his service in appointive positions; he was less a political leader than a gray eminence, a Mycroft Holmes, upon whom political leaders could rely for disinterested counsel.

His approach was at once more modest and more realistic than Henry Adams's. He conceded more to modernity than Adams was willing to do. He did not try to be an Athenian, living always at the highest pitch of genius and poetry. Instead he patiently mastered the mandarin arts of bureaucracy, the highly specialized but often dull work of mobilizing the powers of the modern administrative state: he wrote a lot of memos. In this he resembled one of his heroes, Oliver Wendell Holmes Jr., who undertook the "laborious study" of a "dry and technical system," the common law, in order to serve his country as a judge. Stimson's mind was more pedestrian than Holmes's; he was not, as Holmes was, a philosopher. But he resembled him in his contempt for *mere* specialization, the specialization that ends in the complacencies of the expert. Like Holmes, he looked upon expertise as a means to an end, that of becoming the sort of public servant who never loses sight of human ends. Holmes believed that "a man may live greatly in the law as well as elsewhere." A similar faith inspired Stimson's conviction that one could live largely in the public service. In language reminiscent of Dante, he expressed the sense of liberation he felt in the early days of his tenure as United States Attorney. "I had gotten out of the dark places where I had been wandering all my life, and got out where I could see the stars . . ."

Franklin Roosevelt as a sixth former at Groton, April 1900.

SIXTEEN

Pax Americana

Va, ch'i' son forte e ardito . . .

Keep going, for I am strong and daring . . .
—Dante, *Inferno*

When he rode up the Albany road to Springwood, the Roosevelt estate in Hyde Park, New York, the village men doffed their caps and addressed him as "Master Franklin." The boy grew up surrounded by servants, governesses, tutors, insulated, to a great extent, from the coarseness of the world. He was his mother's only child; his father, James Roosevelt, was a fifty-two-year-old widower when he married twenty-six-year-old Sara Delano in 1880. Her "plump, pink" boy was born two years later. Fretting lest any harm come to him, she and Mr. James educated him at home. Master Franklin was instructed by a series of governesses, the last of whom was a Miss Clay, an Englishwoman. But Miss Clay was not quite up to snuff for so bright a boy as the young master, or so his parents thought. There was, too, the matter of the Groton entrance examination. Master Franklin's name had been set down for the school before it even opened; and Mr. James, concerned that his son might forfeit his place, prudently engaged, first, a Mr. Foley, and afterward Arthur Dumper, a former master in St. Paul's School, as tutors in succession to Miss Clay.

Mr. James was growing ever more feeble. In 1890 he took to his bed with chest pains. He had, as the English say, a "heart"—cardiopulmonary trouble—and together with Sara and Franklin, he crossed to Europe and made the obligatory pilgrimages to Bad Nauheim, with its restorative waters and fin de siècle strangeness, the music of the Kur orchestra, the hot rooms and the douche rooms, the invalids in bath-chairs, the smoking lounges where ailing Englishmen drowsed over the pages of *Punch* and *The Times*.

Mr. James was an old man, Sara a still young woman; the boy gradually became the center of her existence. It was not simply that she was overprotective, ever vigilant to guard Franklin against danger, or even that, as she faintly reproved him, she seemed secretly to delight in the way he lorded over the children of the retainers at Springwood. To her, Franklin was the little prince, and she the woman who had given him life; they were creatures of their own romance. The fairy tale might have proved ruinous. But her idea resembled that of Freud, who said that if a "man has been his mother's undisputed darling he retains throughout life the triumphant feeling, the confidence in success, which not seldom brings actual success along with it."

At the very least, Sara was certain, her darling boy would be most unlike his half-brother, James Roosevelt Roosevelt. Twenty-eight years older than Franklin, Rosy, as he was called, was Mr. James's son by his first wife, Rebecca Howland. He had married Helen Astor, and had grown into a rich epicure, charming and for the most part useless, the image of Gilded Age vapidity. His son, James Roosevelt Roosevelt, Jr., who was known as Taddy, was a still sadder case. More than two years older than Franklin, Taddy was Franklin's nephew, and was said to be "not all there."

Most boys entered Groton in the first or second forms, as twelve- or thirteen-year-olds, but Sara and Mr. James were unwilling to part with their "especial treasure" so soon. It was only in September 1896, when Franklin was fourteen, that the family boarded Mr. James's private railway carriage for the journey to the school, where the apprehensive boy was welcomed by the Rector and Mrs. Peabody at the door of the headmaster's residence in Hundred House. Three days later he wrote his first letter to his parents from school.

Groton School
September 18, 1896

Dear Mommerr & Popperr
    I am getting on finely, both mentally and physically. I sit next a boy named A. Gracie King at meals, he is from Garrisons and knows the Pells and Morgans. Do you know about him? . . . I am all right in Latin, Greek, Science and French; a little rusty in Algebra but not more so than the others . . . . We went to Mrs. Peabody's Parlor last night for half an hour and played games. I got the shoes last night with the tooth-powder; the shoes are just right. We are off to dinner now, so I cannot write more but I will write you Sunday. With lots of love to Pa & yourself

                                                            F. D. R.

It was far from easy for the little prince to adjust to a world in which he was not the object of universal adoration. He had, besides, to make his way among boys who had been two years together at school, and who associated the name Roosevelt with his nephew, Taddy, who was a year ahead of him at Groton. Taddy was in his own way a sympathetic character, a holy fool out of a Russian novel: but he was not the sort of boy who has an easy time in boarding school.

"Uncle Frank," as he was soon called by his form-mates, had his disappointments. He was not especially good at sports, and he did not become one of the top prefects. But he loved Groton and mastered its "subtle, almost masonic marks of distinction." "We always dressed for supper," George Biddle remembered, "that is put on a white shirt and black pumps; and the younger boys wore Eton collars in the evening and on Sundays. . . . It was bad form—though not forbidden—to wear a cap; not to take a cold shower before breakfast; to swear or talk smut." Franklin all but worshipped the Rector, whose influence, he would later say, meant more to him than that of anyone besides his parents. And he was grateful for the teaching of Mr. Gardner. "I can learn better & quicker with him," he said, "than anyone else." Yet it was Sherrard Billings alone, among the Groton masters, who divined his potential, and who was convinced from the first that Franklin was a God-sent man destined for greatness.

That Franklin felt himself something of a failure at Groton was one of the saving features of his career: like his subsequent rejection by the Porcellian, it played a part in stimulating the ambition that carried him on to future triumphs. But already qualities that were to make him the greatest of the WASP statesmen were evident to George Biddle, who was impressed by the "gray-eyed, cool, self-possessed, intelligent" senior who had the "warmest, most friendly and understanding smile." Another quality, not less useful to Franklin than his enormous charm, also revealed itself around this time, a certain flexibility in regard to the truth.

FRANKLIN'S YEARS AT GROTON COINCIDED with the Rector's entrance into middle age. Looking out across the well-tended lawns of his school to the world beyond, he was filled with dismay. "One looks almost in vain," he wrote, "for men who are willing to serve their country. It makes me feel like chucking up everything and making a desperate charge in politics."

He resisted the urge; better to help the country by bringing his boys "into contact with high ideals of life" and "helping them to see the vast possibilities of their country." But could he really make them into citizens devoted to something larger than themselves? He was beset by now familiar doubts. His favorite poem was Matthew Arnold's "Rugby Chapel," in which the poet depicts his father, Thomas Arnold, as the "faithful shepherd" who extends a loving hand to save his straying sheep. It was Peabody's ideal of what a headmaster should be. But how could he be such a shepherd himself, when his own illumination so often failed? "I have been so selfish and so sinful," he lamented. "There is so little of Christ in my own life that I fear I can bring but little to others." "My religious feeling," he confessed, "is spasmodic and dependent on occasions. . . . At times I seem to get a glimpse of the Beatific Vision and then all is earthly and my thoughts as selfish as ever."*

---

* In his spells of dejection, Peabody was consoled by his friend Theodore Roosevelt. "You say that at times you feel depressed," Roosevelt wrote him. "It is the penalty of doing hard and active work, old fellow." "I fairly laughed," he said, "when I came to the line where you said that you sometimes longed to be in the larger world of men. I don't think you understand how much good you are doing. You *are* in the larger world, in the very highest and best service, and I can say quite conscientiously I don't know any one of our generation who I think is making so permanent a mark for good."

The world, after all, was an enticing place, and not even he could always resist its blandishments. In the spring Jekyll Island beckoned, with its famous millionaires' club, and although he jestingly called it "Shekel Island," it was pleasant to go there and be treated with respect by the swells of the day. In the summer there were visits to Maine or Newport. "Sweldom," as he called it, prevailed in the latter place, where he yachted with Amory Gardner and was fêted by the Whitneys. "I rather enjoy a day or two of it," he admitted, "just enough to make me feel thankful that I am not in the whirl." But he *was* in the whirl. When he went to England he stayed with the Joseph Chamberlains at Highbury. (Chamberlain's third wife, Mary, was the daughter of Peabody's cousin, William Crowninshield Endicott.) And when he went down to New Jersey to preach at Princeton, he did so as the guest of Woodrow Wilson, whom he thought "a first-rate man. We made great friends together." It was no wonder the Beatific Vision sometimes faded.

He was, to be sure, gratified that Groton was accounted a success. He was, in the words of sociologist Jerome Karabel, "the leading headmaster in the United States." John Singer Sargent painted his picture, Columbia offered him its presidency, and Harvard made him a doctor of divinity. His school captured the imagination of the most fastidious intellectuals. To be educated at Groton, Professor Santayana said, was to be "brought up in the most select and superior way" in which you very well could be in the America of that time. Nor was the school's name unknown even to the readers of popular magazines. "My Child, Virginia, is a Boy," a satirist wrote, "his application has been sent, already, to Groton; he is going to Yale when he is nineteen; he's going to be Captain of the Crew and he's going to play on the Eleven . . ."

But it all meant nothing, as far as Peabody was concerned, if he was not really reaching his boys. The music of the old canticle, *Non nobis, domine,* resounded in the chapel—

> *Not unto us, O Lord, not unto us,*
> *But unto thy Name be ascribed all honor and glory . . .*

But perhaps the boys did not hear it.

FRANKLIN ROOSEVELT WAS BEGINNING HIS second year at Harvard when Henry Adams, breakfasting in Stockholm, saw a headline in a Swedish newspaper reporting an attempt on the life of President McKinley. The "death of McKinley and the advent of Roosevelt," Adams reflected, were not "wholly void of personal emotion" for him. He had formed with Roosevelt a friendship not untinged with malice, and his first thought on learning of McKinley's death was envy "of Teddy's luck." It was with decidedly mixed feelings that he watched the young president go down to Washington intent on making Americans conscious of the opportunities and the perils of the new century before them.

Ten years before, as America's coal output approached that of the British Empire, Adams held his breath at the nearness of what he had never expected to see, the "crossing of courses" and the "lead of American energies." The courses had since crossed, and the United States was now the greatest economic power on earth. But could Roosevelt be trusted to manage so potent a machine? Adams had his doubts. "Power when wielded by abnormal energy," he said, "is the most serious of facts, and Roosevelt's "restless and combative energy was more than abnormal."

Yet when, in January 1902, President and Mrs. Roosevelt asked him to dine, he accepted, though he claimed to loathe going over to the White House. John and Clara Hay fetched him in their carriage, and they soon found themselves being shown into what Adams called the "hideous" Red Room. Henry Cabot Lodge and Nannie were waiting for them. "We waited twenty minutes," Adams told Lizzie Cameron, "before Theodore and Edith came down, and we went in to dinner immediately with as much chaff and informality as though Theodore were still a Civil Service Commissioner." Cabot, who could be dour, was bright that evening. Hay "was just a little older and a thought more formal than once we were; Edith was very bright and gay; but as usual Theodore absorbed the conversation, and if he tried me ten years ago, he crushes me now."

It did not help that the food "was indifferent" and "very badly served," or that he got nothing to drink but a glass of sherry. The president himself, he thought, "was not exactly forced or unnatural," but he had "less of his old freshness," though "quite as much of his old dogmatism." In fact Adams was unable to see the world as the president did. Roosevelt had read, a dozen years before, Alfred Thayer Mahan's *The Influence of Sea Power Upon History* and digested its alarming thesis that however a strong a nation might be in riches or armies, it could easily find itself at the mercy of any nation that possessed a superior navy. America, it was true, could solve that problem by building a bigger fleet, but Mahan's book pointed to a deeper, less easily soluble difficulty. With its natural resources and commercial wealth, the United States might well build the world's strongest navy. But richly endowed though the North American continent was, it was, in the global scheme of things, an island floating in waters off the much larger Eurasian continent. Should a single power come to dominate Eurasia and command its immeasurably greater resources, there would be no American century.*

Henry Adams shrugged. Roosevelt was apt to become overexcited about great power diplomacy. He "lectures me on history as though he were a high school pedagogue," he complained. For his own part he was willing to abandon the world to its fate. "I incline to let England sink; to let Germany and Russia try to run the machine." He would have America pursue an insular policy and "stand on our internal resources alone." Yet events would show that Roosevelt's apprehension was justified. A policy that left the coming century to Germany and Russia was fraught with peril for the United States.

A FORTNIGHT AFTER HE DINED in the White House, Adams made his way, together with much of the rest of the Washington great world, to the Church of the Covenant to witness the marriage of John and Clara Hay's daughter Helen to William Collins Whitney's son Payne.† The president, who, it was said, wanted to be the bride at every wedding and the corpse at every funeral, arrived dramatically late with Mrs. Roosevelt on his arm. Vows were exchanged in a Wagnerian atmosphere, to the music of *Tannhäuser* and *Die Meistersinger*; afterward there was a reception in the secretary of state's house on Lafayette Square. The president was seated at the same table as the groom's father, whom he looked down on as an unscrupulous sharper just canny enough to stay within the letter of the law.

The Roosevelts returned to the White House only to be awakened, at half past three in the morning, by an usher bearing a cable from Cotty Peabody. Their oldest son, Ted, a second former at Groton, had come down with a bad case of pneumonia. A virus had swept through the school; one boy had died. Edith Roosevelt left Washington the next day on the 4:50 Boston train.

---

* Theodore's cousin Franklin was also to experience Mahan's influence. Mahan's son, Lyle, was in school with him at Groton, in the form of 1897, and the great man himself came up to the campus to address the boys. Franklin dreamed of going to Annapolis after Groton but was persuaded by his father to matriculate at Harvard.

† William Payne Whitney was the younger brother of Harry Payne Whitney.

Young Ted was in many ways his father's son. He had been given a loaded rifle at the age of nine, and when, at twelve, he was "pumped" at Groton—held under a running spigot in the cellar of Hundred House—he had the temerity to remonstrate with his tormentors. Pumping was a Groton ritual somewhat at odds with the family idea of the school; the Rector, in his horror of hazing and fagging, hit upon the curious expedient of solving the problem of the bully by institutionalizing bullying. Boys, he reasoned, had a natural tendency to mistreat other boys, but if a school domesticated the urge and brought it under the sanction of the prefects and the headmaster, sadism itself could be made into a bulwark of order, and homosexual impulses sublimated into water-torture, in which the victim was "pumped" rather than, as in the bad old days of Eton, humped.

And so little Ted had his pumping. He had not, George Biddle remembered, "committed any specific breach of the school code." He was instead selected "after a rather vehement debate and several consultations with the Senior Prefect, as the most typical of his form, the general tone of which we disapproved." Twice he was held under the spigot, each time for eight seconds. "One of the form leaders then explained to him that he was fresh and swell-headed," Biddle recalled. "To our amazement he denied everything, answered back, even started asking all sorts of questions." Shouts arose. "Shut up! Under again! Shut him up! Under with him!"

Ted survived the ordeal, and in his second year he was reported to be a "popular student" and an exemplar of his father's idea of the strenuous life, persuading his chums to join him on ten-mile cross-country runs "in which all the boys were bareheaded." Newspapermen speculated that it was this practice of exercising hatless in the Massachusetts winter that led to Ted's catching cold. When, on Saturday morning, Edith Roosevelt reached Groton, she found her son in the school's Cottage Infirmary, or Pest House as it was more often called, where a number of other boys also languished. Ted was feverish with a temperature of 104°.

The president himself was by this time alarmed. He cancelled a trip to Charleston and a little after midnight on Sunday boarded his private railroad car. Making record time, he arrived at the Groton station in the early afternoon. After a visit to the sick room, he stayed nearby for much of the day, working in the infirmary's office, and it was midnight before he retired to Amory Gardner's house, where a direct line to Washington had been installed; Edith slept in a cot beside her son's bed.

Reporters huddled that night in Shirley Road, fixing their eyes on the windows of Pest House and straining for a glimpse of the nurses and doctors moving about within. One correspondent claimed, perhaps fancifully, to have heard Ted calling for water and concluded that the boy was delirious. The next day the president breakfasted with his wife in Mr. Gardner's house, and after lunch he went for a brisk walk around the Circle. He knew Groton well. In 1884 Cotty had tried to persuade him to teach there, and although he had declined the offer he had over the years visited the school often, delighting the boys with what his cousin Franklin called "killing stories" of his adventures in life, while urging them "not to take champagne or butlers with them on camping trips to the Adirondacks." As "Mrs. Peabody scrambled the eggs and the Headmaster recommended the apples," Roosevelt would "spin his boisterous cowboy yarns," Ellery Sedgwick remembered, and the boys "would shed tears of delight at the culmination of each adventure . . ."

Peabody's Groton embodied the president's own philosophy of unceasing exertion. If in Vienna Dr. Freud was attempting to cure neurosis by getting people to lie on a couch and chatter, he and Cotty, for their part, were trying to get people *off* the couch and doing things. Get action, be sane. Roosevelt marveled at Peabody's devotion to strenuosity, which at times exceeded his own. "Pray do not think me grown timid in my old age," the president had written to his friend in January, but it seemed to him that Ted was being pushed too hard in football. He pointed out that the boy had broken his collarbone, and he was afraid that "if he goes on like this he will get battered out before he can play in college."

But for the most part Roosevelt approved of the Groton regimen, though he found it a trifle strict. One morning in June 1900, Bishop Lawrence, staying at Groton for Prize Day, the day when the senior class (or sixth form) graduated, was startled to see Roosevelt, then governor of New York, "burst into my room half-dressed." "Bishop," Roosevelt exclaimed to the half-awake prelate, "can you tell a bewildered Governor what time it is? My watch has stopped, and if I am late to breakfast in this school, I may be disciplined." Like other WASP reformers, Roosevelt sought not a "sharp change in the social structure, but rather the formation of a responsible elite," one that would help direct the course of the twentieth century in much the way British mandarins had directed the nineteenth.[*] It was

---

[*] WASPs were divided about just how the United States was to exert its power in the new century, whether by means of British-style imperialism backed by diplomacy and military power or by diplomacy and military power without conquest and colonial annexation. Still others favored America's traditional policy of aloofness, whenever practicable, from the military and diplomatic practices of the Old World, and sought, like Jefferson, to foster "peace, commerce, and honest friendship with all nations, entangling alliances with none."

Peabody's own ideal. "If some Groton boys do not enter political life and do something for our land," he said, "it won't be because they have not been urged." He was working to mold the sort of elite Roosevelt sought, educating boys who might one day staff the American Century. If, as the Duke of Wellington believed, the battle of Waterloo was won on the playing fields of Eton, it was just possible that boys trained in Cotty's little seminary might play a part in vanquishing new foes, in an age that would see the elaboration of a Pax Americana.

THE NEXT DAY YOUNG TED was markedly better. Mrs. Roosevelt attended divine service in the chapel, and she and her husband were among the guests at a dinner in Mr. Gardner's house. Everyone "seemed not only cheerful, but jovial," the correspondent for the *New York Times* reported. On Thursday the president left the school. "Ted has improved with such rapid jumps that I am sure he is out of the woods," he told reporters before he boarded the train for Washington.

Pierpont Morgan (gripping a walking stick) wanted to liberate Americans "from the bondage of ugliness."

SEVENTEEN

The Great World and J. P. Morgan

'Perché tieni?' e 'Perché burli?' . . .

'Why do you hoard?' 'Why do you squander?' . . .
—Dante, *Inferno*

In the fall of 1882 the gentlemen who composed the vestry of St. George's Church in Manhattan were in search of a new rector. The Reverend William Stephen Rainsford, a young Episcopalian holy man, presented himself at 219 Madison Avenue, the residence of St. George's most illustrious congregant, the banker John Pierpont Morgan. Rainsford found the gentlemen of the vestry gathered in Morgan's study, a room rather ominously paneled (much like Morgan's own soul) in the darkest of mahoganies. St. George's had long ministered to the rich and the comfortable, but Reverend Rainsford told the assembled gentlemen that this must change. Had not the church a duty to raise up the poor, the lame, the halt, and the blind? For like Vida Scudder and Endicott Peabody, Rainsford was an adherent of the Social Gospel movement. He actually believed that a Christian ought to try to love his neighbor as himself.

Pierpont Morgan, who had been largely silent during the interview, looked the young clergyman in the face. "Mr. Rainsford, will you be our rector? If you consent I will do what I can to help you carry out this plan." Whereupon Rainsford named the conditions on which he would accept vestry's offer, setting forth a plan to "democratize" the church.

"Done," Morgan said as he moved to grasp Rainsford's hand. "Come to us. We will stand by you."

Pierpont Morgan was a faithful Episcopalian who believed in the reality of sin and the obligation of charity; in subsidizing the good works of Reverend Rainsford, he found a convenient way of assuaging the uneasiness a rich Christian is likely to feel if he is not a hypocrite. The two men grew close, and breakfasted each Monday in Morgan's house. But when Rainsford went so far as to propose admitting working men to the vestry, Morgan put his foot down. "The rector wants to democratize the church," he told the vestry, "and we agree with him and will help him as far as we can. But I do not want the vestry democratized. I want it to remain a body of gentlemen whom I can ask to meet in my study."

Yet the motion to democratize the vestry was carried. "Rector," Morgan said darkly as he rose from his chair, "I will never sit in this vestry again." Rainsford, for his part, refused to accept Morgan's resignation, but there was now a coolness between the two men. The Monday breakfasts went on as before, but Morgan was grumpy and often silent. It was not until he was on the point of sailing to Europe that his conscience smote him. Catching sight of Rainsford among the crowd that had gathered to see him off, he led him to his stateroom, where they patched up the quarrel and put the vestry behind them. It is said that Morgan went so far as to throw his arms around the young priest. "Rainsford," he cried, "pray for me, pray for me . . ."

EVEN AS THEODORE ROOSEVELT WAS prophesying a *Pax Americana*, J. P. Morgan, the most powerful WASP in the United States, was forging the steel that would undergird it. (He incorporated the United States Steel Corporation in 1901.) His pharaonic shadow darkened Wall Street as he consolidated the capital on which the WASP ascendancy ultimately rested, yet in character and personality he was in many ways at odds with the myth of the capitalist that was gaining credence in his time. According to this mythology, the capitalist tycoon was a modern version of the Renaissance condottiere and the Elizabethan swashbuckler—a daring, piratical character like the protagonist of Byron's *The Corsair*, an "incarnation of the will to power." The German seer Oswald Spengler would celebrate the "metal-hard natures" of titans like John D. Rockefeller and Cecil Rhodes, men who, Oliver Wendell Holmes said, had a more "poignant" insight into the future than their duller-witted contemporaries. In the culmination of the new mythology Joseph Schumpeter, the Austro-Harvard economist, would depict the capitalist as a romantic hero like Shelley's Prometheus or Milton's Satan, a rebel against conventional order, a master of the arts of creative destruction.

There was a touch of this romantic diablerie in Morgan himself. He had tremendous powers of will; meeting his gaze, the photographer Edward Steichen said, was like looking into the headlights of an oncoming express. His hideous nose only contributed to the impression that sinister forces were at work in his soul. (He suffered from rhinophyma, and the "appalling excrescences" were, Henry Adams said, almost "too terrible to look at": the nose seemed to "spread.") But although Morgan named a succession of yachts *Corsair*, he thought of himself not as a romantic superman but as a well-bred Christian gentleman, and his sympathy for the work of men like Dr. Rainsford shows him to have been a humane figure, with a broader range of sensibility than narrower plutocrats possessed. Much has been made of his interest in art: he was drawn to it and collected a great deal of it—more than a billion dollars' worth in today's money. But it is as easy to exaggerate Morgan's commitment to culture as it is to overpaint his Übermensch qualities. There was, Helen Schlegel says in E. M. Forster's novel *Howard's End*, something missing in his pursuit of the beautiful. "Pierpont Morgan has never said 'I' in his life," for the assertion "I want" must lead to the question "Who am I?" Such a man "only says 'want.' 'Want Europe, if he's Napoleon; 'want wives,' if he's Bluebeard'; 'want Botticelli,' if he's Pierpont Morgan."

Critics were quick to point out that Morgan, with all his appetite for art, had a very nearly "perfect insensibility" to it—was, in his general culture, not much superior to the Vanderbilts, whom old WASPs looked down upon as arriviste philistines. ("I wish the Vanderbilts didn't retard culture so very thoroughly," Edith Wharton said. "They are entrenched in a sort of *thermopylae* of bad taste, from which apparently no force on earth can dislodge them.") Bernard Berenson mocked Morgan's taste; after touring one of his houses he described it as a "pawnbroker's shop for Croesuses." Morgan was avid of acquisition, possessed what Henry James called the "sharpened appetite of the collector," but once the thing was collected, it often ceased to exist for him. Coming across a receipt for a bust of the infant Hercules he had bought, he inquired of his librarian, the lovely Belle Greene, where it was. "This bronze Bust is in your library," she replied, "and faces you when sitting in your chair. It has been there about a year."

THE LIVING FORCE, FOR MORGAN, was not art or beauty but capital. His instinct for it was memorialized in a panel of the choir of St. Thomas, the Episcopal church on Fifth Avenue, where the initials J.P.M. and the image of three money bags are carved into the wood. Yet he was far from being the sort of creator-destroyer whom Schumpeter exalted, the demonic enthusiast who runs enormous risks to realize his ends.* Morgan, if he was capable of daring speculations, was as a rule careful of capital, and did not like to risk it in naked competition. He favored consolidation and cooperation, "Morganatic harmony," as one historian has called it, the principle that underlay his Northern Securities Company, a trust intended to eliminate "ruinous competition" among rival railroads by bringing impertinent speculators like E. H. Harriman into the fold and making them behave. (The trust was dissolved after the Supreme Court found it a combination in restraint of trade in violation of the Sherman Act.)

Government, for Morgan, was another unruly competitor that had to be taught good manners. Theodore Roosevelt was, in his eyes, a "big rival operator" with whom he might bargain as he would any other recalcitrant businessman. "If we have done anything wrong," he told Roosevelt after the administration brought suit against the Northern Securities Company, "send your man to my man and they can fix it up." "That can't be done," Roosevelt replied, and he was privately amused by Morgan's conception of the federal government as merely another big trust, a larger version of AT&T or U.S. Steel. But although Morgan resented the attack on his interests—a "tremendous whack," Henry Adams said, on the unhappy nose—in the end he got from Roosevelt the kind of government

---

* Surely Schumpeter and Spengler exaggerated the romantic vitality of their capitalists. Coming across one of Spengler's paeans to his visionary titans, Santayana scribbled in the margin of the page: "Bosh: I know Jack Morgan & old Rockefeller: they are ridiculous." Santayana's account of a dinner with Rockefeller would seem to lend credence to the maxim that the more money an American makes, the *less* interesting he becomes.

regulation he wanted. Roosevelt's Bureau of Corporations proved not only tolerable but even helpful to Morgan, a form of federal supervision that allowed the masters of capital to work out their problems with Washington in a cooperative rather than adversarial manner. Like so many ostensibly radical plans to regulate capital, the bureau devolved into a bankers' club; the "big rival operator" had been made to see reason.

BUT IT WAS NOT ENOUGH, for Morgan, to bring capital into harmony and equilibrium; one must do the same thing for the possessors of capital. His idea was to promote a WASP big tent that would bring together the old rich, whose capital was wearing thin but whose social prestige* was considerable, and the new rich and their freshly mined gold. He did not, of course, invent the WASP gentleman's club, yacht club, or millionaires' getaway colony, but he helped to turn them into wherever-people-are-rich-together places in which hard cash mattered more than ancient pedigrees or a classical education.

The Metropolitan Club in New York was only the most overt example of Morgan's desire to broaden WASPdom's financial base: he founded it after the Union Club refused to admit some of his newly risen chums to membership. He was a loyal member of the Jekyll Island Club, the millionaire playground on a barrier island off the coast of Georgia; and although he continued be faithful to Cragston, his country house on the west bank of the Hudson—an area that had become unfashionable—he dutifully patronized plutocratic Newport. The charming, rather low-key summer colony that Henry James likened to a "little white hand" had by the turn of the century become grasping and grotesque, the "vulgarest society in the world," in the opinion of Cecil Spring Rice. Springy's friend, Theodore Roosevelt, denounced "Newport cads" who aped the English aristocracy, and James himself spoke of hearing "the chink of money" in the very ripple of the water. Surveying the vast villas, he warned of "prohibited degrees of witlessness" and of "the peculiarly awkward vengeance of affronted proportion and discretion." Morgan, however, was at home in Newport.

"Well, we need new blood and new money," says Mrs. Mingott in Edith Wharton's novel *The House of Mirth*, and Morgan's own openness to strangers

---

* A noun much favored by lax WASPs: high WASPs would have spoken of "reputation," whether for honor, dignity, probity, or respectability. "Prestige" derives from the Latin verb *praestringo*, to blind, dazzle, or confuse. Prestige suggests a vulgar conjuring trick; Mr. Gladstone spoke of that "base-born thing in these last times called prestige."

was in many respects more amiable than the snobbery of WASP humanists who resented the degradation of taste they associated with the new rich. Young George Cabot Lodge deplored this alien "money power," with its "philistine-plutocrat" ideals, and he lamented the way it was ruining his favorite summer colonies, while Edith Wharton (no Mrs. Mingott she) looked down on Gilded Age captains of industry as vulgarians with "gold-fever," the sort of morons who thought they were doing her a favor when they offered her a glass of the "famous Newbold Madeira."* Henry Adam's brother Charles was no less dismissive. "I have known, and known tolerably well," he wrote, "a good many 'successful' men—'big' financially—men famous during the last half-century; and a less interesting crowd I do not care to encounter. Not one that I have ever known would I care to meet again, either in this world or the next; nor is one of them associated in my mind with the idea of humor, thought or refinement."

If Mrs. Wharton mocked the newly rich mogul (in her portrait of Abner E. Spragg of Apex City in *The Custom of the Country*), Morgan extended his hand to him, welcomed him as a friend, and even adopted his manners, going so far, it is said, as to allow money to be talked at his table. In the orgy of club-making that took place after the Civil War, Morgan played a notable part, helping to forge a latitudinarian cult of the WASP millionaire that embraced both old money and new, a civil religion whose worship was concentrated in spaces in which money of different vintages could peaceably mingle, separated from the rest of the country by wrought-iron gates and high-clipped hedges.

"MONEY IS A KIND OF poetry," said Wallace Stevens, and in Morgan's time the tycoon was rapidly becoming its lyrical embodiment. "I don't think there is any doubt but the millionaire is now the American ideal," says a character in William Dean Howells's novel *A Traveler from Altruria*. "It is the man with the most money who now takes the prize in our national cake-walk." The problem was that the golf clubs and summer resorts in which the money-poetry was most in evidence were so mockable. Within a dozen years of Morgan's death, the young F. Scott Fitzgerald was ridiculing Tom Buchanan and the fatuities of Long Island's

---

* "The 'Jones' Madeira (my father's)," Wharton wrote in *A Backward Glance*, "and the 'Newbold' (my uncle's) enjoyed a particular celebrity even in that day of noted cellars. The following generation, interested only in champagne and claret, foolishly dispersed these precious stores. My brothers sold my father's cellar soon after his death; and after my marriage, dining in a *nouveau riche* house of which the master was unfamiliar with old New York cousinships, I had pressed on me, as a treat not likely to have come the way of one of my modest condition, a glass of 'the famous Newbold Madeira.'"

north shore preppies. The lock-jawed dialect of Northeast Harbor, Maine, and the steam-room-and-martinis culture of the Racquet Club became running jokes; *Caddyshack* would deliver the coup de grâce to the dignities of the country club.

Morgan's investment in prep schools was arguably a sounder way of shoring up the new, ecumenical upper class. He was a benefactor of St. Paul's and Groton, two WASP institutions that did much to shape the character of the American boarding school, a combination of muscular rigor (the football field), humane education (the classics), and poetical mysticism (the chapel) that bit deep into the souls of impressionable WASP youths, and instilled in them a keen sense of class identity.*

The Episcopal Church, the American branch of the Church of England, completed what Digby Baltzell called the "Episcopalianization" of the American money aristocracy, as Quaker, Baptist, and Unitarian millionaires made peace with Anglican spiritual orthodoxies. It was the last touch of Morganization—the great man's effort to weld the disparate elements of American capital into a harmonious WASP whole. The boy from a newly rich Presbyterian or Methodist family was sent, at fourteen or fifteen, to Choate or Hotchkiss; he there became friends with some sprig of a venerable though perhaps faded New England or Dutch patroon stock; met the sprig's sister over the summer at Newport or in Northeast Harbor; and a few years later married her, in accordance with the Anglican rite, in a Grace Church or St. Thomas wedding in Manhattan, the headquarters of the new establishment.

For if the Episcopal Church and the New England prep school promoted the Gilded Age marriage of pedigreed blood and plutocratic cash over which Morgan presided, New York was, more often than not, the scene of the actual consummation. Boston, with its hieratic cruelties and its "cold roast" manners, stood aloof from these déclassé transactions and so gradually lost ground. The Lowells, Appletons, and Lawrences of Boston's State Street had been pioneers of modern capitalism, speculating in power looms on the Merrimac River at a time when Wall Street was drowsing over beaver pelts and buffalo skins. The problem was that Boston's nobility was hardly less blood-proud than the Roman

---

* As boarding school became, in the second half of the nineteenth century, a rite of passage for boys whose families sought either to obtain or maintain a place in the WASP elite, new schools were founded to meet the demand, among them St. Paul's (1856), St. Mark's (1865), Groton (1884), Taft (1890), Hotchkiss (1892), Choate (1896), St. George's (1896), Middlesex (1901), and Kent (1906). Deerfield Academy, founded in 1797, was on the point of closing its doors as a result of declining enrollment when, in 1902, it was revived and reorganized by Frank Boyden.

patriciate that produced Julius Caesar and Sulla Felix: it looked upon a "man without ancestors" who aspired to the highest honors as "a scandal and a pollution." Boston's Beacon Street was a closed society, and Boston's Brahmins, in Elizabeth Chanler Chapman's words, were an "absolutely unmixed race," for they shunned the stranger.

New York, with its looser standards, was more accommodating, and as a result it became the city highbred WASPs loved to hate on account of the vulgarity of its wealth and the primitiveness of its culture. For Henry Adams and Henry James, New York was less a city than a brownstone encampment where the assembled barbarians could conveniently barter and profit, a "cramped horizontal gridiron of a town," in Edith Wharton's words, without even a rudimentary civic art, the "towers, porticoes, fountains or perspectives" of traditional urban culture, and cursed with a "universal chocolate-colored coating of the most hideous stone ever quarried." But such carping was vain; New York was the WASP future.

PIERPONT MORGAN, ALTHOUGH HE WAS originally from Hartford, came to embody the brownstone virtues of New York's WASP aristocracy, and even Henry Adams and Theodore Roosevelt, with all their ambivalence about modern capital, conceded that the man was indispensable: he helped make the American machine run. But did he deserve a place in the true WASP priesthood, the order of which Adams himself was unofficial pontifex maximus? This was a more complicated question. Morgan had certain of the authentic qualities of the breed, the distinctive signs and stigmata of the WASP. He was neurasthenic, and knew periods of funk and depression, when he lay prostrate in bed under "a vast despair." He had, too, the WASP sense of civic obligation. Acting for many years as the de facto central banker of the United States, he bailed the Treasury out during the gold crisis of 1895 and masterfully diffused the panic of 1907; in 1902 he helped Roosevelt settle the anthracite coal strike by persuading the mine owners to consent to arbitration.

He set, as WASPs were apt to do, great store by character. "A man I do not trust," he said, "could not get money from me on all the bonds in Christendom." Yet he fell into the luxe hedonism of the age, the sort of life the Prince of Wales, the future King Edward VII, and his Marlborough House set epitomized—cigars and brandy, plushly upholstered steam yachts and railway carriages, soporific dinners of ten courses far removed from the light and choice repasts of a better taste.* Morgan might not have smoked cigarettes rolled in hundred-dollar bills, as some of New York's nouveaux riches did, but he did appear at the grotesque Bradley-Martin Ball in 1897, costumed as Molière, and joined revelers who drank Moët & Chandon and supped on Lobster Newburg while a good many New Yorkers were going hungry. (The ball, which Reverend Rainsford denounced, provoked so much anger in the city that Theodore Roosevelt, then president of the police board, was forced, he told his sister, "to protect it by as many police as if it were a strike.")

Jack Chapman thought Morgan the "apex as well as the type, of the commercial perversions of the era," yet the real problem was not his occasional vulgarity but the steady emptiness of his cult of plundered art. WASPs like Henry Adams and William Amory Gardner tried, however imperfectly, to revive the idea that art is a living force, capable of regenerating communities; Morgan put his whole effort into embalming the dead. Like Henry James's Adam Verver in *The Golden Bowl*, he aspired to "rifle the Golden Isles" of Old World creativity in order to establish New World museums that would liberate the natives "from the bondage of ugliness." But in pillaging the old places and appropriating their plastic and their painted beauty, Morgan, like Verver, only intensified the country's philistinism, making art into a roped-off, Sunday-best sort of thing, incapable of brightening the prosaic day. Adams and Gardner sought the integration of poetry and life in a humane forum; Morgan settled for a gentleman's club, with a visit to the picture gallery at the weekend, squeezed in between the golf and the tennis.

Santayana, that Mediterranean mind accidentally strayed into American pastures, saw the museums Morgan and his fellow WASPs were building as characteristic of a class that feared the interblending of art and life as it had been practiced before the modern era. A "genuine lover of the beautiful," he argued, "would never enter a museum" and sanction that "unwholesome and vain attempt to feed" on "corpses." And on the whole he was right: Morgan's new WASP class was never more comfortable with art than when it was safely shut away in a glass case.

---

* Roger Fry, the Bloomsbury critic who occasionally advised Morgan in his acquisitions of painting, was, his friend and biographer Virginia Woolf wrote, "astonished by the luxury" in which Morgan was perpetually enveloped. "He travelled in the great man's private car tacked on to the end of a private express. It was snowing, and a log fire was lit in the car, which was 'fitted up like a private house in the grandest style.'"

Learned Hand envisioned a welfare state
directed by WASP mandarins.

EIGHTEEN

Mandarinism

sì selvaggia strada . . .

so wild a path . . .
—Dante, *Inferno*

Learned Hand is one of the more appealing figures in the WASP revival. He had the neurasthenic heritage, without which one could not be a true WASP, and he had, too, the horror of failure, the dread of "being merely one of the countless mediocre," which distinguished the breed. He had had, at Harvard, the teaching of James and Santayana, and all his life he would worry that he was living too narrowly, sacrificing his powers to the crossword-puzzle work of the law, and failing to attain to some Greek or Renaissance notion of excellence.

He was fortunate in his obstacles, which were real, but which could be surmounted. He had to escape a domineering mother (Lydia) and a hometown (Albany) which, he said, struck "a kind of deadness in my soul." Lydia Hand was by her own admission "inclined to look on the dark side" of things and was closely occupied with the state of her health. In her letters she catalogued her aches and pains, and she did her best to impose her neuroticisms on her son, that they might have a pool of valetudinarian ailments over which to commiserate. She also did her best to keep him in Albany, a city he had come to loathe. He foresaw himself a "melancholic" failure rotting unloved in the provinces, "hopelessly hypochondriac" and doomed to perpetual monkhood.

It was his friend George Rublee who advised him that liberation would come only through the acquisition of a legitimate sex partner. "Few men seem to me more capable of being happy in marriage than you," he told Hand, "and few seem to need such happiness more." On a summer excursion to Murray Bay in Quebec, Hand met a young woman who, he thought, might rescue him from his unsatisfactory bachelorhood. The problem was that Frances Fincke, the girl in question, had been educated at Bryn Mawr. The college had been founded, in 1885, as a WASP experiment in extending the advantages of liberal education to young women who would otherwise have been condemned to finishing school, and it was a good deal more academically rigorous than Harvard or Yale at the time. Its president, Martha Cary Thomas, part visionary, part ogress, was determined that nothing should stand in the way of her girls' self-realization. Among the obstacles she had in mind were husbands. "Our failures only marry," she said.

Frances had met, at Bryn Mawr, a girl called Mildred Minturn, the daughter of the well-to-do New York family that had a share in creating Edie Sedgwick. Mildred was intelligent and neurasthenic; she was also beautiful. Bertrand Russell thought her "extremely clever" and urged her to study at the London School of Economics, where the randy philosopher perhaps supposed he would have a better chance of getting his paws on her.* At Bryn Mawr, where *amitiés particulières* flourished among the girls, Mildred and Frances were best friends. There were "evening brews & talks & speculations," Frances remembered. "And how we used to wander down to Radnor in the moonlight after teas & be glad

---

* Russell was a visiting professor at Harvard when T. S. Eliot first encountered him. He preserved the impression in his poem "Mr. Apollinax," in which the narrator, hearing Mr. Apollinax's laughter tinkling the teacups, thinks of "Priapus in the shrubbery/Gaping at the lady in the swing."

we were there together." The Bryn Mawr years, Mildred echoed, were "the *best* years of our life." After they graduated they would return to campus to recapture the old life, having "a joyous time, reading & talking hours in the delicious old way, perfectly intimate & perfectly happy at being together," as Mildred recorded in her diary. "Good days, good nights, friendships & freedom & always some new idea to be discussed together."

They contemplated living together in a "Boston marriage," for each seemed to suspect that she would never find so perfect a sympathy in a relationship with a man, that friendship between the sexes must always be, in Santayana's phrase, "a kissing in the dark." Mildred went so far as to purchase, in Mount Kisco, New York, a "rocky corner of land" from her cousin Louisa Shaw Barlow, the wife of Pierre "Pete" Jay, Endicott Peabody's "most perfect gentleman." There she and Frances could have "our retreat together," "perfect independence & our own tiny home." But in the summer of 1901, Learned Hand appeared at Murray Bay, and in August he proposed to Frances.[*]

She put him off, reluctant to break with Mildred and the Bryn Mawr tradition. But he was persistent. She was, after all, the means by which he was to escape the twin dominion of Lydia and Albany. Frances wavered. "I have seen

---

[*] The circumstances of their meeting shed light on just how interconnected the WASP elite was. Hand was invited to Murray Bay by his friend Henry Ingersoll Bowditch, a cousin of Fanny Bowditch Dixwell, the wife of Oliver Wendell Holmes, the future Supreme Court justice. Henry had been at Groton in the same form as Payne Whitney (who married the daughter of Henry Adams's best friend John Hay), Henry and John Adams (Henry Adams's twin nephews), and Joseph Wright Alsop IV (who married Corrine Robinson, the daughter of Theodore Roosevelt's younger sister Corinne Roosevelt Robinson). In Murray Bay Hand visited the Minturn cottage, where his Harvard friend Charles Lowell "Charlie" Barlow (whose sister would marry Pierre "Pete" Jay) was staying. Susanna Shaw Minturn, the sister of Brahmin Civil War hero Robert Gould Shaw and a Sturgis on her mother's side, was the matriarch of the family: Charlie Barlow was her nephew, the son of her sister Ellen Shaw and the "rough diamond" Francis Channing Barlow, another Civil War hero. Susanna's son Hugh Minturn had been in Franklin Roosevelt's form at Groton and was now at Harvard with Franklin: both would serve as ushers in the wedding of Corinne Roosevelt Robinson's son, Theodore Douglas Robinson, to Franklin's niece Helen, the sister of the unfortunate Taddy. Another of Susanna's sons, Robert Shaw Minturn, married the daughter of Howard Potter, the uncle of our old friend Warwick Potter. Susanna's daughter Gertrude would marry Amos Pinchot, the father, by his second wife, of Mary and Tony Pinchot, who under their married names, Meyer and Bradlee, were to become luminaries, together with the journalist Joseph Wright Alsop V, better known as Joe Alsop, in the court of John F. Kennedy. Another of Susanna's daughters, Sarah May, married Theodore Dwight Sedgwick III, the grandfather of Edie Sedgwick. Still another daughter, Edith (after whom Edie Sedgwick was named), married the architect Isaac Newton Phelps Stokes: the couple was famously painted by Sargent. Frances Fincke, Mildred Minturn's guest at Murray Bay, was herself part of this world. Her father, Frederic Fincke, had been at Harvard with Edith Wharton's future husband, Teddy Wharton; her nephew, Reginald Fincke Jr., would be in Joe Alsop's form at Groton.

him every day now for a week," she wrote to Mildred after a visit to Albany in the spring of 1902, "and feel as if I knew him very well and I like him *exceedingly*." Mildred shuddered. She confided to her diary that she had begun to "suspect that Frances was going to take Learned Hand." She would, she said, never "forget how physically sick the thought of losing her made me feel."

In the fall of 1902 Learned moved to New York City, and in December he and Frances were married. But he found the life of a lawyer on Wall Street hardly less insipid than his old life in Albany. Nor did he prosper at the bar. "I was never any good as a lawyer," he later said. "I didn't have any success, any at all." He wanted to become a judge, a step that Frances's father, Frederic Fincke, a lawyer in Utica, New York, resolutely opposed. The cash value of a Wall Street partnership, he told Hand, was a "far worthier" object than the largely illusory prestige of the bench. "The invisible, intangible & largely theoretical honor of the place has no audience with me," he lectured his son-in-law. "It does not buy houses, maintain them, educate children, or afford them a fair start in life." But Hand persevered, and in 1909 President Taft submitted his name to the Senate. A short time later he took the oath as a district court judge in the Southern District of New York.

In migrating from the private to the public sector, Hand followed a path familiar to WASPs. Probably the majority of WASP males in those days, whatever their profession, had the morally unambitious stockbroker mentality; but for high WASPs like Hand and Henry Stimson, moneymaking was a kind of hell to be endured in the hope that they might one day enter the public service, which, they supposed, afforded a larger scope for virtuous activity and human fulfilment. Yet the quarrel between low WASPs who, like J. P. Morgan, pored over their ledgers in the bowels of the banks, and high WASPs who, like Hand and Stimson, left Wall Street to go into government was not, as it has been sometimes portrayed, an antagonism between avarice and idealism. It is better understood as a difference in aptitudes, and the desire of different kinds of men for different types of power.

If Learned Hand had little talent for the unreflective hurry of Wall Street practice, he had precisely the kind of intelligence that would do much to build up a power in its own way as formidable as the stock exchange, the mandarin state. His work on the bench brought him into close touch with the obstacles that judges sympathetic to Wall Street had erected against the emerging welfare state. In 1905, in the landmark case of *Lochner v. New York*, the Supreme Court struck down a law regulating bakers' hours, reasoning that the due process clause of the Fourteenth Amendment protected liberty of contract. A law that interfered with the freedom of bakers and their bosses to make contracts that called for long hours was, for the justices in the majority, unconstitutional. With wit and learning Hand argued, in the *Harvard Law Review* and other forums, that the justices' doctrine—in the jargon of the law it is known as "substantive due process"—had no basis in the language of the Constitution and was instead a reflection of the "prejudices of that economic class to which all the justices belong." He went on to warn that if the justices insisted on reading their personal economic preferences into the Constitution, they would transform the court into a super-legislature in which unelected lawyers acted as arbiters not simply of law but also of policy.

Hand opposed *Lochner* on constitutional grounds, but he also believed in the regulatory and administrative state. In "a vast multitude of cases," he argued, "the State must and should regulate the conduct of individuals for their own welfare . . ." He deplored what he saw as the self-interest and class-bias that led jurists to argue that the due process clauses of the Constitution embalmed the "individualistic doctrine of a hundred years ago." Yet the mandarin state to which he pledged himself had its own class biases. It too would empower a particular social type, and for many years senior appointments in the mandarin establishment would go disproportionately to WASPs who had the same sort of background, training, connections, and even sense of humor that Hand himself did.

THE FACE, IN ITS CONTOURS, was rather plain. But there was something appealing about Dorothy Whitney, an attractiveness that could not be written off as merely the glow that any young millionairess might possess. Unlike her brothers, Harry and Payne, given up to sporting indolence, Dorothy thought her brain a thing to be used. She read books like William James's *Pragmatism* and was disturbed by the plight of the poor. She enrolled in a course in political economy at Columbia that she might better understand social questions, and although she had little faith in priests, she spoke of the "priesthood of conscience," an order to which her father, William Collins Whitney, had never aspired to belong.

Yet she was not a radical. She had been educated at Miss Chapin's and Miss Finch's schools in Manhattan and had been presented to the King at Ascot. She was at ease in the society of Fifth Avenue, and she took pleasure in the company of the numerous well-bred, well-schooled young men who flocked about her.

But try as she might, she could not see a husband in any of them. She confided to her friend May Tuckerman* that she liked Sumner Gerard, who had been one of Theodore Roosevelt's Rough Riders. Yet there was also Bob Bacon, who addressed her as "dearest Dorothy," but who was perhaps not so handsome as his father, Robert Bacon, a J. P. Morgan partner who was now in the State Department serving at the behest of his old Harvard friend, Theodore Roosevelt. Then there was Howard Potter Cary, a cousin of Warwick Potter. "Wonderful ride in the P. M. with H. Cary," Dorothy noted in her diary. "Walked with Howard before lunch, and read aloud with him afterward." In May 1906 she and Howard traveled separately to England, but their relationship went no further. On the day Dorothy reached London, Howard dined with his cousin, Lord Fairfax, and afterward went to the theater; the next morning he was found in his lodgings in Kensington, still dressed in evening clothes, with a revolver "in his right hand and a bullet wound in his right temple."†

Some speculated that Cary was driven to suicide after Dorothy frowned on his proposal of marriage. She was, indeed, beset by suitors, and perplexed by the question of which one she should marry. No parent, certainly, could advise her. Her mother, Flora Payne Whitney, died when she was six; she was nine when her widowed father, William Collins Whitney, remarried. Yet his happiness with Edith Randolph, Dorothy's stepmother, was short lived. The couple went down together to the Whitney plantation in Aiken, South Carolina, for the chase and were mounted in pursuit of a stag when Edith, approaching a bridge, failed to bend sufficiently low to clear the girder. She broke her neck, and after lingering, a paralytic invalid, for many months, she died at the Whitney manor in Westbury, Long Island, in 1899. Whitney himself continued to dance upon the tightrope of stock speculation, and at least once lost his balance, but recovered

---

* May, afterward Mrs. Herman Kinnicutt, would become deeply versed in the tribal prosopography of the WASPs, a *savante de snobisme*. Joe Alsop described her as "a specialist in unlikely identifications" and arcane genealogies. "I don't know if you know them," she would say, "but she was one of those Hazards from Providence, the ones that tend to go a little bit mad." Or again: "She was an Albany Pruyn, but one of the poor Pruyns, you know." Her daughter, Dorothy May Kinnicutt, known as Sister, married Henry Parish II, and became one of the arbiters of mid-twentieth-century WASP taste.

† Nearly all of Dorothy Whitney's suitors came from the same WASP circles and possessed similar social and institutional pedigrees. In addition to Sumner Gerard (Groton and Yale), Bob Bacon (Groton and Harvard), and Howard Cary (Groton and Harvard), her admirers included Sheldon Whitehouse (Eton and Yale), Howland Auchincloss (Groton and Yale), Devereux Milburn (the Hill School, Oxford, and Harvard Law School), Meredith "Bunnie" Hare (Groton and Yale), DeLancey Jay (Eton and Harvard), Lydig Hoyt (Groton and Harvard), and James Breese (Groton and Princeton).

to find himself richer than ever. He died suddenly, at sixty-two, after a botched operation for appendicitis.

In the end Dorothy, who inherited a large part of her father's fortune, married merit. Willard Straight was an attractive young man, tall and slim, with receding hair and an "unusual frankness and charm of manner." He had been born, in 1880, in Oswego, New York; his parents were schoolteachers who died young. After graduating from Cornell he obtained a post in the Imperial Maritime Customs Service in Peking. Next he was a correspondent in Tokyo for Reuters and the Associated Press, then vice consul in the American legation at Seoul, where he impressed the American visitors whom it was his business to escort, among them E. H. Harriman, the railway tycoon, and Alice Roosevelt, the daughter of President Roosevelt by his first wife.

Word of the young man's brilliancy soon reached the president himself. He summoned Straight to the White House and later invited him to Oyster Bay. Much taken with Straight's idea that America should flex its muscles in Asia, Roosevelt made him Consul General at Shenyang, the railroad junction in Manchuria, "the biggest game in the East, save Peking itself," Straight said. There he worked out a plan for an American bank that would invest in Chinese infrastructure, a policy that became known as Dollar Diplomacy. Returning to the United States to serve as acting chief of the State Department's Bureau of Far Eastern Affairs, he found himself in the deepest penetralia of the WASP financial establishment. He was on close terms with E. H. Harriman (who had ceased to be a renegade speculator and was now a respectable member of J. P. Morgan's wherever-WASPs-are-rich-together elite, with a son, Averell, at Groton) and with Henry P. Davison, a partner in Morgan's bank at 23 Wall Street. (He, too, had a son, Trubee, at Groton.) Together they worked to create the American Group, a consortium of New York banks dedicated to overseas investment and what Straight called "the game for an empire." He became the group's representative in China, where he in lived in splendor at Peking.

Dorothy Whitney, on a visit to China in 1909, was impressed by the driving ambition of the young proconsul and also by his quixotic romanticism, for he had suppressed artistic inclinations and liked to play the guitar. She had met him before, in New York, but it was in China that he appeared fully himself, a man of power and mastery. She called him the "Wise Man of the East," and day by day "the magic of Peking grew upon us," she wrote. "Then one day came a trip to the

Great Wall and the Ming Tombs, and after that, things were forever different. The magic of China seemed to fade before the magic of a human personality."

They were married in September 1911 in Geneva, having overcome the opposition of Dorothy's brother Harry, who held it against Straight that he had courted other heiresses, among them Mary Harriman, and had not been to the right schools. After the honeymoon the couple went to Peking, but with the revolution that overthrew the Qing Dynasty and established a Chinese republic, investors panicked and Straight's star fell. He was recalled by his superiors in the Morgan bank to New York, where he watched the loan for which he had worked come to nothing, and where he found himself sullenly leading the life of a junior banker. After the romance of Asia, it was not enough.

LEARNED AND FRANCES HAND, SEEKING a means of escape from the city, chose Mount Kisco, where Mildred Minturn had her cottage. But Mildred went away to Europe, and Mount Kisco lost its charm not only for Frances but also for Learned, who found, among the vacationing bankers and stockbrokers, no one to talk to other than Pete Jay. George Rublee suggested that they come to Cornish, New Hampshire, his own refuge from city life and a watering hole for artists and writers. There Learned met a WASP intellectual who was a good deal more neurotic than he. Herbert Croly had, like Hand, been at Harvard, but a succession of nervous crises had prevented his graduation; he was now living in Cornish and writing a book. He and Hand took to each other instantly, talking excitedly over rounds of golf and during walks in the New Hampshire countryside. When, at length, Croly's book, *The Promise of American Life*, appeared, Hand thought its brief for the emerging mandarin state the best thing "which any man of my acquaintance or anywhere near my age has given forth, with perhaps the exception of Santayana."

Hand had himself drawn attention to one front on which the war for the new state would be fought, a judiciary dominated by what Mr. Justice Holmes called the "comfortable classes of the community." But it was Croly's *The Promise of American Life* which, with a sweep of generalizing power, revealed the entire theater. There were, Croly believed, two elemental strains in American life. The country had inherited, from Jefferson, an agrarian vision of individual dignity for all that was brilliant but in a modern industrial civilization unrealizable: it had inherited from Hamilton an elitist method of governing and a modern approach to economic development, policies which, wherever they were adopted, succeeded brilliantly, but disproportionately benefited the rich. Croly's solution was to stand Hamilton on his head: he would use the powers of a strong central government directed by mandarin expertise to secure the Jeffersonian ends of equality and dignity for all.

The book soon found its way into the hands not only of Willard Straight but also of Theodore Roosevelt.

When Dorothy Whitney used her Gilded Age fortune to promote reform, her brother Harry mocked his "pink sister."

NINETEEN

From Theodore at Armageddon to the *New Republic* on West Twenty-first Street

Tu nota: e sì come da me son porte,
così queste parole segna a' vivi
del viver ch'è un correre a la morte . . .

Take note: and just as I speak these words
to you, speak them in your turn to those
who live a life that runs toward death . . .
—Dante, *Purgatorio*

E xhibiting himself, bodily and acrobatically, on the national stage as warrior, blood-sportsman, and family man (sire of six), Theodore Roosevelt prided himself on his ability to fight and to breed. "Work—fight—breed" became, indeed, one of his mantras; those who did not "breed well or fight well" were "cold and selfish and timid," as well as disposable. Yet in retrospect Roosevelt's ethic of fighting and breeding appears to have been as much a hothouse growth of his age as the foppery of the "mollycoddles," the "tame cats," whose moral decay he deplored. His portrayal of the fighter-breeder as a man of action, the "man in the arena"—a gladiator at the mercy of sadists, his face "marred by dust and sweat and blood"—is as characteristic a specimen of fin-de-siècle overripeness as Aubrey Beardsley's drawings and Oscar Wilde's epigrams; it is bathed in the violet glow of the Mauve Decade.

Give a man a mask, Wilde said, and he will tell you the truth. When, as a boy, Roosevelt discovered that he was an asthmatic weakling, he willed himself to courage. Yet even after he put on the mask of command, all the nervous sensitivity of the child remained, and through a freak of development he carried into adulthood a boyishness undiminished. "The misfortune of man," Nietzsche says, "is that he was once a child." Roosevelt escaped the misfortune; if he posed as the embodiment of an extravagant manliness, he did so by evading many of the complications that beset the grownup. Beneath the masquerade of the warrior-breeder lay a child's exuberance that was seldom abated by the adult's anxious preoccupations. He passed from one thing to the next, his friend Sturgis Bigelow observed, with the unselfconsciousness of a child, and "was just as much interested in the next thing as if the last one had never existed." Woodrow Wilson thought him "a great big boy," as did Cecil Spring Rice. "You must always remember," Springy said, "that the President is about six."

If many found this boyishness endearing, Henry Adams thought it warped. Roosevelt "lived naturally in restless agitation that would have worn out most tempers in a month," and showed a "chronic excitement that made a friend tremble." The torrents of uninterrupted talk had the quality of hysteria. "It has not the excuse of champagne," Adams said: "the wild talk about everything—Panama, Russia, Germany, England, and whatever else suggested itself—belonged not to the bar-room but the asylum." Roosevelt was, Adams concluded, beyond thought: he was, like a child, "pure act." Adams himself was by this time almost beyond act, and he found Roosevelt's temporal cross-dressing—his mixing up of the child and the grownup—as unnatural as any other morbidity being diagnosed in an age transfixed by decadence, a case study for Nordau or Krafft-Ebing. The boy who, in an adolescence protracted into middle age, fantasized about being a gladiator tortured under the eyes of Nero or Commodus—Kaiser Wilhelm, that aesthete in jackboots, had very little on Teddy.

It was precisely because the morbidities of the fin-de-siècle touched him so closely that Roosevelt was so wary of them. To make matters worse, he was deeply affected by poetry. Haunted by the specter of impotence—the tame-cat syndrome to which so many intellectuals succumbed—he took care to keep his knowledge of subjects unconnected with war or statecraft at the level of the precocious showoff. More profound study would have required a suspension of motion, and he had a dread of relaxing the sinews of action. He lived, as a boy did, in a perpetual present that enhanced his life but detracted from his books, which are not much read today. He knew that there is something morbid in intellectual effort, and that books that survive commonly bear the stigmata of solitude and despair. He dictated rapidly and moved on, in a chaos of enthusiasms, and fixing a skeptical eye on the two Henrys—Adams and James—refused to follow their example. They sought to shape knowledge and passion into an artistic whole, the ideal of an older civilization.* Roosevelt was careful to remain American in his indiscipline, his resistance to molds, his anarchies of motion—a "bolting bull calf," in Adams's words, who delighted in the percussive rather than harmonious. The boyish frenzy, the playful energies, were, in a man past fifty, in their own way abnormal: but they were an abnormality of power, what Roosevelt's friends and enemies alike equated with his "magnetism." They allowed him to escape the lethargy that crippled so many of his WASP contemporaries.

THE DIFFICULTY WAS THAT THE man who would be boy eternal had by this time lost his playground, having surrendered the White House, in 1909, to William Howard Taft. Those who have sipped from the cup of power are seldom content with other brews, and Roosevelt was soon looking for a way to win back the presidency. He justified this ambition by pointing to Taft, who in his opinion was no reformer. Taft had brought nearly twice as many antitrust suits as Roosevelt

---

* The "great value" Matthew Arnold found in the Greeks, Lionel Trilling said, was their "sense of the wholeness of the human personality." It grew out of the idea, Wilhelm von Humboldt wrote, that the "true end of man—not that which his transient wishes suggest to him, but that which eternal immutable reason prescribes—is the highest possible development of his powers into a well-proportioned whole." The idea illuminates the higher WASPs, and was not without influence of the lower and middling ones.

himself, the trust-buster, but he had bungled the tariff question, agreeing to duties on imported goods that infuriated both progressives who saw them as a sop to industrialists and consumers who wanted cheaper products. Roosevelt was unimpressed; he believed quite sincerely that the irresponsibility of the "criminal rich," the "malefactors of great wealth," threatened the stability of the Republic. Yet Taft, a WASP of the cautious, high and dry school, seemed to coddle the plutocrats. In doing so he threatened to bring the "gold-ridden, capitalist-bestridden, usurer-mastered" future Roosevelt feared that much closer.

H. G. Wells recalled how in private conversation the "strenuous vehement Teddy" of the platform gave place to "an entirely negotiable individuality," a relaxation of manner that allowed Roosevelt to speak candidly of his fears for his country. He admitted that America's republican experiment might prove, in the end, to be a "a gigantic futility," incapable of balancing the claims of competing groups, regions, and classes. But he chose, he said, "to live as if this were not so," to act in the faith that the American experiment would succeed. "Suppose after all," he said as he put out his hand and made a fist, that Wells's own prophecies "should prove to be right," and that it "all ends" in "butterflies and morlocks"— that is, in the dystopian, class-riven world of Wells's novel *The Time Machine.* "That doesn't matter now," Roosevelt insisted. "The effort's real. It's worth going on with. It's worth it. It's worth it—even then," even if it should fail.

In August 1910 Roosevelt went to the John Brown Cemetery in Osawatomie, Kansas, to continue the effort at regeneration. He had recently finished Herbert Croly's *The Promise of American Life,* and drawing on Croly's ideas and his own state papers, he laid out the New Nationalism, the blueprint for an administrative state that would establish national health care, social insurance for the old and the unemployed, workers' compensation, an eight hour workday, and federal regulation of the securities industry, with costs to be met through taxation of wealth. With the annunciation at Osawatomie, Roosevelt became at once the leading progressive in the country and the hero of such reformist WASPs as Learned Hand and Gifford Pinchot, an early environmentalist whose niece, Mary Pinchot Meyer, would become one of John F. Kennedy's more memorable girlfriends before she was murdered on the towpath of the Chesapeake and Ohio Canal in Georgetown in 1964. Others, however, were skeptical of Roosevelt's motives and still more of his idea of government by experts. To H. L. Mencken, Roosevelt's policy amounted to "rigid control from above, a despotism of inspired prophets and policemen," a nosy paternalism "concerning itself with all things, from the regulation of coal-mining and meat-packing to the regulation of spelling and marital rights."

Old Guard Republicans were even more disturbed by the Osawatomie manifesto, and they worked diligently behind closed doors to ensure that the Republican presidential nomination went to Taft in 1912. Roosevelt responded by running as an independent, the candidate of the newly formed Progressive or Bull Moose Party. Not only had his ideas about the viability of third parties evolved since 1898, when he had thrown over Jack Chapman and the Independents in New York, so too had his taste in rhetoric. Employing the language of the prophets, he described the coming contest in apocalyptic terms, telling supporters in Chicago that "we stand at Armageddon, and we battle for the Lord."

WASPs like Learned Hand and George Rublee, not given to prophecy, nevertheless became happy warriors in Roosevelt's quest for a new mandarinism. But America at large was not persuaded by the former president's apocalypse, and in the general election the Bull Moose Party went down to defeat. Roosevelt's candidacy split the Republican vote, and although he ran ahead of Taft in the three-way contest, Woodrow Wilson, the Democratic candidate, won the White House.

As a boy loses interest in a new toy, Roosevelt soon tired of the Bull Moose Party; seeking fresh stimulants, he decamped to the Amazon to survey the Rio da Dúvida. Herbert Croly, a more faithful New Nationalist, was stung by Roosevelt's loss; he was looking for a way to keep the faith alive when, he said, Willard Straight "hunted me up and asked me to make a report for him on the kind of social education which would be most fruitful in a democracy." Straight was, like Croly, Hand, and Rublee, an ardent Rooseveltian, and hoping that Theodore would yet regain the presidency, he wanted to keep the Bull Moose program before the eyes of the public. He toyed with the idea of using Dorothy's money to acquire a newspaper to advance the Roosevelt interest, but newspapers are expensive. Croly thought a weekly magazine would be more manageable.

In the fall of 1913 the Straights invited Croly to join them at Applegreen, their estate in Old Westbury on Long Island, where plans for a New Nationalist publication assumed a definite shape. Dorothy had, like her husband, been excited by *The Promise of American Life*. If Willard saw in the book a path to power in a future Roosevelt administration, Dorothy was attracted to the author's dream of reforms that would do something for the little people. (Her brother Harry, frowning on her progressive impulses, spoke of her as "my pink sister.") At one point during the visit, Croly began to denounce as anachronistic the editorial line *Harper's Weekly* was taking. Its editor, Norman Hapgood, wanted to break up monopolistic combinations and restore competitive markets; Croly, by contrast, wanted to *preserve* industrial monopolies and at the same time bring them under the control of government planners.

"Why don't you get out a weekly yourself, Herbert?" Dorothy suggested.

"Where would I find the money?" Croly asked.

"I will find it."

"It would take a lot of money," he pointed out. "About a hundred thousand the first year. . . . It might take five years to make the paper self-supporting."

"Yes," she said, "I understand. It may take longer, much longer. But let's go ahead."

THE RESULT WAS THE *New Republic*, a magazine that would become one of the oracles of the American Century. It was, in the early days, a distinctly WASP operation. Learned Hand and Dorothy and Willard Straight played a leading part in its foundation; it was for a time closely identified with Theodore Roosevelt and the cause of WASP mandarinism; Mr. Justice Holmes was one of its earliest fans. The magazine's offices on West Twenty-first Street resembled nothing so much as a good WASP club, with leather chairs in the library and a French chef in the kitchen.

Yet the most original and penetrating of the *New Republic's* early writers was not a WASP. Walter Lippmann's forebears were German Jews who had emigrated to America in the middle of the nineteenth century. But the psychological background was similar. Just as WASPs were threatened by a rising middle class unwilling to defer to self-appointed Brahmins, however well-educated, so cultivated Jews like the Lippmanns were wary of the enterprising but in their eyes uncouth immigrants (refugees from the ghettos and shtetls of Russia and Austria-Hungary) who were beginning to assert themselves in America.

Young Walter was brought up in an atmosphere of fin-de-siècle privilege. He traveled with his parents to Europe to take the waters at Baden-Baden and Marienbad, and he was classically educated at Dr. Sachs's School in New York. An adolescent wallow in Ruskin led him, one summer, to haunt the Louvre, and he was deep in contemplation of Cimabue's *Madonna and Child* when he was approached by an American woman, evidently in the cream of fashion, who was intrigued by the intensity of his concentration. It was Mrs. Jack Gardner, who took it upon herself to act as the young man's cicerone, guiding him through the galleries of the museum.

Quite as much as Henry Adams and Learned Hand, Lippmann dreaded neurasthenic debility, the hysterical terrors, as he called them, that "prepare the soul for weakness." He felt himself, too, as the sensitive WASP was apt to feel, an "antediluvian" making his way in an alien world, a Roman senator clinging to his Horace and his Falernian, shrinking from the barbarism of Goth and Vandal. It was the characteristic mode of the defensive patrician, a sense of estrangement that made the Greek poet Theognis disdain new men who did not know what "is noble and ignoble, because they have no tradition," and that made Evelyn Waugh regret the inundation of Oxford, "submerged now and obliterated, irrecoverable as Lyonesse, so quickly have the waters come flooding in."

Like Learned Hand and John Jay Chapman before him, Lippmann was seduced, at Harvard, by a still potent humanism. He drew close to James and Santayana, and under the latter's supervision applied himself to *literae humaniores*, reading Lucretius in Latin, Dante in Italian, and Goethe in German. Liberal education awakened in him a civic impulse, and he was rapidly converted to socialism, which had expropriated the old language of republican virtue. But by the time he reached the *New Republic* Lippmann was near to breaking with "parlor socialists" and histrionic anarchists: they were not serious. He was drawn instead to "constructive solutions" to "administrative problems," the work of a new managerial state that was to be neither classically liberal nor overtly socialist.

There was, he believed, a good deal of urgency in the work. From Theodore Roosevelt he had learned that America must prepare itself "spiritually and physically" for its "inescapable destiny" as a global power; from Herbert Croly he had absorbed the dogmas of the mandarin state. Yet when he came to sum up the mission of the *New Republic*, Lippmann drew neither on Roosevelt, the impresario of the American Century, nor on Croly, the most faithful apostle of American mandarinism, but on the humanism of Santayana. "If there is any word to cover our ideal," he wrote to Van Wyck Brooks, "I suppose it is humanistic . . ."

Like Hand and the other *New Republic* liberals, Lippmann wanted his fellow citizens to escape what was cramping in modern life, to realize the humane injunction of the Greek poet Pindar, "Become what you are." But he failed to explain how a regulatory state devoted to technical efficiency and the mandarin direction of affairs would accomplish the desired end. Nor was he as alive, at this point, as he would later be to the danger that the omniscient state, in babying people and doing their thinking for them, might stunt the very growth he hoped to foster. Lippmann, the new mandarin, was no more able than Henry Adams, the old mandarin, to see the way to the regenerated Republic that haunted their dreams.

Franklin Roosevelt as assistant secretary of the navy.

TWENTY

Franklin and Eleanor

la sconoscente vita . . .

the unowned life . . .
—Dante, *Inferno*

He was "charming, good-looking, loved by all who came in contact with him," Eleanor Roosevelt said of her father. But Elliott Roosevelt was also troubled. Once, when Eleanor was six or eight and they were walking their terriers together, he stopped at the Knickerbocker Club, then on Fifth Avenue at Thirty-second Street. It would only be a moment. Hours later she watched as he was carried out to a cab; she and the terriers were taken home by the doorman.

Eleanor Roosevelt was, in her background, a more characteristic WASP than her future husband, Franklin, who all his life was to bask in what Edmund Wilson called a "slightly unnatural sunniness." He had been carefully protected by his parents from the rawness of life; she was a child of well-to-do disorder and neglect. Elliott Roosevelt had in his youth been diagnosed with hysteria, and he was prone to headaches and fainting fits, so much so that he was compelled to leave St. Paul's School. As a boy he had outshone his older brother Theodore, the future president, but he soon lost ground; unlike Theodore, he seemed to have no objects in life other than hunting, yachting, and the WASP social round. He married, at twenty-three, a daughter of old New York, Anna Livingston Ludlow Hall, but his bride was not the woman to help him discover a latent sense of purpose: she was a society figure whose "utterly frivolous life," Theodore said, ate "into her character like an acid." Motherhood did nothing to change her. "Eleanor, I hardly know what's to happen to you," she once said to her daughter. "You're so plain that you really have nothing to do except *be good*." When she and Elliott were not living apart, in mutual enmity, they roamed nomadically about Europe fruitlessly seeking amusement and a cure for Elliott's drinking. Periodically he would collect himself and resolve to live soberly, only to fall again into dissipation and even scandal, a "flagrant-man swine," in his brother's judgment.

Elliott and Anna died young, she of despair and diphtheria, he of drink and delirium tremens. The "terrible mixture of madness and grotesque, grim evil," punctuated by "dreadful flashes of his old sweetness," continued to the end, Theodore wrote after Elliott's death. Little Eleanor was now an orphan. Yet she was always to cherish the memory of her father, and she carefully preserved his letters to her; for all his faults he had loved her, in a way her disdainful and contemptuous mother never could. But she would not make her parents' mistakes. If they had been overly absorbed in the trivialities of society, she would be extravagantly purposeful; if they had been thoughtless in their luxurious pleasure-seeking, she would be as grimly conscientious as Charlotte Corday.

Her high-mindedness was reinforced by her schooling. In 1899, when she was fifteen, her aunt and uncle, Tissie and Stanley Yates Mortimer, took her to England and enrolled her in the Allenswood school near Wimbledon Common. The headmistress, Marie Souvestre, combined in her own person the dominating authority of Endicott Peabody and the artistic sensitivity of Amory Gardner. She was nearly seventy when Eleanor first saw her, white-haired, gray-eyed, with "the charm," Beatrice Webb thought, "of past beauty and present attractiveness," and the "dignity of manner and brilliancy of speech" of an "habitué, during middle life, of intellectual society in Paris, Berlin, and London." She had, one of her students thought, "the agility and grace of a humming-bird," and a gift for sharp and epigrammatic speech. But there was another, less easily definable quality in Mlle. Souvestre's inspiration; she seemed to radiate "a Promethean fire which warmed and coloured" her students' souls.

Like Peabody, Mlle. Souvestre "had an eagle eye which penetrated right through you to your backbone" and "took in everything about you." She "always knew more than she was told," Eleanor said.* And like Peabody, she could be severe and even cruel, having little patience for weakness or slovenliness. "I have seen her take a girl's paper," Eleanor remembered, "and tear it in half in her disgust and anger at poor or shoddy work." She could also be remarkably intolerant. Beatrice Webb thought her brilliant qualities undermined by a lack of humility and a certain "narrowness of vision," a "total inability to understand religion," a "dogmatism that was proof against the spirit of scientific investigation," and a "lack of charity to feelings with which she did not sympathize."

But Mlle. Souvestre's faults were more than counterbalanced by her faith in the liberating power of humane education. Her own training, Beatrice Webb said, had been purely literary, and as much as Amory Gardner she wanted to make the humanities live for her students. The curriculum at Allenswood was classical, devoted, Blanche Wiesen Cook writes, to "high culture, literature, and the arts." Reading aloud in her library, Mlle. Souvestre acquainted her girls with the tragic poets; Dorothy Strachey, one of her old girls, would in her novel *Olivia* describe how a character modeled on Mlle. Souvestre gave her, through her reading of Racine, her "first conception of tragedy," of the "complication and pity of human lives."

Whatever the secret of Mlle. Souvestre's teaching, it worked. The scarred, orphaned Eleanor, convinced that she was inherently flawed and irredeemably plain, throve at Allenswood, and became in effect head girl, "the most important person at the school." She sat at Mlle. Souvestre's table at dinner, traveled with her when she went abroad, became her intimate friend. The headmistress spoke

---

* "I do not believe any boy, however crooked his tongue, however deep his sins below the surface, ever lied face to face with the Rector," Ellery Sedgwick wrote. "There was an instinctive, comprehensive understanding about him. He never spied, but he always knew and you knew he knew. Out with it!"

of the "purity" of Eleanor's heart and the "perfect quality of her soul"; to her, Eleanor was "my Totty whom I shall always love."

MLLE. SOUVESTRE WAS ON FRIENDLY terms with such eminent Victorians as Joseph Chamberlain, John Morley, Leslie Stephen, Mrs. Humphry Ward, and Lady Strachey, and at Allenswood Eleanor saw something of the great world of English liberalism in its heyday and the effort of its leading figures to reform politics and society. But Mme. Souvestre was as closely connected to Bloomsbury, the Bohemian stepchild of English liberalism, then still in embryo. She was, in her tastes, at odds with Victorianism; nudes by Rodin and Puvis de Chavannes (who were her friends) could be found in her library, and her unconventionality and freedom from inhibition made a lasting impression upon Lady Strachey's son, the future Bloomsbury eminence Lytton Strachey. Lytton's sister, Dorothy, dedicated *Olivia*, with its candid account of Mlle. Souvestre and the girl-love that flourished in her school, to Leslie Stephen's daughter Virginia Woolf. These Edwardian children of Victorian liberalism would carry their parents' reformist impulse into the once taboo territory of sexual morals, and the very Englishness of their prose would disarm readers who might not otherwise have been sympathetic to their desire to emancipate women and liberate gays.

The patrician liberalism Eleanor found at Allenswood had a good deal in common with the WASP mandarinism of her uncle, Theodore Roosevelt, and his friends Learned Hand, Henry Stimson, and Willard Straight. But there were differences. The most liberal English patrician was by American standards an archaic, almost an ancien régime figure, who sometimes went so far as to chuck mass opinion when he thought it wrong. The WASP reformer in New York or Washington was much more closely pressed by a vigorous and undeferential democracy, and was at the same time constrained by a Yankee hardheadedness that scented decadence and aristocratic languor in learning, reflection, and philosophy. The WASP reformer was just able to make out his case for the mandarin regulatory state—Americans were always ready to entertain a technical argument—but he did not even try to translate his Athenian humanism into policy: there was no market for it. England's Bloomsbury patricians, by contrast, had the patrician self-confidence to pursue their own pet peeves: their beef, for example, with Victorian sexual morality, which they assailed in books like E. M. Forster's *A Room with a View*, Lytton Strachey's *Eminent Victorians*, and Virginia Woolf's *Mrs Dalloway*. The WASP male in America had a different ideal; in his pursuit of human completion he was not especially concerned with lovemaking, with the evils of sexual constraint or the virtues of erotic transcendence. What he wanted was to make use of his various powers and develop them into a well-proportioned whole—the old humane ideal. What he lacked was faith in himself. He readily bowed down before his country's instinctive utilitarianism, and he was often too timid even to try to vindicate the Greek agora he was chasing in his heart.*

WHEN ELEANOR LEFT ALLENSWOOD IN 1902 to make her debut in New York, Mlle. Souvestre was concerned that she would lose her way. "I fear to hear," she wrote, "that you have been unable to defend yourself against all the temptations which surround you; evenings out, pleasures, flirtations."

But Eleanor, with her deep conscientiousness, was proof against what Mlle. Souvestre called the "season of social dissipations." She dutifully joined her friends Mary Harriman and Gwendolyn Burden in the charitable labors of the Junior League, and she went down to the Bowery with Jean Reid, the daughter Whitelaw Reid, the American ambassador in London, to work with slum children in Vida Scudder's College Settlement in Rivington Street. She also acted as surrogate mother to her younger brother Hall. Their grandmother, Mary Livingston Ludlow Hall, was too old to care for the boy properly, and Eleanor worried that her country house, at Tivoli on the Hudson, was no place for him on account of their bibulous Uncle Vallie—Valentine Gill Hall III—a tennis champion who was growing ever wilder in his carouses, and who found amusement in shooting his rifle in the direction of his mother's guests. Little Hall was put into the hands of Mr. Peabody at Groton.

Eleanor did of course make her debut, and indeed confessed that for a time her "sole object in life was society." But by "no stretch of the imagination," she wrote, "could I fool myself into thinking that I was a popular debutante." This was false modesty. "She was always making herself out to be an ugly duckling," her cousin Alice Roosevelt recalled. In fact "she was really rather attractive," a tall, willowy girl, "rather coltish-looking, with masses of pale, gold hair rippling to below her waist, and really lovely blue eyes." Eligible young men sought her hand, among them Nick Biddle of the Philadelphia Biddles and the doomed

---

* The agora was the civic center and marketplace at the heart of an old Greek city: it became for a number of WASPs the model of an ideal forum in which human nature could do justice to itself. Yet the best of these places were always imperfect and in their different ways inhumane.

Howard Potter Cary, whom she thought "a charming man with a really lovely spirit," but who was perhaps a little stiff.

One day she was in the train going up to Tivoli when she ran into her cousin Franklin Roosevelt, whom she had not seen in ages. Some young women were put off by Franklin's ingratiating smiles: they made a little joke that his initials F.D. stood for "Feather Duster," and they took him for the sort of young man who never amounts to much in life. Yet his lighthearted charm may well have appealed to Eleanor as being like her father's, the unfortunate Elliott, even as she was reassured by Franklin's evident sanity and freedom from neurotic shadow. She was, too, perceptive enough to see that beneath the breezy manner lay a certain seriousness of purpose, the very thing her father, who was also Franklin's godfather, conspicuously lacked.[*]

Chaperoned by her Aunt Kassie and Cousin Muriel, she went up to see Franklin at Harvard. They watched the Harvard-Yale game—Franklin in his crimson sweater led the cheers—and afterward he showed them his rooms in Westmorly Court, the most luxurious of Harvard's rich-boy Gold Coast residences. She and her party then went off to Groton to visit Hall; the next day Franklin joined her there. They went to chapel, and later, as they walked down the path that leads to the river, Franklin proposed to her, saying something to the effect that, with her help, he might make something of himself.

Their engagement not only united the two severed Roosevelt lines, Hyde Park and Oyster Bay, it brought together two different WASP approaches to life. Eleanor had, like so many WASPs, been touched by a lingering Puritanism; as a girl she had accepted her mother's disdain as a just punishment for something wrong in herself. But at Allenswood she had been introduced to the liberal faith that one's inward faults were only a symptom of the deeper evils of a corrupt society: the way to escape one's own suffering was to try to save the world.[†]

Franklin had, at this time, a much less elaborate social conscience. Under the Rector's inspiration he had taught Sunday school and worked with the poor, but

---

[*]   Franklin's old Groton master, the Reverend Sherrard Billings, perceived what so many others overlooked. "It has been a dream of mine for some years," he wrote to Franklin after the announcement of his engagement to Eleanor, "that you would be a man widely useful to your country, and a sympathetic wife will be a great help to you on the road to realizing my dream and I am thankful and glad." Billings prayed with all his heart "that men will say of you that he was a man sent from God to help the world in its dire need."

[†]   The liberal or radical, Edmund Wilson observed, evolves "a psychological mechanism which enables him to turn moral judgments against himself into moral judgments against society."

he had no burden of neurotic guilt to expiate. (The seed planted by Peabody, who sought to develop in his boys a Christian social conscience, would not bear fruit in his most famous pupil until later, when pain and polio changed him.) The distinctive element in Franklin's approach to life, at the time of his marriage, was a pragmatic expediency. Pragmatism was in fashion: Eleanor's Uncle Theodore, with his constantly evolving domestic program, was a pragmatist; so too, in a different way, was William James, who judged the truth of an idea not through an appeal to immutable principles but by the conduct the idea "dictates or inspires," its "cash-value in terms of practical experience." Franklin seems to have experienced nothing of James's personal influence at Harvard, nor was he likely to have read any of his books, but already he was working out for himself a version of James's "romantic utilitarianism," in which you believe what you want to believe if it helps you get through the day,* and in which a sublime indifference to past thinking and superseded dogmas, together with an enthusiasm for novelty and experimentation, will lead to greater material and spiritual goods.

Franklin's mother, Sara, was shattered by the engagement and insisted that the couple refrain from announcing it for a year. But she would later deny that she did anything to prevent the marriage, and at last a date was set. Eleanor had recently been a bridesmaid in her friend Flossie Twombly's wedding to William A. M. Burden, at which Endicott Peabody officiated. "It seems quite necessary for a Groton boy to have him," she wrote to Franklin. The Rector and Mrs. Peabody rearranged their schedules to come down to New York for the wedding, which took place in the twin Ludlow-Parish townhouses on East Seventy-sixth Street in March 1905. President Roosevelt gave his niece away.

THE MARRIAGE OF CONTRASTS HAD its ups and downs. Franklin liked to drink, flirt, and have fun. He stayed up to all hours playing poker at the Knickerbocker Club, and he could be "drunk, loud, and silly" at parties. His cavalier pragmatism recognized no moral law against pleasure, and indeed his cousin Alice Roosevelt thought that he "deserved a good time. He was married to Eleanor." Eleanor, for

---

* In an 1879 essay, "The Ethics of Belief," William Kingdon Clifford, the English mathematician and philosopher, said that it "is wrong always, everywhere, and for every one to believe anything upon insufficient evidence." In a talk to the Philosophical Club at Yale in 1896, James replied, with some hedges and qualifications, "that we have the right to believe at our own risk any hypothesis that is live enough to tempt our will." "Objective evidence and certitude are doubtless very fine ideals to play with, but where on this moonlit and dream-visited planet are they found? . . . No concrete test of what is really true has ever been agreed upon."

her part, disapproved all the more fiercely of Franklin's intervals of sybaritic indolence because she was conscious of her own failures of purpose; she was very far from living up to Mlle. Souvestre's belief that one must rise above conventionality and attain to virtue. She was another WASP matron much like the next, perfectly respectable and often perfectly miserable—an unimpassioned wife, an indifferent mother, a sullen daughter-in-law, knitting and embroidering her way through what she thought a morbid and idiotic existence.

She seemed fated to resemble one of the heroines of Edith Wharton's novels, crushed by convention. But in 1910 a group of reform Democrats invited Franklin to run for the New York State Senate. With his winning smile and "patrician carelessness of dress and manner," he was a natural candidate, and although the district was Republican, he won easily. He and Eleanor took a house in Albany, where he played the sympathetic part of an anti-Tammany reformer even as he prudently remained a loyal party man—no whimsical third-party dreams for him. Perhaps to her surprise, Eleanor discovered that she liked being a political wife; she found, in the smoke-filled rooms of Albany and the earthy, uncouth pols, with their spittoons and colorful language, a greasy human warmth unlike anything she had encountered on the Upper East Side or the estates of the Hudson Valley squires. The blithe spirits of the new WASP generation, Mrs. Wharton observed, if they were not going in for Georgian architecture or Pre-Columbian art, were, like Eleanor and Franklin, becoming "absorbed in state politics or municipal reform." Here was a different, more exciting, and possibly more liberating kind of slumming.

Franklin, already a shrewd judge of political horseflesh, was an early supporter of Woodrow Wilson's candidacy for the presidency, and after Wilson defeated Taft and Uncle Teddy in the election of 1912, he accepted the office of assistant secretary of the navy in the new administration. He and Eleanor and their young family took up residence in Washington, where they saw a good deal of the aging Henry Adams. The old man had recently suffered a stroke, and he had little patience for Franklin's ambitions, which must have seemed to him a caricature of his own thwarted aspirations. "Young man," he lectured the assistant secretary over lunch, "I have lived in this house many years and seen the occupants of that White House across the square come and go, and nothing you minor officials or the occupant of that house can do will affect the history of the world for long."

Eleanor was indignant. "Mr. Adams," she said, "that is a very terrible thing to say to a young man who wants to go into politics and be of use to other people." She made, as she remembered, "quite a speech." But Adams, leaning back in his chair, "just laughed at me. We were always good friends."

Eleanor became one of Adams's honorary nieces. "He was such a kind man," Eleanor recalled, so good with the children. "They would crawl all over him when he sat in his victoria. He was very . . . tolerant." For although he professed himself ennuyé to the last degree, he still loved the Madonna in women, and he granted Eleanor the rare privilege of reading a privately printed copy of *The Education of Henry Adams*. (The book would not be given to the public until after his death.) She found it "very interesting but sad to have had so much and yet find it so little."

The shriveled old sage could but have nodded. He had plumbed the depths of knowledge, yet he knew less than when he began. He had sought an agora, and found only Lafayette Square. Coming to Washington to undertake the "steady remodeling of social and political habits, ideas, and institutions" he believed America needed, he had seen everything go "to the devil," not least himself. Yet he liked the young WASP mother who still believed in dreams he himself had forgotten.

Gertrude Vanderbilt Whitney was unafraid to break taboos, and went places where respectable WASPs had never before set foot.

TWENTY-ONE

The WASPs Throw Off Victorianism

Da questa visione innanzi cominciò lo mio spirito naturale ad essere impedito ne la sua operazione . . .

From the commencement of that vision my natural spirit
began to be impeded in its function . . .
—Dante, *La Vita Nuova*

Alice Roosevelt, the only child of Theodore Roosevelt by his first wife, Alice Hathaway Lee, had a girlhood less traumatic than her cousin Eleanor's, but in its own way botched—"awfully bad psychologically," as she was later to say. Her mother died after giving birth to her, and her widowed father fobbed her off on his older sister, Anna. Bye, as Anna was known in the family, was warm in her instincts and, though at the time childless, a natural mother; she devoted herself to the little girl. But in 1886 Theodore married his childhood sweetheart Edith Carow, and in the spring of 1887 three-year-old Alice was taken from Bye, the only mother she had ever known, to live with her father and stepmother. Edith, though by no means a Victorian witch out of Dickens or the Brontës—a Miss Murdstone or an Aunt Reed—was not without Gothic touches. She was prone to invalidish ailments, and like Lady Bertram, the unsatisfactory substitute mama in Jane Austen's *Mansfield Park*, she inclined to "a little ill-health, and a great deal of indolence." She was, too, to have a brood of five of her own to look after, and there was not much tenderness left over for Alice, whose personality was, to say the least, at variance with her own. The girl was high spirited; she "needs someone," Edith said, "to laugh and romp with her." But being herself a "sober and staid person," it was not a part, she felt, that she could reasonably be expected to play.

And so Alice passed her childhood with this "withdrawn, rather parched" gentlewoman, as she described her stepmother, who "had almost a gift for making people uncomfortable." The girl longed to know her father better; Theodore shared her high spirits, and could laugh and romp with the best of them. He might have made good the deficit of love, but he was mostly absent, pursuing politics and war, and Alice, taking the easiest course open to a neglected child, became a rebel. At thirteen, she was raising Cain in the streets of Washington. She rode her bike "with her feet on the handlebars," and playing the Dickensian urchin, she became the leader of a gang of boys. Theodore and Edith dispatched the "guttersnipe" to Aunt Bye in New York, but to no avail. Alice smoked cigarettes, played poker, grew enamored of pistols and fired one of them from the observation car of a train, and drove unchaperoned in a motor-car from Newport to Boston. In those days, when a girl could not allow herself to be kissed by a boy until after he had proposed to her, Eleanor Roosevelt warned her cousin of the disrepute she courted, going so far as to lecture her on the gifts that she might with propriety accept from gentlemen. Flowers, books, and cards "were all possible," Eleanor preached, but "jewelry of any kind" could not be countenanced. Alice listened complaisantly to her cousin's "earnest discourse," all the while fingering a "modest string of seed pearls" which a male admirer had recently bestowed upon her.

ALICE WAS IN REBELLION AGAINST the Victorian constraints and pruderies that
her father accepted and her stepmother positively cherished. But although she
acted the mischievous gamine, she was careful, at this period in her life, not to
transgress the more serious sexual taboos. She was, she said, "greedy for sensation," but it was her misfortune to have been made acquainted with the facts
of life by her father, and to have been initiated in those mysteries by Theodore
Roosevelt might have warped the healthiest female libido; all her life Alice was
to dislike being touched. Yet other WASP women were rapidly discarding the
thou-shalt-nots. Nine years older than Alice, Gertrude Vanderbilt, the great-
granddaughter of Commodore Vanderbilt, had been born into the Vanderbilt
splendors, and her part in life had been ordained at birth. She was to find a
suitable mate, produce a suitable number of heirs and heiresses, appear, suitably
coiffed and gowned, in her box at the opera, and preside, in a suitable manner,
over dull dinners and duller teas in the draughty mock-chateaux favored by her
class.

The only difficulty was that Gertrude possessed an unsuitable sense of purpose. Unlike Isabella Stewart Gardner and Pierpont Morgan, who were content
to acquire art, she actually wanted to make it, an ambition so strange, in one of
her sex and social position, as to be almost scandalous. In the circles in which
she moved, art might be venerated, but artists were suspect. Their manners
were bohemian, their methods indelicate: they worked with undraped models.
Growing up, Gertrude encountered only a few souls who spoke her language.
There was Henry Adams's friend the artist John La Farge, who gave her encour-
agement, and there was Esther Hunt, a wild, interesting girl, the daughter of
the architect Richard Morris Hunt. (After the Breakers—a Vanderbilt summer
"cottage" in Newport—burnt to the ground, Hunt rebuilt it in a style that might
have made Palladio weep.) There was also Howard Cushing, who after Groton
and Harvard stole away to Paris to appease with paint whatever obscure passions gripped him, and for his pains was whispered to be a degenerate. But such
sympathy as Gertrude found could not silence the ticking clock; she was under
intense pressure to marry and reproduce. "Alas," she wrote on her twentieth
birthday, "I am out of my teens today! Alas, I am no longer very young! Alas,
when a girl is twenty she is on the road to being an old maid!"

Harry Payne Whitney, who had frowned on his sister Dorothy's marriage
to Willard Straight, was good-looking, intelligent, and rich. He was also
candid, and admitted to Gertrude that, much as he liked her personally, he was

intrigued by the possibility of uniting their two fortunes. She was charmed by his candor, and impressed by a youthful career that seemed to presage vigor and activity. At Groton Harry had stood near the top of his form, and at Yale he had been elected to Phi Beta Kappa and the board of the *Yale Daily News*. The wedding took place, in 1896, at Newport, in the Gold Room of the reconstructed Breakers, where Bishop Potter, the uncle of Harry's form-mate Warwick Potter, officiated in his capacity as "pontiff to the cream of rich and fashionable America."

From the first there were difficulties. Gertrude wanted to create a school for architects, with provision for classes in painting and sculpture, but Harry, having no sympathy for her artistic interests, opposed the project. "It never has made any difference to him," she said, "that I feel as I do about art and it never will (except as a source of annoyance)." His indifference was maddening. "I feel at times that I must set off a bomb under him or die," she wrote. "Bomb . . . He will not go halfway with me and I will starve." A trip to Europe led to deeper estrangement. She and Harry sailed from New York with their friends Adele and Jay Burden; Jimmie Appleton, another old pal, accompanied them. But scarcely had the party reached London when Harry, fast on his way to becoming a sporting dolt, disappeared into polo. Gertrude crossed to France without him, and in Paris had a flirt with Jimmie Appleton. She confessed to a "deviltry that is not altogether safe," but after all she was in Paris, and Parisians taught one, she said, to "live for the moment." When Harry caught up with her, he accused her of lacking "good principles." She, for her part, referred to him, in her account of the journey, as "Fatty."

They proceeded to Italy like characters in a tale of Henry James, the one being changed by the revelation of the Old World, the other looking forward to the moment he got back to the Racquet Club in New York. In Rome Harry took to his bed with a cold, and Gertrude explored the city with Howard Cushing. Unlike Harry, he sympathized with all that she saw and felt; there was, she said, "no one I would rather see beautiful things with than this man," so "sympathetic and strong and magnetic." She sensed in the old stones "memories of a warm life" at odds with the coldness of the "Anglo-Saxon temperament": they "beckoned me to follow and live and learn." They went on to Naples, where she reveled in the dirt and vice of the city. The Neapolitans, she said, were very bad, "racked by many sins," yet they possessed a "glamour which in the wilderness of my mind shone like stars, distant but strangely bright." A "great passion of selfishness" swept over her: "*my* life, *my* desires." She wanted to "touch the core of life," to overcome the "inexpressible agony of the 'shut in feeling,'" a byproduct of her WASP training. At the climax of this not wholly original vision (Walter Pater's gemlike flame burned now even in those who had never read him) she dared to hope that through art she might become "steeped in beauty" and "make an image" in her heart "that cannot be wiped out."

THE OLD WORLD WAS LIBERATING, but it was Harry himself who stamped Gertrude's passport to freedom. If Europe revealed to her the depth of the gulf that divided her from her husband, in America she discovered a more concrete impediment to their happiness: she caught Harry in an affair with an equestrienne who shared his passion for horses. But she did not ask for a divorce. Instead she made a bargain. She would keep up appearances as Mrs. Harry Payne Whitney. She would attend Harry's polo matches, watch his thoroughbreds at the racetrack, play hostess in their various houses. But when not on duty, she would lead a life of her own and permit no man to "drag her down" until her vitality was "sapped and all her fine possibilities destroyed."

Free, now, to pursue both her vocation as an artist and her instincts as a woman, Gertrude acquired, for use as a sculptor's studio, a carriage house in MacDougall Alley in Greenwich Village, and she took lovers of her own, among them one of the young men who modeled for her. She confessed, in her journal, to looking forward to their sessions together, when "his beautiful bare body will be more beautiful than ever and I will look at him and be glad that I am alive . . ." Rodin himself, who knew Gertrude in Paris, said that "she has the true vocation," the "mysterious gift." She had escaped.

In that prelude to the Jazz Age when, Virginia Woolf said, "human character changed," WASP women, not WASP men, took the lead in smashing the idols. This was partly because they had more opportunity to see what was going on in places where respectable WASPs had never before set foot. WASP males were busy at the office or, if they were sportsmen, consumed by horses and sailboats; it was the WASP woman who ventured into the Village, slummed in the most sordid districts of the Lower East Side, and studied the pictures in Mr. Alfred Stieglitz's Gallery at 291 Fifth Avenue, that "attic kept warm by an iron stove" where Matisse and Cézanne were first exhibited in the United States. From these expeditions the WASP woman brought back tales of ragtime, Freud, Cubism, and the necessity of overcoming archaic taboos.

As much as Gertrude Whitney, though in a different way, Mabel Dodge embodied the new resistance to everything that seemed to make human beings *smaller*. An heiress from Buffalo, she went through men as rapidly as she went through what German sociologists were beginning to call *Lebensstile*, lifestyles. Bored by her first husband, who was as addicted to shooting wildlife as Harry Whitney was to breaking polo ponies, she went to bed with her gynecologist. Later she fled to Europe, where she was pursued by a preppy architect called Edwin Dodge, a "nice young man in tweeds," as she described him before their marriage. They installed themselves in the Villa Curonia overlooking Florence and threw a continuous house party, in Mabel's words, for "pianists, painters, pederasts, prostitutes, and peasants."

Tiring of views of the Duomo and of poor Dodge himself, Mabel decamped to the Village, America's reply to the Latin Quarter, where artists cursed the "damned bourgeois" and young women disrobed at masquerades known as "Cubist balls" and "pagan routs." ("We don't want any uptown rubbernecks sneaking in here," a doorkeeper said as he turned away a curious journalist, "to get a cheap eyeful of Greenwich Village beauty unadorned.") Mabel took the young Harvard radical John Reed for a lover, experimented with peyote, and was psychoanalyzed by Dr. Abraham Brill, the first Freudian witch doctor in the United States. She also played the part of *salonnière*, and her white-painted rooms—they overlooked Fifth Avenue near Washington Square—were soon the most calamitous in the city. Everywhere, she wrote, barriers were coming down and people were reaching "each other who had never been in touch before." She did what she could to foster the "new communications," and styling herself a "collector" of people, she brought her acquisitions together in her salon. Anarchists and poets, labor leaders and birth control advocates, came, drank, made friends and made enemies, for Mabel had a way, the socialist (and later classical liberal) thinker Max Eastman said, of stimulating the passions of her guests. There were "quarrels, difficulties, entanglements, abrupt and violent detachments," but those who engaged in this intellectual street-fighting seldom hesitated to come "back for more."

If Mabel Dodge brought WASPs into closer touch with the larger world by means of conversation and strong drink, Gertrude Whitney did so by means of art. When Roger Fry took Pierpont Morgan to see Degas's *Le Viol* in Paris, the old banker acknowledged its beauty but would not go far as to propose its acquisition for the Metropolitan Museum of Art. American collectors and museum directors had even less interest in the work of contemporary American artists, and in their complacency they looked down on such painters as Robert Henri, Everett Shinn, and George Luks who wanted to bring American art closer to American life—wanted paint to "be as real as mud, as real as the clods of horse shit and snow that froze on Broadway in the winter, as real a human product as sweat, carrying the unsuppressed smell of human life itself." They were known as the Ashcan School, after a writer for *The Masses*, the magazine Max Eastman edited, complained that they painted too many "pictures of ashcans and girls hitching up their skirts on Horatio Street" in the West Village. Despised by the establishment, these artists found a patroness in Gertrude Whitney, who bought their pictures and who founded the Whitney Museum of American Art, an institution that would teach WASP connoisseurs to embrace what they had long held at arm's length.

IN THEIR REBELLION AGAINST AUTHORITY, WASP women like Alice Roosevelt, Gertrude Whitney, and Mabel Dodge were in harmony with the spirit, if not of the age, of the well-to-do rebels who found their manifesto in Lytton Strachey's 1918 book *Eminent Victorians*, in which the Bloomsbury mandarin used an irony modeled on that of Gibbon to ridicule the Victorian age, its religious hypocrisy, its imperialist fantasies, its suppression of Eros. But the books and ideas that blew up the old order—Ibsen and Nietzsche, Freud and D. H. Lawrence—had less to do with the changes that overcame the WASPs than an alteration in their social and sexual manners.*

The love affair became respectable—a great relief to WASP women who were famished sexually because they found themselves matched with unsuitable breeding partners. The traditions of preppy endogamy obliged them to marry within their class, and this severely restricted the choice of mates. "There were," Edmund Wilson said, "very few people that one could marry." The result of such exclusiveness was, naturally enough, inbreeding, both moral and genetic, with the circle of acceptable bulls and heifers further shrunken by the mental defectives, depressive valetudinarians, narcissistic wastrels, and melancholic drunks who made up a good part of the WASP beau monde. This was the downside of

---

* A change in habits of dress played a part in this revolution in manners, as a trend toward simpler and less constraining fashions for women accelerated. The encumbrances of Victorian and Edwardian couture made the lady of fashion a creature of the pedestal or the gilded cage, ridiculous in all active employments; but stiff corsets and floor-sweeper dresses were beginning to give way to more natural styles, to undraped ankles and less constricted figures, to clothing that allowed for greater freedom of motion.

the effort to form a patrician class capable of dominating the state by means of connections and family alliances secured by matrimony. The old boys' network and the blood ties on which it rested worked well enough for . . . the old boys: it enabled them to turn institutions like the State Department and Wall Street into private clubs. But it made a hell of many marriages, with the women paying the steeper price: under the Victorian double standard, a woman who was unfaithful to her vows risked a good deal more than an errant male. (Compare the different outcomes in the case of the Prince of Wales and Lady Mordaunt.) Isabella Stewart Gardner's love for Frank Crawford had been doomed from the start, and Lizzie Cameron had taken a great risk in going to bed with young Trumbull Stickney. But as love affairs and divorce court became staples of WASP life, sexual freedom no longer meant social ostracism for the women who took advantage of it.* Learned Hand's wife, Frances, conducted her affair with Louis Dow (a professor of French at Dartmouth) quite openly; and Learned was a good sport about it.

The cocktail party, an institution that went hand-in-glove with the love affair, was another innovation that changed the temper of WASP life. The ritual of predinner drinks (in which dinner was often an afterthought) played its part in revolutionizing the relation between the sexes. Men and women drank together now, on empty stomachs,† and talked over their drinks. Such old-fashioned WASP matrons as Sara Delano Roosevelt frowned on the cocktail hour, and visitors from England had mixed feelings about it. "We can't make cocktails in England as they do in America," said a young officer in the Royal Field Artillery who toured the United States. He found the drinks themselves enticing and their names "attractive: Jack Rose, Clover Club, Manhattan, Bronx, and numerous others." But "I rather suspect that they are bad things," he continued, and he found it "unpleasant to see girls drinking" them. "Our breeding," he argued not

---

* There was also the pleasure of getting even. WASP women had long been the victims of what was goatish in WASP men, as many even of the best of the males looked on females, not as ends in themselves, but as carnal candy, *das Ewig-Weibliche*, the eternal M&M. Once only men could with a degree of propriety be sexual consumers of this kind, but in the new era respectable women entered the market as erotically acquisitive customers in their own right. Everyone might now be reduced to their sex appeal or lack of it.

† "You Americans have a savage habit," Winston Churchill was heard to say during one of his visits to the United States, "this drinking before your meals." "I didn't know you drank cocktails, Elliott," Somerset Maugham says to Elliott Templeton in *The Razor's Edge*, which opens in Chicago in 1919. "I don't," Templeton replies, "but in this barbarous land of prohibition what can one do?" He sighed. "They're beginning to serve them in some houses in Paris. Evil communications corrupt good manners."

implausibly, "gives us all a certain reserve of strength to stick to our ideals. A few cocktails, sometimes even one, helps to knock this down and the results are often regrettable." But it was just this "knocking down" of reserve that attracted the liberated WASP hostess, in part, no doubt, because it made her more powerful. After all, it was she who took the lead in drawing up the guest lists for bacchanals in which old reticences fell away. It was she who brought together people who in previous ages would never have met, or who having met would never have gotten to know one another without the relaxant of the cocktail. In deciding who should be admitted to the luminous circle she became formidable in her own right. "We had a couple of drinks and . . ." Few things loom larger, in the memoirs of twentieth-century WASPs, than drinks and the encounters they made possible; it has been seriously argued that they influenced the course of history. "The hand that mixes the Georgetown martini," Henry Kissinger observed, "is time and again the hand that guides the destiny of the Western world." But after all, it was the hand that wrote out the invitation that decided who would consume the Georgetown martini.

As a result of this sexual and social iconoclasm, WASP women gained a new ascendancy, and the cross-pollination made possible by so many cocktail hours and love affairs enlarged the WASP trade in ideas, perhaps compensating for the side effect of broken homes and spells in rehab. Yet there was also a falling off, a retreat from earlier aspirations. The newly liberated WASPs did not, like the humanists whom they pretended to emulate, try very hard to integrate Aphrodite and Dionysus into a larger idea of human potential. The whole point of Plato's *Symposium* (in Greek, a drinking-together) is to show that wine and Eros may lead the aspirant to something higher. Dante carried the business further: he distinguished between good wine, which produces crust in the cask, and bad wine, which only makes mold, and in his ultimate apprehension he saw love (*amor*), which "moves the sun and the other stars," as the way to *l'alta fantasia*, the high fantasy of ideal order. But this vision, which had meant a good deal to Jack Chapman and Henry Adams, was becoming less real to the WASPs who came after them.

ON A SATURDAY IN MAY 1914 seventeen-year-old Henry Dwight "Halla" Sedgwick and his fifteen-year-old brother Minturn, uncles of the as yet unborn Edie, took advantage of the break between classes and lunch at Groton to go down to the river to row. Afterward, afraid that they would be late, they ran up to the Circle under a hot sun. "My brother had a ravenous appetite and bolted his food," Minturn remembered: "it disagreed with him." Soon Halla lay in the infirmary, dying of pneumonia. His family gathered around the sickbed. Minturn knelt on one side, holding his brother's hand; their parents, Henry Dwight "Babbo" Sedgwick, a man of letters who wrote a book on Dante, and Sarah May Minturn Sedgwick, knelt on the other. "Mr. Peabody read from the prayer book," Babbo remembered, "and we repeated the daily prayers we had always said with the boys. It was a bitter cold night, and the windows were wide open to give Henry air. Toward morning a bird sang on the little tree close beside the window." Halla died at dawn. "He looked very handsome," his father thought, "as he lay there in his white linen, with sprigs of many coloured snapdragon about him." His coffin was covered with a deep red pall, and his form-mates bore it to the chapel. In the Gothic dimness the Rector intoned the Order for the Burial of the Dead. "I am the resurrection and the life, saith the Lord; he that believeth in me, though he were dead, yet shall he live . . ."

Even as the WASPs threw off Victorianism, they found Peabody, one of their household gods, an inescapable figure, overpowering and at the same time faintly ridiculous. He "changed singularly little" as he aged. "His hair was grayer, his face less pink and white. But he had the same vitality, the same clear eye, the same indestructible dominance and untiring energy. He looked more than ever like some splendid eleventh- or twelfth-century crusader; the militant Christian, half warrior, half priest." They accused him of being theatrical, the manipulator of a puppet show that mesmerized WASP youths and scarred them for life. When, robed and surpliced in the chapel, with candles burning on the altar, he preached of St. George slaying the dragon,* there was, one of his old boys said, "something phony" about his dragon. Yet WASPs could not get enough of the spectacle, a showmanship that led one observer to call him the Cecil B. DeMille of American education. For Peabody, though he had no great love of the arts, was in his way an artist, or rather a conjurer, determined to make a living drama of his school. Even as he grew older he was involved in every aspect of Groton's life, and he devoted his afternoons to inspecting his handiwork, visiting every part of the school during the course of a fortnight, for he could "never bear to see the school or a boy anything but shipshape."

---

* A stained-glass window on the north side of Mr. Gardner's chapel depicts St. George's confrontation with the dragon.

The bad boys themselves, those who were never shipshape, were part of the drama. Peabody grieved over them, playing the part of the pained, Christlike shepherd a little too melodramatically, or so his detractors thought. "I can forgive you," he told one of his old boys, "but I don't know if God can." To which the graduate replied, "If you can forgive me, I'm sure God can." The rebels, in turn, taunted him with the gap between his ideals and the reality. "Of the fifty-six members of my two Groton forms," George Biddle wrote, "the names of seven have been listed in *Who's Who in America*. Nearly twice that number could, I suppose, be listed as absolute failures—not in economic terms but in terms purely of manhood: parasites on the community, cheats, drunkards, lechers, panhandlers, suicides." When Peabody bore such taunts patiently, they accused him of being ostentatious in his forbearance, the star of his own overwrought drama of redemption.

To the greater number of his graduates his philosophy seemed quaint. Peabody disapproved of cocktails and spirits, and he urged his old boys, if they were going to drink, to have wine or beer with meals. Sexual mores were a more serious matter. He sensed the erotic sea change and fulminated against the evils of adultery and divorce. "I feel obliged to tell you that the contents of your letter from Bermuda have brought me great distress," he wrote in reply to a graduate who asked him to bless his marriage to a divorced woman:

> I have been informed that Mrs.—obtained a decree of divorce from her husband for some reason other than that of unfaithfulness on his part. This being the case, she was not in my judgment free to contract another marriage. The step is directly contrary to the teaching of Christ and strikes at the very foundations of family life. . . . I wish I could write differently. Indeed it hurts me, my dear—, to withhold my blessing—but I am compelled to do so under the circumstances.

His graduates rolled their eyes, but although Peabody could never quite it articulate it, he seems to have felt that guiltless sex threatened to make the whole business shallow, that as men and women became more casually carnal, carnality would become routine, hardly more sacred than the coupling of dogs.*

---

* T. S. Eliot was to argue that the idea that sex was evil "was less boring than the natural cheery automatism of his contemporaries." Curiously enough Maynard Keynes agreed: the generation that came after his own was "trivial: like dogs in their lusts. We had the best of both worlds. We destroyed Christianity & yet had its benefits."

WASPs who had emancipated themselves from Victorianism were drawn to various kinds of radicalism, but only a few saw that Peabody, in his very archaicism, with his monastic cubicles and his medieval chapel, was as radical as they were, reviving, in a small way, forgotten techniques of reaching the mind. Flaubert and Pater recreated the soul-culture of antiquity and the Middle Ages in their fiction, in stories like "La légende de Saint-Julien l'hospitalier" and "Denys L'Auxerrois." Peabody, a much simpler character, made the old music live, if only in a school. "I'm going to punch Cotty Peabody's head some day," one of the Groton masters heard Jack Chapman say when he visited the school. He resented Peabody's success in being a more radical reformer than he was.

"When I see changed men," Emerson says, "I shall look for a changed world." Peabody knew that renovation is impossible unless you first renovate the renovators. His poetry of cloister and liturgy was, in comparison to the psychological refinements of Charcot and Freud, wholly primitive, yet it fingered the nerves of a certain kind of boy, who in later life could never be quite satisfied with himself unless he knew "what it really is that God wills that he shall do, the idea for which he is willing to live and die." The Groton boy who, like Harry Payne Whitney, fell into polo and horse racing, was thought a failure, and though the stockbroker would be honored with a trusteeship in exchange for his checks, he really wasn't the point, either. It was a graduate like Franklin Roosevelt, carrying his boyish purposes into the tasks of real life, who seemed to vindicate Peabody's idea of a school, in part because those purposes had been shaped by the school. "As long as I live," Roosevelt wrote, "the influence of Dr. and Mrs. Peabody will mean more to me than that of any other people next to my father and mother."

Beneath the sentimentality, the inspiration of Dante is again evident; a really inspired vision, Dante says in *La Vita Nuova*, breaks your natural buoyancy, destroys your equanimity. Suffering under this visitation, you are tempted to break off the pursuit, to turn to things that promise immediate relief. Thus in the demise of Victorianism a good many WASPs devoted themselves to the pleasures of iconoclasm, to finding the easiest, most obvious way to discharge their passions and (as they fondly hoped) disperse their goblins: "nothing is true, everything is permitted." But when the last idol is smashed, the last tablet broken, what then?

"Hobey" Baker at Princeton shortly before the war that put WASPs ideals to the test.

TWENTY-TWO

The New Patricians in War

Noi pur giugnemmo dentro a l'alte fosse
che vallan quella terra sconsolata . . .

We came within the deep-cut trenches
that are the moats of this disconsolate land . . .
—Dante, *Inferno*

Toward the end of June 1914 Edith Wharton stopped in the garden of the painter Jacques Blanche at Auteuil on the periphery of Paris. "It was a perfect summer day. . . . the air was full of new literary and artistic emotions, and that dust of ideas with which the atmosphere of Paris is always laden sparkled like motes in the sun. I joined a party at one of the tables, and as we sat there a cloud-shadow swept over us, abruptly darkening bright flowers and bright dresses. 'Haven't you heard? The Archduke Ferdinand assassinated . . . at Sarajevo . . . where *is* Sarajevo? His wife was with him. What was her name? Both shot dead.'"

Henry Adams was also in Paris, staying in a flat near the Eiffel Tower. But the wrinkled old seer failed to foresee the catastrophe, and even as the clouds thickened he made his leisurely way to the castle he had hired for the summer, the Château de Coubertin in Saint-Rémy-lès-Chevreuse. It was within driving distance of Chartres, where he could pray to the Virgin, and also of various social watering holes, where he could fulfill the social obligations of a good WASP. The Robert Blisses were installed in the Château de Bombon (he was first secretary in the Paris Embassy, she heiress to a laxative fortune, Fletcher's Castoria), and the Île-de-France as a whole was scarcely less congested with WASPs than Mount Desert Island itself.

Europe trembled on the precipice of hell, but Henry Adams fancied himself in the twelfth century, the springtime of Europe, when the troubadours were singing and the towers of Chartres were rising. It was true that "Paris looked grubby" and that his own contemporaries were dull. "It is astonishing to me," he said, "that no one of rank and breeding has ever said anything worth repeating—except me, of course . . ." But his spirits were sufficiently good that he told Lizzie Cameron that he was unlikely to return to America before the fall, for "I rather like November in Washington, and don't much care for it here." Armageddon seemed comfortably remote.

Mrs. Wharton was as unconscious of the crack of doom, and after Jacques Blanche's garden party she left Paris for a "quick dash" into Spain. She was fifty-two, rich, haughty, talented, and in certain moods oddly obtuse. She had painted, in her fiction, the limitations, the sterility and unnaturalness, of the old New York world in which she had grown up: an upbringing that had done something to supply her with those nervous afflictions that are so useful to a writer. Yet she had little sympathy for more up-to-date WASPs who, with whatever tincture of hypocrisy (for of course they craved power), were trying to cure their souls with "reforms and 'movements,' with fads and frivolities." But in pursuing her own writing cure, she may have come closer to what these reformist WASPs really sought. Newland Archer, the hero of her novel *The Age of Innocence*, knew what "he had missed: the flower of life." But Edith Wharton found a means of getting hold of at least a few of the petals.

After some radiant days in the Pyrenees, she descended to the burning summer of Catalonia. The Spanish air had never seemed so "saturated with pure light." But Barcelona proved too hot, and there were no berths on the steamer to Majorca. She and her party went back up into the Pyrenees, passing shining days in a mountain country where questions of war and peace "seemed as remote as the moon." But no sooner did she reach the Atlantic coast than she "felt the chill of the same cold cloud which had darkened the Blanches' garden-party" at Auteuil. Toward the end of July she was in Poitiers, where she lay in bed listening to citizens singing "La Marseillaise" in the square in front of the hotel. In the morning she drove on to Paris, where she found everyone "paralyzed with horror." The next day—it was Saturday, August 1—Germany declared war on Russia. It all "seemed strange, ominous and unreal, like the yellow glare which precedes a storm." On Monday, Germany declared war on France.

"EVERYTHING BLACKENED OVER," HENRY JAMES scrawled in his appointment book, "blighted by the hideous Public situation. . . . horrible suspense and the worst possibilities in the air." With all his "imagination of disaster," he, no more than Henry Adams or Mrs. Wharton, had expected the conflagration. But when, on August 4, Great Britain declared war on Germany, he knew at once what "monstrosities" must follow. It was, he wrote to Mrs. Wharton, the "crash of our civilization."

James was not technically a WASP. His grandfather, an Ulster Protestant, had come to America from County Cavan in Ireland and made a fortune in Albany. T. S. Eliot, in the security of his own breeding, would describe the family as "comparatively parvenu." But in his fiction James often depicted a recognizable WASP type, the sensitive rentier with a modest income, a disinclination for business, and a vague desire to get something more out of life, an urge that leads him to art or Europe or both. But he has also, with all his aspirations, certain reticences and timidities, and he finds himself confined, impotently, to the edges of life, an observer rather than a partaker of the human feast.

It was once thought that James had more than a little in common with the emotionally stunted figures he portrayed in his books. Like Kate Croy in his novel *The Wings of the Dove*, he "always saw," but in his case this perpetual seeing seemed to have gotten in the way of his actually living. His manner, "portentous" and "oracular," reinforced the impression of strangeness, the uncanniness of one not in an ordinary relation to life. The novelist Ford Madox Ford remembered house servants who swore that James's "eyes looked through you and through you until you could feel your own backbone within you." In Rye, in the English seaside county of East Sussex, where in 1897 James took a twenty-one-year lease, the townspeople, mystified by his literary voodoo, held that he "practiced black magic behind the high walls of Lamb House." More recent critics, on the contrary, have suggested that James's weirdness was a bit of a pose. If he played the part of artistic voyeur, looking on life rather than living it, it was only a part, adopted from prudence. If he was sometimes clumsy in handling sexual relation-ships in his books—if, as E. M. Forster said, the clothes do not come off—it was a feint, intended to obscure his robust homosexuality in an age when the Wolfenden Report was a long way off, and the possibility not merely of scandal but of criminal prosecution sufficiently real.*

The debate over the uses to which James put what he called his "well-meaning old trunk" will go on till doomsday, but it can do little to illuminate his imagina-tion of disaster, the belief, at the core of his art, that life is something "ferocious and sinister." He is never more likely to rouse his reader from complacency than in his portrayal of characters who, like the narrator of *The Sacred Fount*, the governess in *The Turn of the Screw*, and John Marcher in *The Beast in the Jungle*, have somehow touched the horror and been put out of their natural relation to existence. Whether or not, as Edmund Wilson believed, James shared the neurasthenic estrangements of his characters—"dramatized his own experience immediately in terms of imaginary people"—his books illuminate the psychology of the higher WASPs whom he knew so well, and do more than any formal history can to explain their longing for regeneration, the magic key that would restore them to complete humanity.

James passed for an American, but although he had been born in New York, he had spent much of his boyhood abroad, and as a young man he had gone back to Europe. He eventually settled in England, but he remained unplaced; his brother William quipped that insofar as he had a nationality, he was a "native of the James family." He felt, it is true, a throb of passion for his forsaken birthland when, in 1904, he saw America again after an absence of twenty years. Giving

---

* One of James's biographers, Sheldon Novick, believes that James was "actively gay," and suspects that he "jacked off" Oliver Wendell Holmes in the spring of 1865. The evidence is uncertain. Somerset Maugham said that the novelist Hugh Walpole once propositioned James and "met with shocked if regretful refusal." Yet another story is told of how as an old man James kissed Walpole, leading one of Oscar Wilde's friends to say, "If only we had known, we could have found him someone better."

up, for the moment, his old horror of commercial vulgarity, he was impressed by the vigor of the country's republican civilization. But he could not overlook America's "bewildered taste." "There is NO 'fascination' *whatever*, in anything or anyone," he wrote, "that is exactly what there *isn't*." The war deepened his attachment to Britain. "However British you may be," he told Edmund Gosse, "I am more British still." (Gosse replied that nobody wanted him to be British.) He confessed to an overwhelming sympathy for "the sole, the exquisite England, whose weight now hangs in the balance," and although he had never before been much of a public man, a sitter on committees, he took up war causes and, with a nod to Walt Whitman, comforted wounded soldiers in in the hospital. In 1915 he became a subject of King George V.

The war brought James into a different relation with the world. He had been, during much of his grownup life, a haunter of English country houses and London dinner parties, and the aridity of this life may have found expression in some of the less penetrable stuff of his later work, that of a strong mind feeding on trifles.* On the other hand, Edmund Wilson argued that morbidities in James's own inner experience had all along frustrated a more direct and easygoing relation to life. There was, Wilson conjectured, an "innocent little girl" inside James whom he sometimes "cherished and loved" and at others times wanted "to violate," "rape," and "destroy," a psychic drama cryptically replayed in the vacancies of the later books.† Wilson was perhaps looking at James too exclusively through the prisms of Karl Heinrich Ulrichs and Marcel Proust, who taught him to "solve" a case like James's by finding a woman's psyche imprisoned in a man's body. Yet he touched the mystery of a magus who concealed the autobiography of his art in the not easily penetrated medium of his fiction, even as he made

---

* Theodore Roosevelt is said to have invented the jest that he knew someone who "could read James in the original," and Rebecca West spoke of Jamesian sentences as "swathed in relative clauses as an invalid in shawls." "But why won't you," William James wrote Henry, "just to please Brother, sit down and write a new book, with no twilight or mustiness in the plot, with great vigor and decisiveness in the action, no fencing in the dialogue, no psychological commentaries, and absolute straightness in the style?" He complained that his younger brother's books were formed "wholly out of impalpable materials, air, and the prismatic inferences of light, ingeniously focused by mirrors on empty space," and he was convinced that "poor dear Harry" had lost touch with the "vital facts of human nature."

† "I once gave *The Turn of the Screw* to the Austrian novelist Franz Höllering to see what impression he would get out of it," Wilson wrote: "he said to me, after he had read it: 'The man who wrote this was a *Kinderschänder*'; and I remembered that in all James's work of this period—which extends from *The Other House* through *The Sacred Fount*—the favorite theme is the violation of innocence, with the victim in every case (though you have in *The Turn of the Screw* a boy as well as a girl) a young or little girl."

vivid the poignance of a sufferer who wrote his last chapter, not in a book, but among the maimed Tommies of St. Bartholomew's Hospital, where the little girl, long immured in art, found herself released into life.

IN PARIS THE BANKS STOPPED making payments, and Edith Wharton was in the unaccustomed state of not having money. She borrowed a small sum from Walter Van Rensselaer Berry, the tall, worldly WASP whom she had long loved yet never married, even after her divorce from Teddy Wharton left her free to do so. But others were also assailing Berry's purse, and she wired to Frederick Whitridge, an American friend who had married Matthew Arnold's daughter. "Very sorry," he replied from his country place in England. "Have no money."

Henry Adams, too, was in difficulties, a "senile and decrepit Childe Roland," as he called himself in an allusion to Browning's poem. He had come once too often to the Dark Tower and now found himself trapped "like an octogenarian rat." Should the Germans encircle Paris as they had in 1870, the Château de Coubertin itself might be overrun, and together with his niece Elsie Adams and his honorary niece Aileen Tone, he sought safety in the French capital, eager, he said, to witness the "crumbling of worlds." But the German armies were advancing with astonishing rapidity, and their guns were soon heard in Paris itself. An age that had embraced "a religion of high explosives," Adams concluded, was no age for him.

He and his nieces made their way, slowly and arduously, to Dieppe, where they saw wounded soldiers being taken off the trains. They crossed to England and found shelter at Stepleton in Dorset, the country house of Lizzie Cameron's daughter Martha, the little girl on whom Adams had once doted. She was now grown up and married to the British diplomat Sir Ronald Lindsay. Bernard Berenson and his brother-in-law, the aesthete Logan Pearsall Smith,* came down from London to see them. Berenson was pleased to find Adams "quite as Anti-Prussian" as he, and together they went into the nearby town of Blandford for news of the first Battle of the Marne. A little later Henry James arrived, and he and Adams talked into the night. Berenson thought Adams in "good form" and "looking extraordinarily well," but James saw only a shattered old man, "more changed and gone" than had been reported, with a "surviving capacity to be very well taken care of."

---

*   William Amory Gardner's older brother, Joseph Peabody Gardner Jr., was said to have killed himself because his love for Logan Pearsall Smith was not returned.

Mrs. Wharton, too, escaped to England. She motored to Calais and crossed to Folkstone, where James met her boat. She spent the night at Lamb House and afterward went up to Stocks in Hertfordshire, the country house of Mrs. Humphry Ward, the English novelist and niece of Matthew Arnold. Her principal impression was of the splendid way Mrs. Humphry Ward's servants ministered to her delicacy amid the disintegration of war. "To the honour of the British race," she wrote, "Mrs. Ward's upper housemaid (whom I had taken with the house) kept every room filled with bowls of flowers arranged with the most exquisite art . . ." You go back over the sentence, looking for the ironic wink; but, no, she meant it.

ON AUGUST 4, 1914, AS Europe was descending into war, Woodrow Wilson issued the first of a series of proclamations to preserve the neutrality of the United States. But many WASPs refused to sit on the sidelines, and London was soon swarming with them. Some, like Henry P. Davison, the Morgan banker, came to profit (there was money to be made purchasing American goods for France and Great Britain). Others came to serve. Dorothy Whitney Straight, who was in London with her husband, Willard, ran into Theodore Roosevelt's younger daughter, Ethel, and her husband, the surgeon Dick Derby. The couple were preparing to cross to France to care for wounded soldiers.

Gertrude Whitney was as unwilling to stay home. She was canoeing in the Adirondacks, meditating on the plight of France, when she decided to go. Her husband—"just-send-a-cheque" Harry—scoffed at the idea, but she brushed him aside and got in touch with Robert Bacon, who was by this time the former American ambassador to France. She wanted to set up a field hospital near the front, and in November she and Bacon, together with a group of Red Cross nurses and doctors, sailed for England on the *Lusitania*. Stepping off the boat train in London, they were met by a knot of reporters and officials. Leaving Bacon to contend with them, Gertrude slipped away in the fog. The sight of recruiting posters—images of Lord Kitchener's accusatory finger urging Britons to enlist had begun to appear in September—made the war real to her as it had not been before. England really "*is* fighting then," she wrote in her journal. In France she came that much closer, and in a big Packard she and her party made their way past posts and sentries to the lines east of Abbeville. She shuddered at the "deadly cold winter trenches" and the thought of "bayonets wielded by soldiers bent on death." The "face of the world is black," she wrote, and she saw the racing ambulances and sad-eyed nurses "with a sick heart." Her hospital was eventually established at Juilly, northeast of Paris, in a college founded in the seventeenth century by the Oratorians, the order to which John Henry Newman had devoted himself. The place was agreeably ghost-haunted: Montesquieu, the political philosopher, had studied there, and Napoleon had been a guest. The dormitories, once they were fitted with steam heat and electric lighting, made ideal wards. Dick Derby, who as a surgeon in the U.S. Medical Corps was to work in the hospital during the war, described it as "one of the best organized and equipped institutions" of its kind in France.

Other WASPs were putting themselves in greater danger, signing up to fight for countries not their own. Norman Prince, six years behind Derby at Groton and Harvard, persuaded the French government to allow him to form the Lafayette Escadrille, a unit that recruited American pilots to fly alongside French aviators. Among the volunteers were Victor Chapman, who had followed in his father "Mad Jack" Chapman's footsteps at St. Paul's and Harvard, and William Thaw II, grandson of the Pittsburgh railroad magnate and half-nephew of the Harry Thaw who shot Stanford White. Tommy Hitchcock Jr., the polo star, left St. Paul's in his sixth form year to join another American unit, the Lafayette Flying Corps, though he is remembered today less for his heroism in combat than for being one of the models for Tom Buchanan in *The Great Gatsby*.

War was putting the ideals of the WASPs—their notions of shame and honor, their larger morality of public-spiritedness—to the test. Schools like St. Paul's and Groton were not simply a nerve ganglion of the old WASP elite, they sought to remodel aspiration and translate ideals into action. As one of the inventors of the preppy cult of service, Endicott Peabody could be excused for looking on the gallantry of his boys as a vindication of his experiment. (In the late summer of 1914 nearly everyone other than Lord Kitchener believed that the war would be short, and none guessed the ultimate price of the butcher's bill.) In the Civil War many top-drawer Bostonians and New Yorkers (among them Pierpont Morgan and Theodore Roosevelt's father) had showed no compunction in purchasing substitutes to do their fighting for them, but in the new crisis a large proportion of preppies were ready to make sacrifices. Dillwyn Parrish Starr, who was a year ahead of Norman Prince at Groton, went to England and was commissioned an officer in the Coldstream Guards. Arnold Whitridge, the American-born grandson of Matthew Arnold, obtained a commission in the British Field Artillery, while Henry Farnsworth, a year behind Arnold at school, sailed for Europe "before his family could object" and enlisted in the French Foreign Legion. Kermit Roosevelt, Farnsworth's classmate, joined the British Machine Gun Corps and was seconded to its 14th Light Armoured Motor Battery to fight in Mesopotamia, with its oil reserves; Arthur Bertram Randolph, the son of Edith Randolph Whitney and stepson of William Collins Whitney, followed his stepbrothers Harry and Payne to Groton and Yale, and in August 1914 joined the 1st Battalion Welsh Guards. If Henry P. Davison, making money for the house of Morgan, was one of the "hard-faced men" who did well out of the war,* his son Trubee devoted his own best efforts to training pilots for active duty, and as a freshman in New Haven he formed the First Yale Unit with cash from his father and Harry Whitney. Among Trubee's recruits were David Ingalls, the only ace among America's naval aviators in the First World War, and Robert Lovett, who after flying with the British Naval Air Force and commanding a U.S. naval air squadron went on to serve as secretary of defense under Harry Truman. (He had the good sense quietly to fade into the woodwork when Vietnam went south.)

But it was Hobey Baker who, though he did not die in combat, was to be the only garlanded WASP hero whose name survived the war and was carried down to a time within the memory of preppies still living. Hobart Amory Hare Baker, one of the greatest of America's early ice hockey players, the star of St. Paul's School, quarterback of the Princeton football team, "the blond Adonis of the gridiron," moved, even before he joined the 13th Aero Squadron, in an atmosphere half mythical, the beautiful youth whom the jealous god must strike down. He had, not merely glory and ability, but what is less common in a preppy stud, modesty, dislike of swagger, the "punctilio of an honor the most sensitive." We are told how, after an especially brutal contest, he limped into his opponents' dressing room "to shake hands and thank them for a wonderful game . . ." On the "rare occasion when he was forced to admit he had been deliberately fouled," he was "driven to tears." Surely his schoolmates must have hated him! Not a bit of it. At Princeton Scott Fitzgerald admired him, as did at least half the student body, though doubtless there were envious souls who sniggered and said to themselves, "Well, he's probably queer."

---

*   To be fair, Davison "gave back," as we say now, and raised large sums for the Red Cross.

THE INSPIRATION OF SERVICE PLAYED a part in the WASP rush to join the colors; war fever did the rest. In 1896 the aged Mr. Gladstone had warned of the "growth of that dreadful military spirit" which was coming over the West. A product of the rivalry of the Great Powers and the glorification of empire, war worship was exacerbated by new philosophies of force, some grounded in a misapplication of Darwin's theory of the survival of the fittest, others growing out of an exaltation of the will, the tropically rank second-growth of romanticism of Wagner and Nietzsche. A year after Mr. Gladstone uttered his warning, Theodore Roosevelt, in an address to the Naval War College in Newport, asserted the supremacy of the warrior over the statesman: no "triumph of peace," he declared, "is quite so great as the supreme triumphs of war." Two years before, Oliver Wendell Holmes, speaking at Harvard, uttered his own war cry, proclaiming as "true and adorable" the faith "which leads a soldier to throw away his life in obedience to a blindly accepted duty, in a cause which he little understands."

Holmes and Roosevelt, like the Greeks before them, admired not so much victory as heroism. The vanquished warrior was in some respects greater than the victorious one; Hector has a pathos that Achilles lacks. The death of the hero was beautiful because the hero's "natural instinct for self-assertion" found its "highest expression in self-sacrifice." The sword might have given way to the Maxim gun, the chariot to the tank, but the ideal was, for Holmes and Roosevelt, as valid now as it had been when Leonidas and his Spartans died in defense of the pass at Thermopylae. The question Roosevelt confronted was whether the war in Europe justified the sacrifice of American warriors. He had himself stared death in the face many times, in the Badlands, in Cuba, in Milwaukee, where a lunatic shot him in the chest in 1912. His most recent encounter with his own mortality had occurred during his expedition to the Amazon Basin to survey the River of Doubt, where an infected wound festered and nearly killed him; a burden to the rest of the party, he wanted to be left behind to die. But if Roosevelt's cult of the hero (whose willingness to die proves his worthiness to live) was steeped in poetry and mysticism, his theory of when the United States should expend its own blood and treasure was grounded, rationally and prosaically, in concepts that would have, if often only covertly, a large place in WASP diplomacy, the national interest and the balance of power.

In September 1914 the French victory at the first Battle of the Marne halted the German advance on the Western Front, but it did not end the war, and Roosevelt doubted whether the United States could safely remain neutral in a prolonged conflict, one that promised to alter the distribution of power in Europe. If Germany collapsed, Russia, he believed, would become over-strong, and would threaten America's tranquility. But he thought it more likely that Germany, already the most formidable economic and military power on the Continent, would emerge victorious, with unpleasant consequences for the United States. "Do you not believe," he wrote his friend Hugo Münsterberg in October 1914, "that if Germany won this war, smashed the English Fleet and destroyed the British Empire, within a year or two she would insist upon taking the dominant position in South and Central America . . . ? I believe so. Indeed I know so." The difficulty was that Americans could not be made to see that the emergence of either Russia or Germany as a Eurasian superpower was likely to blight the fortunes of the United States. "Thanks to the width of the ocean," he wrote Rudyard Kipling, "our people believe that they have nothing to fear from the present contest, and that they have no responsibility concerning it."

FROM THE NORTH SEA TO the Swiss frontier, the digging of trenches went on. Sailing from England in August 1915, soldiers of the 1st Battalion Welsh Guards docked at Le Havre, a war town now, where pimps shadowed soldiers in the street. "I take you to my sister. She very nice. Very good jig-a-jig. . . ." Troops traveled by train to the front lines, where old hands laughed when they dropped on all fours at the sound of a shell. "You're wasting yourselves, lads. Listen by the noise they make coming where they're going to burst." The trenches cut through the red clay of the Artois; they were filled with rodents and the stench of unrecovered corpses in no man's land. "Survivors," as they were called, were pointed out with awe. "See that fellow. That's Jock Miller. Out from the start and hasn't got it yet."

Lieutenant Arthur Bertram Randolph gave his first name as Julien when he joined the Welsh colors, possibly because he identified with Julien Sorel, the tragic glory-driven hero of Stendhal's novel *Le Rouge et le Noir*, possibly because he thought the allegiance he swore to King George V would jeopardize his American citizenship. (It was noted in his paybook that he was also known as Arthur; British recruiters, eager for volunteers, did not ask too many questions.) Arthur or Julien was to be part of the "big push" in 1915 by the Allies on the Western Front, which had been largely stationary for months. General Joffre, commander in chief of the French armies, envisioned a thrust in the Artois, with the British First Army attacking German positions in and around the village of Loos while the French pushed toward the bloody heights of Vimy Ridge south of the coal town of Lens. Sir Douglas Haig, the commander of the First Army, remonstrated with Joffre; the terrain around Loos, he pointed out, was flat and open, and would afford his soldiers no cover from the German guns. He wanted to delay a major offensive until 1916, when his forces would be more numerous and better equipped. But Joffre appealed to Kitchener, the British war secretary, who believed that an Allied thrust on the Western Front was necessary in order to relieve German pressure on Russia in the east. He told Haig to defer to Joffre.

British forces had been fighting for two days when, on September 26, 1915, Lieutenant Randolph and the Welsh Guards moved forward to Loos, and on the next day advanced toward their objective, Hill 70, amid intense shelling, some of the shells being filled with shrapnel, others with high explosives. Clouds of smoke obscured the field, and the Guards were, one observer said, "dropping like flies." But those who were not hit went on "as if they were marching up the Mall" in London for a parade. The attempt to capture Hill 70 began in earnest around six o'clock, just as daylight was fading. But no sooner did the Welsh Guards take the hill than star shells burst in a blaze of light and German gunners raked the Guardsmen with machine-gun bullets; the result was slaughter that sickened the Germans themselves. The surviving Guards were ordered to fall back; not all their dead could be recovered. "After the first day or two the bodies swelled and stank," the poet Robert Graves, an officer of the Royal Welch Fusiliers, remembered. "I vomited more than once while superintending the carrying. The ones that we could not get in from the German wire continued to swell until the wall of the stomach collapsed, either naturally or punctured by a bullet; a disgusting smell would float across. The colour of the dead faces changed from white to yellow-grey, to red, to purple, to green, to black, to slimy."

Lieutenant Randolph was among those who died in the struggle for Hill 70, as was Second Lieutenant John Kipling, the poet's son, who was fighting nearby with the 2nd Battalion Irish Guards—two of nearly 60,000 casualties suffered by the British in three days of battle or, as some would call it, abattoir-butchery.* The next day, farther south, Lieutenant Randolph's schoolmate Henry Farnsworth

---

* "I don't know what is to be done," Kitchener said of the trenches. "This isn't war." Some have argued that the result at Loos would have been different if Field Marshal Sir John French, Commander in Chief of the British Expeditionary Force, had kept his reserves closer to the front and brought them up sooner. After Loos he was sacked as chief of the B.E.F. and replaced by Haig; yet the stalemate continued.

was killed by machine-gun bullets as he fought with the French Foreign Legion in Champagne, in the battle of Fortin de Navarin.

❦

In August 1916 Flora Whitney, daughter of Gertrude and Harry, made her debut in Newport, where she danced with Quentin Roosevelt, the youngest son of the former president. Two years ahead of Flora's brother Cornelius "Sonny" Whitney at school, Quentin had inherited not only his father's toothy grin but a good deal of his charm and intellect. Yet he was drawn less to power and politics than to poetry and machinery, to cars, motorcycles, and airplanes. He and Flora fell in love; the uncertainty of their future gave piquancy to their romance. Quentin was predestined for war service; it would, he told Flora, be "pretty sordid" if he and other Americans kept "looking on while England and France fight our battles and pan gold into our pockets." But the fates of those of his classmates at school and college who had gone "over there" only to pay a soldier's debt did not augur well for his own longevity. In June 1916 John Jay Chapman's boy Victor was shot down north of Douaumont in France. In September Dillwyn Parrish Starr fell at Démuin. A month later Norman Prince was returning from a raid on the Mauser rifle works at Oberndorf when his plane struck a telegraph cable and crashed.

There would be more. When, on the evening of April 2, 1917, Woodrow Wilson went up to Capitol Hill, his mood was somber. He knew that the address he was about to deliver "was a message of death for our young men." Standing before Congress jointly assembled, he asked the lawmakers to declare that a state of war existed between United States and the German Empire. He did not rest his case merely on German submarine warfare, the U-boats that had sunk ships like the *Lusitania* and killed scores of Americans, among them Flora Whitney's uncle, Alfred Vanderbilt. Still less did he speak of the need to maintain a balance of power in Eurasia. He argued instead that authoritarian or semi-authoritarian regimes like Germany could not in their nature peaceably coexist with democratic nations: in the presence of their power, he argued, "there can be no assured security" for free governments. The world, he declared in words that would both inspire and bedevil American diplomacy, "must be made safe for democracy."

Theodore Roosevelt, who had come to despise Wilson for failing to stand up to the Germans, shifted his ground at once and praised the president's address as one of America's "great state papers." He also offered his services as warrior, asking to be permitted to raise a division of infantry with a brigade of cavalry attached. Wilson refused. Should Roosevelt's unit succeed, he would have advanced the career of a rival who might evict him from the White House if he stood for election a third time in 1920. In the more likely event that the unit failed— the Western Front in 1917 had little place for the adventurist whimsies of Cuba—he would have raised questions about America's military competence.

"I don't understand," Roosevelt is supposed to have said to Edward M. House, the small, soft-spoken Texas intrigant who had become President Wilson's soulmate and éminence grise. "After all, I'm only asking to be allowed to die."

"Oh," Colonel House is said to have replied. "Did you make *that* point quite clear to the President?"*

The old lion would have to be content with the service of his cubs. All of Roosevelt's boys would fight in the war; Quentin, posted to Long Island, was training as a pilot. Yet whenever he could he drove up from Hazelhurst Field† to Old Westbury to see Flora, or Fouf, as he called her. He did not, he confessed to her, see "how you can love me." He felt "as tho' it were all a dream from which some time I will awake . . . with nothing left to me but the memory of beauty and the wonder of it all." She assured him that there was nothing to worry about: "it's absolute worship on my part."

They announced their engagement in June 1917, and shortly afterward Quentin was commissioned a first lieutenant in the Aviation Section of the Signal Corps. In July, having spent his final night in America on the Whitney yacht with Flora, he sailed for Europe, where he was to join the 95th Aero Squadron.

HENRY STIMSON, JUST SHY OF fifty when the United States entered the war, also volunteered for active duty, and was commissioned a lieutenant colonel in the Field Artillery. He was ordered to the line with the 77th Regiment at Baccarat, a "quiet sector" on the Western Front. Stimson had lived his life in the shadow of the Civil War heroes, and he yearned for the test of combat. He would not prob- ably have minded the distinction of a wound like one of those his friend Oliver Wendell Holmes had incurred as a Union officer, a red badge of courage. But

---

* Colonel House's military title was honorary, a reward for political services rendered to a Texas governor.

† It was afterward named Roosevelt Field in Quentin's memory. It is now a shopping mall.

the American high command had little interest in throwing a former secretary of war into the cauldrons to the north, and Stimson by his own confession never saw, at Baccarat, "the hideous side of war."

Willard Straight was also in uniform; in May 1917 he was commissioned a major in the adjutant general's Reserve Corps, and in December he sailed for Europe to oversee the operations of the War Risk Insurance Bureau, which provided federal insurance for enlisted men. Reaching Paris after Christmas he was billeted in the Hôtel de Crillon and found the city swimming with WASPs. Daisy Harriman, the widow of banker J. Borden Harriman and tireless advocate of worthy causes (in 1963 President Kennedy would award her the Citation of Merit for Distinguished Service), was assisting the Red Cross and was "in a state," Straight told Dorothy, on account of her affair with Colonel Frank McCoy, a West Pointer serving on the American General Staff. Straight dined out most evenings, breaking bread with Quentin Roosevelt, "whose smile was so like his father's," Edward "Pete" Bowditch, the Harvard football star who was now aide-de-camp to General Pershing, Edith Wharton, Colonel Stimson, Dick Derby, the Robert Blisses—the *Social Register* was remiss in not publishing a wartime supplement of Parisian dilatory domiciles. "Too much food and good wine," Straight complained. "Must cut it out or I will get fat headed."

Alice Roosevelt could not, like her brothers, put on a uniform, but in her own way she tried to do her duty, taking part in a Keystone Cops operation to detect German spies. She was by this time married to Cincinnati preppy Nicholas Longworth, the bibulous congressman. ("Nick and I are both members of the Porc, you know," her father told the Kaiser after the betrothal.) But the marriage was not happy; Nick, in addition to being a drunk, was also a lecher, and Alice, bored both by the drinking and the infidelities, was only too happy to help her cousin, Assistant Secretary of the Navy Franklin Roosevelt, plant listening devices in the house of Washington hostess May Ladenburg, who was suspected of wheedling secrets out of her lover, Bernard Baruch, the chairman of the War Industries Board. Alice's and Franklin's bugging of the Ladenburg house revealed much kissing, but no betrayal of secrets.

Sherrard Billings, on leave from Groton to serve as an army chaplain in France, was making his hospital rounds when he was startled to hear a soldier in traction greet him with the familiar words *"Ulmi sunt gloriae Grotonae,"* the formula Billings used to teach his students the Latin double dative: "the elms are for a glory to Groton." It proved to be one of his old boys, Captain Archie

Roosevelt, who had been wounded as he led his platoon against a German position. Visiting the American 42nd Division on the front lines at Toul east of Paris, Willard Straight watched with awe and envy as a young colonel named Douglas MacArthur ("a corker—the best in the business I should think") set off one night with a French officer to raid the German trenches. They came back with a German officer's spiked helmet. It was, Straight wrote Dorothy, a "damn fool—but a ridiculously brave thing to do." Eager to fight himself, Straight attended the Army General Staff School at Langres, southeast of Paris, with Henry Stimson ("Hotspur Hal," the younger officers called him), and afterward applied for combat duty. But his habit of pestering superiors for showy assignments betrayed him, as did his own physical constitution. He was susceptible to colds, fevers, and fits of coughing, and he found himself reduced to the less than heroic task of observing operations from the rear—he was deeply impressed by the heroism of the marines at Belleau Wood—and interrogating enemy prisoners. "Everybody with their tails up," he lamented, "and I'm not in it."

THEODORE ROOSEVELT WAS DICTATING TO his secretary, Miss Josephine Stricker, in the summer of 1918 when one of his friends in the press burst in and showed him a cable from Paris: WATCH SAGAMORE HILL IN EVENT OF [DELETED BY CENSOR]. "Something has happened to one of the boys," Roosevelt said. A telegram from General Pershing soon followed: REGRET VERY MUCH THAT YOUR SON LT. QUENTIN ROOSEVELT REPORTED AS MISSING. The newspapers announced that the young pilot had been shot down and was dead, but there was no official confirmation.

"Now, Colonel," an acquaintance said to Roosevelt as he came into the Harvard Club in Manhattan for a previously scheduled lunch, "you know it may not be true."

"No, it is true," Roosevelt replied. "Quentin is dead."

A telegram from President Wilson removed all doubt. Roosevelt hid his sorrow beneath his customary fighter-breeder rhetoric. The warriors who fell in the war "dared the Great Adventure of Death" and drank "the dark drink proffered by the Death Angel." More eloquent, perhaps, were the words he was heard to utter in the stables at Sagamore Hill, his face buried in the mane of his son's pony.

"Poor Quenty-Quee."

THE GERMAN EMPIRE, NEAR TO collapse, was temporarily restored to life by the revolution in Russia. The Tsar was deposed, and the Provisional Government under Kerensky ambushed. At Brest-Litovsk in what is now Belarus, the Germans negotiated with, or rather dictated terms to, the Bolshevik rulers of Russia. The resulting treaty ended the war on the Eastern Front; the Germans were now free to throw their superfluous divisions at the West. They made quick gains, but were eventually repulsed by the Allies, freshly reinforced by American doughboys. By September the German position was hopeless, and in November the Armistice was signed.

Amid the general rejoicing, Hobey Baker, a pilot flying with the American 13th Aero Squadron, was strangely sullen. It is said that he dreaded to go back to America to work in a bank. After receiving, a few days before Christmas, his discharge papers, he wanted to take a last flight, and going toward his old plane he saw a recently repaired one in need of a test flight. He took it up. Shortly after takeoff, the plane went nose-first into the ground; the mystery has never been cleared up. But there were those who, surveying the pilot and the wreckage, thought of Aristotle's words. Some men "would prefer short intense pleasures to long quiet ones; would choose to live nobly for a year than to pass many years of ordinary life; would rather do one great and noble deed than many small ones."

In Paris, Willard Straight was billeted in the Crillon, where young WASPs got their first taste of empire.

TWENTY-THREE

The New Patricians in Peace

Molti son li animali, a cui s'ammoglia,
e più saranno ancora, infin che 'l Veltro
verrà, che la farà morir con doglia.

Questi non ciberà terra, né peltro,
ma sapïenza, e amore, e virtute;
e sua nazion sarà tra Feltro e Feltro.

Many are the souls she mates with and many
more will she ensnare until the *Veltro* (Wolfhound)
comes to give her death in pain.

That Hound will feed neither on land nor pelf,
but on wisdom, love, and virtue,
and his nation shall be between fabric and fabric.
—Dante, *Inferno*

In January 1918 Daisy Harriman's daughter Ethel married Henry Potter Russell, grandson of old Bishop Potter, in the American Church in Paris; Sherrard Billings officiated. Willard Straight helped to make the festivities possible by writing a few checks even as he wondered how Daisy could be so "utterly irresponsible" as to have left a trail of debts in America for Dorothy to settle. Dorothy replied mildly that Daisy was "a luxury." Afterward everyone went to Daisy's suite in the Ritz, where Cole Porter played the piano; the Yale graduate had not long before dropped out of Harvard Law School to compose show tunes on Broadway, and he was now in Paris doing a little relief work and exaggerating his services to the French military. He was attracted both to Parisian high society and to its intimate relation, the underground life of the city, a netherworld that intrigued WASPs precisely because, as one observer said, "Vice is rampant . . ." For Paris had gone much further than any American city in smashing idols and breaking taboos. The art of Diaghilev, Stravinsky, Picasso, Nijinsky, Cocteau; the bohemian dissipations of the Café du Dôme, the Nègre de Toulouse, and the Lapin Agile; the homosexual demimonde Marcel Proust was to depict in *Sodome et Gomorrhe*; the louche obscurities of the *cafés chantants* and the nightclubs—Americans ate it up. It was an American, Elsa Maxwell, who gave a dinner at the Ritz to that consummate British patrician, Mr. Balfour, which would have been forgotten had not she afterward persuaded the diners, among them Grand Duke Alexander of Russia, Mrs. George Keppel, mistress of the late Edward VII, and the Princesse de Polignac, an American sewing-machine heiress, to visit a *boîte de nuit*. Mr. Balfour had never before been to such a place. "My dear Miss Maxwell," the Prime Minister of Edward VII said, "allow me to thank you for the most delightful and degrading evening I have ever spent."

It was not, however, the decadence of Paris that interested Major Straight, but its possibilities as a field of glory, for he believed that the Peace Conference soon to be convened there presaged the "dawn of a new era," as a French officer enthusiastically exclaimed to him one night over champagne and Havana cigars. Yet as the day of peace approached, Straight was gloomy. He "felt like saying Oh Hell to it all," he wrote Dorothy. He had been assigned to the headquarters of Marshal Foch, who was now generalissimo of the Allies, but he did little more there than report the gossip of Foch's staff to the staff of General Pershing. "I am afraid it is a sort of diplomatic liaison job," Straight's friend Grayson Murphy said. "Poor Willard—he tried so hard, and he is so fine and able. He would have been invaluable in the right place . . ." The man who had once seemed to hold the destiny of

China in his hands was reduced to coding messages, relaying information over the telephone, and showing Daisy Harriman around Foch's chateau. Her cheerfulness annoyed him; she was, he wrote sourly to Dorothy, "having such a wonderful time & gossiping & wearing a uniform around—& is really such a damned fool . . ."

Dorothy tried to console her husband, telling him that "even though you didn't get all the fighting you wanted, or the promotion you hoped for—the actual accomplishment is there." He was not persuaded; members of his own little WASP club, "the Family," as it was called, gloated over his fall from the heights.* When Dorothy went to 1718 H Street, the Family's clubhouse in Washington, Basil Miles, a rising Russia expert in the State Department, teased her about how her husband "has been holding Marshal Foch's hand so successfully," while Bill Bullitt, the wild Philadelphian, observed that Straight seemed to be "covering himself with glory these days." Dorothy dutifully worked her WASP connections in an effort to retrieve Willard's fallen star; she sounded out Frank Polk about a place in the State Department, and she lunched with William Phillips, another preppy State Department figure who was also a member of the Family. Upon learning that Colonel House thought Straight might be useful to him, she rang him up and told him how much she hoped Willard would have "the opportunity of helping" him in the "tremendous world game" to be played in Paris.

How the Straights went about using their contacts to advance Willard's career showed how far the WASPs had come since the Civil War in using blood, marriage, and the old school tie to form a cohesive and self-aggrandizing patriciate. Willard had more raw talent than many of the WASPs who had the power to decide his fate, and more winning human qualities; he was married to a great WASP heiress; he had passed muster with Theodore Roosevelt himself and, though more ambiguously, with Henry P. Davison and the house of Morgan. But it was by no means certain that he would find a place at the Peace Conference. He was not descended from one of the old tribal families, and he had not been to one of the old tribal schools. It did

---

* The Family was an example of the Cosa Nostra principles by which the WASPs banded together to outmaneuver their rivals in the struggle for power: the club numbered, among its members, David K. E. Bruce (married into the Mellon family, Georgetown grandee, ambassador, successively, to France, Germany, Britain, and NATO), William Phillips (Noble and Greenough, Harvard, undersecretary of state), Joseph Grew (Groton, Harvard, ambassador to Denmark, Switzerland, Turkey, and Japan), Andrew James Peters (St. Paul's, Harvard, mayor of Boston), Benjamin Strong (Princeton, governor of the Federal Reserve Bank of New York), Leland Harrison (Eton, Harvard, spymaster who directed the State Department's Bureau of Secret Intelligence), Joseph P. Cotton (Harvard, Cravath, undersecretary of state), and Norman Armour (St. Paul's, Princeton, "the perfect diplomat," in the words of the *New York Times*).

not help that Harry Whitney, his Groton, Yale, and Skull and Bones brother-in-law, never wholeheartedly embraced him, though this in itself was not decisive. When Frank Polk (Groton and Yale) and William Phillips (Nobles and Harvard) declined to plump for Straight, it was not for tribal reasons but rather because he was close to Roosevelt, and Polk and Phillips worked for Woodrow Wilson.

Colonel House also worked for Wilson, but he was fond of the Straights, particularly of Dorothy, and shortly after he arrived in Paris he invited Willard to lunch. It was one of a series of tests by which the establishment informally took the measure of a man; House and his son-in-law, Gordon Auchincloss (Yale and Groton, a classmate of Dillwyn Parish Starr) wanted to make sure Straight was the right sort, and declining, at lunch, to offer him a serious post, House intimated, Straight remembered, "that he had various niches any of which I might fit—etc., etc.—but he never knew, etc., etc." The old man spoke vaguely of Straight's heading an information service for newly liberated "Czechs and Jugoslavs," hardly the plum Willard sought. Later that day he dined at Larue near the Place de la Madeleine, doing his best to cover his dejection. His fellow diners, after all, though they were still young, were influential and might vouch for him: Edward "Pete" Bowditch (Harvard and Groton, aide-de-camp to Pershing), Warwick Greene (Harvard College and Harvard Law School, junior proconsul under Cameron Forbes at Manila, director of the War Relief Commission of the Rockefeller Foundation), and Perry Osborn (Groton and Princeton, a lawyer at Winthrop & Stimson before he was tapped to head the War Credits Board; as a lieutenant colonel in the Army in 1918 he was instrumental in reorganizing the General Staff). Louisine Havemeyer (she of the spurious Titians), Ogden Reid (Yale College and Yale Law School, publisher of the *New York Herald Tribune*), and Lloyd Griscom (shipping heir, former ambassador to Italy, partner in the New York law firm of Beekman, Hemmens & Taylor) all mixed socially with Straight in Paris, and their opinion of him, as it got around, helped him, for they all liked him. Yet what astonishes the historian is not so much the extended nature of Straight's job interview but how, within half a century of Lincoln's proclamation of a new birth of democracy in America, a fresh labyrinth of blood and privilege should have grown up so intricate in its connections, so formidable in its institutional power, that the most accomplished prosopographist, a Sir Lewis Namier or a Sir Ronald Syme, might hesitate to the thread the devious maze.

In the end Straight was hired, and he was soon working with "with Joe Grew on the organization of the Peace Commission," a "whale of a job," as he described it to

Dorothy. He was in touch with the great; House sent him to tell the French prime minister, Georges Clemenceau, that President Wilson would sail in December to be personally present at the Conference. Straight remembered how the French leader put aside all Gallic hauteur and spoke to him earnestly in English. (His English was excellent; as a young man he had taught school in Stamford, Connecticut.) Rising above his customary posture of fatigued cynicism, the old Tiger grasped Straight by both arms and told him how much he liked America.

In hiring Straight, House was conscious of the utility of Dorothy, and he urged the couple to take a house in Paris. He envisioned Dorothy presiding over a brilliant salon, one in which "people could be brought together." It was arranged that she and the children (Whitney, six, Beatrice, four, and Michael, two) would cross in early December on the *George Washington*, the confiscated German ship on which President Wilson was also to sail. Straight, in the meantime, was engrossed in the intricacies of peacemaking. But one Sunday in November he took time off to join House and Auchincloss for a motor tour of the old lines and battle places. Returning to Paris that night, he dined at Voisin's with Captain Walter Lippmann, his *New Republic* employee, and Dwight Morrow, the Morgan partner whose daughter Anne would one day marry Charles Lindbergh.

The next morning Straight woke with a chill and kept his bed. Daisy Harriman, forsaking her Red Cross duties, came to sit beside him, and various American military doctors attended him; Sherrard Billings visited daily. Lippmann, too, was by this time suffering from influenza, as were House and Grew. They would recover, but Straight's condition worsened, and symptoms of pneumonia were detected in one of his lungs. His temperature rose to 104° and he became delirious. "He thinks that he is at the front," Daisy wrote, "and talks all the time about divisions, machine guns and the like." Thanksgiving Day found him still conscious. "Did you say this was Thanksgiving?" he asked Daisy. "Look in my dressing table . . . take out all the money you want to get turkeys, and give everybody a good time. I love people to be happy." On the Saturday after Thanksgiving she and Lippmann "realized that he was going fast. We sent a motor for Billings of Groton. . . . He came quietly into the room, stood beside the bed, made three beautiful prayers, and two minutes after he stopped Willard quietly stopped breathing." Daisy cabled Frank Polk at the State Department: PLEASE HAVE HERBERT CROLY . . . OR SOMEONE ELSE CLOSE TO DOROTHY STRAIGHT DELIVER THE FOLLOWING MESSAGE TO HER: "WILLARD STRAIGHT PASSED AWAY VERY PEACEFULLY AT 12:45 A.M. DECEMBER 1ST."

❧

WHEN WOODROW WILSON REACHED EUROPE in December 1918 crowds pressed round his carriage, and he found himself hailed as a "God of Peace," a "prophet risen in the West," the anointed one who would "give to the whole world a new message and a more righteous order." When, a month later, he was driven to the Quai d'Orsay for the opening of the Peace Conference, the curtain rose on the American Century. Yet the first act in the drama was little more than a series of blunders, and Wilson's failures would long haunt WASPs who wanted America to have a greater say in the world.

Part of the problem, as WASPs saw it, lay in Wilson's cast of mind, which was to them uncongenial. The British diplomat Harold Nicolson pointed out that the president was the descendant of Covenanters and Cameronians, Scottish Presbyterians whose fire-and-brimstone Calvinism figures, not very sympathetically, in one of the romances of Sir Walter Scott. It is in most cases fanciful to trace a person's character to remote ancestors, and Wilson himself was a complicated man, not easily reduced to formulas. He admired the British Whig tradition, and he numbered Edmund Burke and Walter Bagehot among his heroes. But Nicolson saw that, beneath Wilson's veneer of urbanity, the old Calvinist modes lingered. His "thought and his temperament," John Maynard Keynes believed, "were essentially theological not intellectual, with all the strength and weakness of that manner of thought, feeling, and expression."

Wilson remains one of the more extraordinary instances of the messianic temperament in the history of the United States, a nation not innocent of the attractions of new heavens and new earths; he was never quite happy unless drawing up a gospel and working the reformation of something or other. Previously he had sought to renovate smaller units, beginning with his attempt to purify Princeton, where he served as president of the university. Now he found himself called to use the moral authority of a much greater office to reorder nothing less than the world itself; by exporting American ideals of democracy and fair dealing into foreign parts, he would lead mankind to a better place.[*]

---

[*]   Dean Acheson, a WASP who would learn from Wilson's mistakes but could not escape his influence, pointed out that the author of the Fourteen Points was hardly alone in his excessive optimism, and that he shared with others of his time a "faith in the perfectibility of man and the advent of universal peace and law." This belief in "all the wonder that would be," was, Acheson wrote in *Present at the Creation: My Years in the State Department*, already "dying in Europe, as 'Locksley Hall Sixty Years After' sadly recalls, when it crossed the Atlantic to inspire American idealists, and none more than Woodrow Wilson."

Wilson set forth his vision in the January 8, 1918, address to Congress in which he elaborated his Fourteen Points. The worldly Clemenceau was appalled. "Fourteen? The Good Lord had only ten." The commandments Wilson brought back from his own sojourn on Mount Sinai were in a vatic style, apparently simple and clear, yet on closer inspection painfully ambiguous. The famous phrases— "open covenants of peace, openly arrived at," "absolute freedom of navigation," "equality of trade," "national armaments . . . reduced to the lowest point consistent with national safety," the "autonomous development" of suppressed nationalities and ethnic groups—amounted collectively, Theodore Roosevelt said, to a "visionary" muddle, being couched "in such vague language" that they might "mean anything or nothing . . ." Colonel House, closer to Wilson than any other man at the time, was negotiating the Armistice with the Germans when he summoned Walter Lippmann to ask what the master's prophecy actually meant. "You helped write these points," he said to Lippmann. "Now you must give me a precise definition of each one."

Each point had its place in Wilson's vision, but it was the fourteenth point, concerning the establishment of a "general association of nations"—a parliament of the world—into which the prophet poured his mystic fervor. So persuasive was the vision that it touched the imaginations of millions who were convinced that the old régime, with its cynical diplomacy and innumerable wars, would be swept away, and the blessings of perpetual peace secured by a world government. As the Peace Conference itself degenerated into factious squabbling and threatened to produce an unsatisfactory peace, the League of Nations (as the world assembly was christened) became the talisman that would right every wrong.

It was, indeed, necessary for Wilson and his supporters to look beyond the Peace Conference, for every day the Peace Conference was revealing the limitations of the messianic approach. The prophet works in visions, and the very nature of his inspiration makes it difficult for him to convert exalted inspiration into mundane policy. Wilson shrank from the task of applying his nebulous ideas to an exceedingly complex reality, and he was unable to withstand adversaries determined to twist his revelations into shapes that bore little resemblance to his own intention. Unpracticed in what Keynes called "the agilities of the council chamber," having none of the pliancy of a skilled negotiator, he lacked, too, that "dominating intellectual equipment" which might have enabled him to contend with such masters of statecraft as Clemenceau and the British

prime minster, David Lloyd George, as they brought him by degrees to sanction a peace that, in treating the German people harshly, could only lead to
further strife.

Yet even as he showed himself a novice diplomat, Wilson was reluctant to
draw on the abilities of his experts. He had brought with him to Paris a group
of State Department WASPs who saw and lamented his "slowness amongst the
Europeans." As trained diplomats or experienced lawyers, men like Robert Lansing, Frank Polk, Joe Grew, and William Phillips had precisely the experience
Wilson lacked. But the president distrusted his State Department. He arrived
in Paris, Grew remembered, in an "ugly mood" toward Lansing, his secretary of
state. An authority on international law with a large experience of negotiating
treaties, Lansing had asked his advisors to apply the theory of the Fourteen
Points to the concrete problems before them in a draft treaty; Lansing hoped
that the paper might serve, during the negotiations, as a kind of "chart marking
out the course," the work of pilots who knew something of the channel. But
the president "at once showed his displeasure" and said that he did not "intend
to have lawyers drafting the treaty of peace." The prophet looked on the State
Departments preppies as narrow and unimaginative, incapable of grasping the
truth of his visions, and they, for their part, shrank from his messianic blindness
to matters of fact.

UNLIKE PRESIDENT WILSON, IN THE grip of his humorless destiny, the WASPs
at the Peace Conference practiced a Stoic philosophy of their own devising,
the art of having a good time in the face of adversity. Franklin Roosevelt was
not about to miss the party, and he soon found a pretext for coming over from
Washington in his capacity as assistant secretary of the navy. (He pretended he
needed to oversee the dismantling of American naval installations in Europe,
a task the responsible admiral already had well in hand). Eleanor accompanied
him; she had recently discovered love letters documenting his affair with their
social secretary, Lucy Page Mercer, and under the circumstances he could hardly
go off by himself to Paris to keep bachelor's hall.

Bernard Berenson, who had lived so long among WASPs as to have in some
measure become one, was as loath to miss the fun. War and peace were more
gripping than old paintings, and after touring scenes of devastation with Edith
Wharton, he wanted to be a part of it. Mrs. Wharton asked her friend Walter
Berry to see what he could do, and he procured for Berenson a place as translator

for American Army Intelligence. He took a flat in the avenue du Trocadero, acquired a mistress, Baroness La Caze, and was soon caught up in the social and artistic life of Paris. He dined regularly with Mrs. Wharton before she fled the city—she found it too full of Americans—and also with Walter Berry. It was during one of Berry's dinners that a "dark rather long-haired man . . . obviously of letters," came in at a late hour. It was Berry's friend Marcel Proust, who assured Berenson that his books "had been bread and meat to him." Proust politely refrained from asking how an aesthete devoted to Renaissance painters contrived to live with so much splendor, but in fact Berenson's opulent style had long piqued the novelist's curiosity. "Have you any idea," he wrote to a friend, "of Monsieur Berenson's fortune (in the most vulgar sense of the word)?" Berenson's transactions with men like Joseph Duveen, the art dealer, were evidently unknown to him.

Daisy Harriman thought Berenson "one of the most charming of the everybodies" then in Paris, and Joe Grew arranged for him to lunch with the Franklin Roosevelts and Secretary and Mrs. Lansing. The dining room of the Ritz was electric with the euphoria of people pleased to be in the midst of great events. There were so many "everybodies," as Mrs. Harriman called them, and so few nobodies, that all the diners, Berenson remembered, were "looking and craning their necks at everybody else." But few eyes in the room can have been more acute than his own. He found Lansing "a very average man, far from stupid, but equally far from brilliant." Franklin, however, was something very different: "a radiant youngster of thirty-seven, and not looking that, keen and piercing and jolly." He only wondered why this splendid young patrician had burdened himself with "one of the most hideous . . . females ever seen."

In the midst of so much excitement one young American was melancholy. The Peace Conference had hardly begun when Captain Lippmann, serving both as a military propagandist and Colonel House's representative to the Allied intelligence bureaus, fell prey to disillusionment, and not simply because he been given no "definite and sizeable job" at the Conference. He had experienced firsthand the "intrigue and bluster and manufactured rumor of Paris," and he doubted Woodrow Wilson's ability to evade the traps that were everywhere being laid for him. Berenson remembered coming to see Lippmann in his office in the rue Royale and asking him whether he knew that the Americans were being betrayed, that "no attention was being paid to our aims in the war," and that a "most disastrous peace treaty was being forged." The young man said nothing, but his eyes filled with tears. He soon laid down his commission and returned to America, the *New Republic*, and book writing.

BUT LIPPMANN WAS THE EXCEPTION; the greater part of the American elite found themselves enjoying a class reunion. The Franklin Roosevelts were staying in the Ritz; Eleanor said she had never seen anything like the Paris of the Peace conference. The city "is full beyond belief," she wrote her mother-in-law, Sara Delano Roosevelt, "and one sees many celebrities and all one's friends!" Sub-ordinates took care of most of the actual work Franklin had ostensibly come over to do, the details of which he knew very little. Free to see and be seen, he lunched with the King of the Belgians, gathered souvenirs from the battlefields, and partied with his Harvard friend Edward Livingston "Livy" Davis. One day he and Livy dined with Joe Grew and other members of the Fly, their Harvard club; Eleanor was not pleased when her husband lurched back to the Ritz in the early hours of the next morning.

But if Paris was a WASP reunion, it also brought different elements within WASPdom into touch with one another. Even those who, in their privileged circles, thought they knew everyone found themselves stimulated by new acquaintance. Berenson, oppressed by the WASP inundation of Paris, sought refuge in the Villa Trianon, the neoclassical retreat of his friend Elsie de Wolfe near the palace of Versailles; it was a place, he said, where his "real self" could come to life amid a richness of "visual values that call back all that I have striven and lived for." Yet it was during this escape from the press of WASP visages that he found something arresting in the physiognomy of one Elsie's own recent dis-coveries, an "enchanting . . . youth named Cole Porter," who delighted him with "improvised ragtime music and words really droll." Louise Cromwell Brooks, a highbred New York divorcée, was as avid of fresh faces—in her case, handsome ones in uniforms with stars on the shoulder marks. Setting up shop in the rue des Saints-Pères, in the aristocratic Faubourg Saint-Germain, she went to bed with both General Pershing and Brigadier General Douglas MacArthur. (She would marry MacArthur in 1922 and divorce him seven years later.)

Joe Grew was beginning his life's work as a diplomat devoted to bringing WASP faces together. Born to a Boston family in the Back Bay, he had been, as he told the story, a "thoroughly inconsequential" boy at Groton until, one morning in the May of his junior year, he found himself "despondent about his lack of academic and athletic success." Going out for a walk before breakfast into a countryside vivid with spring, he was seized by the "truth that the only way to get your teeth into life is to bite hard." By 1919 he was a rising young State Department man, his dark hair combed back from a handsome face, "a terribly nice fellow," fond of Monaco and the gaming table, a deft host who knew his wines. (Wine, he said, is the "backbone of diplomacy.") He was *très aimable et serviable*, an obliging chap who delighted to be helpful, either by assisting others in their careers or introducing them to new personalities in whom they might take pleasure. It was through Grew's offices that future secretary of state Christian Herter, a young Harvard graduate recently married to heiress Mary Pratt, came to Paris as private secretary to Henry White, one of the American plenipotentiaries to the Peace Conference. (White's ambitious wife, Margaret "Daisy" Stuyvesant Rutherfurd, had some years before turned the old fox-hunting gent into a diplomat.) Grew was helpful, too, in getting young American officers posted to the Ceremonial and Liaison Bureau, where they could be in the whirl of things, though he was criticized for favoring preppies like Grafton Winthrop Minot in these appointments. Grew replied that Minot was selected from prudence, given the power that his wife's grandfather, Senator Henry Cabot Lodge, was likely to exercise over the peace treaty when it came before the Senate.

There were, to be sure, rebels like Bill Bullitt, who grew up in Rittenhouse Square, the heart of Philadelphia's WASP ascendancy, yet scorned its prosaic ideals, for he had, George Kennan said, an aversion to "dullness and dreariness." His parents obtained his admission to Groton, where he would have been in Averell Harriman's class and two years ahead of Grafton Minot, but on the day he was to go up to the school, he expressed a passionate opposition. "Every Groton fellow I know," he said, "is a snob," and his parents, who could not very well dispute the fact, sent him instead to the Delancey School in Philadelphia. At Yale he and Cole Porter founded the Mince Pie Club in a jab at the pretensions of Skull and Bones, and as a junior diplomat in Paris he harried his superiors with unsolicited memos urging them to recognize Lenin and the Bolsheviks as the government of Russia. Bullitt believed that the Russian Revolution represented a "great spiritual awakening," but in making his case he suppressed radical enthusiasms and pointed out that an accommodation with the Communists would be in the West's interest if, in return, Lenin agreed to honor debts the late Tsar and his government had run up in London, Paris, and New York. Colonel House, for his part, was intrigued, and in March he dispatched Bullitt and Lincoln Steffens, the reforming journalist, on a mission to Moscow. But Woodrow Wilson rejected a rapprochement with

Bolshevism out of hand, and an embittered Bullitt resigned his office; all that survives of the Bullitt Mission is Steffens's observation that in Russia he had "seen the future and it works."

Standing outside the Hôtel de Crillon in 1919, where much of the American delegation to the Peace Conference was billeted, an observer would have seen a long line of limousines painted olive-drab and groups of chauffeurs standing around in olive-drab coats as fresh-faced young Americans went through the revolving doors. Gazing into those faces, the observer, if he were a prophetic Lombroso, might have perceived the emerging physiognomy of the American Century. Passing through the portals were future secretaries of state, intelligence chiefs, jurists, ambassadors, spies—the brothers Dulles (Allen and John Foster), Christian Herter, Edward Stettinius, Joe Grew, and a score of others who got their first taste of empire in Paris.

In retrospect it is remarkable that these WASPs should have sought satisfaction in directing the destinies of distant nations and puzzling out the feuds of remote peoples in insalubrious climates. But statesmanship, if it is an expensive form of therapy, is not, Pascal long ago observed, an ineffective one.* Yet beneath the WASPs' pursuit of those twin balms, power and pleasure, there was a desire to make a civic contribution. They had all been expensively educated in a tradition that descended, ultimately, from Athens, and they regarded "the man who takes no part in public affairs, not as a man who minds his own business, but as a man who is good for nothing." Public service, they were taught, not only bettered the res publica, it was an essential element of self-realization.

At the same time there was something less creditable at work in this zeal for civic virtue. Complex webs of privilege enabled the WASPs to live spacious, many-sided lives even as so many of their fellow citizens performed monotonously dull tasks to get their bread. The WASPs persuaded themselves, as they negotiated their treaties or sailed about their harbors in Maine, that their lives were of service to those forgotten millions who toiled away in occupations that made a mockery of their potential. Self-deception is evident. So far were the

---

* "What else does it mean to be Superintendent, Chancellor, Chief Justice," Pascal asks in the *Pensées*, "but to enjoy a position in which a great number of people come every morning from all parts and do not leave them a single hour of the day to think about themselves? When they are in disgrace and sent off to their country houses, where they lack neither wealth nor servants to meet their needs, they infallibly become miserable and dejected because no one stops them thinking about themselves."

WASP mandarins from seeking to enlarge the civic playground, so that others might play there, too, they seemed to rejoice in their possession of the high places in the state. In the recesses of their hearts, they seem even to have derived pleasure from looking down on their less fortunately developed and less well connected fellow citizens.

THE TREATY THAT WOODROW WILSON and the other potentates signed at Versailles in June 1919 was the outcome of a bargain, the consequences of which would long perplex WASPs who, in pursuit "of fame, of empire, of success," sought to pour the twentieth century into an American mold. Wilson let Clemenceau and Lloyd George have their way with Germany, and in exchange Clemenceau and Lloyd George let Wilson have his League of Nations.* The treaty's economic clauses were onerous: they were meant to impoverish the German people even as they required them to pay large sums to the victors in the form of reparations. Yet at the same time the treaty reconfigured Europe in a way that inadvertently improved Germany's geopolitical position. Instead of confronting two great empires in the east, Russia and Austria-Hungary, Germany now looked down on a host of smaller, more vulnerable states. France, to the west, was growing ever weaker than her rival on the Rhine, yet she could not compensate for her weakness, as she had in the past, by forging a defensive alliance in the east with Russia, for Russia under the Bolsheviks was committed to the destruction of bourgeois states like France, and was in any event less of a threat to Germany now that the two countries were separated by the buffer states of Poland and Czechoslovakia. The Versailles Treaty, too vindictive to pacify an aggrieved Germany, was at the same time too forgiving to prevent her from recovering her old prepotency; and when she did recover it, there would be very little in Europe to stand in the way of her ambitions.

---

* Clemenceau and Lloyd George were on the same worldly page. "It was part of the real joy of these Conferences," Lloyd George wrote, "to observe Clemenceau's attitude towards Wilson during the first five weeks of the Conference." If Wilson "took a flight beyond the azure main, as he was occasionally inclined to do without regard to relevance, Clemenceau would open his great eyes in twinkling wonder, and turn them on me as much as to say: 'Here he is off again!'" Once Wilson in his advocacy of the League of Nations ventured to speak of the "failure of Christianity to achieve its highest ideals." "Why," he asked, "has Jesus Christ so far not succeeded in inducing the world to follow His teachings in these matters? It is because He taught the ideal without devising any practical means of attaining it. That is the reason why I am proposing a practical scheme to carry out His aims." Clemenceau, Lloyd George said, "slowly opened his dark eyes to their widest dimensions . . ."

Wilson was unconcerned by the danger: the League of Nations, he believed, would keep the peace. Having settled for the Treaty in order to establish the League, he now looked to the League to correct the imperfections of the Treaty. It was this quasi-magical body* that was to prevent a revivified Germany from seeking revenge and wrecking the peace of the world. But the League operated on the principle of collective security: in order to undertake any important action, the agreement of all the nations represented in its Council or, in certain cases, all the nations represented in its larger Assembly, had to be obtained. This alone made the League visionary; any one nation could cripple its ability to act. It was, Santayana said, "the old Polish system of an individual right of veto," one that made "impotence not only constitutional but expressly intended and prized." But Wilson persuaded himself that a spirit of enlightened benevolence would animate the participating states, and that each nation would cooperate altruistically with the others to suppress the aggression of warlike states without regard to its own stake in a particular conflict.† In practice, of course, nations were reluctant to involve themselves in quarrels that appeared remote from the immediate interests of their own anxious publics; and even in those cases where governments might agree that a strong line was necessary, it was not easy for them to agree on just what that line should be, or to do so quickly enough to forestall a determined aggressor. If "collective action is to be a reality and not merely a thing to be talked about," the British prime minister Stanley Baldwin would observe, "it means not only that every country is to be ready for war," it means that every country "must be ready to

---

* Keynes saw at once that the League was likely to be "a body merely for wasting time," an "unequaled instrument for obstruction and delay," an "unwieldy polyglot debating society." "It is not a sufficient explanation," Nicolson observed, to contend that President Wilson was "conceited" and "obstinate" in Paris: he was a man "obsessed by the conviction that the League Covenant was his own Revelation and the solution of all human difficulties. He was profoundly convinced that if his new Charter of the Rights of Nations could be framed and included in the Peace Treaties it mattered little what inconsistencies, what injustice, what flagrant violations of his own principles, those Treaties might contain."

† In eschatology a Calvinist, seeking to reform a sinful civilization, Wilson was in moral sentiment a disciple of Rousseau, who held that human beings, so far from being tainted by original sin, are naturally good: they become corrupt only under the influence of evil institutions. It was self-evident to Wilson that as virtuous democratic institutions replaced cynical oligarchical ones, human beings would become more beneficent and more humane. The League of Nations was to figure decisively in the transition from a malevolent to a benign world order, from an aristocratically corrupted to a democratically purified humanity.

go to war at once," anywhere in the world. The dream of Wilson proved to be unrealizable in practice.*

But Wilson was possessed—"obsessed," Harold Nicolson believed—by his inspiration, and he returned to America to stump for both the Treaty and the League. His mind, however, was by this time enfeebled by his hardening arteries, and during his long months in Paris he had lost touch with the mood of his own people. Americans were already beginning to tire of the world: they were agitated by rising prices at home. As Henry Cabot Lodge worked adroitly to turn public sentiment against the Treaty, Wilson boarded the presidential train to take his case to the country. But his head throbbed, and after speaking in Pueblo, Colorado, in late September, he collapsed; an aide saw him sitting in the compartment of his train "with one side of his face drooping" and "saliva running out of the corner of his mouth." He returned to Washington, where in early October he suffered the stroke that undid him. He recovered sufficiently to be wheeled, white-bearded, about the White House, weeping and reciting limericks, while at night he lay awake in Lincoln's bed, afraid of the dark. He spent many hours in the East Room, where the curtains were drawn so that he could watch silent movies; when he had gone through all the Westerns, he called for Signal Corps footage of his reception in Europe, and in his desolation watched flickering images of himself at the top of fortune's wheel, adored by delirious crowds. Yet even in his broken state he had just enough willpower to reject any compromise with Lodge. The Senate voted down the Treaty of Versailles, and the United States never joined the League.

IN THE *DIVINE COMEDY*, DANTE envisioned a noble *veltro* (wolfhound) acting the part of a good emperor, promoting a stable world order through wisdom and virtue. WASPs as a rule wanted America to play a similar role. In forming their ideas about how the United States might function as a benign superpower,

---

* Instruments of collective security differ from the traditional alliances that Wilson sought to do away with. Traditional alliances are "directed against specific threats" and define "precise obligations for specific groups of countries linked by shared national interests or mutual security concerns." Collective security, by contrast, "defines no particular interest, guarantees no individual nation, and discriminates against none." It "is theoretically designed to resist *any* threat to the peace," but because it "leaves the application of its principles to the interpretation of particular circumstances when they arise," it unintentionally puts "a large premium on the mood of the moment and, hence, on national self-will," with different nations favoring different approaches and unable to agree on the concerted action that might deter an aggressor.

they naturally studied Wilson's policy, and found that it taught an ambiguous lesson. They were convinced that Wilson was naïve in believing that foreign affairs could be based primarily on altruism and disinterested benevolence. Yet they saw, too, how adept Wilson had been in inspiring a nation inclined to isolation to act in the world. He had portrayed America's intervention in the war, not as an exercise in the pursuit of geopolitical advantage but as an enterprise in exporting democracy to people oppressed by tyrants. Jefferson and Lincoln had interpreted the history of the American Republic as a providential exercise in the enlargement of liberty, but it was Wilson who universalized the vision. America, he believed, must make the world "safe for democracy."

"We live by poetry, not by prose," Wilson said, "and we live only as we see visions." It would be truer to say that we live by poetry and by prose, and that we get into trouble whenever we confuse the one with the other. The WASP statesmen who were to shape the American Century were, by and large, realists in the tradition of Theodore Roosevelt, versed in the language of geopolitical interest. But Woodrow Wilson taught them to clothe this realistic prose in an ideal rhetorical poetry. As statecraft, the WASPs' mélange of the two presidents' policies was ingenious, but not without disadvantages. The WASPs intended Wilson's poetry to be the servant of Roosevelt's prose. But poetry is a potent, as well as an unpredictable thing. What if the servant should become the master?

Harry Payne Whitney around the time he discovered Gertrude's affair with a friend. "Are you all a lie? Are you all false?"

TWENTY-FOUR

Lost in the Jazz Age

Per tutt' i cerchi de lo 'nferno scuri . . .

Through all the circles of deep hell . . .
—Dante, *Inferno*

With Quentin's death, the boy in Theodore Roosevelt died, leaving behind an old man with a white moustache. At sixty he described himself as "an elderly literary gentleman of quiet tastes and an interesting group of grandchildren." He suffered from intermittent fevers, his joints ached, and he was apt to become lightheaded; shortly after the signing of the Armistice, he was taken from Sagamore Hill to Roosevelt Hospital in Manhattan, where he was kept six weeks by his doctors. Flora Whitney, who mourned Quentin as much as he did, was his stenographer whenever he was well enough to compose.

He was discharged at Christmas, and coming home to Sagamore Hill he took to his bed in a spare room that looked to the south and west and the afternoon sun, low in a winter sky. He was by this time dying, and his old valet, James Amos, was summoned to tend and bathe him. The next day he was a little better, and as the sun sank, he lay on a sofa before the fire, watching the flames. He was given morphine, and as the night wore on his breathing became labored. Edith was wakened and came to his side. "Theodore darling!" He was dead.

Many years later Walter Lippmann, when he was himself close enough to death to tweak its nose, would tell Arthur Schlesinger that presidents "in general are not lovable. They've had to do too much to get where they are. But there was one President who was lovable—Teddy Roosevelt—and I loved him."

The WASP old guard—the original crew inspired by an idea of reform and a vision of human completeness—was in decline. Henry Adams suffered a stroke in 1912; a thirty-four-year-old maiden woman, Aileen Tone, came to Lafayette Square as his "secretary-companion and adopted niece" with instructions "to keep him alive." When Adams discovered that she could sing medieval French songs, he insisted that he could not do without her. "You must write your mother," he said, "and tell her you are never coming home."

Uncle Henry, as Miss Tone called him, was attached to his routine. "We always walked for an hour before breakfast," she told Louis Auchincloss many years later, "which we ate on trays in the living room by a fire." Dawson, the coachman, would bring the purple victoria around and they would drive to Rock Creek Park for another walk. Lunch was served at noon, and "afterward Uncle Henry would sleep until three." They always dressed for dinner; Robert and Mildred Bliss and Frank and Lily Polk would sometimes join them. Uncle Henry "insisted that I should have good clothes and look well—and there was always champagne, which he would drink in such rapid gulps that I was sometimes afraid he would choke. 'It's the only way to taste good champagne,' he would retort if I protested.'*

It was Miss Tone who introduced her honorary uncle to Father Cyril Sigourney Fay, the "delightful Father Fay," as Adams called him, "who has an Irish love for the twelfth century." Fay, who had been ordained in the Episcopal Church before being received into the Catholic Church, tried to bring Adams into the Roman fold. "As far as possible," Adams wrote, "I do nothing but talk about the Council of Trent with Father Fay, and the Day of Judgment with Aileen." He was not, however, converted. Yet he carried with him a motet of his own composition—a "Prayer to the Virgin of Chartres"—which embodied his own idiosyncratic faith, and which was found in his wallet after his death.

Oliver Wendell Homes said of Adams that he was fond of "posing to himself as the old cardinal" for whom everything was "dust and ashes." He was no less a glutton of doom in old age. Life, he told Miss Tone, had "become intolerable." The world, he wrote Lizzie Cameron, was "waiting to drop into some *new* bit of darkness that it can't escape . . ." But in the meantime, he said, "we try to be cheerful and whistle our twelfth-century melodies." For his pessimism was by this time little more than the humorous crotchet of a largely serene old man who "was kindly, courteous, and sarcastic to the last." As he waited "for what the final void will show," he was far from spleen and anger, and it was in a placid frame of mind that he felt himself drawing near to the end (or fulfillment) of all desires.†

The moment of illumination he had, many years before, experienced at Chartres remained with him to the end, just as it remained imprinted in the poem in his wallet. Yet if the vision remained, so probably too did his sense

---

* One piece of advice that Adams gave Aileen Tone was very much in the WASP mold. Some "old but not very interesting acquaintances of Uncle Henry's had proposed themselves for dinner," and the "conversation was going very slowly." Adams "was obviously bored, and rather thunderously silent, and I tried, in my nervousness, to save the party with small talk. The next morning in the victoria, Uncle Henry said gruffly and suddenly: 'My dear, you were a bore last night.' I shall never forget the pain of that moment! To be called a bore, of all things! By Uncle Henry, who could never suffer bores! I was almost blinded by the soreness of it; I was like some desperate hurt creature; I even tried to get out of the carriage. Then Uncle Henry grabbed my wrist and said, very clearly and firmly: 'Listen to me, and I will tell you why you were a bore, and then you need never be one again. You were a bore last night because you talked about yourself. There! It's as simple as that! And now we shan't have to worry about it in the future.'"

† *E io ch'al fine di tutt' i disii*   And I, who was now drawing near
   appropinquava . . .   to the end of all desires . . .
                                              —Dante, *Paradiso, Canto XXXIII*

of failure in having been unable to make it useful to others by counteracting the shattered multiplicity of his age, the fragment-lives of people unable "look beyond the piece-work" of their circumscribed tasks. Surely a greater figure, prophetic, inspired, could have shown Americans what they were missing. But Adams was resigned: a WASP whose heart had been "cankered" by his Boston breeding could never be a prophet. He envied the vitality of Walt Whitman, who was one of the few Americans, he said, who understood the power of sex. Whitman knew the erotic power of both god and goddess, the male energy that erected dynamos and machines, and the "force of the female energy" that (as Adams believed) brought forth such things as Chartres. But Whitman was not the prophet Adams sought or (in his opinion) America needed. There is in Whitman's *Leaves of Grass* a procession of democratic faces, but community in the older sense was remote from a poet carried to ecstasy by his own hands only, whose song was solitary, like that of the thrush in his elegy of Lincoln:

> *The hermit withdrawn to himself, avoiding the settlements,*
> *Sings by himself a song . . .*

Adams wanted a more comprehensive music, but in his ember days he was unembittered by his failure to have realized it. Dining one night in March 1918 with Miss Tone and Elsie Adams, his brother Charles's daughter, he was "unusually bright and cheerful and laughed a good deal." "Good night, my dear," he said to Miss Tone after she saw him to his room. The next morning she found him lying dead in his bed.

JOHN JAY CHAPMAN WAS NOT yet dead, but he was going downhill. Shortly after Theodore Roosevelt spurned him by refusing to run for governor of New York on the Independent ticket, he suffered a nervous collapse. He spent the greater part of a year lying in bed in a darkened room at Rokeby, the old Chanler place on the Hudson, where his wife Elizabeth had grown up. During his sickness he underwent a mystical experience, a "midnight visitation" in which he discovered that he was a "unity" and a "creature of divine power." Even after he rose from his sickbed, he remained emotionally fragile. A sunset in the Catskills was more than his inflamed nerves could bear. In 1902 he and Elizabeth went to Europe with their baby, little Chanler Chapman, and Jay and Victor, two of Chapman's sons from his marriage to Minna. "I never saw children like them," Chapman said, "they are King's children in disguise, and I am stepfather to them." He was taking the waters at Römerbad, with its thermal springs, when Jay was drowned in the river. "I would rather it had been you," he said to Elizabeth; and she said she understood. Back in America, he spent some two years mostly by himself at Edgewater, another Chanler house on the Hudson, occupied with music and the company of a local eccentric, Mr. Plass, who lived in a houseboat on the river.

"What do you talk about?" Elizabeth asked.

"I don't talk to him. I just sit there."

"Well, what do you think about while you are sitting?"

"Oh, I keep wondering whether the black things in his beard are melon-seeds or cockroaches."

Jack himself grew a long beard, and he found it difficult to be "socially agreeable" to the Hudson River gentry. "If some one comes to dine, I go into a cold sweat—lie awake after it and resolve never to see anybody." He was uneasy in his place as one of the "patriarchs" of the "River families," the Hudson Valley squirearchy, and when Mrs. Wharton's *The House of Mirth* appeared, he spoke of being "so glad to have this social set torn to pieces." Yet he shuddered at the "close analysis of evil" in her book, and he expressed the hope that she was able to keep the novel's failure of benevolence from poisoning her own soul. "Mrs. Wharton," he wrote to William James's son Henry, "is probably *not* so malicious or bad-hearted as we would think."

Some of his old power yet remained. In August 1911 a man called Zachariah Walker was taken to the hospital in Coatesville, Pennsylvania, the day after an altercation in which a security guard working for the Worth Brothers Steel Company—his name was Edgar Rice—was shot and killed. The next day a mob dragged Walker, who was Black, from the hospital. "For God's sake," he said as the pyre was kindled, "give a man a chance! I killed Rice in self-defense. Don't give me no crooked death because I'm not white!" He was burned alive. A number of suspects were arrested, but all of the accused were ultimately acquitted by juries of their peers.

The horror of Zachariah Walker's death made a deep impression on Chapman. "I was greatly moved at the time the lynching occurred," he said, "and as the anniversary came round my inner idea forced me to do something. I felt as if the whole country would be different if any one man did something in penance . . ." He had long believed that something was wrong in America that could not be fixed by mere progress, as Americans understood it—better laws, better schools, more effective hygiene and readily available groceries. The "important work of the present," he told William James, "was to be done more by sack-cloth and ashes." There was too little of Dante in American life—too little recognition of the necessity of suffering and atonement in the struggle to reach a better place. There was instead only a callow optimism, what Chapman called a "Hurrah-for-us Americanism," such as he saw embodied in the public career of his old Porc brother Theodore Roosevelt.

In August 1912 Chapman left Quick Freshes, his summer place on Seven Hundred Acre Island at Dark Harbor, Maine, and went to Coatesville to hold what he called a Prayer Meeting in memory of Zachariah Walker. Four people assembled in the rented hall—Chapman himself, Edith Martin (a friend of Chapman's from New York), an old Black woman, and a man whom Chapman suspected of being a police informer. He delivered himself of his prayer. "We are met to commemorate the anniversary of one of the most dreadful crimes in history," he began, "not for the purpose of condemning it, but to repent of our share in it." That no one was successfully prosecuted for the crime was, he said, "only proof of the magnitude of the guilt, and of the awful fact that everyone shares in it." He told how, on first reading in the newspapers of "the burning alive of a human being" with no one trying to stop it in the "name of Christ, of humanity, of government," he seemed "to get a glimpse into the unconscious soul of this country. . . . I have seen death in the heart of this people." For the "great wickedness that happened" was not that of "Coatesville nor of today." A nation could not condone human bondage for nearly three hundred years "and then suddenly throw off the effect of it." The "marks of that vice" were in all of our American faces. Books and resolutions "will not save us, but only such disposition in our hearts and souls as will enable the new life . . ."

Yet Chapman's lucidity in quest of the new life, the vita nuova, would soon give way to morbidity. His hero was Emerson, who seemed to him "a younger brother of Shakespeare," and who gave him the confidence to believe that it "is just as well that there should be one person like *me* in the world." But he knew that Emerson was an insufficient prophet: his "aloofness" from fellowship, from communion with others, showed the "anæmic incompleteness" of his character.*

---

* Though "I prize my friends," Emerson said, "I cannot afford to talk with them and study their visions, lest I lose my own." Or as the Emersonian neighbor in Frost's poem says, "Good fences make good neighbors." "If an inhabitant of another planet," Chapman wrote, "should visit the earth, he would receive, on the whole, a truer notion of human life by attending an Italian opera than he would by reading Emerson's volumes."

Too exclusively pursued, Emerson's ideal of self-reliance abetted all that was least healthy in America's unmusically mechanical way of living. Chapman admired the "beautiful and complete" wholeness he found in such remains of older, un-Emersonian communities as he chanced to encounter in his travels, and he deplored the destruction of what was "medieval" (his word for cohesive and humane) in places like Harvard. But he saw no way either to revive that artistry or to use its music to enable the new life he desired for his country, and toward the end of his life he retreated, as the disappointed WASP is apt to do, into the little oases of preppy order in which he had been bred. His interests, Edmund Wilson wrote, came "to be almost entirely confined to the horizons of his old Harvard circle. It is all Harvard College and St. Paul's School, Porcellian Club and Tavern Club." In the last decade of his life, saddened by grief yet giddy with the caprice of age, he fell into anti-Catholicism and anti-Semitism, and he became involved in an organization called the Aryan Society. The reformer who many years before had thrust his hand into the fire as a pledge of his desire for a new life had come to an unsatisfactory end.

THE ANNALS OF WASPDOM IN this period are redolent of decay. In 1919 Harry Payne Whitney came upon letters composed during the heat of Gertrude's affair with their mutual friend William Stackpole. "By the worst piece of luck in the world," Harry wrote to his wife, "I would have given ten million dollars if it had not happened—I ran across your Stackpole letters last night in the country. You are the only person I have ever really loved, the only person that means more to me than anyone else, man or woman. . . . Now the bottom is kicked out of life. It's all lies. Are you all a lie? Are you all false?"

Yet Gertrude and Harry grew closer as they aged, and Harry himself became a more sympathetic figure as his health decayed. Although he was scarcely fifty, he thought himself an old man. Weakened by liver disease, he seemed a sweeter character than he had been in his prime. He was affectionate and thoughtful, and much devoted to his family. In 1925 he broke his collarbone playing polo and never completely recovered. In the same year his daughter Flora's marriage to Roderick Tower ended in divorce. A stockbroker and oilman by way of Exeter and Harvard, Tower had been a friend of Quentin Roosevelt, but he was "unstable, temperamental, and withdrawn": he was also not Quentin. He would commit suicide in 1961 in Locust Valley.

Much like the Whitneys, the Oyster Bay Roosevelts, too, were in a slump. Ted, the oldest son of Theodore, could not shake the idea that he was unworthy of his father. His brother Archie, whom his mother, Edith, called a "beautiful idiot," suffered on account of his mental dullness. "I'm stupid," he would say after a few drinks. "I'm just stupid." Both Ted and Archie were tainted by the Teapot Dome scandal in the early twenties, and although they were cleared of wrongdoing, the revelation of corruption contributed to Ted's loss to Al Smith in the 1924 New York gubernatorial race.*

Kermit, the other surviving brother, was the most solitary and contemplative of Theodore Roosevelt's boys, and the closest to his mother. He was drawn to poetry, and was much struck by Edward Arlington Robinson's poem "The Wilderness" when one of his Groton masters, Henry Howe Richards, read it aloud. Learning from Richards of the poet's poverty, Kermit bought two copies of Robinson's book *The Children of the Night* and presented them to his mother and father. The volume impressed the president, who reviewed it in *The Outlook* and obtained for the poet a low-show job in the Customs Service. But Kermit's discovery of poems like Robinson's "Richard Cory" was a rare bright moment in his career at Groton, where he was otherwise unhappy. He sought relief in drink and opium, and he was said once to have appeared in the Rector's study drunk. His melancholy deepened with age, as did his tendency to seek solace in drink.

Theodore's daughter Alice was also unhappy. Her husband, Nick Longworth, was an amiable drunk and philanderer who in 1925 became Speaker of the House of Representatives. Alice took a lover of her own, Senator Bill Borah of Idaho, a rugged man of the West very different from the WASP males in her circle. (When she bore his child, Paulina, Nick genially accepted the fiction of his own paternity.) As Washington's preeminent hostesses, Alice became a power in her own right. Much involved in the political machinations of the city, she appeared, in 1927, on the cover of *Time* magazine. Fine-boned, attractive, intelligent, and cynical, she was in many ways Henry Adams's successor in the capital. Each came from a family that had once held the White House but was now out of power; each presided over a notable salon; each was amused by the comic

---

* Ted was serving as assistant secretary of the navy when President Harding ordered oil leases for the navy's petroleum reserves in California and Wyoming—among them the Teapot Dome field—to be transferred from the Navy Department to the Department of the Interior. In 1922, the secretary of the interior, Albert Fall, oversaw the leasing of the Teapot Dome field to oilman Harry F. Sinclair in exchange for a cash bribe. Archie Roosevelt was employed by Sinclair at the time, in a position obtained because he was Ted's brother and a Roosevelt. Fall was convicted and sentenced to a year in jail; Sinclair received a shorter sentence for contempt of Congress and jury tampering.

spectacle of politics, knew the players, fed on their gossip, and laughed at their follies. Alice's tongue was sharper than Henry's; Joe Alsop said that lunching with "Cousin Alice" was like breaking bread with a scorpion, so envenomed with malice were her accounts of the Washington personalities of the day. She "came close to disliking simple human goodness as a boring quality," Alsop thought, and she "had a mortal horror of anything or anyone with the least savor of gush or sentimentality, earnest dullness, or overly ostentatious virtue," in fact anyone who resembled her cousin Eleanor.

Yet for all Alice's success in the capital, Alsop sensed in her a "basic unhappiness." She read much of the night, widely and for the most part seriously, her favorite reading being the Greek philosophers. "I am quite certain," Alsop said, "that if her mind had been disciplined in any way, she would have made her mark as a scholar or a thinker"—the by now familiar WASP theme of unused potential. For all his professions of failure and dilettantism, Henry Adams worked with a vengeance to live up to his own. Amid the oysters and champagne he labored to make a moralist's point about the limitations of American democracy. The salon on Lafayette Square was a source not merely of private amusement but of material—first-hand reporting—for his book *The Education of Henry Adams*, in which he employed a highly artificial, aristocratic, and world-weary style modeled on the French aphorists (La Rochefoucauld, La Bruyère, Vauvenargues) to produce the antithesis of the natural, democratic, and hairily exuberant poetry of Whitman. The *Education* is superficially a joke Adams tells on himself—a man mis-fitted by his troglodytic education for life in the American Republic. But if you read the *Education* carefully you find that the joke is on you; you are made to understand that there is a range of experience that your own American education has overlooked.

In Adams, the would-be reformer of the Republic still lingered, in the cénacle on Lafayette Square, beneath the mask of the cynic; but in Alice's salon on Massachusetts Avenue, even the memory of regeneration has faded.

HENRY STURGIS CROSBY SOUGHT A different path to reanimation. His background was high WASP: his father, Stephen Crosby, was a Boston banker descended from the Van Rensselaers, patroons of Rensselaerswyck on the Hudson and models for the Van der Luydens in Edith Wharton's novel *The Age of Innocence*—founding members of the social set John Jay Chapman, who belonged to it, wanted to see torn to pieces. Harry's mother, Henrietta Marian Grew, was the cousin of Joe Grew (the diplomat) and Jack Morgan (the son of Pierpont). At all events young Harry passed from Boston's Back Bay to St. Mark's School in Southborough; in 1917 he crossed to France to serve in the ambulance corps. He saw unspeakable maimings—"agonies of hell"—and was awarded the Croix de Guerre for bravery under fire. Afterward he returned to America to complete his course at Harvard. But Cambridge and Boston seemed to him, much as they did to Henry Adams, a dead and "sexless" civilization.

At a Fourth of July picnic in 1920, he met and fell in love with Mary Peabody. Known as Polly, she, too, was in a high preppy mold: colonial descent, Miss Chapin's School in New York and Rosemary Hall in Connecticut. She had large breasts and as a debutante designed a brassiere that allowed her to dance more easily at balls. She was decidedly not sexless, and she willingly gave herself to her "ruthless" yet "most vivid" lover, as she described Harry. Scandal followed. For Polly was married; five years before she met Harry, she had wed Dick Peabody in a ceremony officiated by Dick's uncle and old headmaster, Endicott Peabody. Dick was chiefly interested in chasing fire engines and watching the firemen extinguish fires; he was also an alcoholic. (He would write *The Common Sense of Drinking*, which became an important text in the Alcoholics Anonymous movement.) He and Polly divorced in February 1922, and in September of the same year she married Harry Crosby. Two days later they sailed to Europe, where Jack Morgan obtained for his nephew a place in the Morgan Harjes bank in Paris.

The couple took a flat in the Île Saint-Louis, and when Harry went to work in the morning, Polly would row him down the Seine in a little skiff to the Place de la Concorde, a short walk from his office in the Place Vendôme. But Harry soon tired of the bank, and the couple abandoned themselves to the new Jazz Age poetries that were invading certain sections of WASPdom with the promise of a new life, much as, many centuries before, the cult of Dionysus would arrive in some old, respectable, and bored Mediterranean town to overturn its verities.

The new god, like the old one, brought with him wine and ecstasy, as well as a relaxation of sexual inhibition; and the copious quantities of champagne the Crosbys served at their parties were in time supplemented by opium, hashish, and cocaine; their marriage was open. Polly thought to take a new Christian name to signalize the revolution in their manner of living, and after considering the possibilities of Clytoris, she and Harry settled on Caresse. "Most people die of a sort of creeping common sense," Harry wrote in his journal, borrowing the words from Wilde's *The Picture of Dorian Gray*, "and discover when it's too late that the only things one never regrets are one's mistakes." In accordance with this philosophy, he cabled his father in Boston: PLEASE SELL $10,000 WORTH OF STOCK. WE HAVE DECIDED TO LIVE A MAD AND EXTRAVAGANT LIFE.

Jazz revivified the Crosbys. Harry was particularly keen on Bessie Smith, the Jazz Age singer, and a single line in *Lady Chatterley's Lover*—"Fellows with swaying waists fucking little jazz girls with small boy buttocks"—appealed to him as nothing else in D. H. Lawrence's novel did. But WASPs like the Crosbys experienced jazz in a vacuum, as a music divorced from the culture that created it; its rhythms, which made for transcendence in the communities in which they evolved, did not bring a comparable wisdom to those who experienced them artificially in night clubs. In any case Harry had need of stronger wine and madder myths. Inspired, perhaps, by the example of Julius Bassianus, whom Gibbon describes as "consecrated to the honorable ministry of high priest of the Sun," Harry resolved to become such a priest himself, though scarcely an orthodox one. The avatar of what he called "a New Sun World" and "a New Copulation," his penis ("the rod of the Sun") became the emblem of his sacerdotal office. He described himself as a "sun worshiper in love with death," for he adored not the conventional sun, an agent of life, the "Demiurgos of everything sensible," but a sun "black as sackcloth of hair," the *sol niger* of the alchemists, a counter-sun, or star in eclipse.

It was not all eccentricity and extravagancy. Harry's cousin, Walter Berry,* encouraged the Crosbys to write, and they were soon caught up in the expatriate literary crowd in Paris, the American writers who rushed out each evening in *l'heure verte*—the green hour—to join a mass of native poets in the search for inspiration (or oblivion) in absinthe. The couple also established a publishing house—it was eventually called the Black Sun Press—that printed the work of James Joyce, Hart Crane, Ernest Hemingway, Henry Miller, and Anaïs Nin. But Crosby's own sun had hardly risen before it began to set. Visiting the Lido in the summer of 1928, he encountered a young WASP woman shopping for her wedding trousseau. Josephine Noyes Rotch had attended Bryn Mawr and was a member of the Junior League; Harry anointed her a "Princess of the Sun," and the two became lovers. The following year she married Albert Smith Bigelow of

---

* Berry had a sharp nose for what was doing in the republic of letters; the close friend, as we have seen, of Edith Wharton and Marcel Proust, he lived to see the Lost Generation of the Jazz Age before his death in 1927. He seems only narrowly to have missed Melville, his Van Rensselaer cousin, with whose mother and sister he vacationed as a boy.

Boston in a ceremony at Old Lyme, Connecticut. But she and Harry were not done with one another. He returned to America in November 1929 to watch the Harvard-Yale game, and afterward he eloped with Josephine (now Mrs. Albert Bigelow) to Detroit, where they registered in the Book-Cadillac Hotel as Mr. and Mrs. Harry Crane. They went next to New York, where on December 7 Harry was present at a party in Hart Crane's apartment in Brooklyn. Malcolm Cowley, Walker Evans, William Carlos Williams, and E. E. Cummings were among the literary revelers; Crane had recently finished his poem "The Bridge," which the Black Sun Press was to publish, and they celebrated the achievement with a certain amount of gin.

On December 9 Harry rejoined Caresse in the Savoy-Plaza Hotel in mid-town. "One is not in love," he wrote in his diary, "unless one desires to die with one's beloved"; and he spoke cryptically to Caresse of meeting "the Sun-Death together." But she seems not have been overly concerned; her husband was, after all, always saying strange things. At five o'clock she and her mother-in-law, Henrietta, went to Uncle Jack Morgan's for tea; Harry was also invited. Morgan was fond of the Crosbys, notwithstanding Harry's desire, expressed in one of his poems, to burn businessmen "alive with *Wall Street Journals*." Harry did not, however, come to tea with Uncle Jack. This was unlike him; the pallid young voluptuary was, with all his eccentricities, beautifully mannered, and faithful in appointments. Caresse and Henrietta went on to the Caviar Restaurant, where they had a 7:30 dinner reservation; Hart Crane and his friend Margaret Robson joined them, but again Harry did not appear. Caresse telephoned Harry's friend Stanley Yates Mortimer Jr., a painter whose mother was Eleanor Roosevelt's Aunt Tissie; Harry had the key to Mortimer's studio in the Hotel des Artistes on West Sixty-seventh Street, where he occasionally stayed. As Caresse and her party were preparing to leave the Caviar—they had tickets to the theater—she was summoned to the telephone. It was Mortimer, who said that his studio seemed to have been bolted from the inside.

At length the door was broken down, and Harry and Josephine were found dead, each with a bullet hole in the head; a .25 caliber Belgian automatic was found in Harry's hand. His toenails were painted red, and on the sole of his right foot was imprinted an emblem of the sun.

Amory Gardner (seated beside Cotty Peabody and Sherrard Billings) took up the aging Plato's belief that poetry and play are the molders of community.

TWENTY-FIVE

In the Secret Parts of Fortune

la santa voglia. . .

the sacred longing . . .
—Dante, Paradiso

M r. Gardner in his sixties was greatly aged. His blue eyes were still child-like in their naïveté, but his hands were stained yellow by tobacco, the result of years of rolling cigarettes, and he suffered from an unreliable heart. To protect it he used, while going up stairs, to pause at each step and recite a line from the *Iliad*, a performance once "watched with fascination" by his former student Franklin Roosevelt.

One spring day in the 1920s two Groton boys found him absorbed in a book and vaguely talking to himself. The book was Plato's *Laws*, the work of the philosopher's old age. It taught playfulness, which men and institutions lose as they age, but need quite as much as they do the spring. From the first Mr. Gardner had a "fanatical, wild devotion" to Groton, but he saw both the good and the bad in the place. "I love the School just as much as ever," he wrote to his cousin the Rector, "but in some ways I positively disapprove of it. It is a complex thing I can't express clearly."

It was his persistent worry that Groton was becoming too rigid, routine, metallic: spring and summer had given way to fall and winter. In the old days a master "passing the door of the Senior Prefect's study, on his way from dinner to Faculty Coffee," would be "pulled by the coat tails into said study and find himself quite as much at home as in the Master's Den—save that he is dying to smoke." Such confraternity was now much rarer, and he professed himself "out of sympathy" with the "codes and systems" that had replaced the old playfulness. There had, moreover, been a hard period in his cousin's headmastership; during the teens and early twenties, the school had become less supple, and boys as different as Dean Acheson, the future lawyer-diplomat, and Oliver La Farge, the future prize-winning author, had been unhappy, if not miserable.

Plato, in the book Mr. Gardner was reading on that spring morning in the twenties, says that man "is God's plaything, and that is the best thing about him." It was a theory to which Mr. Gardner himself had long been attached. He believed that a school succeeds only if it is in conspiracy with the playfulness of its charges, and deepens it imaginatively. To this end he built, on the edge of Groton's campus, a playground called the Pleasure Dome. The building itself was designed in a beaux arts style by Warwick Potter's older brother Robert, who after Harvard had studied in the École des Beaux-Arts in Paris. There was a squash court, a swimming pool, and a stage for theatrical productions, as well as a garden with a maze of clipped arborvitae hedges. Here Mr. Gardner gave chocolate parties and "feeds," at which a sugary drink called google was served: but there were also readings from *The Odyssey* and the sort of desultory talk that enlarges young minds.

Yet the school seemed to Billy Wag to have become less playful over time; it was in danger of forgetting that rules and regulations are but a secondary and imperfect form of order. For he thought, as Plato did, that we have "been strung together by our choirmasters (the gods) on a thread of poetry and play, of singing and dancing." The idea sounds strangely in our American ears; we children (or adopted children) of the Puritans instinctively shrink from the idea, expressed by Plato in the *Laws,* that if a community is to retain both its cohesiveness and its vitality, it must resort to poetry, and find a way to embody that poetry in its ways of getting through the day. Hence rituals and traditions, games and festivals—little pieces of ceremony and stage-drama, of musical levity, of dressing up to act a part—that do something to lift the day above its inevitable prose. Plato, indeed, insists that we make these games, this play-acting, as *perfect* as possible, and he seems, in his *Laws,* to rebuke the naïveté of an earlier self, the younger philosopher who devised, in the *Republic,* an imaginary city called Callipolis, more fitted for "gods or sons of gods" than for all too human mortals. Scarred by life and experience, an older and perhaps wiser philosopher takes up the ideal rationality of the *Republic* and in the *Laws* softens it into the sweet compulsions of rhythm and harmony ritually elaborated. Like the aging Mr. Gardner, the aging Plato saw the shadow of the cypress grove, and looked to music and poetry as embodying a reason which, if it was not deeper than that of the rational intellect, was yet more accessible to the human heart.[*]

In 1928 Mr. Gardner published a slim volume, *Groton Myths and Memories,* in which he attempted to distill the essence of the poetry of his school, the little world that revolved around the Circle. To a "far greater degree" than in most institutions, he wrote, the "real essence" of Groton was the "result of a thousand little manners and customs and traditions which have grown out of a thousand little episodes of its daily life." This pageantry amounted, he said, to the "mythology" of the school, and it was this poetry alone that could counteract the "stiffening of joints" of the institution as it aged. *Groton Myths and Memories* is a quaint book, the atmosphere it evokes so much *Goodbye, Mr. Chips* sentimentality. As you turn its pages you seem to hear the prefect's cry, "Brooks House go by," as the Rector and Mrs. Peabody shake each boy's hand before bed; in the morning you listen to Palestrina and Mozart in the chapel, and afterward, taking your seat at one of the desks in the schoolroom, witness the little dramas of roll call, which culminate in the senior prefect's dismissal, "sixth form may go." There is the reading of *A Christmas Carol*

---

[*] "*Le cœur a ses raisons que la raison ne connaît point,*" says Pascal: and Plato in his old age seems to have found this "reason of the heart" latent in certain kinds of poetry and music, which he made into a principle of civic order. "With mankind," says Melville's Captain Vere in *Billy Budd,* "forms, measured forms, are everything; and that is the import couched in the story of Orpheus with his lyre spell-binding the wild denizens of the wood." Schiller says that the playfulness that goes into the creation of these forms is essential to their beauty, in which a large part of their fascination lies. "We shall never be wrong," he says, "in seeking a man's ideal of Beauty along the selfsame path in which he satisfies his play impulse."

by the December fire, and the procession of the Magi at Epiphany; there are the games in Mrs. Peabody's parlor and the songs of farewell beneath the apple trees in the June twilight, when the odor of the lilacs foreshadows the white flannel trousers and straw hats of Prize Day, the day the sixth form takes its leave. Yet running through the myths and memories is Plato's thread of poetry and play, giving life a form and coherence that touched the imaginations, not perhaps of all, but of some of those who experienced it.

OTHER EDUCATORS WERE ALSO ATTEMPTING to create humane forums within aging, bureaucratizing institutions, but with less comprehension of the arts Plato described in his late account of the foundation of a fortunate community. As president of Princeton, Woodrow Wilson proposed the creation of quadrangles within the larger university modeled on the colleges of Oxford and Cambridge. Princeton's trustees rejected Wilson's Quad Plan, but in the 1920s both Yale and Harvard were drawing up plans for college or house systems on the Oxbridge model, plans that would be brought to fruition in the thirties. Yet with all their virtues, the new residential institutions were in one sense failures. An Oxford or a Cambridge college has its magic even now in its institutional mysticism, its poetry and ritual—precisely what is missing in the spiritually antiseptic institutions of New Haven and the American Cambridge.

A more fruitful WASP experiment in education was undertaken at Columbia, where in 1920 John Erskine, a professor of Renaissance literature, established, after much bickering, a General Honors course in which students read, each week, a classic text and discussed it in a weekly seminar.* Separately, the War Department in Washington asked Columbia, during the First World War, to develop a "war issues" course for college students in the Army Training Corps, one that would give them a sense of the civilization their country was in theory fighting for. Erskine's General Honors course and the war issues course or, as it was later called, Contemporary Civilization, were over time expanded into a group of courses known as the Core Curriculum, in which students studied and talked about Great Books and other works of art under the guidance of their

---

* Devoted as he was to highbrow literature, Erskine was better known in his time for his historical romance *The Private Life of Helen of Troy*, which outsold Anita Loos's *Gentlemen Prefer Blondes* to become the most sensational novel of 1926. Its spirit, perhaps, was not Arnoldian: "When the war ended in Troy, with the fall of the city, Menelaus went looking for Helen, with a sword in his hand. He was undecided whether to thrust the blade through her alluring bosom, or to cut her swan-like throat. . . ."

teachers: an Arnoldian exercise in transforming or liberating the mind by means of the best that has been thought and said in the world. The Core Curriculum at Columbia bore some resemblance to the course in *literae Humaniores* (more humane letters) at Oxford, which was known as Greats, but there were differences. Columbia's Core was not limited, as the Oxford Greats course traditionally was, to the literature of Greco-Roman civilization, and (a grave but pardonable defect) the books were not read in the original tongues.

Columbia's Core was intended to be a course in Western civilization, but any reasonably alert student began to sense, as he read the books, that most of them were products of cultures very different from his own American one, in some ways better, in some ways worse. In many cases the books awakened desires that could not easily be requited in a conventional career in New York or Chicago: they also threw an unexpected light on the humane forums that so many WASPs were unconsciously chasing, as perhaps Erskine himself was. The critic Lionel Trilling, who took the General Honors course in the 1920s, pointed out that Erskine "had been the pupil of George Edward Woodberry,* who at Harvard had been the pupil of Charles Eliot Norton, who had been the friend of Carlyle, Ruskin, and Matthew Arnold. This lineage makes clear the provenance of the idea that was at the root of the General Honors course—the idea that great works of art and thought have a decisive part in shaping the life of a polity."

A WASP experiment in civic humanism, Columbia's Core enabled the student to eavesdrop on the life of the polities from which so many of the Great Books came, books that were produced under the direct inspiration of places that served not only as centers of commerce and government but as seminars in life and its possibilities, the humane forum in its prime. The Athenians spoke of the hour of the full marketplace (*agora plethousa*), a time when the sun was at its zenith and the citizens "in good agora form," when business and conversation "mingled with delightful loafing and standing around together." Talk that began in chaffing

---

* Woodberry was a WASP humanist. A mentor to a generation of Columbia students, both in the classroom and in his office in Fayerweather Hall, he was a descendant of New England sea captains who was somewhat out of place in Gotham. He believed that classic works of art and poetry both awaken various potentialities in the soul and show how they might be harmonized in a coherent whole. "He was the first teacher," Erskine said, "from whom I got the notion that the public life of the citizen is important as an expression, even as a test, of his private aspirations, and that the business enterprises of a country cannot in the long run be separated from its essential religious or spiritual faith. Having learned from him that poetry is the flower of life but still an integral part of it, we went on to learn that all human activities are related, and—unless one is stupid or a hypocrite—must be harmonious."

and gossip might end in literature and philosophy, in speculation about what human beings were and what they might be. The Core attempted, in a small way, to recreate that experience.

Today we may *read* Great Books, but in the old civic forums, it was possibly easier to live them. Greek tragedy—the poetry that culminated in the plays of Aeschylus and Sophocles—began as drinking music for an Athenian wine festival; the choruses of the early Greek tragic dramas made music in the corner of the agora known as the *orkhestra*, which translates as the "space where the chorus dances." Homer sang of the old Phaeacian city, Virgil of the fall of the Trojan one and the foundation of what was meant to be Troy's new and improved successor in Latium, which became Rome. Dante, in the *Vita Nuova*, encounters Beatrice, the girl whom he loves, in the public spaces of Florence and goes back to his room to dream; in the *Divine Comedy* he traces the corruption that undermined his city, telling of a purer time when the naked beauty of women needed no girdle as they turned with unpainted faces from their looking glasses. Rabelais reveled in a market carnival still medieval in essence, Goethe in the "unfolded tapestry" of Venice: Shakespeare found such stuff as dreams are made on in a London a bit smaller than Athens under Pericles.

Perhaps it was cruel of the WASPs to acquaint students, as the Core Curriculum did, with these overhearings, these books (pale vestiges of a thing once living!) that introduced them to a way of life so different from their own.* The other half of the books the students read were, indeed, written by authors who, coming after the fall of the old forums, regretted the triumph of a new and different way of life, even when it brought peace and plenty in its train. So far from being contented with the revolutions that overthrew the agora, they felt its loss as a wound, one that they imperfectly assuaged with fantasy. Machiavelli and Rousseau dreamt of new or refurbished city-states. The intellectual "clerisy" envisioned by Samuel Taylor Coleridge and John Stuart Mill was intended to be a modern version of the choruses of Sophocles that challenged the pretensions of the powerful. (The new clerisy, alas, ended up producing not poetry but

---

* Classic texts and traditions liberate you from the provinciality of your time and place, yet they emerge from and are shot through with the most pungent local attachments: Athens, Florence, Jerusalem, Medina, Shiraz, Tumbutu, Banaras, Pratishthana, Nalanda, Lu, Kyoto. Our modern Western way of being, Ira Katznelson observes, has been less successful in reconciling the universalism which its Enlightenment philosophy celebrates with "the local attachments, the historical particularities" that embody the "plurality" and "heterogeneity" that an Enlightened liberalism ideally seeks. It is a problem that in different ways perplexed the WASPs.

opinion columns, the grey prose of the newspaper.) John Ruskin fell in love with Venetian Gothic, John Keats with Mediterranean classicism, the arts of "Dance, and Provençal song, and sunburnt mirth." But readers who admired the writing politely overlooked the moral suggestion. Karl Marx had a half-baked notion that under socialism the civic generalism of the Greek cities would flourish again in all the splendor of the *eutrapelia*—many-sidedness—that Matthew Arnold sought as unrealistically to revive.* Even Nietzsche, whose Zarathustra despises the poisonous flies of the marketplace, was half in love with its aesthetic forms. He was a sympathetic student not only of the tragic poetry of the civic play-spaces, but of the architecture, the dancing, the feasting—the whole effort to build up a humane common space. "Whenever I look for another word for *music*," he once said, "I only ever find the word *Venice*." But readers largely ignored this strand in his thought.

The Core Curriculum was criticized for being superficial, so much intellectual tourism. The real danger, however, was not that most students would take the mysticism of the Core too lightly, but that a few would take it too seriously. They might then find themselves, as Edmund Wilson said of an earlier generation that took its liberal education too closely to heart, "launched on careers of tragic misunderstanding." But on the whole the Core was probably a good thing, and performed at Columbia a function somewhat analogous to the teaching of Mr. Gardner at Groton. Making use of transcriptions of a superseded way of life, it supplied a poetry that did something to awaken a student's powers, even as it brought a degree of coherence to them, and ripened them for the service of some perhaps noble end.

IN THE LATE SUMMER OF 1920, as thirty-eight-year-old Franklin Roosevelt crossed the country as the Democratic nominee for vice president, many Americans mistook him for the son of Theodore. "I voted for your father," citizens shouted. "You're just like your old man!" Franklin did not try very hard to correct

---

* *Eutrapelia* was a quality the Greek citizen needed in order to contribute to the maintenance of his city. The word *eutrapelos* means originally good turning (or turning round): it came to mean an ingenious versatility, not unlike that of our "well-rounded" person, and it implied what Arnold, in a lecture at Eton, called "a happy and gracious flexibility." A citizen who has been so educated as to be able to "turn," easily and gracefully, from one task to another perhaps very different one will not, Thucydides has Pericles say in the Funeral Oration, be *idiotes*—an idiot—imprisoned in a fragmentary part-life. On the contrary, such a citizen will be sufficiently broad-souled to contribute to various aspects of the city's life. "I say that our city is the school of Hellas," Thucydides makes Pericles say, "and that each individual among us could in his own person, with utmost grace and *eutrapelos*, prove himself self-sufficient in the most varied forms of activity . . ." Quite as much as Marx and Arnold, the higher WASPs sought to resurrect *eutrapelia*.

the mistake; he knew that it was to his advantage to persuade Americans that he was the political and spiritual heir of his cousin and uncle-in-law, who in death was at least as popular as he had been in life. Yet as the running mate of Ohio's Governor James Cox, the Democratic nominee for president, Franklin proved an appealing candidate in his own right. "The physical impression leaves nothing to be asked," wrote a *New York Post* reporter who covered the campaign. The candidate seemed the "figure of an idealized college football player, almost the poster type in public life," and he was so often surrounded by adoring women that Eleanor, a little peeved, spoke of the "worshippers at his shrine." Frances Perkins, who would later serve as his secretary of labor, said that he had become "better looking than he used to be" as well as "more amiable." Eleanor once remarked that her husband was "not at ease with people not of his own class," but he had found a way to make strangers with whom he had little in common feel as though he cared about them. "I'm sure he didn't start out being attracted to people as people," Perkins said. Indeed she was not sure if he ever really *was* attracted to people as people. But he learned to assume a virtue though he had it not. The engineer of one of the trains that pulled his railway carriage spoke for many when he said, "that lad's got a 'million vote smile.'"

As the original WASP reformers, with their dream of restoring a purer government and establishing a more humane culture in America, passed from the scene, and as their heirs and assigns lost their way in the Jazz Age, Franklin Roosevelt emerged as a radiant figure, one who promised to carry on the WASP effort at regeneration. He had been schooled by the Rector, Mr. Gardner, and Reverend Billings in an ideal of service and civic virtue, and he was eager to promote social change, telling an audience that he was a statesman in the reforming mold of Theodore, "a progressive Democrat, with accent on the word 'progressive.'" He and Cox lost the election; Americans wanted to return to normalcy under Warren Harding. But Franklin's own future appeared bright.

Yet something was missing. Franklin took life as a game, and though he was shrewd in playing it, he seemed not serious enough about it; he had smiled and laughed his way to a high place in the Republic with the help of his uncle-in-law's name and his mother's cash. Steve Early, the Roosevelt advance man and publicist, said that in 1920 Franklin was "just a playboy." Such gloom as he knew he kept to himself, and in fact his setbacks had been mild, if not risible. Returning to America in 1919 on the *George Washington* with Woodrow Wilson, he told Eleanor's cousin Sheffield Cowles Jr. that the "greatest disappointment" in his life to date was his failure to have been admitted to the Porcellian. The cheerful levity of his nature set him apart from the typical WASP reformer: there was no Dante in him, no thought of going through dark places to find the stars.

AFTER HIS DEFEAT IN 1920, Franklin obtained, through the good offices of his friend Van Lear Black, undemanding but lucrative work drumming up contracts for the Fidelity and Deposit Company, a surety firm that wrote bonds guaranteeing the work of government contractors as well as government and union officials. Black, an officer of the F&D with an ownership interest in the *Baltimore Sun*, thought that Franklin would prove useful in a business that depended for its profits on political influence and indeed political corruption, the kickbacks that greased the wheels of the industry. Presumably Roosevelt the reformer held his nose as he pushed his friends in the party machine for bond work, but at all events his chores at the F&D were light, and largely relegated to the afternoons; his mornings were devoted to what he called his law practice, but in fact were mainly given over to politics, correspondence, and arranging a calendar heavy with speaking engagements and meetings of the various boards and committees on which he sat. Yet he still had time for fun, and a reunion of the class of 1904 at the Harvard Club in May 1921 left him, much to Eleanor's dismay, in bed till a late hour the next morning.

The warm weather came, and with it the promise of a long spell at Campobello Island in New Brunswick, where Roosevelt had spent his summers ever since he was a child. He arrived at the family cottage* overlooking Friars Bay on July 10, only to learn, three days later, that he must depart at once to defend his good name. Four years before, his former boss, Secretary of the Navy Josephus Daniels, had discovered that there was vice in Newport, where sailors from the Navy's Atlantic Fleet were known to visit grog shops and even to patronize bordellos. As if this were not troubling enough, Daniels (who, it is perhaps unnecessary to add, had never served in the Navy) heard more disturbing reports of "dens where perverted practices are carried on," of men with men "working that which is unseemly." The indignant secretary ordered the Newport commandant to "clean the place up." There followed a purgation in which Franklin himself, the dutiful assistant secretary, took a leading part; and young sailors were sent out to entrap the guilty.

---

* It was decidedly a WASP cottage, with some thirty-four rooms.

A Senate subcommittee eventually took up the question of why naval personnel had been ordered to compromise their own virtue in the effort to ensnare offenders, and in July 1921 the Republican majority on the committee issued a report that concluded that Franklin himself had either approved the "deplorable, disgraceful and unnatural" methods of entrapment or had been "most derelict in the performance of his duty" by failing to keep an eye on his subordinates. The Republicans did not hesitate to express their own opinion that Franklin "must have known" that sailors had been instructed to allow "beastly acts" to be "performed upon them" in order to secure convictions—a claim that made for a lurid headline in the *New York Times* concerning "unprintable" conduct. Franklin, who went down to Washington to salvage his reputation, issued a statement denying the accusations. Naturally it received less coverage than the charges themselves.

Afterward he went up to New York City, angry at the way the Republicans had treated him, fearful of the effects of the majority report on his political future, yet hopeful that the whole affair might, as scandals often do, fail to outrage an inattentive public. On July 28 he sailed up the Hudson River to visit the Boy Scout camps near Bear Mountain, where he inspected troops of boys, witnessed their feats of skill, and ate fried chicken with them by the campfire. A week later, feeling oddly tired, he boarded Van Lear Black's yacht, the *Sabalo*, to steam up to Campobello. After the *Sabalo* dropped anchor at Welshpool, the harbor on the western side of the island, Black hosted a dinner for Franklin and Eleanor on the fantail. The next day Franklin took his boss fishing; at one point he lost his footing and fell into the waters of the Bay of Fundy. In the evening his legs ached.

After lunch the next day he, Eleanor, and their two oldest boys, James and Elliott, went on a long sail, beaching the boat to put out a fire burning among the pines of one of the coastal islands. When he returned to the cottage he felt unwell, but he nevertheless went with the children to a nearby freshwater pond to swim. Afterward they plunged into the Bay of Fundy and then raced back to the cottage. Franklin sat down in his wet bathing suit to read his mail, "too tired," he said, "even to dress." Beginning to shiver, he took to his bed. Dinner was sent up on a tray, but he found that he had no appetite. The next morning his left leg gave way. He was by this time in pain, and Eleanor, taking his temperature, found that he had a fever of 102°. As for his leg, he could move it only with difficulty. Presently "it refused to work" at all, and "then the other collapsed as well."

Distressed by "the broken city," T. S. Eliot advanced a theory about how art repairs it.

TWENTY-SIX

The Waste Land

Qual fortuna o destino
anzi l'ultimo dì qua giù ti mena?

What chance or destiny
led you here before your last day came?
—Dante, *Inferno*

In 1922 eighty-two-year-old Isabella Stewart Gardner sat once more to her old friend John Singer Sargent. He had famously painted her many years before, in her sensual prime, with lips suggestively parted and a décolletage so naked (for the time) that Mr. Jack Gardner ordered the canvas to be removed from the St. Botolph Club in Boston with instructions that it never again be exhibited publicly. But all that vanity had passed away, and in her last portrait, painted in an apartment in her museum, she appears a wraithlike figure, an apparition of Virgil or Dante, a Delphic priestess who has chewed her last laurel leaf.

But to a new generation of WASPs Mrs. Gardner was a less than clairvoyant seer. Her museum in Boston was a temple of art, but it was also art's coffin and burying place. A young Harvard student called T. S. Eliot saw that, in common with much of genteel Boston, Mrs. Jack was in an unsatisfactory relation to the creative life. She invited Eliot to tea in her house in Beacon Street, an atmosphere he afterward recreated in his poem "Mr. Apollinax." In the palace of Mrs. Phlaccus (as he calls Mrs. Jack), the Muses do not appear; and Mrs. Phlaccus herself and two of her guests, Professor and Mrs. Channing-Cheetah (a Harvard couple), are dismissed by the poet as "a slice of lemon, and a bitten macaroon."

There were more morbid WASPs in T. S. Eliot's Boston than Mrs. Phlaccus and Professor Channing-Cheetah, but they were just as futile. Four wax candles burn in a darkened room on Beacon Hill as the aging spinster greets the young Harvard man:

> *'I have saved this afternoon for you'* . . .

In his poem "Portrait of a Lady," Eliot paints the sterility of the WASP effort to live life through waxwork substitutes. There is the phony cult of art:

> *We have been, let us say, to hear the latest Pole*
> *Transmit the Preludes, through his hair and finger-tips.*
> *'So intimate, this Chopin, that I think his soul*
> *Should be resurrected only among friends*
> *Some two or three . . .'*

And there is the WASP vampirism of the old lady, cut off from life, feeding on the younger and more vital spirit:

> *Now that lilacs are in bloom*
> *She has a bowl of lilacs in her room*
> *And twists one in her fingers while she talks.*
> *'Ah, my friend, you do not know, you do not know*
> *What life is, you who hold it in your hands';*
> *(Slowly twisting the lilac stalks)*
> *'You let it flow from you, you let it flow . . .'*

In his early poems, Eliot, though not out of his twenties, compresses a quantity of WASP morbidity—the dowagers with their footmen and housemaids, the spinsters who live through the pages of the *Boston Evening Transcript*, the lonely men in shirtsleeves leaning voyeuristically out of windows—into brief images of despair, like those in the *Inferno*. For the poetry of the WASPs is, Eliot thinks, inadequate, and their prophets are false. Matthew Arnold and Ralph Waldo Emerson wanted to liberate potential, but their books now rest on glazen shelves. "Matthew and Waldo" are for Eliot guardians of a faith that has failed. Yet he sees, too, that the rebellion of younger WASPs is as unfruitful, and he makes fun of "Cousin Nancy," who "smoked/And danced all the modern dances," as she vainly rides to hounds over barren hills and muddy cow-pastures.

A KNOWLEDGE OF T. S. Eliot's background—he was in heritage and family connection a WASP—is not necessary for an appreciation of his poetry. But a knowledge of his poetry illuminates his background. He was descended from an Englishman called Andrew Eliot who came to America in the seventeenth century from East Coker in the southwest of England. The Eliots had, by the time Thomas Stearns himself was born 1888, produced a large number of respectable WASPs, among them Charles Eliot Norton, the Harvard aesthete, and Charles Eliot, the Harvard anti-aesthete. T. S. Eliot's grandfather, William Greenleaf Eliot, had been adventurous and gone west. He became a leading citizen of St. Louis, where he impressed upon his family the importance of public virtue and civic obligation. But just as Eliot saw through the genteel culture of the WASPs, so he perceived the flaw in their ideals of civic benevolence and political reform. Coming to the East (for school and summer vacations) from Missouri, he was able to look upon the tribe to which he belonged with a degree of disinterestedness that would have been more difficult to achieve had he been bred entirely on the Atlantic coast. In his essay on Rudyard Kipling, he observed that the outsider, if he happens to be "alarmingly intelligent," has a "peculiar detachment and remoteness" that enables him to see the places through which he passes more clearly than the natives do. When Eliot, the transplanted New Englander, came to catalogue the weaknesses of his fellow WASPs, he exhibited them pinned and wriggling on their drawing room walls in a way no purely New England Brahmin could have done.

But Eliot had the advantage, too, of coming later in the WASP cycle than men like Henry Adams and John Jay Chapman. He was born after Chapman

beat Percival Lowell with a stick and had the fit in Cambridge that led to the
loss of his hand, and after Adams fell in love with Lizzie Cameron and set out
on the road to Chartres. Coming of age at the end of Theodore Roosevelt's
presidency, he was conscious of just how *little* the WASP reformers had achieved.
Their idea of regeneration—a program of political reform that was to prepare the
way for cultural renewal—had borne meagre fruit. He had only to pass through
the gate of Harvard College and wander about North Cambridge—"sinister,
sterile and blind," with its bottles and broken glass, its ashes and tins in piles,
the mere "débris of a city" rather than a city itself—to know that the land was
unredeemed. And he had only to return to Harvard Yard to know that his class
could not redeem it.

Eliot rejected the WASP vision of service in the renovation of America, yet one
aspect of his environment stayed with him long after its other inspirations faded.
From Oyster Bay and Southampton on Long Island to the preppy archipelago of
Fishers Island, Martha's Vineyard, and Nantucket, from Newport to Cohasset,
from Prides Crossing and Beverly on the North Shore of Massachusetts to Dark
Harbor and Mount Desert Island in Maine, WASPs monopolized the choicer por-
tions of the Northeastern sea coast. Eliot was eight when his father, Henry Ware
Eliot, built a summer house for his family on Cape Ann overlooking the outer
harbor of Gloucester, Massachusetts. The memory of that life, where the salt was
on the briar rose and the fog was in the trees, imprinted itself upon his imagination,
and remained long after his other associations with WASPdom lapsed.

"My idea," Eliot wrote to the poet Richard Aldington in November 1921, "is
to consult, and perhaps stay some time under, Vittoz, who is said to be the best
mental specialist in Europe—now that I have a unique opportunity for doing so.
I am satisfied, since being here, that my 'nerves' are a very mild affair, due, not
to overwork, but to an *aboulie* and an emotional derangement which has been a
lifelong affliction." Eliot broke away from the WASPs, but like so many of them,
he was, by his own confession, a neurasthenic whose *aboulia* or want of will led
to a diminished desire to live. His difficulties were exacerbated by the disorder of
his personal affairs. In the decade between his graduation from Harvard College
in the spring of 1910 and his nervous breakdown in the autumn of 1921, Eliot
struggled with a chaos of potential destinies; he attempted to understand himself,
by turns, as philosopher, mystic, saint, blasphemer, prophet, clown, lecher, and
ineffectual WASP. "Faust complains of having two souls in his breast," Otto von

Bismarck said. "I have a whole squabbling crowd. It goes on as in a republic." So it went on in Eliot. He tried to be a poet in Paris, a philosopher at Harvard and Oxford, a banker in London. He also attempted to be a husband. He was studying philosophy in Oxford in the spring of 1915 when, punting on the Thames with his Harvard friend Scofield Thayer, he met an Englishwoman called Vivienne Haigh-Wood; later they all lunched together in Thayer's rooms in Magdalen. On June 26 Eliot and Miss Haigh Wood wed. The marriage was not happy. Vivienne was, like Eliot himself, a basket case, yet unlike him she was not merely neurotic but at times palpably crazy, or so Tom's admirers have contended; she would end her life in an asylum. He, for his part, was unable to get on with her sexually, or so Lyndall Gordon, in her study of Eliot's early life, supposes.

Amid all this chaos Eliot was trying to work out, in poetry, a formula that would express the thoughts and feelings that oppressed him, an idiom that would convey with force and precision the nature of his predicament. He was drawn, as those who suspect in themselves a vocation for prophecy or sanctity sometimes are, to scenes of wantonness and degradation. In Paris he wandered in the streets of Montparnasse observing the harlots and the *maquereaux* who pimped them; in London he explored the "disreputable suburbs" south of the Thames. What he said of Baudelaire was as true of him: his *ennui* was a "form of *acedia*, arising from the unsuccessful struggle toward the spiritual life." For the "hatred of life," he believed, "is an important phase—even, if you like, a mystical experience—in life itself." But if Eliot sought out hellishness in the hope that his inner world of nightmare, "some horror beyond words," would eventually be "reconciled among the stars," he also derived pleasure from his hell-diving, finding among the outcasts and spiritual lepers the blood-vitality, the passion that murders and creates, that lay dormant in himself.

To convey this not simple experience, Eliot looked to the Elizabethan dramatists, who distilled beauty from the macabre, and to such nineteenth-century French poets as Jules Laforgue and Tristan Corbière who found a contemporary way to piece together poetry out of apparently unrelated fragments of mood and feeling, mixing up the different tones and inspirations so that a line of prophetic intensity or classical dignity might be found cheek by jowl with the earthily scabrous or the comically mundane. "The form in which I began to write, in 1908 or 1909," Eliot recalled in 1928, "was directly drawn from the study of Laforgue together with the later Elizabethan drama; and I do not know anyone who started from exactly that point."

≈

"Tom has had rather a serious breakdown," Vivienne wrote to Scofield Thayer in October 1921, "and has had to stop all work and go away for three months." Just as Eliot's despair neared its height, neurasthenia came to the rescue; pleading breakdown and the need of a rest-cure, he took a leave of absence from Lloyds, the bank in which he was employed, to sit by the sea at Margate in Kent. He did not precisely rest, but instead worked on a long poem that had so far refused to be written. In Margate the composition went rapidly: the numbers came. By Christmas, when he was in Lausanne under the care of Dr. Vittoz, Ezra Pound could say of one of the drafts, "Complimenti, you bitch. I am wracked by the seven jealousies . . . . It is after all a grrrreat litttterary period . . ."

There is no one way to read *The Waste Land* any more than there is any one way to read any poem worth reading. Yet though it may not be the most illuminating way to approach the poem, *The Waste Land* can be read as a form of WASP confession, as well as a response to other works in the same mold. Eliot, who reviewed *The Education of Henry Adams* in 1919 shortly after it was published, dismissed its author (to whom he was related) as a butterfly, the wings of his "beautiful but ineffectual conscience beating vainly in a vacuum jar." (Eliot liked to examine human beings clinically, as a species of higher insect.) Adams, he concluded, was stunted: because he was unable to surrender to anything, to believe in anything, neither his senses nor his intellect "flowered or fruited." He was yet another Bostonian "predestined" to failure, one who had more than a little in common with the protagonist of Eliot's own poem, "The Love Song of J. Alfred Prufrock."* Like Prufrock, Adams was constrained by the scruples of his Puritan conscience and by the genteel traditions of class, and was one of those sensitive WASPs who, in Eliot's words, "want to do something great," but who are "dogged by the shadow of self-conscious incompetence," martyrs to missed chances and unrealized potential.

With the confession of *The Waste Land*, Eliot exorcised the demon that incubated in Adams and Prufrock, or so he dared to hope. The poem describes a journey through hell that ends in belief and a vision of potential fulfilled. In

---

* Adams, like Prufrock, loves or wants to love a woman (in Adam's case, Lizzie Cameron) but is unable to pull the trigger, and like Prufrock he is too respectable and too timid to be faithful to his moments of illumination. "I am no prophet," Prufrock declares: "And in short, I was afraid." Adams ends the *Education* with an admission of his "sensitive and timid" nature.

contrast to the nervous ironies of Adam's *Education*, Eliot made *The Waste Land* boldly out of words archaically rank, fragments of poetry that lodge in the imagination like the after-vision of roots and tendrils that remains in the mind following the weeding of a garden. The poem "is tongued with fire beyond the language of the living," and the words are atavistic: the dead tree amid the barrenness of stony places; the garden of Hyacinth, slain by his lover Apollo yet come to life again as the lilac does, in the lover-fever of the flowers; the Jacobean dog of Webster that would dig up the unfriended corpse; the Hanged Man in the Tarot deck, occultly connected to divination and prophecy.

But this primeval imagery is made by Eliot to illustrate a modern WASP hell. Madame Sosostris, "famous clairvoyante," wielding her wicked cards is in reality Mr. Apollinax, Bertrand Russell: it was he who fatally lured Eliot to Oxford, where the poet encountered Belladonna and was led by her into the deadly nightshade of a miserable marriage. Dante's astonishment that death should have unmade so many has been transferred by Eliot from a canto in the *Inferno* to the London of an expatriated WASP's daily commute to the bank. Shakespeare's Cleopatra, drowned in perfumes unguent, powdered, and liquid in "A Game of Chess," foreshadows the checkmate of matrimony gone wrong; Tiresias, in the "Fire Sermon," has walked among the lowest of the dead, but in the modern metropolis he foresuffers a novel horror, the loveless coupling of a typist, home at teatime to eat tinned food, and a house agent's clerk.[*]

Yet at the end of the poem there is a "flash of lightening" and a "damp gust bringing rain," and the cracked earth is redeemed. It is not simply that the poet has surrendered to "What the Thunder Said." It is that in embracing this poetry he has found (as Henry Adams never did) the vegetation god who revives the parched land.

⊗

---

[*] The integration of archaic poetry and modern experience in *The Waste Land* gives the reader the sensation almost of reading a foreign language, one with which he is not very well acquainted. This was in keeping with Eliot's belief that "that genuine poetry can communicate *before* it is understood." It is, he thinks, easier to experience a "direct shock of poetic intensity"—to come closer to the "objective 'poetic emotion'" being expressed—if there is some barrier between the reader and the literal meaning of the poem's words: the reader is forced to grapple with the strangeness, the unconscious mysticism, that inheres in the words themselves, a quality, indeed, of all words, but one that familiarity makes us overlook. Elizabethan poetry stirs us in part because we do *not* fully understand it: and the familiarity and remoteness in a phrase of Horace or Virgil may speak to a reader who has only a little Latin. "I was passionately fond of certain French poetry," Eliot said, "long before I could have translated two verses of it correctly."

THE WASTE LAND WAS HAILED as the expression of the "disillusionment of a generation," and its success was profound. But it did not extricate Eliot from his immediate difficulties. His wife, Vivienne, lay in their flat in Clarence Gate Gardens near the Regent's Park "a helpless and unspeakable wreck of drugs, fear, and semi-paralysis." She soon developed colitis, and Eliot was harried by doctors' bills. It was only in 1925 that he left Lloyds Bank to begin a new life as an editor in the publishing firm that became Faber & Faber. Two years later he was received into the Church of England and became a subject of King George V; in 1933 he separated from his wife.

Eliot alluded in *The Waste Land* to Greek and Near Eastern vegetation gods, but it was the Christian vegetation god whom he ultimately embraced. His conversion to Anglo-Catholic poetry was a private matter, but his public reflections on the way otherworldly poetry makes community possible in a fallen world incidentally shed light on the humane forums WASPs had long but not very successfully sought. He was himself attracted to such places. With whatever contempt or subtle envy, he makes Bleistein, in the poem "Burbank with a Baedeker: Bleistein with a Cigar," stare with his dead eyes at dying Venice, a "perspective of Canaletto" in the smoky candle end of time; and in his pageant play *The Rock* he makes the chorus condemn, a little lugubriously, the uncentered, agora-less life, destitute of civic inspiration:

> *And now you live dispersed on ribbon roads,*
> *And no man knows or cares who is his neighbour*
> *Unless his neighbour makes too much disturbance,*
> *But all dash to and fro in motor cars . . .*

Eliot was distressed by what he called "the broken city," and he advanced a theory about how poetry repairs it. In September 1921, just before he suffered his nervous breakdown, he finished what he called an "unsatisfactory" essay on the English metaphysical poets of the seventeenth century in which he spoke of the poet's power of "amalgamating disparate experience." The ordinary man's experience, he said, "is chaotic, irregular, fragmentary." He "falls in love, or reads Spinoza, and these two experiences have nothing to do with each other, or with the noise of the typewriter or the smell of cooking." But in the mind of the poet "these experiences are always forming new wholes." Certain kinds of poetry, Eliot believed, performed the office of "forming new wholes" in a more public sphere, not least dramatic poetry, the staged art that had so important a place in the old civic centers that Sophocles and Shakespeare knew. Eliot put a good deal of effort into trying to restore verse drama to its old preeminence, but he was never able to revive it in anything like its old amalgamating power.

Religious poetry was another such art. He was drawn to the *Upanishads* and the *Bhagavad Gita*: "Hinduism," Sonia Chumber writes, "was not alien to Eliot." But he was more intimately familiar with the poetry of his own Anglo-Catholic confession. Its rituals, music, and liturgy were called the Divine Office, but they also undertook, he believed, a very human one in helping people to get through the day, lifting them above its chaos or showing it in the light of a higher order. Emerson said that the question of how "to spend a day nobly, is the problem to be solved, beside which all the great reforms which are preached seem to me trivial." Eliot replied that certain kinds of poetry, when experienced as part of the infrastructure of daily life, do something to produce this effect of nobility or grace. The liturgy of the Mass, he pointed out, is a stage drama, indeed "the perfect and ideal drama," just as it is also a ballet, "one of the highest forms of dancing" he knew. A richly developed liturgical art, he was certain, is among other things a machinery for organizing experience and transmuting its anarchies into wholeness: it supplies one of those threads of poetry and playfulness that knit up the life of a community.

YET ELIOT'S OWN CONVERSION TO this divinely inspired poetry did not bring him the serenity he sought: it did not even make him a more charitable human being. What is striking about his 1934 book *After Strange Gods: A Primer of Modern Heresy*, which grew out of lectures he delivered in the University of Virginia, is its malice. The peace which passeth understanding in which *The Waste Land* culminates ("Shantih shantih shantih") has given way to so many hatreds: of the "foreign races" that have "invaded" America and disestablished the culture of the English settlers, and of the "free-thinking Jews" who are "undesirable" because they threaten traditions founded on Christianity and "blood kinship."

After Strange Gods smolders with the heat of imperfectly suppressed hatred, but what was icily cold in Eliot was no less forbidding. Many of those who were closest to him found themselves, after he tired of them, shut out of his life: his first wife, Vivienne, his sometime soulmates Emily Hale and Mary Trevelyan, and his close friend John Hayward, with whom he lived in Cheyne Walk, were among those who got the Eliotian pink slip. He could, Lyndall Gordon has written, be "genial" and "jokey"; he was, indeed, a man of immense charm. "Manners is an obsolete word these days," his Harvard friend the poet Conrad Aiken said, "but he had them. He did things with an enviable grace." But his graciousness masked detachment and even contempt. The ideal of loving one's neighbors is of course aspirational: but Eliot could not bring himself to love even his friends.

Can light be derived from one so imperfect? Eliot drew attention to something that WASPs in their quest for regeneration too often overlooked, that without "the music of some inspired Orpheus was no city ever built." Eliot knew that a certain kind of poetry *does* do something to keep a community in working order, but he never even tried to show how the religious poetry he favored could perform its office in a modern pluralist society. Quite the opposite: in *The Idea of a Christian Society* he sketched a post-pluralist regime. Still he kept a debate alive. He was, at different points in his career, in a dialogue not only with Henry Adams but also with George Santayana, who had been his teacher at Harvard, and with Henry James, whose work had greatly influenced him. Santayana maintained against Eliot that it is not the religious truth of a particular poetry that enables it to intervene effectively in life, but rather its natural wisdom, its accumulation of practical insight into the needs of human beings. James, in his dream-vision in the Galerie d'Apollon in the Louvre, saw life raised to its "richest and noblest expression" through "beauty and art and supreme design," and in his novel *The Princess Casamassima* he showed Hyacinth Robinson, the hero of the book, transfigured by his apprehension of the poetry of Venice. But in making his case he imposed no religious test.

Ernest Hemingway, left, in Pamplona.
"The things that happened could only
have happened during a fiesta."

TWENTY-SEVEN

Young Men Who Would Return to the Provinces

ditemi de l'ovil di San Giovanni
quanto era allora . . .

tell me of the sheepfold of St. John,
how great it was . . .
—Dante, *Paradiso*

In the late summer of 1927 Edmund Wilson, a writer on the staff of the *New Republic* who was living in Greenwich Village, went out to dine alone. On the way to the restaurant he stopped in a bookstore and bought an eighteenth-century edition of the poet Persius, a satirist in the age of Nero. Wilson was twenty-seven at the time and at work on the book that eventually became *Axel's Castle*, a study of the revolution in letters being then carried out by such writers as James Joyce, William Butler Yeats, Gertrude Stein, and T. S. Eliot. (Marcel Proust was recently dead.) They were known, these writers, as Modernists, but Wilson, although he lived in the Village, did not think of himself as a Modernist; already he was beginning to feel himself as "more or less in the eighteenth century—or, at any rate, not much later than the early nineteenth." He disliked such innovations as the radio, the movies, and the automobile, and he did not find the 1920s—a decade in which WASP ideas of reform were in abeyance and the vulgarly prosperous went about in their "Buicks and Cadillacs" drinking "bad gin" and worse Scotch—an improvement on the 1820s.

Sitting down to dine that evening, Wilson saw the vices of the period embodied in his fellow diners. In the middle of the room "was a party of men and women, all pink and of huge size, who were uncorking loud sour laughter; across the room was a quiet pretty young girl, of an obviously simple nature, who had some sort of keen professional interest in pleasing a rather defective-looking half-aquiline man, whose eyes one couldn't see through his eyeglasses."

A bottle of yellow wine was set before him, and Wilson addressed himself to Persius. The very design of the volume, brought out by the young publisher John Wright in 1797, spoke of forgotten craftsmanship. An "attractive duodecimo," it "was bound in green morocco and stamped in gold," and "had the aspect of a little casket in which something precious was kept." As he waited for the antipasto, Wilson began to read the preface, and he soon found himself admiring the sentiments of its author, the translator of Persius, Sir William Drummond of Logiealmond, a member of Parliament who would serve as George III's envoy to Naples and Constantinople. "Jefferson might have thought and written so," Wilson mused, and indeed some "of the logic, some of the elegance, some of the moderate and equable qualities" found in the preface to Persius had gone into "the announcement of our national policies and the construction of our Constitution."

Wilson was at home here. He professed an old-fashioned American patriotism, adhering to what he called the country's "republican tradition," a "social ideal which had survived from the founding of the Republic," one that inspired "at once a certain all-around humanism and a serious and dignified attitude toward life." But there seemed to him less of this sort of dignity in the America of his own time. Glancing at the fat people at the other table, he reflected that "the only element in sight which had anything in common with Drummond on Perseus was the Italian dinner itself, of which a bowl of minestrone, with its cabbage, big brown beans and round noodles, had just reached me as the second course, and in the richness and balance of whose composition I could still see the standards of a civilization based on something more comfortably human than commercial and industrial elements."

It was the old WASP grievance. The industrial expansion that followed the Civil War had altered the character of the country. It had, among other things, made it harder, Wilson believed, for a man "who had been educated for the old America," and "who might once have served the Republic or followed an interesting profession," to find a place for himself that offered both "stability and leisure." Such a man had either to become "the slave of Business at one extreme or drink himself to death at the other . . ." The bottle of yellow wine was less full. That even college men should be forced to surrender a little of their old leisure might suggest that the Republic was spreading the hardships of life as well as its dignities a little more liberally. Wilson, as he raised his glass, would as readily have replied that when even fortunately situated souls have difficulty in doing justice to their gifts, something is rotten in the res publica.*

He had in mind his dead father. Edmund Wilson, Sr., had been educated at Andover and Princeton, and he had aspired to a life of public service. He became, in fact, a brilliant trial lawyer who served as attorney general of New Jersey and was on Woodrow Wilson's short list for the Supreme Court—a rather satisfactory outcome, one might think. But the pressure of trying to live up to an older ideal while keeping a wife and child in WASP upper-middle-class comfort broke him down. "By the time he was thirty-five," Wilson wrote, he began to suffer "neurotic eclipses." He followed the rest-cure regimen devised by Weir Mitchell, the leading head-case man of the day, but he was never cured, and he was, in his later years, in and out of sanitaria. The problem, Wilson believed, was that the "old-fashioned lawyer" his father sought to be, an independent figure beholden to no one, was being forced to become "a corporation lawyer whose principal function was to keep Business from going to jail." In the same way, Wilson thought, the old-fashioned doctor "was on his way to becoming a modern 'specialist,'" whose job was to send neurotic professional men to the sanitarium. As for those

---

* Wilson had what he called his "theory of American Presidents—the able and idealist politicians carrying on the tradition of the Republic (Lincoln, Wilson, the Roosevelts), the machine party politician (Harding and Truman), and the completely non-political expert put in by the big-business interests on the strength of a popular reputation achieved in some non-political field (Grant, Eisenhower, Hoover)."

other refuges of the liberally educated, the church and the university, they "were beginning to be abandoned by first-rate men altogether." As a result humanism "went by the board; moral scruples were put to rout; and seriousness about man and his problems was abrogated entirely in favor of the seriousness of Business about things that were not serious."

As HE ATE HIS DINNER Wilson caught sight of E. E. Cummings, another solitary diner; and when he found Drummond censuring the willful obscurity of Persius, he was reminded of Cummings's own poems. If the eighteenth-century critics thought Persius obscure, what, he asked himself, "would they have thought of Cummings? And what was the use, in the eighteenth century, of the critics having cultivated those standards, if Cummings was what the future had in store?" But where "life is disorderly," he reflected, "the poets will express themselves in nonsense." In an age of civic wholeness, an artist might, as in old Athens, fulfill his nature by adorning his city, chiseling the stone, painting the frescoes, tuning the choirs. But in a broken age, he will become a romantic rebel, estranged from the life of the city; he will find, as Cummings did, a refuge in the artistic ghetto of the metropolis, making a poetry that reflected the brokenness he saw around him: somewhat in the way Persius, in an age in which the unity of the city-state had given way to the chaos of Nero's Rome, wrote poems that, with their abrupt transitions and deliberate crudeness, were at once savagely colloquial and elliptically fractured.

Wilson found it extraordinary that Drummond, with his polite literature and eighteenth-century taste, should yet have felt a certain "solidarity with Persius," so much so that he lamented the poet's early death "as if it were that of some able young man whom he had known in his time in London, some young man who had been educated in the same institutions and shared with him the same values." In fact Drummond and Persius had been similarly educated; they had both been nourished, as Wilson himself had been, on the literature and poetry that grew out of the old civic forums. At the Hill School, a boarding school in Pennsylvania, Wilson had studied Greek under Alfred Rolfe, a native of Emerson's Concord with a "benignant incandescence" of mind, and at Princeton he had found a humane mentor in Christian Gauss, the image, Wilson thought, "of that good eighteenth-century Princeton which has always managed to flourish between the pressures of a narrow Presbyterianism and a rich man's suburbanism." (As a result of this schooling, the classical humanist in Wilson could never reconcile himself to progressive education, and he was, he said, "appalled by the slackness of the training" he found in many of these ostensibly liberating institutions.)

But the glimpses that Wilson had, through his friends at school, of the larger WASP world only strengthened his conviction that as a class the WASPs would never effect the kind of regeneration the young Henry Adams and the young Theodore Roosevelt sought.* The older sister of his Hill roommate Larry Noyes had married the railroad man Henry deForest—they were to be the maternal grandparents of Edie Sedgwick—but although Wilson found their estate at Cold Harbor to be in every detail "perfect: house and grounds, pictures, furniture and dinners," he thought the family preoccupied with trifles. At the same time he was struck, in visiting the houses of his friends, "by the extent to which such families constituted a genuine 'Establishment.' They were likely to be intermarried, and they seem to have had more or less in their hands all the more respectable public activities." But it was so much respectable impotence.

Wilson rejected a conventional WASP career, but he was not reconciled to bohemian disorder, and as he finished his wine on that summer night in 1927, he had a fleeting vision of working "with the dead for allies, and at odds with the ignorance of most of the living," to rebuild the old humane "edifice" that had been "so discouragingly reduced to ruins." Warmed by the thought, he was on the point of leaving the restaurant when he collided with the "bulky pink people who had stopped laughing and were dancing to the radio."

WILSON HAD GOTTEN HIS JOB at the *New Republic* because Walter Lippmann wanted to give up editorial chores and devote himself to writing books. In the summer of 1927 the prodigy whom Theodore Roosevelt had once pronounced "on the whole the most brilliant young man of his age in the United States" was working on a book and writing editorials for the *New York World*, the paper he had joined in 1922. Lippmann was a meticulous man, orderly in everything from his clothing to his prose style. "Really, nothing more correct could be imagined than the home life of the Lippmanns," Wilson wrote after dining with Walter and his wife Faye, and disheartened by their "extreme conventionality," he "fled to the Village and assisted at the latter phases of an ignoble studio party, where a mixed and ribald company were doing a little serious drinking." Lippmann, for his part, shrank from bohemia. He would rise at five, work on his book in a

---

* Wilson described the young, reform-minded Roosevelt as an "attractive and even inspiring" figure.

sound-proofed study with the desk facing away from the window, write an editorial for the newspaper, go into the office, and come home to turn once more, after a bath and dinner, to the book; on weekends he would escape to Wading River on the north shore of Long Island. He was, in early middle age, good-looking, engrossed in his work, in touch with the powerful, and looked up to as a sage. Yet he felt a "vacancy" in his life.

In his books *Public Opinion*, published in 1922, and *The Phantom Public*, which appeared in 1925, he had been perplexed by the problems of democracy. "My own mind has been getting steadily anti-democratic," he wrote Learned Hand in 1925. "The size of the electorate, the impossibility of educating it sufficiently, the fierce ignorance of these millions of semi-literate, priest-ridden and parson-ridden people have gotten me to the point where I want to confine the actions of majorities." He toyed with the idea of an *élite*: superior souls capable of correcting the passions of the "bewildered herd." This, of course, was a long-standing WASP preoccupation, and Lippmann himself was something of a WASP in spirit: "through his marriage, his social life, his professional contacts," his biographer Ronald Steel observed, he saw himself as part of the "dominant white Protestant culture." In *Public Opinion* he envisioned a "specialized class" of mandarin experts capable of managing problems too complicated for the mass of misinformed citizens to grasp; in *The Phantom Public* he spoke of intelligent "insiders" whose access to superior information would allow them to make the complex machine work. These benevolent "insiders" had more than a little in common with the class of public-service preppies WASP educators like Endicott Peabody were trying to form; the Harvard and *New Republic* liberal Bruce Bliven pointed out how much Lippmann's insiders resembled, too, the "new order of samurai" proposed by H. G. Wells in *A Modern Utopia*, "an aristocracy of mind and character" whose members were "dedicated to making democracy work for the best, whether the populace wants it or not . . ."

But in his new book—it would be published in 1929 as *A Preface to Morals*—Lippmann went beyond his old concerns to seek the intellectual's Holy Grail, a solution to the problem of "modern man's discontent." The rebels and emancipators had promised that the "dissolution of ancient habits" would "restore our birthright of happiness." But those who had been liberated from conventions, taboos, gods, and priests were not as "serene and composed" as they had expected to be. Man had defied God, and had "become very nervous." Women had "emancipated themselves from the tyranny of fathers, husbands and homes," and with the "expensive help of a psychoanalyst" were "enduring liberty as interior decorators." The young were "world-weary at twenty-two," and the masses drugged with inferior pleasures.

Lippmann identified the problem, but his solution, what he called a "religion of the spirit," one that human beings would be moved to practice as science made them more rationally disinterested, was pretty thin gruel: it was his mentor Santayana's poetic conception of the spiritual life debased into the prose of a gifted wonk. Santayana argued that spirit, if it grows out of our organic, fleshly life, also liberates us from it, allowing us to participate in what he calls an ideal realm "infinite in extent and variety." Anyone may experience this "continual sense of the ultimate in the immediate." A saint will deliberately cultivate spirit, yet spirit may also "crop out marvelously in the sinner, as it may in the child or the poet." But most people, if they are to touch the eternal—if they are to attain to this "play-life" which is also our "true life"—require imaginative stimulants: thus "established morality and religion, by protecting the eye from too much distraction and fixing it on noble objects, may make a better soil for spirit" than more profane ways of living. Some of these poetries, Santayana thought, are more satisfactory than others, and he felt pity for a young English clerk of his acquaintance whose desire for spiritual insight led him to embrace the Irvingites, a religion recently invented by Thomas Carlyle's friend Edward Irving. Had the clerk's "connections and education been more fortunate," Santayana said, "he might have become a high Anglican or a Catholic . . ."

Santayana saw at once that Lippmann's new-made religion was anemically inward: it divorced the spiritual life from all that ritual wine and moral poetry* that enabled most people to find it. By confining his religion to the "ultimate reaches of contemplation," Lippmann had puritanically severed spirit from the music that mediates between the two realms between which we are all crawling, the *vita activa* and the *vita contemplativa*. He "rises at once," Santayana wrote, "from the ruins of Christianity into the empyrean," and the empyrean, if it might, for some, be the ultimate end of the moral life, can hardly be its foundation. Lippmann's gospel of nerdery was, Santayana thought, less a prologue to morals than an epilogue. It was not the sort of thing that could reinspire what

---

* By morals Santayana meant not merely ethical commandments but the larger tapestry of customs and manners, *mœurs* and *mores*, myth and memory, that do something to reconcile people to the constraints of life: the higher forms of morality were for him a kind of poetry that enabled human beings to get through existence with a degree of dignity.

the German sociologist Max Weber called a disenchanted world: there was no chant, no cantation, in it.

Yet *A Preface to Morals* impressed such high WASPs (native or honorary) as Bernard Berenson and Mr. Justice Holmes. Edmund Wilson admired it as a foil to the High Church prose of T. S. Eliot's *For Lancelot Andrewes: Essays in Style and Order*, which had excited Tories that year with its brief for royalism, classicism, and Anglo-Catholicism. At the same time Wilson recognized that there was a "certain unreality" in Lippmann's book, a bloodless abstraction from life. It did nothing to answer Emerson's question of how to live a day nobly. It was no less blind to what another student of regeneration, Lippmann's Harvard contemporary Van Wyck Brooks, called "that intensification of the poetic view of life" that had in the past made it possible for citizens to revive a despairing city. Lacking such a mysticism, America was, Brooks said, littered with communities that had never become much more than transient camps, places that, after the first "current of enterprise" passed over them, grew "old as nothing else anywhere in the world is old, old without majesty, old without mellowness, old without pathos, just shabby and bloodless and worn out."

IF VAN WYCK BROOKS SAW what Walter Lippmann could not, it was because his own quest for a remedy was more desperate, and therefore more searching. He bore the wounds of his WASP upbringing in Plainfield, New Jersey, and the "sadness and wreckage" of his family's life there: a failed father, a mother who kept up appearances with money borrowed from relations, a brother who would later kill himself by walking in front of the commuting train. Brooks envied the newly arrived in America because, poor and despised as they often were, they had something Plainfield lacked. They had been "bred in a richly poetic, a richly creative soil," but although they desired "to live poetically and creatively" in their adopted country, they were like the "detached limbs of a tree." They might eventually become prosperous after the fashion of Plainfield, and at any rate they got enough to eat. But they were foredoomed to rot in some other department of the spirit, the part that requires form, the art which (another soul in search of regeneration has written) is "not a decorative adjustment, but a cup into which life can be poured and lifted to the lips and be tasted."

At the same time Brooks, in spite of his own Anglo-Catholic background and tendencies, had no patience for the poetry being pushed by Eliot, who was another of his Harvard contemporaries. (The Yard could be cruel; Brooks once expressed the wish that Eliot would "contract cancer and die in agony.") What Brooks wanted was a "national poetry," an American poetry, and he looked on Eliot almost as a traitor, one who had, in his European morbidity, "rejected the American tradition in toto." The problem, as Brooks saw it, was that the two greatest poets America had produced, Emerson and Whitman, both suffered from the Puritan aloneness: theirs was not a music that could build a city or keep it in working order.*

"WE HAD COFFEE AT THE Iruña, sitting in comfortable wicker chairs looking out from the cool of the arcade at the big square. After a while Bill went to write some letters and Cohn went over to the barber-shop. It was still closed, so he decided to go up to the hotel and get a bath, and I sat out in front of the café and then went for a walk in the town. It was very hot, but I kept on the shady side of the streets and went through the market and had a good time seeing the town again . . ."

A barbarian from the North and the West, Ernest Hemingway came down to the old civic places of Southern Europe (which began for him at Paris) to penetrate their mysteries. His people were originally from Yorkshire in the north of England, where Constantine assumed the purple in July 306 and afterward, as emperor, hastened the conversion of the Roman Empire to a Christian poetry not unmixed with remnants of the superseded pagan one. In time the family that became the Hemingways forsook Yorkshire for the New World. Anson Tyler Hemingway, Ernest's father's father, was born in East Plymouth, Connecticut, his family having come to America in the seventeenth century from Doncaster in the West Riding. Ernest's mother's father was also from Yorkshire, having been born in Sheffield in the West Riding. Ernest himself was born, in July 1899, in Oak Park, a suburb of Chicago. His father was a doctor who had attended Oberlin College and committed suicide; his mother, Grace, was musical.

---

* Brooks overlooked Emily Dickinson, but she, if anything, lived more deeply than Emerson and Whitman in the American aloneness: none of the three is a poet of civic communion in the way, for example, Aeschylus or Dante is. Americans have, of course, the civic poetry of the visionary presidents, but if the orations of Jefferson or Lincoln or Reagan changed the way Americans saw their country and conceived it imaginatively, it was not the kind of music that could help them to get through the day or live it nobly. The poetry of the mystic presidents is a poetry of the American nation, and not of the innumerable communities that compose it.

WASPs may be pure (Cotty Peabody), ornate (Henry Adams), or grotesque (Pierpont Morgan). The Hemingways were casual. They summered not in Maine but at Horton Bay in Michigan; and Ernest was sent not to a WASP seminary in New England but to Oak Park High School. Yet probably no one ever took the WASP fear of neurasthenic effeminacy more closely to heart than Ernest, and eschewing the ivory-tower daintiness of college boys he went, not to Oberlin or Harvard, but to a job covering cops and hoodlums as a reporter on the *Kansas City Star*. But there was a war on and he wanted to be in it. He volunteered as a Red Cross ambulance driver, for he was (much like a too-bookish Harvard sissy) myopic and could not be admitted to regular service. He was commissioned a second lieutenant in the Army and posted to an ambulance unit on the Italian front, where he was badly wounded; in the hospital he and his nurse, Agnes von Kurowsky, fell in love.

Coming home he found work on the *Toronto Star Weekly* and married a girl called Hadley Richardson. Always impatient of Henry James and his "snobbish, difficultly written shit," he was yet faster than James in quitting inartistic America; as soon as practicable he and Hadley decamped to Paris, where Ezra Pound, fresh from midwifing Eliot's *The Waste Land*, took him up. "Hats off, gentlemen, a genius!" For in spite of his sporting exterior, Hemingway was a daemonic poet, one whose power was felt even before he published his first serious work.* "The only [other] person I have ever known," his fellow poet, Archibald MacLeish, remembered, "who could exhaust the oxygen in a room the way Ernest could was Franklin Delano Roosevelt." He crushed Scott Fitzgerald and unnerved James Joyce. "Well, here comes James Joyce the writer, drunk again with Ernest Hemingway," Nora Joyce said when the two men came in after a spree. The raw force of Hemingway depressed Joyce and made him wonder whether his own art was not "too suburban." Mrs. Joyce smiled. "Ah," she said, "Jim could do with a spot of that lion hunting." Bernard Berenson, who would become Hemingway's pen pal, felt himself a pretentious "muff" in comparison; and Lionel Trilling, after reading Lillian Ross's profile in the *New Yorker* ("How

---

* "Most people don't think of Hemingway as a poet," Wallace Stevens wrote, "but obviously he is a poet and I should say, offhand, the most significant of living poets so far as the subject of EXTRAORDINARY ACTUALITY is concerned." Stevens, whom Hemingway punched out at Key West in 1936, proposed his sparring partner for a lectureship in poetry at Harvard.

Do You Like It Now, Gentlemen?"), all but flung the magazine at his wife, Diana. "And you expect *me* to be a novelist?"[*]

HEMINGWAY WOULD HAVE MOCKED HENRY Adams had he known him personally, and he once spoke of his readiness to see T. S. Eliot "ground to a fine powder." But in his first book, *in our time*, he was as preoccupied as any pure or ornate WASP with the unregenerate.

> They shot the six cabinet ministers at half-past six in the morning against the wall of a hospital. . . .

> The picador twisted the stirrups straight and pulled and hauled up into the saddle. The horse's entrails hung down in a blue bunch and swung backward and forward as he began to canter, the *monos* whacking him on the back of his legs with the rods. . . .

> They hanged Sam Cardinella at six o'clock in the morning in the corridor of the county jail. . .

"We have lived very quietly, working hard," Hemingway wrote Edmund Wilson from Paris shortly after *in our time* was published, "except for a trip to Spain, Pamplona, where we had a fine time and I learned a lot about bull fighting, inside the ring." The next year he went to Pamplona again—it was his third visit—with Hadley and a group of friends. There was Bill Smith, whom he had known since he was a boy in Horton Bay, Donald Ogden Stewart, a Yale graduate who would write the screenplay for *The Philadelphia Story*, and Harold Loeb, a Princeton alumnus who ran a literary magazine called *Broom*. Loeb's friend Lady Twysden

---

[*]   Hemingway tried to reassure Berenson that his writing was worthwhile even though it had emerged from a sissified life. But when he was being candid he said that the only modern writer who was man enough to take him was Tolstoy. Lillian Ross, in her *New Yorker* profile, remembered Hemingway mentioning a would-be war writer who "was apparently thinking of himself as Tolstoy, but who'd be able to play Tolstoy only on the Bryn Mawr field hockey team. 'He never hears a shot fired in anger, and he sets out to beat who? Tolstoy, an artillery officer who fought at Sevastopol, who knew his stuff, who was a hell of a man anywhere you put him—bed, bar, in an empty room where he had to think. I started out very quiet and I beat Mr. Turgenev. Then I trained hard and I beat Mr. de Maupassant. I've fought two draws with Mr. Stendhal, and I think I had an edge in the last one. But nobody's going to get me in any ring with Mr. Tolstoy unless I'm crazy or I keep getting better.'"

was keen to join them. An "alcoholic nymphomaniac," as Hemingway described her, she was the daughter of a solicitor in the North Riding of Yorkshire who had acquired her title through her second marriage to Sir Roger Twysden, baronet.

"Everybody's sick. I'm sick, too," says Georgette, the prostitute in *The Sun Also Rises*. But in the Basque country there is health. There "was a big river off on the right shining in the sun from between the line of trees, and away off you could see the plateau of Pamplona rising out of the plain, and the walls of the city, and the great brown cathedral." Pamplona was a walled town and Hemingway, in a dig at Santayana, said that he did not idolize a walled town. He knew "how much human shit there is on the ramparts and under the towers." But in *The Sun Also Rises* he conveyed the feeling people have when they reach such a place that it is the sort of place for which they have been reaching. Henry Adams felt it at Chartres and Henry James in any place where there were "old forms and pleasant rites" and "queer crooked silent corners behind cathedrals." What Hemingway wanted to know was how much in this feeling was real and how much mirage or speculative fable, the delusion of littérateurs and pansies.

As merely a report on civic infrastructure and its effect on the brain, *The Sun Also Rises* surpasses the briefs filed by Ruskin in *The Stones of Venice* and Burckhardt in *Griechische Kulturgeschichte*; Hemingway has a firmer grasp of the relation between the civic center and the countryside that feeds it, of the way in which the pastoral rhythms of the outlying villages and farms have been carried into the city, a place nourished not only physically by wine and cattle and grain, but mythically and spiritually. But he makes you feel, too, the way in which the builded poetry works on you, in the colonnades and arcades, the plazas and alleys, the wine shops and cafés: you are happy to linger there, with the result that you see things you would not otherwise have seen.

Jake Barnes, Hemingway's mouthpiece in *The Sun Also Rises*, says that the first meal in Spain is always a shock. Some memory of the old sacramentalism of life lingers in the feast Montoya gives the travelers after they reach the hotel. "You have to drink plenty of wine," Barnes says, "to get it all down." The ritual poetry reaches its peak in the fiesta of San Fermín the martyr, with its commedia dell'arte tug at the passions. "The festival requires style," the Dutch historian Johan Huizinga has written. "If those of modern times have lost their cultural value, it is because they have lost style." But style survives in the fiesta of San Fermín, not yet wholly stomped out under the cloven hoof of the tourist; the mysticism of masks, incense, chaunts, and effigies, of minstrel and jongleur, is still potent. "The things that happened could only have happened during a fiesta," Jake Barnes says.

"Don't look at the horses, after the bull hits them," Jake says to Brett Ashley, as Hemingway calls Lady Twysden in the book, while they wait for the bullfight to begin. "Watch the charge and see the picador try and keep the bull off, but then don't look again until the horse is dead if it's been hit." At the center of every sheepfold is the tragic circle, the sacrificial ring. It was rawer in Pamplona than in classical Athens, where during the festival of the bull-god, Dionysus, the procession of bulls was followed not by a bullfight but by the dramas of Aeschylus and Sophocles. In Pamplona human blood might be actually as well as artistically spilt, for bullfighting, Hemingway said, "is the only art in which the artist is in danger of death," is a participant in the blood-sacrifice he offers up. An air of tragic fatality overhung the city as the poetry approached its climax and "the music broke wildly" over the populace, a "feeling of things coming that you could not prevent happening."

Charles Sweeny, the soldier of fortune, said that Hemingway, with all his Yorkshire and Illinois breeding, was a Mediterranean type. More probably than any other poet, he interpreted the experience of the old forums for the neurotic suburbanite. Still he was an honest reporter who did not exaggerate the cathartic benefits of his cure. Jake Barnes and his friends are at the end of *The Sun Also Rises* unhealed and unredeemed. But Hemingway himself continued to spend much of his life in places like Pamplona. He felt better in them, even though he knew they could not readily exorcise the incubi and succubae of a certain kind of damaged soul.

IT IS REMARKABLE HOW OFTEN you find the modern artist or intellectual (fragments of a personality originally whole) homesick in the way the way WASPs like Hemingway and Henry Adams were for spaces in which a living poetry was made: Cyril Connolly slouching wistfully about Provençal towns, William Morris catching his first glimpse of Rouen ("then still in its outward aspect a piece of the Middle Ages: no words can tell you how its mingled beauty, history, and romance took hold on me"), Proust wandering in the *calli* and *campi* of Venice, feeling himself "like a character in the Arabian Nights." Picasso was always returning, in imagination, to the play-centers of Andalusian villages, to the magic-lantern world of the guitar and the strolling player, the market whore and the masked comedian. He went so far as to conceive an imaginary village that he called Navas de Malvivir, the Vale of Evil Living, working out to perfection the prurient gossip of the villagers, the cynicism being, one must conclude, but the loincloth of his love.

Such misplaced characters were drawn to clowns, acrobats, jugglers, and *saltimbanques,*[*] to strolling players and the stock characters of the commedia dell'arte: Watteau's Pierrot, Fellini's Zampanò, the sad clowns of Daumier, Picasso's Harlequins, Goya's comedians. Sometimes the figures are masked, and often they are slightly sinister; in the painting of Watteau, they have a childish innocence that is perhaps more disconcerting. In one mythology they are a remnant of the Romany-gypsy diaspora, in another they descend from the priests and seers of antiquity, who in the fall of paganism assumed the garb and manner of circus performers and itinerant players, of jugglers and mimes, charlatans and magicians. Mysterious crimes were not infrequently attributed to the players, and gave rise to legends that endowed them with the lurid powers of goblins, witches, werewolves, or vampires, the forms of which they were said to be able to assume at will. Such legends appealed to a vein of morbid sentiment in those who were estranged, as high WASPs themselves were, from their own way of living. But surely Baudelaire was right when (in his meditation on the degradation of an old *saltimbanque*) he fingered the chief element in the clowns' appeal: beneath the mask of gaiety they are sad. He found in the *clown triste* an image of his own displacement.

WASPs who were attracted to the old commedia dell'arte spaces felt a similar displacement, an estrangement from an age that had little use for what they conceived to be their gifts. Yet the revolution that left them feeling disinherited was for the most part a benign one. Moveable type and printed books freed people from the tyranny of place. A person who has learned to read, and who can get hold of books, ceases to be dependent solely on his immediate community for information, diversion, and imaginative escape. This was liberating, and at the same time isolating. With the appearance of the printing press, the playground began its migration away from the play-space in the center of town. In a short time the old civic forums became, in Balzac's words, as "stale as stagnant water."

---

* *Saltimbanques* and *saltimbanchi* (bench leapers) were itinerant showmen (*banquistes*): together with *tumbestres* (dancers, tumblers), *funambules* (tightrope walkers), magicians and fortune tellers, they contributed to the atmosphere of the old civic place.

Subsequent innovations—the railway, the telegraph, the moving picture—made them staler still.

Balzac himself told the story of talent's escape from the rotting provinces. Lucien de Rubempré, the young hero of *Illusions perdues*, was born in Angoulême, a city of some 28,000 souls in the southwest of France. His father, before his death, had been a pharmacist called Chardon; Lucien took his mother's name, Rubempré, in order to claim an aristocratic lineage. His talents were such as might have been the ornament of a small place. But provincial centers like Angoulême were by this time culturally obsolete, and young Lucien went to Paris, where he ends by hanging himself. Five or six centuries earlier, it might have been different: a town of some 30,000 souls was for Dante the center of a world, a place from which he had no desire to escape, and from which he was parted only under a de facto sentence of death. After he was banished from Florence, he was, indeed, able to *live* at Verona and Ravenna. But he longed to return to the place where he says (with the pardonable exaggeration of a patriot) that, before the wolves came, the citizens (*cittadini*) lived beautifully in the ancient circle (*cerchia antica*) of faithful citizenship (*fida cittadinanza*)—a "fair sheepfold, where a lamb I slumbered."

In their own yearning for that defunct sheepfold, WASPs like Ernest Hemingway and Henry Adams were quarrelling with history, a history that had outgrown the old places and their magic circles, just as it had outgrown the need for the people whose artistry *made* them places. A handful of metropolitan virtuosi now supplied myths for millions. The high WASP could not accept this; he or she could not be easy in a world in which *no* place mattered in the way the old places mattered, in which no place could be what Florence was for Dante, the center of a world. For if history has outgrown such places, the human soul has not. Or so the high WASP believed. He or she was, at heart, a young person who wanted to return to the provinces.

Franklin Roosevelt delivers his sixth fireside chat in September 1934.

TWENTY-EIGHT

Fear Itself

*Quella medesma voce che paura
tolta m'avea*

That very voice that took
away my fear . . .
—Dante, *Paradiso*

After Eleanor Roosevelt discovered Franklin's affair with Lucy Mercer, she went regularly to Rock Creek Cemetery in Washington to sit before the grave of Clover Adams. Face to face with the shrouded figure sculpted in Clover's memory by Augustus Saint-Gaudens, she pondered the similarities between her own life and that of Clover, each betrayed by a man unfaithful in mind or body or both.

Eleanor came away from these meditations determined to find a new life for herself, though Franklin, the betrayer, would remain part of it. It is said that she offered him "his freedom," a divorce that would allow him to marry Lucy, whom he undoubtedly loved. It is possible that he would have liked to do just that. But he could not leave Eleanor without sacrificing both his future in politics and his income, for divorce was unacceptable in a public man in those days, and his mother, Sara, threatened to cut off his funds should he abandon his wife. And Eleanor was willing to stay.

The marriage survived; and when Franklin was stricken, in the summer of 1921, by the virus at Campobello, Eleanor nursed him in the hours when not only his legs but even his bladder and bowels failed. It was as close as he was ever to come to knowing the despondency that afflicted so many of his tribe. Dante was of no use to him in the crisis, but his old headmaster, Endicott Peabody, seems to have been. John 17:19 was the text on which the Rector preached most frequently: "And for their sakes I sanctify Myself, that they also may be sanctified by the truth." Sanctification, Peabody told his boys, was "not a question of just resisting evil" for one's own sake, but of striking out against it for the sake of others. This, he pointed out, is what the hero of Matthew's Arnold's poem, "Rugby Chapel," does. Arnold of Rugby (the poet's father) suffers, but in spite of his wounds he gives his hand to others. For the very dejection that tries one's spirit enlarges one's sympathies; it enables one to comprehend the plight of those whom one is obliged to help.* As for the trials one undergoes, they come, Peabody believed, from God. ("For whom the Lord loveth he chasteneth.") The idea that the chastened and sanctified soul is better able to meet its appointed destiny—to be of service in the pursuit of a larger end—consoled Roosevelt in his own ordeal. He would later tell Frances Perkins that when he was first struck down by the virus he was "in deep despair, feeling God had abandoned him." But he came to believe that he had been "shattered and spared for a purpose beyond his knowledge."

---

* Dostoevsky similarly pointed to the difference between a merely passive acceptance of Christ's vision of faith, hope, and love and the active use of these gifts in the service of others. "Dostoevsky distinguished in the end between the yearning love which does nothing and submits," Alexander Boyce Gibson wrote in his study *The Religion of Dostoevsky*, "and the active love which has the power to save." In *The Brothers Karamazov*, Alyosha embodies this "vigorous and active" gospel of love, and the novel culminates in the schoolboys whom he has mentored embracing the idea of service and sacrifice envisioned in John 17:19.

The champagne in his nature reasserted itself. He and Eleanor fell into what has been variously described as an armed truce and a political partnership founded on mutual respect. She, for her part, obtained not merely a room of her own but a cottage—it was built with Franklin's assistance at Val-Kill in Hyde Park, and it symbolized her new life: a place where she could pursue her causes in the company of friends who, contemptuous of convention, embodied the spirit of the New Women of the era. It was her own version of Gertrude Whitney's studio and Virginia Woolf's "quiet room," with its dignities of "luxury and privacy and space." It even had a swimming pool. Franklin, too, fashioned a space of his own, or rather several. He spent much of his time on boats in Florida, where sun and rum and fishing with old school chums were his medicines, and in a clinic at Warm Springs in Georgia, where he took the therapeutic waters. At the same time he attempted, with less success, to be a capitalist, investing in enterprises that mostly failed. His genius lay not in finance but in politics, and in 1928 he was elected governor of New York. A year later the stock market crashed.

ON NOVEMBER 8, 1932, ENDICOTT Peabody voted for Herbert Hoover. ("I do not consider personal relations when I am casting my vote for a Government official," he told Ellery Sedgwick.) He stayed up late into the night listening to the election returns on the radio, and early the next morning he made his way to the corridor that adjoined his house and opened the door to the suite of the senior prefect.

"Roosevelt, wake up!" he barked as he switched on the light.

"Yes, sir," the young Franklin D. Roosevelt Jr., replied.

"Your father was elected president of the United States yesterday. The first Groton student to be so honored and very much in the tradition of Groton School . . ."

The hope of Grover Cleveland, whom the boy Franklin had met in the White House many years before, was unfulfilled. "My little man," President Cleveland is supposed to have said as he placed his hand on little Franklin's head, "I am making a strange wish for you. It is that you may never be president of the United States." The botched laying on of hands contributed to the aura of inevitability in which Roosevelt's career became enveloped, that of a man of destiny. But at the time of his elevation to the presidency many were skeptical of his actual abilities, among them Walter Lippmann, who dismissed him as an "amiable boy scout," a "pleasant man" without "any important qualifications for the office" he was to hold. (Reproached, later, for this apparent error of judgment, Lippmann said that he would maintain to his "dying day" that what he said "was true of the Franklin Roosevelt of 1932.") The critics were so far right: the new president had no deep understanding of the intricacies of policy or of the rival claims of different schools of political economy. But as he rode up to the Capitol on March 4, 1933, to take the oath of office, Franklin Roosevelt had a keen insight into his country's needs in the disaster that had befallen it.

"FROM A DISTANCE, THE DOME of the Capitol looks like gray polished granite, and against this bleak sky of March, it has a sort of steel-engraving distinction." So Edmund Wilson thinks as he stands among the crowd waiting for a glimpse of the new president. "The people seem dreary, even apathetic," with the "numbness of life running out," for the "prosperity of America has vanished; even the banks don't know where the money is; even the banks say they have not got it; so they are simply shutting up, no more checks cashed; general dismay and blankness. . . ."

"What are those things that look like little cages?" someone in the crowd asks. "Machine-guns," a woman giggles. (The Army has set up machine-gun nests on the tops of buildings.) Soon Roosevelt's figure appears dimly on the platform moving through the mass of dignitaries. Somewhere among them, unknown to the crowd and (one hopes) to Eleanor, is Lucy Mercer. She is now Mrs. Winthrop Chanler Rutherfurd, and Franklin himself has arranged for her to be present at his investiture.[*]

Gripping the arm of his son James, he moves slowly to the rostrum in the stiff-legged, marionette-like movements he has mastered to simulate walking. He raises his right hand; his left rests on an old Roosevelt Bible printed in Dutch and opened to 1 Corinthians 13:13. After the chief justice, Charles Evans Hughes, administers the oath, Roosevelt turns to address his people. He has been shaped by WASP reformers and educators who believed, in William James's words, that the "mark of the beast" is fear, and who taught that grace is a quality of not being afraid. It is a faith that the new president himself put to the test, a decade

---

[*] After her engagement to Wintie Rutherfurd, Lucy asked Lily Polk to tell Franklin of the approaching marriage; she did not want him to learn of it from the newspapers. Lily and her husband, Frank Polk, were having tea with the Roosevelts when she mentioned the betrothal to Eleanor. Overhearing the words, Franklin, it is said, "started like a horse in fear of a hornet."

before, in the great trial of his life. Now the country itself is listless with dread and apprehension. And so he speaks.

"This great Nation will endure as it has endured, will revive and will prosper. So, first of all, let me assert my firm belief that the only thing we have to fear is fear itself—nameless, unreasoning, unjustified terror which paralyzes needed efforts to convert retreat into advance. . ."

DISCUSSING MONETARY POLICY WITH A group of senators, the president tossed back his head and laughed. "I experimented with gold and that was a flop. Why shouldn't I experiment a little with silver?" Roosevelt's New Deal policies were admittedly imperfect; the need for cash and credit, for lending and spending, to lubricate the seized-up gears of a broken economy was not so well understood in 1933 as it is today. But if Roosevelt was not, as Maynard Keynes thought, very "literate, economically speaking," he was an acute psychologist. What was needed, he believed, was action, even action that might later prove to have been mistaken; for action was the only way to restore confidence. "It is common sense," he said, "to take a method and try it: If it fails, admit it frankly and try another. But above all, try something."

The centerpiece of the early New Deal, the National Recovery Act of 1933, was in economic terms a mistake. A system of wage and price controls, the N.R.A., the historian Alan Brinkley writes, "utterly failed to stabilize industrial prices and production; its administrative structure dissolved in chaos; its legal authority was struck down by the Supreme Court . . ." Yet the N.R.A. Blue Eagles that appeared in shop windows throughout the country gave the impression that something revolutionary was being done. And the new president's extravagant optimism made it seem as though the revolution was working.

What Edmund Wilson called F.D.R.'s "unnatural sunniness," the cigarette holder at the jaunty angle, the exuberant laugh, the infectious blitheness, was part of his nature; he was one of those men who, William James said, "seem to have started in life with a bottle or two of champagne inscribed to their credit; whilst others seem to have been born close to the pain-threshold, which the slightest irritants fatally send them over." Sir Oswald Mosley, in the days before he became head of the British Fascists, sailed with Roosevelt in Florida and was struck by the way "this magnificent man with his fine head and massive torso, handsome as a classic Greek," radiated charm, though he was "completely immobile.'"* But if optimism was innate in Roosevelt, it was also a discipline at which he worked. Making his way, in 1936, under the spotlights to address the Democratic National Convention, he nearly fell on his face. The knee-lock on one of his leg-braces sprang open, the leg gave way, and the pages of his speech scattered on the ground. "There I was," he afterward said, "hanging in the air, like a goose about to be plucked, but I kept on waving and smiling, and smiling and waving." Out of the corner of his mouth he asked his son Jimmy to fix the brace. "Dad," he replied, "I'm trying to pick up the speech." "To hell with the speech. Fix the God-damned brace. If it can't be fixed there won't be any speech." And yet through it all, Roosevelt said, "I didn't lose a smile or a wave."

The actress Lillian Gish thought him a child of light, "dipped in phosphorous." "There is a sort of angelic sweetness about him," John Jay Chapman observed to his wife after encountering Roosevelt in New York. He was "calm, sparkling. . . . debonair and witty." "It's not possible," Nicholas Roosevelt said to himself as he watched his cousin splash about in the new White House pool: "This delightful, youthful-looking man in this pool cannot be President of the United States." Franklin was a past-master in enhancing the mood of those who came within his immediate orbit, yet it remained a question whether he could revivify an entire nation. As governor of New York he had experimented with radio broadcasts, and now, as president, he broke through rhetorical tradition to talk to his fellow citizens over the airwaves in a way that seemed as though he were sitting beside them. Eight days after taking office he gave the first of his presidential radio addresses. "I want," he said, "to talk for a few minutes with the people of the United States about banking. . . ." The fireside chats were easily the greatest innovation in presidential talk since Lincoln's orations in the Civil War. Roosevelt was not a master of English in the way Lincoln was; in his formal oratory the striking phrase often emerges from a clumsily assembled sentence. But in the fireside chats he deliberately eschewed the conventions of high oratory in favor of a simple conversational style; he gestured as though his listeners were physically present in the room. "His face would smile and light up," Frances Perkins said, so much so that he might have been "sitting on the front porch or in the parlor" with his auditors. The addresses were in fact carefully prepared, having

---

*   Moseley's taste in character is open to question; he found Hitler a compelling, even attractive figure, a "calm, cool customer, certainly ruthless, but in no way neurotic . . . with a gentle, almost feminine charm."

gone through numerous drafts: but they *seemed* unrehearsed. Nor was the voice less important than the words; it was confident, soothing, strong. It filled the room.

Yet the voice was unmistakably patrician. The young Saul Bellow, walking in Chicago and hearing it over the radios of cars whose drivers had pulled over to listen to the president, thought that the "odd Eastern accent" would in anyone else "have irritated Midwesterners." Instead they were reassured by it. F.D.R. was the most progressive leader to occupy the White House in the twentieth century: he was also the most deeply archaic. Not only did he speak after the fashion of a lord of the manor, he acted like one. When he declared that he was going to be "President of all the people," Edmund Wilson said, he "meant that, as lord of the nation, he was going to take responsibility for seeing that all the various ranks of people, as far as was in his power, were going to be given what was good for them." Dean Acheson, who was not without his own patrician conceit, disliked Roosevelt's airy, Whig magnifico condescension; it was not pleasant, he said, to receive from the squire of Hyde Park the "easy greeting which milord might give a promising stable boy and pull one's forelock in return." A morning briefing in the presidential bedroom was, Acheson thought, like a *levée du roi* at Versailles; a public servant intent on transacting the nation's business was expected to be amused when a Roosevelt grandchild, "leaning innocently against her grandfather, would suddenly clap her hand over his mouth in the middle of a sentence, smothering the rest of it." Acheson found the president's seigneurial style trying, but most Americans, theoretically egalitarian though they were, could not get enough of it. The progress of the American Republic from Ben Franklin to Franklin Roosevelt seemed itself to refute the founders' Enlightened theories of self-government. Roosevelt, every inch a king, was a good deal more naturally, instinctively royal than George III.

In 1939 Margaret Delano, the daughter of Roosevelt's cousin Lyman Delano, married a young Philadelphian called Anthony Joseph Drexel Paul Jr., who had been a classmate of Roosevelt's son Franklin at Groton and Harvard. During the reception that followed at Steen Valetje on the Hudson, Lewis Stuyvesant Chanler Jr., the nephew of Jack Chapman's wife Elizabeth, took his son Bronson aside. He wanted the teenager to shake the hand of the president. They found F.D.R. remote from the revelry, sitting almost alone, but for his bodyguards, on a terrace looking out over the river. Years later Bronson could not remember just what they had talked about; he rather thought Roosevelt joked about the rivalry between their respective schools, Groton and St. Paul's. But what made a deeper impression on him was the president's exit. As the open-topped car drove past the guests on the lawn, Roosevelt smiled and waved his hat. And to Bronson's astonishment, some of the guests began to boo, a chorus that grew steadily louder. The president, he said, "couldn't have missed it."

As the Depression diminished the capital of the WASPs and the New Deal taxed what remained of it, Roosevelt became a scapegoat for the anxiety of a class that found itself going downhill. Many WASPs failed; a few disgraced themselves trying to stave off failure. The most spectacular of the descents was that of Richard Whitney, the Groton and Harvard banker who had risen to be president of the New York Stock Exchange, but who had speculated unwisely, and being unable to meet his obligations had embezzled money from, among other institutions, the New York Yacht Club, of which he was treasurer. "No, not Dickie Whitney!" Roosevelt exclaimed when he learned that his old acquaintance had been charged by Thomas E. Dewey, the New York County district attorney. It was afterward claimed that when Whitney was taken to Sing Sing in the custody of the police, a gold Porcellian pig could be seen dangling from his watchchain. (The photographs in *Life* do not bear this out.) In jail he was visited by his old headmaster, Endicott Peabody, who also sent him a left-handed baseball mitt. (Once the captain of the Groton nine, Whitney now played on the Sing Sing team.) He "did wrong," the Rector said, "but he has paid the penalty. He needs help and friendship and is entitled to a fresh start."

If Whitney betrayed the *mores* of his class, Roosevelt himself was for many WASPs the greater apostate, the figure whom they would have liked to go down to the Trans-Lux to hiss, as the upper-crust characters in Peter Arno's *New Yorker* cartoon propose to do. It was Peabody who pointed out that Roosevelt was, in fact, carrying on the reformist traditions of his class. Though the Rector was a Republican and the founder of a school that depended on capital, he came to support the New Deal even though, as he conceded in a letter to Roosevelt, his "knowledge of economic principles" was not "sufficient to enable me to form an adequate judgment of all the policies of your government." A student of John Frederick Denison Maurice, the Anglican theologian and Christian Socialist who influenced Vida Scudder, Peabody wanted Groton to be an instrument of reform in a society that would yet preserve all that was useful in capitalism, and he saw in Roosevelt's program the embodiment of his own ideals of service and mindfulness of the needs of others. (John 17:19 again.) "I do most heartily rejoice," he wrote to Roosevelt, "that there should be throughout the land a greater emphasis laid upon the duty of the citizen to the community and this even among those who were formerly considering only their own interests."

But the gulf between reform WASPs and Wall Street WASPs was now much wider than it had been in the days when Theodore Roosevelt and J. P. Morgan quarreled about the *Northern Securities* case. Differences in policy had once coexisted with gentlemanlike courtesy, but under the pressures of the thirties good manners failed. WASPs hostile to Roosevelt might not have wanted to see his head on a pike, but they did make it expedient for him to resign his membership of the Knickerbocker Club.* The aged Peabody did what he could to smooth the waters, and after one of his visits to Dick Whitney at Sing Sing, he defended the president at a Groton dinner in the Union Club. "I believe Franklin Roosevelt to be a gallant and courageous gentleman," he told the assembled graduates. "I am happy to count him as my friend."

His words were met with silence.

ONE EVENING IN THE FALL of 1936 a young WASP entered the precincts of that choicest of academical habitats, King's College, Cambridge, and in the shadow of its apparently irreconcilable masonries, perpendicular Gothic and the eighteenth-century classicism of Gibbs, made his way to Webb's Building, where he climbed the staircase to the rooms of Maynard Keynes.

Michael Straight, the youngest child of Dorothy and Willard Straight, was about to be inducted into the Conversazione Society, better known as the Apostles. By birth an American, Straight had passed much of his life in England. Seven years after his father's death, his mother married Leonard Elmhirst, a Yorkshire gentleman and a disciple of the Bengali mystic Rabindranath Tagore. Afterward the couple devoted themselves to the restoration of a medieval manor in Devonshire called Dartington Hall, where Tagore detected a healing virtue in the springs and water beds. Here the Elmhirsts attempted to create an ideal community, an English Brook Farm; Michael remembered it as a sort of Greek city-state with terraced gardens and readings from Shakespeare. There was a progressive school, a farm, and provision for arts and crafts, all the work of the

---

* It was during Roosevelt's presidency that the Pot and Kettle Club at Bar Harbor, the fifty members of which were believed to control a not inconsiderable portion of the nation's wealth, replaced the club's toast to the president of the United States with a toast to the Constitution of the United States.

place being carried on amid a happy smashing of idols that went beyond anything Dorothy's sister-in-law Gertrude Vanderbilt Whitney or her friend Mrs. Franklin D. Roosevelt dreamed of. There were mixed-sex dormitories and showers, and in the first years of the school, the scholars were largely free to do as they pleased; the drama program, which was first rate, was directed by Michael Chekhov, the nephew of Anton.

Dartington Hall was evidently Dorothy's way of expiating the guilt that her fortune had fastened on her: it was meant to be an alternative to the kind of society in which her father, William Collins Whitney, had flourished and made his money. But there was, in the naïveté of the chatelaine, a whiff of Marie Antoinette playing the milkmaid, and the new idols she established in the pantheon of Dartington had their own drawbacks. There was the sexual mysticism of Freud (two of whose grandchildren were in the Dartington school), and there was the economic mysticism of Marx. Bernard Shaw, who was to proclaim Stalin "the greatest man alive" and Russia the "only country in the world in which you can get real freedom," came to Dartington, and Ivan Maisky, the Soviet ambassador to the United Kingdom, was a guest. After young Michael completed the school course in 1933, he went up to London to study in the School of Economics, where he rapidly fell under the spell of Soviet Communism, "carried along," he said, "in a powerful current."

The following year he entered Trinity College, Cambridge, where he studied economics under Keynes. He was, a contemporary remembered, "handsome, gifted, versatile, precocious, virile," a "combination of playboy and Sir Galahad," and his virtues were signalized by his induction, in Keynes's rooms, into the Apostles. The Society dated from the 1820s, when Tennyson and Hallam were initiated, and it soon became one of the proving grounds of the English intelligentsia. Doors opened easily to Apostles, who were known as Angels when they left Cambridge, but rather like the more intellectual WASPs across the ocean, these English scholars were perplexed by the problem of maintaining a humane way of life in an altered world. The cloisters of Cambridge had long been consecrated, Lytton Strachey said, to poetry and common sense; but a rift had opened up; the common sense of the technicians seemed to have got the better of the poetry of the artists. Alfred Marshall, a Cambridge man though not an Apostle, believed that his technical work as an economist would make the world more equitably prosperous. Yet to many Cambridge men there was something ominous in the new conquering discipline of economics, so closely bound up with the steamship, the railway, and the other innovations that were shaking mankind. As the world spun ever more rapidly down the grooves of change, the Apostle G. E. Moore, a young fellow of Trinity, stood up for poetry. In a book called *Principia Ethica*, he endeavored to prove that those "highly complex organic unities," art and friendship, are the most beautiful of life's goods, and that one need not feel guilty in cultivating them at the expense of the more prosaic ideals preached by men like Marshall.*

But the new poetry cultivated by the Apostles had its own limitations. Until the 1970s only men could be Apostles, and for many years what Keynes and Strachey liked to call the "higher sodomy" dominated the imaginations of Society at the expense of other ideals. And by the time Michael Straight swore his Apostolic oath of secrecy, a number of Apostles were less interested in constructing a humane forum for the cultivation of beauty than in furthering the causes of the Soviet Union. Straight was one of them. From the moment he joined the communists, the eyes of Moscow were on him; a rich, well-born, well-connected American could be useful to the Kremlin. Scarcely had he arrived in Cambridge when John Cornford, scion of an old Cambridge family connected by blood or marriage to Darwins, Sidgwicks, Balfours, Wedgwoods—the names of the intellectually distinguished "clerisy" families go on and on—asked him to join the Cambridge Socialist Society, which was controlled by the British Communist Party, itself controlled by Moscow.

Michael was soon a member of the Socialist Society and one of twelve students in the communist cell in Trinity College. Not for him a dull bourgeois career like that of his cousin John Hay "Jock" Whitney, the son of Michael's uncle Payne and aunt Helen (daughter of Henry Adams's best friend John Hay). Jock was a good boy, the best boy, "gentle, graceful, and wealthy," or so Ben Bradlee thought him. He was senior prefect of Groton, crew-cutted oarsman at Yale, star polo player with a four-goal handicap; at twenty-five, though he had just inherited twenty million dollars, he went dutifully to work as a clerk in Lee,

---

* Maynard Keynes was an Apostle divided between prose and poetry: the most influential economist of his age, he was at the same time a cultivated humanist and patron of the arts, and he was devoted to the little "collectivity," as he called it, of the Apostles, a forum of "contemplation and communion" consecrated to "beauty and truth." He spent his life, his biographer Lord Skidelsky has written, "zig-zagging between the two poles." Keynes seems to have been genuinely fond of Michael Straight, but unlike Straight he was far from seeing a solution in what he called the "complicated hocus-pocus" of Marxism, an "insult to our intelligence," a preposterous religion "founded on a silly mistake of old Mr. Ricardo's." The "class war," he said, "will find me on the side of the educated bourgeoisie."

Higginson, the firm in which his old headmaster, Endicott Peabody, had been employed before he was consecrated a priest.* While Jock was mastering the art of investing capital, Michael was exploring the art of destroying it, visiting the Soviet Union with a group of young communists on an Intourist trip arranged by a shadowy *mitteleuropäische* character, the Soviet agent Arnold Deutsch. Straight wore shabby clothes and asked one of his companions if he looked like a proletarian. "No," came the reply, "you look like a millionaire pretending to be a proletarian."

Another Trinity man on the Intourist trip made an impressive figure. He was tall, courteous, with a long face that tapered down to a sharp chin, the skin stretched tightly over a girlish overbite. With his concave chest and wax-paper complexion, Anthony Frederick Blunt had something of the appearance of an elegant cadaver. At twenty-seven he was a rising art historian; he appeared to be a creature of the British establishment. His father, an Anglican clergyman of evangelical tendency, descended from a cadet branch of the Blunts of Crabbet Park in Sussex; his mother, the daughter of a magistrate in the Indian colonial service, was second cousin of the Earl of Strathmore, the maternal grandfather of Queen Elizabeth II, and a friend of Queen Mary, the consort of King George V. Blunt himself, a bachelor don, had rooms in Nevile's Court in Trinity; his friend the poet Louis MacNeice thought them "coquettishly chaste," with "white panelling and Annuciation lilies," the setting for amusing parties with plenty of gin. Isaiah Berlin found Blunt charming and civilized; others thought him "slightly camp."

Blunt "took a close interest in me," Straight remembered. The young American was now entering his second year at Trinity and had been given rooms in Whewell's Court. An old, white-haired recluse lived above him. He would "feel his way like an old crab" down the staircase before venturing on a "brief outing in the winter sunshine, a long scarf covering his mouth and nose . . ." When the noise of Straight's gramophone disturbed him, he would rap the floor with his cane. But as winter gave way to spring, the rapping grew fainter, and after the old man died, two college porters bore his corpse away. It was only as one of the college bedders began to paint over the name beside the door that Straight realized who he was. But he "did not pause to mourn" A. E. Housman. The

---

* He also refused to allow his name to be printed in the *Social Register*, on the ground that the publication was undemocratic.

Victorian poet of *A Shropshire Lad* had nothing to say to a young WASP besotted with the new heaven and new earth of the Soviet Union.

As FRANKLIN ROOSEVELT WORKED TO preserve the democratic free state, Michael Straight, an exemplar of the fashionable radicalism that seduced so many WASPs, was drawn deeper into the Stalinist underworld. His college, Trinity, was the "center of Communism" in Cambridge, having spawned such characters as the bibulous *Zanni* Guy Burgess, who was mad for the proletariat and "intoxicated by Marxism," the historian Miranda Carter has written. "If you want to know about dialectical materialism," the Holy Grail of the Marxists, "come to me," Burgess would say. Burgess's friend Anthony Blunt was convinced that Marx's theories would not only solve the economic problem, they could also instruct the historian of art, illuminating such things as the way in which the foot of a Chippendale chair embodied the class struggle of Georgian England.

"Cambridge was still full of Peter Pans," MacNiece said after a visit to Blunt, "but all the Peter Pans were now talking Marx." Some were doing more than talking. In June 1934 Kim Philby, a twenty-two-year-old Trinity man and son of the Arabist St. John Philby, was propositioned by Arnold Deutsch on a bench in the Regent's Park in London. "You are a bourgeois by education, appearance and origin," Deutsch said. "You could have a bourgeois career in front of you—and we need people who could penetrate into the bourgeois institutions. Penetrate them for us!" Philby agreed to penetrate, as did Donald Duart Maclean, another Cambridge scholar and the son of the British Liberal politician Sir Donald Maclean. Burgess, who was not tapped by Moscow, resented having been left out in the cold; he "must have been one of the very few people," Philby said, "to have forced themselves into the Soviet special service." The N.K.V.D. in the end accepted him on the theory that, in the words of spymaster Alexander Orlov, the "majority of this country's most polished sons are pederasts," and he might prove useful in recruiting them. Burgess was instrumental in persuading Anthony Blunt to become a spy, and Blunt, after his recruitment, went to work on Michael Straight.

On a Wednesday in March 1931, Edmund Wilson wrote in the *New Republic*, three people tried to kill themselves in Brooklyn. There was Otto Reich, a nineteen-year-old German émigré who could not find work and was down to his last four dollars; he turned on the gas in his room in Bay Ridge. There was

Irma Meyer in Brownsville, two months behind with her rent and owing all the tradesmen money. "For food she had to go to the police station, where they gave her, once a week, some potatoes and onions and canned goods." Her children "were too young for this kind of food—they needed milk; but they told her at the police station she could feed them on boiled cabbage." She, too, turned on the gas. And there was Mr. Dimiceli, an electrician from Sicily who had lost his job. His family was "listening to the radio in the apartment of the woman below" when the youngest Dimiceli boy, coming up the stairs, "heard a shot from their own apartment."

In Lawrence, Massachusetts, where the power looms established in the 1840s by Abbott Lawrence and his partners in the Essex Company had paid dividends to generations of WASPs, Wilson found "hunger and cold and fatigue and hopelessness." The textile companies had announced a ten percent wage cut, and the workers struck. "The poverty of their homes is wretched," Wilson wrote. "The children who are old enough for school often cannot go for lack of shoes. If each child has a pair of his own—usually handed down from the next oldest one—the parents consider themselves lucky. Some of the families buy stale bread in bags . . ." In Ward, West Virginia, Wilson came upon coal miners living in company towns in "little flat yellow houses on stilts that look like chicken-houses." They seemed to him reduced "to the conditions of serfs," and their children had "so little to wear that they are sometimes more or less naked." They had "hardly ever eaten fresh meat or vegetables," and their diet consisted mainly of "sow belly, potatoes and pinto beans."

If WASPs in the Union Club in New York and at Steen Valetje on the Hudson opposed F.D.R. as too radical, other WASPs, among them Wilson and Vida Scudder, faulted him for being too mild.* In 1931 Wilson brought out *Axel's Castle*, his study of how Joyce and Proust, Yeats and Eliot, had through their writing "broken out of the old mechanistic routine" of modernity and momentarily revived the "hope and exaltation" of the Renaissance. But he was by this time as deeply absorbed in studying conditions in the United States and the lives of those of his fellow citizens who were suffering under the economic catastrophe. He welcomed the boldness of Roosevelt's first hundred days, the flurry of initiatives with which the president sought to relieve the emergency, but by 1934 the

---

* "The 'gradualism' of the New Deal, so absurdly dubbed socialistic, saddens me more than it cheers," Scudder wrote. "I am tired of hacking at the branch on which I sit; we must destroy the roots of that poisonous Upas Tree, the Profit System, and plant the Tree of Life—if only we can find its seeds."

"first splendor of the New Deal," he believed, had faded. The "President is still handling things so suavely, still showing himself so accomplished a politician," he wrote in *Modern Monthly*, "that it is hard to tell how firmly he grasps the problems involved in the experimentation which constitutes the New Deal." But like an anxious liberal to whom he spoke, Wilson doubted whether Roosevelt had any "far-sighted policy at all."

At the same time he believed, much as Michael Straight and Vida Scudder did, that "a fundamental 'breakthrough' had occurred" in Soviet Russia, and "that nothing in our human history would ever be the same again." It was the old WASP dream of regeneration, only with a new sheepfold as its object. The Soviet Union, Wilson contended, was creating a society "which will be homogenous and cooperative" in a way "our commercial society is not," a way of life that would make possible the "first really human society" in history.* In the 1932 election he voted not for Roosevelt or Hoover but for the communist ticket; around the same time, as he was walking in the East Fifties in Manhattan, it occurred to him "that nobody had ever presented in intelligible human terms the development of Marxism," the philosophy to which he looked to replace what seemed to him America's outmoded ideals of private initiative and individual liberty of action.

He set himself to study the intellectual origins of the Russian Revolution, and in 1935—the same year Michael Straight visited Russia—he made his own journey to the Soviet Union on a Guggenheim fellowship. There was some difficulty about the visa; Wilson's "freewheeling leftism" was suspect in Moscow. But in May he sailed from London on the steamer *Siberia*, and in Russia he worked hard to see what he wanted to see. Coming upon a beggar in the street, he concluded that "people who don't work they won't compel to work." Russians were permitted "to do as they please—not checked up by petty officials as in Germany and America." There was everywhere a "feeling of freedom," a "lack of self-consciousness." The Soviet policemen were "quite unlike grim domineering or stiff cops elsewhere," and they dealt with one in "friendly fashion." Indeed "relations between the police and the public" seemed to him "almost ideal." He knew that there was a secret police, but after all, he pointed out, workers in industrial America were "spied upon every moment," and a person who is "known to be engaged in pro-labor work" may be "followed on the train by a detective" and very likely "run out of town."

---

* Trotsky, in *Literature and Revolution*, envisioned the foundation of "the first truly human culture" on socialist principles.

In the diary he kept in Russia and in his book *Travels in Two Democracies*, published the following year, Wilson shrank from admitting the sinister aspects of a regime he everywhere saw. Stalin's face was ominously postered in all the streets and squares, yet the American tourist did not like to think that Russians trembled before their new Tsar.* A totalitarian exercise in which a banner was carried aloft—THANKS TO COMRADE STALIN FOR THE GOOD LIFE—seemed to Wilson "more sincere and impressive than any American parade" he could recall The same voluntary blindness colored his relations with D. S. Mirsky, the critic and man of letters whom he found living in "almost Dostoevskian lodgings" in a remote quarter of Moscow. Mirsky, who was descended from the prerevolutionary aristocracy, seemed to Wilson to embody the "permanent Russia." The world of Tolstoy's *War and Peace* still lived in him, and "Kiev and Novgorod and the Golden Horde (from whom he must have got his Tartar eyes) were not entirely remote." His "learning and information were enormous, exact, and wide-ranging," and he had written, in English, what Vladimir Nabokov would call the "best history of Russian literature in any language including Russian." Yet Wilson found Mirsky oddly "stiff and rather shy," with a reserve that made for "constraint" in conversation. Reading Wilson's diary, you see what its author did not want to see, that Mirsky was, in fact, terrified. He was doomed. He was descended from one of the ancient princely families known as *Ryurikovichi* that claimed descent from Rurik, the legendary founder of the Russian state; his father had been minister of internal affairs under Nicholas II, in which capacity he had supervised the Tsar's secret police; he had fought with the White Russians against the Bolsheviks in the civil war that followed Lenin's revolution; and—if all this were not sufficient to consign him to Lubyanka and the Gulag—he was an intellectual who in 1921 emigrated to England, returning a decade later after his conversion to Marxism. At their last meeting, Virginia Woolf, watching Mirsky's "eye brighten and fade," could not help thinking: "soon there'll be a bullet through your head." (If only his end had been so merciful.) Not long before Wilson encountered him, Mirsky had been accused, in *Izvestia* and *Pravda*, of deviating from the official line.

It is true that Wilson could not be wholly candid in the diary he kept in Russia for fear of police spies. (That in itself ought to have sobered him up.) But when,

---

* Visited by Stalin in 1935, his mother, Katherine, is said to have asked him, "Joseph, what exactly are you now?" "Well, mama, do you remember the Tsar? I'm something like a Tsar." "You'd have done better to become a priest."

safe in America the next year, he published an account of his trip in *Travels in Two Democracies*, he continued to sanitize the regime. He did, indeed, acknowledge "the Terror" under Stalin. The "atmosphere of fear and suspicion," he wrote:

> is really pretty oppressive. It has evidently become more tense since the Kirov assassination. A foreigner cannot talk to [Russians] about politics at all, least of all, about the Kirov affair. If you venture to ask anybody about it, they either refer you to the official statements, which are certainly extremely implausible, or start to explain and then break down, protesting that it is all very difficult for a foreigner to understand. If Americans discuss these matters at a gathering where there are Russians present, the Russians pick up books and begin to read. I came away from Russia knowing almost as little of Russian politics as I had when I had arrived.

But he went on to make allowances. Russia was "no worse" than the United States, and with an unwillingness to admit that the sheepfold he sought was less fair than he had supposed it to be, he said that "you feel in the Soviet Union that you are at the moral top of the world."

"POLITICAL TYRANNY," FRANKLIN ROOSEVELT DECLARED as he opened his campaign for reelection in 1936 at the Democratic convention in Philadelphia, had been "wiped out" in that city a hundred and sixty years before, on July 4, 1776. But a "new despotism," he told the delegates, had since arisen. A class of "economic royalists" had carved out fresh dynasties for themselves, impressing the "whole structure of modern life" into their "royal service."

It was not, Roosevelt later said, "until I reached the line about 'economic royalists' . . . and heard the mighty roar from the crowd that I knew I had them, so I gave them the business." Frances Perkins, who was present at Franklin Field for the address, was uneasy. "This is going to be used against him," she thought. The rhetoric was out of character; it was generally Roosevelt's custom, whether in his own house or in politics, to ease tensions with a charming geniality. (There was no shortage of tension in the Roosevelt household. Eleanor resented her mother-in-law, Sara, and the children resented both their father, who was overly absorbed in being Franklin Roosevelt, and their mother, who was overly absorbed in being Dickens's Mrs. Jellyby, full of philanthropic solicitude for others while neglecting her own offspring at home.) Yet now, as he prepared to run for a second term, F.D.R. deliberately stoked the fires. He did so partly to rally the faithful in what some believed would be a close race against Alf Landon of Kansas, and partly because he worried that his left flank was vulnerable. (Huey Long, with his "Share Our Wealth" plan, was dead, but a host of lesser figures sought to challenge the New Deal from the Left.) Yet Roosevelt spoke as he did, too, because he had been startled by the depth of opposition he had encountered from people of his own background. When he denounced, in Philadelphia, the "privileged princes" of capital, he knew very well that he was attacking the very sort of people whom he had known all his life, in the Hudson Valley, at school, in his clubs. He had expected his fellow WASPs to understand his fidelity to those ideals of Christian charity that they all theoretically shared. But instead he found them bitter against him. It was as though he were being rejected all over again by the Porcellian, was once more failing to become class marshal at Harvard and senior prefect of Groton.

In October he went further, identifying himself, at Madison Square Garden, with the "millions who never had a chance—men at starvation wages, women in sweatshops, children at looms," and he rebuked a WASP-dominated upper class that looked upon "the Government of the United States as a mere appendage to their own affairs." They "are unanimous in their hatred of me," he said, "and I welcome their hatred." For it was the hatred of those sunk in "selfishness" and "lust for power."

This passionate oratory did not, however, foreshadow an equally impassioned policy. The New Deal had crested the previous year with the passage of the Labor Relations Act of 1935. Better known as the Wagner Act, it altered the balance of power in America by endowing labor with new bargaining leverage—a "good democratic antidote," Roosevelt said, "for the power of big business." It is true that after he was reelected (in a landslide) he made a bold attempt to defang the Supreme Court—which had held various New Deal programs to be unconstitutional—with a proposal to enlarge the number of justices. Walter Lippmann accused the president of being "drunk with power," and in his 1937 book *The Good Society* he pointed to the dangers of the mandarin state for which the New Deal seemed to him to be laying the groundwork, the very sort of state he himself had once advocated in the pages of the *New Republic*.

The attempt to pack the court failed, and Roosevelt himself seemed to sense that he had gone far enough. Ever the sailor,* he tacked again. After an effort to forestall inflation led to another downturn—the recession of 1937–38—he worked toward a compromise between private initiative (favored by Wall Street WASPs) and government mandarinism (advocated by WASPs in the Theodore Roosevelt mold). It is a compromise that in some measure prevails to this day: a safety net or welfare state as embodied in the Social Security Act; the enforcement of antitrust law (as pioneered by trust-busters like the New Deal lawyer Thurman Arnold) to prevent anticompetitive monopoly; fair dealing in financial markets as policed by various regulatory bodies (staffed mostly by once or future Wall Street people); and Keynesian fiscal policies which, in Roosevelt's words, use the "public wealth" to "help our system of private enterprise to function" in times of distress.

The Rooseveltian compromise between capitalism and socialism has been much criticized. But whatever else it might have been, it was a retreat from the days when New Dealers such as Rexford Tugwell dreamt of "doing America over," of nationalizing the banks and corporations, of regimenting the economy along the lines of the Soviet Gosplan. Roosevelt sought not a true revolution but a middle way between those who, like his fellow WASPs Vida Scudder, Edmund Wilson, and Michael Straight, wanted a socialist state, and those who, like the WASPs who booed him at Steen Valetje, were pledged to an unregulated market.

---

* Along with golf clubs and tennis rackets, WASPs are enamored of sailboats. Anyone who has sailed with them must be impressed by the curious pleasure they derive from the deviousness by which they reach their ends. They can only rarely attain their goal by the shortest and most obvious way; the winds and the tides are too often in conspiracy against them. The sailor becomes used to indirection; he develops a certain guile and cunning. It must have been obvious to Roosevelt that Woodrow Wilson, with his landsman's intransigence, had never sailed a boat. And he suggested that Lincoln himself, the child of the prairies, lacked the requisite nautical patience when captaining the ship of state. Lincoln, he said, was a "sad man because he couldn't get it all at once—and nobody can."

A WASP radical, Whittaker Chambers helped mobilize forces that would doom the ascendancy of his kind.

TWENTY-NINE

The Terrors of the Earth

quand' io feci 'l mal sonno
che del future mi squarciò 'l velame . . .

when I dreamt the evil dream
that rent the veil of my future . . .
—Dante, *Inferno*

By this time Eleanor and Franklin lived mostly apart, with their own courts and harems. Her seraglio was dominated by her private secretary Malvina "Tommy" Thompson and by Lorena "Hick" Hickok, the poker-playing journalist: his by his assistants Marguerite "Missy" LeHand and Grace Tully, and by his cousins Daisy Suckley and Laura "Polly" Delano. Yet the couple, though they led separate lives, continued to have a good working relationship, and Eleanor was in many ways useful to Franklin. Her outspokenness made her a lightning rod, attracting thunderbolts that might otherwise have struck the president himself, even as her more fervid politics appealed to New Deal constituencies he could not afford to overlook. As a roving emissary, she reported to him about Blacks, Latinos, Native Americans, and others whose difficulties might not in the ordinary course of things have come to the attention of the president of the United States. He exercised, indeed, considerable ingenuity in finding remote places to which to dispatch her, leaving him free to drink and smoke after hours amid the humorous bantering he found relaxing, and to flirt with attractive women, among them the heiress Dorothy Schiff and Princess Märtha of Sweden, who through her marriage to Prince Olav of Denmark, heir to the throne of Norway, was the crown princess of the Norwegians.

But the peace between the president and his wife was somewhat precarious. Eleanor's incessant do-gooding and what Cousin Daisy called "a certain lack of humor on her part" wrought upon Franklin's nerves, and the barrage of virtuous "phone calls and letters distracted and upset him." Their daughter, Anna, who was known as "Sis," remembered how once her mother had the temerity to interrupt one of her father's cocktail hours. "Now, Franklin," she said as she came into the room with a stack of papers, "I want to talk to you about this." "Oh, God," Anna remembered thinking, "he's going to blow." And he did. "He took every single speck of that whole pile of papers, threw them across the desk at me and said, 'Sis, you handle these tomorrow morning.'" It was no wonder, as Cousin Daisy said, that Franklin "was easier" when Eleanor was away.

For unlike Franklin, Eleanor was a creature of guilt. Only she had by this time turned her conscience into a means of accusing other people's sinfulness. The New Deal was for her too timid, left too much evil untouched. The Soviet Union had gone further. As late as 1939 she looked on its innovations "as a positive force in world affairs," and she extended her patronage to the American Youth Congress, a communist front organization. But if Eleanor was what her biographer, Blanche Wiesen Cook, calls a "democratic socialist," she was also a WASP who had been educated by Mme. Souvestre in the poetry and high ideals of Allenswood, and who had known the rival White House on Lafayette Square over which Henry Adams presided as anti-president much as Clement VII presided at Avignon as antipope, with a rival court and rival ideals that mocked those of the impostors across the way.

One of her more curious projects, the model town of Arthurdale in West Virginia, was influenced by the two strands in her being, the one puritanical and altruistic, the other growing out of a desire to escape mere utility through culture. Arthurdale, a community for miners and farmers and their families, was conceived in the utilitarian spirit of Robert Owen's New Lanark in Scotland and the planned cities of the Soviet Union, but it owed something, too, to the WASP dream of humanely ordered space, as embodied in Henry Adams's equation of Chartres with a social ideal. Unfortunately Arthurdale, which was built with federal funds as well as donations from philanthropists such as Dorothy Whitney Straight Elmhirst, was to have more in common with a Soviet town than with Chartres. It was not simply that the flimsy houses did not fit their foundations. Arthurdale was meant to resemble a self-governing New England community, but in much of what they did the residents were subject to the mandates of remote administrators. They were obliged to raise their own crops, which proved difficult and left them dependent on government relief. And although most of them wanted a traditional education for their children, Eleanor imposed a progressive school in accordance with John Dewey's theories. Yet even putting to one side the mandarin regimentation, something was missing. Like Viola, the old civic places to which WASPs were drawn spoke in many sorts of music. But in Arthurdale there was only so much bureaucratic prose.*

In the spring of 1937 Michael Straight and his stepfather, Leonard Elmhirst, had tea with Franklin and Eleanor in the White House, and the four of them discussed the possibility of Michael's going to work in Washington, perhaps on the staff of the Federal Reserve Board or as a private secretary to the president himself. Elmhirst observed that Michael was both a student and friend of Maynard Keynes, whose stock was high in New Deal Washington, and the president seemed to think that the National Resources Planning Board was the "best place" for a young economist.

Afterward Straight returned to England to complete his course at Cambridge, and in June he drove down to London. He stopped in Oxford Street,

---

* Together with the so-called Greenbelt Communities—Greenbelt, Maryland, Greenhills, Ohio, and Greendale, Wisconsin—Arthurdale came eventually under the authority of Rexford Tugwell's Resettlement Administration, which skeptics described as the New Deal's Department of Utopia. The town was privatized in the 1940s.

where Anthony Blunt got in the car. They drove off to what Straight described as a roadhouse on the Great West Road near the aerodrome that is now Heathrow Airport. There Blunt introduced him to a man he called George, but who was in fact Arnold Deutsch. He ordered a beer and instructed Straight in such precautions as telephoning from public booths to avoid detection; he also explained to him the manner in which he would be contacted once he returned to America.

In October Straight was staying in his mother's apartment in Manhattan when the telephone rang.

"Mr. Straight?" said a thickly accented voice. "I bring you greetings . . . from your friends in Cambridge University . . ."

Straight was told to go to a nearby restaurant, where he presently found a small, puffy-lipped man with a warm smile.

"My name is Michael," the stranger said, "the same as yours . . . Michael Green."

Iskhak Akhmerov was an agent of the N.K.V.D. and was keen on Straight's finding work in Washington. The difficulty was that the young man's employment counselor, President Roosevelt, had in spite of his musings about the National Resources Planning Board been unable to find a place for him. Another expedient was hit upon. Straight drove to Arthurdale, West Virginia, where, as if by chance, he ran into Mrs. Roosevelt, who was making one of her periodic tours of the model village. Her Packard limousine became stuck in the mud, and Straight joined a group of miners in extricating it. Afterward she asked him to join her. "I would be a Communist," she said as they drove to meet a train she hoped to catch, "if I thought that Russia was comparable to America." He told of her of his interest in working in the State Department, and she, in turn, wrote a letter to Under Secretary of State Sumner Welles, an old friend of hers who had been a year behind her brother Hall at Groton and who had been page boy at her wedding to Franklin. He was now her husband's most trusted diplomat.

Straight was soon working as a temporary unpaid assistant in the Office of the Economic Advisor in the State Department and feeding government documents to Akhmerov. At the same time he insinuated himself in the social life of Washington. He dined with Dean Acheson and lived in his father's old clubhouse at 1718 H Street—the headquarters of the Family—where he got to know Joe Alsop. It was Alsop who helped him to find his next job, as an assistant to Thomas Corcoran—"Tommy the Cork," as F.D.R. called him—a prominent New Dealer and one of the president's speechwriters.

WASHINGTON WAS BY THIS TIME swarming with young idealists who, like Straight, were inspired by the Soviet example. The Depression seemed to them the death knell of capitalism, and with the collapse of the American economy the "great drift" of educated communists "from Columbia, Harvard, and elsewhere" had begun. So Whittaker Chambers would later write. He had himself anticipated the trend. In 1925, four years before the Crash, he joined the American Communist Party.

If the family of Henry Adams represented the higher verges of WASPdom and that of Edmund Wilson the respectable middle, the family of Whittaker Chambers belonged to its ragged lower fringe. His mother, Laha Whittaker, felt herself to have come down in the world. She had grown up in a house near Milwaukee's Yankee Hill, and she had later attended the Home School in Racine, which prepared its "students for Eastern Colleges," the graduates being "received at Smith and Wellesley without examination." But her father's business failed and she went, not to Smith or Wellesley, but on the provincial stage, touring with traveling theatrical companies; she later joined her parents in Manhattan, where they ran a lunch counter on West Twenty-third Street. It was here that she met her future husband, Jay Chambers, a young artist who was then working as an illustrator for the *New York World*.

Believing that she had married beneath her, living in the memory of former grandeurs, real or imagined, Laha "buried herself" in Lynbrook, the village on Long Island where she and her husband lived with their two boys, Whittaker (or Jay Vivian, as he was christened) and Richard. She made efforts to find a place among the "nice people" of the town, but with so little money it was hard for her to hold her head up among the local gentry. She was much alone, dreaming, in her shabby house, of a more genteel way of life, and looking to her boys to find a way back "to that upper-middle-class world which was, for her, the earthly paradise." So isolated that she held "desperate monologues with the walls," she insisted the more fiercely on her culture and breeding, which she did her best to transmit to her children. "The voices around me in my early childhood," Whittaker Chambers remembered, "were all gentle voices. Outright rudeness or meanness were unthinkable. Ours was a highly decorous life." Laha insisted as vehemently as Endicott Peabody ever did on grace of conduct. So thoroughly did she impress her code upon Whittaker that he was, he said,

never quite able to shake off its rigors. She began by explaining
to me that a gentleman, or, as she would say, "a man of breeding,"
is known not so much by what he does as by what he will not do.
First and foremost, he never imputes a base motive to anyone else.
If someone is rude to him, he assumes that the rudeness is unin-
tentional. If he knows that it is intentional, he acts as if it were not.
He never insulted anyone himself except by intention. He never met
anger with anger . . .

Proust's Marcel, studying the medieval quarterings of the Guermantes's scutch-
eons in *Remembrance of Things Past*, fantasizes that the Duchesse de Guermantes
will herself emerge from the feudal mists and take a fancy to him. But Whittaker Chambers had no desire to scale the social heights of WASPdom. His
estrangement was profound. "I am an outcast," he told himself when he was
still a teenager and spent days by himself wandering in the woods of what was then
the Brooklyn reservoir system. "My family is outcast. We have no friends, no
social ties, no church, no organization that we claim and that claims us,
no community. We could scarcely be more foreign in China than in our alien-
ation from the life around us."

His situation was at least as bitter as that of the young Van Wyck Brooks.
His father left the family for a time, sending slender remittances from New
York; his brother, like Brooks's, died by suicide. "We're hopeless people," Richard
Chambers said before he died. "We can't cope with the world. We're too gentle.
We're too gentle to face the world." Whittaker was entranced by the natural
beauty of western Long Island, with its tides and meadows and second-growth
woods, but the peaceable refuge it afforded him was tainted by its steady corruption. Visiting his brother's grave on New Year's Eve, he saw cars hurtling
"down the Merrick Road, filled with hooting, singing people. A bottle, tossed
from one car, shattered against the cemetery wall." The Merrick Road itself,
once lined with cherry trees that in the spring blossomed in fragrant whiteness,
was succumbing to the slovenliness of what Chambers called the Neon Age.

Other influences reinforced his sense of belonging to a dying breed in an
altered world. His grandfather James Chambers, a Philadelphia journalist,
was an acquaintance of Theodore Roosevelt who sympathized with Roosevelt's
opposition to the trusts that both men believed were subverting a better America;
Whittaker Chambers himself would later maintain that the trust provided "the

logic of all totalitarian organization." And he was much taken with Henry Adams's *Education* when it was published in 1918, with its depiction of "sensitive and timid" souls confronting a world in which the "stupendous acceleration" of history was, as Adams believed, everywhere creating chaos, hysteria, and social disequilibrium. When, in 1919, Whittaker snuck off to Washington and New Orleans on an attenuated *Wanderjahre*, he used the name Charles Adams as an alias, the surname having been inspired by Henry and the *Education*. The following year he entered Williams College, which Laha saw as step on the ladder to upper-middle-class respectability. But he left almost immediately: "one or two days on that beautiful but expensive campus told me that Williams was not the place for me." He took the night train to New York, and was later admitted, after taking a general intelligence test, to Columbia College, where the student body was less stultifyingly WASP. He proved a dazzling if erratic student. He read Great Books in John Erskine's General Honors colloquium, where his performance, according to Mortimer Adler, the future Great-Books maven, "was simply brilliant." The course made a deep impression on him, and it is likely that his first sustained encounter with Dante, the poet who would influence his memoir *Witness*, took place under its auspices.

At the same time he lost his faith in the Republican Party as an instrument of reform. Having been a staunch supporter of Calvin Coolidge, the party's candidate for vice president in 1920, he became as convinced as T. S. Eliot or Edmund Wilson that he lived "in a world that is dying." The kind of existence "that could destroy so gentle a nature" as his brother's seemed to him "mean-ingless." But Chambers sought regeneration not, as Eliot did, in Christ, but in Marx. And unlike Wilson, he was not content to be a fellow traveler: he joined the Communist Party outright, and in his own name. He was as appalled by the garishness of the 1920s as Henry Adams had been by the gilded puddle of the 1880s, but where Adams sought solace in the Virgin of Chartres and her rose window, Chambers was attracted by the "ascetism (or puritanism)" of Bolshevism, and by that "denial of the values of the world as it is" that lies "close to the heart of Communism, as of all great faiths."

Chambers, Lionel Trilling said many years later, "was the first person I ever knew whose commitment to radical politics was meant to be definitive of his whole moral being, the controlling element of his existence." This commitment accounted for the "quite exceptional respect" in which he was held by his friends at Columbia, "young men of intimidating brilliance." But Trilling did not count himself one of Chambers's friends: there "was indeed something about him that repelled me." He was "short of stature and very broad, with heavy arms and massive thighs . . . His eyes were narrow and they preferred to consult the floor rather than an interlocutor's face." When he opened his mouth, "it never failed to shock by reason of the dental ruin its disclosed, a devastation of empty sockets and blackened stumps." The mouth seemed to Trilling the "perfect insigne of Chambers's moral authority." It "annihilated the hygienic American present—only a serf could have such a mouth, or some student in a visored cap who sat in his Moscow garret and thought of nothing save the moment when he would toss the fatal canister into the barouche of the Grand Duke."

With his gnomic utterances and sense of himself as a portentous figure, a man of history, Chambers was, Trilling thought, a disturbing character, and at the same time a faintly ridiculous one, a "tragic comedian." But it is the brilliant, unsettling Chambers who overmasters Trilling's novel *The Middle of the Journey*, which was published in 1947. In it Trilling portrays Gifford Maxim, the character modeled on Chambers, as a natural aristocrat, his voice "filled with the politeness of centuries of humanistic culture, with the bows and curtsies, the fauteuils and carpets of many civilizations . . ." It was Chambers, almost alone among a host of liberally educated dilettantes with an "impassioned longing to believe" that Soviet Russia was creating a republic of "reason and virtue," who acted on the longing, and followed it to its logical conclusion.

It is true that, in his first incarnation as a communist, Chambers did little more than write for the periodicals he helped to put out, the *Daily Worker* and the *New Masses*. But in 1932 he discovered, much as Michael Straight discovered, another dimension of his faith when he was recruited by Soviet military intelligence—the G.R.U.—and summoned "into crypts of Communism" that he "scarcely dreamed existed, into its deep underground, whose door was about to close noiselessly behind" him, almost as if he "had never existed." A portentous figure indeed. For when, eventually, Chambers emerged from those subterranean depths, he would play a part in mobilizing forces that would doom the ascendancy of his fellow WASPs.

AT TWENTY MINUTES TO THREE on the morning of Friday, September 1, 1939, a buzzer sounded on the White House switchboard. Russell "Mac" McMullin, the switchboard operator, plugged in the line. "Paris calling . . ." Another voice broke in. "May I speak to the president?" Mac, recognizing the upper-crust

Philadelphian accents of William Christian Bullitt, rang Missy LeHand and told her that the American ambassador to France was on the line.

Bill Bullitt was, at this time, one of a handful of people privileged to speak, "without explanation, at any hour of the day or night," to the president. "Put him through," Missy said. (Bullitt was supposed to be in love with Missy, though others thought he feigned desire in order to maintain a channel to their mutual boss.)

Roused from sleep by his valet, Franklin Roosevelt reached for the telephone.

"This is Bill Bullitt, Mr. President."

"Yes, Bill."

"Tony Biddle* just got through from Warsaw, Mr. President. Several German divisions are deep in Polish territory, and the fighting is heavy. Tony said there were reports of bombers over the city. Then he was cut off. He'd tried to get you for half an hour before he called me."

"Well, Bill, it's come at last," the president said. "God help us all."

PANZER DIVISIONS SPED EASTWARD TOWARD Warsaw and Stuka dive-bombers soared above them as Adolf Hitler brought blitzkrieg—lightning war—to Poland. Behind the Wehrmacht divisions followed S.S. Death's Head units with orders to extirpate civilians. In France the rose window of Chartres was boxed up and put away, and in England the King's forces were mobilizing.

In Washington Franklin Roosevelt lit a cigarette—he smoked some forty Camels a day—and placed calls to his secretaries of state, of war, and of the navy, as well as to his top general, George Marshall, and his top diplomat, Sumner Welles. He then took up pencil and paper, noted the date and time (3:05 A.M.), and described how, having learned of the invasion from Bullitt, he ordered that all Navy ships and Army commands be notified at once. The notation made, he went back to sleep.

He told Henry Morgenthau, his secretary of the treasury, that he liked it "when something is happening every minute," and later that morning he was found lying in bed relaxed among the pillows. There was a blue bed cape around his shoulders and a cigarette in the ivory holder he clenched between his teeth. The truth is that domestic politics had begun to bore him. He had accomplished most of the internal reforms higher WASPs had long sought, and he now found himself invigorated by a fresh challenge, and perhaps also by a fresh justification for holding on to power, the need to persuade Americans to take a stand in the world crisis.

---

*   Anthony Joseph Drexel Biddle Jr., the American ambassador to Poland.

He had for some time been steadily, stealthily, trying to wean his country from the isolationist habits to which it had reverted after the curtain rang down on Woodrow Wilson's appearance on the world stage. He had listened to recordings of Hitler's broadcasts (translating the Führer's German for the benefit of his aides), and he had found both the man and his policies abhorrent. He had also seen in them a threat to the United States. As early as 1935 he privately expressed his desire "to do something" about Hitler, even as he knew that most Americans had other things on their minds.

His policy was not, like Woodrow Wilson's, disinterestedly altruistic. Alfred Thayer Mahan and his own Cousin Theodore taught him that the splendid isolation so many Americans desired was impossible in a world of economic interdependence and modern military technology. Should Germany and its allies obtain dominion over the natural and human capital of the Old World—a treasure considerably greater than that of the New—America, Roosevelt believed, would be at their mercy.

Speaking in Chicago in October 1937, he told his fellow citizens that they could no longer escape the world "through isolation or neutrality." In January 1939, talking to members of the Senate military affairs committee, he was blunter. "About three years ago we got the pretty definite information that there was in the making a policy of world domination between Germany, Italy, and Japan." If Hitler and Mussolini were to put France and Great Britain "out of business," the "next step" would be Central and South America. "Do not say it is chimerical," he warned the senators, "do not say it is just a pipe dream."

Roosevelt's effort to make the American people understand the dangers of the gathering storm—Henry Kissinger would call it the greatest foreign policy achievement of a twentieth-century American statesman—culminated in his address at the University of Virginia in June 1940. It was there that, on the occasion of his son Franklin's graduation from the law school, he rejected what he called the "delusion that we of the United States can safely permit the United States to become a lone island, a lone island in a world dominated by the philosophy of force. Such an island may be the dream of those who still talk and vote as isolationists. Such an island represents to me and to the overwhelming majority of Americans today a helpless nightmare of a people without freedom—the nightmare of a people lodged in prison, handcuffed, hungry, and fed through the bars from day to day by the contemptuous, unpitying masters of other continents."

Cotty and Fannie Peabody in old age, when the headmaster grappled with the tension between the WASP ideals of virtue and power.

THIRTY

Joy Lane

al Cerchio che più ama e che più sape . . .

the Circle which most loves and most knows . . .
—Dante, *Paradiso*

In June 1940, at the age of eighty-three, Endicott Peabody retired as headmaster of Groton, and he and Fannie moved into a newly built house on Joy Lane, a few minutes' walk from the Groton Circle in a fringe of second-growth woods on the crest of Joy's Hill.

He was the only survivor of the triumvirate that had come to Groton in 1884 drawn by the vision of a school that would be different from other schools. Mr. Gardner died in 1930, mourned by "such a host of impassioned friends," John

Jay Chapman said, "that his funeral, which took place in the Gothic Chapel that he had given to the school, lives in my mind as the most impressive religious service that I ever attended." It was "the only real pageant I ever was at—like *Parsifal*, only real—everyone on the verge of tears—and great majesty and beauty. . . . It was an hour of heaven . . ."

Three years after Mr. Gardner was buried in a crypt beneath the chapel, Sherrard Billings lay dying in his chamber in Brooks House. "His tiny shrunken body looked as Gandhi looks," Ellery Sedgwick said of his old teacher. "He had no longer strength to raise his head from the pillow, but he laid both his hands over mine, and with the barest ghost of his familiar smile slowly withdrew one hand and from beneath the bedclothes brought forth my own letter and pressed it against my palm. Dear old Billings! There is no teaching like a good man's life."

Peabody carried on alone. A year after Billings died, he enjoyed his greatest worldly triumph when, in June 1934, Franklin Roosevelt motored onto campus as president of the United States to celebrate the fiftieth anniversary of the school's founding. The relation between the overpowering headmaster and the nervous third former of 1896 had long since ripened into friendship. "Franklin I am very fond of, have been ever since he was a small boy," Peabody wrote Ellery Sedgwick. "I have been in close touch with him ever since he left School, married him, and have done what we could for his boys at Groton." On the morning of Franklin's inauguration in 1933, Peabody assisted at the order for morning prayer in St. John's Church on Lafayette Square, where he "rejoiced" to join the new president "in prayer for the strength which you would need in meeting the solemn responsibilities of your office."

"Our love and prayers are always with you," he assured the most illustrious of his old boys, yet with all this pastoral solicitude, the appearance of Franklin at Groton on that June weekend in 1934 had been anticipated with some apprehension. Would there be unkind words, failures of courtesy, even, God forbid, a scene? Those of Franklin's schoolmates who had been perplexed by his rise to power were now disturbed by the policies his power enabled him to pursue. "I can't understand this thing about Frank," Fuller Potter, one of old Bishop Potter's nephews, was heard to mutter. "He never amounted to much at school." What was worse, in Potter's view, than Frank's success was the crypto-Bolshevik program he was pursuing. So vehement, indeed, was the stockbroker's opposition to the New Deal that his son Jeffrey, who had recently graduated from Groton, urged him to forgo the celebration. But Fuller Potter resolved to be present, and to tell the president what he thought of him.

Escorted by police motorcycles, the open Packard blazoned with the presidential seal passed through the Bacon Gate and drew up to Hundred House. The sight of old Mrs. Peabody, as she came down the steps to greet the president, softened all but the most obdurate hearts. "Franklin, dear boy," she said as, in violation of all protocol, she threw her arms around him. "My! But it is good to have you back." Tears were shed, but Fuller Potter, as he waited in the receiving line, was determined to act as spokesman for all those Grotonians who loathed the New Deal. His son, dreading the confrontation he foresaw, closed his eyes. He had begun to pray when he heard Roosevelt, seated under one of the Hundred House porticos, "shouting Father's name—and his *first* name at that. . . . The president called to him to come up here and give him the hand that won the St. Mark's game." Fuller Potter was soon lost in smiling reminiscence with Franklin Roosevelt and Endicott Peabody.

PEABODY WAS BY THIS TIME "unquestionably" the "outstanding private school Headmaster in the United States," or so Roosevelt told Robert Worth Bingham, his ambassador to the Court of St. James's. Educators were curious to understand the nature of his experiment at Groton and the reasons for its success. "Intelligent and expert persons," one graduate recalled, "repaired to the school and examined the process and made reports." Peabody himself wrote a piece "which was duly published, explaining the system: with the result that everyone agreed that he himself did not understand his own technique." Yet the experts had no deeper insight, and exhausting "all the stock phrases about 'orientation, integration, motivation,' etc.," failed to penetrate the mystery.

He had become a name, but for all his renown, it was generally conceded that his time had passed. The theories of John Dewey were now ascendant, and when, at a conference of educators, the Rector stood up to say that he had heard "a great deal of talk about self-expression and creativity" but that in his "experience a single life based on the principle 'for their sakes I sanctify themselves' was worth the whole lot of it," everyone was embarrassed for him.

Groton itself seemed the relic of a vanished age. The boys worshipped God each morning in the chapel. They were animated, from the pulpit, for the gravest duties of the citizen, and opened, through the choir, to "graces human and divine," the "love which from our birth over and around us lies . . ." Greek,

Latin, and modern languages had still the largest place in the curriculum, and no boy was made to hew wood or draw water, to wait on table, make his bed, or clean his cubicle. All the chores were undertaken by maids and janitors, and all the shoes were shined during the night by the watchmen; in the evenings the boys dressed for dinner, and wore stiff collars and patent leather shoes.

It is true that the Rector had, during his long headmastership, brought to campus men and women who challenged the boys' complacencies, Booker T. Washington, Julia Ward Howe, and Jacob Riis among them. He expanded the arts program, and he invited John Jay Chapman to come up to Groton to help the boys to put on better plays. (The school itself seemed to Chapman a theater: "Groton a splendid place to start a school of speaking. It can spread to the other schools afterwards. Groton so small—no reason why the whole place should not speak like good actors.") But for all that the critics were right; Groton was archaic; Peabody himself was an ancien régime, even an antediluvian figure, devoted, in the age of John Dewey, to the soulcraft of the old Greek and Renaissance *paideia*, to "a set of social technologies designed to alter minds and hearts" not only through "formal educational routine," but by means of "customs, ritual, the plastic arts, music, theater, and oratory."

Peabody used the old artistry to try to persuade his boys to do justice to their gifts and undertake lives of civic virtue. So incessantly, indeed, did he preach on the importance of public service that it was "God's mercy that all of us didn't go into it," Ellery Sedgwick winked. For most "Grotonian consciences never twinged properly," the historian Waldo Heinrichs believed: the greater number of graduates became bankers or corporation lawyers. Yet Peabody's preaching "pervaded the impressionable years of Franklin D. Roosevelt, Averell Harriman, Dean Acheson, and Joseph C. Grew; who can say it failed?"

Franklin himself never forgot that he was a guinea pig in the Rector's experiment and an exemplar of what the economist John Kenneth Galbraith was to call the "Groton ethic" of public service. "More than forty years ago," Franklin wrote his old headmaster in 1940, "you said, in a sermon in the Old Chapel, something about not losing boyhood ideals in later life. Those were Groton ideals—taught by you—I try not to forget—and your words are still with me and with hundreds of others of 'us boys.'"

PEABODY RESISTED BEING PUT OUT to pasture, but at eighty, during a visit to Paris, a careless taxi driver sent him to the hospital with broken ribs, and for the first time he seemed old. He knew that the "Groton family," as he called it, was apprehensive for its future, and in 1939 he announced his intention to retire the following year, giving the trustees time to elect a successor. At his last Prize Day as headmaster, an emotional occasion, he spoke of "whatsoever things are true, whatsoever things are honest, whatsoever things are just, whatsoever things are pure, whatsoever things are lovely, whatsoever things are of good report." He also insisted that Groton was a "Church School" with "a spiritual atmosphere which we all breathe and are consciously or unconsciously affected by." Afterward he and Fannie traveled to Arizona, where as a young man he had preached the Gospel to the outcast, to enjoy its sunshine while their new house on Joy Lane was being built. Franklin, who was unable to be present at Prize Day, expressed the hope that they would derive benefit from the desert air, and he assured them that he wanted "to see the new house" on Joy Lane "just as soon as" he possibly could.*

It was only in retirement that Peabody had leisure to reflect on both his successes and his failures as an educator and as an architect of the WASP revival. He was assisted in this stocktaking by Malcolm Strachan, an intense young instructor in the school's English department who had recently taken holy orders. He discerned in Peabody the complexity that others missed, and aspired to write a book that would capture it in a way that Peabody's authorized biographer, the brilliant Frank Ashburn—senior prefect of the form of 1921, chairman of the *Yale Daily News*, tapped for both Skull and Bones and a Rhodes Scholarship (he turned the latter down)—was unlikely to do, not because he lacked ability but from a too fastidious sense of the fitting and the decorous: he could never acquiesce in the lèse-majesté of a warts-and-all portrait of his hero.

Peabody showed Strachan a side of himself he revealed to few others, and in long hours before the fireplace in the house in Jay Lane he took up an old theme in confessing his doubts and lamenting his mistakes as a headmaster and a priest. Had he not, in his obsession with discipline, too often failed to be

---

* In another letter Roosevelt said that regretted that the Peabodys' sojourn in Arizona would prevent the Rector from officiating at morning prayer on the occasion of his third inauguration as president, but he added that "I shall be recompensed in part if you and Mrs. Peabody derive benefit from your stay in Tucson. Let us hope you will return to Groton with real zest for life in your new home. . . . I am deeply touched by your reference to the old days at Groton. I count it among the blessings of my life that it was given to me in formative years to have the privilege of your guiding hand and the benefit of your inspiring example."

a good shepherd to his boys? Had not worldly temptations—his desire to have a school with gleaming buildings, a soaring chapel, an influence to rival Arnold's Rugby—gotten in the way of his mission to make Groton a place unlike other places, a community devoted to success not as the world measures it but as Christ does, concerned with the immortal soul of each boy who passed through it? It was a question that laid bare the ambiguity at the heart of the WASP revival, the tension between its ideals of virtue and power.

STRACHAN'S BOOK, WHICH WAS TO have brought to light the hidden drama of the Rector's soul, kept not getting written, and in September 1960, on the day the boys were to return to school, Strachan himself was found dead. He had been, at Groton, the teacher and mentor of Louis Auchincloss, and over the years they had often talked about the book he proposed to write. But now Strachan was gone, and the book unwritten. Auchincloss decided to write it himself, only he would write it in his own way, what he called "my idea of it."

The result was *The Rector of Justin*, one of the best-selling novels of 1964. In it Auchincloss freely mixed incidents drawn from Peabody's life with elements of character drawn from Learned Hand, whose law clerk he had been. At the heart of the novel is Francis Prescott, who like Peabody has been educated in England, chucked business to answer the call of God, and founded a church school in New England, but who has at the same time been endowed by Auchincloss with all the wit and intellect of Learned Hand. During the course of the novel, Peabody and Hand struggle for the soul of Prescott, but by the end of the book, when Auchincloss depicts Prescott in retirement, Peabody has pretty clearly won, and Hand has retreated before the old man whom Strachan visited in Joy Lane.

The urbane Hand was unlikely to have been troubled by a boy's saying "My God," as Prescott in *The Rector of Justin* is. Peabody, on the contrary, *would* have been troubled: one must never take the Lord's name in vain.* He tolerated no profane or vulgar talk on his campus. In the late twenties, he was on horseback near the school's golf course when he heard the word "shit" issue from the lips of one of his boys, disappointed after having driven his "third consecutive ball into Lake Romaine." He immediately suspended the boy and sent him down

---

* Pierre "Pete" Jay, the first chairman of the Federal Reserve Bank of New York, was taken aback when he heard that Peabody had pronounced him the "most perfect gentleman" he knew. "My God," he exclaimed, "did the Rector say that?" When Bishop Atwood repeated Jay's words to his old headmaster, Peabody replied, "I wish Pierre Jay were not quite so profane."

to New York. When the boy, Kent Sanger of the form of 1930, reported to his father in Manhattan, he found him "incredulous." He "drove me back to school and we went in to see the Rector. The Rector said to Dad, 'Prentice, I have not heard that word used since I heard the street cads of London curse.' To which my father responded, 'Mr. Peabody, are you aware that my son plays in the streets of New York where the boys he plays with use this and much worse language regularly?' The Rector paused in thought for some time and then turned to me and said, 'Kent, I have done you an injustice. I apologize.' And to Dad, 'Prentice, thank you for caring enough to set the record straight.'"

It is still less easy to imagine Hand in the temptation-on-the-mount scene in which *The Rector of Justin* culminates, when Francis Prescott realizes that, unlike Christ, he has been unable to resist the devil's inducements, and that having been beguiled by all the kingdoms of the world, he has allowed his school, Justin Martyr, to become merely another factory of "snobbishness and materialism," a passport to "good society," a stepping stone to "the brokerage house, the corporation law firm, the place on Long Island, the yacht, the right people," with "no life whatever of the higher faculties, no faith, no hope, no aspiration . . ."

The religious mode was remote from the spirit of Learned Hand, who in maturity was an agnostic, but it was the authentic note of Endicott Peabody, as Strachan heard it as he sat beside the fire in Joy Lane. To this earnest young priest the Rector confessed his suspicion that Groton was not, perhaps, so very different from other fancy schools, that it was only another lamasery of the elite consecrated to money and power, to the idols of Wall Street and the *Social Register*—the sort of school caricatured in Wallace Morgan's *New Yorker* cartoon, in which the complacent millionaire in spats and a Panama hat gestures, in Grand Central Station, to a slip of a boy standing beside a chauffeur bent under a burden of luggage, "Remember, son, we old Grotonians have a saying that the fourth form makes or breaks a man." If a few Grotonians happened to turn to statesmanship at some point in their careers, it was only because statesmanship promised a still more rarified form of power.

This, indeed, was to be David Halberstam's verdict on Groton, "the greatest prep school in the nation, where the American upper class sends its sons to instill the classic values: discipline, honor, a belief in the existing values"—as embodied in Protestant Christianity—"and the rightness of them." Such were the school-catalogue pieties; what really mattered, Halberstam wrote in *The Best and the Brightest*, his book on the suicide of the WASP elite, was that at Groton "one starts to meet the right people" and make "connections which will serve well later on—be it Wall Street or Washington." Above all, one learns, at Groton, "the rules of the game, and even a special language: what washes and does not wash." *Cui servire est regnare*, Halberstam noted, is Groton's motto: "To serve is to rule," as he translates it.* Service to God, according to Halberstam, is the school's "overt teaching," but its "covert teaching, far more subtle and insidious," is that "strength is more important" than virtue, that "there is a ruling clique," and that "there is a thing called privilege and you might as well use it."

Halberstam mocked both the Athenian humanism of Groton and its Christian idealism. The title of his book is a rough translation of an idea at the heart of old Greek culture: *kalos kagathos*—the noble (or best) and the beautiful (or brightest). But culture is one thing, Emerson said, and varnish another. The humanism of Groton, Halberstam suggested, was ornamental, and the sanctification it preached hypocritical: the real end was always power and domination.

Peabody would have been appalled by this conception of his school as an institution in the Lord Chesterfield mold, teaching the morals of a whore and the manners of a dancing master. Yet he might have perceived a degree of truth in it. The civic virtue he preached was intended to build up communities in which people might better realize their God-given talents and purposes in the light of a love that never dies.† But public service as actually practiced by his graduates was

---

* The earliest use of the phrase *cui servire est regnare* has been traced to a fifth-century sermon on Matthew 6 (the Sermon on the Mount), in which a "sweet obedience" to God is held to free the soul from earthly cares and the bondage of evil: by serving God and trusting in His grace, one rules one's unruly self. The phrase formed part of the Sacramentary of Gregory the Great, a breviary which in the sixth century was brought to England by Augustine of Canterbury, and it was sung in English churches for a nearly a millennium when, at the Reformation, Thomas Cranmer translated it into English and incorporated it in the collect for peace in the order for morning prayer: "O God . . . *whose service is perfect freedom* . . ." Whatever Halberstam might urge, Endicott Peabody never taught or implied that the words *cui servire est regnare* contain a cryptic assurance that Christian service leads to worldly rule: he understood the phrase rather as describing the power and freedom that come with the extinction of self in service to God, and he would have looked upon a cynical construction of the words as being in the worst possible taste. He believed with St. Paul that Christians are "called unto liberty," but that they are to use their liberty not "for an occasion to the flesh, but by love serve one another." For "he that is called in the Lord, being a servant, is the Lord's free man: likewise also he that is called being free, is Christ's servant."

† *Bene è che sanza termine si doglia*   It is good that he should know grief without end,
   chi, per amor di cos a che non duri   who for the love of things that do not last,
   etternalmente, quella amor si spoglia . . .   forsakes the love that lasts forever . . .
                                              —Dante, *Paradiso*, Canto XV

arguably more concerned with worldly pleasure and worldly falseness, with finding a place in the ruling clique (through the knowledge of what washes) and with the passing-brave pleasures of riding "in triumph through Persepolis," than it was with concern for the needs of others. Arthur Schlesinger would later observe that his own school, Exeter, produced nothing like Groton's roster of statesmen and diplomats. "Compared to Groton (Franklin D. Roosevelt, Averell Harriman, Dean Acheson, Sumner Welles, Francis Biddle, Bronson Cutting, Joseph C. Grew or, in my own generation, Douglas Dillon, Joseph and Stewart Alsop, F.D.R. Jr., McGeorge and William Bundy, Richard Bissell, Jonathan Bingham, Bill Blair, Frank Keppel), Exeter's representation in public leadership in the twentieth century," Schlesinger wrote, "was negligible. Groton was a much smaller school with much richer and more snobbish boys, yet its role in the days of F.D.R. and, later, John F. Kennedy was far greater than Exeter's." But did such service really transform the world, as Peabody hoped that it would, and lift it, if only temporarily, above its mundane preoccupations? Or was it merely another form of the old unregenerate politics, a politics, moreover, that enabled a class already privileged to arrogate yet more power to itself?

There is no simple answer to the question. Peabody was divided against himself. He valued humility and sacrifice, but he knew the importance of authority and strength, and at times he mixed up the proportions. If in certain moods he resembled Dostoevsky's Alyosha, talking as tenderly of Christian compassion to his boys as Dostoevsky's hero does at the end of *The Brothers Karamazov*, in other moments he had more than a little in common with the novel's Grand Inquisitor. He would never have consciously encouraged his boys to look upon service cynically, as mere "actions that a man might play." But a part of him knew that the *un*conscious temptation was always there, and in Joy Lane he lamented his failure to make Christ really live for his boys.

THE LAMENTATION IN JOY LANE has long been connected, in the school's mythology, to an episode that occurred late in the Rector's headmastership. In 1930 there were a series of vandalisms at the school. The chapel was desecrated in "a minor, but mean way," and various items were smashed or stolen, among them a silver "milestone" on the Rector's desk that had been bestowed on Mr. Gardner for his services to the school. It was a little profanation of Groton's lares and penates that "grieved the Rector and Mrs. Peabody deeply," for the vandals seemed to strike, in Ashburn's words, at "the heart of the school," and while the damage they did was in purely material terms not very great, it seemed motivated by a "venomous" hatred.

In due course the vandals were caught. Three graduates from the form of 1927 had come up from Harvard and under cover of darkness committed the acts that shocked the Groton family. Whether or not the incident, which Auchincloss incorporated in *The Rector of Justin*, really did trouble Peabody in his retirement in Joy Lane cannot now be known with any certainty. But it lives in the myth of the school as a parable of the Rector's humility, that of an old man who regretted those sheep that, uncaught, went over the edge of the cliff. Arnold of Rugby had turned in the storm and beckoned to the lamb that would otherwise have been lost, fallen into one of the mountain gorges.

> *O faithful shepherd!* . . .
> *Bringing thy sheep in thy hand.* . . .

Peabody was pained by the thought that he had not always been able to give his hand. Amory Gardner's prophecy, uttered so many decades before, was in some sense true. "It is because I care so terribly," he had told Cotty in 1888, "that I say it over and over again. If they learn to hate the school, it will go the way of all other schools and that is far worse than useless. They didn't use to hate . . . Why should they ever do so?" The acts of the three vandals would seem to have been more in the nature of an undergraduate prank than an expression of philosophic hatred for the school. But as myth the vandalisms represent both a truth, that every school, however rich in pastoral care, will lose some of its sheep,* and to a fact, that the Rector could never bear to accept this truth, and blamed himself.

"You know he would be an awful bully," little Averell Harriman said of Peabody, "if he wasn't such a terrible Christian." But he *was* a terrible Christian, and it made a difference. How often he had stood, in the pulpit, trying to *reach* them, pawing the air with his hand "as though he were digging into us." "That's it," he would say, "that's it, my boys . . ." He was, in his disillusionment, unfair to himself. Something remarkable *did* happen on the campus he created, and if at times

---

* "God forgive us," Mr. Gardner had written, "if by anything we have done or left undone any boy goes away from this school worse than if he had never come. And yet there will be such boys. I fear they will form the majority when the school is large. They do at most schools. Why not at Groton unless we differ as we do now from any in England or America?"

the worldly disciplinarian predominated, at other times the self-sacrificing priest loomed largest, catching those who might otherwise have gone over the edge.

In 2019, at the age of ninety-seven, John Goodenough was awarded the Nobel Prize for chemistry in connection with work that helped to make possible the rechargeable lithium-ion battery, the power that drives those devices without which we can now scarcely live. He is probably the last of the Rector's boys still active in the world, and in his remarkable memoir *Witness to Grace* he testifies to the Rector's terrible or, some might say, beautiful Christianity. Goodenough came to Groton as a first former in 1934, the year Louis Auchincloss entered the sixth form, and he graduated in 1940, the year the Rector retired. One would think that he of all people—a scientific genius—would have found the school's emphasis on the humanities stifling. (When a science wing was added to Groton's Schoolhouse in the 1970s, it connected to the cellar, and for many years science and math classes were taught in the basement while humanities classes were held upstairs, in classrooms with tall windows, fireplaces, and wood paneling.) But Goodenough found the humanities liberating. As a boy he had never, he said, "been able to appreciate more than the rhythms and sounds of a poem," and in his fifth form poetry class he found himself helpless before Shakespeare's sonnet, "Let me not to the marriage of true minds . . ." But during the course of the year he "discovered the art of metaphor," which opened the world of poetry. When he reached Yale, his own intellect and his Groton training stood him in good stead. In his first year he was allowed, such were his accomplishments, to take a junior course in ethics and aesthetics in lieu of freshman English, a junior course translating Greek plays, a sophomore calculus course, and a qualitative analysis course. The only disappointment in New Haven was freshman psychology, "an intellectual insult; I found Freud totally unconvincing in many of his assertions, and Pavlov's dog seemed to be more trivial than made out."

That Goodenough was a scholarship boy at Groton might, like the school's emphasis on the humanities, have been expected to blight his experience, but it did not. "The Rector made no distinction in the School between scholarship and paying students," Goodenough wrote: "the distinctions between those from wealth and social status and those of us from middle-class homes arose only in discussions of vacation activities." But he was not left out, and he spent many of his vacations with his well-to-do schoolmates. He sailed with them to Maine, danced with their debutantes in New York, and yachted with Morgans and Princes. But although he enjoyed himself, the life of these WASPs held no attraction for him. "I knew that this was not my world and I had no desire to make it my world."

What struck him was the culture of pastoral care in which he was enveloped, one that manifested itself both in small ways and large. He remembered how, when he came down with jaundice, the Rector and Mrs. Peabody visited him each day in the infirmary, and how Mrs. Peabody took him "for a morning drive to see the autumn colors on a beautiful Indian-Summer day when the foliage was as brilliant as I have ever experienced it." He had "never before ridden in a chauffeur-driven car," and it "was a kindness" that remained "vivid with me." Later, when he was at Yale, the Rector helped him to make ends meet by arranging for him to tutor his grandson Harry Sedgwick, the child of his daughter Helen and Minturn Sedgwick (Edie's uncle) at Murray Bay, in the Minturn cottage where Learned Hand had, many years before, courted Frances Fincke.

In his third form year Goodenough underwent an awakening. He came to realize "that the words of the prayer book with which I had become familiar carried a meaning that was hidden from me." He was baffled by Leviticus 19:2. ("Ye shall be holy: for I the Lord your God am holy.") Then he "realized that holiness is a word that cannot be defined; it must be experienced." He decided to be baptized in the hope that baptism would "lift the veil" between words and their meaning, but although the Jordan's water brought him into a new community of spirit, "it did not reveal the meaning of the symbols and metaphors" that perplexed him. Next he was confirmed and experienced the sacrament of communion, but still he remained confused. Then, in his fifth form year, he had a dream. A series of ancient images appeared before him, and at each one he cried out, "That's not God!" At last the head of a hound appeared, and again he cried, "That's not God!" The "hound smiled; behind the smile was a warm light; and I cried out, 'God is Love!'"

The Rector took a deep interest in Goodenough's spiritual development, and "one spring day as we were walking together to lunch from the School House," he urged him to enter the ministry. Goodenough replied that he would rather proclaim the Gospel as a layman. The Rector was afraid that as a layman he would lose his "Christian witness," and said that he hoped that he would at least become a teacher.

For all his "aristocracy of character," or perhaps because of it, Peabody was, Goodenough said, "my emancipator." A teacher who inspired a "young man struggling to find himself" in the storm, Peabody extended his hand and helped him on what he called his "journey to grace," that "action of the Spirit of Love," as he defines it in *Witness to Grace*, which has the power to transform, "to make one a new creature." The Nobel laureate dedicated his book to three individuals, his wife Irene, his mathematics professor at Yale, Egbert Miles, and Endicott Peabody.

Franklin Roosevelt at Warm Springs on April 11, 1945.

THIRTY-ONE

The Death of Men

Pur a noi converrà vincer la punga . . .

We had better win this battle . . .
—Dante, *Inferno*

On June 12, 1940, Henry Stimson boarded the Boston train in Grand Central Station. Having served as secretary of war under President Taft, governor-general of the Philippines under President Coolidge, and secretary of state under President Hoover, he was now a private citizen practicing law in the firm of Winthrop, Stimson, Putnam & Roberts in lower Manhattan. But briefs and pleadings were momentarily forgotten as he embarked on a sentimental journey, intent on paying a debt of gratitude to two institutions that shaped him.

He made his way, first, to Andover, Massachusetts, where, on the morning of June 14—the day German troops entered Paris—he rose in the Cochran Chapel to address the graduating class of Phillips Academy.

"You are leaving Andover in what is certainly a very dark hour for the civilized world," he told the young men assembled before him. "But as I look into your faces and realize your responsibilities, I am filled, not with pity for you in what you are facing, but with a desire to congratulate you." For it had been given to this young generation, he said, to play a part in one of the great crises of history. The human race confronted "the clearest issue between right and wrong" that had ever been presented to it on such a scale, the question of whether the world was to be a free one or a slave one. It was the duty of the young men of Andover, Stimson believed, to help to make it a free one.

His words were greeted by more than perfunctory applause, and they made an impression on a young WASP in the Cochran Chapel who, though he was not graduating that day, would soon be flying in combat over the Pacific. George H. W. Bush, who two days earlier had turned sixteen, was to find in Stimson an inspiration for his own public service. But the old man's work was not done, and after a weekend's rest at Highhold, his country house on Long Island, he and Mrs. Stimson went to New Haven to attend the commencement exercises at Yale, where he had taken his Bachelor of Arts degree fifty-two years before and where his friend and colleague Harvey Bundy's boy McGeorge was about to graduate, the cleverest youth the place had seen since Jonathan Edwards finished his course in 1720. At Yale Stimson exhorted the Elis to support compulsory military service (the draft) in the face of the global emergency, and in a national radio address delivered from his niece's house on Prospect Street he urged the American people to reject "defeatist arguments" about the "unconquerable power of Germany" and to send munitions to Great Britain and France in their struggle against Hitler.

The next day the Stimsons were taken in a chauffeured car to the Pierre in New York, where they had a pied-à-terre. He was in his office in Liberty Street that afternoon when the telephone rang. It was Franklin Roosevelt. He wanted to know whether Stimson would serve as secretary of war. Stimson replied that he was almost seventy-three years old. Roosevelt countered that if he took the job he would be free to name as his assistants whoever could best help him manage the burdens of the office. Stimson asked for time to discuss the matter with his wife and his professional associates, but his answer was not in doubt.

He could never bear to let the bugle-horn go unheeded, and that evening he told the president he would serve.

On December 7, 1941, Stimson was lunching in Washington when he was summoned to the telephone. Franklin Roosevelt sounded "rather excited." "Have you heard the news?" the president asked. Stimson thought he was referring to Japanese advances in the Gulf of Siam. "Oh no," Roosevelt replied, "I don't mean that. They have attacked Hawaii. They are now bombing Hawaii."

His "first feeling," Stimson wrote in his diary, was one "of relief that the indecision was over and that a crisis had come in a way which would unite all our people." At the same time the Japanese attack on Pearl Harbor made his task in building the American war machine that much more urgent. When, in July 1940, he became secretary of war, the army of the United States, with some 174,000 soldiers, was smaller than Portugal's. (It was a little larger than Bulgaria's.) He was charged with turning this tiny force into a phalanx of more than ten million men and women capable of defeating the Axis powers. The challenge would have staggered a much younger man, but not only was Stimson not young, he continued to suffer from insomnia and gastric complaints that would once have been described as neurasthenic but were now put down to the vagaries of infantile sexuality. His solution to the problem was to limit himself, so far as possible, to formulating the general objectives to be pursued by the War Department while leaving talented subordinates to undertake the laborious business of implementing them. He generally left his office in the old State, War, and Navy building next to the White House early enough in the day to ride on horseback with Mrs. Stimson at Woodley, his estate in the neighborhood of the Cathedral Church of Saint Peter and Saint Paul, the Anglican edifice better known as Washington National Cathedral. (WASPs were so bold in those days as to envision their microscopic Episcopal communion as the national church.) On other days he would swim and play golf at Chevy Chase, and there were frequent long weekends at Highhold, as well as occasional expeditions to South Carolina to hunt quail or to the Ausable Club in the Adirondacks to fish and trailblaze.

In this comparative leisure he could rely on the exertions of such aides-de-camp as Harvey Bundy, whom he had first brought into the public service when he was secretary of state under Hoover. Bundy, like Stimson, had gone to Yale College; after a brief career as a teacher at St. Mark's, he had gone on to Harvard

Law School, a clerkship in the chambers of Mr. Justice Holmes, and a career as a trusts and estates lawyer. Married to a daughter of old Boston, he was a careful, meticulous man whom Stimson trusted implicitly. Robert Lovett was another of Stimson's War Department dynamos. The son of a lawyer for railroad tycoon E. H. Harriman, Lovett had gone to the Hill School and Yale, where he was tapped for Skull and Bones and flew in Trubee Davison's First Yale Unit. A naval aviator during the First World War, he spent much of his peacetime career at Brown Brothers Harriman, the private bank. In Henry Stimson's War Department, he oversaw the expansion of the Army Air Corps, the predecessor of the United States Air Force. John J. McCloy completed Stimson's trinity of War Department stars. Educated at the Peddie School and Amherst, he had commanded an artillery battery in the First World War. After graduating from Harvard Law School, he went to Wall Street, becoming a partner in the Cravath firm. In Stimson's War Department he was charged with creating a new intelligence-gathering unit, the Office of Strategic Services, a forerunner of the C.I.A. He also helped implement one of the most egregious policies undertaken on Stimson's and Roosevelt's watches, the forcible internment of American citizens of Japanese descent.

IF STIMSON HAD AN EYE for talent, he also had talent for eyeing WASPs, actual or, in the case of Jack McCloy, aspirant. (McCloy was a Scots-Irish Presbyterian from a family in "reduced circumstances," as the saying went.) The institutional pedigrees of his War Department recruits were Stimsonian. Bundy and Lovett were Yale-educated Bonesmen; Bundy and McCloy were graduates of Harvard Law School. Bundy was connected through marriage to the old Brahmin families of Boston, to Putnams, Bigelows, and Lawrences: his mother-in-law was the sister of A. Lawrence Lowell, the president of Harvard, Percival Lowell, the astronomer whom Jack Chapman beat up, and Amy Lowell, the Imagist poet. Lovett was connected through his father to the new plutocratic wealth of the Harrimans and to the Brown Brothers firm, where bankers like Ellery Sedgwick James, George Herbert Walker, and Walker's son-in-law, Prescott Bush, managed it.

Stimson was hardly alone in dispensing preppy patronage; Franklin Roosevelt, though he was more open to outside talent than Stimson, was assiduous in promoting the fortunes of those whose backgrounds were similar to his own. Dean Acheson and Averell Harriman are often cited as Groton's two most eminent public servants after Roosevelt himself, but without Roosevelt's patronage in the early phases of their careers they might never have risen so high. Harriman, unsatisfied with the life of a rich playboy, entered public service in 1934 with a position in the New Deal's National Recovery Administration; Roosevelt later used him as a special envoy, entrusting him with sensitive missions to Churchill and Stalin, and in 1943 he made him ambassador to the Soviet Union. Roosevelt brought Acheson into government in 1933 as under secretary of the treasury. A brilliant lawyer, he resigned over a difference with the president concerning monetary policy, but did so in so graceful a fashion that Roosevelt was keen to have him again in harness. Acheson spoke of the "generous attempts by the president to lure me back to public service" during the 1930s, but it was only in February 1941, with the approach of war, that he left his law partnership to report for duty as assistant secretary of state. When, in January 1943, Harvey Bundy's son Bill* married Dean Acheson's daughter Mary, the two lines of preppy patronage, the one deriving from Stimson, the other from Roosevelt, touched.

Nowhere were Roosevelt's tribal loyalties more evident than in his relation to Sumner Welles, the unsmiling toff who was for more than half a decade his top diplomat. It was in some ways a curious choice, for Welles was not a particularly endearing figure or even, for all his undoubted intelligence, an especially distinguished practitioner of his craft. If he could take much of the credit for F.D.R.'s Good Neighbor Policy in Latin America, his work as ambassador to Cuba prepared the way for the Grau San Martin-Batista dictatorship. A scarcely less grave defect, he lacked a sense of humor, or possessed one so rarefied as to be almost undetectable. When Acheson's wife, Alice, once made him laugh, he immediately apologized. "Pardon me," he said. "You amused me." When he was not being pompous and aloof, he was likely to be drunk and lecherous, for his stuffed-shirt demeanor concealed passions that he tried, not always successfully, to keep in check; Arthur Schlesinger described him as a "frosty patrician who drank too much" and who, when drunk, "made passes at everyone, fish, flesh or fowl." The stock-in-trade of a diplomat is his ability to judge character, but Welles's judgments are open to question; on a fact-finding mission for Roosevelt in 1940 he dismissed Winston Churchill as a hopeless drunk. Yet his own drinking

---

* William Putnam Bundy served as assistant secretary of state for East Asian and Pacific affairs under Lyndon Johnson, an office in which he was succeeded by his Groton form-mate Marshall Green. Among the other members of the form of 1935 were Stanley Resor, secretary of the army under Johnson, and Louis Auchincloss, the chronicler of the WASPs.

was reckless; in September 1940, coming back on the presidential train from the funeral of Speaker of the House William Bankhead of Alabama, he threw back "one whiskey after another" and propositioned several Pullman porters. Roosevelt, apprised of his lapses, arranged for a minder to watch over him when he was in his cups, but as the story of the Pullman affair reverberated in the whispering gallery of Washington, he regretfully allowed his old friend to resign from the State Department. Yet he was loath to hold Welles accountable for his indiscretions, and he cast the blame instead on those who, like Bill Bullitt, used Welles's peccadillos to intrigue against him.

Roosevelt treated Welles in his ordeal with rare generosity of spirit, but his humane qualities were less evident when the victim came from outside the charmed circle. When David Ignatius Walsh, an Irish-Catholic lawmaker who represented Massachusetts in the Senate, was (falsely) implicated in a similar scandal, F.D.R. put aside his Christian charity. He told future vice president Alben Barkley that in the Army they would have left a man like that alone in a room with a loaded revolver.

SHORTLY AFTER PEARL HARBOR WINSTON Churchill came to Washington to spend Christmas with the Roosevelts. ("You should have told me!" Eleanor shrieked when her husband informed her of the prime minister's imminent arrival.) Franklin arranged a press conference with Winston in the White House, introducing his guest to "my wolves—my beloved pack of wolves," as he called the assembled journalists. Winston glowered so fiercely at the hungry pack that the British reporter who asked the first question was concerned.

"Mr. Prime Minister, are you of good cheer?"

F.D.R. laughed so hard that "he nearly choked on his cigarette holder."

The two prima donnas got on well, in part because Churchill suppressed his own egotism in order to win over the egotist who, as president of the United States, held all of the cards. "No lover," he said, "ever studied every whim of his mistress as I did those of President Roosevelt." Yet secure in the freemasonry of great men, each could take pleasure in the other's personality without envy or resentment. Franklin told Winston that it was "fun to be in the same decade" with him, and Winston said that meeting Franklin "was like opening your first bottle of champagne; knowing him was like drinking it." Besides these billets-doux, they had in common their mutual connection to old New York, to which both the president and the prime minister owed something of their fortune in life. Their mothers had been born in the state in the same year, 1854, Sara Delano in Newburgh, Jennie Jerome in Brooklyn. But in those days people like the Delanos and the Roosevelts, with their colonial pedigrees, looked down on people like the Jeromes as gaudy arrivistes. As the friend and partner of the Vanderbilts, Leonard Jerome—he was Jennie's father, Winston's grandfather—was just the sort of newly risen man who gave the old mercantile, Mugwump elite out of which the WASPs arose moral indigestion. Lord Randolph Churchill, a younger son of the Duke of Marlborough, was less fastidious, and his marriage, in April 1874, to Jennie Jerome brought him not only a handsome wife, with "more of the panther than of the woman in her look," but also a substantial dowry—that byproduct of a New York financier's speculations without which Winston Leonard Spencer Churchill would never have come into being.

There was also a mutual fondness for drinking and smoking, and in the White House the two men stayed up late into the night over brandy and cigars. Such, indeed, was their bibulous conviviality that Eleanor, like an anxious mother suspicious of her son's new college chum, worried that Winston was corrupting the president. "It was astonishing to me," she said of her guest, "that anyone could smoke so much and drink so much and keep perfectly well."

WINSTON COULD OUTDRINK FRANKLIN; ON coming to the White House he is said to have informed Alonzo Fields, the White House butler, that he "must have a tumbler of sherry in my room before breakfast, a couple of glasses of scotch and soda before lunch and French champagne and ninety-year-old brandy before I go to sleep at night." But if he was the deeper drinker, he was also the more conventionally disciplined public man, and he was annoyed by what seemed to him Franklin's laziness and indecision. The president, he said, was "a charming country gentleman" with no habits of business. Stimson was as frustrated by what he called Roosevelt's "topsy-turvy, upside-side down" manner of conducting his government. "Conferences with the President are difficult matters," he complained. "His mind does not follow easily a consecutive chain of thought but he is full of stories and incidents and hops about in his discussion from suggestion to suggestion and it very much like chasing a vagrant beam of sunshine around a vacant room." Stimson deplored, too, Roosevelt's evasive, even mendacious glibness, and once went so far as to say to his face, "Mr. President, I don't like you to dissemble with me."

It was true. Roosevelt was reluctant to obligate himself, either by giving straightforward answers to questions or by making definite decisions in unpropitious moments.* Few statesmen can have so sedulously avoided premature commitment in the faith that ripeness is all. He was always "calculating the future," the New Dealer Paul Appleby said, "but seeing the future in terms of a variety of alternatives always developing out of a set of current alternatives." Subordinates found this slipperiness vexing, but it enabled him to navigate some of the trickiest crosscurrents ever confronted by an American leader without coming to grief. Stimson himself admitted that, for all his indirection, Roosevelt was "a superb war President—far more so than any other President of our history."

His motto might have been that of Augustus, *festina lente*—hasten slowly. He seems almost to have believed that when it was not necessary to make a decision, it was necessary *not* to make a decision. Yet this superstitious reluctance to decide was counterbalanced by an almost mystical assurance of the rightness of the decision once the die was cast. Francis Biddle, who had known him since their Groton days, said that he "had more serenity than any man I have ever seen." This preternatural tranquility perplexed even those who were closest to him. "There's something he's got that eludes me," Harry Hopkins, who was for a time his de facto prime minister, once said to Frances Perkins. "It seems unreasonable at times, but he falls back on something that gives him complete assurance that everything is going to be all right, that he isn't able to share with me, or to explain to me. Why should he be so sure that it will be all right?" "Why Harry," Perkins said, "it's clear that he's got a relationship to God." "I think that's it," Harry reflected. "But by gosh, I can't find out what it is or how he gets this relationship."

IF F.D.R. HAD A CLOSE relation to God, he had a hardly less intimate connection to the gatherers of intelligence. He always wanted to *know*; and if many of those who served him were skeptical of his habits of decision, few were anything other

---

* Roosevelt could be direct when he wanted to be. In November 1943 a cargo plane carrying American medical personnel, among them twelve women, crashed behind enemy lines in Albania. Frustrated by the slowness of the rescue operation, Roosevelt personally called the headquarters of the British Special Operations Executive in Cairo. "Captain Naar here," the duty officer answered. "Please hold for the President," said the operator. "This is Franklin Roosevelt. Why the fuck is it taking you so long to get those nurses out?" He did not pause for explanations. "Captain, if any one of those girls is so much as *touched*, there'll be serious consequences. . . . They are the flower of American womanhood. They must be saved . . ."

than impressed by the extent of his information. His practice of giving several people similar assignments meant that he was rarely dependent, in important matters, on a single person's knowledge and point of view. But he had, too, other, more devious ways of finding out. Gentlemen might not, as Henry Stimson said, read other gentlemen's mail, but they were free, at Roosevelt's direction, to listen to their telephone calls. The Federal Bureau of Investigation had, under J. Edgar Hoover, been tapping the wires for years when Attorney General Robert Jackson, citing the Supreme Court's interpretation of the Communications Act of 1934, forbade the practice. Roosevelt overruled him, and government agents were once against listening to the calls of suspected "spies, saboteurs, and traitors," as Roosevelt called them. They were also listening to the calls of the president's law-abiding opponents.

The degree to which F.D.R. was lord of the phones is suggested by Winston's Churchill's experience when, after his visit to the White House at Christmas, he was staying in Palm Beach. Wendell Willkie, whom Roosevelt had defeated in the 1940 presidential election, left a message for Churchill, and the prime minister responded by putting a call through to him. "After some delay," Churchill remembered, "I was told, 'Your call is through.' I said in effect, 'I am so glad to speak to you. I hope we may meet. I am traveling back by train tomorrow night. Can you not join the train at some point and travel with me for a few hours? Where will you be on Saturday next?' A voice came back: 'Why, just where I am now, at my desk.' To this I replied, 'I do not understand.' 'Whom do you think you are speaking to?' I replied, 'To Mr. Wendell Willkie, am I not?' 'No,' was the answer, 'you are speaking to the president.' I did not hear this very well, and asked, 'Who?' 'You are speaking to me,' came the answer, 'Franklin Roosevelt.'" Churchill got the message.

Francis Biddle, who succeeded Robert Jackson as attorney general after Jackson was elevated to the Supreme Court, was surprised that Roosevelt and his chief eavesdropper, J. Edgar Hoover, should have "liked and understood each other" so well. How odd, Biddle thought, that the man whom he had known for so many years should have become fond of a dour apparatchik who held the equivocal office of director of America's secret police. Where Eleanor thought that Hoover's techniques seemed, as she bluntly told him, "to smack too much of the Gestapo methods," Franklin winked at his transgressions. When Hoover confessed to him that one of his agents had been caught in the act of tapping the phone of a labor leader, the president laughed and clapped him on the back.

"By God, Edgar, that's the first time you've been caught with your pants down!" He "enjoyed Hoover's intimate gossip," Blanche Wiesen Cook writes, and he "loved reading his secret documents." He found Eleanor's own F.B.I. dossier highly diverting, telling a friend that if it were ever made public it "would make her appear to be the worst enemy of the United States." (Whatever else Hoover might have been, he was a man who knew how to be certain of keeping his job.)

"Do you realize," Churchill asked his wife, Clementine, on the night of June 5, 1944, "that by the time you wake in the morning twenty thousand men may have been killed?" The night before, Dwight Eisenhower, whom Roosevelt had made his supreme commander in Europe, had ordered the landings in Normandy to begin on the morning of the sixth.

Conscious of the momentousness of the event that was about to take place—the largest seaborne invasion in history—Roosevelt in the days before D-Day took up his prayer book. Studying the Elizabethan language of Thomas Cranmer, he wanted to find a way to talk to his fellow citizens that would do justice to the gravity of the occasion. As news of the landings reached America, church bells rang, and Roosevelt, drawing on the inspiration of Cranmer, addressed the nation in words of prayer. "Almighty God: Our sons, pride of our Nation, this day have set upon a mighty endeavor, a struggle to preserve our Republic, our religion, and our civilization, and to set free a suffering humanity . . ."

Oliver Wendell Holmes said that all societies rest ultimately on the death of men—on people's willingness to die for what they believe in. But theory is one thing, practice another: the "future slaughters" that Holmes prophesied would come with the clash of world-visions were now taking place. More than four thousand Allied warriors died on D-Day, and that figure was but a drop in an ocean of blood greater (to borrow Dante's figure) than that which stained Arabia's waters red. Amid so much dying, any one man's mortality might seem a trifle. But as the shadow of death began to creep over Roosevelt's own once ruddy face, those familiar with the state of his health began to prepare for his disappearance. In the weeks before the Democratic convention in Chicago that summer, party leaders, anxious over the succession, urged him to dump his current vice president, Henry Wallace, whom they looked on as a kook with a naïve faith in the virtues of the Soviet Union. Senator Harry Truman of Missouri became Roosevelt's running mate instead, and in August the president invited him to the White House. They lunched alfresco, in the shade of a magnolia tree, and

Roosevelt suggested that, so hot was the day, they might take off their coats. The next morning photographs of the two men in shirtsleeves appeared in newspapers across the country. Yet what shocked Truman was not the president's departure from decorum, but his trembling effort to pour cream into his tea: "he got more cream in the saucer than he did in the cup." He had not known that the president "was in such a feeble condition."

The state of the president's health was, in wartime, closely guarded as a national secret, and many of the relevant documents have vanished. Dr. Frank Lahey, founder of the Lahey Clinic in Boston, examined Roosevelt in 1944 and found him suffering from advanced cardiovascular disease; in his opinion the president did not have the "physical capacity" to complete another term of office. Others have speculated that he suffered not only from high blood pressure but from some form of cancer, a cancer of the stomach, perhaps, or a metastasizing melanoma. (A pigmented lesion above his left eye disappeared in the 1940s.)

Whatever the causes of Roosevelt's decline, he was now easily fatigued, and visitors found him, at times, groggy and listless. "Have you noticed that the President is a very tired man?" Winston Churchill asked his physician, Lord Moran, in 1943. "His mind seems closed; he seems to have lost his wonderful elasticity." It is true that, much of the time, he was as he had ever been, full of force and charm. But suddenly he would go dark. Senator Joseph O'Mahoney of Wyoming, having just seen Roosevelt, assured a colleague, Senator Frank Maloney of Connecticut, that he "was absolutely terrific . . . funny . . . charming . . . just like old times." But Maloney on going into Roosevelt's presence found his eyes "fixed in a glassy stare." He seemed to have "no idea who he was, or even that anyone was there." Afraid that the president had suffered a stroke, he made haste to inform General Edwin "Pa" Watson, the officer in charge of the president's appointments. "Don't worry," Watson said. "He'll come out of it. He always does." Turner Catledge of the *New York Times* had a similar experience. Having not seen Roosevelt in several months, he was "shocked and horrified" by his appearance, so much so that his "impulse was to turn around and leave. I felt I was seeing something I shouldn't see." The president sat in his chair "with a vague, glassy-eyed expression on his face and his mouth hanging open," and his "shirt collar hung so loose around his neck that you could have put your hand inside it." He "would start talking about something, then in mid-sentence he would stop and his mouth would drop open and he'd sit staring at me in silence."

As his last election approached, F.D.R. sought to dispel any impression that he was no longer up to the job, and to simulate good health, he allowed himself to be driven through the streets of New York in a cold October rain. At intervals along the route the president's car would be driven into a heated garage. The president would be lifted out of the car by Secret Service agents and set down on blankets on the concrete. The agents would then strip off the president's clothing, towel him dry, and give him a rubdown before dressing him in fresh clothes. Having been put back into the car and fortified with brandy, F.D.R. would return to the parade. More than a million people straining to catch a glimpse of the rain-soaked leader saw not a sickly old man but a gallant figure braving the elements.

THE EMPEROR VESPASIAN, SENSING THE approach of death, drolly remarked that he seemed to be becoming a god. (A sufficiently virtuous emperor might in death be deified by the Senate and enrolled in the Roman pantheon.) Those closest to Franklin Roosevelt in his last days acted as though they were tending a dying god, filled with consternation and something like awe as the great dominating spirit they had known was gradually extinguished before their eyes.

If he was among the most radical of American presidents, Roosevelt was also among the most traditional, a Tory radical. As such he had more patience with death than the conventional radical, who being unmoored in the past has less sense of death as a thing growing out of life and intimately involved in it.* For Roosevelt the passages of death were not, as they are for the conventional radical, merely a biological dead end. A Tory radical, being rooted in the very traditions he seeks to reform, is always in a dialogue with the dead; he moves as though in the presence of his forebears, in an atmosphere of canonized bones, ancestral voices, portraits in dark frames on dark walls. Roosevelt in his most progressive acts was conscious of upholding the standards of those who came before him, just as, he supposed, those who came after him would one day seek the inspiration of his own shade: much in the way Dante, in *Paradiso*, is nourished by his encounter with his ancestor, the great captain Cacciaguida, the "root" from which he sprang.

But not even the consolations of tradition, that knitting together of the living and the dead, could entirely take away mortality's sting. His mother, Sara Delano Roosevelt, had always been the preeminent woman in his life; his principal

---

* Roosevelt once defined a conventional radical as "a man with both feet firmly planted—in the air."

residence, Springwood, was her house; the land that held so much meaning for him was her land. Sara always said that Franklin was more a Delano than a Roosevelt, and he himself attributed his vitality and energy of character to her Delano blood; their bond, so close in his childhood, was hardly diminished with age, and though he was now the president, she still listened in on his telephone calls. "Mama, will you *please* get off the line," he was heard to say. "I can hear you breathing . . ." As she declined he spent much time alone in his bedroom; Eleanor compared his mood to Sara's "delicate Dresden china, which had to be handled with very great care." When she died at Springwood in September 1941 he was by her side. Afterward he shut "himself off from the world more completely than at any time" since taking office. Going through her things, he came upon some mementoes she had preserved, a lock of his baby hair, his first pair of shoes, gifts he had made her as a child. As tears started in his eyes, he asked to be left alone. She was buried beside her husband, Mr. James, in the churchyard of St. James's Church in Hyde Park. "In the midst of life we are in death," said the priest. Yet as the coffin was made ready to be laid into the earth, Franklin Roosevelt looked away.

Another cord was snapped in November 1944. Ten days after Franklin was elected to a fourth term as president, Endicott Peabody finished his lunch in Joy Lane and offered to drive a departing guest to the train station in Ayer. As they were going down Joy's Hill, Peabody observed that "Franklin Roosevelt is a very religious man." These were his last words. He pulled over to the side of the road and slumped in his seat.

Roosevelt was "shaken by Peabody's death." "I have leaned on the Rector all these many years," he said, "far more than most people know," and when, on January 20, 1945, he was inaugurated a fourth and final time, he paid tribute to his teacher. "I remember," he said in his last inaugural address, "that my old schoolmaster, Dr. Peabody, said in days that seemed to us then to be secure and untroubled: 'Things in life will not always run smoothly. Sometimes we will be rising toward the heights—then all will seem to reverse itself and start downward. The great fact to remember is that the trend of civilization itself is forever upward; that a line drawn through the middle of the peaks and the valleys of the centuries always has an upward trend.'"

The last inauguration found the president himself not on a peak but in a valley. It took place on the terrace of the south portico of the White House, and after the ceremony an exhausted Franklin retired to the Green Room while Eleanor received their guests. There was a stabbing pain in his innards. "Jimmy," he said to his oldest son, "I can't stand this unless you get me a stiff drink." Jimmy brought him a tumbler of whiskey and watched him drink it down straight. "It was the first time in my life," Jimmy said, "I ever saw father take a drink in that manner."

TWO WEEKS LATER THE *SACRED COW*, the presidential airplane, landed on the airfield at Saki in the Crimea. After greeting Churchill and the other dignitaries F.D.R. was driven past scenes of devastation—the Germans had abandoned the peninsula some nine months before—to Yalta and to Livadia, the palace of white limestone which Tsar Nicholas II had built on the site of an earlier residence, that of his grandfather, Alexander II, the liberator of the serfs.

"To a doctor's eye, the President appears to be a very sick man," said Lord Moran, the physician who attended Churchill. "He has all the symptoms of hardening of the arteries of the brain in an advanced stage, so that I give him only a few months to live." In the courtyard of Livadia Roosevelt sat for photographs with Churchill and Stalin; in his gauntness and elegance of style, the dark cape with velvet collar, the voluble cigarette, he was the image of an American patrician. But too little blood was now flowing through the thickened arteries to the patrician brain. The statesman who had so astutely perceived the evil of Hitler failed to discern the truth of Stalin. The master of the Kremlin was, Edmund Wilson had come to be believe, "the most cruel and unscrupulous of the merciless Russian tsars." But Roosevelt insisted that Stalin "doesn't want anything but security for his country," and that "if I give him everything I possibly can and ask nothing from him in return, noblesse oblige, he will not try to annex anything and will work with me for a world of democracy and peace." Bill Bullitt pointed out to Roosevelt that Stalin was not "the Duke of Norfolk" but "a Caucasian bandit, whose only thought when he got something for nothing was that the other fellow was an ass." But it was in vain; the president was determined, in his words, to "play my hunch."

Playing the hunch meant separating himself from Churchill, who found himself, at times, ignored by the American leader and mocked by the Soviet one. "There I sat," Churchill said, "with the great Russian bear on one side of me with paws outstretched, and, on the other side, the great American buffalo." He thought of himself as the "poor little English donkey . . . the only one who knew the right way home." "Germany is finished," he had told Harold Macmillan, the

British minister resident in Algiers, in 1943. "The real problem now is Russia. I *can't* get the Americans to see it." Yet he bore Roosevelt no ill will; indeed he became "angry when he heard criticism" of his friend, whose declining health once moved him to tears. "I love that man," he said.

Stalin, for his part, worked artfully to detach the president from the prime minister. The great commissar "particularly distinguished himself," Milovan Djilas tells us, "by his skill in exploiting people's weaknesses," and he soon discerned F.D.R.'s. The president was vain of his personal charm, with which he had won over so many opponents and pacified so many quarrels. He believed that he could sit down with Uncle Joe for what Harry Hopkins called a "heart-to-heart talk," appeal to their common humanity, and convince him to work disinterestedly to forestall aggression.* The Soviet leader had without scruple condemned millions of his own people to death, yet Roosevelt professed to believe that Stalin's youthful experience in the seminary had shaped him rather in the manner of Groton. "I think," he said, "that something entered into his nature of the way in which a Christian gentleman should behave." A similar naïveté underlay Roosevelt's faith that the new world parliament he envisioned, when duly established, could manage the territorial aspirations of Russia, and he was willing to make extravagant concessions to Stalin in order to ensure his cooperation in setting up the United Nations. But not even the most inspired lawgiver could have arranged an institutional machinery that would be at once acceptable to Stalin and at the same time a bulwark against the philosophy of force he embodied.

Quite as much as Woodrow Wilson, Roosevelt, in his last days, misread the world, and he misread human nature. Wilson had consigned such concepts as national interest and the balance of power to the ash heap of history.† But although F.D.R. would have been loath to admit it, those allegedly outmoded

---

* Yet Walter Lippmann detected cynicism even in Roosevelt's benevolence: "He distrusted everybody. What he thought he could do was to outwit Stalin, which is quite a different thing." Henry Kissinger dryly observed, "If that was his intention, he did not succeed."

† Churchill, as the inhabitant of a small island floating off Eurasia, had lived his whole life in the light of these concepts. For centuries, the English sought to preserve a balance of power in Europe that would prevent any single state from commanding resources sufficient to build a navy that could rival England's own. The policy underlay Churchill's resistance to Hitler; it is the burden of his biography of his ancestor, John Churchill, first Duke of Marlborough, the captain-general of the second Grand Alliance against Louis XIV; it led him to perceive the danger of Stalin when the oxygen-starved brain of his friend Franklin had succumbed to sentimentality.

ideas had guided his own response, in the 1930s, to the threat posed by Hitler, Tojo, and Mussolini. It was not in America's interest, he believed, to allow the Axis powers to upset the balance of power in Europe and Asia and thereby obtain mastery over their vast resources. But in his dealings with Stalin, he ceased to be a WASP realist in the tradition of Cousin Theodore: he reverted to the faith of the younger self who had, many years before, succumbed to the illusions of the League of Nations.

"THE PRESIDENT WAS THE WORST looking man I ever saw who was still alive," said the station master in Warm Springs as a much shrunken Franklin Roosevelt was taken from the train to the waiting car. It was his practice to help the Secret Service agents by gripping the car door so that he could thrust himself in, but on March 30, 1945, he was, agent Mike Reilly remembered, "absolutely dead weight."

Warm Springs seemed to revive him, and the sun took away the death pallor in his face. He worked in the mornings at a card table in his cottage, slept after lunch, and in the afternoons drove through a countryside coming to life with the spring, clotted with peach-blossom. "He sits a little straighter in his chair," Cousin Daisy wrote in her diary, "his voice is a little clearer and stronger, his face is less drawn & he is *happier!*" On April 5, he lunched with the president of the Philippines, and in the afternoon he held a press conference with the three press association reporters who had been permitted to accompany him. "Have a cig?" he asked as he pushed a pack of Camels across the card table toward the wire-service reporter Merriman Smith. Yet so palsied were his hands that, when he himself wanted a cigarette, he had difficulty extricating it from the pack, and no less trouble lighting it. "It was an intense thing," Smith remembered. "I wanted not to watch." But a moment later he was "waving his long cigarette holder jauntily" and cracking jokes. He had "a good suntan," Smitty said, but his face was "unusually drawn," and he had a cough.

He had, gathered about him in Warm Springs, the little harem that consoled and amused him whenever Eleanor was safely out of the way. In addition to Cousin Daisy, there was Cousin Polly Delano and Grace Tully, his secretary. But the principal ornament was missing, and one day he drove to Macon, Georgia, in search of Lucy Mercer Rutherfurd. He did not find her, and he was returning in disappointment to Warm Springs when he stopped at a drug store for a Coca-Cola. It was there that Mrs. Rutherfurd, who had been recently widowed, came upon her old lover sitting in his car, draped in his dark cape, sipping a Coke, and surrounded by a crowd of onlookers gasping at the unexpected sight of the president of the Republic. The artist Madame Shoumatoff, who had accompanied Lucy, was struck by the "expression of joy on F.D.R.'s face" when he saw Mrs. Rutherfurd.

The days went by. Smitty, the wire reporter, was on horseback when F.D.R. motored past him. "Heigh-O, Silver," the president cried. On the ninth Henry Morgenthau came to dine in the president's cottage. He was startled to find that Roosevelt had "aged terrifically" since he had last seen him and could only with difficulty mix the drinks. "His hands shook so that he started to knock the glasses over," Morgenthau said, "and I had to hold each glass as he poured the cocktail." At dinner Lucy was seated on his right, in the place of honor. She has "*so many* problems & difficulties," Cousin Daisy remembered the president telling her, and "no other person like him—a friend of such long standing—to whom to go for the kind of sympathetic understanding which he always gives." At night they all drew closer to the fire, and F.D.R. laughed and joked, doing his imitation of Churchill and calling Stalin "a jolly fellow." When the doctor told him it was time for bed, he begged like a child to be allowed to stay a little longer.

On the morning of Thursday, April 12, Madame Shoumatoff went to her easel to work on the portrait of the president she was painting. He was seated at his card table while Lucy and Daisy sat nearby on the sofa. Lizzie McDuffie, the maid, passed through on her way to make the beds. "The last I remember," she said, "he was looking into the smiling face of a beautiful woman." (Presumably it was the face of Mrs. Rutherfurd, for that of Cousin Daisy is in all the extant records described as plain.) A little after one o'clock, Madame Shoumatoff saw the president pass his hand across his forehead. Cousin Daisy thought that he seemed to fumble for something. "Have you dropped your cigarette?" she asked him. He said that he had a "terrific pain" in the back of his head. Later that afternoon a wire operator in the capital pressed the bell key four times and typed the shortest flash in the history of the wire service. FLASH WASHN—FDR DEAD.

THE GREATEST OF THE WASP reformers, Franklin Roosevelt was not a representative specimen of the breed. He had none of the neurasthenic longing that led his acquaintance Henry Adams to Chartres or his teachers Endicott Peabody and William Amory Gardner to Groton. He was never a lamb in search of a sheepfold, but ever the master of the manor, ending his days as liege lord of a sizable one. For Charles de Gaulle, he was "this artist, this seducer," for George Kennan, who served in his State Department, he was "a very superficial man, ignorant, dilettantish, with a severely limited intellectual horizon." Missy LeHand, his private secretary, believed that he "was really incapable of a personal friendship with anyone," for his real love was power, that most intense of narcotics, and one to which he was thoroughly addicted. "When you are in the center of world affairs," Eleanor said, "there is something so fascinating about it that you can hardly see how you are going to live any other way."

Few statesmen can have had so much of "that penetration of judgment," as Francis Bacon called it, by which a leader discerns "what things are to be laid open, and what to be secreted, and what to be shewed at half-lights, and to whom and when . . ." He was, says Geoffrey Hodgson, the biographer of Henry Stimson, "perhaps the most gifted political and strategic genius his country has produced." He devoted himself to reform on the grand scale, for with all his nonchalance, Franklin Roosevelt was as ambitious of patriotic distinction as they come. The WASP cult of public glory in which he had been schooled was hardly less fanatical than that of the Romans, and the man who established mandarin government in the United States even as he laid the cornerstone of the American Century had his own romance of lawgiving. Yet for all the magnitude of the achievement, something was missing. The greatest of the WASP statesmen died a sphinx with too many riddles, and left his fellow citizens few clues to that deeper regeneration which had long beguiled his class.

The Skull and Bones "Tomb" at Yale, a totem of the WASP power to keep everyone else out.

THIRTY-TWO

Pour le Mérite

Quell' è 'l più basso loco e 'l più oscuro . . .

That is the deepest and darkest place . . .
—Dante, *Inferno*

The egregious cases—Henry Adams, Edith Wharton (whose depiction of Simon Rosedale in *The House of Mirth* is a tissue of anti-Semitic clichés), T. S. Eliot fixing as Milton had done on "the dark idolatries of alienated Judah"—are perhaps less troubling than the milder, unexpected ones: Theodore Roosevelt, in a fit of pique, denouncing the *New Republic* as the work of "three anemic Gentiles and three international Jews," Louis Dow, Frances Hand's lover, writing of a "sickening sense of Jewdom about the Brandeis household," Eleanor

Roosevelt describing a "Jew party" in Bernard Baruch's house that seemed to her "appalling."

There were, to be sure, WASP philo-Semites, headed by Mr. Justice Holmes, who tried to overcome prejudice by dwelling on those things that the two groups had in common. WASPs were products of a Puritan tradition that derived at least as much inspiration from the Old Testament as from the New, and their forebears regarded themselves as a chosen people selected by providence to found a new Zion in the American wilderness.* Both groups, therefore, lived with a perfectionist heritage that induced hysteria. (Mutual neurosis as a potential bond.) WASPs noted, too, that they shared with Jews a respect for intellect and education, as well as a capacity for application and industry. The problem was that they suspected that Jews might, on the whole, surpass them in these things. The supposition seemed not unsupported by data. By 1922, the percentage of the student body of Harvard College that was thought (by apprehensive WASPs) to be Jewish had risen to some twenty-one percent. President Lowell (great-uncle of McGeorge Bundy and brother of Percival Lowell who had been beaten up by Jack Chapman) believed that such numbers would "ruin the college." "The summer hotel that is ruined by admitting Jews," he wrote by way of analogy, "meets it fate, not because the Jews it admits are of bad character, but because they drive away the Gentiles, and then after the Gentiles have left, they leave also." When Lowell demanded a quota of fifteen percent, Franklin Roosevelt, a member of the Harvard Board of Overseers, supported him. So intense was anti-Semitic feeling in some quarters of the university that when, in 1920, Francis Biddle asked Felix Frankfurter, the future Supreme Court Justice, to come to a banquet in the Fly Club in honor of Roosevelt, "several of the members of the club would not go to the dinner," and one refused to speak to Biddle because of the invitation he had extended to Frankfurter.

---

* The Puritans from whom so many of the WASPs descended identified strongly with the Jews of the Bible: of the two Testaments in that book, the Puritans, Macaulay wrote, felt for the Old one "a preference which, perhaps, they did not distinctly avow even to themselves, but which showed itself in all their sentiments and habits. They paid to the Hebrew language a respect which they refused to that tongue in which the discourses of Jesus and the epistles of Paul have come down to us. They baptized their children by the names, not of Christian saints, but of Hebrew patriarchs and warriors." "The Puritanism of New England," Edmund Wilson believed, "was a kind of new Judaism transposed into Anglo-Saxon terms. These Protestants, in returning to the text of the Bible, had concentrated on the Old Testament, and some had tried to take it as literally as any orthodox Jew."

Whether Roosevelt himself was closer to the philo- than to the anti- camp may be debated. The New Deal relaxed the WASP grip on the public service and opened the door to talented outsiders. F.D.R. not only worked closely with but enjoyed the company of men like Felix Frankfurter, Henry Morgenthau, and Ben Cohen, the New Deal lawyer and speechwriter. (Some of my best friends . . .) But lunching in 1942 with the economist Leo Crowley, who was Roman Catholic, he showed a different side of himself. America, he declared, "is a Protestant country, and the Catholics and the Jews are here on sufferance." It is possible that Crowley misheard or misrepresented the president's words—F.D.R. as a rule avoided unnecessarily antagonizing those to whom he was speaking. It is possible that he was letting off steam as opposed to saying what in the depths of his conscience he really thought.* One cannot imagine him saying, as Harold Nicolson did, that "although I loathe anti-Semitism, I do dislike Jews." Yet one senses in him those mixed feelings that long bedeviled the WASPs.

"I was a stranger, and ye took me in." The WASPs knew their Gospel, yet their cartel was premised on keeping the stranger out. Not from prejudice alone, but because they knew that their pursuit of power and effort at reform would fail without an intense tribal solidarity, one that would allow them to become a force in the world. The family tie, the club tie, the old school tie would allow them to band together to do good. In the bargain they made with themselves, they would obtain power, and pay for it in the coin of virtue.

But there were those who doubted their virtue even as they acknowledged or even exaggerated their power, and WASPs soon came to have a high place in the fantasies of what Richard Hofstadter called the paranoid imagination. The journalist Richard Rovere, in a May 1962 *Esquire* essay, "The American Establishment," satirized the naïveté of the conspiracy theorists. He pretended that he had gotten the name of the "chairman" of the WASP elite when John Kenneth Galbraith—who had "for some time been surreptitiously at work in Establishment studies"—confirmed his guess that it was John J. McCloy. (In the imaginations of the credulous, McCloy often figured as the real power in the state, the mayor of the palace, a dignity in which he was succeeded by David Rockefeller.) But in fact WASPs had only themselves to blame for their

---

* Roosevelt believed that he was to go before a judge who was "no respecter of persons"—that is, a God who looked at the soul itself and not its external trappings. "For there is no difference between the Jew and the Greek: for the same Lord over all is rich unto all that call upon him."

reputation for cryptic manipulation and intrigue. In a commercial democracy, where preeminence is brief as woman's love, an elite is bound to be insecure; those on top today will likely be submerged tomorrow. Insecurity breeds snobbery, a noli me tangere aloofness; and snobbery in turn breeds institutions like the Porcellian, St. Paul's School, and the Racquet Club, which in keeping out the hoi polloi (as they once did) can only provoke the excluded.* An organization like Skull and Bones, bathed in the lurid rumor of secret handshakes, nakedness in coffins, vast landholdings, purloined skulls, Mithraic rituals, and house courtesans, would seem to have been invented precisely to antagonize ingenuous souls who want to believe that the world really is romantically conspiratorial after the fashion of Stevenson's *New Arabian Nights* or Balzac's *La Comédie humaine*.

The reality of both Bones and the WASP elite as a whole was much duller, yet not so dull as to be unattractive to those looking in from outside. It is all very well for Edith Wharton and Joe Alsop to say that the WASPs never constituted anything like a true aristocracy, for by whatever name you call it, their ascendancy was seductive, even to those who in theory opposed it. "The moral attitudes of dominant and privileged groups," Reinhold Niebuhr wrote in his 1932 book *Moral Man and Immoral Society*, "are characterised by universal self-deception and hypocrisy." And yet in the 1940s he sent his son Christopher—to Groton! (He must have put it down to original sin.) By 1962 Niebuhr had so far made peace with the "dominant and privileged groups" that Rovere was able to jest that he was the Establishment's official theologian, the Pope of its Vatican. For however full of hypocrisy, arrogance, or mere dullness WASP institutions might have been, one disliked being excluded from them; they had something about them that made some part of you wish that you belonged to them.

THE MYSTIQUE OF THE WASPs derived from their power to exclude. The problem was that they could not hope to maintain the mystique without relaxing their exclusiveness. For with all their antipathy to the stranger, they soon recognized that cronyism and nepotism too rigidly pursued produced imbecility. It was evident fairly early in the WASP revival that an old boys' network was doomed if a certain number of exceptional new boys were not admitted to leaven the stupidity of the hereditary lump; a patriciate without the means of change was without

---

* Snobbery is, to be sure, the perversion of a passion originally virtuous. The choicer forms of order grow out of so many repulsions and disgusts: the snob errs only in carrying these salutary nauseas into trivial realms.

the means of survival. Groton, for all its reputation for wealth and snobbishness, saw the difficulty and in the 1890s began to admit by competitive examination a number of boys for whom "tuition was an insurmountable obstacle." The "rivalry for places is severe," Frank Ashburn wrote, "and the standard for the successful candidates very high." These merit-based admissions not only gave the school "a wider social spread" and raised its "scholastic standard," they also acted as a brake on the legacy preference. Groton, Ashburn wrote, knew all the "sorrows" which came from excluding some portion of "its own flesh and blood" from its fields and halls. But by doing so it was able to take in promising newcomers like John Goodenough.

Young Henry Chauncey had a foot in both worlds, hereditary privilege and threadbare merit. His father, Egisto, was a graduate of the Groton form of 1892, two years behind Frank Polk and Ellery Sedgwick and two years ahead of Payne Whitney and Henry Adams's nephews John and Henry. But Egisto was called to the Anglican priesthood, and Henry's Groton tuition was paid only with the help of relatives. The future curtailer of legacy admissions was one of just two sons of graduates in the Groton form of 1923, in which he rose to be senior prefect. (The other hand-me-down was Alfred Mahan, the son of Lyle Mahan '97 and grandson of the admiral.) But Chauncey, looking at the forms immediately below him, saw the writing on the wall: they were filling up, at an alarming rate, with the second possessors of foolish faces. The question to which he was to devote much of his life was how schools could best promote genuine merit by discerning the most luminous minds.

Older methods of separating the wheat from the chaff were, he saw, either haphazard and amateurish or biased. (Even a great natural genius had little hope of performing well on the old Harvard entrance examinations if he had not studied under a capable teacher of Greek and Latin.) The public schools from which novel talent might be derived were so various in their standards that it was not easy to tell the really intelligent student from the mediocre one. Chauncey, who followed his father to Harvard and later became an assistant dean in the university, found a solution to the problem in standardized tests that allegedly measured raw intelligence with a much greater degree of accuracy than other methods. He went on to become one of the founders of the Educational Testing Service, which gave America the Scholastic Aptitude Test or S.A.T.

The result was a meritocracy that did as much as anything (other than the New Deal wealth tax) to undermine the WASP ascendancy, for it broke the WASPs' near monopoly of schools like Harvard, Yale, and Princeton. The new regime was decidedly fairer than the old one, but it had the unintended effect of hindering those salutary projects which WASPs, for all their shortcomings, had long cherished. Henry Adams and John Jay Chapman believed that America's hysterically competitive society was destroying the very things that made existence something other than an organized bore—the old civic artistry of place, techniques of learning that broadened the soul and developed its latent possibilities, all that moral and spiritual refinement which constitutes the unbought poetry of life. The new science of merit, by contrast, seemed to exacerbate the rat race, to reduce life to a mechanical checking of boxes, a crude Pavlovian system of rewards that, so far from developing human potential, seemed to stunt it.* A present-day critic of meritocracy, Daniel Markovits, has gone so far as to cast a languishing glance at the world in which children of people like the WASPs once grew up, so different from the life of "meritocratic children" today who must relentlessly "calculate their future—they plan and they scheme, through rituals of stage-managed self-presentation, in familiar rhythms of ambition, hope, and worry." Professor Markovits has, I suppose, no wish to revert to the old system that allowed a few privileged souls, a Henry Adams, a Franklin Roosevelt, a certain margin in life in which their deeper character could ripen. His point is that Chauncey's system has its own drawbacks.

Yet for all that, Chauncey and his tests did something to forge the broader, ecumenical elite that governs America today. With changes in admissions policies at the more selective schools, much else changed, and changed fast. A WASP of the old school might have had reservations about the young Harvard man of doubtful provenance who was courting his daughter at Radcliffe. But he soon enough relented; he walked his daughter to the altar, and afterward was not about to try to keep his son-in-law out of the yacht club or the country club. WASP blood-pride died hard, but it *did* die, and soon enough novelist John P. Marquand Jr., the son of Ellery Sedgwick's niece Christina, was inviting Norman Podhoretz to the old Sedgwick house in Stockbridge. The visit was not without its awkward moments; Podhoretz and his wife, Midge Decter, were said to have

---

* Judge Calabresi, when he was dean of Yale Law School, tried to resist what was robotic and mechanical in the meritocracy by urging his students to look on their time at Yale as a "break from the treadmill." But this was easier said than done.

felt as though they had entered Cossack territory. But that the visit happened at all was a sign of change.

THE BINGHAMS OF HARVARD, RADCLIFFE, and the *Louisville Courier-Journal* were staunch liberals. Robert Worth Bingham, a lawyer in Louisville who married Mary Lily Flagler, a Standard Oil heiress, was Franklin Roosevelt's first ambassador to the Court of St. James's; his son Barry Bingham and his wife, Mary, vigorously supported the civil rights movement and were closely allied to Adlai Stevenson. One hot summer day in 1945 their son, thirteen-year-old Worth, invited George, the son of the gardener, to swim in the pool at Melcombe, the Bingham estate in Louisville. "Mother screamed at us," Worth's younger brother Barry remembered. "She began to go on and on about polio and syphilis and the germs that colored people have. . . . Then she drained the pool. This was the first sense Worth and I ever had that our parents were really hypocrites. The newspapers could stand for one thing in public, but in private it was a different story entirely."

Eleanor Roosevelt, a guest of the Binghams at Melcombe, had her own manner of racial condescension. "Darky servants came," she wrote in her journal in March 1919 after she dismissed her white servants: "heaven knows how it will all turn out!" She had been told that, "properly trained, the colored people were the most faithful and efficient servants in the world." So, apparently, it proved, as far as she was concerned. "Amid a world of people who are having fearful domestic trials," she wrote her friend Isabella Selmes, "I seem to be sailing along peacefully," for her "darky household," as she called it, was a success.*

When, during her husband's presidency, Eleanor published an installment of her memoirs in which she adverted to these domestic felicities, people of color were stung. "Alas as I was reading," Esther Carey of Chicago wrote her, "I came across two mentions of 'darky.' I couldn't believe my eyes. Surely no one of the

---

* As mistress of a great WASP household, Eleanor seemed at times oblivious of how different her own "fearful" trials were from those of the greater number of her fellow citizens. During the First World War, she was interviewed by a *New York Times* reporter about the management of her household in wartime and was quoted in the paper as attributing her economizing skill to "making the ten servants help me to do my saving . . ." It was not the sort of publicity Franklin found helpful in his public career. "I am proud to be the husband," he wrote to Eleanor at Campobello, "of the Originator, Discoverer and Inventor of the New Household Economy for Millionaires! Please have a photo taken showing the family, the ten cooperating servants, the scraps saved from the table, and the handbook. I will have it published in the Sunday Times."

Roosevelt blood could be guilty of using this hated term, and we do hate it, as much as the Jew hates 'sheeny' and the Italian 'dago' or 'wop.'" A graduate of the Tuskegee Institute in Alabama, Mrs. Carey said that she looked upon Eleanor's "Uncle Theodore with reverence and thought that the blood of a Roosevelt could not hurt and humiliate Negroes who live and struggle under such dreadful handicaps." When the "First Lady of the Land dubs us 'darkies' it hurts . . ."

To be sure, Eleanor was, by the 1930s, putting aside prejudice against "darkies" * and urging the country to acknowledge the rights of African Americans. In 1939 she resigned her membership of the one of the more snobbish of the WASP syndicates, the Daughters of the American Revolution, when Marian Anderson was refused permission to sing in Constitution Hall in Washington, where the D.A.R. held its annual conventions. Later in the year she invited Miss Anderson to perform at the White House, and afterward presented her to King George VI and Queen Elizabeth. But although WASPs were coming to pique themselves on their freedom from prejudice, there was a whiff of slumming in their kindness; Henry James's Princess Casamassima lived on in their virtuous condescension. It was they who were doing the outsiders a favor, they who were allowing strangers into their institutions, to show them how they did things. There was no relaxation of their pale dominion; virtue, for them, was power, as well as a pleasurable form of self-aggrandizement. Patricians in the past distributed alms to gaping plebs and got themselves adored; WASPs promised to lead people of color to a better place and did not mind getting themselves worshipped in the process.

Yet in one of the matters closest to their own hearts, the artistry of community, WASPs had more to learn than to teach. The ancestors of African Americans, who as slaves had been denied a civic life, "created songs in community," Cheryl A. Kirk-Duggan writes, "incubating the music until the singing helped to liberate them." The blues people who made a common life in the face of whips and bloodhounds knew a good deal more about poetry as the molder of community than any WASP did. But WASPs were incapable of learning from those whom

---

* Eleanor's friend Henry Adams also used the word, observing that Lizzie Cameron's husband, Senator J. Donald Cameron, who had bought a house on Saint Helena Island in South Carolina, was "supporting the darkies, who are all washed out of their sand-holes, by paying them fifty cents a day to make a shell road as far as Ward's store . . ." Adams came from an antislavery family, but persons of color figured for him largely as beings who, like Dawson, his coachman, and Gray, his manservant, were created to take care of people . . . like him. He did not, he said, like to "cross the color-line" in the matter of domestic service, or indeed in any other sphere.

they looked on as protégés. They acted, Ernest Wilson said, "as if we were a Black tabula rasa ready to be filled with New England education and high culture."

WASPs did know something about the liberating power of humane education, but even here they were patronizing, oblivious of the fact that Blacks were already pursuing the ideal more passionately in their own schools than Franklin Roosevelt had done at Harvard or Henry Stimson at Yale. In 1897 W.E.B. Du Bois, who had been educated at Fisk University and Harvard, where he studied under William James and was the first African American to obtain a doctorate from the university, became a professor of history and economics at Atlanta University in Georgia, an historically Black institution. The beauty of the place, he said, lay in the "simple unity" of the life lived on its hilltop: a "broad lawn of green rising from the red street and mingled roses and peaches; north and south, two plain and stately halls; and in the midst, half hidden in ivy, a larger building, boldly graceful, sparingly decorated, and with one low spire." One "never looks," Du Bois said, "for more; it is all here, all intelligible." The reader will will perhaps search in vain for a more powerful expression of the virtues of humane education—its effect on the soul, the fair sheepfold it seeks—than Du Bois gives. "There I live," he wrote:

> and there I hear from day to day the low hum of restful life. In winter's twilight, when the red sun glows, I can see the dark figures pass between the halls to the music of the night-bell. In the morning, when the sun is golden, the clang of the day-bell brings the hurry and laughter of three hundred young hearts from hall and street, and from the busy city below,—children all dark and heavy-haired,—to join their clear young voices in the music of the morning sacrifice. In a half-dozen class-rooms they gather then,— here to follow the love-song of Dido, here to listen to the tale of Troy divine; there to wander among the stars, there to wander among men and nations,—and elsewhere other well-worn ways of knowing this queer world. Nothing new, no time-saving devices,— simply old time-glorified methods of delving for Truth, and searching out the hidden beauties of life, and learning the good of living. The riddle of existence is the college curriculum that was laid before the Pharaohs, that was taught in the groves by Plato, that formed the trivium and quadrivium, and is to-day laid before

the freedmen's sons by Atlanta University. And this course of study will not change; its methods will grow more deft and effectual, its content richer by toil of scholar and sight of seer; but the true college will ever have one goal,—not to earn meat, but to know the end and aim of that life which meat nourishes. The vision of life that rises before these dark eyes has in it nothing mean or selfish. Not at Oxford or at Leipsic, not at Yale or Columbia, is there an air of higher resolve or more unfettered striving; the determination to realize for men, both black and white, the broadest possibilities of life, to seek the better and the best, to spread with their own hands the Gospel of Sacrifice,—all this is the burden of their talk and dream.

George Kennan advanced the cause of the American
Century even as he was nauseated by its culture.

THIRTY-THREE

Centurions of an American Century

tra tirannia si vive e stato franco . . .

between tyranny and a free state . . .
—Dante, *Inferno*

In February 1946 George Kennan, minister-counselor in the American embassy in Moscow, lay in bed, feverish under one of his periodic sieges of illness. The ambassador, Averell Harriman, was not then in residence, and it was left to Kennan, suffering under his various *douleurs*, as he called them, to attend as best he could to the press of business. Among the items brought to his attention was a cable from Washington requesting "interpretative guidance" concerning a speech Marshal Stalin had recently made at the Bolshoi Theater in Moscow. After tumultuous cries of "Long live great Stalin . . . . Cheers for our beloved

Stalin!" the master of a large swath of Eurasia* declared from the rostrum that it was "impossible under the present capitalist conditions of world economic development" to prevent future "catastrophic wars." In such an environment, the "Motherland," he said, must be insured "against all contingencies."

Washington was baffled. Hitler was dead and Tojo immured in Sugamo; Germany and Japan lay vanquished amid the smoking ruins of their cities. Yet Stalin, America's ally in the struggle against the Axis powers, the leader whom Franklin Roosevelt looked on as a partner in the creation of a "world of democracy and peace," was now baring his fangs and prophesying war. What, America's policymakers wanted to know, lay behind it all?

Kennan, bedridden though he was, resolved not to "brush the question off with a couple of routine sentences," the sort of easily digestible, easily forgettable prose favored by the busy technicians of bureaucracy, that giant power, as Balzac called it, wielded by pygmies. "It would not do," he said, "to give them just a fragment of the truth. Here was a case where nothing but the whole truth would do. They had asked for it. Now, by God, they would have it." Though he knew his response to the State Department's query—it ran to some five thousand words—was an "outrageous encumberment of the telegraphic process," he believed that the questions involved were "so intricate, so delicate, so strange to our form of thought, and so important to the analysis of our international environment" that he could not dispose of them briefly without yielding to a "dangerous degree of over-simplification."

He began by stating the obvious, that the Soviet leadership believed that it was threatened by a "capitalist encirclement" with which it could never peacefully coexist. But the deeper difficulty, he said, was that Stalin, the inheritor of the empire of the tsars, felt the vulnerabilities of that empire in precisely the way the tsars themselves had felt it. "At bottom of Kremlin's neurotic view of world affairs," he wrote (dropping his articles for the sake of telegraphic economy), was Russia's "traditional and instinctive" sense of insecurity:

> Originally, this was insecurity of a peaceful agricultural people trying to live on vast exposed plain in neighborhood of fierce

---

* Santayana was struck by the way Stalinism, with its "systematic extermination of all other ways of thinking," had come "to cover vast regions of Europe and Asia like a blanket of Siberian snow." "The depth of it," he said, "is unknown, but the silence is impressive."

nomadic peoples. To this was added, as Russia came into contact with economically advanced West, fear of more competent, more powerful, more highly organized societies in that area. But this latter type of insecurity was one which afflicted rather Russian rulers than Russian people; for Russian rulers have invariably sensed that their rule was relatively archaic in form fragile and artificial in its psychological foundation, unable to stand comparison or contact with political systems of Western countries.

The precariousness of Russia was both geographic, for it lay at the crossroads of Eurasia, and technical, for it languished under the dead hand of despotism (the natural government of the geographically precarious). Its rulers lived in a double fear of those at home, whom they ruled, and those abroad, who might rule them; they therefore shunned "compacts and compromises" with more safely situated and technically advanced powers (that could crush Russia or overturn its government) even as they sought constantly to take advantage of any weakness or distractedness those powers showed.

Not even the most inspired diplomatic overtures, Kennan believed, could alter these distinctly Russian habits of thought and action. The task of American policy was rather to restrict the scope of the evil, to counter the provocations of a country ruled by suspicious, cunning masters in the mold of Ivan the Terrible. Russia was, Kennan believed, "undoubtedly the greatest" challenge American diplomacy had "ever faced." But it was a challenge that could nevertheless be overcome. In his Long Telegram, as it came to be called, he was groping his way toward a policy that would (in words he would use in a State Department meeting in September 1946) "contain" the threat posed by the Soviet Union "both militarily and politically."

THE MAN WHO STOOD GODFATHER to the Cold War doctrine of containment had been born in Milwaukee in 1904. His mother died of a ruptured appendix nine weeks after giving birth to him; his father was a tax lawyer. The family descended from emigrants from Scotland and the north of England who, imbued with the old Puritan culture of the north Britons, came to America in the eighteenth century to farm the land and worship God. In addition to a lingering Puritanism, there was in the family heritage a notable example of intellectual achievement and adventurous romance, that of a cousin of George

Kennan's grandfather who was also called George Kennan, a man who devoted much of his life to the study of Russia. "The life of this elder Kennan and my own," Kennan wrote in his memoirs, "have shown similarities that give, to me at least, the feeling that we are connected in some curious way by bonds deeper than just our rather distant kinship."

Inspired by Scott Fitzgerald's recently published novel *This Side of Paradise*, Kennan went to Princeton. He found it difficult to fit in; as an outsider from the Midwest, he had no entrée into the circles of graduates of the fashionable boarding schools. Fitzgerald, too, had been an outsider, but where he had happily thrown himself into the effort to scale the WASP hierarchies, Kennan, a "thin, tense, introverted" young man, as he remembered himself, had "no idea how to approach boys from the East," and during bicker week, when students were invited to join eating clubs, his pride kept him away from vanity fair.* An acquaintance nevertheless sought him out and persuaded him to join a club. He did so, but unwilling, he said, "to make social prestige" the "sole aim of life," he subsequently resigned, and thereafter took his meals "among the nonclub pariahs" in the gloomy refectory known as upper-class commons. In truth he was not fitted for the life of a country club, which in that era Princeton largely was; and some part of what he called his gloomy, puritanical nature shrank instinctively from the callow sons of Belial, "flown with insolence and wine."

After Princeton Kennan was accepted into the American consular and diplomatic service, having gone before a panel headed by the solicitous Joe Grew. He "rather loved" consular work, and found that public service offered an escape from the neurasthenic self. I "discovered that in this new role as representative (however lowly) of a government rather than of just myself, the more painful personal idiosyncrasies and neuroses tended to leave me, at least in the office."

---

* Fitzgerald's own view of WASPland would darken, and he would later dwell on all that separated him from the preppies of the Northeast. In *The Great Gatsby* he makes Nick Carraway reflect on how he and his friends from the West differed from those with whom they went to school in the East: "I see now that this has been a story of the West, after all—Tom and Gatsby, Daisy and Jordan and I, were all Westerners, and perhaps we possessed some deficiency in common which made us subtly unadaptable to Eastern life. Even when the East excited me most, even when I was most keenly aware of its superiority to the bored, sprawling, swollen towns beyond the Ohio, with their interminable inquisitions which spared only the children and the very old—even then it had always for me a quality of distortion." In a curious reversal of fortune, Kennan, who never consciously sought to join the WASP ascendancy, found himself, as an adult, in the center of it, much loved and admired by its best known figures, while Fitzgerald, forgotten by the nabobs of Princeton, died obscurely of drink in Los Angeles.

With his relative, the elder George Kennan, much in his mind, he trained for the State Department's Russia service, studying the language in Berlin and in the Baltic capitals of Tallinn and Riga. When, in 1933, the United States and the Soviet Union established diplomatic relations, Kennan accompanied Bill Bullitt, the American ambassador, to the Kremlin, where Bullitt presented his credentials to the Old Bolshevik Mikhail Kalinin; afterward the two Americans set up the new embassy.

THE RUSSIAN LANGUAGE SEEMED TO Kennan like one he had known in a previous existence, and he found in its grammar a means of expressing aspects of his nature that were unrenderable in the Western idioms with which he had grown up. He had, from boyhood, "habitually read special meaning into things, scenes, and places—qualities of wonder, beauty, promise, or horror—for which there was no external evidence visible, or plausible, to others." The mysticism of old Russia—the Russia of the *moujici* (peasants), *startsi* (holy men), *skomorokhi* (wandering minstrels), and *kalyeki* (crippled singers)—appealed to something in his own nature. He had an intuitive perceptiveness akin to that of the misfits and holy fools of primordial Muscovy; the diplomat who experienced visionary ecstasy in the birch woods was the spiritual cousin of Dostoevsky's Makar Dolgoruky and Leskov's Alexander Ryzhov. But he was, finally, *only* a cousin, and during his second posting in Russia he would reflect in sorrow that "I will never be able to become part of them, that I must always remain a distrusted outsider, that all the promise of the white nights, of the lovely birches," could "never be realized" by a forty-year-old American foreign-service officer.

Kennan liked nothing better, he said, than "to drink in impressions of Russia . . . of its life, its culture, its aspect, its smell." His love of the old Russia, a Russia which endured even under Stalinism in "the apogee of its horror," coincided with his deepening dislike of the culture of the modern West and more especially modern America. He came to hate "the endless streams of cars, the bored, set faces behind the windshields, the chrome, the asphalt, the advertising, the television sets, the filling-stations, the hot-dog stands, the barren business centers, the suburban brick houses." He resented "the ruthless destruction of setting" that was everywhere going on, an obliteration of place that weakened all the sinews of common life. At the same time a "sickly secularism" and a readiness to prefer vacuous social science to "the more subtle and revealing expressions of man's nature" in the Bible and Shakespeare was subverting the cultural infrastructure of the West, the wisdom that had enabled Old Western peoples to balance individualism and commonalty, the claims of the flesh and the claims of the spirit, more ingeniously (in some respects) than their descendants. In place of the older arts and wisdoms, Kennan said, were solipsistic technologies that invited people to withdraw into neurotic cocoons—into "private lives" so "brittle" and "insecure" that those who lived them "dared not subject them to the slightest social contact with the casual stranger." The diplomat whose theories would do much to advance the cause of the American Century wanted to escape from the culture the American Century would deepen and extend.

AFTER THE PRIVATIONS OF WAR, the revival of the Washington dinner party seemed to Joe Alsop and his Georgetown circle of WASPs a paradise regained. There were, of course, the formal dinners, often given in honor of some visiting potentate, but there were, too, the more purely tribal meals, the WASP version of the mess halls (*syssitia*) of old Crete, by which they maintained their caste fellowship in the democratic capital. On Sunday evenings, when they were largely without servants, the WASPs would gather, at one house or another, for a potluck affair they called Sunday Night Supper or, as Alsop styled it, Sunday Night Drunk. At any given meal one might find, among the diners, Marie and Averell Harriman, Alice and Dean Acheson, Annelise and George Kennan, Adele and Bob Lovett, Tish and Stewart Alsop. "They would all argue at the top of their lungs," Tish remembered, and the arguments were often fierce. Chip Bohlen, a Sunday night regular and the second most brilliant Russia man in the State Department (after his friend George Kennan) was a handsome WASP who had come up through St. Paul's, Harvard, and the Porcellian; as a young man he had fortified himself for his appearance before the panel that was to determine his fitness for the Foreign Service by drinking gin. (One of the examiners, smelling it on his breath, wanted to turn him away, but another State Department eminence, William Castle, took pity on his fellow Harvard man.) Two decades later Chip was still priming his eloquence with gin. Growing impatient, after a few of Joe Alsop's martinis, with one of Joe's specious arguments, he shouted, "Get out of my house!" This Joe could not consent to do, for, as he pointed out, they were in fact in *his* house.

Marietta Tree, née Peabody, was another source of postwar WASP merriment. "I was staggered," Arthur Schlesinger said, when a "stunning tall blonde girl in a smashing red dress swept" into a dinner party in Paris. Slipping into the (for him) uncharacteristic idiom of a bodice-ripping romance, he confessed that "I fell in love with her the first second I saw her." Yet to do him justice, Marietta might well have *been* the heroine of a bodice-ripper. The granddaughter of the Rector of Groton, she was a shapely blonde who aspired to be the mistress of a great salon. Shortly after her grandfather's death she divorced her husband, the swashbuckling C.I.A. preppy Desmond Fitzgerald, to marry Ronald Tree, an English gentleman of leisure whose mother's father, Marshall Field, the founder of the Chicago department store, had left him enough money to support his new wife's ambition, that of making a great center and gathering-place of the American Century, much in the way Mme. Geoffrin had made a great center and gathering-place of the eighteenth century. But Mme. Geoffrin left Paris only once, to visit Warsaw; Marietta's salon was in perpetual motion as she made her progresses from her London residence to her pied-à-terre in Manhattan, and from thence to her villa, built of coral stone in a Palladian style, at Heron Bay in Barbados. But there were difficulties; Ronnie seemed more interested in boxer shorts than corsets. ("Poor Marietta, with all her luscious flesh unappreciated . . .") The graver problem was that Ronnie was a Tory, and Marietta, who inclined to the Whig reform side, wanted a range of opinion. She solved the problem by taking Adlai Stevenson as her lover, much to the chagrin of Joe Alsop, who thought Adlai the embodiment of starry-eyed, impractical liberalism. Casting a jaundiced eye on Marietta's voluptuous figure, he dismissed her political passions as a case of "beautiful bosoms beating for beautiful causes."

Yet with all this glamour, the postwar years were a bit of a drop for the WASPs. The new tax regime deprived many of them of that margin of capital on which their public service depended; their schools were meritocrasizing; their children were marrying strangers. The Cold War revived them and gave them a new sense of purpose. They were not by nature enthusiasts; they were never engagé in the way that French intellectuals are engagé; but when they saw that by fighting the good fight against communism they might run the world, they gave Sartre himself a run for his money. If Sartre was committed to Stalin, the WASPs were as profoundly on the other side. Their internationalism had, as early as 1921, possessed a temple, the Council on Foreign Relations, but it was only with the arrival of George Kennan's Long Telegram that they found a creed. Containment was their credo, and under Dean Acheson's generalship they were quick to give it expression in such world-altering policies as the Marshall Plan and NATO, even as the cloak-and-dagger institutions of the national-security state extended their lease on public life.

They quibbled about the details. Containment, as Acheson's boss, Harry Truman, understood it, was disturbingly uncontained. The Truman Doctrine committed the United States to support all "free peoples" who were "resisting attempted subjugation by armed minorities or by outside pressures" anywhere in the world. Walter Lippmann pointed out that so broad a policy of engagement would lead to over-extension. George Kennan agreed. Why, he asked, must Americans invoke Woodrow Wilson's shade and use "universal formulae" to "clothe and justify particular actions"? The answer, Dean Acheson knew, was that Americans, if they *had* to give up their old isolationist habits and act in the world, were determined to act virtuously. Theodore Roosevelt's theory of geopolitical interest would have seemed to them too cynical; it was much prettier to think, as Woodrow Wilson did, that the United States, in going forth to slay monsters abroad, was providentially extending the blessings of its own city on a hill to a suffering humanity.

In deferring to the sentimentality of their countrymen, WASPs like Alsop and Acheson found themselves in a curious position. For they themselves had lost some essential part of John Winthrop's faith in the city on the hill. They had, as a class, been invented by people like Henry Adams and John Jay Chapman who believed that America's free state, if it was an economic success, was a cultural failure. As a *civilization* it did not come up to Chartres or Venice or Athens; Henry James made a notorious list of the ways in which it failed to measure up even to philistine England. One might, James said in his study of Nathaniel Hawthorne, enumerate

> the items of high civilization, as it exists in other countries, which are absent from the texture of American life, until it should become a wonder to know what was left. No State, in the European sense of the word, and indeed barely a specific national name. No sovereign, no court, no personal loyalty, no aristocracy, no church, no clergy, no army, no diplomatic service, no country gentlemen, no palaces, no castles, nor manors, nor old country-houses, nor parsonages, nor thatched cottages nor ivied ruins; no cathedrals, nor abbeys, nor little Norman churches; no great Universities nor public schools—no Oxford, nor Eton, nor Harrow; no literature, no

novels, no museums, no pictures, no political society, no sporting class—no Epsom nor Ascot!

George Kennan, echoing Henry, went so far as to say that he had found, in the mud and absolutism of Russia, a civilization which, even after twenty years of Bolshevism, was a good deal richer than that of the America of chewing gum and hot-dog stands.

It has long been commonplace to say of the WASP proconsuls of the American Century, from Averell Harriman to David Rockefeller, that they pursued their internationalist policies out of a passion for power and profit, from a love of dominion and a desire to open lucrative markets. The reality was more complicated, and considerably sadder. The WASP wanted to escape from America as from a much loved friend who has yet begun to be a bore. Thirty years ago a member of the Cravath firm, after lunch in the little club at the top of the Chase Manhattan building, pointed out the landmarks of the city below and then turned to the west, bathed in a sunlit haze that stretched to the horizon. "And out there's America," he said softly, reflectively, as though pondering the reality, after decades spent counseling great banks and investment concerns—a career as a superb technician of capital—that America "out there" was scarcely known to him, an immense but strange, essentially foreign country. He then took the elevator a few floors down to resume his labors. The country that lay beyond the precincts of Manhattan, the Federal District, and the various suburbs, watering holes, and finishing schools of the seaboard was for many WASPs not merely terra incognita, it was terra that they were for the most part content to let remain incognita. What they longed to experience was not America but those parts of the world that were not yet Americanized.

IN 1948 WHITTAKER CHAMBERS WAS on the staff of *Time,* and in the opinion of Henry Luce the best writer the magazine ever had. A journalist visiting him in his office high above Rockefeller Center mentioned a woman who had recently gone to the F.B.I. with a tale of Soviet espionage. The woman's name was Elizabeth Bentley, and that summer Chambers learned from the newspaper that she was to testify before the House Un-American Activities Committee. Showing the story to his wife, Esther, he said, "I think that I may be called to testify too."

"What will you do?" she asked.

"I shall testify."

Ten years before Chambers had broken with the Communist Party and ceased to be an agent of Soviet military intelligence, the G.R.U. (He had, he said, heard the screams.) In August 1939, when the nonaggression pact between the Soviet Union and the German Reich was concluded, he had just started at *Time*, was making good money, and was finding success in his new, post-communist life. But he was unable to forget the "tigerish smile" on Stalin's face as he became the ally of Hitler and "unloosed upon mankind" the "horror of world war." He flew to Washington, where he informed Adolf A. Berle, a New Deal lawyer who as assistant secretary of state for Latin American affairs was advising President Roosevelt on security matters, of the existence of Russian espionage networks in the United States. (Chambers was afraid that the Soviet Union would share the intelligence it gathered with the Nazis.) The Roosevelt administration sat on the information.

It was different in 1948. The Iron Curtain had fallen across Europe, and Soviet spies had penetrated the Manhattan Project, the venture Franklin Roosevelt had on his personal authority undertaken to build the atomic bombs that were exploded over Japan in 1945. When, in August 1948, Chambers presented himself in the committee room of the House Un-American Activities Committee to bear witness before the country that Americans were "at grips with a secret, sinister and enormously powerful force whose tireless purpose is their enslavement," the country was ready to listen.

Eccovi l' uom ch' e stàto all' inferno . . . See, there is the man that was in hell. So Dante was pointed out in the streets of Verona, and so Chambers looked under the lights of the House Un-American Activities Committee, a tormented figure struggling under the burden of his revelation, as it was sympathetically elicited by a young congressman from California, Richard Milhous Nixon. Chambers's testimony led to the fall of Alger Hiss, the talented Harvard-trained lawyer who had clerked for Mr. Justice Holmes and served in high positions in the State Department. In 1950 Hiss was convicted in federal court of the crime of having perjured himself when he said, under oath, that he had not passed secret government documents to Chambers in his capacity as a Soviet spy.

Chambers did not "self-identify" as a WASP; he left Williams College because he shrank from the gig of WASP respectability his mother wanted for him. But he could not escape either his class or its preoccupations; he was a liberally educated man shaped by the humane idea of doing justice to whatever it was he had in him. As much as Henry Adams and George Kennan, he was convinced that America's contemporary culture stood in the way of this kind of human fulfillment. It was for this reason that he lived on a farm in Maryland, "beyond the smog of the great cities, seeing few newspapers, seldom hearing the radio, seldom seeing motion pictures, untouched by the excitements by which the modern world daily stimulates its nervous crisis." He had once sought a solution to the nervous crisis in secular progress, and since it was not in his nature to do anything by half-measures, he had become a communist. Now, having broken with communism, he went to what some would see as the opposite extreme. Endicott Peabody, speaking at his last Prize Day, said that the age was one in which "freedom is threatened by tyranny, Christianity by paganism." This was Chambers's own mature view; human beings, in their "mortal incompleteness," could not live freely and humanely without God.

The communist evil against which Chambers bore witness has long since dissipated, but his testimony survives, in part because he left, in his memoir, a remarkable revelation of self. "At least four classics of European autobiography," the Princeton medievalist John V. Fleming writes, have left their "formal traces" on the book Chambers called *Witness*: "the two very different *Confessions* of Augustine and of Rousseau; Goethe's *Wahrheit und Dichtung*; and Newman's *Apologia pro vita sua*." Simply from the "artistic point of view *Witness* is worthy to be mentioned in their company."

At the same time, *Witness* is, Fleming argues, the "very emblem of a liberally educated mind," and one remembers the intellectual genealogy Lionel Trilling traced—descending from Matthew Arnold through Charles Eliot Norton and George Edward Woodberry to John Erskine—that produced Columbia's General Honors colloquium, in which the young Chambers was initiated in a tradition that stretched back, in time, to Florence and Athens. When he speaks, in the first chapter of *Witness*, of the "journey of my life" and says that it "would be hard to tell how hard it was," he recapitulates the opening of *Inferno*. The interest of his book lies partly in its account of a journey through hell, and partly in the way it reproduces, in a contemporary context, Dante's longing for the fair sheepfold. Chambers's farm in Maryland, with its brood sows, dairy heifers, Shropshire sheep, was his own version of Dante's *beato chiostro* or blessed cloister: a sanctuary of necessity private because a more public forum, a Florentine Mercato Vecchio or an Athenian agora, was beyond the power of his age. But if Pipe Creek Farm was, for Chambers, a green isle in the "deep wide sea of misery," it was also a place in which to seek God. What is humane in the soul, Chambers believed, craves union with God; man without God is a beast,

> never more beastly than when he is most intelligent about his beastliness. *"Er nennt's Vernunft,"* says the Devil in Goethe's *Faust*, *"und braucht's allein, nur tierischer als jedes Tier zu sein"*—Man calls it reason and uses it simply to be more beastly than any beast.

On the farm he lived, he said, in the presence of eternal wonder and knew awe before the births of the lambs. Those who farmed the land complete "the arc between the soil and God," because to labor is to pray (*laborare est orare*) and the farm a form of witness:

> It is a witness against the world. By deliberately choosing this life of hardship and immense satisfaction, we say in effect: The modern world has nothing better than this to give us. Its vision of comfort without effort, pleasure without the pain of creation, life sterilized against even the thought of death, rationalized so that every intrusion of mystery is felt as a betrayal of the mind, life mechanized and standardized—that is not for us.

Chambers's idea of rooting himself and his family in the soil is, I suppose, easy enough to ridicule, or to distort. (*"La terre et les morts* . . . the European tradition of blood-and-soil chauvinism.) But Pipe Creek Farm owed nothing to Maurice Barrès or Charles Maurras. It was the attempt of a neurasthenic WASP to find order and sanity in a nervous world, and the effort of a highly educated WASP to bridge the gap between his own cultivation and the different backgrounds of most of his fellow citizens. Chambers wanted to root himself and his family not only in the soil but "in the nation—that part of the nation each of whose days is a great creative labor." That is the "part of the nation to which by choice I belong," the America of the farmers and the small-town people who live "out there," in what we now call flyover country, and whose virtues he contrasted with the falsity and decadence of much of the rest of the country.

As a formula for national regeneration, it was of course hopeless. Not that Pipe Creek Farm was a vanity project; Chambers was not George III pretending to be a farmer, nor was his wife Marie Antoinette playing the milkmaid. He and his family worked hard, milked cows, baled hay, plowed fields. But the farm was nevertheless subsidized by money a highly gifted man made in a skyscraper in New York as a writer for *Time*, a way of life out of reach of most people. Chambers's marriage of primitive Christianity and Jefferson's agrarian ideal ("Those who labour in the earth . . .") was outmoded in the America of 1800, and could scarcely redeem it in 1950.

Still he yearned for regeneration, and in his yearning he was a product of the WASP tradition. Yet he was almost universally loathed by WASPs. It is true that, when he testified in the 1940s, he had not yet written the apologia by which he endeavored to explain himself. But even after *Witness* was published in 1952 WASPs were unforgiving. It was not simply that Alger Hiss, the handsome Harvard graduate, was more clubbable. Chambers, in taking up the mantle of prophet, appointed himself spokesman for America "out there," and WASPs had mixed feelings about that America. They shrank from what John Ruskin called the "taint of American ways," from life as it might be lived (in the words of one of Henry James's characters) in "some beastly American town," and from their club windows they looked down on a mass of fellow citizens sunk, as it seemed to them, in moronic darkness, and as helpless, in their confrontation with a higher culture, as a "Danubian Hun before a statue of Alcibiades." It is a question whether a high WASP ever supported a fashionable cause without some secret pleasure in the knowledge that the cause was abhorred by the vulgarians. The graduates of Bryn Mawr and Yale disliked Chambers less because he peached on Hiss than because he was admired by sort of people who liked Nixon. In siding with the country against the court, Chambers became, for the WASPs, a pest eating away at the privet hedge that separated them from the yahoos.

CHAMBERS'S CRITICISM OF THE WASP elite helped to create a new movement in American politics. Dean Acheson was a patriot and a dedicated Cold Warrior, but when, after Hiss was convicted, he cited Matthew 25:36 ("I was in prison, and ye came unto me") and said that he would not turn his back on the man, Chambers pointed to the existence of a shadowy conspiracy in Washington that sought to minimize Hiss's treason and subvert American liberties. There were, he said, "powers within the Government" that "wanted the Hiss case stilled," and for a definite reason. The "simple fact is that when I took up my little sling and aimed at Communism, I also hit something else. What I hit was the forces of that great socialist revolution, which, in the name of liberalism, spasmodically, incompletely, somewhat formlessly, but always in the same direction, has been inching its ice cap over the nation for two decades." Chambers would later change his mind about Franklin Roosevelt's welfare state; he became an Eisenhower Republican who made peace with the Social Security Act and the other New Deal laws. But by that time his testimony had helped to mobilize a conservatism he could not fully share, one that was energized by an antipathy to those sinister WASP cabals he had deplored in *Witness*. The man who had once sympathized with the loathing that the fiercer populists felt for *Social Register* traitors versed in "the Groton vocabulary of the Hiss-Acheson group" now saw their politics as so much "crackpotism."

WASPs were not, of course, in conspiracy against America. They were, however, out of touch with it: F.D.R. was the last, and with the exception of his uncle-in-law Theodore, perhaps the only WASP to have had a genuine mass following. What was more, WASPs never mastered the art which a viable elite must incessantly practice, that of hiding its contempt for those who seem to it vulgar. In provoking popular revulsion they got what was coming to them. Yet it is curious that the two men who did so much to finger the arrogance of the patricians, Chambers and his close friend William F. Buckley Jr., had themselves been educated in WASP institutions. Chambers, we have seen, was one of the original guinea pigs in what became Columbia's Core Curriculum, that WASP experiment in civic humanism; Buckley came up through Millbrook, Yale, and Skull and Bones, and his manners and address were those of a highly cultivated WASP. Each man had, in his way, taken to heart the *eutrapelian* ideal, Chambers in his intimacy with great books, which were for him primers in the art of living humanely, Buckley in the dazzling variety of his pursuits, as man of letters, intellectual provocateur, Catholic humanist, iconoclastic wit, savorer of human quirkiness and possibility, a man who, in his friendships, found as much to interest him in such an obscure eccentric as Charles Wallen, the letter-writer and bibliophile, as he did in John Kenneth Galbraith and Allard Lowenstein, Henry Kissinger and Vladimir Nabokov. But neither Chambers nor Buckley had any faith in the WASP establishment through whose portals each had passed, and both cherished a skepticism of elites that found its classic expression in Buckley's saying that he "should sooner live in a society governed by the first two thousand names in the Boston telephone directory than in a society governed by the two thousand faculty members of Harvard University."

In their decrepitude, WASPs looked to Kennedy (pictured with
Averell Harriman) as an Osiris who could turn their winter into spring.

THIRTY-FOUR

Burnt Offerings:
The Ember Days of the WASPs

li splendor mondani . . .
the splendor of the world . . .

La dolorosa selva . . .
The wood of sorrow . . .
—Dante, *Inferno*

I can't relax," Jack Kennedy said when, late in the night that followed his inauguration, he dropped by Joe Alsop's house in Georgetown. "I came over to
have a few drinks and talk about the last few days." As a convert to a faith is apt

to be a more zealous communicant than one born in it, Jack, though in heritage an Irish Catholic, was the most WASP-oriented of the American presidents, more respectful of WASP *mores* than the maverick Roosevelts or the transplanted Bushes, pushing their fortunes amid the alien corn of Texas. Seeking to unwind, he unwound with WASPs.

Old Joe Kennedy, the father, had no doubt that the WASP ascendancy was real; he wanted his boys to be first assimilated to it, and afterward to master it. Rose Kennedy, the mother, placed Jack and Bobby in Catholic boarding schools (Canterbury, Portsmouth Priory). But Joe soon put an end to *that* and moved the boys to WASP seminaries (Choate, Milton). "The next regular step was Harvard College." So Henry Adams had said of his own course in life, and the same step was now no less regular for Kennedys than it was for Adamses.

Jack, having been assimilated to the WASP ascendancy, for a time dominated it, but he also liked it. Dave Powers, one of his Irish Catholic fixers, was amused by his boss's fondness for WASPs, though he admitted that some of the eminent figures were quite personable, and he joked that Leverett Saltonstall, the senator from the Porcellian Club, was Irish on his chauffeur's side. Certainly no other president ever surrounded himself with so tight a preppy cabal. There was Mac Bundy, his national security advisor, who as "clerk of the world" was a more potent force than the State Department, and there was C. Douglas Dillon, his secretary of the treasury, a banker, diplomat, and philanthropist who, having been a year ahead of Joe Alsop at Groton and Harvard, spoke preppy as well as anyone, though, like Jack, he had an outsider heritage. Henry Cabot Lodge, the son of the dead poet George Cabot Lodge, represented Kennedy in Saigon, Adlai Stevenson was his envoy to the United Nations, and G. Mennen "Soapy" Williams made his case to Africa; Averell Harriman, his ambassador-at-large, was his plenipotentiary to the world as a whole, and in practice a solver of puzzles like that of Laos which baffled less worldly diplomats. Kennedy of course relied, as all modern presidents do, on cadres of specialized technicians, but the only technocrat who carried a large portfolio in his administration was Robert McNamara, his secretary of defense, a man who, Joe Alsop said, had no "feeling for history and how it works," but had instead "this sort of computer-like mind," this "illusion that you could win a war with a computer . . ."

Kennedy *spoke* WASP and was a convert to the WASP faith in public service, but he never thought of himself as being a WASP, even in an honorific sense. "We got on the subject of family backgrounds," Ben Bradlee, a journalist of Brahmin descent, said of an evening with the Kennedys, "and the President noted with pride that he and his brothers and sisters were one hundred percent pure Irish," naming the family names, "Kennedy, Fitzgerald, Hickey, and Hannon . . ." When Edmund Wilson, in conversation with Kennedy, mentioned a statue recently placed before the Massachusetts State House in memory of Mary Dyer, a Quaker hanged by Puritans, the president replied sharply, "*That* took them three hundred years." The WASPs who descended from the Puritans were still "them" to Kennedy, not "us." But the line was blurring; Kennedy had more in common with Harvard preppies like Alsop and Bradlee (or "Benjy," as he called him) than he did with Eugene McCarthy, the poet-statesman who had been educated by the Benedictines, and whom Jack likened to an Irish-Catholic pol who ostentatiously read his missal in the trolley car. When Jack and Benjy get together we are back in the Protestant prep school dorm, as when Jack persuaded Benjy to call up Jack's old Harvard roommate, Torb Macdonald, the congressman, on the pretense that *Newsweek* (Bradlee's employer) wanted to know about Torb's (wholly imaginary) involvement in the bribery scandal then consuming Bobby Baker, a crony of Lyndon Johnson's. "Lay it on old Torb good," Kennedy urged, and listening on the extension as his old friend squirmed, he cupped the mouthpiece to tell Bradlee that "Torb's hurting. Tuck it to him some more." The president, Bradlee remembered, "slumped over on his back on the sofa, he was laughing so hard," as three men relived their youth.

For even in its pranks and inanity WASPdom could be seductive, and through his wife Jacqueline, Jack was connected to quite a lot of it. Among the preppies who were in some measure family were our old friends Louis Auchincloss, Frank Polk, and Wintie Rutherfurd, all related to Jackie and her stepfather, Hugh D. Auchincloss Jr., by a network of blood and marriage. (Gore Vidal, who, like Jacqueline, was a stepchild of "Hughdie," said that the man's originality was revealed when, after Groton, he discovered that "*he was unable to do work of any kind*. Since the American ruling class, then and now, likes to give the impression that it is always hard at work, or at least very busy, Hughdie's sloth was something of a breakthrough.") As a matter of course Jackie commissioned WASP interior designer Sister Parish, the daughter of Dorothy Whitney Straight Elmhirst's girlhood confidante May Tuckerman, to refurbish the family quarters of the White House, which had been much neglected by the cavalier Roosevelts and the downmarket Trumans and Eisenhowers. But iron-souled Sister proved too tough a WASP chairs-and-curtains arbiter for Jackie, and she was dismissed, in the midst of her redecorative exertions, for having kicked little Caroline Kennedy. (Would Sister really have done *that*? "I wouldn't have put it past her," her granddaughter said, though she thought the root of the problem was "money and Jackie's belief that not everything had to be paid for.") As Sister's star fell, that of French interior designer Stéphane Boudin rose, but WASPs remained on the scene, and Boudin's work in redecorating, or as Jackie preferred to say, restoring, the state rooms of the White House was overseen by a WASP all-star committee that included Joe Alsop's beard, Susan Mary Alsop, the architect Nathaniel Saltonstall, Henry Francis du Pont, Babe Paley and her sister Minnie, and Minnie's second husband—he replaced Vincent Astor—the painter and art historian James Fosburgh. Yet the Tuckermans had still a place in Camelot; Nancy Tuckerman, Jackie's friend at Chapin and Miss Porter's, proved a more congenial assistant than Sister, and as White House social secretary she assisted the magicians in conjuring the illusions and casting the spells of that memorable if insubstantial pageant.

Henry James laid the scene on a Sunday afternoon in the Faubourg Saint-Germain, the old aristocratic quarter of Paris. Lewis Lambert Strether, a New England WASP in middle age, finds himself in the garden of the sculptor Gloriani, a place intended by James to stand for all those WASP dreams of a sheepfold in which one is revivified and becomes what one is. Gloriani's garden, the focal point of James's novel *The Ambassadors*, is a symbolic compendium of the old forums, walled centers, porticoed heights, "enclosures green"—Athens, Chartres, Florence, and their innumerable lesser cousins. The garden is a "treasure dug up," a sanctuary bespeaking "survival, transmission, association, a strong indifferent persistent order," a "great convent" famous for one "scarce knew what," a "nursery of young priests, of scattered shade, of straight alleys and chapel-bells," a place "of ghosts at the windows, of signs and tokens, a whole range of expression . . . too thick for prompt discrimination."

In the center of the garden are two of the more potent of James's potential revivifiers, Gloriani himself, "with the light, with the romance, of glory" playing about his person, and the no less penetrating radiance of Madame de Vionnet, who in "her slim lightness and brightness" seems a "goddess still partly engaged in a morning cloud," a "sea-nymph waist-high in the summer surge," a Cleopatra with "aspects, characters, days, nights" that show the completeness of a "woman of genius."

For a trembling moment Strether threatens to ripen under this aggressive nurture; he opens, for a "happy instant, all the windows of his mind" to the revelation of possibility, and lets his "rather grey interior drink in for once the sun of a clime" unmapped in any New England cartography. He feels the erotic tug of the life that he, in his New England depletion, has missed. But he is not, finally, reanimated. All he can do is urge another WASP whom he encounters in the garden—hardly more than a boy—to take hold of what he has missed. "Live all you can," he urges John Little Bilham, the "happily and hatefully young" ingénu: "it's a mistake not to. It doesn't so much matter what you do in particular, so long as you have your life. If you haven't had that what *have* you had?"

James leaves in ambiguity the nature of Gloriani's garden, whether it is a forum for completion or a scene of temptation, a humane sanctuary or a place "covertly tigerish" with the carrion waft of the jungle. An "aesthetic torch" illuminates the garden, but there is also, as in the aboriginal one, the "trail of the serpent." *The Ambassadors* is probably James's greatest meditation on the defect of soul that prevents the WASP from taking the cup of life to the lips, but its power lies, too, in its prophetic intensity; the scene in Gloriani's garden was to be acted over by people who, in 1903, the year the novel was published, were not yet born, and James himself would have found much to ponder in the way his fable retold itself in the ember days of the WASPs, with the president and Mrs. Kennedy figuring as the potentially revivifying characters. Jack had the radiance, the touch of Prospero, that Gloriani possesses, and Jackie rivaled Mme. de Vionnet in her lightness and brightness. Jack, if anything, overdid the Prospero bit about the rough magic of poetry, the artistry that creates the humane forum with its cloud-capped towers and temples and palaces. In his address at Amherst in October 1963 he showed that he knew all about the WASP cult of the humanities, and alluding to Aristotle and Matthew Arnold he declared that when "power corrupts, poetry cleanses," when "power narrows the areas of man's concern," poetry works for his completeness, "reminds him of the richness and diversity of his existence . . ."

Whether Kennedy had been converted to humanism or merely pretended to be, his invocation of poetry had its end mostly in talk and (still more doubtfully) the establishment of federal arts bureaucracies. The poetry that would have interested James inhered in the presidential couple themselves. Crusty old Walter Lippmann, who had been part of the WASP revival in the days of Theodore

Roosevelt, paid tribute to the Kennedys' reanimating power. "This is a most Presidential country," he opined. "The tone and example set by the President have a tremendous effect on the quality of life in America." With the coming of the Kennedys there was, he said, "a curious exhilaration in Washington. . . . people are beginning to feel that we can *do* things about problems after all—that everything is possible."

Others fell harder, drank more deeply of the vitality of the vegetation god who promised to turn winter into spring. Isaiah Berlin, visiting Washington in the early sixties, was uncomfortably reminded of the romance between Napoleon and his marshals; Kennedy's courtiers were "physically in love with him."

THE WASPs THEMSELVES WERE BY this time much changed from what they had been. Freud had replaced Dante as the reigning WASP prophet. WASPs were as neurotic as ever, but they now turned not to the *Divine Comedy* for a path to regeneration but to the psychoanalyst's couch. It is not evident that this was an improvement. If Dante inspired WASPs to seek a fair sheepfold, a forum in which they could realize their various gifts and keep alive the idea of the complete human being, Freud, on the contrary, persuaded them to become absorbed in the mysteries of their infant sexuality. They still sought regeneration, as we all do, but there was an element of desperation in their belief that they could effect it through their adoration of Kennedy, who, after all, was not Osiris, but a rather conventional if unusually attractive American politician.

Yet as WASPs became less serious, they became more fun. Once again, gossip must be our guide, gossip, which, like a flash of lightning in a dark sky, reveals motive and desire, the virtue and the sordidness of souls, with a clarity unattainable by the most patient historical analysis. In these retrievements out of the night, Edmund Wilson becomes an indispensable guide. A "cheerful, corpulent, chuckling gentleman," the critic Elizabeth Hardwick remembered, "well dressed in brown suits and dry martinis," he was attuned to the gossip of the time even as he was productive of it himself, still vigorous, in his old age, in different beds of lust. The novelist Penelope Gilliatt, thirty-seven years his junior, drove him one day to the Princeton Club, where he was to meet the writer Anaïs Nin to go over passages in the latest installment of the diary she was perennially publishing. "It's strange," Wilson wrote in his account of the visit, "now that I'm seventy-five and can only get an erection at half-mast, two such attractive women as [Penelope Gilliatt and Anne Miller*] should offer themselves to me." Gilliatt came up to his room and afterward, as she got up to go and was putting mascara on her eyes, said, "I look like a woman who's been fucked." "Not enough," Wilson lamented.

But he was not on such easy terms with the age as his erotic life might suggest. The Princeton Club itself had ceased to be congenial to him. After visiting it in March 1963 he pronounced it "a horror," "full of tacky-looking people." "One of the boys had brought a rather disreputable-looking blonde," and there was a "vulgar inscription" at the entrance to the bar. "I doubt whether I'll go there again." He did go there again, but the Greenwich Village radical of the twenties had by now settled into the curmudgeonly patrician of the sixties, and the former Marxist now openly mourned the passing of the cultivated haute bourgeoisie. "My reaction to all things that I disapprove and dislike," he wrote, "is that of a member of a once privileged class which is being eliminated all over the world and has very little means any longer of asserting its superior 'values.'" All around him he saw "anarchy and what seems to me stupidity." He supposed he ought not to complain of the changing tenor of American life, "of the many cars, the 'mobile homes,' of the movies and television sets, of the grills for outdoor cooking." But none "of these things seem to me attractive." He deplored the coarseness of American civilization, the tyranny of its bureaucracies, the dearth of young people "ambitious of meeting, outside the fields of technology, the higher standards of competence and culture." His very editors at the *New Yorker*, he discovered, could not read Greek.

He was by this time avoiding as much of America as he could, retreating into private gardens, little self-fashioned principalities remote from the polluting multitude. One of these centered around his house at Wellfleet on Cape Cod, which his fourth and final wife, Elena Mumm Thornton, made into a refuge where he could do his work with a minimum of interruption. He spent the greater part of his days in his study "uncombed, unshaven, in his pajamas and bathrobe—the daylong uniform of his work." It was only around five o'clock that he would emerge, "freshly shaved, with a cherubic glow on his Roman features, fully dressed, wearing a jacket and tie set into a crisp shirt ironed by his wife, ready for the evening bottle of whiskey in the parlor," or so his friend Leon Edel,

---

* Anne Miller was the wife of Wilson's dentist. Wilson helped her with her poetry and enjoyed watching her swim naked in the Sugar River in upstate New York.

the biographer of Henry James, remembered. But summer brought tourist hordes to the Cape, and Edmund had himself driven—for, like Joe Alsop, he never learned to drive a car—to another miniature polity, his family's ancestral fief at Talcottville in the lower Adirondacks. "I sit here in this old house alone," he wrote, a trifle solemnly, for after all he had at least two girlfriends upstate. But although Wilson was less detached from the world than he pretended to be, the man who had once delighted in the bohemian anarchy of the Village had indeed returned to the provinces. Talcottville represented stability and endurance; it had "changed very much less since I first knew it as a child," he said, "than any other part of this country I know . . ." Enchanted by the romance of memory and of patrimony, he found that the America of his ancestors interested him more than the America in which he was actually living. His 1962 book *Patriotic Gore*, a study of the literature of the Civil War, was the happy result of this looking backward, but he was much of the time anything other than pleased with himself. "The day was marred at the end," he wrote in April 1957, "by my drinking too much whiskey and stupidly reproaching Elena." In December 1966 he described how he got up in the morning to "make a brief toilet. While sitting on the W.C., I read the folders of old reviews of my books, in order to support my morale—though this only makes me realize again how slipshod and incompetent most reviewing is." "I spent the day in sloth and the doldrums," he wrote in May 1969. "Champagne at lunch . . . Had some drinks and went to sleep very early, but had bad dreams and woke up feeling horrible. . . . read Macaulay and somewhat regained my equanimity and my inspiration to live."

Literature was, indeed, the only faith that remained to him, and he found it quite "fortifying" to find Macaulay sustaining it: "Though he was dying, he more or less rounded out" his history. Certainly the faith in Russian socialism that once animated him and found expression in his 1940 book *To the Finland Station* had long since died. His friend D. S. Mirsky had been arrested by the N.K.V.D. in 1937 and sent to Kolyma, possibly the cruelest of Stalin's death camps; it is believed that he died in January 1939 after having gone "violently insane." Wilson himself went behind the Iron Curtain in 1964 to visit Hungary and was appalled by the evils of the regime. "I came to feel an *absolute hatred of the Soviet system*," he wrote, "its mechanical stupidities imposed on an intelligent Western people," the "simpleminded cant of Soviet Marxist terminology . . ." But no other dream of regeneration took the place of the dead one to inspire or console him: for great as his devotion to literature was, he had no faith, as his light waned, in its power to alter the world. Those whom he saw around him seemed as bereft. In their shrunken lives they had ceased to ache, as the neurasthenic satraps in Cavafy's poem do, for the other things, "the Agora, the Theatre, the Crowns of Laurel. . ."

IN THEIR DISILLUSIONMENT A NUMBER of WASPs, among them Wilson himself, made their way to Rome as to an oracle, to sit at the feet of one of the touchstones of their now diminished faith. On the Caelian Hill, in the convent of the Blue Nuns, "crowned with all the snows and wisdom of extreme old age," lay George Santayana, reclining, Wilson remembered, on a kind of chaise longue with a blanket over his legs. Coming to Rome just after its liberation in 1945, Wilson felt a "sacred awe" at seeing him: "a shell of faded skin and frail bone, in which the power of intellect, the colors of imagination, still lived . . ."

The old philosopher could scarcely see now, and with squinting eyes he turned his wrinkled face to visitors like Wilson and the poet Robert Lowell, a neurasthenic WASP who, though still young, saw already the skull beneath New England's skin, a culture dying before his eyes much as he saw his uncle Devereux Winslow dying, in white trousers and a coat like a blue jay's tail, "as brushed as Bayard, our riding horse," one summer at the Winslow farm, called "*Char-de-sa*/in the Social Register . . ."* Santayana took an instant liking to Lowell. "Your name, the aspect of your book, the discreet inscription, and the form of your verses, even before I had read them, made a strong impression on me," he wrote in thanking the young Bostonian for his poems. Lowell stirred old WASP memories in Santayana, evoked the faces of other Lowells he had known, the once famous poet James Russell Lowell and the Harvard grandee A. Lawrence Lowell, whose brother Percival had been cudgeled by Jack Chapman. Always in search of a replacement for the vanished Warwick, he now fastened on Lowell, "my *new* young friend," as he called him, whose poems were the first since those of Trumbull Stickney "that belonged at all to my moral and poetical world . . ."

Edmund Wilson was startled by how self-sufficient Santayana was in his monk's cell: he "absorbs, enchants, and satisfies" himself in his seclusion. But the "thought of his spending night after night, so far from Harvard and Spain, alone in that little bed, with its simple white pillow of which I could see a corner from

---

* Lowell, "My Last Afternoon with Uncle Devereux Winslow." The second "r" in the word "Register" in the poem should be pronounced in non-rhotic WASP fashion.

behind the concealing screen, came back to me in my own solitude, my rather lonely evenings of writing and reading, actually to appall me."

Wilson somewhat misjudged Santayana's feelings about Harvard. At fifty he had resigned his professorship in the university to live in Europe. He spent the years of the First World War in the United Kingdom, where he wrote his *Soliloquies in England* and his *Egotism in German Philosophy*; later he lived mostly in Rome, the "anthropological centre" of the world, as he called it, "where nature and art were most beautiful, and mankind least distorted from their complete character." With the income of his Sturgis legacy—club membership had its benefits—he could live and work conveniently in hotels, and when, like the discontented man in Lucretius's poem, Rome or his own spirit oppressed him, he could escape in a swift, though now coal-propelled, chariot, to Paris or Venice, Ávila in Spain or Cortina d'Ampezzo in the Dolomitic Alps. He wanted no regular companion; for constant company he had, he said, "enough, and too much, with myself." A daily routine established itself, "which I could carry with me wherever I went; it gave me abundance of private hours" in which to work, "and for relief and refreshment, I liked solitude in crowds, meals in restaurants, walks in public parks, architectural rambles in noble cities."

With the coming of the Second World War, being unable either to leave Italy or to draw on his American funds, he found refuge in the nunnery on the Caelian. (It was in fact a medical clinic staffed by the Blue Nuns, so called from their azure habits.) Slight and shrunken in his brown bathrobe, he looked, Wilson thought, "rather like a monk," but in fact he was a philosopher, and Wilson was impressed by his readiness "to receive anybody and start talking," imparting wisdom. The young Gore Vidal, who visited him just after Wilson, "felt like Phaedo with Socrates."

Santayana had been long and rather fruitlessly trying to persuade WASPs to keep open more ample lines of communication with the classical and Mediterranean civilization of the West. A too impassioned attachment to the psychology of the Germanic north, whether it took the form of religious Puritanism, secular commercialism, or Prussian militancy in statecraft and theoretic speculation, was the surest way to an imbalanced psyche. In an age philosophically in thrall to Teutonic egotists holding forth on their solitary mountaintops, Santayana stood for the sanity of the common life of the Latin plain and the Mediterranean littoral. In his own person he revived the tradition of sages who dwelt not on the peaks with Zarathustra but in the agora with Socrates, in the compactness of the old civic center. He quoted with approval the words of Dante's ancestor Cacciaguida in praise of an older, not yet swollen Florence, the chaste city that lay within "the narrow circuit of her walls," and in his own writing he recreated, in the epigrammatic concision of his phrasing, something of the same inward tightness.*

But each pursues his star in his own way, and Santayana, who had long smiled at human folly, was now ready to forgive it. "My old age judges more charitably and thinks better of mankind," he said, "than my youth ever did. I discount ideal-isations, I forgive onesidedness, I see that it is essential to perfection of any kind. And in each person I catch the fleeting suggestion of something beautiful, and swear eternal friendship with that." One pauses at the word eternal. Santayana's naturalist, Epicurean philosophy admitted of no conventional immortality, no paradiso such as Dante sought, in which friendship might go on forever. But as much as Dante's teacher Brunetto Latini, Santayana taught

> come l'uom s'etterna . . .
> how a man makes himself eternal . . .

We are, he believed, children of matter, "captive spirits" imprisoned in "the toils of time, place, person, and circumstance." But moments of liberation are avail-able to those who master liberation's esoteric art. Existing in nature, we may yet, he says, learn "to digest, to refine, to dominate" that existence spiritually and philosophically, so that, like the runner in Canto XV of *Inferno* who wins the green cloth at Verona, we may outrun nature herself to touch the eternal.

MAKING ONE'S THREADLESS WAY THROUGH the labyrinth of a dying WASPdom, one comes upon Jack Chapman's son Chanler, making off with John Singer Sargent's portrait of his mother, Elizabeth, "Queen Bess," as she sat to the artist in Tite Street in the nineties. He appeared at Rokeby one day in 1963 "unan-nounced, took the painting off the wall, put it in the back of a farm truck, and drove away." The painting was his, now that Aunt Margaret, the old Rokeby dowager, was dead, and needing money, he took it back to Sylvania, the house his

---

* Santayana's Latinizing English is very different from the Latinizing periods of the English writers of the eighteenth-century, the style of Gibbon and Dr. Johnson: he writes rather from the living Latinity of the south of Europe, and exhibits the same lucid compression one finds in Horace and Virgil.

parents had built to the north of Rokeby, intent on selling it to raise funds. (He was eventually persuaded to donate it to the Smithsonian in exchange for a tax break.) "Chanler was one person who could be rough on his mother," according to Aunt Margaret's daughter, Margaret Aldrich Rand. When Elizabeth "was dying he yelled at her to go over and pray by her bedside, though she was unconscious by then anyway." At all events there was a certain roughness in the way he handled his mother's image.

Edmund Wilson, who had a touch of the Jacobin in him, was uncharacteristically impressed by the Hudson River squierarchy, with its "cupolaed castles on their towering dark-wooded hills" and its "tradition of public responsibility," one "which Hamilton Fish shares with Franklin D. Roosevelt." In their general culture they were "likely to range so much more widely and to seem to have more authenticity" than the inhabitants "of most wealthy communities in America." They possessed, besides, a "naturalness and amiability which merge quietly and not unpleasantly with smugness," that of aristoi "walled-in from the rest of the United States and alone with the noble river."

Reading Wilson you would not guess that perhaps a third of the aristoi beside the noble river were mad as hatters. The scions of the Chanlers, indeed, vied with one another for the title of "most eccentric man in America." There was no shortage of competition. Chanler Chapman's uncle, William Astor Chanler, insufficiently attended to by a waiter at Maxim's, took off his peg leg and flung it at him. Another uncle, Archie, was said to have believed that he was Napoleon, but this, according to Chanler Chapman, was wrong: he "told me he was the reincarnation of Pompey." When Archie's brother, the artist Robert Winthrop Chanler, married an opera singer who promptly made off with a large part of his fortune, Archie, hard at work defending his own sanity, telegraphed, "Who's looney now?"

Chanler Chapman's burden was that of a survivor. One of his father's sons (Chanler's half-brother John) drowned as a child, another (Chanler's half-brother Victor) was among the glorious dead of the First World War. Chanler felt himself a disappointment in the very fact of remaining alive. To make matters worse he disliked St. Paul's School, going so far as to write a book about how its masters expected too much of him, and though he succeeded at Harvard, it was not the sort of success with which John Jay Chapman could sympathize. "He ran a gambling den there," his cousin Peter White said. "He had a bootlegger, and all the gilded aristocracy from St. Paul's, St. Mark's, and Groton as his customers.

Chanler and his partners took in $300 to $400 a week. They didn't drink until their customers left at three in the morning, but then they drank themselves blind." Chanler eventually became a pig farmer at Sylvania and published a local newspaper, the *Barrytown Explorer*, which he edited with a certain flair. "Close the blinds at night and lower the chances of being shot to death in bed," he wrote. "That goes for the district attorney who wants to be a judge." And who will not sympathize with the headline, "Kingston Attacked by Giant Mall"? His first wife, Olivia James, a grandniece of Henry and William, bore him a son, John Jay Chapman II, who after Harvard became a mail carrier in Puerto Rico devoted to his vocation. Chanler's cousin Winty Aldrich, who lived at Rokeby, twitted Chanler about this. "Isn't it remarkable, Chanler, that Edmund Wilson called your father the greatest letter writer in America, and now your son may be the greatest letter carrier!" Chanler, in turn, disparaged Winty as "the essence of nothing. . . . He has the personality of an unsuccessful undertaker and he uses semicolons when he writes. He knits with his toes." Yet Winty's son was a good fellow who delighted in iceboats and interested himself in Slavic grammar. "The most obvious fact about Ricky," a visitor to Rokeby wrote, "is that he seldom bathes." "Ricky would give you the shirt off his back," a friend said. "But who would want it?"

In 1973 Chanler married his third wife, the psychiatrist Ida Holzberg. "It's convenient," Cousin Winty said, "for Chanler to have his own psychiatrist in the house." Like Chanler's second wife, Helen, Ida was Jewish, and once, when they were quarrelling, he said, "Jesus Christ, maybe I should have gone Chinese the third time around." Saul Bellow, who rented an apartment above the carriage house at Sylvania, loathed the WASP gentry, or so Gore Vidal remembered. (He would have known; he bought Edgewater, another Barrytown property that for a time had been owned by Chanler's parents.) Saul had reason to dislike Chanler, who failed to provide enough wood for his stove, but in his novel *Henderson the Rain King* he did as much justice to the WASP pathos of the man, the "absurd seeker of high qualities," as is ever likely to be done it. "I was one of three children and the only survivor," Bellow makes Henderson (Chanler) say. "In my own way I worked very hard. Violent suffering is labor, and often I was drunk before lunch. . . . Shall I start with my father? He was a well-known man. He had a beard and played the violin . . . . Of course, in an age of madness, to expect to be untouched by madness is a form of madness. But the pursuit of sanity can be a form of madness, too . . . So tell me, did your fiancé go to Choate or St Paul's? Your last husband went to President Roosevelt's prep school—whatchumajigger. . ."

The Roosevelts themselves were a Hudson River family in disarray. If Eleanor throve as the embodiment of progressive liberalism, those around her wilted. Her brother Hall became an assistant professor of engineering at Harvard and later worked at General Electric and various other firms until he was disabled by drink and a dysfunctioning liver. His sister installed him in a cottage at Hyde Park, but by 1941 he was dying the death of their father, the doomed Elliott. "It's such an unattractive death," Eleanor wrote as she sat beside his bed in Walter Reed Hospital in Bethesda. "He is mahogany color, all distended, out of his head most of the time. . . ." "My ideal of hell, if I believed in it," she wrote, "would be to sit or stand & watch someone breathing hard, struggling for words when a gleam of consciousness returns & thinking 'this was once the little boy I played with and scolded. He could have been so much and this is what he is.'" He was "always a little my child and the waste of a life seems a bitter thing."

Her actual children, corrupted by the temptations of their situation in life, were too inured to its pleasures to find any other way of living bearable, and their lives, at times, seem little more than a register of disappointment, divorce, and deterioration. Eleanor was full of anguish over the wreckage, and in her distress she turned to the Freudian shaman Lawrence Kubie, who believed that she was "on the verge of a breakthrough" in comprehending the "role of the dark forces of the unconscious in human behavior . . ." In fact it was the brightness of the uncannily conscious Franklin that warped the children; like others who were too long exposed to that irradiating glow, they found themselves poisoned by it. Anna, the oldest child, very sensibly tried to wean her own children from the addictive but corrosive narcotic of being a Roosevelt. Her son Curtis, who thought to emulate his grandfather, once said that when he grew up he "wanted to be like Papa." He long remembered his mother's reaction. "Mummy looked at me very seriously, as if I had said something quite rude and offensive, and then she said with finality: 'You can never be like Papa.'"

When, in 1960, Eleanor was cool to Jack Kennedy's presidential aspirations, the candidate ascribed it not to his failure to have censured his family's friend, the scaremonger Joe McCarthy, but to her regret that her own offspring were not more satisfactory: "She hated my father and she can't stand it that his children turned out so much better than hers." Chappaquiddick was still in the

Kennedys' future, but even so there was truth in Jack's remark. The Roosevelt boys were brave in war, but in civil life there were so many missteps. James, the oldest son, spent his life trading on the Roosevelt name; he was eventually elected to Congress from California. His brother Elliott's course was similar, only he had five wives to James's four; he later served as mayor of Miami Beach and published ghostwritten mystery novels in which his mother figures as Sherlock Holmes in drag. Franklin, Jr., who most resembled his father in charm, was called the "sunshine boy," but his arrogance was his undoing. Elected to Congress at thirty-four, he "coasted instead of working at his job," his brother James said, and "considering it beneath him" sought bigger game. But he failed in his quest for office in New York State. Misjudging the power of the Roosevelt name, he neglected to cultivate the Tammany sachem Carmine DeSapio, who worked instead to install Averell Harriman as governor; and in his race for attorney general he was defeated by Jacob Javits, leading Eleanor to lament that her son "was defeated because they put a *very good Jew* against him." In 1961 he became under secretary of commerce, in part because Jack Kennedy liked to be reminded of how far the Roosevelts had fallen; in later years he owned a car dealership and interested himself in horse racing, cattle farming, and philandering, once startling his brother Elliott's fifth wife, Patricia Peabody, by telling her that she was "the only sister-in-law I haven't had." John alone seemed to escape the poison of Caesar's laurel crown. The youngest child and the least like his father, he was content to lead the humdrum life of a businessman and a Republican; he never sought public office. But it may be that the oddest of the Roosevelts, the holy fool Taddy, the son of F.D.R.'s half-brother James, was the wisest of them all, and he seemed to know what he was about when, turning his back on the Roosevelt splendors and his mother's Astor fortune, he moved to Queens, where he worked as a car mechanic and lived over the garage.

EDMUND WILSON WAS HAVING A nap in the Princeton Club when Arthur Schlesinger rang him up and invited him to a couple of parties. He had difficulty finding the address, telling the friend who drove him that the host had "some name like Vanderweevil." "Oh, Vanden Heuevel," the friend said, and deposited him at the Dakota on Central Park West, an "antiquated and somber" structure, Wilson said, with an iron gate and a shadowy courtyard. Hardly had he reached the drawing room when "Arthur emerged with two handsome and rich-looking ladies," followed by Jackie Kennedy and Tennessee Williams. He shook hands with Mrs. Kennedy, and she, on hearing his name, gave him an "interested look." But although he "should have liked to talk to her," she "curled up in the corner of a couch and talked all the time to Tennessee Williams." Then "Arthur announced to me that we were going 'to a better party.'" They crossed the courtyard, and by "gloomy corridors and turning stairs," reached another apartment. It was a housewarming party for Amanda Burden, the daughter of Babe Paley and Stanley Mortimer in their unhappy marriage, and her husband Carter Burden: the couple whom Tom Wolfe was to describe as the most glamorous in New York in the age of radical chic that was then dawning. "The first thing that confronted you on entering," Wilson said, "was one of Francis Bacon's yelling popes, with a drawing by Vertès beside it." Everyone "was in evening dress—the women, even when insipid, very well and expensively turned out—like the Vanderbilt lady, who had come from the other party." "These children," as the guests called the newlyweds, seemed to Wilson have assembled an entertaining group, "a combination of New York society with a dash of café society and, when we arrived, a sprinkling of Kennedy intellectuals." At one point the bride sat beside him, and he asked her about two Pop Art figures standing beside the piano, a girl and a boy made of wooden boxes.

"So and so makes them," she replied helpfully.

He inquired after his host, and a slender blond figure bearing a tray of drinks said, "I'm the host," and put the tray down so that they could shake hands. In the distance Wilson saw Jock Whitney, whose wife, Betsey, was the bride's aunt, but he did not speak to him. Jock was now publisher of the *New York Herald Tribune*, a paper in which he had a controlling interest and which gave him something to do now that he was no longer Eisenhower's ambassador to the Court of St. James's, where his grandfather John Hay had been McKinley's. The Queen and the Duke of Edinburgh had thought him delightful, and had gone so far as to address him as "Jock," but he had not liked the job. An ambassador, he said, is "a cross between a butler and a pimp for senators."

Jock's cousin Michael Straight sat glumly during a meeting in the offices of the *New Republic*. He had made former vice president Henry Wallace, a dupe of the communists, editor of the magazine, and the junior editors were haranguing Arthur Schlesinger for supporting the anticommunist line of the newly formed Americans for Democratic Action. Straight, Schlesinger remembered, had a look of "profound dejection" on his face as he listened to Teddy White, the future scholar of presidential elections, argue that America's Cold War policy was more menacing toward the Soviet Union than "the present U.S.S.R. policy toward the U.S." The magazine that once defined American liberalism was now retailing Stalin's talking points. Schlesinger would later suspect that Straight was unhappy precisely because he knew from his own experience how successful Moscow had been in coopting elements of the American Left. But he could say nothing without compromising his own past, for although he had broken with the N.K.V.D., he shrank from exposing his former treachery.

After Wallace left the *New Republic* to run for president on the Progressive ticket in 1948, Straight began to turn the magazine around, endorsing Harry Truman rather than Wallace for president and supporting the Marshall Plan. But the Whitney fortune was not what it had been, and the family was forced to sell Applegreen, the estate in Old Westbury where the idea of the *New Republic* had been hatched, decades before, by Herbert Croly and Michael's mother Dorothy; the magazine itself was sold in the 1950s to Gilbert Harrison and his wife Anne, a descendant of Cyrus McCormick, the founder of the company that became International Harvester. By the sixties the *New Republic* was again readable, so much so that President Kennedy was once seen carrying a copy as he climbed the steps to his airplane.

Giving up journalism, Michael Straight became a novelist, a collector of art, and a patron of worthy causes. His dilettantism was rewarded when in 1963 Kennedy asked him to chair his new Advisory Council on the Arts, the forerunner of the National Endowment for the same. "We're convinced that you're the best man for the job," the president's friend Bill Walton, the painter, told him. "You're a novelist in your own right and a damned good one. You're respected by the arts organizations. You have many friends in Congress. Above all, you and the president will get along well together. You come from the same backgrounds; you share the same interests; you're bound to like each other. . . . The president is ready to go, but we'll have to clear you with the leaders in Congress. Then there's the F.B.I. check. . ."

"The F.B.I. check," Straight remembered thinking. "I hadn't thought about that." Lying in bed in the night, he reflected on his predicament and resolved to confess his secret. He went first to Arthur Schlesinger and then to the F.B.I. Whatever else Kennedy's arts program accomplished, it led eventually to Anthony Blunt's admission that he had been a spy for the Soviet Union and one of the Cambridge Five, the "ablest group of British agents ever recruited by a foreign power," or so the authorized historian of the British Security Service has written.

"ABOUT KENNEDY," EDMUND WILSON WROTE Alfred Kazin, "I think you somewhat overrate his literacy. His historical allusions are likely to be inaccurate in a way which suggests he cannot really have read much history. I suspect that his pretensions to 'culture' are largely worked up by Arthur Schlesinger." But unpersuaded though he was by Kennedy's gestures of cultural renewal, he accepted an invitation to the dinner in May 1962 at the White House in honor of his old friend André Malraux, the French intellectual and man of action who, in common with the higher WASPs, was an anti-bourgeois bourgeois who looked to art to recover a lost wholeness, and who was now serving as de Gaulle's minister of culture. Jacqueline Kennedy adored him.

Elena Wilson was seated next to Chip Bohlen at a table over which one of the president's sisters presided; Edmund was seated at the president's own table opposite "a rather queer portrait of Lincoln" which "must have been a modern production." (The Healey portrait of Lincoln was painted in 1869.) When the president asked him about *Patriotic Gore* and its conclusions, he said that he "couldn't very well answer him then and there and referred him to the Introduction," a reply that somewhat dampened the conversation. The food, however, was, Wilson thought, excellent, particularly the soup, with its *double crème* and dab of caviar. The oratory was another matter. Malraux, in his toast, seemed to Wilson to carry diplomatic politeness to the point of absurdity, and he said to Mme. Malraux, "*Dites à Malraux que je n'en crois rien.*" He was startled to find that Kennedy understood him. "You don't tell us what *you* think," the president said. When he bade the Wilsons goodbye, he brought up *Patriotic Gore* again. "I suppose I'll have to buy it," he said.

"I'm afraid so," Edmund told the president.

It was a giddy and an ominous time. Ten days after the Malraux dinner Lieutenant Colonel John Paul Vann arrived in the Mekong Delta to advise the Army of the Republic of Vietnam in its struggle with the Viet Cong, and in June President Kennedy's status as honorary WASP was confirmed when, in the company of Dean Acheson and Prescott Bush, he was made doctor of laws at the hands of Yale's president, Alfred Whitney Griswold, in the Old Campus in New Haven.

In October 1963 Wilson flew with Elena to England. There were the usual literary parties, with everyone "talking so loudly that any real conversation was impossible," and the usual round of engagements with men of letters: champagne and luncheon at the Ritz with Cyril Connolly, who stuck Wilson with the bill, tea at Claridge's with Compton Mackenzie, who said that his "principal ambition was to outlive Somerset Maugham," and lunch with Wystan Auden in the Café Royal, the only place in London, the poet said, that never changes. Ever alert, in this phase of his life, to the choicer sanctuaries, Wilson was impressed by Headington House in Oxford, where his old friend Isaiah Berlin had been luxuriously installed by his French wife Aline. It was a large comfortable place "with servants, many pictures and lots of books," as well as "gardens, well-kept grounds, a gazebo, and a black retriever who had grown so fat that they had to put him on a diet."

Wilson thought that the "humanity" of Headington House "must be unique in Oxford," but if older standards were in a few places being kept up, there was much deterioration, and he was conscious of the deformities of mind and spirit into which he found his old friends slipping. Cyril Connolly's "feeling of frustration and envy of other writers" was "making him overtly nasty about his friends," and he seemed to be living "more and more in a little self-centered world" of his own. Isaiah himself, when he stepped out of his dukedom in Oxford, was hysterically voluble, shooting down everyone and everything in sight like a gamekeeper gone mad. He would not, Wilson said, "allow anyone else to talk: you have to cut down through his continuous flow determinedly, loudly and emphatically, and he will soon snatch the ball away from you by not waiting for you to finish but seizing on some new association of ideas to go off on some new line of thought."

He and Elena crossed to France, where he found that it was not merely the individuals but the country itself that was failing to live up to its potential, surrendering its ancient dignity as it became part of a "more uniform and increasingly Americanized world." The people "were small and dreary—you rarely nowadays see women dressed with chic." Nelly de Vogüé, he claimed, was "the only good-looking soignée woman" he had seen. At Versailles the insipid French visitors seemed "completely alien" to the grandeur of the château, and belonging as they did to "a much flatter world," had no "vital relation" to the gardens and galleries and works of art.

He and Elena were suffering from head colds in their rooms in the Hôtel de Castille when they learned of the death of President Kennedy. In the days that followed they sat about dismally, "surrounded by the ghastly newspapers." "The whole thing is sickening," Wilson wrote: the "sordidness of the assassins," Oswald and Ruby, the one "a schizoid boy who thought he was a Marxist rebel," the other "a boastful crook who ran a small nightclub." There was, too, the "ineptitude of the Dallas police" and the "humiliating position of the American President who has to chase all over the country appealing for votes." What he had not expected was that Europe should have felt the loss as keenly as America. He was "surprised at the reaction in France and apparently in Europe generally—which showed how much they have been counting on us as represented by Kennedy."

WASPs, too, had been counting on Kennedy, and after his death his preppy aides-de-camp were stricken, so many "male widows," Joe Alsop thought. The Cravath partner Roswell Gilpatric, who served under Bob McNamara in Kennedy's Pentagon and was a considerable ladies' man, offered up his own drop of homoerotic perfume for the grave of him he loved, telling Alsop that he felt about Jack as "I've never felt about another man in my life." But Osiris was dead, and neither tamarisk nor lilac sprouted from his blood. Three years after Dallas his shade overhung Truman Capote's Black and White Ball for the *Washington Post's* Katharine Graham, a strange funereal rite, part wake, part Walpurgisnacht, in which those who had hitched their wagons to WASPery's drooping star mourned obliquely for Jack, and still more for themselves. A great WASP fête of the night, the last in a long black trail, it masked so many griefs and uneasinesses; there was (according to those who left a candid record of the passing hours) no gaiety in the thing. Blood and death were in the mourners' minds, and now that their king was dead, they laughed openly about their own impending journey to the guillotine.

AT PARTIES IN GEORGETOWN, GEORGE Kennan would play his balalaika. Joe Alsop, who ordinarily would have raised his eyebrows at such a crotchet, was impressed by his friend's mastery of the Russian instrument. The balalaika was for Kennan a talisman, an antidote to all that he found unsympathetic in an American civilization he had come to detest. "I hate democracy . . . I hate the 'peepul,'" he had written as a young man, and as an old man he was not more enamored. For "my own country, I have not a shred of hope, not one," he said in the 1950s. By the seventies and eighties he was describing the United States as a "vast polyglot mass . . . one huge pool of indistinguishable mediocrity and drabness," "a wasteland, a garbage dump, a sewer." "The America I know and love and owe allegiance to," he said, was the America "of John Hay and Henry Adams and [Theodore] Roosevelt." The America, that is, of the high WASPs.*

If by the late 1960s the WASP elite was mostly ashamed of itself—the most disestablishmentarian establishment on record—Kennan made so bold as to stick up for a dying patriciate. He insisted that only a more potent mandarinism—a "strong central power"—could save the Republic. He toyed with extra-democratic "councils of state" that would take a "decent account" of the "feelings and opinions" of the masses, yet would "assure a sufficient concentration of governmental authority" and "a sufficient selectivity in the recruitment of those privileged to exert it" to permit the "implementation of hopeful long-term programs of social and environmental change. . ."

Unlike more equivocal WASPs, who talked like democrats and acted like Whig grandees, Kennan was forthright in expressing his conviction that egalitarianism was ruinous. "The trouble with this country," he told Joe Alsop, "is that we are a democracy and instead should be ruled by aristocrats." (Alsop, who was firmly in the equivocal camp, said that he "was very nearly sick.")† Yet Kennan was only advocating openly what WASPs had long covertly sought, an "enlightened and responsible" class of WASP males who, endowed with the proper "character, education, and inclination," could serve as unofficial guardians of the Republic. What is odd is that he hardly bothered with the question that has bedeviled all the more thoughtful advocates of government by the best and the brightest. Who will guard the guardians? How will the elite remain

---

*　Kennan might disagree with the WASP mandarins about questions of foreign policy, but he "should be most unhappy" if anything he said "should seem a mark of disrespect for such men as John Hay, Elihu Root, Charles Evans Hughes, or Henry Stimson. These men embodied that pattern of integrity of mind and spirit, moderation and delicacy of character, irreproachable loyalty in personal relations, modesty of person combined with dignity of office, and kindliness and generosity in the approach to all who were weaker and more dependent, which constitutes, it seems to me, our finest contribution to the variety of the human species in this world and comes closest to embodying our national ideal and genius."

†　The equivocal nature of Alsop's egalitarianism is evident in Ben Bradlee's account of the manner in which he took the pulse of the common people, the American *demos*. An "enormously stylish man with great taste" who was also "a serious snob," Alsop, in his quest to comprehend character and opinion in the United States *circa* 1956, went out into the fields of Minnesota in "a green tweed jacket, tailored gray slacks, and highly polished English Peal shoes" to talk to those who labored in the earth. When, at last, he came upon a farmer, he nudged him with his walking stick and asked him, "What do you make of it all, old boy, eh?" The WASP patriciate was, in comparison to that of, say, England's, what a child's sketch is to the work of some master: but even so flagrant a toff as Alsop, with his walking stick and his English shoes—John Lobb, not Peal, was his bootmaker—had a guilty conscience about it.

virtuous amid the temptations of power? Plato, in the *Republic*, dragooned all the ingenuity of a vast intelligence into the effort to solve the problem. But by the time he composed the *Laws*, he all but conceded defeat. Where Plato failed, not only did Kennan not succeed, he seemed unconscious of the problem.

Another member of the WASP establishment was as conscious of the perils of elitism as Kennan was oblivious. Once the apostle of the mandarinism of Theodore Roosevelt and the early *New Republic*, Learned Hand had, after the failure of the Theodoric crusade, submitted to the psychic tonsure of the judge, and under the cowl of judicial humility he abjured politics to devote himself to his work in the district court. In 1924 he was elevated to the Second Circuit Court of Appeals, which became, largely because of the quality of his opinions, one of the most luminous appellate bodies in the annals of American jurisprudence. His work as a judge, which required him, among other things, to determine whether democratically fashioned laws violated the Constitution, made him familiar with the temptations and the dangers of mandarinism, and he made short shrift of his friend Bernard Berenson's faith in the virtues of aristocracy. When, in the 1930s, Berenson spoke contemptuously of democracy, arguing that "we are hierarchical animals with pyramidical societies" who need Platonic guardians to "hold down" the hoi polloi, Hand replied that Plato's theory of a virtuous elite in the *Republic* was "desperately unconvincing," and that there never has been a brace of aristocratic rulers who "did not abuse their powers before long."

Ever since his days as a student in Harvard Law School, Hand had wrestled with that most ambiguous prerogative in the American constitutional system, the power of unelected judges to overturn the acts of popular government. His teacher James Bradley Thayer, "one of the great masters," as he called him, imbued "us with a scepticism about the wisdom of setting up courts as the final arbiters of social conflicts." In the nineteenth century judges had been cautious in exercising their power to declare laws unconstitutional, but Thayer foresaw an age in which courts would "make themselves into what is really a legislative body." As Thayer's prophecy came true, Hand anguished. What was to become of a society that evaded its responsibility to resolve disputes by thrusting that responsibility on the courts?

Anguish was, to be sure, an element of Hand's nature, that neurasthenic part of his soul that made him a great and uncomplacent judge. He thought of himself as a "twisted introvert," yet as he aged he came to know a degree of serenity, one that not even the constitutional difficulties raised by Thayer could entirely disturb. After his wife's lover, Louis Dow, died in 1944, his marriage revived, bringing him unexpected happiness. With no remaining rivals for Frances's heart—Dow and Mildred Minturn being in their graves—he was soon writing love letters to the woman whom he called his "pearl without a price."

In 1951 he retired from regular active service as a judge of the Second Circuit court of appeals. But he continued to hear and decide cases, and his essays and occasional writings, gathered together in a volume called *The Spirit of Liberty*, were hailed as the work of "a great American humanist," one whose "style and view of life" were, in the words of *The Economist*, "as far removed from the common, trivial, and the undercivilised mass-mind as it is conceivable . . . to be." Yet amid all these encomiums, the memory of his teacher, Thayer, continued to goad him, and in February 1958, at the age of eight-six, he undertook the last of his civic labors when he returned to Austin Hall at Harvard to deliver the Oliver Wendell Holmes Lectures. Speaking to a crowded house, he warned that too great a faith in elites, even judicial elites, the *noblesse de robe* of the Supreme Court itself, might well undermine a people's capacity for self-government. The court over which Chief Justice Earl Warren had presided since 1953 threatened, Hand said, to become a "third legislative chamber" with a veto over the other two. Nine unelected lawyers might now give laws to a nation. Hand's lectures were principally concerned with the temptation of judges "to pour their personal preferences into vague constitutional phrases" (the sin of *Lochner* transplanted into new realms) and with certain technical difficulties in construing the Constitution, but they touched, too, the broader question of government by patriciate. Others might welcome the rule of philosopher kings, but for himself, Hand said, "it would be most irksome to be ruled by a bevy of Platonic Guardians, even if I knew how to choose them, which I assuredly do not. If they were in charge, I should miss the stimulus of living in a society where I have, at least theoretically, some part in the direction of affairs."

Yet different as their positions were, both Learned Hand and George Kennan, each a civic humanist who had been shaped by the WASP tradition, were evidence of how far the higher WASPs had come from the aspirations that originally animated their kind. Henry Adams's elitism had been inspired by a dream of cultural regeneration, a renovation "not only in politics, but in literature, in law, in society, and throughout the whole social organism of the country." Hand, foreswearing such visionary ideas, made peace with the reality of an unreconstructed *demos* and the "wayward vagaries of popular assemblies."

Kennan, pledged to aristocracy, envisioned the power of the magnificos not, as Adams did, as a means of ennobling the citizenry, but as a kind of duke's horsewhip to keep the proles and rednecks in line.

THE DREAM HAD DIED, AND with its death the pursuit of the fair sheepfold—the charmed zone or magic circle in which the soul ripens—was given up for good. In its place WASPs contented themselves with the cocktail party, ideally to be conducted on a patch of emerald lawn at Nantucket, with a glimpse of sea, or on a promontory in Maine, with the woodthrush singing through the fog. The lesser WASPs, with their golf and tennis, their gin-and-tonics and their oddly colored leisure clothing, were all that remained of the breed, so much so that you would hardly know that there had been any other kind.

For the great personages of WASPdom, pure, ornate, or rebel, were dead or dying. Ernest Hemingway shot himself in 1961, the same year in which Whittaker Chambers's heart gave out and Learned Hand was laid in his grave; Eleanor Roosevelt expired the following year. T. S. Eliot vanished in January 1965, Bill Bullitt in February 1967, Dorothy Whitney Straight Elmhirst in December 1968. Dean Acheson, dismayed to have lived into a period in which "there are mediocre men everywhere" and leaders "are made in the image of the masses," spent an afternoon in October 1971 in his garden. (In the days before Viagra, aging WASPs took up gardening as a substitute for sex, deriving a vicarious pleasure from the orgies of pollen, the fertilizing stamens, the receptive pistils—the exuberant display of all that voluptuousness we ourselves are at pains to conceal.) He afterward suffered a stroke in his study, where his butler found him dead. Edie Sedgwick perished the following month, poisoned by drink and barbiturates: half a year later, at Talcottville, Edmund Wilson disappeared, much as he had predicted, like "a puff of smoke." Joe Alsop's syndicated column and the Republic of Vietnam were extinguished at about the same time. Joe's cousin, Alice Roosevelt Longworth, died in 1980, two years after Babe Paley went to her grave; Joe himself departed in the summer of 1989, though not before delivering a couple of memorable performances on C-SPAN, a diverting exhibition of the high WASP manner in all its eccentric perfection.

With the death or disgrace of so many of their luminaries, WASPs lost their grip on power, and they were soon doing penance for having been in power at all. The class that had once inspired fear and loathing had the mortification to find itself looked down upon as amiably goofy. Yet it was in their decrepitude that WASPs came to be emulated or parodied. With the exception of the Bushes, who, having emigrated to Texas, went native and abjured their tribal inspirations, and a few relics such as Cyrus Vance and John Kerry, WASP mastery of the high places in the state came to an end in 1966 when McGeorge Bundy, undone (as his Yale College friend Kingman Brewster helpfully pointed out) by his mistakes on Vietnam, resigned as national security advisor to become head of the Ford Foundation. As a cultural force WASPs were by this time quite as spent; the failure of their effort at regeneration was neatly recapitulated by Robert Lowell (whose heart gave out in a New York City cab in September 1977) in his poem "For the Union Dead," with its image of a disemboweled Boston Common (fenced off for the excavation of a parking garage) mocking the WASP idealism of Colonel Robert Gould Shaw, whose Civil War valor in pursuit of regeneration had been memorialized by Augustus Saint-Gaudens, that embalmer of high WASPs. (*Omnia relinquit servare rem publicam*—he gives up everything to save the Republic.) In the post-WASP America Lowell depicts in his poem, Colonel Shaw has been ostracized—"He is out of bounds now"—by citizens who, in their "giant finned cars," have forsaken the old civic inspirations and become so many "cowed, compliant fish" in the "downward and vegetating kingdom" of a technically advanced but otherwise sterile Republic. Yet it was just as the WASPs ceased to be a power in the country that the more superficial qualities of their style were taken up by middle America, as books like Lisa Birnbach's *The Official Preppy Handbook* and movies like *Dead Poets Society* retailed a culture that was appealing precisely because no one took it seriously. Henry Adams would have enjoyed the joke.

HE WAS THIRTEEN WHEN HE came to the school in September 1979, to enter the second form. (The first form had been abolished in the 1960s.) His mother brought him up to Groton, for his father was dead, and the headmaster and his wife stood at the door of their residence in Hundred House to greet them. Afterward they were shown to the second form dormitory in Brooks House, a long, dreary hall of heavily varnished oak, largely unchanged since the reign of Edward VII. It opened, to the east, on a threadbare common room, and to the north on a bathroom with soapstone washbasins like horses' troughs. On either side of the hall were cells called cubicles, each of which contained a bed, a chest of drawers, and a small window. There were no doors; each cubicle had instead a corded red linen curtain.

The master of this monastic domain, Mr. Gula, a scholar of many languages and disciplines, said that he had been anxious about Rob in those first hours, for he had remained by himself in his cube after his mother left. "His family *owns* the newspaper I delivered." So another boy said on one of those first September mornings. Rob's father, Robert Worth Bingham, whose name he bore, had been killed in an accident on Nantucket shortly after his birth; his great-grandfather had been Franklin Roosevelt's first ambassador to the United Kingdom. But this, had they known it, would not have meant very much to the other thirteen-year-olds.

Were it not for its high New England associations and its large endowment of capital, that touchstone of WASP respectability, the school would have seemed, to the casual outsider stumbling upon it, the manifestation of a strange, possibly sinister cult. Surely a place where young people were made to sleep in bare cubicles, and who were roused by bells to sing hymns, study dead languages, and recite poetry under the compulsion of black marks ought to have been investigated by the responsible authorities.

The hymns were sung each morning in chapel. The service was short—twenty minutes—and enlivened by what was called a chapel talk, delivered by a student or teacher from the pulpit, typically humorous, though in theory inculcating a moral lesson. The talk was followed by a moment of silence, and afterward by the peal of the organ. The "boldest lyric inspiration," Emerson says, "should announce and lead the day's work." Few people today find themselves, for any length of time, in places where the entire community *sings* to itself each morning, and may find it difficult to comprehend the psychological effects of such a discipline, a rather potent grooming ritual; in later years you pondered Dr. Johnson's saying of his Oxford college that it was "a nest of singing birds." For Polymnia lived in the chapel, and her music shadowed you through the day, touching all its little ceremonies with the note of the nightingale.

By such means, for good or ill, the school wrought upon you. It was a place, such as few places in America now are. You take it for granted today that you may travel two or three thousand miles, from one end of the continent to the other, and find, when you have reached your destination, the same shops, the same architecture, the same opinions. Gerald Brenan, the scholar of Spain, went so far as to speak of death "by monotony, by sameness, by loss of identity." But in the school the art of identity was potent, perhaps too potent, so that you developed for it something of the feeling of the Greek for his city. "His city was the only city, and her ways the only ways. He loved every rock and spring in the folds of her mountain, every shrine and haunt within the circuit of her walls. . ." Ernest

Renan said of his hometown, Tréguier in Brittany, that it was "enveloped in an atmosphere of mythology as dense as Benares." It was something like that in the school. The shrines were unshattered and the myths uneffaced.

IN THIRD FORM THE CID arrived, preceded by a reputation much exaggerated by hearsay and the human fondness for fable. He was only fourteen, but (so vicious is Fama) he was said to possess an extensive knowledge of human degeneracy, and a nose for depravity that might favorably have impressed Madame de Merteuil, the witch in de Laclos's novel.* He had, it was generally believed, lost his virginity to a sun-withered matron in a preppy summer colony, and young as he was, he was reputed to have ingested the fashionable narcotics of the age—it was the era of "Studio 54"—and pronounced them insipid. (In fact he was abstemious.) He was credited (here the reports were closer to the truth) with having been passionately loved by the prettiest Brearley girls, and with having been as jealously abhorred by their mothers, who, it was said, were in love with him themselves.

Yet when you first saw him, you were perplexed. The Cid seemed, in his blond slenderness, the image of innocence. Surely the reports were false; the angelic child who, unpacking his trunk, placed a Bachrach photograph of his mother on the bureau of his cubicle could hardly be the changeling whose deviltries had made him the despair of his teachers and the terror of half a dozen summer resorts.

Rob was among the first of the old second formers to greet him. In the musty corridor of Brooks House where, as a third former, you were entitled to a study in addition to your cubicle, he extended his hand.

"I'm Rob."

The Cid smiled. "How you doin', Bob?"

"Don't ever call me Bob." Known by all who were close to him as "Rob" or "Robbie," he had often spoken of his distaste for the downmarket "Bob."

The Cid touched his arm and with an impish look in his eye began to stroke it. "Whatever you say, Bob."

Bob, as he was now rechristened, burst out laughing.

---

*   In this section and in the last chapter of the book the author has recreated from memory certain scenes from the past. To preserve the privacy of individuals he has, in several instances, altered names, nicknames, and other incriminating details.

Friends are born, not made. In the strong light of the Cid's fantasy Rob was lifted out of his prosaic self and invested with a succession of comic costumes. First he was "Bob," then "Brother Biff," then "Caker," at last "Angel Boy." Bob figured, in the ascensions of the Cid's wit, as an awkward giant. It was a part for which he was fitted, for he had, and would retain even into early manhood, an indifference to the more obvious graces of manner and carriage. Though he was a natural athlete, his métier, as a teenager, was an endearing clumsiness, a vocation that was revealed plainly enough in his physical makeup, in the thick brown hair, which was very little combed, in the unsharpened nose and the lazy muscles of the mouth, which in repose was not always accurately closed. To this ungainliness the Cid opposed a swifter, more skillfully organized force. He was the clumsy giant's foil, the picador who goads the bull. The humor was as old as that of the *miles gloriosus* of the Roman stage; Bob was the swaggering soldier at the mercy of his sharp-witted slave. But to third formers the Cid's genius was as fresh as that of Plautus must once have been to the Romans.

THERE WERE THE STONES AND the shrines, "altars to the Naiads, or Faunus, or some deity of the place." In an alcove in the Schoolhouse a window stained by Louis Tiffany (a relic of the school's first chapel) depicted the seraphic features of a sleeping youth against a background of angelic figures in an Art Nouveau style. Studying the dark-robed figure in the glass, as you waited for something or other to begin, you became acquainted with Warwick Potter, beloved of Santayana, and in the tablet under the portico you came upon Dillwyn Parrish Starr exhorting his Coldstream Guards, *Come on, 12 Platoon, come on*, before he fell in the Battle of the Somme. But it was at the end of chapel, as you moved past the names carved in the stone to the strains of the recessional, that you were most conscious of something else. (There are times when it is better to curse the candle than light a darkness.)

HELEN SEDGWICK 1890–1948
OF SUCH IS THE KINGDOM OF HEAVEN

As Bach sounded in the dimness, a thirteen-year-old pictured an ethereal figure enwrapped in clouds, for he knew nothing of the Minturn cottage in Murray Bay, where John Goodenough once tutored Helen's son Harry, the cousin of Edie, and where Learned Hand once courted Frances Fincke.

FRANKLIN DELANO ROOSEVELT 1882–1945
OF THE SIXTH FORM OF 1900
PRESIDENT OF THE UNITED STATES 1933–1945

What the school had was a thickness of poetry, the kind that (in the old Greek theory) draws out whatever powers are in you. It was the tradition of Rob's own family, which was high WASP with touches of Southern Gothic. He was as conscious as Balzac that beneath every fortune was a crime, and years later, at a party in his loft in Tribeca, he alluded to the original sin that underlay his own. A middle-aged, *mitteleuropäische* character sank into an armchair as Rob poured out Cretan raki. (I reproduce the gist of the conversation.)

"Your grandfather. He was the ambassador, was he not?"

"Great-grandfather."

"A gruesome character."

"It *was* convenient that the rich widow left him some of the Standard Oil money."

"He killed her, no?"

"Not proved. She was a drunk. Did he make sure the bottles kept going up to her room? Maybe."

He went off and returned with some clippings and a book or article about his family by a mud-mongering journalist.

"Oh yes, here he is. The Ambassador. Ghastly. But I can see you in him, Robbie. I really can. Of course he is fair and you are dark. But the set of the jaw, the line of the hair, the modeling of the nose—it's wonderful. And here is the house he built after he got hold of the money—"

"The Big House we call it."

"The Big House. I picture horses in the background. Flowering magnolias. But what's this?"

"That's the Greek theater. The line from *Hamlet* is carved over the stage. *To hold as 'twere the mirror up to nature.* My grandmother would make us recite poetry. I had to recite the chapter from First Corinthians. *When I was a child, I spake as a child, I understood as a child, I thought as a child: but when I became a man, I put away childish things. . . .*" He took a sip of raki. "And d'you know? I never did put away childish things."

His grandmother had been a formidable "Grecian" or classicist at Radcliffe. His grandfather was an all-around man in the civic humanist sense, a reforming liberal who had helped to organize the Americans for Democratic Action, the friend of Arthur Schlesinger and Adlai Stevenson, a journalist who made the Louisville *Courier Journal* into one of the most respected regional newspapers in the country, a man who had, withal, a most courtly, charming, intensely decent way about him. It was the environment in which Rob grew up. If ever there was a late-twentieth-century child of *eutrapelia*, the Greek ideal of many-sidedness that Matthew Arnold sought to resurrect, it was he.

Groton reinforced this intensive culture. He read Shakespeare and rowed crew under Mr. Jesdale, a teacher of prophet-like intensity who worked to train both a boy's body and his mind. Rob was soon as conscious as anyone of the challenge that Tertius Lydgate confronts in *Middlemarch*, that of keeping one's soul alive in a world that has abandoned the very idea of the soul. The school in those days was full of teachers like Mr. Jesdale whose vocation, one might almost say whose passion, was the pastoral one of helping young souls to ripen, so many Brunetto Latinis and Jane Brodies in their prime.

To HAVE A BEST FRIEND is the privilege of youth. In middle age the relation is much rarer. The way we live now, Santayana pointed out, conspires against it.* But probably nowhere does it flourish more intensely than in a boarding school, where the ordinary ties of domestic intimacy have been cut, or artificially suspended; the relation with the best friend bears the whole of an emotional weight that in ordinary cases is more equally distributed, is borne alike by mothers and fathers, by sisters and brothers and the family dog. There must have been a certain amount of suppressed erotic feeling in these Platonic couplings. But at Groton the relationships were not sexual, as jailhouse hitchings, or as Etonian and Harrovian betrothals, are said to be. Rob early became infatuated with a delicately featured girl whose eyes, as ingenuously blue as Mr. Gardner's, contrasted agreeably with her dark hair. His passion, unabated and unrequited, for Cynthia, as I shall call her, was protracted until the end of his school days, when it became even more completely hopeless; for in sixth form Cynthia fell in love with Blagden.†

---

* "The ancients, so long as they were free, spent their whole life in forum and palæstra, camp, theatre, and in consequence could live by friendship even in their mature years." But modern men, Santayana believed, too often find themselves "parted by unbridgeable chasms" from those who might be their friends.

† The first girls had been admitted to Groton four years before Bob arrived.

One day, not long after Cynthia and Blagden began to go out, the conversation at the lunch table turned to sex.

"I like it," Cynthia said.

The Cid raised his eyebrows. "Do you? *Do* you?"

"Why do you doubt it?"

"Because of your own severe virginity."

A few days later, as we walked to morning chapel, Bob related the upshot of the conversation at the lunch table.

"Last Saturday Blagden . . ." He looked you in the eye and nodded as it was his habit to do whenever he made a significant avowal. Yet his bond with the Cid was stronger than a merely carnal coupling could be, for without an element of spiritual interest, a mingling of souls, such an attachment rarely survives the gratification of the passion that prompted it. The love that the Cid roused in Bob lasted until his death. A friend of both observed how each seemed to know the other's thought before he uttered it, for there was an unspoken sympathy between them. Rob was a lover of women, yet I am not sure he ever loved a girl more than he loved the Cid.

JUST BEFORE THE SCHOOL BROKE for Christmas the aged Jack Crocker, who had succeeded Endicott Peabody as headmaster forty years before and was now in retirement, climbed the steps of the pulpit to read the lesson, wisps of white hair illuminating his aquiline face. *Now when Jesus was born in Bethlehem of Judaea in the days of Herod the king, behold, there came wise men from the east to Jerusalem . . .* The voice was so rich, so archaic, as to be almost otherworldly. In fact Jack Crocker had had a hard time in his first years as the successor of Peabody, and he had been accused by McGeorge Bundy, who had what amounted to a genius for getting things wrong, of being incompetent. ("Mr. Crocker is not a bad Headmaster. He is not, basically, a Headmaster at all. . .") Yet it was Jack Crocker who, preserving what was best in the old Groton, charted a modern course for the school. He believed in civic engagement informed by humility, and he drew inspiration both from his friend Reinhold Niebuhr and from Dr. Martin Luther King Jr., who came to Groton in 1963 to spend two days preaching and teaching in the school. It was under Jack Crocker that the first boy of color was accepted. Endicott Peabody had himself contemplated such a step, but had dreaded a parental and alumni revolt. Jack Crocker had more confidence in moral man. When the *New York Times* got wind of the news and prepared a front-page story, he told the reporter that the development was not noteworthy. "My dear sir," he said, "the only real news would be if Groton did *not* admit Blacks." Such opposition as he encountered was mild, civil, and easily overcome, with a single exception, that of an alumnus who sent out a letter to the Groton family which, purporting to come from the school itself, was crudely intended to undermine the headmaster. The culprit proved to be Edie's father, Fuzzy Sedgwick. Yet Crocker treated his old schoolmate humanely. Fuzzy was crazy; his various erratic actions around this time were, Crocker saw, "the fruit of anguish," and turning the other cheek he assured him that if "it were possible for us by mutual forbearance to establish confidence in each other again, it would mean more to me than I believe you would surmise . . ."

Jack Crocker was by the early 1980s fading into senescence, but his theory of a school was carried on by his old student Bill Polk, Rob's headmaster, who worked to make Groton more diverse even as he sought to preserve its ideals of Christian charity and pastoral care. In Rob's form—it was the form of 1984, the centenary of Cotty Peabody's first coming to the place—were descendants of Saltonstalls, Lowells, Frelinghuysens, Wilmerdings, but there were more new people than old. It was only on alumni day that you saw the graying hair of aboriginal WASPery, as the last of the Rector's old boys returned to the Circle for their anniversaries. It was then that you might spy McGeorge Bundy sipping a cocktail under the tent, or the younger Kermit Roosevelt, grandson of Theodore, agreeing with his form-mate Francis Keppel, as they watched a losing battle against St. Mark's on the baseball diamond, that the trees had grown up to the west, obscuring the mountains.

"Groton, again and again, Groton," groaned Harrison Salisbury of the *New York Times* as he found the fingerprints of its boys all over mid-twentieth-century American life. But by Rob's time it was no longer so. The school had ceased to be a shaper of the governing patriciate; its significance, such as it was, lay in its style of order, so different from that of most other places in the America of that time, its life closer to that of a Greek village than to the America of suburbs and shopping malls and the six o'clock news. (The methods of the WASP "anti-modern vitalists" remained surprisingly . . . vital.) In New York, encountering the Hasidim, you had the same sense of affinity, for they, too, were connected to one another by such a thickness of poetry as hardly existed anywhere else. It was not for nothing that the troubadours called it the joyous science.

❧

THE LILACS BLOOMED EARLY THAT spring, and the odor left its elegiac stain. You sauntered about in an easy and perhaps too exquisite idleness, seeking out the choicest places at the richest hours—the nooks behind Hundred House in the late afternoon sunlight, or the terrace in front of the chapel just before you dressed for dinner, when the sun played on the glass of the window in the western wall. The lassitudes into which you fell were broken only by the rituals of the school, and by your quickened expectation that you were about to leave. Otherwise you were very nearly absolute in your mastery of the place. All the sixth form were prefects, and all possessed the prerogatives of prefectship; yet the restraints on conduct were every day weakening, and you were startled to find yourself practically on a footing with the masters, who were by this time your friends. After five years of labor and discipline, the school granted you this brief interval of irresponsible authority.

THE SCHOOLHOUSE BELL TOLLED TEN o'clock, and you went out into the night, searching for him. He had not appeared at handshaking in the dorm, a grave offense at Groton. You looked everywhere you could think of, without result. At last you found him. He was with a girl. You saw their moonlit faces emerge from the door of the chapel, where old Mr. Gardner, best man at Jack Chapman's wedding, lay in his coffin. Only then did you remember that it was in that somber undercroft, moist with rat-droppings and rotting reredos, that Rob most liked to have sex, for of all the places in the school, it was there that you were least likely to be disturbed.

She went back to her dorm. But he was restless, and there was the sixth form privilege of midnight curfew. You were beside him as he passed rapidly over the last of the lawns to the wood. The contrast was always violent. The school was Georgian in style, with a Gothic chapel. No trace of archaic Massachusetts lingered there, among the box-hedges and whitewashed porticos, lilac and chapel and star. But the forest, in a moonshine night, was the forest of the seventeenth century. The erotic phantasms of a primitive Puritanism were vivid. Every misshapen rock seemed a cloven hoof, every meadow a shadowy conventicle.

Down to the river, the moon running fast between tufts of cloud. You had not yet learned to hide yourself behind the fences and screens of maturity; every man was his brother's confessor.

"I don't really have a family," he said. "Certainly not a father. The school is the closest thing I have to that."

He was an infant when his father died, and he had passed a vagrant childhood, now with his mother, now with his grandparents, in Washington, New York, Paris, Patmos, Nantucket, and other such places. The family seat was in Louisville, but they were nomadic millionaires, and he had learnt early to savor the fragrances of their habitual way-stations. But it was what he found in the school, with its strange religion of friendship—the "controlling principle which underlies the whole system of the school," George Rublee said, "is the principle of love"—that most interested him that night, in the forest, as the moon touched the oak trees.

ROB'S GRANDFATHER CAME UP TO the school on the eve of Prize Day. You saw him sitting quietly by himself in a chair on the terrace of the headmaster's residence, remote from the chatter of the party. You had at first an impression of diffidence, but this, when you saw more of him on Nantucket, was certainly wrong. He was a man who would have been at ease in any society. He had in his time wielded power; was a newspaper magnate; Bob spoke of the strange fascination he had exerted over Adlai Stevenson. He had clear blue eyes, and the jaw and dignity of a Roman senator, as history has idealized the type.

The outgoing prefects and the incoming ones led their forms in rival cheers, and afterward the sixth form sang the farewell hymn. Prize Day dawned. A heat wave had come over New England, and the mercury stood above ninety. Bob, in his white trousers and blue blazer with brass buttons, was tall and loose-jointed. You would not have called him handsome, but he had force, a dark-starred mastiff power. Did you sense how much in him was lurid and foredoomed?

No, you didn't.

IT WAS AROUND THE TIME people began to use the verb "craft" to give a touch of spurious poetry to their shriveled lives and mundane, nose hair–trimming tasks. A troubadour of capital was hailed for the élan with which he "crafted" the acquisition of a pharmaceutical company, a mayor of a large city praised for "crafting" a settlement with the sanitation workers. The verb could only be used in these ways when all sense of its meaning was lost.

While the Cid was studying law in New Haven, Bob took a loft in Tribeca in order to pursue his vocation as a writer. He met with much success; a number of his stories were published in the *New Yorker*, and his loft became a gathering place for the *jeunnesse dorée* of literary New York. He was himself becoming something of a literary celebrity in the city; he dined with old lions like Schlesinger and was on closer terms with Plimpton; his parties were filled with young literatuses severely costumed in black, their haughty eyes, sensitive to the subtlest gradations of fashion, glistening with a disdain like that of the high-booted grandees painted by van Dyck.

The loft itself was vast, its accent bohemian. On the kitchen counter cartons of takeout food lay beside invitations to charity dinners and faded issues of the *Cambodia Daily*; on the table trays of cigarette stubs rested alongside shards of ancient pottery. Going down a dimly lit hallway you found a blackboard on which Bob had scrawled, in chalk, *Divorced, beheaded, died; absolved, beheaded, Survived*. The hallway led to a bedroom. You pushed the door and found a dark, shuttered chamber with a large funereal bed.

Here was the predicament of the literary craftsman. In his life of George Cabot Lodge, Henry Adams pointed out that art and poetry were now in "reaction against society" rather than its natural outgrowth. The very nature of the artist's position made him a rebel, and in some measure an outcast. Bob felt the estrangement. At a friend's party, he encountered the friend's father, a financier who sat in the Cabinet. The great man went through the room asking the young people about their jobs. "And what do *you* do? And what do *you* do?" Bob remembered how, when his turn came, he lied and said that he worked for a fund. You thought of George Cabot Lodge, his desire to "work with the tide and not against it," his wish to "adapt myself to my time and become a moneymaker," all these accommodating impulses being in a grapple with something else, the inability to "stifle my own self."

It would be extravagant to pity one so fortunately situated in life, nor was pity in Bob's case called for, for the dominant note of his existence was an exuberant happiness in his powers, in those of his friends, in the feast of life. But his nature and upbringing combined to nourish aspirations that could not easily be satisfied. He found, as George Cabot Lodge had before him, that the effort to become what you are was more difficult than you could have foreseen.[*]

THE DEAD CITY LIES ON a plain near the sea, a cross-work of shallow walls and narrow alleys, seat or citadel of a mysterious race. The Egyptians called them

---

[*] Bob had chucked the family tradition of Harvard and gone to Brown: but he was in some respects a late-born contender for the laurels of the Harvard Pessimists.

Keftiu, but no one knows what they called themselves. They adored bulls and dolphins, and inspired a bloody mythology. A sharp wind blows but it is still very hot. Hugh Sackett, sandaled and white-haired, presides as, beneath him, the other archaeologists crouch in their holes, sifting historic sediment. After weeks in the sun they have grown as golden as the defunct race they labor to untomb, the people they know as Minoans, the name fastened on them by Sir Arthur Evans, a child of the Mauve Decade who fancied them peaceful and Parisian, the sensuous vassals of Minos.

Bob traveled widely, but there were fixed points in the compass of his expatriate existence. One was Crete, where Mr. Sackett, his old schoolmaster, was excavating a Bronze Age town. In the old stones you saw the shadowy origins of the culture of grape and lyre and agora that seduced the high WASPs. Plato set his dialogue the *Laws* amid the vines and olives of Crete because community, born of the lyre and the grape, is a twining of poetry and play and imagination: they draw the citizens in and stimulate their imaginations, which in turn feed the city. A community runs on fantasy, is an exercise in cooperative daydreaming.

A FIVE-MINUTE RIDE ON A moped brought you from the dead town to the living one, a Greek village that revolved around its *plateia*. Amid these agora inspirations Bob and his friends could recover their old playfulness in a second school, fed now by a Greek rather than an Anglican poetry, and by raki, that distillation of the dregs of the grape which carried you away in its carotic undertow.

Dante in the *Inferno* intimates that dreams dreamt close to dawn are true, and so it seemed in Crete, where the olive plain was ringed, to the east, by the sea, and to the north, the south, and the west by the mountains. They rose up in a geometry of limestone pyramids, smashed spheres, fractured cubes: an amphitheater of the gods and mute chorus in the drama enacted in the *plateia* below, where on a feast day you saw such a commedia dell'arte spectacle as Fellini or Watteau might have conceived, an art that constantly aspired to the quality of dream.

A rich feast for an artist, and Bob profited from it. But the garden of living art, which died among English-speaking peoples with Shakespeare, was one from which the artist has been cast out. Evelyn Waugh mocked the sea-change (when he made Mr. Hornbeam say, "There is no place for the Artist in the Modern World") only because he himself felt the truth of it so intimately, as he drank his way to an untidy death. When art was embedded in the infrastructure of life, the artist, even the artist not of the upper ranks, had a place and performed a service. He chiseled the stone, tuned the choirs, gilded the domes, composed the masques or the dithyrambs.* But with the coming of new technologies the old order failed. There is a reason that Shakespeare, who never took much trouble to print his own work, makes Hamlet take pleasure in his theatrical players, "the tragedians of the city," and mock the printed bookishness of Wittenberg. He must have dreaded the alteration he foresaw as the artist ceased to engage the community face to face even as the old civic or common life to which he might have contributed withered and died. No longer a player in the community, the artist became a long-haired rebel in the impersonal metropolis, pushing his chances among a thousand other unbarbered *âmes condam-nées*, the misfits of the garret: a bohemian hell from which only a few famous might hope to emerge with livelihood and self-respect.† Bob saw all this cannily enough; he knew that his literary future lay, not in Crete, with its dated agora imaginations, but elsewhere, in places closer in spirit to the morbidity of his age.

IN 1997 HE PUBLISHED A volume of stories, *Pure Slaughter Value*, which enjoyed a considerable success, but was superficially read as merely a Grand Guignol exercise in shocking the innocent. And it is true that a writer will often be tempted to exaggerate the horror or bleakness of things in order to attract readers, for human taste in all ages runs to the macabre. But the preppy desperado who narrates the stories in *Pure Slaughter Value* is, with his gift of comic mayhem, a true poet of the devil's party, one who has found and mapped a new territory of estrangement, a new hell. The WASPs, in their last disintegration, provided Bob with a rich source of material, so many lives that mocked, and were mocked by, the old ideal of completeness. He shows the WASPs to be more neurasthenic now than they were when such characters as Henry Adams and Theodore Roosevelt, Jack

---

* It is anachronistic, where agora civilization is concerned, to speak of the artist in our modern sense of the word, since there was under the old regime no rigid demarcation between the artistic and the civic personality. The ordinary citizen, in Athens, had a role in maintaining the artistry of the community, its myths and its cultic life. Whether the citizen sang in the choirs, judged the dramatic competitions, or contributed to the festivals, he (and to a lesser degree she) was in some sense a poet, a ποιητής, a maker and imaginer of order. Hence Pericles's insistence, in the Funeral Oration, that the citizen be sufficiently *eutrapelian* to perform a wide variety of tasks.

† Since we are all now entertained, to the degree that we *are* entertained, by remote virtuosi, only artists who have attained to fame or something approaching it can assuage their *amour-propre*. Santayana's Harvard friend Herbert Lyman would have liked to devote himself to music, but music would have been an acceptable profession, Santayana said, only if "you could begin by being famous. It was not acceptable if you were to begin at the foot of the ladder, and perhaps remain there." Bob spoke of what he called flashbulb fame, and he knew that without some wide notoriety his fate would be that of a crank.

Chapman and Endicott Peabody, invented them as a class, a gigantic version of the hospital in Minnesota he entered in 1993 and about which he wrote in the story "Preexisting Condition":

> "What the fuck do you think this is?" he hissed. "Boarding school? I can't believe you're drunk. This is a hospital filled with drunks. Fuck-ups, get it. We're all fuck-ups trying to figure out how it is we got so fucked up. You can't fool a fuck-up at his own game, Jean."

We're all fuck-ups trying to figure out how it is we got so fucked up: Henry Adams did not put the basic WASP proposition more succinctly. Each of the characters in *Pure Slaughter Value* is an "expensive example of moral decay, of shit." Each, in his shallowness, is the reverse of the *eutrapelian* ideal he was educated to embody: preppy libertines who reek of the morgue, ex-lacrosse studs and crew jocks who have fallen from boarding school grace and whose chief amusement lies in degrading themselves and humiliating their women, the private-equity dominatrixes, husband-hunting maenads, and coke-sniffing Circes who with their voodoo sexuality seek to unman them. He fixes them all, male and female, for eternity as Dante might: "*You* will be dead soon. Your portrait is frozen. It's entitled 'lush.'" The solemn horror of Dante's damned is that they might have known paradise; the hell of *Pure Slaughter Value* is a laughing hell because no paradise was possible. A joke rather than a tragedy.

Pure Slaughter Value showed Bob to be deeply, even painfully, au courant, and fastidiously discriminating in his perception of the different shades of modern cynicism. But the modernity was a façade. Behind it lay the archaism of his nature and heritage. He shrank from accepting a stunted place among the ruins; was haunted, as Henry James was haunted in the Galerie d'Apollon, by the possibility of something better. He was conscious, as he retailed the sordid fates of his characters, of the happier destinies he saw for them in a world different from what it is. In this he was unlike his friend the Cid, who not unreasonably looked on the whole *eutrapelian* business—the broad-souled life of imperishable deeds—as dangerous even when you discounted it as a delusion. "We're all going to be mediocrities," the Cid said. Not only were we not Prince Hamlets (nor meant to be), we were highly unlikely even to be attendant lords. It was unwise, the Cid believed, even to toy with the possibility of such fates. But Bob held fast to his idea that you must try to live largely, even in a smallish age. His great-grandfather, the ambassador, arriving at court in satin breeches and silk stockings to present his letters of credence to King George, could scarcely have been more antiquated.

"Mao got down into his crouch and began cooking. He took the utensils out of the beaker and applied a small ball of opium partially wrapped in an olive leaf to the oil lamp, twisting and turning it for a short time . . ."

He found, in Cambodia, an escape from all that was demoralizing in America. In his novel, *Lightning on the Sun*, he evokes the sirens and lotus eaters east of Suez, their innumerable seductions. The brooding sunshine, the inscrutable natives, the saffron-robed monks, the rattan chairs and ceiling fans of the Foreign Correspondents Club, where the expat journalists and dilettantes drink in the tropical heat, the nights of boiling tea and "snorting heroin and playing backgammon and falling asleep and waking up and lighting candles and playing music and telling soft tales . . ." Phnom Penh was as far as Bob could very well get, this side of the hunter gatherers, from what oppressed him in his own Republic.

The floodplain of the Mekong, scene of the great debacle of the American Century, was by this time a destination for burnt-out Westerners in search of Shangri-la. Cambodia, he wrote in his novel, drew out "the sadness that lingered in the hearts of the strangers who chose to make this strange place their home." But the main character in his book is not a person but a flower: *papaver somniferum*, its mauve petals, freaked with purple, standing tender guard over the ovary, from which comes the nectar that slowly embalms the still living flesh. But before it lulled him to his last sleep it liberated an unsuspected vein of insight.

> *Weave a circle round him thrice,*
> *And close your eyes with holy dread*
> *For he on honey-dew hath fed,*
> *And drunk the milk of Paradise . . .*

He was enchanted by what he called the "departing from care," a more profound tranquility than Henry Adams knew in his own blossom, the rose of Chartres. When the Cid, who frowned upon drugs, chided him, as though the juice of the poppy were a thing anyone might easily dispense with, his eyes flashed. It was no joke. The repose he knew in the "snug cocoon" of opium was, he saw, a synthetic reverence: a counterfeit sheepfold rather than the real thing. But it was nevertheless powerful, clarifying, illuminating; it helped him, among other things, to give a remarkable account of WASPdom in its ember days.

He was an artist, unconstrained by reticences that cripple so many WASPs; he reached out to a larger world of poets and intellectuals; he wanted, like the Ulysses of Dante, to sail beyond the conventional seas. But for all his reprise of Baudelaire and Nerval in the Club des Hashischins, he bore the stigmata of his kind. His long-term girlfriends were graduates either of Groton or St. Paul's; the Cid was his best friend; he spoke fluent preppy. The social regime of the WASPs, it is true, meant little to him; it surprised and a little saddened him when people whom he hardly knew asked him to escort their debutantes or write letters for clubs, so much futility.* Yet he admired, and not altogether in irony, the kind of WASP who turned up at the tennis courts in Phnom Penh "in whites with a racquet of his own. . . . Now that was something to ponder, arriving in Phnom Penh with a tennis racquet. A man with a passion or a splendid illusionist?" He paid tribute to the Racquet Club and George Plimpton, and recorded a deeper debt to what he called the alchemy of Groton, where Mr. Jesdale taught him to row and read Shakespeare, giving him a "clarity of purpose," he said, that he would never know again. In the tedium of later life, whenever he found himself in places where "mediocrity and boredom reigned," he would return in imagination to the water, to the "shell running out from beneath him, sliding beyond . . ."

But there was the other side of the coin. *Eutrapelia* was a demanding thing. "That's what this place did to you," he said of Endicott Peabody's school, "it planted guilt in your heart forever." His novel, a happiness, was also a burden, that of expectations to be lived up to; he found writing it more difficult than writing the stories, as though he were being weighed in the balance. For there was always the Viking prow on the horizon, the black sail of failure. The cryptic postcards you received were not always reassuring. *Saigon, Aug. 9. I broke my pinky on a moto driver's face so writing difficult. Am under vaulted ceiling of French Colonial Post Office, which is still a post office but with an expanded DHL presence and a huge portrait of Ho Chi Minh. Matthew, well we're not sure who Matthew is fucking, but*

---

* When the Cid was practicing law in New York and rooming with Rob in Tribeca, the questionnaire concerning his listing in the *Social Register* came to the apartment. Rob took the liberty of filling it out for him, inventing spurious marriages and nonexistent offspring, which were duly printed in one of the *Registers*. When the impostures were exposed, the Cid, much to his amusement, found himself banished from the pages of the preppy study book.

since he forgot to bring his camera on our [illegible] Your presence on Crete was sorely missed. love, Rob. It was not promising; yet he found, in that ominous sunshine, the power he needed to write the books that are the epitaph of his kind.

ONE DAY, NOT LONG AFTER he returned from an interval in Indochina, the telephone rang.

"I haven't read my Bible," he said, "and I'm comin' down on the very last pages of my book." The Louisville lilt was new, and seemed to speak of recovered freedom, a new access of creative power.

At the climax of the book one of the characters, a missionary in the Far East, cites scripture. Did you have any ideas for chapter and verse? In fact you didn't; someone else supplied him with the passage from the Book of Revelation, *I shall come upon you like a thief, and you will not know the hour of my coming.* But when you saw him you were startled by the change that had taken place. There were more flecks of gray in his hair, but what was curious was that his face also seemed gray, as though it were covered with a fine powder. His eyes were larger than you remembered them, the pupils smaller. You attributed this partly to the hollowness of the orbits, where the skin was stretched thin over the cheek bones. He was more handsome than he had been before, but you had a curious impression of skull pressing out from beneath the flesh.

"I was a mess when I got to L.A." His voice was sunken and remote. "For two days I had the chills and slept all the time. Then I went wild. I saw Grayson. He gave me his sober-up-get-yourself-some-help routine. Personally I think he was coked to the gills. And then to Kentucky to this miserable turkey. My family could tell I was drunk. The level of conversation since my grandmother died has dropped off a cliff. What with the drooling screaming babies and Aunt Edna's children playing 'Puff the Magic Dragon' with an electric guitar. I spent most of my time drinking at the track, then found this wonderful band of rockers. And everyone was worried because I didn't call for four days! When actually I was having a fabulous time going to the recording studio every day to help this band called Asphalt . . .

"I have been close to getting in fights—have gotten in fights—and now there's talk of putting me in the hospital again. Even Celia Riquer wants to have me committed which is certainly calling the kettle black. But I have quelled that committee . . .

"You see I was trapped inside the song of my book, and it made me temporarily quite insane, though there was very little life-threatening activity . . . Though had I kept it up for another month or two who knows . . . Though you never know do you? In L.A. I was just run, run, run around. After Thanksgiving I had rendezvous with Medusa Mellincourt. Did you ever know her? She was throwing a party and it was going to be the most gorgeously reactionary affair since Metternich and the Holy Alliance. It turned out to be a bunch of Tory pederasts and sowish English girls trying to start N.G.O.s. Afterward we went out and drank Crack Babies. I bolted . . .

"So many things scare the shit out of me. Something I have to do at Racquet Club tomorrow. And I won't have slept, or slept well, and . . . Oh shit. I have a book party. It'll be horrible but in a way funny. Come on, we'll have a drink at the Baby Doll first. . . ."

He died in November 1999.

Henry James found the key to the revivification
WASPs craved in a superseded plasquagórazza culture.

THIRTY-FIVE

The *Eutrapelian* Imagination, or WASP Neurasthenia—and Ours

*Comincia dunque: e dì ove s'appunta
l'anima tua . . .*

Therefore begin: speak of the end to
which your soul is directed . . .
—Dante, *Paradiso*

*"S'egli han quell' arte," disse, "male appressa,
ciò mi tormenta più che questo letto . . ."*

If they have learned that art badly,
It torments me more than this hellish bed . . .
—Dante, *Inferno*

IT HAS BEEN SLYLY SAID that the finest nineteenth-century prose was composed in the 1940s by Lionel Trilling. It was not simply the style of the Columbia professor's essays that recalled the work of such writers as Matthew Arnold and George Eliot. So, too, did the sentiments, alive with the fear, as Arnold expressed it, that under modern stars the individual was "being stunted and enfeebled in his own development." Trilling phrased *The Liberal Imagination*, published in 1950, in the accents of the nineteenth-century humanists, with words like "various-ness," "possibility," "wit," "flexibility," "imagination," "poetry," and "intelligence," in a death-grapple with their nemeses, "mechanical," "narrowness," "prosaic," "stupidity," and "peasant stubbornness."

Trilling was, in other words, a convert to *eutrapelia*, the Greek idea of human completeness that Coleridge, Arnold, and the high WASPs sought to revive, and he had been got to early. When, in 1921, he entered Columbia College at the age of sixteen, he found a school just entering its renaissance. As the rest of the Ivy League pursued elective anarchy, Columbia embraced the humane methods of Athens, and set its scholars to study the best that has been thought and said in the world. The Core Curriculum was, Trilling believed, "a fundamental criticism of American democratic education," a reversion to older techniques of broadening and elevating the mind, that it might do justice to its gifts. Possibility and poetry were to overcome stupidity and small-mindedness.

Trilling would later be conscious of how narrow an escape he had. In a chapter he contributed to the history of Columbia College, he described how, at the end of the nineteenth century, his alma mater was very nearly done away with. Columbia's leadership wanted the school to become a modern research institution devoted primarily or even solely to graduate and professional studies. Liberal education in the older sense, the making of minds broadly equipped for life, was thought to be outmoded; the "Renaissance ideal of the whole man . . . the honorable and responsible citizen of enlightened and gracious mind," was, Trilling wrote, to make way for a more "productive" specialization that would show "results." Frederick A. P. Barnard, the tenth president of Columbia, pro-posed that the "college proper," as it was called, be abolished outright; others urged that it be turned into a kind of cramming school, one in which students would, by means of drill and textbooks, acquire enough rudimentary information to pass, after a couple of years, into the professional schools or graduate research.

But the college survived, not as a cramming school but as a place devoted, in Trilling's words, to the belief "that humanistic studies were of the first

importance in collegiate education." To him the most striking expression of
"the Columbia College *mystique*" was its "course in the Humanities," in which
were studied "the classics of the Western World, the Great Books, beginning
with Homer and coming down through the nineteenth century—in those days
there were as yet no recognized twentieth-century classics. . . . We were assigned
nothing else but the Great Books themselves, confronting them as best we
could without the mediation of ancillary works." That the methods of Athens
should have been resurrected in Morningside Heights in all their "primitive
simplicity," as Trilling called it, might seem a *eutrapelian* miracle, but in fact
the Core Curriculum was the result of so much teaching and mentorship in the
spirit of Dante's Brunetto Latini. Trilling, as we have seen, traced an apostolic
descent from Matthew Arnold through his fellow humanists, Harvard's Charles
Eliot Norton and his student, George Edward Woodberry, to Columbia's John
Erskine, who studied under Woodberry at Columbia and who established the
Core Curriculum in order to vindicate the Athenian idea that art and poetry are
essential to the creation of a satisfying common life.*

The Core was, in the beginning, very much in the WASP mold, an effort
at regeneration: young people whose minds had been properly nourished and
ennobled would go out into the nation and do it good. But it bore fruit among an
elite no longer exclusively WASP. Trilling himself, the child of immigrants, was
decisively shaped by it, and in maturity he would devote a good deal of energy
to upholding its idea of *eutrapelian* completeness in the face of new agents of
shrinkage. In his effort to bring ideas that had long absorbed the WASPs to a
larger audience, he was much influenced, as the WASPs themselves had been, by
Arnold, the subject of his first book. But he could not help but see that Arnold's
twin watchwords—poetry and culture, those bearers of sweetness and light in a
philistine age—were a bit shopworn. Too Victorian, too precious, too apt to be
on the tongues of the sort of people who talked of sunsets and Michelangelo.

---

* When Trilling spoke of the "humanistic versatility" that the Core Curriculum was intended to develop,
he had very much in mind the *eutrapelian* humanism of Arnold, Norton, and Woodberry, educators
who, he wrote, believed that citizens "who were in any degree responsible for the welfare of the polity and
for the quality of life that characterized it must be large-minded men, committed to great ends, devoted to
virtue, assured of the dignity of the human estate and dedicated to enhancing and preserving it; and that
great works of the imagination could foster and even institute this large-mindedness, this *magnanimity*."
Hence the effort, in such WASP experiments as the Columbia Core, to put before young people "great
models of thought, feeling, and imagination," that they might better understand "the close interrelation
of the private and the personal life with the public life," the life of the city.

Trilling subsumed them under his own trademark idea of imagination. The liberally educated mind, he argued, was being corrupted by narrow, mechanical habits of thought, by "agencies and bureaus and technicians." The thing to do was to recall it to "its first essential imagination of variousness and possibility." Humane education had a part to play in the business; its poetry challenged and enlarged what Trilling, borrowing the phrase from Edmund Burke, called the moral imagination.

Imagination was, for Trilling, the school of possibility and the vanquisher of dullness, but all too often it was itself vanquished. ("Variety of imagination," Henry James wrote, "what is that but fatal in the world of affairs unless so disciplined as not to be distinguished from monotony?") The point of Trilling's book *The Liberal Imagination*, in which he repackaged the WASP idea of regeneration for a broader readership, is that the modern American world and its dominant liberal culture lack imagination. Like James and Emerson before him, Trilling believed that imagination must be "cared for and cherished," and he feared that without the superbness and arbitrariness of potent imaginers "the idea of life raised to the richest and noblest expression will quite vanish."

IN EVELYN WAUGH'S STORY "SCOTT-KING's Modern Europe," the aging schoolmaster is told by his headmaster that fewer boys were reading classics and that he should consider teaching economic history. "As you know I'm an old Greats man myself," the headmaster says. "I deplore it as much as you do. But what are we to do? Parents are not interested in producing the 'complete man' any more. They want to qualify their boys for jobs in the modern world. You can hardly blame them, can you?"

"Oh yes," Scott-King replies. "I can and do. . . . I think it would be very wicked indeed to do anything to fit a boy for the modern world."

"It's a short-sighted view, Scott-King."

"There, head master, with all respect, I differ from you profoundly. I think it the most long-sighted view it is possible to take."

Perhaps it is, but neither Scott-King nor, perhaps, the WASPs themselves sufficiently grappled with the objection raised by the headmaster. Harvard's Steven Pinker dismisses the humane approach as so much archaic "literarism," and putting tradition and sentimentality to one side, there are good reasons to think that the *eutrapelian* idea of developing the various aspects of one's nature is little more than a mystical mumbo-jumbo justification for what was once a practical necessity. In the Greek city-state, where liberal education began, populations were small, and a citizen was required to be competent in tasks that today are left to specialists and professionals. The Athenian citizen was at once soldier, lawmaker, artist, and (in some measure) priest of a civic cult. He (the she's were largely left out) contributed not only to the defense of his city and to its civil government, but to its festival and liturgical culture: he fought in the wars and sang in the choruses. Such a citizen had as much immediate practical incentive to be many-sided as we have to be one-sided; and his education was the natural outgrowth of his necessities.

In the Athens of Pericles there were too few citizens to make a rigorous specialization possible; what was needed, rather, was civic generalism. To this end the citizen applied himself to the study of the poets, for he believed, as we have seen, that "a poet was in the broadest and deepest sense the educator of his people." Poetry was the school of versatility. It impressed upon the mind notions of fitness, proportion, balance, and harmony that could then be applied both to the practical life of a city and to its artistic and cultural infrastructure. It would, indeed, startle Aristotle or Euripides to learn that our civic life today has almost nothing to do with art or poetry. The modern civic person, from the member of the zoning board to the Speaker of the House, is typically a technician, by profession a lawyer or accountant or banker; there has not been a poet in politics since Goethe's service as privy councillor in Weimar. Yet in the old communities the two vocations, civic and artistic, were closely interwoven. Sophocles was an Athenian commissioner, Aeschylus fought the Persians at Marathon, Dante rose high in the politics and diplomacy of Florence. They brought to their civic patriotism not only educated competence but aesthetic longing, a desire to make the city beautiful.

Liberal education grew out of this need for multitasking; it taught the student to cultivate various gifts and (in Matthew Arnold's words) to conceive "true human perfection as a harmonious perfection, developing all sides of our humanity . . ." The way of human flourishing, whether in a person or a city, was "of like spirit with poetry," followed "one law with poetry." Which was all very well in classical Athens, with some 30,000 fully active citizens (out of a total population of perhaps a quarter of a million).* But it is likely to be ruinous in the modern nation-state, where one's fortune in life typically depends on one's

---

* J. H. Plumb, the Cambridge historian, spoke of the "astonishing array of genius" which Florence produced in the Quattrocento: no city "of so small a compass has ever before, or since, made a greater contribution to arts and letters." But it was just *because* the compass of places like Athens and Florence was at once so small and so intensively cultivated that a culture flourished there which drew forth the powers of the citizens.

mastery of an all-absorbing specialty. Pericles commended *eutrapelia* in an age that knew nothing of moveable type, the Protestant Bible, the Industrial Revolution, the rise of the nation-state and its overarching metropoli, the immense growth in numbers—of people, goods, and areas of specialized knowledge—that have so greatly altered the character of life.

THE WORLD NO LONGER NEEDS *eutrapelia*. It was the soul, the high WASPs contended, that could not do without it. They based their contention on their own experience. They had what are called "advantages" and could command every luxury modernity had contrived, yet for all that many of them found themselves experiencing, in words Henry James applied to his friend Constance Fenimore Woolson, a "tragic and latently insane *difficulty in living*." It was not that they were unprepared to suffer. They were hardly so naïve as to think that anyone, least of all themselves, could escape that portion of misery and discontent which is the lot of mortals. And they would no doubt have conceded that the infinite commodities which progress has bestowed upon the world have alleviated much suffering. But certain salves were missing.

"Travel over every road," says the Greek sage Heraclitus, "you cannot discover the frontiers of the soul—it has so deep a logos." The problem with our modern manner of living, the high WASPS believed, was that it made use of only a slender part of this soul-territory; large regions lay uncultivated, and being left uncultivated grew rank. The result, in their self-understanding, was neurasthenia, in which the unused appetites, deprived of sustenance, feed upon themselves. And so the WASPs frantically sought to do justice to the different aspects of their nature; possibility frustrated was, for them, possibility become poisonous.

Eros was one of the frustrated possibilities. High WASPs readily admitted, as so many of the leading lights of modernity did, a connection between the neurasthenia of the age and its diminished or frustrated sexuality. "In any previous age," Henry Adams said, "sex was strength," but in Boston "sex was a species of crime." As might easily have been predicted, a spurned Aphrodite had her revenge, and under the inspiration of those modern masters of the macabre, Sade and Robespierre, the neglected passions were diverted into the unhealthy channels of mass pornography, on the one hand, and mass politics on the other, so much so that it is not easy to know where the one ends and the other begins. But high WASPs differed from those hygienists who naïvely supposed that more readily available sex would by itself restore Eros to its rightful place. Gertrude

Vanderbilt was, in comparison to her forebears, sexually liberated, but she had the good sense to see that the revival of Eros must be part of a larger restoration, one that she connected to the recovery of the cathartic powers of art. The way to a healthy life, erotic and otherwise, lay along Plato's thread of poetry and play, in the commedia dell'arte allurements of a forsaken civic (plasquagórazza)* culture. This was very much Henry James's position: when he portrayed an instance of conversion from a modern flat-souled civilization to the older *eutrapelian* way of living, he made the transformation depend on his hero's response, not to a particular piece of flesh, but to Venice itself, experienced as a whole. In *The Princess Casamassima*, James's hero, Hyacinth Robinson, is initially pledged to mass revolutionary politics, but in a little Venetian square he is changed; the cracked marble, the ancient fountain, the gliding girls with their copper water-jars, the magenta divan on which he reclines in the hot light, smoking cigarettes and reading Leopardi—by these and a hundred other sensualities the young man is converted, and this in a Venice in decline, already a tourist trap, and far from the Veronese pageant Goethe had known a hundred years before.†

High WASPs differed from the modern prophets of sex in another way, in their insistence that Eros is but one among many underused gifts of the spirit. In Thomas Mann's *Death in Venice*, Gustav von Aschenbach, in thrall to Dionysus, worships at a single shrine, and is destroyed in the shadow of a city that is itself the relic of a richer complexity of desire. WASPs sought in *eutrapelia* an art of balancing the different gifts, and were drawn to places that ministered to that variousness. Henry Adams's Chartres, Ernest Hemingway's Pamplona, John Jay Chapman's Rothenburg ("It ought to be put under glass") were the originals of Gloriani's garden, where more than one dead place in the soul is recalled to life.

---

*   A portmanteau term that draws on a few of the many words—plateia, platz, agora, plaza, piazza—that once defined the civic focal point and the humane forum.

†   Few people today read *The Princess Casamassima*, and to the degree that the novel is known, it is known largely from Lionel Trilling's essay in *The Liberal Imagination*, in which he consciously or unconsciously misread the book in an effort to wean the philistine Left from its extravagant faith in an unimaginative utopian politics. James makes Hyacinth Robinson repudiate the revolutionary mirage precisely in order to embrace the *eutrapelian* completeness to which he has been converted in Venice. When, in his last interview with the Princess Casamassima, she repeats the revolutionists' mantra that the "ferocious selfishnesses must come down . . . must be smashed," he can only reply, "I wish to God I could see it as you see it." Trilling, however, could not admit that Hyacinth rejects the Princess's fantasy in all its intolerable shallowness: he feared to lose the trust of those earnest middle-class intellectuals whom he was seeking to convert to a nobler ideal. He therefore pretended that Hyacinth dies poised between the two ideals, that of mass politics on the one hand and humane artistry on the other.

YOUNG KENNETH CLARK WATCHED AS Bernard Berenson, "small, beautifully dressed, a carnation in his buttonhole," made his way through the daily round at I Tatti, his villa overlooking Florence. Ever the magician, this survivor of the WASP revival captivated those around him with a stream of beguiling talk. "The flow of ideas, the range of historical reference, the intellectual curiosity and unexpected human sympathy," Clark remembered, "were certainly beyond those of anyone I have met." Then there was the "intense gaze" of his "beautiful grey eyes, with their long lashes," which could only be described as "caressing." Of course they were all hypnotized, not least Clark himself, who had agreed to serve as the sorcerer's apprentice.

But Berenson was not easy in his good fortune, or so Clark (who was to bring art to the masses in his televised series *Civilisation*) believed. The great man was haunted by his failure to have achieved the dream of his youth, when as a poor scholar studying under WASP humanists at Harvard he had conceived the ambition of becoming "a poet, philosopher, and universal man," a second Goethe. Art-jobbing, Clark thought, got in the way. He believed that Berenson, in certifying the authenticity of Old Masters for rich collectors, sold his soul for the pleasures of a fortune and a sycophantic court, the little Olympus of the Villa I Tatti, where (as Clark believed) he figured as Zeus. The degrading transactions worked their deformations of spirit, the "subtle corruption," Clark wrote, "which attacks almost everyone when he can no longer be contradicted or prevented from doing things, and when everyone except a few old friends kow-tows to him." "He's really only a charlatan," Charlie Bell, the Keeper of Fine Art in the Ashmolean at Oxford, said of Berenson, "and all that business of attribution is pure guesswork." The old wizard himself felt the truth of these imputations, and he was always a little shamefaced under the gaze of his old Harvard friend Learned Hand. "Mr. Berenson admired him more than any man alive," Clark wrote. "Judge Learned Hand did not admire Mr. Berenson."

Goethe says that every human being is "a whole, a unity of manifold, internally connected powers." Berenson reproached himself for having failed to do justice to his own wholeness, but he never doubted the truth of Goethe's belief that it is to this wholeness that the "work of art must speak." If he spent much of his life ministering to the vanity of tycoons, helping them to procure the paintings they collected like golf trophies, in his better moments he performed a higher service by showing that art, when not shut away with the golf trophies, speaks to possibilities that might otherwise be lost, for it holds up "the noblest models for mankind to attain, models of realizable and never impossible states of being and ways of living." This was not, or not wholly, late Victorian sentimentality.* Berenson, a creature of the WASP revival, saw that a painting like Raphael's *School of Athens*, the product of an age when wholeness still seemed possible, is one of the great depictions of what the *eutrapelian* imagination seeks: one of the "clearest and most convincing visions of the perfect existence for which we yearn, and which we hope to attain," a hedge against that dullness, that denial of one's potential, which we are always trying to escape.

THE LITTLE DEMON-WHISPER, TO BE elsewhere . . .

Emma Bovary heard it. "She longed to travel; she longed to go back and live in the convent. She wanted to die. And she wanted to live in Paris." The heroine of Flaubert's novel would rather have been in any place, in any time, other than the time and place in which she was. "If only," Flaubert wrote, "she could lean over the balcony of a Swiss chalet, or enclose her melancholy in a Scottish cottage, with a husband wearing a long black velvet cloak . . ."

How do you counteract the demon-whisper? For we are, the high WASPs saw, all Emma Bovaries now, trying to escape both our unsatisfactory presents and the places in which we experience them by leaping into fantasies of other people's places, other people's presents. Hitch your wagon to somebody else's star. The WASPs knew nothing, of course, of our own itching fingers, so often seeking, as they do, for those little Mephistophelean devices by which we try, and fail, to escape the ennui of the here and now. But they, too, were conscious of vacancy, and of the temptation to escape it by living every life but their own. They tried to counteract the temptation through a recovery of Dante's concept of the fair sheepfold, the artistry that makes a place the center of a world and in doing so stimulates the soul's possibilities. In their pilgrimages to Venice and Chartres and Athens, they were searching for thereness, a way to live "not in another place but this place, not for another hour but this hour . . ."

Sitting in the Place Saint-Germain-des-Prés, in the Latin Quarter of Paris, you seemed to come closer to what it was the WASPs quixotically sought. The old stone in a strong sunlight, the multitude of passersby who yet never became

---

* If Santayana was, at times, able to overlook Berenson's less savory qualities, it was because the man's desire for *eutrapelian* completeness was, he believed, genuine: "his vigour and many-sidedness make me entirely forgive his mendacity, which is too abundant to deceive."

a crowd, the Merovingian shadow of the abbey-church, where the kings and queens of the line of Childebert slept in their sepulchers—some juice of balm was at work, though it was not easy to say what it was. Saint Germain-des-Prés, where Vautrin, in Balzac's *Splendeurs et misères des courtisanes*, watches holy water being sprinkled over the corpse of Lucien de Rubempré, the young man from the provinces who hanged himself in a cell of the Conciergerie, defied every dogma of modernist decency. Segregation of function, antipathy to ornament, abhorrence of the poetically archaic—all the canons of current orthodoxy were outraged in the market square of the Merovingians. With a voluptuous abandon they created a space that mixed business with pleasure, the commercial with the artistic, the sacred with the profane. But the result of this various, apparently unconnected activity was not, as might have been expected, chaos. It was unity.

High WASPs were drawn to these civic hearths: play-spaces that drew you in, touched parts of your brain that might otherwise have lain fallow, made possible encounters that widened inward barriers and enlarged your sense of possibility. Nor was it only the five-star Michelin culture-kitchens of Athens and Florence that did this, but humbler sheepfolds where vestiges of plasquagórazza culture survived, the Place de la Maison Carrée in Nîmes, the Piazza del Campo in Siena, the Place de la République at Arles, a hundred, a thousand, such "community centers," to use a term that betrays our ignorance of both words. In fact they were so many civic jewel-boxes, their plastic art—the builded and sculpted ornamentation—being a scaffolding which, in its prime, was clothed by music, poetry, liturgy, festival: the Fêtes Dieu of Aix and Evian, the mystery and mumming plays of Nürnberg and Salzburg, the flower-games of Toulouse, where the golden violet of the poetical academy of that city (the *Sobregaya Companhia dels Sept Trobadors de Tolosa*—the Very Joyous Company of the Seven Troubadours of Toulouse) was awarded to the poet who emerged victorious in them.

But the idea of the polity as a work of art died away. What Johan Huizinga in his book *Homo Ludens* called the "play-circle" shrank almost to nothing. The poetry of the civic hearth lost its "primary play-quality" and no longer invited the citizen, by means of its spells and enchantments, its intimations of "beauty, sacredness, magic," to enter the kingdom "of dream, enchantment, ecstasy, laughter." The music that had once its "full value in the *playing* of a community" succumbed to a modernity that had little interest in the higher forms of play (as opposed to mere rules and regulations) as makers of order. "Even in the eighteenth century," Huizinga wrote:

> utilitarianism, prosaic efficiency, and the bourgeois ideal of social welfare—all fatal to the Baroque—had bitten deep into society. These tendencies were exacerbated by the Industrial Revolution and its conquests in the field of technology. Work and production became the ideal, and then the idol of the age. All Europe donned the boiler-suit [and] the shameful misconception of Marxism could be put about and even believed, that economic forces and material interests determine the course of the world.

As a result of such changes, music and poetry no longer had a recognized place in ordering the hours and amusements of the day. Quarantined in the culture-ghettos of the museum and the concert hall, art became enervated and curatorial. It was the beheading of Orpheus: the death knell of the humane forum as a piece of civic artistry that ministered to the different aspects of one's being.

AND SO WE COME BACK to Henry Adams, looking out of his club window on Fifth Avenue, astonished that modernity, for all that was benign in her revolutions, should have created so much nervous dread.

> The city had the air and movement of hysteria, and the citizens were crying, in every accent of anger and alarm, that the new forces must at any cost be brought under control. Prosperity never before imagined, power never yet wielded by man, speed never reached by anything but a meteor, had made the world irritable, nervous, querulous, unreasonable and afraid.

In the Galerie des Machines in Paris, Adams found himself praying to the generators known as dynamos, which embodied the spirit of the new age much as the Virgin embodied the spirit of the old one. But where the Virgin represented, for Adams, unity and coherence, the dynamo fomented anarchy and hysteria. Probably he put the case too strongly, but like his fellow WASPs Jack Chapman, Learned Hand, Endicott Peabody, and Theodore Roosevelt, he saw neurasthenia as the byproduct of a fractured civilization, one composed of individuals imprisoned in so many part-lives, "shrouded and coffined out of the way," their neurotic complaints a symptom of the stunting and cramping that had disfigured their souls.

Dante spoke to Adams and his fellow WASPs because he was, for them, another sick soul lost in the beastly wood, one who identified well-being with the *eutrapelian* city, that mortal sheepfold that foreshadows an eternal one, just as (in the Dantean eschatology) the love-vessel of Beatrice foreshadows the everlasting rose (*rosa sempiterna*) of salvation. Hamlet (as WASPs read him) was a neurasthenic young man who saves himself by means of playacting and stage drama, the creative work that puts him on the path to balance and serenity. The creative madness of Don Quixote was for high WASPs sanity, just as neurasthenia was for them the sane response to a way of life marked by the absence of imagination and its power to transform life, and to heighten it.

In *Democracy in America,* Tocqueville argues that not only does our narrower way of living constantly undermine "the pleasures of imagination," it also isolates the individual: it "makes every man forget his ancestors," it "hides his descendants and separates his contemporaries from him; it throws him back forever upon himself alone and threatens in the end to confine him entirely within the solitude of his own heart." The more prosperous, safe, and free we become under our modern stars, the more anxious, dejected, and miserably alone we seem to Tocqueville to be; there are aspects of our nature that are not being done justice to.* High WASPs wanted to repair this fragmented manner of living without sacrificing its material blessings: they wanted to reconcile Adam Smith's *The*

---

* Jefferson, too, had been perplexed by the narrowing of the American mind. Concerned that his fellow citizens, foregoing the higher possibilities of their nature, would "forget themselves, but in the sole faculty of making money," he entertained various ideas about how the *eutrapelian* ideal (which he, in his eighteenth-century way, sought to live up to) might flourish in America. He toyed with the idea of dividing America into communities called "wards" or "hundreds," after old English models. Each ward or hundred, he said, would be "a small republic within itself, and every man in [these little republics] would thus become an acting member of the common government, transacting in person a great portion of its rights and duties." "As Cato, then, concluded every speech with the words, '*Carthago delenda est,*'" Jefferson wrote, "so do I every opinion with the injunction, 'divide the counties into wards.'" The same civic vision underlay the University of Virginia: he wanted the school to be an "academical village," a civic humanist experiment in making a college resemble a town, a marketplace, a Greek agora, with the buildings grouped around a central lawn. Making ingenious use of the arts of classical Greece and Rome, he created one of America's more memorable common spaces, one that he hoped would foster the "Attic" (Athenian) forms of interconnection he had known in his own student days in the College of William and Mary.

Wealth of Nations with Plato's *Laws*, to introduce, into a technically advanced commercial Republic, with all its chaotic sprawl and empty noise, little oases of order of the kind Bernard Berenson envisioned, in which "poetry, music, ritual, the visual arts, the theater" would recreate the Dantesque sheepfold.

They knew that there is a deep relation between the heart of any place—town, village, city, school, asylum—and the souls of those who live there. WASPs made the calculations, and dreaded what they told about their country. According to the Viennese scholar of plasquagórazza culture Camillo Sitte, the old civic centers of the West could be understood only if they were studied as aesthetic wholes, instances of what he called artistic synthesis or *Gesamtwerk*. It was, he said, the concentration of different kinds of art—the cooperation of the frozen and the fluid music—that enabled these places to awaken or restore a corresponding wholeness in the mind itself.* WASPs went further. There was a connection, they believed, between the inadequacy of America's common life and the neurasthenic anxiousness of its citizens, the "neurosis in the air which the inhabitants," Evelyn Waugh said, "mistake for energy."

WERE THE WASPs RIGHT IN this? *Is* there a connection between our way of living and our neurasthenic entropy? Look into the mirror held up in our TV advertisements, where you see reflected the image of a sick, sleepless, depressed, and impotent people, and you are likely to think that the WASPs were onto something. (Consult your health-care provider if after swallowing your pills you experience thoughts of suicide or mass-murder . . .) As the pharmacy becomes our agora, one is tempted to take another look at the case high WASPs made

---

* Would something so vital to the humane tradition as the philosophy of the Greeks, with its "civilising ethics and charming myths," have been possible without the agora? Yet the word itself is a stumbling block: in Greek agora means the place where people gather. Although the concept is less familiar than it ought to be, it encompasses a good deal of what the WASPs were striving for: a forum—at once marketplace, civic center, spiritual sanctuary, communal gossip trough, and artistic showcase—that is itself a facsimile of human completeness. By whatever name you call it, the agora was, until the day before yesterday, one of the basic building blocks of the civilization, or, to alter the metaphor, one of the cells, the primary structural units, of the cultural organism. It was by no means a purely Greek phenomenon, and indeed the Greek word is to an ear trained in English awkwardly pronounced: the accent is on the *first* syllable. But there is no obviously better word. The Roman *forum* emphasizes the political and administrative aspects of the space at the expense of its artistic and cultural ones. The post-Roman *marketplace* acknowledges the living qualities of a place where people shop and drink, gossip and pray: but its emphasis on commerce fails to do justice to the Rabelaisian playfulness of the thing and its intense, life-heightening theatricality.

for the cathartic benefits of the old plasquagórazza arts. A century after Henry Adams said that for the American "work, whiskey, and cards" were life, it is not all that different. That our routine labors and occupations too rarely engage us fully is perhaps excusable; there is a certain amount of drudgery in most work. But that our leisure is so soullessly trivial, with less artistry than the Athenian knew twenty-five centuries ago, is unforgivable.

To be sure, the causes of these morbidities are many and complex; it is not a case of a "secret which lies in a single word, and which, the word being spoken, will secure the kingdom against all danger." Our neurasthenia is rather in the state of the atmosphere, the vibration all around. WASPs, in their preoccupation with the decline of the *eutrapelian* imagination, chanced on a couple of pieces of the puzzle. What is maddening is that they failed to build on their collective insights. Henry Adams knew both Cotty Peabody and Amory Gardner, and his nephews were in their school, but he did not see that he and they were working along similar lines, trying to understand how to create places and institutions that command the heart and vitalize the soul. Jack Chapman and Isabella Stewart Gardner, had they pooled their resources with those of Berenson, could have shown the world what a modern sheepfold might look like. Edmund Wilson once vowed to restore the old humane edifice, but although he gave Lionel Trilling's book on Matthew Arnold a career-starting review, the two men, who saw each other socially over several decades, never got together to turn bookish meditations on the relation between the provinces and the metropolis into something more substantial: an insight into how the failure of local culture and local salves has played a part in the rise of mass hysterias, as so many unplaced Emma Bovaries look for consolation to nationalist and other mass-identity poetries, much as Emma herself sought it in a debased Romantic poetry.

Frederick Law Olmsted, the WASP landscape architect who designed Groton's Circle, *tried* to introduce a bit of the agora into New York City, with his plan for squares and promenades. He blamed the city's grid-iron plan (that prison-house of perpendicularity) for his failure, but he might as easily have fingered the indifference of the citizens themselves to *eutrapelian* space. That the dream of the sunlit portico and the humanizing forum should have yielded (in T. S. Eliot's words) to the asphalt road and a thousand lost golf balls was perhaps to be expected. But the WASPs hardly put up a fight.

They were patrons of colleges and humane learning, but although they endowed hundreds of professorial chairs, they were too diffident to insist that some of the beneficed scholars should study what was nearest their own hearts. For it was obvious that the *eutrapelian* ideal of the WASPs could be comprehended only if it were studied in the context of a wider culture. But this the orthodox scholars conspicuously failed to do. Each specialist knew a fragment of the mosaic: the education of the young in Athens, the architecture of Venice, the festivals of Florence, the plays of the Elizabethans, the attempts of philosophers and divines to understand what human beings are and what their ends should be. The scholars handled the fragments, and never put them together. As a result the thing has never been recognized as a distinct field of inquiry as for instance the English Sonnet is, or the Ming Dynasty. There is no catalogue raisonné to take stock of its treasures, or speculative essay to elucidate its cryptic wisdom.

WASP generalists might have helped the narrower scholars to perceive the figure in the carpet, but they were very much in the tradition of the Edwardian tourist, addicted to dilettantism; they made singularly little study of the actual infrastructure of the humane culture they professed to love.* Henry Adams, for all his close study of Chartres, tells us almost nothing about the people who lived there. Had the WASPs been bolder, or less sunk in preppy lassitude, we might now not only have a better understanding of the relation between the arts of the old civic spaces and the *eutrapelian* imagination they nourished, we might be in a position to say whether this highly evolved culture of civic grooming owed anything to the grooming techniques of earlier hominids, the simian arts by which they knitted together their primeval packs: a debt which, if established, might either vindicate or cast doubt on the claims of the humanist philosophers. If man is simply a more elaborate ape, their talk of the soul was bosh—or evidence that the species has the capacity to develop its potential, to approach more closely to what the Greeks called excellence or *areté*.

---

* The most insightful work on agora or plasquagórazza culture has been done almost entirely by Europeans, and almost entirely in the years between 1790 and 1940: Burke's theory of the "little platoon," Wordsworth's evocation of provincial Cumbria and the "high value he set upon customariness, upon all that is habitual, local, rooted in the ground," Coleridge's vision of the provincial nucleus "round which the capabilities" of a place "may crystallize and brighten," Ruskin's studies of Venice, Pater's "Denys L'Auxerrois" and his other agora fantasies, Fustel de Coulanges' work on the Roman city and Jacob Burckhardt's studies of Greek and Renaissance culture, the agora scholarship of Camillo Sitte, Johan Huizinga, and Werner Jaeger. (Hannah Arendt's *The Human Condition* was published in 1958, but belongs in spirit to the earlier period.) With the possible exceptions of Lewis Mumford and Jane Jacobs (whose work was devoted rather to the large urban center than to the plasquagórazza forum) and of such expatriates as T. S. Eliot and Hemingway, no American has made a comparable contribution.

❈

ADMITTEDLY, NO ONE, HOWEVER INGENIOUS, could have revived the artistry of Florence and Athens in their prime: nor perhaps would anyone have wanted to bring it all back, for it may be that the poetry and the pillars and the cult of *homo universalis* were of a piece with the parochialism that condemned Socrates to death and Dante to exile, and with the hierarchies that excluded so many from the richer forms of citizenship. Chartres embodied for Henry Adams a culture that "penetrated and enriched the recesses of the whole being," but any effort to recreate it could only produce, he admitted, "a more or less effaced or affected echo of a lost emotion which the world never felt but once and never could feel again."

There is no stepping in the same city twice. But what appalls Farinata degli Uberti in the *Inferno* is not that his descendants have failed to master the art of returning to *his* city—the Florence he knew—but that they have failed to make their way back to a Florence that might have become *their* city: a failure that tormented him, he said, more than all the pains of hell. The WASPs were as unable to master the art of *tornare*, the art of return. They might, like Ptolemy summoning his seventy sages, have gathered their experts and succeeded in adapting at least some of the older techniques to a changed world. This was the project Leopardi commended to civic humanists when he said that a man must learn how to "build himself a little city within the great one." But in spite of the fervor of the WASPs' desire to vindicate the *eutrapelian* imagination, the little cities went unbuilt.

The Roosevelts with the clergy (and King George VI and Queen Elizabeth)
outside St. James's Church in Hyde Park, New York.

THIRTY-SIX

Recessional:
The WASP and God

Bestemmiavano Dio . . .

They reviled God . . .
—Dante, *Inferno*

Of all the conditions of his youth which afterward puzzled the grown-up man," Henry Adams wrote, "this disappearance of religion puzzled him most." As a boy he "went to church twice every Sunday; he was taught to read his Bible, and he learned religious poetry by heart; he believed in a mild deism; he prayed; he went through all the forms; but neither to him nor to his brothers or sisters was religion real."

That the "most powerful emotion of man, next to the sexual, should disappear" was a puzzle to Adams, though of course he exaggerated religion's demise. If he heard only the "long, withdrawing roar" of God, the sea of faith was in fact quite real to many of his fellow WASPs in the first innings of the twentieth century. Isabella Stewart Gardner, Vida Scudder, Endicott Peabody, and Franklin Roosevelt, to name only a few, declined to be mourners in what Thomas Hardy called "God's Funeral." (Adams himself, we have seen, flirted with Catholic conversion in his dotage, spurred on by his friendship with Father Cyril Sigourney Fay.)* The Authorized Version and the Book of Common Prayer were still part of the fabric of WASP life, but as the century wore on, God for many WASPs—probably indeed for most of them—ceased to be a faith and became instead a whimsy, an exercise in keeping up the forms.†

Yet there was an undercurrent of devotion. T. S. Eliot, WASP counter-revolutionary-in-chief, was probably the most illustrious figure in the resistance; he had gone to school to Dante, and when he recited the Athanasian Creed he meant every word. He wrote movingly of Dante's ultimate apprehension, in *Paradiso*, of *legato con amore in un volume*, of divine love binding in one volume the scattered pages of the universe. It was a vision that embodied for him "a principle of order in the human soul, in society and in the universe." Yet for all that something was missing in his idea of a Christian society; it was somehow colder, less caring, than, say, Cotty Peabody's. His version of Anglo-Catholicism—in contrast to that of John Henry Newman at the height of the Oxford Movement—converted very few. Eliot was, at least until Anthony Julius threw the spotlight on his anti-Semitism in the nineties, the poet laureate of the WASPs; they all learned, in prep school, about J. Alfred Prufrock and the Objective Correlative. But they declined to take his Christianity seriously—to them it was he, with his faith, not they, in their want of it, who was "after strange

---

* A mentor to Scott Fitzgerald, Fay was the model for Monsignor Darcy in *This Side of Paradise*.

† Joe Alsop, in his seventies, "wanted to begin going to church regularly once more," for in his old age he found "church moving and rewarding." He blamed his failure to do so on the barbarous iconoclasm of his age, one that shattered the poetry of the Authorized Version and the Book of Common Prayer. There "seems to be no church in Washington," he wrote, "that regularly uses the King James version of the Bible or the magnificently lovely old Episcopal prayer book." When he heard the liturgy in its new "castrated" form, he found himself, he said, committing "the sin of anger," and was "out of temper for the rest of the day." It should perhaps be added that, although he disliked religious enthusiasm and was contemptuous of the more saccharine forms of piety, when he lay dying in Georgetown in 1989, he was heard by his housekeeper to moan, "Is there a God?"

gods"; and in the years since his death in 1965, they have gone in more and more for agnosticism, atheism, various travesties of Hinduism, Buddhism, Sufism, and the like, or (most characteristically) simple indifference.

WHAT, THEN, OF THE FAIR sheepfold the WASPs sought, the image of their idea of regeneration? Was such a thing possible without God? T. S. Eliot, following Dante, said no. Henry James said yes: he does not portray Hyacinth Robinson's conversion, in Venice, to humane culture as a religious awakening. Santayana took a position that differed from that of both. He did not believe in God, but he nevertheless believed that religion, as poetry intervening in life, had a part to play in a well-ordered community. "Always bear in mind," he told his friend Daniel Cory, "that my naturalism does not exclude religion; on the contrary it allows for it. I mean that religion is the inevitable reaction of the imagination when confronted by the difficulties of a truculent world. It is normally local and always mythical, and it is morally true." He was himself partial to the liturgies of Catholicism and high Anglicanism, poetries sufficiently rich at once to engage the imagination and to pacify it, reconciling it to life's limitations even as it genially obscured life's horrors.

We are today likely to think of ourselves as being compelled to check a box, as on a census form or a standardized test: religious, secular, or not sure. Santayana offers another possibility, that of the nonbeliever who yet recognizes the utility of religion. Some will dismiss his position as so much spiritual hermaphroditism, but he points to a compromise that would preserve our pluralism in matters of faith (and the denial of faith) but would not force us to resign ourselves to the sterility that characterizes a society in which all the most poignant spiritual poetry has been shut away. (It may be possible to get through life without Bach's Mass in B Minor, but who would be willing to essay so dangerous an experiment?) You need not believe in Greek Orthodoxy to find the festival of the Virgin in a Greek village more life-enhancing than the tediousness of our own pedestrian civic calendar.* Nor must you subscribe to the religion of the Koran to find the poetry of Fez a relief after the spiritual vacuity of New York. We interpret pluralism as a commandment to keep one's religion out of the way; faith in public becomes,

---

* In *Die Cultur der Renaissance in Italien*, Jacob Burckhardt saw the old festivals as representing "a higher phase in the life of the people, in which its religious, moral, and poetical ideas took visible shape." The festivals in their highest form "mark the point of transition from real life into the world of art."

like farting in the same situation, a thing in bad taste. But it would do pluralism no harm and might do the body politic considerable good if the poetry of various spiritual disciplines were more palpably present in public space. Jefferson said that it did him no injury if his neighbor said there are twenty gods or no God. It does me no injury if I find the representatives of five or fifteen faiths making music in the public square. I am enriched by the music, whether it be that of the mass or the muezzin. It would be a great advantage if we were to encounter, in our daily rounds, spiritual wares as frequently as we do material ones: so many examples of longing and beatitude to counterbalance the monotony of getting and spending, the excessive worldliness that made Wordsworth say he would rather be a pagan suckled in a creed outworn than a modern Briton living in the shallows of her soul.

WE MAY ENJOY THE POETRY of the fair sheepfold without believing in the shepherd himself. But when we come to the achievement of the WASPs, their public service, their standards of conduct, their faith in the possibility of regeneration, we find that it owed a good deal to their conviction that there *is* a shepherd, a divinity that shapes our ends, rough hew them how we will. "He believes that he communicates with God and God communicates with him." So Rebecca West said of Whittaker Chambers. Chambers was, according to his detractors, a crank: yet the words were no less true of Franklin Roosevelt, whom it is less easy to dismiss as a crank. "Why Harry," Frances Perkins said to Harry Hopkins, "it's clear that he's got a relationship to God." The idea of the good shepherd animated the little seminary in Massachusetts in which Roosevelt was educated, perhaps the most successful of WASP efforts to impress upon the soul the virtues of civic obligation and service to others. The "active love" that Endicott Peabody tried to make real for his boys—the same love that Alyosha, in Dostoevsky's novel, tried to make real for his boys after the death of little Ilyusha—remained with many of them to the end:

> And whatever happens to us in later life, even if we don't meet for twenty years . . . even if we are occupied with most important matters, if we attain to honor and high place or fall into great misfortune— still let us remember how good it was once here, when we were all together, united by a good and kind feeling which made us, for the time we were loving that poor boy, better perhaps than we are . . .

WASPs at Water Mill on Long Island, circa 1999.

When We Are Gone

Più lunga scala convien che si saglia . . .

A longer ladder still to be climbed . . .
—Dante, *Inferno*

S ome years ago I was invited by a friend to the beach club—it is formally known as the Bathing Corporation—in Southampton. There, on a half-acre of Long Island sand carefully demarcated from the merely plebeian strand by an array of cables and pennants, a portion of what remains of the WASP ascendancy lounges warily under its turrets.

It is not easy to be admitted to membership of the beach club, even, perhaps especially, if one is very rich. George Soros has been let in; but other Croesuses have drawn the black ball. My friend, a young man of genius who has risen from obscurity to become a mogul in California, tells the story of a hedge fund king who bought a large property on Lake Agawam, the polluted pond behind the beach club. He expected, as a matter of course, to be admitted, but was soon disabused of that quaint notion. The beach club did not cotton to him. The members thought him gauche and his family vulgar.

It is true that, in the eyes of the beach club, all new money is gauche. And yet some of the freshly minted coin—indeed, quite a lot of it—gets in. My friend expatiates. The most astute new money cultivates gatekeepers. My friend tells me of an acquaintance of his—let us call him Jonathan Oldbuck V—who does a brisk business in club memberships. Oldbuck is a gatekeeper. Four or five of his closest chums *happen* to be billionaires. He has superintended their candidacies for membership in the old WASP clubs, and they, in return, have rewarded him with scraps from the deal table—no mean gift in the eyes of a young man who, like an impoverished nobleman reduced under Nero to exhibiting himself on the stage, is struggling to build an asset management business with which to retrieve his family's sagging fortunes.

Thus does the WASP ascendancy expire, its scions, bereft of purpose, stooping to pimp their patrimony. The vision that inspired Henry Adams and Henry Stimson, Learned Hand and Vida Scudder, the desire to develop one's powers and realize one's potential, has dwindled into the fatuities of Southampton.

FAILURE IS A WORD AT the heart of Henry Adams's *Education,* that key to all WASP mythologies. Adams believed that he had failed, that his generation had failed, that America itself had failed—failed to live up to Jefferson's prophecy that "under our democratic stimulants" progress would be made "on a great scale, until every man is potentially an athlete in body and an Aristotle in mind." Could Adams have foreseen the remnants of his class, lounging on the beach at Southampton, he would have found a new field in which to indulge his fascination.

High WASPs strove in their own lives to avert failure, to realize what Jacob Burckhardt, the friend of Nietzsche and scholar of the humane ideal, called the "highest individual development," a regimen in which the cultivation of a "powerful and varied nature" and a mastery of "all the elements of the culture of the age" would combine to produce the "'all-sided man,' '*l'uomo universale*.'" They believed that this sort of development, if carried out on a wider scale, could regenerate the waste spaces of their country. *Hoc opus, hic labor est.* Only the task, the labor, of creating places in which the old soulcraft could flourish was more difficult than the WASPs foresaw, would, indeed, have taxed the powers of figures much greater than they themselves were. What the poet Hölderlin calls the road to Olympia's pillars is the more arduous because the old play-circles were sustained by myths and beliefs that, with all the ingenuity in the world, cannot simply be imported into a modern environment or reproduced to order. You can set up one of Henry Ford's factories anywhere, but try to build the Erechtheion or the Temple of Nike without inhabiting the myths out of which the Athenians evolved them, and you will produce only a lifeless copy, a waxwork rose. This was Ruskin's criticism of the Renaissance itself: its classism was, he believed, a half-hearted imitation of the achievement of others rather than an organic growth.

It is not merely that it takes a lot of time to distill even a little civic nectar: it is that, even if you succeed in distilling the nectar—in creating places that live by their shaping myths—they will, in their very intensity, be cut off from the larger civilization of which they are a part. You may indeed find the Chartres of your heart's desire, but having found it, you will never again be at ease in Peoria, if you happened to have been at ease there in the first place. Separatism is a high price to pay even for *eutrapelian* flourishing and a richly imagined common life. In theory you might find a place in both worlds, might, for example, commute between a plasquagórazza community and a job in the modern metropolis or corporate park, doing your living in the one and earning your living in the other. But the tension is likely to be great; you will be under strong compulsions to choose between the two. An ingenious spirit, it is true, might work a genuine compromise between the two ways of living, integrating the different visions. But such a synthesis would be the work of a high imagination, akin, perhaps, to the divine madness that Socrates, in the *Phaedrus,* ascribes to poets and prophets—a thing beyond the power of our poor WASPs.

There were other obstacles. For more than a millennium, history, in the West at any rate, was a struggle between castles and agoras, between the old Greek aristocracy and the new democratic citizenry of the polis, between the medieval barons in their feudal strongholds and the artisans and guildsmen of the walled towns, the market squares of the Meistersinger. But with the emergence, in the seventeenth and eighteenth centuries, of modern rights, liberties, and opportunities, anyone might obtain a castle. Why bother keeping up the poetry of the town square when you might soon find yourself installed amid the luxuries of a castle? What Americans admired and envied in the WASPs was not their *eutrapelian* dream of the civic play-circle, but the apparently more substantial reality of their castles, their mansions and estates and summer houses. It is the WASP castle that Jay Gatsby seeks, and although Scott Fitzgerald intended Gatsby's tragicomedy to be a cautionary tale, his more naïve readers embraced it as a how-to manual. We all want castles now, and though few of us will attain one, and fewer still will find it fulfilling once attained, the idea itself has a fascination in our eyes that its rival lacks.

Beyond this, the plasquagórazza forums the WASPs sought made demands on the citizen that we are unlikely to find congenial. If they promoted the development of the soul's possibilities, they also taught that some possibilities are better than others. They were schools of what Santayana called insight, which he defined as a "steady contemplation of all things in their order and worth." But the problem of order and worth has become for us a much simpler calculus: the question of good and evil today is largely reducible to calculations of material loss and gain. Socioeconomic utility is the only widely accepted moral coin we honor; questions that cannot be reduced to dollars and cents become matters of personal preference, of mere opinion. Both our elites and those who challenge them defend their ideas of human thriving not through appeals to the good, or to a higher conception of excellence, but by promises of greater or more widely diffused material abundance; given a certain income, the requirements of flourishing are largely met. Matter and utility triumph over the longing for virtue and beauty and *areté*. Tocqueville said that the modern mind will "habitually prefer the useful to the beautiful." Such a mind can have little patience with Aristotle's belief that to "be always seeking after the useful does not become free and exalted souls," or with the conviction of Victor Hugo's Bishop of Digne that the "beautiful is as useful as the useful. . . . More so, perhaps."* Yet if each of us could, on the morrow, be installed in a modern castle with every circumstance of material opulence, every device of ingenious utility, we would still confront Emerson's insistence that how "to spend a day nobly, is the problem to be solved, beside which all the great reforms which are preached seem to me trivial."

---

* The civic artistry that was once so closely connected to the pursuit of beauty and *areté* is now looked upon as so much inefficiency, so many unjustifiable trifles. The modern mind, for all its mostly phony interest in museums and concert halls, is that of the onlooker who asked Michelangelo why he took so many pains with his statue. "Trifles make perfection," came the reply, "and perfection is no trifle." It is not an assertion that would survive modern cost-benefit analysis.

The WASPs' search for a higher life while economic grievances persist—while people are cold or hungry or working in those absurdly named forums, the Amazon Fulfillment Centers—may seem so much intellectual caviar, a daydream of the ivory tower. But the point of Henry James's novel *The Princess Casamassima* is that "a fresh deal of the social pack" that concentrates relentlessly on material wants at the expense of other kinds of poverty will beget evils no less real than the socioeconomic ones it seeks to remedy. Lionel Trilling, taking up James's point in *The Liberal Imagination*, argued that a program of reform that is overwhelmingly materialist in its aspirations, that looks upon the old humane artistry as a sentimentality or even as "one of the great barriers in the way of human freedom and decency," will in its own way be ruinous. Earnest reformers might claim that it is not a question of the one or the other, "that [economic] security can be imagined to go with richness and nobility of expression." But Trilling demurred: "we have not seen it in the past and nobody really strives to imagine it in the future." The imagination that might accomplish a double renovation was wanting.

IN AN ESSAY ON DAVID RIESMAN's book *The Lonely Crowd* and its account of the decline of certain kinds of aspiration in the modern world, Trilling said that his own experience as a teacher confirmed Riesman's findings. "For some time I had been increasingly aware that my students had no very great admiration for Stendhal's *Le Rouge et Le Noir*, gave it nothing like the response it had had from my college generation. Then one day a whole class, almost all its members gifted men, agreed in saying that they were bored by Julien Sorel and didn't like him. Bored by Julien Sorel! But didn't he, I asked, represent their own youthful desires for pre-eminence, their own natural young ambition? They snubbed me with their answer and fixed between themselves and me the great gulf of the generations: they did not, they said, understand ambition of Julien's self-referring kind: what they wanted was a decent, socially useful co-operative work to do."

Sorel's grandeur of passion and lofty ambition (that last infirmity of noble mind) grew out of desires and longings that humane culture has long sought to guide and educate. Trilling feared the loss, or suppression, of these desires in his students, the atrophy of the instinct to develop one's powers. It was another evidence, he thought, of the emergence of a culture composed of large numbers of "other-directed" people, as Riesman called them: people who, far from following

Pindar's injunction to become what you are, conform to the imperatives of the ascendant groups in order to become what everyone else is.

Long before our antisocial social media mobs came into being, the civilization was, Trilling thought, unconsciously working toward the casual mediocrity of so much of life today, the world of the smiley-faced emoji, in the stupidity of which we all now in some measure live. Yet some of the highest intellects of modernity welcomed this vacuity. Alexandre Kojève, who was born into a well-to-do family in Moscow in the waning days of the Romanovs and later emigrated to France, foresaw a world in which human striving would give way to bovine tranquility and in which human beings themselves would degenerate into mere "automata," interchangeable nonbeings. "In the final state," Kojève wrote, "there can be no more 'human beings' in our sense of an historical human being. The 'healthy' automata are 'satisfied' (sports, art, eroticism, etc.), and the 'sick' ones get locked up." What is distinctively human disappears; the race survives merely as a species of soulless creatures chewing the most rudimentary cud. "Everybody wants the same, everybody is the same."

What Santayana feared, the "universal hygienic hypnotisation" of the citizenry, the molding of individuals into a monotonous sameness, that "striking homogeneity of language, spirit, and manners" that he found characteristic of the United States, Kojève professed to welcome: a "vacant freedom" that "leaves all in the same anonymous crowd." Trilling and Riesman were, with Santayana and the WASPs, all on the other side, defenders of the culture Kojève sought to bury. But it is suggestive of the extent of the WASPs' failure that, although both Trilling and Riesman were in some degree shaped by WASP institutions, neither took up the WASPs' theory of civic regeneration. In his investigations of mid-twentieth-century America, Riesman studied three categories of citizens, the "other-directed" individual, a conforming herd animal; the "tradition-directed" individual, a dying breed, typically the product of an old-fashioned cultural-religious upbringing; and the ever scarcer "inner-directed" individual, who lives in the Puritan-Yankee tradition of the inner light and who seeks satisfaction in personal achievement: a solipsist who paddles his own canoe, following Emerson in culture and the nineteenth-century individualists in commerce and industry. Riesman entirely overlooked the civic-agora (plasquagórazza) personality that Henry Adams, Amory Gardner, Vida Scudder, and Jack Chapman in their different ways sought to nurture or promote: minds enlarged by humane artistry, brought up, ideally, in a sort of miniature Greek agora, and urged to live up to their potential even as they were to be conscious of civic obligation. This agora-directed personality, a blend of egoistic striving and *eutrapelian* cultivation placed in the service of the community, transcended the self-aggrandizement of Ries-man's "inner-directed" personality and the self-erasure of his "other-directed" one. The type found exemplars in Franklin and Eleanor Roosevelt, in Learned Hand and George Kennan, indeed in Trilling and Riesman themselves, who yet failed to make anything of it in their work.

FOR THIS FAILURE THE WASPs themselves must be blamed: they were unable to make their vision sufficiently vivid. They defended the humane tradition but failed effectually to reply to those who looked upon it as so much "literarist" rubbish. As a result liberal education, long at the heart of that tradition, is tacitly acknowledged by just about everyone today to be outmoded. The liberal arts survive not because anyone actually believes in the civic humanist culture they once underwrote, still less because we have confidence in their ability to prepare the mind for the active work of life. The charade is kept up only because the more selective colleges look upon liberal education as you might the tarnished silver service your grandmother left you, a hoary heirloom you don't really need but can't bring yourself to put on eBay. Something has to be done with all those chairs in the humanities that WASP bankers and businessmen and their descendants endowed.

The critics of liberal arts education are so far right. If the broad-souled citizens that this education was meant to nourish have no place in a modern culture of specialization, the effort to introduce young people to Sophocles and Shakespeare, the Bhagavad Gita and the Tao Te Ching, is not only a crime but a cruelty, acquainting them with something that may do them actual harm without doing society any good. Abolish it now, before it brings about more of those tragedies that Edmund Wilson, looking back on his father's generation, lamented: the tragedies of people educated for a world that no longer exists.

AT A PARTY IN Ox Pasture Lane in Southampton, in a garden where once the bovids grazed, bankers in velvet opera slippers stand with flutes of champagne in their hands. A society lady, expiating the sins of a now vanished preeminence, modestly plays the part of event photographer, much as, in old France, a *grande dame* who had lost her salon and her beauty might shut herself up in a convent, and by such abasement atone for former vanities. Birds of fairer plume, oblivious of the withered wren beneath them, dart about the pasturage, and amuse the tycoons. They flit from luminary to luminary, and with the sweet compulsion of honeybees rubbing their bellies on the stamens of a hydrangea, assuage an exquisite itch.

If you doubted that the fair sheepfold the WASPs sought was dead, even as an idea, Southampton showed you the tombstone. What remained of the old patrician elite of the East Coast was scarcely distinguishable from the new technical one of the West Coast. Both establishments sought the millennium by means of source codes, price-to-earnings ratios, and more poignant algorithms. In their prime the WASPs, with their faith in human potential and civic interconnection, were a hedge, however feeble, against the narrowness of the technicians. They read Tocqueville's prophecy of the last American—imprisoned in a life that throws "him back forever upon himself alone and threatens in the end to confine him entirely within the solitude of his own heart"—and shuddered.* But now the WASPs, too, were technicians. The hedge had withered.

You thought, naïvely, that the colleges might take up where the WASPs left off, play the part that Learned Hand and Edmund Wilson once played, figures who, in the very way they lived, bore witness to the virtues of the older faith. But although individual scholars have written, with much cogency, in defense of the humane tradition, the university itself (once faulted for being out of touch) has come to embrace every passing fad with a zealotry rivaling that of the faddists themselves.† Above all, Nietzsche said, the philosopher needs a rest from "anything to do with 'today.'" Diotima, who instructed Socrates in philosophy as well as in sex, taught that the nobler a person is, the more he or she will be in love with the eternal. But such commerce with eternity is the more difficult to achieve in institutions that give philosophers every incentive to wallow in the commonplaces of the moment.

---

* The United Kingdom has been compelled to appoint a Minister for Loneliness, who now sits in the Cabinet.

† There are, of course, exceptions. Harvard's Danielle Allen, who has devoted much of her life to the study of Athens, has defended, as Santayana once did, the sort of humane education that seeks happiness (*eudaimonia*) in the old Greek sense, an "ethical outlook," as she describes it, "organized around the efforts of individuals to achieve their full human flourishing by means of the development of their internal capacities." It is noteworthy, too, that Louis Menand and Stephen Greenblatt should have recently established the Humanities 10 course in Harvard College, a seminar or colloquium inspired, in part, by Columbia's approach to humane education. Whether it fills the void that opened up when Santayana ceased to give his own informal humanities course beside the fire in Stoughton Hall remains to be seen.

֍

ONE COMES BACK TO THE insecurity of elites in a democracy. Under a democratic regime a power establishment has hardly got its moat dug, and its escutcheons discovered or fabricated by the heralds, before it finds its ascendancy assailed by a new troop of moneyed barbarians. The WASPs felt the precariousness of their position, and if they were happy to govern their fellow citizens, they were afraid to mingle with them. Prince Hal, with all his royal pride, could "sound the base string" in the Boar's Head Tavern in Eastcheap, but the tremulous patrician under egalitarian stars fears loss of caste and takes refuge in snobbery. WASPs could create for themselves those little Greek democracies Richard Hofstadter admired: they could not create them for others. Confronted with the vigorous reality of a forum that mixed not only the commercial with the artistic and the sacred with the profane, but also the patrician with the plebeian, Henry Adams would have pined for his H. H. Richardson masonry. (*Odi profanum vulgus*: as much as Horace before him, Adams dreaded the stink of the crowd.) WASPs yearned for the old civic openness, but as a rule sponsored cultural institutions enclosed by thick casings of bricks and mortar. The concert hall, the museum, the college Great Books seminar, each carefully walled off from the living world beyond, collectively betrayed not the humanist but the culture-philistine.* WASPs were always to patronize these little mausoleums of embalmed culture, hid from the sun; they did very little to integrate a living art into the midst of the everyday America Walt Whitman and Louis Armstrong knew. Santayana's notion of "poetry intervening in life" was, outside their own little circles, beyond them.

Drawn as they were to the humanizing center but afraid to make it a reality, high WASPs could only watch with dismay as a cruder materialism came to dominate American life. From the cattle-pen spaces inspired by Le Corbusier's theory of functional segregation to the lightly dressed hog troughs of the sub-urban shopping center, Americans pass a good deal of their lives in nonplaces that rot the soul. The modern dream of conquering nature in order to overcome our animal frailties—our susceptibility to hunger, disease, and death—ends paradoxically in our becoming more purely animal than ever.

---

* Nietzsche's *Bildungsphilister* who, in his "easy self-complacency" and "self-contentment," is the "antithesis of a son of the Muses, of the artist, of the man of genuine culture."

❧

You remembered Bob, uncharacteristically quiet, sitting by himself on a settee in the anteroom, remote from the merriment of the party. The Cid was engaged to be married, betrothed to the daughter of an old WASP family much like his own, but of greater worldly consequence. In a crimson library high above the museum and the park that stretched beyond it, you watched as the stepmother of the Cid's fiancée led him up, as a turf baron might a prize filly, to some aging society dowager. Beneath varnished bookcases surmounted by marble busts were gathered those who had inherited what remained of Mrs. Wharton's New York. There was a partner in Frank Polk's old law firm, a brace of Harvard and Yale private equity bucks, a journalist who had made his name gratifying the desire of the city's beautiful people (a titular designation) for notoriety. The bride's mother was more formidable. A woman of the highest fashion, she seemed, like many such women, to cherish an inner secret. The solution to the mystery has never been found. You saw her, from a distance, conversing with charming animation. Her smiles alternated with girlish tosses of the head, and she seemed, at fifty-five, to be a pert schoolgirl. You looked longer, and would as soon have trifled with the Sphinx.

They had to go of course, along with their trophies and their taste, amply displayed in the splendid apartment, "possessions not vulgarly numerous, but hereditary cherished charming." Yet the images of that evening impressed themselves on the mind: of the Cid being led up to the old dowager, of Bob, sitting quietly by himself, not having had a drop to drink, so as not to embarrass his friend. It was the closing of a chapter, and you saw the last pages in a long history of missed chances being written. WASPs had by this time less power and less fame than they once did, but they were still blessed or burdened with opulence and authority. You might mock them at a distance, but in their own houses they were, when they chose to be, formidable; class was more real than you had supposed. Only it was not what the WASPs did with their power now, as it ran into the sands, that got you to musing, much as, long before, another historian sat musing amid the ruins of a fallen patriciate and contemplated its demise. No, what struck and a little pained you was what they failed to do with that power in their prime, when they might have made their theory of regeneration live outside their private snobberies, their clubs and their secret societies, their fenced-off schools and their own, happily *eutrapelian* careers.

You wanted to blame the WASPs' failure on the constraints of their Puritan-Yankee background, with its paralyzing effect on artistic and cultural vocation. How can you liberate others by means of culture and poetry when you belong to a group that, as Emerson said, is itself afraid to sing? (Strether in Gloriani's garden.) Yet kicking the Puritan in the WASP gets one only so far. John Ruskin, with the same Calvinist-mercantile background, tried to live his poetry, in projects like the Guild of St. George. The Guild, an exercise in service and civic conscience, was ridiculous, but it was the sort of ridiculousness the world needs more of.

THE WASPs PRODUCED LAWYERS, BANKERS, and diplomats in abundance, but neither a prophet nor a saint (if one excepts Phillips Brooks and Vida Scudder, with feast days in the Anglican calendar); and probably only a prophetic or saintly boldness could have done what in their hearts the WASPs would have liked to do. Failing sanctity or clairvoyance, might not a strong sense of self-possession have done in a pinch? Perhaps, but in comparison, say, to the English upper crust, WASPs lacked self-trust. If English feudalism died as an economic system with the repeal of the Corn Laws in the 1840s, its spirit lived on much longer, and is perhaps not quite dead even now. The old feudal alchemy bred a confidence, and commanded a deference, that the WASP could only envy. The ruined English squire, Bagehot says, struggling under a load of debt, will get "five times as much respect from the common peasantry as the newly made rich man who sits beside him."

The WASPs did not have this instinctive conviction of their own worth. With all their shyness and reserve they could not, finally, follow their star, and so did not find the "glorious harbor" of which Dante speaks, the new life which they sought. Where they failed, it is unlikely that a future power establishment will succeed: today's elites, morbidly technical, beguiled by rockets, spaceships, and synthetic ventures in immortality are not on the path to the fair sheepfold.

YET IF THE WASPs FAILED in their highest purposes, it was no mean thing to have shown how much a certain kind of education *can* do to awaken the soul and promote the civic virtues, an achievement that bore fruit in a culture of public service and sober patriotism that did something to ensure that the twentieth century was neither a National Socialist nor a Stalinist one. Yet one can easily make too much of this. America might well have defeated the Nazis and resisted the Soviet Union without the WASPs, as it would certainly have established a mandarin welfare state, which was not in the least a WASP invention. (Disraeli, Bismarck, and Lloyd George, after all, got there long before Franklin Roosevelt did.)

But however one ultimately judges the WASPs, there can be little doubt that the habits of civility which their education and upbringing implanted in them were an essential part of what they accomplished and valuable in themselves. Good manners were for WASPs more than a fussy code for society people, though they produced a number of books in that line, some of them even now in print. Their system was by no means so elaborate as the 3,300 rules of old Chinese etiquette, but it had a similar object in promoting self-restraint. Henry Adams said that he "never labored so hard to learn a language as he did to hold his tongue," and there is in his *Education* more than one tribute to the virtues of that well-nigh impossible art. The self-effacing manners of the WASPs were closely connected to their sense of humor, which had the same effect of forestalling grandiosity, for it led them to laugh at themselves. Honor was another restraint on conduct; it obliged WASPs, on certain occasions, to make sacrifices, and together with their humor and their tact (that other word for politeness), it made for a courtesy which, when they carried it into public life, did something to soften the fierceness of their country's politics. When the national interest required it, WASPs like Henry Stimson (a Republican who went to work for Franklin Roosevelt) and Dean Acheson (a Democrat who late in life counseled his old nemesis Richard Nixon) put partisan differences aside to work for the common good.

But the real decency of the WASPs was too often debased into the service of mere self-interest. Knowing, à la McGeorge Bundy, "what washes" and what doesn't, a WASP could tell in an instant, on meeting a man or woman for the first time, whether he or she was (in a phrase the WASPs would never have used but is expressive of the underlying feeling) "one of us." The manners of the WASPs and the peculiarities of their humor amounted to a private language, a system of psychic walls and trenches that made it easy for them to keep the stranger out—of the school, the club, the bank, the State Department.

Still it would be a pity if their incurable snobbery were to erase what was perhaps their greatest service, their attempt to show how a certain kind of education does enlarge the horizons of the mind. It is so easy in life to fall into one or two rigid grooves and live in a certain narrowness of fixation. We Americans seem as a people to devote too much energy to too few things, about which we are apt to become hysterically impassioned, while great tracts of possibility lie undiscovered around us. Heraclitus, in one of his paradoxical sayings, says that we go through life as though we are asleep, and forget what we do when we are not awake. Yet for all their patronage of *eutrapelia* and the much mocked "well-rounded" ideal, WASPs made very little progress in awakening their country's dormant possibility, and hardly had they begun to arouse it when they themselves proceeded to nod off.

FAILURE, THEN, IS THE WASPs' epitaph. But it was an illuminating failure. Their longing for a place, a city, a sheepfold forms an interesting if neglected chapter in our history. It was a desire like that of Jude for Christminster in Hardy's novel, and that of Dante when he said that he no longer saw Florence "save in dreams." WASPs were lesser cousins of Leopardi, whose *noia* was, like theirs, a despair for the lost city, and of Trollope's Josiah Crawley, that noble agora character wounded and almost destroyed by the nineteenth century.

They felt, the best of them, what Hölderlin felt for Eleutherai and the old civic world, but one must not think of them as prophets of community, which becomes an ever less helpful word. One uses it, but one is aware that it is a piety, invoked with too little understanding of the artistry that commands the heart and makes a place the center of a world. Nor will it do to reduce the WASPs' longing for *eutrapelian* space to their encounter with Europe. That encounter, preserved in Henry James's fiction, too often makes the WASPs seem not quite American. "Improvised Europeans, we were," Henry Adams said in a letter to James, "and—Lord God!—how thin!" Others were harsher. WASPs were spiritual traitors, snobs who exchanged a red-blooded connection to their country for an anemic Europeanism that left them, finally, in a moral no man's land. At the other extreme, T. S. Eliot praised WASPs for *trying* to be good Europeans. In his essay "In Memory of Henry James," he said that it "is the final perfection, the consummation of an American to become, not an Englishman, but a European—something which no born European, no person of any European nationality, can become."

Ernst Robert Curtius, the scholar and humanist, saw the WASPs' encounter with the Old World in a light different from that of either Adams, who deplored WASPs as cultural hybrids, or Eliot, who idealized them as so many potential Europeans. He found a "deep spiritual meaning" in Adams's pilgrimage to

Chartres, the journey of a man "trying to get at the roots of the civilization to which he belonged." Adams was, he believed, "in the position of a man who has never known his mother." (A shrewd insight into that fetishist of the Madonna.) High WASPs, in Curtius's reading, were American patriots who yet sensed the incompleteness of the civilization for which America was preparing the way. They did not discount America's achievement: they knew that in certain kinds of ingenuity—in the arts of free government and political economy, individual rights and rational self-interest—the United States led the world with a way of life that liberated millions. But they felt what was missing more poignantly than their contemporaries. Travel, leisure, *taste*, all indulged from an early age, enlarged or, depending on your point of view, corrupted their imaginations. WASPs feared the human consequences of a way of life that was inadequate precisely because it had been founded on too narrow a conception of human flourishing. In this they differed profoundly from Kojève, who saw the products of the new civilization as shrunken but satisfied. Kojève's human "automata," like Nietzsche's last men, are stupidly happy, or at any rate nauseatingly content. WASPs, to the contrary, suspected that Tocqueville was closer to the truth when he depicted his own last man as gnawed by unhappiness and miserable in his narrowness and aloneness.

There is a curious parallel in Plato. His *Republic* is a portrait of a city which, utterly different from the American Republic though it is, is nevertheless a product of the highest conscious human ingenuity. But Plato came in time to see that with all this ingenuity, something at the heart of being human was missing. In his old age he glimpsed another possibility. The way to a balanced life lay in the recognition that, if human beings were creatures of rational necessity—the necessity of getting their bread and of living up to their rational natures—they were also creatures of no less rational fantasy and imagination, strung together by their "choirmasters (the gods) on a thread of poetry and play." Whether Plato thought this thread really and truly divine, as he seemed to, or whether he thought it a human projection, one that grew out of some truth of the soul, may be debated by philosophers. The point is that on his pilgrimage (real or imagined) through the Cretan hills he saw a way of integrating the two rationalities, and of finding a manner of being that did justice, not to this or that part of the soul, but to the whole. The high WASPs, if I have read them right, were reaching for something similar, were patriots who really did want the best for their country in seeking a deeper reasonableness. But they lacked the grandeur of imagination that could distill that nectar.

∽

Louis Auchincloss wrote perhaps the best book there is on the longing for wholeness that, more than anything else, invented the WASPs as a force in American life. The author of *The Rector of Justin* used to describe his subject as the "decline of a class." Yet he harbored no illusions about its virtues and accepted with serenity its decay. "I used to say to my father, 'Everything would be all right if only my class at Yale ran the country.' Well, they did run the country during the Vietnam War, and look what happened!" The books in which Auchincloss chronicles the decline of the WASPs are notably unsentimental; there is in them nothing of the romantic nostalgia for a waning patriciate one finds in Waugh and Lampedusa, in Proust and Faulkner (in his portrait of the Sartorises). But he did say to me once, in connection with the withering of the WASP ascendancy, "When we are gone, they will miss us."

He was right.

Orpheus's Head

Εγώ φρονώ ότι πρέπει το μεν σπουδαίον να το σπουδάζωμεν, το δε
μη σπουδαίον να μη το σπουδάζωμεν. Εκ φύσεως δε ο μεν θεός είναι
άξιος πάσης της αξιομακαρίστου μελέτης, ο άνθρωπος όμως, καθώς
είπαμεν προηγουμένως, είναι εν παιγνίδιον εφευρημένον από τον
θεόν, και βεβαίως αυτό το έργον αυτού είναι το ανώτερον από όλα.
Λοιπόν αυτόν τον τρόπον πρέπει να ακολουθή και να παίζη όσον το
δυνατόν ωραιότερα παιγνίδια έκαστος ανήρ και εκάστη γυνή εις όλην
των την ζωήν, σκεπτόμενοι αντιθέτως από ό, τι συνηθίζουν τόρα.

I say that a man should be serious about that which is serious, and
not about that which is not serious. For while God is the natural and
worthy object of our most serious and blessed endeavors, man, as we
said previously, is a plaything created by God, and this playfulness
really is the best thing about him. It follows that we should play the
most beautiful games, every man and woman, all through life, and
be of another mind from what we now are.
—Plato, *Laws*, 803c

WASPs have been studied, usefully but imperfectly, through the prism
of sociology: which is to say in the light of that which they tried to
resist, a way of looking at things that has little room for many of the things they
cared about. I have tried to look at them instead in the light of the poets and
philosophers who shaped them. Their masters, particularly Plato, Dante, and
Shakespeare, have been for me indispensable guides, interpreters of the experience of people whom they never met, but whom they understood—understood as
souls frustrated by their failure to do justice to themselves, as though unfaithful
to some deeper music.

"We are all of us very near to sublimity," Emerson says. This sublimity, according to him, is within us. It is the logos of Heraclitus, the way (tao) of Lao Tzu, the "depth of the spirit" which, St. François de Sales says, some "call the Kingdom of God." The eye, Lao Tzu says, "gazes but can catch no glimpse of it"; it perishes in being uttered; we can but call it "the Mystery," or "rather the 'Darker than any Mystery,'" the "secret of being mated to heaven." WASPs were not, as a rule, either mystics or philosophers, but they were consumed by the fear that much of their own potential lay dormant within them, in those fathomless depths of being of which the sages speak. They were by no means unique in this preoccupation; we have seen that they were indebted to Coleridge and Arnold and a number of other British thinkers who, as Raymond Williams has shown in his book *Culture and Society*, looked to art, poetry, and humane culture to bring about (in Coleridge's words) "the harmonious development of those qualities and faculties that characterize our humanity." A similar desire or anxiety to develop the "culture of the inward man" is found in the Germans whom W. H. Bruford studied in his book *The German Tradition of Self-Cultivation: 'Bildung' from Humboldt to Thomas Mann*, though it was the misfortune of the Germans to have failed to connect *Bildung* (education, cultivation, poetry, *paideia*) to civic life in any reasonable way.

Eutrapelia or well-roundness was for WASPs the art of waking what was asleep. It was less a matter of surface accomplishments (the rather showy achievements of the Renaissance virtuosi) than an attempt to reach the elusive untapped reservoirs of being. As such it was bound up with other artistries that find out the hidden, unvisited places:

The artistry of place. How many places to which you go, however often you do go, cause your heart to leap up? The artistry that creates such places in all their thereness has grown exceedingly rare. WASPs sought to recover a dying placefulness; they were sensitive to the "genius" of places, and in their institutions they favored a voluble architecture, what Nietzsche calls the "symbolism" found in the "lines and figures" of the builded environment. "Everything in a Greek or Christian building originally signified something," he wrote, "and indeed something of a higher order of things: this feeling of inexhaustible significance lay about the building like a magical veil." The façade of Henry Adams's house at 1603 H Street, the interior of William Amory Gardner's chapel at Groton, were meant to appeal to something latent in the minds of those who beheld them. Such places are in contrast to the prefabricated, antiseptic space—"place so unsanctified"—in which American life is now largely lived, scrubbed of anything that might speak to the heart.

The artistry of play. For all the vastness and variety of the modern leisure economy, what is most striking about it is its psychological crudity. Almost all the higher intelligence of the civilization goes into work, leaving play to the dunces. The delicate apprehension that led Plato see that in our games we are God's playthings, the depth of spirit that moved Dante to find in play a memory and an apprehension of paradise—all this refinement is for the most part absent from our coarser entertainments. Paradise is for Dante a feast of *giochi* and *canti*, of games and songs: a recovery of what was lost when, after the expulsion from the earthly paradise of Eden, man exchanged laughter and games (*onesto riso* and *dolce gioco*) for tears and anguish (*pianto* and *affanno*). We think of WASPs as traditionalists, ritualists, in thrall to complicated etiquettes, from the proper manner of dressing for dinner to the right way of mixing a martini. In fact their manners were so much stylized playacting. In frowning on their stuffiness, we ourselves lose in playfulness. Why does the judge don her robe, the priest his surplice, the scholar her gown, the barrister his wig, the queen her crown? It is all a piece of (perhaps not very impressive) stage acting, yet it has its effect in endowing life with the quality of play.

The artistry of the poet. Plato in the *Laws* says that the gods are our choirmasters: they "string us together one by one on a thread of singing and dancing, knitting us together in bodies called choirs (χοροι, *choroi*) on account of the joy (χαρᾶς, *charás*) they give." The result of this divine gift—"the power to perceive rhythm and melody"—is the *dolce lira*, the sweet lyre, which Dante makes a principle of sanity in life. Poetry remains the most effective means of getting at the soul: its rhythms and harmonies (in Plato's words) sink "farthest into the depths of the soul and take hold of it most firmly by bringing it nobility and grace." It is true that Plato, who distinguished between good poetry and bad, believed that the latter should be banished from a healthy community. But good poetry was essential to its soulcraft: by developing the powers of the soul it enabled it to go up higher even as it relieved it of the burden of its unused power. Poetry in the *Laws* is shown to embody a rational mysticism, one that, when it is made palpable in the living forms of music and play, hallows a place and enables it to command the heart. It is the lyre of Orpheus that creates the humane (plasquagórazza) forum and the fair sheepfold the WASPs sought,* places that in their lyric reasonableness keep alive the cantatory and incantatory virtues† and resist what Nietzsche called the "atrophy of the melodic sense" characteristic of life in so many of the places in which we live now.

The artistry of time. Old WASP institutions had not only their myths but also their memories, their ancestral portraits, their little shrines and altars of the dead, that brought alive the different phases of the institution's growth, so that the past was always obtruding on the present, and the present was continuously throwing an unsuspected light on the past. It was Emerson's "Carnival of time," when the "Ages went or stayed," and it momentarily relieved you from the trivialities of the moment. You thus escaped the shallow present of such a character as Henry James's Mrs. Worthingham, who "was 'up' to everything, aware of everything—if one counted from a short enough time back (from week before last, say, and as if quantities of history had burst upon the world within the fortnight)." Where time is honored, eternity is possible.

HIGH WASPs WANTED TO KEEP alive parts of the soul that were endangered amid so many beneficent revolutions in our way of living. Every material and technical advance in human life, however benign, must be met with a countervailing force if equilibrium is to be preserved. With the advent of Roman engineering or the Apple iPhone something valuable is put at risk; a flanking movement is needed if the balance of the soul is to be maintained.

In seeking to prevent soul shrinkage, WASPs like Henry Adams and Jack Chapman had something in common with thinkers who in the name of an older soul-culture led what Isaiah Berlin called the counter-Enlightenment against

---

*   In their quest for such places, high WASPs found inspiration in the examples with which they were most familiar, which were mostly, though not exclusively, Western. Yet I read them as being, in this respect, only incidentally apologists for the West: driven less by cultural chauvinism than by the desire to find a way to live up to what was in them. Confucius's emphasis on music, poetry, ritual, and tradition would have been immediately intelligible to Henry Adams, who undertook to study Chinese; and John Jay Chapman and William Amory Gardner would instinctively have sympathized with Claude Lévi-Strauss's reaction to the poetic myths of supposedly primitive peoples. "But are they really superstitions? I see these preferences rather as denoting a kind of wisdom which savage races practiced spontaneously and the rejection of which, by the modern world, is the real madness." And yet it is a vexed question; one might with some justice make the WASPs out to be radically blind to the virtues of those with whom they had not many haplogroup markers in common.

†   "Our songs," Plato says, "are really spells for souls." *Laws*, 659e.

those Enlightenment sages who, contemplating modernity's mastery of matter and the abundance it made possible, thought the older wisdoms obsolete. Challenging the complacency of the new children of light, the counterrevolutionists argued that the soul of man under prose was no nearer perfection than it had been under poetry, even as inward provinces of being that the old artistries routinely nourished withered and died. The rich depths of the soul, with all that music which, according to Plato, is divinely lodged there, came, under duller stars, to be reduced to the unconscious *id* of Freud and the pedantries of depth psychology. "No heart is dark when that moon shines": but only in the catacombs of sleep, in the underworld of dreams, does one now regularly encounter the buried treasures. One's waking life is too often little more than the prosperous treadmill.

Sir Isaiah, though he had a sneaking sympathy for the prophets of counter-Enlightenment, whom he wrote about more piercingly than he did the modern sages, nevertheless characterized them as, for the most part, "irrationalists" or "anti-rationalists." He seems (for he was, his friend Edmund Wilson pointed out, a lazy reader who never got through Dante) to have overlooked Plato's intimation, in the *Laws*, of another aspect of rationality no less profound than that favored by the rationalists themselves, of whom Plato himself was, in his earlier career, among the foremost. In his last work Plato sought to reconcile the rationality of his *Republic* with another, no less illuminating rationality, that we might bind up the two kinds of reason—the two logoi—in a richer conception of human experience. A rationality of the surface, one that fails to tap, as the rationality of the *Republic* fails to tap, the depths of logos, will never, the Plato of the *Laws* suggests, produce anything adequately human, let alone really beautiful and noble.* You can't live wholly in the shallows and expect to see what Dante and Shakespeare and Heraclitus did.† Veil upon veil conceals the

---

* Plato's insight has been largely ignored by thinkers who would seem to be less interested in discovering truth than in perfecting the art of failing to find answers to problems you never knew you had. Yet Burke, who said that "art is man's nature," grasped the essence of the perception, as did Henry Adams, who preferred the lyrical wisdom of Dante, St. Francis, and the Virgin of Chartres to the surface rationality of Thomas Aquinas.

† Tertullian apparently never meant to be understood to say, in *De carne Christi*, "I believe because it is absurd" ("*credo quia absurdum*.") But to say, "I believe it, not because it is absurd, but because it embodies a reason deeper than my merely superficial rationality comprehends," has its place in the thought of Hamann, Burke, and Kierkegaard. (It was Hamann who put surface rationality in its place when he said: "Only love—for a person or an object—can reveal the true nature of anything.") "Should we mark someone down for believing in a way that they take to be irrational?" the philosopher Brian Weatherson has asked. He argues, in his book *Normative Externalism*, that we should not.

beauty the sages uncovered, that of Beatrice, Diotima, Cordelia, Maryam, the "Mysterious Female" of Lao Tzu,* things hidden from those whom Katágaios calls the spiritually overdressed.

Plato, the magus of Enlightenment, was also the first philosopher of counter-Enlightenment. Yet Sir Isaiah was surely right when he pointed out that a number of the counter-Enlightenment divers who followed in his wake found, in their explorations of the depths of logos, some very dark places indeed, even as they preached (as Plato never did) the rejection of conscious reason altogether, doing away with the tools that help us to distinguish between the dark places and the light, the worse and the better. "Nothing is true," says Nietzsche's Zarathustra, "all is permitted. . . . Alas, my animals, man needs what is most *evil* in him for what is *best* in him . . ." Nietzsche strove for the forbidden: he opposed older moralities of good and evil (and the Platonic rationality that sustained some of them) because he was convinced that they stood in the way of a new, higher humanity, one that would find "a thousand paths that have never yet been trodden—a thousand healths and hidden isles of life."†

This was going too far for most people, but in a curious twist, the irrational-ists of counter-Enlightenment who followed Nietzsche rather than Plato found allies in Enlightenment thinkers who had as little use for the old moralities and their attendant poetries. According to these *lumières*, notions of good and evil have been superseded by a new scientific understanding of man: a conception of human beings, not as playthings of God, but as puppets of biology, reducible to so many biological drives and urges. A way of looking at things that works up to a point—the point where it fails to account for the distinctively human. When a cat torments a rodent, it is true to its biologically evolved nature; when a human being tortures a living thing, it betrays its human nature, however much biology may have gone into the act. But the human difference goes deeper. Each year a number of books appear explaining that we do this or that because natural selection has selected this or that trait of our nature. But if biology can explain why we sing and why we build, it cannot account for the distance between, say, the Muzak in the supermarket and the late quartets of Beethoven, between the

---

* See Arthur Waley's translation of the *Tao tê Ching*, which he dedicated to Dorothy and Leonard Elmhirst.

† But *Zarathustra* is the *surface* of Nietzsche, as the *Republic* is the surface of Plato. The philosopher who, seeking another word for music, found it in Venice, felt the power of the deeper reasonableness that Zarathustra, seeking his alpine cure among ice and high mountains, denied.

local community center and Chartres. And yet that space—the gulf that separates Colley Cibber from Keats, Disney World from the Parthenon—is part of the mystery of what it is to be human, the striving for ends that transcend biology. It is the human difference, and none of our modern masters can really account for it; some of them were quite miserable over it.[*]

THE WASPs WHO FIGURE IN this book were neither irrationalists nor biologists. They sought rather to keep the human difference alive in an age in which it was being eroded. To modern thinkers they must seem priggish and boring: they did not seek to go beyond good and evil—to do away with the rational arts (such as those Socrates and Plato practiced) of distinguishing between the better and the worse. Nor did they seek to make themselves slaves to biology, to processes that are innocent of ethics and know nothing of right and wrong. On the contrary, WASPs would seem to have believed that human beings have evolved (biologically) beyond biology, and that their rational arts of seeking the good are an essential part of the (supra-biological) beings they have become. Only WASPs believed, as the old Greeks did, and as Plato himself (in the shadow of the Cretan cypresses) admitted, that art and poetry embody their own reasonableness: are as good, as rational, and as useful as, say, corporate finance or computer science or the studies of Professor Pinker in a Harvard purged of Santayana's spirit.[†]

But WASPs never worked out, or even tried to work out, the difficulties of the stand they took. They embraced the deeper (or unconscious) reasonableness of the poetry that informed institutions like Columbia's Core Curriculum and created places like Groton. But they could not say why those particular poetries were good (and rational and true) while other poetries, the myths, say, of Pol Pot or Dr. Francia, were bad and irrational and false. Who is to judge? The philosopher? Perhaps; but it is not obvious that the conscious rationality of Socrates is

---

[*] Even so luminous a child of light as Diderot felt the incompleteness of his philosophy. "I am furious," he wrote to his mistress Sophie Volland, "at being entangled in a confounded philosophy which my mind cannot refrain from approving and my heart from denying." If, during Holy Week at Roissy in 1659, the Abbé Le Camus did not actually christen a pig and say a Black Mass over it, "scandalizing a court not scrupulous," the story is suggestive of the animus that the luminary is likely feel in the face of a deeper, because more lyric and poetic, reasonableness.

[†] The thought has something in common with Santayana's intuition that religious wisdom may be literally false but morally true. Not a noble lie, but an acknowledgment of the truth of a deeper mystery. To concede that we are continuously touched by mystery is not obscurantism, it is sanity. Without mystery we should die of boredom.

capable of judging the unconscious reasonableness (or lack of it) in the poetry of Aeschylus or Dante. Yet if the philosopher is ill-equipped for such a task, who is better able to judge? The economist? The politician? The democratic citizen? We may instinctively feel that certain kinds of poetry (without which we cannot reasonably live) are benign, and express some perhaps obscure but worthwhile truth of our being: and that others are evil and reflect aspects of our nature that are to be resisted. But how do we know? How *can* we know?

The Romantic artists, whose poetry the WASPs (other than T. S. Eliot after he passed from adolescence into premature old age) read with keen delight, were conscious of the problem. They wanted to recover provinces in the soul that were being lost under an Enlightened regime, much as the WASPs themselves did. And yet their deep-souled heroes have a diabolic or infernal quality: Byron's Manfred, Balzac's Vautrin, Melville's Ahab are the descendants of Milton's Satan, and for all their grandeur of soul, they seem more in love with evil than with good. Plumb the depths of the soul, in other words, and you might find, not Melville's "insular Tahiti, full of peace and joy," but instead his doomed *Pequod*, "freighted with savages," plunging into the "blackness of darkness." In this reading, the WASPs' insistence on the dignity and potential of homo sapiens was largely a delusion, the conceit of fabulists determined to pretend that the species is less brutal than it in fact is, that human beings are something more than pitiable creatures born, as Augustine says, *inter fæces et urinam*, between piss and shit, and doomed to live in the dread of suffering and death. As for the humane forum the WASPs sought, it was, when viewed in this light, so much ludicrous make-believe, a Xandu, a Cleopolis, a Land of Cockaigne or Garden of Irem, in which you might forget that horror, mitigated by boredom and misery, is so closely interwoven with life as be at times its essence.

Is the human difference the WASPs tried to assert an illusion? The question has become more pressing now that the old humane ideal is itself slipping away. It takes an effort, today, to understand how human beings could ever have conceived themselves as being at once "a little lower than the angels" and at the same time on terms of intimacy with devils. In our shrunken self-knowledge, we find ourselves, on the contrary, to be little more than biologically evolved brutes whose salvation lies either in evading our nature or in transcending it through a mating with machinery.

IN THIS THRENODY FOR FALLEN toffs (composed by one who was, for better or for worse, influenced by them), I have tried to illuminate what was worthwhile in their effort to do justice to the humane ideal in an unsympathetic age. Most people, it has been said, die with their music still in them. WASPs saw this as a tragedy: not only for those who died without having flowered, but for the places in which they lived, that might have benefited from the blossoms. Hence the fair sheepfolds to which they were drawn as though by Plato's golden cord. From Fuzzy Sedgwick's corrupted duchy in the California hills to Dorothy Elmhirst's ingenuous Dartington in Devonshire, from Henry Adams's Chartres to Mrs. Jack Gardner's Venice and her Venetian museum in Boston, from Bernard Berenson's Villa I Tatti in Fiesole to the rose-garden of T. S. Eliot in *Burnt Norton*, from Marietta Tree's gossip-leavened political banquets at Heron Bay to Joe Alsop's civic dinner parties in Georgetown, with their nostalgia for the *symposia* or drinkings-together of the Athenians, the WASPs (actual or honorary) created (or aspired to create) places in which different aspects of the soul could ripen. They saw the need for regeneration, but tragically or comically lacked the gifts of the regenerator. They were unable to produce a potent imaginer, a Prospero whose rough magic could remake a larger portion of the world, that more of us might "be of another mind from what we now are."

Even so I am grateful to them.

Picture Credits

Eleanor Roosevelt, Sara Delano Roosevelt, Franklin Roosevelt, and Fannie Peabody in Washington on March 4, 1940: Library of Congress. Dean Acheson and John F. Kennedy in Georgetown in November 1960: Library of Congress. Nathaniel Hawthorne: Library of Congress. Isabella Stewart Gardner by Anders Zorn: Library of Congress. Henry Adams: Getty Images. William Amory Gardner, Cotty Peabody, and Sherrard Billings circa 1884: collection of the author. The Grand Canal and the Palazzo Barbaro in Venice: Library of Congress. John Jay Chapman: collection of the author. Cotty and Fannie Peabody circa 1885: collection of the author. Lizzie Cameron: Library of Congress. Hollis Hall, Harvard: Library of Congress. Theodore Roosevelt: Library of Congress. Vida Scudder: collection of the author. The Adams Memorial, Washington D.C.: Library of Congress. St. John's Chapel, Groton School: collection of the author. Henry Stimson: Library of Congress. Franklin Roosevelt at Groton in April 1900: Franklin D. Roosevelt Presidential Library and Museum. Pierpont Morgan circa 1907: Library of Congress. Learned Hand: Library of Congress. Dorothy Whitney: Library of Congress. Franklin Roosevelt as assistant secretary of the navy: Library of Congress. Gertrude Vanderbilt Whitney: Library of Congress. "Hobey" Baker: Library of Congress. Willard Straight: Library of Congress. Harry Payne Whitney: Library of Congress. William Amory Gardner, Cotty Peabody, and Sherrard Billings at Groton in 1924: collection of the author. T. S. Eliot in 1926: National Portrait Gallery, London. Ernest Hemingway in Pamplona in 1925: John F. Kennedy Presidential Library and Museum. Franklin Roosevelt delivers his sixth fireside chat in September 1934: Library of Congress. Whittaker Chambers: Library of Congress. Cotty and Fannie Peabody at Groton, circa 1940: collection of the author. Franklin Roosevelt at Warm Springs, April 11, 1945: Franklin D. Roosevelt Presidential Library and Museum. Skull and Bones in New Haven: Library of Congress. George Kennan in February 1966: Library of Congress. Averell Harriman and John F. Kennedy at the White House in July 1963: John F. Kennedy Presidential Library and Museum. Henry James: Library of Congress. The Roosevelts with the clergy in Hyde Park, New York, in June 1939: Franklin D. Roosevelt Presidential Library and Museum. WASPs at Water Mill on Long Island, circa 1999: collection of the author.

Notes and Sources

PREFACE

p. xiii *their mistakes*: Whatever it is that makes for an attraction to boards and committees, to commissions and blue-ribbon panels, the WASPs possessed it. Whenever they found a problem to be addressed, they established a panel or ad hoc committee to make inquiries and issue a report; and for many years few great national commissions were without one or more eminent WASPs among the commissioners. (The Warren Commission, with a membership of seven, numbered two WASPs, Allen Dulles and, in a semi-honorary capacity, John J. McCloy, among its members.) (For McCloy and WASPdom, see chapter 33 above, "Centurions of an American Century.") A WASP advisory committee was even established to inquire into the justness of the convictions of Sacco and Vanzetti for the offense of murder, its most illustrious member being A. Lawrence Lowell, the president of Harvard. The two anarchists were thus enabled to go to their graves in the knowledge that their deaths had the WASPs' stamp of approval. And yet, strangely enough, the WASPs never appointed a panel to inquire into their own errors, or their own fitness as a leadership class. The author has therefore taken the liberty of constituting himself such a committee. This book is the result, and in composing it the author has tried to live up to the example of scrupulous impartiality set by President Lowell.

p. xiii *The term WASP*: As early as the 1950s the acronym formed part of what the political scientist Andrew Hacker called the "cocktail party jargon of the sociologists." See Hacker, "Liberal Democracy and Social Control" (*The American Political Science Review*, December 1957, 1010). Its rise as a term of explanatory art coincided with what was perhaps the apogee of the sociological imagination in the American university and in the country's larger intellectual life, a time when it seemed that the social sciences would demystify the world. Today we are likely to be conscious of the *limits* of the sociological imagination, and certainly there was, in the life and culture of the WASPs, much that the sociologist was ill-equipped to bring to light. Hence this effort.

p. xiii *Saxon or Anglo*: As opposed to, say, Jutish-Frisian, Romano-British, Beaker-Folkish, or any other strain of genetic material that has been incorporated in the English people.

p. xiv *stars*: "*E quindi uscimmo a riveder le stelle*." "And then we came out to see the stars again." Dante, *Inferno*, XXXIV, 139. A grammarian, living in the perpetually illuminated northeastern corner of his Republic, sees few stars, and those with difficulty; not since he was, many years ago, more than he cares to count, in the kingdom of Minos has he beheld a mantle so "rich with jewels hung, that night/Doth like an Æthiop bride appear."

1. TWILIGHT OF THE WASPS

p. 2 *"My parents owned"*: Jean Stein, *Edie: An American Biography*, ed. George Plimpton (London: Jonathan Cape, 1982), 69.

p. 2 *light and feeling of the gods*: Ibid., 56.

p. 2 *"After breakfast"*: Ibid., 83–85.

p. 2 *"stood at the windows"*: Ibid., 85.

p. 2 *"raffish and violent"*: Ibid.

p. 2 *"enormous thorax"*: Ibid.

p. 2 *"priapic, almost strutting"*: Ibid.

p. 2 *"immediately ushered"*: Ibid., 88.

p. 2 *"It was sort of like the emperor"*: Ibid., 89.

p. 3 *"a fauve"*: Ibid.

p. 3 *"strutting out"*: Ibid.

p. 3   *"so thin"*: Ibid.

p. 3   *"just humping away"*: Ibid., 105.

p. 3   *"laughter and conversation"*: Ibid., 56.

p. 3   *"life of Greek Gods"*: Ibid.

p. 3   *some improbable garden of Apollo*: What explains the attraction which the inquirer—the one who says "ἱστορέω," "*historéō*," "I inquire"—feels for the thing into which she inquires? All the higher forms of inquiry reveal what Proust calls those "precepts of the heart" to which "every profound work of the spirit brings us nearer, and which are unknown only to imbeciles." The Enlightened inquirer, Gibbon or Voltaire, conceals this soul-work: the Romantic inquirer—Carlyle or Ruskin or De Quincey—perhaps too ostentatiously flaunts it. (De Quincey said that he wrote his history of opium-eating to vindicate the power of the soul "to dream magnificently," to "reveal something of the grandeur which belongs *potentially* to all human dreams.") But even the slightest work of inquiry—of ἱστορία, *historia*—may show traces of a buried impulse, the woods and meadow in the lowlands of a suburb in which the roads and gardens of a childish city were fashioned with rude art. On the lowland of χαναάν, see Edward Robinson, *A Greek and English Lexicon of the New Testament* (Boston: Crocker and Brewster, 1836), 887.

p. 3   Mayflower *screwballs*: Robert Lowell, "Waking in the Blue."

p. 4   *"very attractive"*: Diana Cooper, *Trumpets from the Steep* (London: Rupert Hart-Davis, 1960), 15.

p. 4   *"tradition-ridden"*: Ibid.

p. 4   *"as for a nuptial night"*: Ibid.

p. 4   *"only one fault"*: Stephen Gundle and Clino T. Castelli, *The Glamour System* (Houndmills: Palgrave Macmillan, 2006), 132.

p. 5   *omitted to shave*: David Grafton, *The Sisters: The Lives and Times of the Fabulous Cushing Sisters* (New York: Villard, 1992), 445.

p. 5   *"wonderfully warm"*: Ibid., 56.

p. 5   *"beautiful, kind, loyal"*: Gloria Vanderbilt, *It Seemed Important at the Time* (New York: Simon & Schuster, 2004), 60.

p. 5   *"nothing mean or hard"*: David Halberstam, *The Powers That Be* (Urbana: University of Illinois Press, 2000), 124.

p. 5   *"abandoned her sexually"*: Grafton, *The Sisters*, 219.

p. 5   *opulence, when governed by taste, could raise life to a higher and nobler plane*: Lionel Trilling would perhaps have agreed with the sentiment: in his essay on Henry James's novel *The Princess Casamassima*, he pointed to the surprise and delight of John Stuart Mill "when he discovered that a grand and spacious room could have so enlarging an effect upon his mind . . ." Lionel Trilling, "The Princess Casamassima," in Trilling, *The Liberal Imagination: Essays on Literature and Society* (New York: New York Review Books, 2008), 84.

p. 5   *colors*: Grafton, *The Sisters*, 156.

p. 6   *"living work of art"*: This, according to Truman Capote, was the aspiration "of my friends among the so-called Beautiful People." They had "the freedom to pursue an aesthetic quality in life," to be "your own living work of art." *Truman Capote: Conversations*, ed. M. Thomas Inge (Jackson: University Press of Mississippi, 1987), 90.

p. 6   *"not unpleasant little monster"*: Edmund Wilson, *The Sixties: The Last Journal, 1960–1972*, ed. Lewis M. Dabney (New York: Farrar Straus Giroux, 1993), 438.

p. 6   *Proust*: Grafton, *The Sisters*, 198.

p. 6   *"campy high-pitched"*: George Plimpton, *Truman Capote* (New York: Anchor, 1998), 291.

p. 6   *"She might have been"*: Grafton, *The Sisters*, 150.

p. 7   *"too rich or too thin"*: Ralph Keyes, *The Quote Verifier: Who Said What, Where, and When* (New York: St. Martin's, 2007), 180.

p. 7   *"fly where others walk"*: *Truman Capote: Conversations*, ed. Inge, 90.

p. 7   *"My God"*: Stein, *Edie*, 87.

p. 7   *"This boy doesn't need a nanny"*: Ibid., 38.

p. 7 *"he just didn't have"*: Ibid., 99.

p. 7 *"Duke"*: Henry Dwight "Halla" Sedgwick, the oldest of the brothers, was the first to be called "Duke" at Groton. Stein, *Edie*, 35.

p. 7 *Cotty*: The name has been spelled both Cotty and Cottie, just as his wife's name has been spelled both Fannie and Fanny. The author has settled on Cotty and Fannie.

p. 7 *"If you put"*: H. H. Richards, "My First Year at Groton," in *Views from the Circle: Seventy-five Years of Groton School* (Groton, Mass.: Trustees of Groton School, 1960), 59.

p. 7 *"most powerful personality"*: Carol Gelderman, *Louis Auchincloss: A Writer's Life* (Columbia: University of South Carolina Press, 2007), 34.

p. 7 *"I don't think"*: Ibid.

p. 8 *"You know, I'm still scared of him"*: Stein, *Edie*, 33.

p. 8 *"end as far as his financial possibilities"*: Ibid., 41.

p. 8 *"to develop his artistic side"*: Ibid., 50.

p. 8 *"I think he was ashamed"*: Ibid.

p. 9 *"ideal world"*: Ibid., 55.

p. 9 *Arcadia*: Ibid.

p. 9 *"surface looked so good"*: Ibid, 57.

p. 9 *"brought his children"*: Ibid., 60.

p. 9 *"I was Miss Mozart"*: Ibid., 87.

p. 10 *coy*: Asked by Elspeth Rostow in 1964 whether he had expected Kennedy that night, Joe replied: "No, not at all. I nearly fell off my chair. [Laughter] I couldn't fall off my chair because I wasn't in a chair. This is very funny. I neither expected him nor had invited him." Joseph W. Alsop Oral History Interview, June 18, 1964, John F. Kennedy Presidential Library. But Joe's stepson, Bill Patten observes that while "Joe liked to characterize the presidential visit as 'impromptu,' it was, of course, far more choreographed. Given the security concerns, it would have to have been carefully planned." William S. Patten, *My Three Fathers: And the Elegant Deceptions of My Mother, Susan Mary Alsop* (New York: PublicAffairs, 2008), 205. There was, too, the spirit of well-bred nonchalance to be upheld before history; it would have been altogether non-U to have *arranged* such a thing, rather as though Raleigh had concerted in advance with the Queen to lay his cloak before her.

p. 10 *"several more bottles of champagne"*: Joseph W. Alsop, *"I've Seen the Best of It": Memoirs*, ed. Adam Platt (New York: Norton, 1992), 434.

p. 10 *"butt of teasing"*: Robert W. Merry, *Taking on the World: Joseph and Stewart Alsop—Guardians of the American Century* (New York: Penguin, 1997), 26.

p. 10 *toff*: Strictly speaking, an English usage, a corruption of *tuft*, the gold tassel that adorned the caps once worn by undergraduates of noble lineage at Oxford and Cambridge. Hence a *tuft-hunter*, one who, like the Oxford youth in Thackeray's novel *A Shabby Genteel Story*, followed "with a kind of proud obsequiousness all the *tufts* of the university."

p. 10 *Benson & Hedges cigarette*: Edwin M. Yoder Jr., *Joe Alsop's Cold War: A Study of Journalistic Influence and Intrigue* (Chapel Hill: University of North Carolina Press, 1995), 6.

p. 10 *would beat him down*: "Tales of his bullying and rhetorical excesses (even at his own dinner parties, and certainly at others) swirled about him. Yoder, *Joe Alsop's Cold War*, 4.

p. 11 *"nightmare"*: Merry, *Taking on the World*, 490.

p. 11 *"American, since no other"*: Ibid., 491.

p. 11 *"Boy, get me a pencil"*: Merry, *Taking on the World*, 44.

p. 11 *"style of life"*: Joseph Alsop, *F.D.R.: A Centenary Remembrance* (New York: Viking, 1982), 157.

p. 11 *"like a rather old-fashioned"*: Ibid., 156.

p. 11 *"extreme puritanism"*: Ibid., 157.

p. 11 *"being the President's department"*: Ibid., 156.

p. 12 *"power and resources"*: Joseph Alsop and Robert Kintner, *American White Paper: The Story of American Diplomacy and the Second World War* (London: Michael Joseph, 1940), 132.

p. 12 *Persians and the Greeks*: Merry, *Taking on the World*, 166–67, 568.

p. 13 Yellow Book: "Although Wilde never wrote for *The Yellow Book*, he was generally identified with it, partly because of the reputation he enjoyed as the arch-decadent of the movement and partly because of his association with the art editor, Aubrey Beardsley, who had earlier illustrated his Salome." Gertrude Himmelfarb, *The De-Moralization of Society: From Victorian Virtues to Modern Values* (New York: Vintage, 1996), 212.

p. 13 *piped with lilac*: Rosemary Mahoney, *A Likely Story* (New York: Anchor, 1999), 262.

p. 13 *2720 Dumbarton Avenue*: The account of Alsop's life there is derived principally from Merry, *Taking on the World*, Alsop, *I've Seen the Best of It*, Patten, *My Three Fathers*, and Gregg Herken, *The Georgetown Set: Friends and Rivals in Cold War Washington* (New York: Vintage, 2015).

p. 13 *His mind was baroque*: On Alsop's "baroque personality," see Yoder, *Joe Alsop's Cold War*, 10.

p. 14 *"high Oxonian"*: So his stepson, Bill Patten, characterizes Joe's dialect in his elegant memoir. See Patten, *My Three Fathers*, 201. But Joe never studied at Oxford; I should think his manner of speaking better described as old WASP or Groton-Porcellian.

p. 14 *"two or three best"*: Merry, *Taking on the World*, 477.

p. 14 *"Isaiah"*: Ibid., 360.

p. 14 *In fact everybody did not know*: Bill Patten tells of encountering his godfather, Charles Devens, who was Alsop's friend and classmate at Groton and Harvard, in the Somerset Club in Boston in the 1990s. Devens had recently read Robert Merry's *Taking on the World*. "My God," he exclaimed to Patten. "I had never realized until I read this book that Joe was a homosexual! Is it true?" Patten, *My Three Fathers*, 229.

p. 14 *"Oh, he's one"*: Merry, *Taking on the World*, 362. As a young man, David Satter, a former Rhodes scholar who has spent much of his career studying Russia, worked closely with Alsop. "Years later," Satter said, "people asked me if there was a homoerotic element" in his relationship with the older man, "but during those years when I was 19 to 28 years old, I was totally unaware of any." On the contrary, "I assumed that Joe was homophobic because he frequently ridiculed gays in private conversation. It was only later that I understood that that was his way of concealing his orientation and warning people off any attempt to hint at it." James Kirchick, "Joe Alsop and America's Forgotten Code," *The Atlantic*, February 15, 2017.

p. 14 *"sweep of a popular gay"*: Herken, *Georgetown Set*, 421; Merry, *Taking on the World*, 361.

p. 14 *graver consequences*: The account of Alsop's entrapment is derived principally from Merry, *Taking on the World*; Herken, *Georgetown Set*; and Kirchick, "Joe Alsop and America's Forgotten Code," *The Atlantic*, February 15, 2017.

p. 15 *could not long remain undetected*: K. A. Cuordileone, *Manhood and American Political Culture in the Cold War* (New York: Routledge, 2005), 65.

p. 15 *wide circulation*: Merry, *Taking on the World*, 363.

p. 15 *real or affected*: Harold Bloom believed that Whitman was tormented by "his quasi-autistic psychosexual sufferings." The "rough self" was a "persona or mask . . ." Bloom, *The Western Canon: The Books and School of the Ages* (New York: Harcourt Brace, 1995), 267, 271.

p. 15 *four days straight*: Merry, *Taking on the World,* 306.

p. 15 *preppy lassitude and impotent liberalism*: Alsop had at one time been impressed by Stevenson, but he soon changed his mind. See Yoder, *Joe Alsop's Cold War*, 89–93.

p. 15 *"sickness of the soul"*: Merry, *Taking on the World*, 167.

p. 16 *"I can still summon"*: Alsop, *I've Seen the Best of It*, 434.

p. 16 *"Jackie and the President"*: Alsop, *I've Seen the Best of It*, 436–38.

p. 16 *"sought a beard"*: The account of Alsop's marriage is drawn primarily from Patten, *My Three Fathers*.

p. 16 *shrewd of Arthur*: Patten, *My Three Fathers,* 186.

p. 17 *"tough & appreciative little guest"*: *The Letters of Nancy Mitford and Evelyn Waugh*, ed. Charlotte Mosley (Boston: Houghton Mifflin, 1996), 313–15.

p. 17 *"very shy, complicated, brave and fine man"*: Patten, *My Three Fathers*, 186. Susan Mary seems initially to have been cold to Joe's suit, even as he piqued her interest by making much of his closeness to John F. Kennedy, who was then running for president. "I tell him," she wrote to a friend, "that much as I enjoy his letters I really don't want to marry him." Patten, *My Three Fathers*, 184. A cynic might note that, with her love of glamour and proximity to the great, she accepted Joe's proposal only *after* Kennedy won the White House. "If my mother was susceptible to any aphrodisiac," her son wrote, "it was political power." Had Nixon won the election, might she not have taken her chances and remained in Paris?

p. 17   *"large bumpers of goodish wine"*: *Letters of Nancy Mitford and Evelyn Waugh*, 189.

p. 17   *"cold mutton"*: "The first these ten years, and it will be the last. It was like cold mutton." So Oscar Wilde told Ernest Dowson after a visit to a French whorehouse. "But tell it in England, for it will entirely restore my character." See *The Autobiography of W. B. Yeats* (New York: Collier, 1965), 219.

p. 17   *Joe and his fellow WASPs were only too delighted*: The "Kennedy style," E. Digby Baltzell observed, "acted like a magnet" in drawing high WASPs to Washington. E. Digby Baltzell, *The Protestant Establishment: Aristocracy & Caste in America* (New Haven, Conn.: Yale University Press, 1987), 306.

p. 18   *Early in 1965*: The account of Edie Sedgwick that follows is drawn principally from Stein, *Edie*.

p. 20   *commonplace*: See accounts of the 1966 Black and White Ball, which a number of contemporary observers compared to the decadence of the French aristocracy in the latter days of the old regime.

p. 20   *"was just* watching*"*: Stein, *Edie*, 209.

p. 20   *Sade*: Emile de Antonio, an acquaintance of Edie's, said that "Andy's like the Marquis de Sade in the sense that his very presence was a releasing agent which released people so they could live out their fantasies and get undressed . . ." He also liked to humiliate people, prevailing on one young woman to be filmed "blowing a guy and being buggered by another guy at the same time. It may be what she had always wanted to do, but I doubt she wanted to do it on the couch at Andy's studio with a camera on hand." Stein, *Edie*, 239.

p. 20   *atone*: "I'd like to recall a side of his character that he hid from all but his closest friends: his spiritual side," the art historian John Richardson said in his eulogy of Warhol in St. Patrick's Cathedral in New York in April 1987. "Those of you who knew him in circumstances that were the antithesis of spiritual may be surprised that such a side existed. But exist it did, and it's the key to the artist's psyche." Richardson pointed out that "this secret piety" led to "at least one conversion" and inspired Warhol to subsidize his nephew's studies for the priesthood. "Andy's religion didn't surface in his work until two or three Christmases ago," concluded Richardson, who called the Last Supper series "a major breakthrough in religious art." See Richardson, "Eulogy for Andy Warhol," in *Great American Catholic Eulogies*, ed. Carol DeChant, Gregory F. Augustine Pierce, and L. C. Fiore (Chicago: ACTA Publications, 2011) (ebook available online).

p. 21   *"Fate, the Press, the Congress, the Intellectuals"*: Kai Bird, *The Color of Truth: McGeorge Bundy and William Bundy: Brothers in Arms* (New York: Simon & Schuster, 1998), 338.

p. 21   *"I blew my top"*: Walter Isaacson and Evan Thomas, *The Wise Men: Six Friends and the World They Made* (New York: Touchstone, 1988), 652.

p. 21   *"to land war"*: Isaacson and Thomas, *Wise Men*, 653.

p. 22   *"You've got to do it"*: Ibid., 650.

p. 22   *"can be argued"*: Bird, *Color of Truth*, 403.

p. 22   *"do it his way"*: Ibid.

p. 22   *"Did it ever occur to you"*: Ibid., 275.

p. 23   *"I didn't think"*: Merry, *Taking on the World*, 406.

p. 23   *"You haven't put"*: "Telephone Conversation between the President and Mr. Joe Alsop, November 25, 1963, 10:40 a.m.," typescript in the Lyndon Baines Johnson Library and Museum.

p. 23   *"like a very old dog"*: Merry, *Taking on the World*, 428.

p. 23   *"Oh, my word"*: Ibid., 425.

p. 24   *"a little old war"*: Bird, *Color of Truth*, 274.

p. 24   *"didn't ask questions"*: Merry, *Taking on the World*, 429.

p. 24   *"You're the epitome"*: Ibid., 424.

p. 24   *Sham briefing*: Isaacson and Thomas, *Wise Men*, 686.

p. 24   *"we can and will win"*: Douglas Brinkley, *Dean Acheson: The Cold War Years, 1953–1971* (New Haven, Conn.: Yale University Press, 1992), 254.

p. 24   *Joe Mayflower*: Art Buchwald maintained, perhaps not very convincingly, that he did *not* have Alsop in mind when he composed his 1969 comedy *Sheep on the Runway*: he pointed to another journalist, Joe Kraft. Yoder, *Joe Alsop's Cold War*, 22–23.

p. 24   *joined the jacquerie*: See Capote's story, "La Côte Basque, 1965," *Esquire*, November 1, 1975.

p. 25   *"as a Jew"*: Ibid.

p. 25   *"Of course it wasn't an accident"*: Ibid.

p. 25   *"Well, that's that"*: *Vanity Fair's Writers on Writers*, ed. Graydon Carter (New York: Penguin, 2016), 95.

p. 25   *"The story about the sheets"*: George Plimpton, *Truman Capote* (New York: Anchor, 1998), 347.

p. 25   *"Truman with total loathing"*: Gerald Clarke, "Bye Society," *Vanity Fair*, April 1988.

p. 27   *"He was a very disagreeable man"*: John Eligon, "Fight for Astor Estate Mirrors Battle 50 Years Ago," *New York Times*, April 25, 2009.

p. 27   *"American aristocrat"*: Alsop, *F.D.R.*, 157.

p. 28   *"never went out at night"*: Michael Knox Beran, "The Aristocracy and Its Discontents," *Wall Street Journal*, July 23, 2009.

p. 28   *"that bitch"*: Ibid.

2. A DYING RACE

p. 31   *"tendency to suicidal mania"*: Natalie Dykstra, *Clover Adams: A Gilded and Heartbreaking Life* (Boston: Houghton Mifflin, 2012), 210.

p. 31   *"dismal tidings"*: *The Journals and Miscellaneous Notebooks of Ralph Waldo Emerson 1852–1855*, ed. Ralph H. Orth and Alfred R. Ferguson (Cambridge, Mass.: Belknap Press, 1977), 177.

p. 31   *"the family disease"*: John Sedgwick, *In My Blood: Six Generations of Madness and Desire in an American Family* (New York: HarperCollins, 2007), 9–10.

p. 31   *"queerness"*: M. A. DeWolfe Howe, *John Jay Chapman and His Letters* (Boston: Houghton Mifflin, 1937), 21.

p. 31   *"mysterious gestures"*: Ibid., 22.

p. 32   *"thought seriously"*: *The Selected Letters of Louisa May Alcott*, ed. Joel Myerson, Daniel Shealy, and Madeleine B. Stern (Athens: University of Georgia Press, 1995), xxi.

p. 32   *"wrestle with nature"*: Henry Adams, *The Life of George Cabot Lodge* (Boston: Houghton Mifflin, 1911), 16.

p. 32   *"shrouded in a blackness"*: Melville's description of Hawthorne's art.

p. 33   *"scarcely have earned . . . ornamental"*: Henry Adams, *The Education of Henry Adams* (Boston: Houghton Mifflin, 1918), 238.

p. 33   *"parasites"*: George Santayana, *The Middle Span* (New York: Scribner's, 1945), 113.

p. 33   *"our strongest"*: Theodore Roosevelt, *An Autobiography* (New York: Macmillan, 1916), 210.

p. 34   *"trained and public-spirited caste"*: Edmund Wilson, "John Jay Chapman," in Wilson, *The Triple Thinkers and the Wound and the Bow: A Combined Volume* (Boston: Northeastern University Press, 1984), 150.

p. 34   *"grey debris"*: Walt Whitman, "When Lilacs Last in the Door-yard Bloom'd."

p. 34   *"mediocre drabs"*: Lewis Mumford, *The Brown Decades: A Study in the Arts of America 1865–1895* (New York: Dover, 1955), 5.

p. 34   *"a dying race"*: Adams, *Life of George Cabot Lodge*, 130.

p. 34   *plutocracy that had outstripped it*: Seymour Martin Lipset believed that WASP Progressives were "American Tory radicals—men of upper-class backgrounds and values, who as conservatives helped to democratize society as part of their struggle against the vulgar *nouveaux riche* businessman." Seymour Martin Lipset, *Political Man: The Social Bases of Politics* (New York: Doubleday, 1960), 299. Lipset drew on Richard Hofstadter's *The Age of Reform*, in which Hofstadter argued that the resentment of Mugwump WASPs like Henry Adams played a part in the WASP quest for civic and political reform. See chapter nine above, "The Madonnas of Henry Adams."

p. 34   *"beating his head"*: Wilson, "John Jay Chapman," in Wilson, *Triple Thinkers*, 151.

p. 35   *"detective"*: Richard B. Hovey, *John Jay Chapman: An American Mind* (New York: Columbia University Press, 1959), 48.

p. 35   *"effort at the Perfect"*: See Emerson's "Lecture on the Times."

p. 35   *"hideous weeks"*: Adams, *Life of George Cabot Lodge*, 33.

p. 35   *"losing my grip"*: Ibid., 31.

p. 35   *"work with the tide"*: Ibid., 34.

p. 35   *"adapt myself"*: Ibid. "I work five hours a day or six, and what on—a miserable little poetaster. . . . I said to myself that I ought to go home in order to get into the tide of American life if for nothing else; that I oughtn't to be dreaming and shrieking inside and poetizing and laboring on literature here in Paris, supported by my father, and that I ought to go home and live very hard making money. I said to myself that I knew I could not be very quick at money-making, but that at any rate in the eyes of men I should lead a self-respecting life and my hideous, utter failure would only be for myself and you, who understand. But somehow all the while my soul refused to believe the plain facts and illogically clung to the belief that I might do some good in creative work in the world after all, and so I struggled with the facts and my faiths and loves and there was the Devil of a row inside me and I most wretched." Adams, *Life of George Cabot Lodge*, 32, 34–35.

p. 35   *"the most brilliant"*: Edith Wharton, *A Backward Glance* (New York: Touchstone, 1998), 149.

p. 35   *"a hot-house"*: Ibid., 150.

p. 35   *"turning sick and cold"*: Adams, *Life of George Cabot Lodge*, 43.

p. 36   *"bewildered efforts"*: Van Wyck Brooks, *New England: Indian Summer 1865–1915* (New York: Dutton, 1937), 426 (note).

p. 36   *"lack of nerve-force"*: George M. Beard, *American Nervousness: Its Causes and Consequences* (New York: G.P. Putnam's Sons, 1881), 5ff.

p. 37   *hell was good*: "To reach Heaven, you must go through hell, and carry its marks on your face and figure," says a character in Adams's novel *Esther*.

p. 37   *"philosophic depression"*: Adams, *Life of George Cabot Lodge*, 22.

p. 37   *barbarians*: The "*Nation* & Harvard & Yale College," Charles Eliot Norton said, "seem to me almost the only solid barriers against the invasion of modern barbarism & vulgarity." Richard Hofstadter, *Anti-intellectualism in American Life* (New York: Knopf, 1963), 174.

p. 38   *"is formless"*: *Emerson in His Journals*, ed. Joel Porte (Cambridge, Mass.: Belknap Press, 1982), 372.

p. 38   *possibilities we seem to have lost*: The conviction of eminent WASPs that they were failing to live up to the higher possibilities of their being might well have been a symptom of the psychological phenomenon *Humanitis civici*, in which individuals labor under the delusion that there are aspects of their nature that are not being done justice to. See Phillippe Bléterie, *L'illusion humaine* (Nîmes: Éditions Onomacrite, 1956), 14–26. What is needed is a better understanding of the conditions in which *Humanitis civici* thrives and of the stimuli that exacerbate it. Sensitive to the sufferings of others (some of whom are, indeed, very near to him), the inquirer asks himself whether there are not more effective cures (perhaps pharmaceutical in nature) than those proposed by the characters who figure in this book. The WASPs' dream of a cure for their morbidities by means of "regeneration," a search for human "completeness" through the creation of humane forums, fair sheepfolds, Athenian *agorai*, revived Florences, etc., seems, perhaps, to have been not entirely realistic.

p. 38   *lukewarm bath*: This was George Orwell's characterization of Eton College.

3. MRS. JACK GARDNER AND HER UNLIKELY SWAN

p. 40   *Proper Bostonians*: See Cleveland Amory, *The Proper Bostonians* (New York: E.P. Dutton, 1947).

p. 40   *she had to be lifted*: Douglass Shand-Tucci, *The Art of Scandal: The Life and Times of Isabella Steward Gardner* (New York: Harper Perennial, 1997), 15.

p. 40   *"neither friends, nor lovers"*: Henry James to Grace Norton, August 2, 1884, in *The Complete Letters of Henry James, 1883–1884*, ed. Michael Anesko, Greg W. Zacharias, and Katie Sommer (Lincoln: University of Nebraska Press, 2018), I, xl.

p. 41 George Apley: John P. Marquand, *The Late George Apley* (New York: Back Bay, 2004), 3. Marquand's
       Apley has, to be sure, Strether-like moments when he is tempted to rebel against his environment, when
       he regrets that his "life has been governed by blue-nosed bigots who have been in their graves for a century . . ."
       "Have any of us really lived? Sometimes I am not entirely sure . . ." Marquand, *The Late George Apley*, 17,
       176. But as a Proper Bostonian he does his best to suppress such dangerous thoughts.

p. 41 *become what you are*: The words from Pindar's second Pythian Ode have been variously mistranslated:
       "Become the one you are" (Nietzsche), "Become such as you are, having learned what that is" (William
       Race), "Be what you know you are" (Barbara Fowler). See Babette E. Babich, *Words in Blood like Flowers:
       Philosophy and Poetry, Music and Eros in Hölderlin, Nietzsche, and Heidegger* (Albany: State University of
       New York Press, 2006), 75. At the other end of the spectrum, Buddha would have you overcome and
       transcend what you are. And what if what you are is not good? In that case you had better not become what
       you are. See on this point a book by the philosopher Brian Weatherson, *Normative Externalism* (Oxford,
       U.K.: Oxford University Press, 2019).

p. 41 *rare flower*: Telephone conversation with Louis Auchincloss, 2003.

p. 41 *"C'est mon Plaisir"*: It was Mrs. Jack's motto. See Hilliard T. Goldfarb, *The Isabella Stewart Gardner
       Museum: A Companion Guide and History* (New Haven, Conn.: Yale University Press, 1995), 18.

p. 41 *"queenliness"*: Leon Edel, *Henry James: A Life* (New York: Harper & Row, 1985), 579.

p. 41 *"not a woman"*: Shand-Tucci, *Art of Scandal*, 46.

p. 41 *"one of the handsomest men"*: Ibid., 44.

p. 42 *knew Italy*: Knew it, a contemporary said, "as a man might know the rooms of his own house." Shand-
       Tucci, *Art of Scandal*, 50.

p. 42 *Urdu*: Ibid., 49.

p. 42 *"yes" to life*: Mrs. Gardner's friend, Professor Santayana of Harvard, deplored the modern inclination to say
       "yes" to everything, to insist, as we so often do today, that "it's all good," rather than to discriminate the
       more perfect and the more choice. He looked upon such yea-sayers as Nietzsche and Whitman as hairy
       barbarians who preferred a romantically wild and unruly chaos to the classical virtues of reason, order, and
       harmonious proportion.

p. 42 *"gloom-dispeller"*: Shand-Tucci, *Art of Scandal*, 23.

p. 42 *"He was a rash man"*: Edmund Gosse, *The Life of Algernon Charles Swinburne* (New York: Macmillan, 1917),
       71.

p. 43 *brilliant*: Henry James to Isabella Stewart Gardner, July 22, 1879, in *The Complete Letters of Henry James:
       1878–1880*, ed. Pierre A. Walker and Greg W. Zacharias (Lincoln: University of Nebraska Press, 2014), I,
       244.

p. 43 *"bright eyes"*: Ruskin, *Præterita: Outlines of Scenes and Thoughts Perhaps Worthy of Memory in My Past Life*, in
       The Complete Works of John Ruskin, ed. E. T. Cook and Alexander Wedderburn (London: George Allen,
       1908), XXV, 519.

p. 43 *"an example of integrity"*: Shand-Tucci, *Art of Scandal*, 38.

p. 43 *"mixture of devotion and rigor"*: *Gardner Memorial: A Biographical and Genealogical Record of the Descendants
       of Thomas Gardner, Planter*, ed. Frank Augustine Gardner (Salem, Mass.: Newcomb and Gauss, 1933), 219.

p. 43 *"the best educated man"*: Howe, *John Jay Chapman*, 35.

p. 43 *"best scholar"*: Ibid.

p. 44 *"fairy tales"*: Ellery Sedgwick, "Three Men of Groton," in *Views from the Circle*, 15.

p. 44 *suspicious*: Shand-Tucci, *Art of Scandal*, 55.

p. 44 *learned that a cousin*: "The future headmaster of Groton had been setting forth to Billings his concept that
       it should be possible to direct a boys' school upon a plane of well-nigh ideal human relationship between
       masters and students, traditional friction giving way to mutual respect in a close and vital fellowship in
       study and in all daily pursuits. In this view Billings warmly shared . . . They approached Amory Gardner
       with the suggestion that he join with them as a teacher, and the proposal met with ready acceptance."
       Gardner Memorial, ed. Gardner, 220.

4. HENRY ADAMS FAILS TO REFORM AMERICA

p. 45   *"You'll be thinkin'"*: Adams, *Education*, 16.

p. 46   *rather the reverse*: The "old man was in a high degree obnoxious to me," Adams said, and he urged his
brother Brooks not to publish an admiring portrait of "this slovenly German *gelehrte* whose highest delight
is to lecture boys about a rhetoric [John Quincy Adams had been Boylston Professorship of Rhetoric
and Oratory at Harvard] of which he never could practice either the style or the action or the voice or
the art, and then gloating over his own foolish production in print, instead of rolling on the ground with
mortification as his grandchildren would do—this picture grinds the [indecipherable] into my aesophagus . . ."
A long passage of vituperation follows. See Garry Wills, *Henry Adams and the Making of America* (Boston:
Houghton Mifflin, 2005), 13.

p. 46   *"was a matter of course"*: Adams, *Education*, 46.

p. 46   *"passionate outburst"*: For the story of Adams being escorted to school by his grandfather, see Adams,
Education, 12–13.

p. 46   *"like white Greek temples"*: For Adams's boyhood visit to Washington, see Adams, *Education*, 44–49.

p. 47   *"half thought he owned it"*: Ibid. 46.

p. 47   *"Tall, largely built"*: For Adams's relations with the Harvard Virginians, see Adams, *Education,* 57–59.

p. 48   *"on the correctness of his estimate"*: Ibid.. 107.

p. 48   *"melancholy function"*: Ibid., 57–59.

p. 48   *Garibaldi*: Adams first met Garibaldi in Sicily before he encountered him again in London.

p. 48   *"to half the dukes and duchesses"*: Adams, *Education*, 203.

p. 48   *instructing the philosopher*: Mill embraced the "infant industry doctrine" justifying protection in 1848 in
the first edition of his *Principles of Political Economy*. He later changed his mind. But he was familiar with the
arguments on both sides of the question, and it is unlikely that Adams could tell him very much that he
did not already know.

p. 48   *encounter with Milnes and the society of the Old World*: After his graduation from Harvard, Adams spent
some two years in Europe. But it was later, during his service in London as private secretary to his father,
that he ceased to be a tourist and became something like a participant in the life of a European country.
The effect of such encounters on the mind of a young American is apt to be great, and Adams himself never
forgot a garden party at Chiswick. See Adams, *Education*, 118. Farther up the Thames, near the walled
physic garden (*paradaijah*) of Sir Hans Sloane, who purchased the manor of Chelsea from Lord Cheyne,
on whose walk Coffee-house Miller died (April 27, 1744) discontented in his lodgings, "as if some over-
ruling Planet hung over his Destiny, and determined to banish Success entirely from him," were others
from beyond the sea come to London with New World conceit. Yet they were soon chastened; and in a
Queen Anne house a young grammarian might know things unknowable in a low-lying suburb. He swept
up the leaves that fell that fall anxiously, for the lease entered into with Lord Cadogan required that the
forecourt of Number Two be kept scrupulously clean.

p. 49   *"scandalized his parents"*: The European "idea of attaching one's self to a married woman, or of polishing
one's manners to suit the standards of women of thirty, could hardly have entered the mind of a young
Bostonian, and would have scandalized his parents." The pun is consummate Adams. See Adams,
Education, 40.

p. 49   *"grove of barren fig-trees called London Society"*: James Pope-Hennessy, *Monckton Milnes: The Flight of Youth
1851–1855* (New York: Farrar, Straus & Cudahy, 1955), 46. At all events it was not the *barrenness* of
London that was likely to strike a young American, then or later. On Lord Cheyne's walk, George was
Four, and the ghosts of Barrymore (thespian) and Brittain (nurse) haunted Two, where (when it was a
rooming house) Jane, retiring from the intensity of her historian at 24 Cheyne Row, would pass a few
peaceful hours in a room temporarily of her own. The grammarian finds himself turning in memory to
that encounter with an older civilization, to the iron boot-scraper at the front of Two, the sinister (by
this time disused) coal-pit in the cellar, the artist's studio at the back of the small garden. In that derelict
space, with the discarded Victorian chimney-pieces and the moldering bottles of linseed oil, you could

smell the Pre-Raphaelite model: a voluptuousness that found its counterpart in the old carved chimney-piece in the attic bedroom, the image of a sensuousness unknown in the land of χαναάν. The grammarian knew nothing, at the time, of his confreres in such initiations, but their shades squeaked and gibbered beside him on the Forty-Nine bus he rode up from the King's Road to school each morning, the bus old Tom rode when he lived in the walk (in Carlyle Mansions), much haunted by the ghost of another habitué of that place, old Harry himself, the artist of these hysteria-making encounters. See Barbara Hardy, *Henry James: The Later Writing* (Liverpool: Northcote, 1997), 11; "Reflections: Mr. Eliot," *Time,* March 6, 1950. ("He left his flat . . . wearing an impeccable dark blue suit and carrying a tightly rolled umbrella, and walked one block to the No. Forty-Nine bus stop. When the bus came, he mounted to the upper deck, unfolded his London *Times* to the crossword puzzle, and fell to . . .") [The inquirer must here differ from the grammarian in his estimate of the virtues of this ancient régime voluptuousness. "Thus it was that the little Jameses not only bore themselves proudly through their childhood as became those who had lived as babies in Piccadilly, and read *Punch* with a proprietary instinct, but were also possessed in spirit by something that was more than the discontent with the flatness of daily life and the desire for a brighter scene that comes to the ordinary child. From their father's preoccupation they gained a rationalised consciousness that America was an incomplete environment, that in Europe there were many mines of treasure which they must find and rifle if they hoped for the health of their minds and the salvation of their souls." Rebecca West, *Henry James* (Port Washington, N.Y.: Kennikat Press, 1968), 13. This romantic adulation of Europe was, the inquirer believes, precisely the original sin of the WASPs: it underlay their refusal to comprehend the poetry of their own country, and led them to lose themselves in a tepid romance with a foreign one.]

p. 49   *British patricians*: Here was another way in which Adams's encounter with the Old World altered his point of view: after his exposure he shrank from the narrow career of a lawyer. One could hardly "pass five years in Europe," he wrote, "and remain a candidate for the bar." His new object was to be a "philosophical statesman." Ernest Samuels, *Henry Adams* (Cambridge, Mass.: Belknap Press, 1989), 66, 74. For the "sacred rage," see James's *The Ambassadors* and Robert Dawidoff, *The Genteel Tradition and the Sacred Rage: High Culture vs. Democracy in Adams, James, and Santayana* (Chapel Hill: University of North Carolina Press, 1992).

p. 49   *a movement of his own*: On Adams's vocation as a "social and political reformer," one whose "mission" could give significance to his "literary and political action," see Samuels, *Henry Adams*, 64–66.

p. 49   *"we want"*: Henry Adams to Charles Francis Adams Jr., November 21, 1862, in *Henry Adams: Selected Letters*, ed. Ernest Samuels (Cambridge, Mass.: Belknap Press, 1992), 51.

p. 49   *"capital, banks"*: Adams, *Education*, 240.

p. 50   *habitable for civilized people*: Ibid., 239.

p. 50   *"twenty-million horse-power"*: Ibid., 375.

p. 50   *"mere private citizens"*: Henry Adams, "The New York Gold Conspiracy," in C. F. Adams Jr., and Henry Adams, *Chapters of Erie, and Other Essays* (Boston: Osgood, 1871), 134.

p. 50   *"smirched executive"*: Adams, *Education*, 271–272.

p. 50   *"one of reform"*: Adams, *Education*, 263.

p. 50   *"evidence enough to upset Darwin"*: Ibid., 266.

p. 50   *"political camp"*: Adams, *Education*, 256.

p. 50   *"introduced Cæsarism"*: Charles Francis Adams Jr., "A Chapter of Erie," in Adams and Adams, *Chapters of Erie*, 12.

p. 51   *"overpowering beauty"*: Ibid., 255.

p. 51   *"loved it too much"*: Ibid., 268.

p. 51   *"command attention"*: Ibid., 258.

p. 51   *"in a coil of political intrigue"*: Samuels, *Henry Adams*, 85.

p. 51   *"party of the centre"*: Ibid., 117; Ari Hoogenboom, "Henry Adams and Politics," in *Henry Adams and His World*, ed. David R. Contosta and Robert Muccigrosso (Philadelphia: The American Philosophical Society, 1993), 35.

p. 51   "Mayflower *screwball*": Lowell, "Waking in the Blue."

p. 51   *"madman possessed"*: John Adams to Abigail Adams, October 12, 1799, Adams Family Papers, Massachusetts Historical Society.

p. 52   *"legitimate politics"*: Samuels, *Henry Adams*, 119–120.

p. 52   *"altogether too much"*: William S. Robinson, *"Warrington" Pen-Portraits*, ed. Mrs. W. S. Robinson (Boston: Lee and Shepard, 1877), 420.

p. 52   *"My disease"*: Edward Chalfant, *Better in Darkness: A Biography of Henry Adams, His Second Life 1862–1891* (Hamden, Conn.: Archon Books, 1994), 588. Adams's nervous discontent was sufficiently real at times to make him question the reformist enterprise to which he had pledged himself. Having begun to make a literary reputation for himself by publishing historical essays in the *North American Review*, he fell into a funk and told his brother Charles that he would never "make a speech, never run for an office, never belong to a party. I am going to plunge under the stream. For years you will hear nothing of any publication of mine—perhaps never, who knows. I do not mean to tie myself to anything, but I do mean to make it impossible for myself to follow the family go-cart." The mood passed. See Samuels, *Henry Adams*, 71–72.

p. 52   *Voltaire*: Dykstra, *Clover Adams*, xiii.

p. 52   *"Heavens!—no!"*: *Henry Adams: Selected Letters*, ed. Samuels, 187.

p. 52   *"seventies"*: Samuels, *Henry Adams*, 205.

p. 53   *died hard*: Adams was far from being ready to sympathize, at this period in his life, with the apolitical instincts of his older brother John, who "laughed at the idea of sacrificing himself in order to adorn a Cleveland cabinet or get cheers from an Irish mob." Henry Adams to Charles Milnes Gaskell, September 27, 1894, in *The Letters of Henry Adams 1892–1918*, ed. Worthington Chauncey Ford (Boston: Houghton Mifflin, 1938), 55.

p. 53   *"the only place in America"*: Henry Adams to Charles Milnes Gaskell, November 25, 1877, in *The Letters of Henry Adams 1868–1885*, ed. J. C. Levenson, et al. (Cambridge, Mass.: Belknap Press, 1982), II, 326.

p. 53   *"most to block his intended path"*: Adams, *Education*, 332.

5. COTTY PEABODY LEAVES THE BANK

p. 54   *"wonderful specimen"*: Frank Ashburn, *Peabody of Groton: A Portrait* (Cambridge, Mass.: Riverside Press, 1967), 34.

p. 55   *"poetic blue-water phase"*: George Santayana, *Persons and Places: The Background of My Life* (New York: Scribner's, 1944), 59.

p. 55   *"a most audacious fellow"*: Ashburn, *Peabody of Groton*, 15.

p. 55   *"a nameless sadness"*: Ibid., 110.

p. 55   *"doesn't lead to anything"*: Ibid., 36.

p. 55   *"the ugliness of everything"*: Howe, *John Jay Chapman*, 48.

p. 55   *"colouring of other times"*: Wordsworth, *The Prelude*.

p. 55   *"barren of romance and grace"*: Henry James, "At Isella," in James, *Travelling Companions* (New York: Boni and Liveright, 1919), 144. The grammarian himself experienced a drop when he returned to his native lowland of χαναάν. Leafless trees, shingled colonials of varying degrees of spuriousness, an encompassing drabness. There stood the condo of the fat boy they once teased, there was the spot where the school bus ran over the dog, there stood the house where a mother and her children were burnt to death in Betsy's Lane on Thanksgiving Day. The grammarian concedes that he can hardly separate his idea of the WASPs from his own personal experience, insofar as it was intertwisted with theirs. While making no pretense to virtue, he wishes that others who dabble in the pack of tricks we call history would as candidly confess their own predispositions.

p. 55   *"What a horrible day"*: Ashburn, *Peabody of Groton*, 60.

p. 56   *"I turned to Phillips Brooks"*: Ibid., 39.

p. 56   *"to do some good in the world"*: Ashburn, *Peabody of Groton*, 106.

p. 56   *"a dominant and dominating"*: Frank Ashburn, *Fifty Years On: Groton School 1884–1934* (New York: Gosden Head, 1934), 9.

p. 56   *"an impenetrable cloud"*: Ashburn, *Peabody of Groton*, 63.

p. 56   *"was not really backsliding"*: Santayana, *Middle Span*, 102.

p. 57   *"the rottenest place"*: Paula Mitchell Marks, *And Die in the West: The Story of the O.K. Corral Gunfight* (Norman: University of Oklahoma Press, 1989), 323.

p. 57   *"hoodlums"*: For Peabody's experience in Tucson, see Benjamin Welles, *Sumner Welles: F.D.R.'s Global Strategist* (New York: Palgrave Macmillan, 1997).

p. 57   *"a parson who doesn't flirt with the girls"*: Ashburn, *Peabody of Groton*, 49.

p. 57   *"largely legendary"*: Ashburn, *Fifty Years On*, 12 (note).

p. 57   *"I am feeling somewhat blue"*: Ashburn, *Peabody of Groton*, 52–53.

p. 57   *"It is a grand gift"*: Ibid., 60.

p. 58   *not even a man of the cloth*: Ashburn, *Fifty Years On*, 13.

p. 58   *English schools*: Peabody "disapproved strongly of many features of the English schools, particularly the House System." Walter S. Hinchman, "My Groton Years," in *Views from the Circle*, 157. He did, however, believe that the English public schools, with all their "glaring defects," were better at promoting character and instilling qualities of leadership than American "prep" schools, narrowly concentrated on readying boys for college entrance exams. See Ashburn, *Peabody of Groton*, 73.

p. 58   *"live together"*: Ashburn, *Peabody of Groton*, 15.

p. 58   *"inner heart"*: Owen Chadwick, *The Victorian Church: Part I 1829–1859* (Eugene, Ore.: Wipf and Stock, 1987), 43.

p. 58   *"ruled remotely"*: Lytton Strachey, *Eminent Victorians* (New York: G.P. Putnam's Sons, 1918), 214–215.

p. 58   *"satirical remarks"*: Ashburn, *Peabody of Groton*, 20.

p. 58   *three of his siblings*: John Endicott Peabody married Gertrude Lawrence; Francis Peabody married Rosamond Lawrence; and Martha Peabody married John Lawrence.

p. 58   *" far from God"*: Ashburn, *Peabody of Groton*, 63.

p. 59   *"It is our purpose"*: Ashburn, *Fifty Years On*, 17.

6. MRS. JACK SEEKS A HUMANIZED SOCIETY

p. 60   *"perpetual youth"*: Shand-Tucci, *Art of Scandal*, 153.

p. 61   *"brash and pushy"*: Ibid., 117.

p. 61   *"monstrous vanity"*: Ernest Samuels, *Bernard Berenson: The Making of a Legend* (Cambridge, Mass.: Belknap Press, 1987), 36.

p. 61   *"the biggest and deepest"*: Shand-Tucci, *Art of Scandal*, 153.

p. 61   *"I am not as stupid"*: Ibid., 183.

p. 62   *"to show Boston"*: Santayana, *Middle Span*, 124.

p. 62   *"literally false"*: see Irwin Edman's preface to his selections from Santayana's works, *The Philosophy of Santayana* (New York: Scribner's, 1953), vi.

p. 62   *"almost by heart"*: Ernest Samuels, *Bernard Berenson: The Making of a Connoisseur* (Cambridge, Mass.: Belknap Press, 1979), 75.

p. 62   *"and meaning to glance"*: Rachel Cohen, *Bernard Berenson: A Life in the Picture Trade* (New Haven, Conn.: Yale University Press, 2013), 39.

p. 62   *"ear and toe-nail school"*: John Brewer, *The American Leonardo: A Tale of Obsession, Art and Money* (Oxford, U.K.: Oxford University Press, 1979), 51.

p. 63   *"our palms and fingers"*: Bernard Berenson, *The Florentine Painters of the Renaissance* (New York: G.P. Putnam's Sons, 1902), 14.

p. 63   *"keen activity"*: Ibid., 71.

p. 63   *"the best vehicle"*: Ibid., 87.

p. 63   *onions and anchovies*: Kenneth Clark, *Another Part of the Wood: A Self Portrait* (New York: Ballantine, 1974), 137; Bernard Berenson, *The Passionate Sightseer: From the Diaries 1947 to 1956* (London: Thames and Hudson, 1960), 44.

p. 63   *"How much"*: Samuels, *Berenson: The Making of a Connoisseur*, 193–94.

p. 63   *"fatal moment"*: Ibid., 308; Shand-Tucci, *Art of Scandal*, 172.

p. 64   *"picture-habit"*: Christina Nielsen, et al., *Isabella Stewart Gardner Museum: A Guide* (New Haven, Conn.: Yale University Press, 2017), 11.

p. 64   *"a terrible row about you"*: Samuels, *Berenson: The Making of a Connoisseur*, 300; Shand-Tucci, *Art of Scandal*, 190; Cohen, *Berenson*, 126.

p. 64   *"mendacity"*: John McCormick, *George Santayana: A Biography* (New York: Knopf, 1987), 240.

p. 64   *"We may between us"*: Shand-Tucci, *Art of Scandal*, 197.

p. 64   *"poetry, music"*: Bernard Berenson, *Aesthetics and History* (Garden City, N.Y.: Doubleday, 1948), 269.

7. THE LOST HAND OF JOHN JAY CHAPMAN

p. 66   *"full of voices, demons"*: Howe, *John Jay Chapman*, 104.

p. 66   *"freedom of limb and motion"*: Ibid., 57.

p. 66   *trifling with her affections*: Hovey, *John Jay Chapman*, 46–47.

p. 66   *"to step on the lawn"*: Howe, *John Jay Chapman*, 59.

p. 66   *"I took off my coat"*: Ibid., 59–60.

p. 67   *"nothing diabolical or insane"*: Ibid., 82.

p. 67   *"There was fire in everything"*: Ibid., 81.

p. 67   *"troublesome handicap"*: Wilson, "John Jay Chapman," in Wilson, *Triple Thinkers*, 150.

p. 67   *"all-around humanism"*: Edmund Wilson, "A Vortex in the Nineties," in Wilson, *The Shores of Light: A Literary Chronicle of the 1920s and 1930s* (Boston: Northeastern University Press, 1985), 110.

p. 67   *"banal in a bourgeois way"*: Edmund Wilson, "The Author at Sixty," in Wilson, *A Piece of My Mind: Reflections at Sixty* (New York: Farrar, Strauss and Cudahy, 1956), 213.

p. 67   *"tragic misunderstanding"*: Wilson, "John Jay Chapman," in Wilson, *Triple Thinkers*, 150.

p. 67   *"a Puritan dread"*: John Jay Chapman, *Memories and Milestones* (New York: Moffat, Yard, 1915), 172.

p. 67   *"as there was in Jay Gould"*: Howe, *John Jay Chapman*, 97.

p. 67   *"to make Harvard large"*: Chapman, *Memories and Milestones*, 174.

p. 68   *"being picked out"*: Chapman, *Memories and Milestones*, 183.

p. 68   *"I confess to having always trespassed"*: Ibid., 19–20.

p. 68   *"a deep sadness about James"*: Ibid., 26.

p. 68   *"horrible fear"*: William James, *The Varieties of Religious Experience: A Study in Human Nature* (London: Longmans, Green, 1905), 160. The sufferer to whom James referred was James himself.

p. 68   *"a tacit understanding"*: Chapman, *Memories and Milestones*, 167–168.

p. 68   *"domestic and approachable"*: For Chapman's account of his Harvard teachers, see Howe, *John Jay Chapman*, 190–94.

p. 68   *"to do with* education": George Santayana, *Character and Opinion in the United States* (New York: Scribner's, 1921), 55 (emphasis added).

p. 68   *"a living angel"*: Gerald Gunther, *Learned Hand: The Man and the Judge* (Cambridge, Mass.: Harvard University Press, 1995), 36.

p. 69   *"That is for you to find out"*: Ibid., 60.

p. 69   *"struggle toward something like reality"*: Hovey, *John Jay Chapman*, 54.

p. 69   "Yours, *yours, I am"*: Hovey, *John Jay Chapman*, 53.

p. 69   *"unfortunate young man"*: Howe, *John Jay Chapman*, 62.

p. 69   *"hardly other than pathological"*: Ibid., 61.

p. 70   *"young soul"*: Werner Jaeger, *Paideia: The Ideals of Greek Culture: Archaic Greece, The Mind of Athens* (Oxford, U.K.: Oxford University Press, 1965), 21.

8. A GLORIOUS AND MOST INTENSELY INTERESTING LIFE

p. 71   *Cotty Peabody's school*: Groton is one of the institutional prisms through which the author has viewed the WASPs in the effort to understand what they were about. Other prisms—the Racquet or Colony clubs in New York, St. Paul's School or Mount Desert Island—would doubtless have offered no less illuminating views of the subject; Groton happened to be the institution with which the author was most familiar. It is an institution which, though it has been studied with much insight by a great number of scholars, is not easily understood by the outsider. Thus Mr. Gardner: "Groton School is perfectly incomprehensible to those who have not belonged to it: only partly comprehensible to those who have belonged to it or still belong. . . . The praise and blame bestowed on it by the world are often ludicrously undeserved. It is in almost equal measure over-praised and under-praised, over-blamed and under-blamed." William Amory Gardner, *Groton Myths and Memories* (Groton and Concord: Rumford Press, 1928), v–vi. What is more, in even the most searching scholarly accounts of the school, the place and its characters never seem the least *alive*. One may hope to say something worthwhile simply because one was there, and knew the place as a living thing: the "I was the man, I suffered, I was there" bit.

p. 72   *"the usual objects of political ambition"*: Adams, *Education*, 347.

p. 72   *"most perfect gentleman"*: Ashburn, *Peabody of Groton*, 128.

p. 72   *"a very attractive and winning personality"*: *Harvard College: Class of 1893 Secretary's Report No. 1* (Cambridge, Mass.: privately printed, 1898), 127.

p. 72   *"Every endeavor"*: Ashburn, *Fifty Years On*, 17.

p. 72   *"vigor and manliness of character"*: Jerome Karabel, *The Chosen: The Hidden History of Admission and Exclusion at Harvard, Yale, and Princeton* (Boston: Mariner, 2006), 25.

p. 72   *"doubt, fear, worry"*: James, *Varieties of Religious Experience*, 95.

p. 73   *"mark of the beast"*: Ibid., 98.

p. 73   *Kentish Manor*: Ashburn, *Peabody*, 91.

p. 73   *"was the first to make friendship"*: Ibid., 256.

p. 74   *"among the very first"*: Santayana, *Persons and Places*, 183.

p. 74   *"became discouraged"*: Marc Eric McClure, *Earnest Endeavors: The Life and Public Work of George Rublee* (Westport, Conn.: Praeger, 2003), 13.

p. 74   *"truly a common life"*: Ibid.

p. 74   *"controlling principle"*: Ibid.

p. 74   *"a glorious and most intensely interesting life"*: M. K. Beran, "A Glorious and Most Intensely Interesting Life," *Groton School Quarterly*, May 1984, 20.

p. 74   *"black mark"*: Gardner, *Groton Myths and Memories*, 18.

p. 74   *"like cramming for the Last Day"*: Sedgwick, "Three Men of Groton," in *Views from the Circle*, 18.

p. 74   *"a more tender-hearted man"*: Richards, "My First Year at Groton," in *Views from the Circle*, 60.

p. 75   *"whole top of Wachusett"*: Ashburn, *Peabody of Groton*, 82.

p. 75   *"Keep innocency"*: Sedgwick, "Three Men of Groton," in *Views from the Circle*, 19.

p. 75   *"Pierpont Morgan"*: Ibid., 14. Sedgwick was mistaken: Morgan was never president of Groton's board of trustees. Phillips Brooks was president until his death in 1893. He was succeeded by William Lawrence.

p. 75   *"oligarchy of a dozen youths"*: Strachey, *Eminent Victorians*, 41.

p. 75   *"older and more positive leaders"*: Ashburn, *Peabody of Groton*, 75.

p. 75   *"little Greek democracy of the elite"*: Richard Hofstadter, *The American Political Tradition: And the Men Who Made It* (New York: Vintage, 1974), 415.

p. 75   *Edward Perkins Carter*: He was the son of Franklin Carter, the president of Williams College. After his expulsion from Groton, he became a student at Williams; he later studied medicine at the University of Pennsylvania and became a doctor. He and the Rector were eventually reconciled, and both his son and one of his grandsons went to Groton: Edward Perkins Carter Jr. graduated in the form of 1924 and Christopher Sherman Carter graduated in the form of 1948.

p. 76   *"to see a girl"*: Henry Howe Richards, *A Schoolmaster's Scrapbook: Half a Century at Groton* (Groton, Mass.: Groton School, 2010), 62.

p. 76   *"become opposed to the school"*: The account of Ed Carter and the prefect revolt of 1888 is drawn primarily from Beran, "A Glorious and Most Intensely Interesting Life," *Groton School Quarterly*, May 1984, 17–21, based on materials in the Groton School archives. Certain details were omitted from the article when it was printed for fear of offending various constituencies. It appeared just twenty years after Louis Auchincloss's novel *The Rector of Justin* was published, a book that angered a number of Grotonians, not least Frank Ashburn, who thought it portrayed Peabody and Groton in an unflattering light. "A lot of [Grotonians] didn't like it," Auchincloss said of the novel. "I was very much criticized." For the relation between Groton's Rector and Auchincloss's fictional Rector, Francis Prescott, see chapter 30 above, "Joy Lane."

p. 76   *"fagging" at Groton*: Conversations with Kent Sanger, 1983, and Louis Auchincloss, 2003. Kent Sanger graduated from Groton in 1930; his father, Prentice, was a member of the form of 1901; Kent's cousin, Jack Crocker, was the school's second headmaster. Kent worked with the author's father at McGraw Hill in the 1960s and '70s. In the early and middle 1980s the author and Sanger exchanged numerous letters and had many conversations, some of them prompted by an article in the *Groton School Quarterly* in which the author, then a student at Groton, portrayed the Rector somewhat unsympathetically as a Victorian disciplinarian whose cult of the gentleman was at odds with his professed Christianity. Sanger contended, on the contrary, that Peabody was not in the least a hypocrite. Like "many men of the cloth," he wrote the author in a 1983 letter, "he undoubtedly had grave doubts about his faith as well as his ability to live up to it. But he was a man of true humanity as well as the possessor of a glorious sense of humor." The author did not respond to these criticisms of his *Quarterly* essay, perhaps from laziness rather than wounded feelings. In a letter dated August 25, 1983, Sanger wrote that "[y]our silence since my last letter suggests that in some way I have hurt your feelings. If so, I'm very sorry. That was not my intent. I'm very proud of your achievements at Groton and your position of school leadership this coming year. I care deeply that this position be held by someone who demonstrates an understanding of the basic principles on which the school was founded and the character of the founder. This was why I was prompted to offer to you critiques of your essay by old friends, [Jack] Crocker and Paul Wright [the fourth headmaster of the school]. I could have added Ted Chase, a classmate, who was a trustee for many years and is presently a member of the Board of Overseers at Harvard. If I have distressed you, let me know, and I'll try to make amends. With concern, Kent Sanger." Such was Kent's concern that he telephoned the indolent author, and in trying to put the Rector's concern with discipline in perspective he described the understanding of his father's generation that there had been a fagging incident in the early years of the school, and that this had opened the Rector's eyes to the need for a greater degree of vigilance and a stricter regimen at Groton. Kent Sanger died in 1992. A decade later, in 2003, the author, who was bringing out a book, spoke over the phone to Louis Auchincloss, whom he had known since the 1980s, and who now offered to give his book a blurb. The conversation covered various topics of WASP interest. There was Davis Polk & Wardwell, a law firm in which the author had worked and in which Auchincloss's father, Howland, had been a partner, and there was the matter of Charles Spofford's divorce, which, many years before, split the Davis Polk partnership into two camps, those partners and their wives who, in their social relations, remained loyal to Spofford's ex-wife, and those who consented to be entertained by Spofford and his second wife in their new establishment. The talk got around to Groton and the prefect revolt of 1888, about which the author had written, in the *Groton School Quarterly*, yet another essay, one which Auchincloss, in a May 1984 letter to the author, said that he had read with much interest. The author mentioned the theory of Prentice Sanger's Groton generation about fagging in the early years of the school, and Auchincloss recalled that his friend and teacher, the Reverend Malcom Strachan, who had been close to Peabody in his old age, had mentioned to him a conversation in which the Rector (who at the time was near death) spoke of the great charm of one of his first students, Warwick Potter, and of his fear that he had let Warwick down, for he had learned that a sixth former, who had been expelled, had been heard by one of the masters to say, "Miss Ryan's my fag." Auchincloss said that he, too, had heard Groton old-timers say that fagging had cropped up in the 1880s, was swiftly stamped out, and never reemerged in the more regimented school of the nineties. Auchincloss pointed out that Warwick Potter's nickname at Groton was "the Biddy," and although he had not previously connected any of this with the prefect revolt of 1888, it now seemed, both to him and to the author, that the two events were almost certainly connected.

p. 76   *schools like Eton and Harrow*: In his novel *The Rector of Justin*, Auchincloss alluded to Peabody's abiding fear that the practices of English public schools, if adopted at Groton, would lead to sexual corruption. Francis Prescott, the Rector in the novel, observes that the cruelty of English schools (in which the younger students or "fags" were brutalized by their fagmasters) went "hand in hand with a certain intensity of friendship between boys," and he admits that he "discouraged close friendships between boys" in his own school, Justin Martyr, because he "did not think a hundred examples of David and Jonathan were worth one of sodomy . . ." Auchincloss, *The Rector of Justin* (Boston: Mariner, 2002), 43. "At Groton there was no straight fagging by a younger for an older boy," George Biddle wrote. "The Rector probably realized the incitement to homosexuality in such a relation." Biddle, "As I Remember Groton School," in *Views from the Circle*, 112. Auchincloss himself believed that there was a good deal in the early history of Groton that was incomprehensible unless one took into account what his friend and relation Gore Vidal (discussing his own experience of Exeter) called "American hysteria about homosexuality." See Gore Vidal, *Palimpsest: A Memoir* (New York: Penguin, 1996), 87. On the relation between fags and fagmasters at Eton, see Cyril Connolly's *Enemies of Promise* (New York: Persea, 1983), 178–189.

p. 76   *"Miss Ryan"*: The use of "girls' names for handsome little boys" was another practice that was common in English boarding schools and was associated with practices that Peabody did not want to see adopted at Groton. See Eve Auchincloss, "The Making of an Englishman," *Washington Post*, October 29, 1978.

p. 76   *misbehavior*: One of the reasons Peabody made his boys live in cubicles (rather than in ordinary rooms) was to discourage the secrecy in which fagging and other forms of misconduct might flourish. In the 1960s and '70s most of the dormitories at Groton were renovated and cubicles were replaced by rooms. But lower school students (eighth and ninth graders) at Groton still sleep in cubicles. These "cubes" were, however, modernized in the 1980s, and are not nearly so spartan as the ones they replaced. In yet another effort to prevent fagging, Peabody discouraged friendships between boys in different forms (grades). Though these prohibitions disappeared long ago, the form has remained the principal social unit at Groton.

p. 77   *"sinfulness in boys"*: Beran, "A Glorious and Most Intensely Interesting Life," *Groton School Quarterly*, May 1984, 19. "How fascinating," Louis Auchincloss wrote the author in connection with this article, "to find the Rector speaking so candidly of the evil in boys." Louis Auchincloss to the author, May 21, 1984.

p. 77   *"try to do better"*: The account of Amory Gardner's opposition to Peabody's plan to enlarge the school is drawn from Beran, "A Glorious and Most Intensely Interesting Life," *Groton School Quarterly*, May 1984, 17–21.

p. 78   *"a boy's real self"*: Gardner, *Groton Myths and Memories*, 100.

9. THE MADONNAS OF HENRY ADAMS

p. 80   *a loss so great*: The marriage is a mystery no historian is likely to penetrate. But it *has* been sentimentalized, not least by Adams himself. He and Clover had, in his words, "twelve years of perfect happiness." Perfect is a strong word, and Adams, who in many ways was a perfectionist, was not blind to what he took to be his wife's blemishes, or so the portrait of the heroine in his novel *Esther* suggests. He deferred, it is true, to Clover's criticism of his writing—because she epitomized, he said, the "average reader." At all events the truth of both the marriage and Adams's grief is perhaps more complicated than it has been made to seem.

p. 80   *"very dangerously fascinating"*: Samuels, *Henry Adams*, 268.

p. 80   *"bored to death with ourselves"*: Dykstra, *Clover Adams*, 181.

p. 80   *"fully express"*: Ibid.

p. 80   *"obviously felt tremendously guilty"*: Stacy A. Cordery, *Alice: Alice Roosevelt Longworth, from White House Princess to Washington Power Broker* (New York: Penguin, 2007), 22.

p. 81   *"more than I can have"*: *Henry Adams: Selected Letters*, 268.

p. 81   *"you are Beauty; I am the Beast"*: Ibid., 271.

p. 81   *"old enough to be a tame cat"*: Ibid., 268.

p. 81   *"I have passed a bad* quart d'heure": Ibid., 267.

p. 81   *"sudden spasm came over me"*: Ibid., 214.

p. 81   *"only to sleep forever in the trade-winds"*: Adams, *Education*, 316.

p. 81   *"combing his golden hair"*: Howe, *John Jay Chapman*, 253, 360.

p. 81   *"If the country had put him on a pedestal"*: Brooks, *New England: Indian Summer*, 273.

p. 81   *"A word from him went far"*: Adams, *Education*, 124.

p. 82   *"as odd as can be"*: Ernest Samuels, *Henry Adams: The Middle Years* (Cambridge, Mass.: Belknap Press, 1958), 325. Springy told the story of how one of the Adams siblings "wrote a book of which a review appeared so bitter and strong that he wrote the Editor to ask who had done it. He was told, his brother." This would appear to be garbled account of Charles Francis Adams's review of his brother Henry's *Life of Albert Gallatin* in the *Nation*. "There is no evidence," Samuels wrote, "that Henry ever learned the identity of his *Nation* critic," though it is possible that he "hit upon the secret" and enjoyed the jest. Samuels, *Henry Adams: The Middle Years*, 66.

p. 82   *"as a son"*: Michael Burlingame, *The Inner World of Abraham Lincoln* (Urbana: University of Illinois Press, 1994), 177.

p. 82   *"a judgment"*: William Roscoe Thayer, *The Life and Letters of John Hay* (Boston: Houghton Mifflin, 1915), II, 7.

p. 82   *"incessant bribery and attentions"*: Samuels, *Henry Adams: The Middle Years*, 329.

p. 83   *sorrow songs*: Patricia O'Toole, *The Five of Hearts* (New York: Ballantine, 1991), 213.

p. 83   *"haunting melody"*: This was W.E.B. Du Bois's characterization of the sorrow songs in *The Souls of Black Folk: Essays and Sketches* 3rd ed. (Chicago: A.C. McClurg, 1903), viii.

p. 83   *"pleasant gang"*: Thayer, *Life and Letters of John Hay*, II, 78.

p. 83   *"dispensers of sunshine over Washington"*: Adams, *Education*, 332.

p. 83   *"as queens ought to look"*: John Arthur Garraty, *Henry Cabot Lodge: A Biography* (New York: Knopf, 1953), 101.

p. 83   *"waste places"*: Adams, *Education*, 354.

p. 83   *"a little walk together"*: John Taliaferro, *All the Great Prizes: The Life of John Hay, from Lincoln to Roosevelt* (New York: Simon & Schuster, 2014), 268.

p. 83   *"Cabot has to be the fourth man"*: O'Toole, *Five of Hearts*, 220. As for the adultery, it cannot be known now with any certainty whether it was of the flesh or only of the heart.

p. 84   *"sucked the lifeblood of poor Henry"*: Leon Edel, *The Life of Henry James* (Harmondsworth, U.K.: Penguin, 1977), II, 270.

p. 84   *"I do not know how he would wear"*: O'Toole, *Five of Hearts*, 338.

p. 84   *"excursions"*: Ibid.

p. 84   *"Mrs. Cam and Joe flirted"*: Ibid., 343.

p. 84   *"real Parisian spree"*: Ibid., 228.

p. 84   *"we dined in cabinet particulier"*: Ibid.

p. 84   *"gaily, with a heart as sick as ever a man had"*: Samuels, *Henry Adams*, 270.

p. 85   *"all the human interest and power"*: *Henry Adams: Selected Letters*, ed. Samuels, 272.

p. 85   *"seclusion and peace"*: *Henry Adams: Selected Letters*, ed. Samuels, 272.

p. 85   *defeats in politics and love*: John Patrick Diggins has pointed out the wrongheadedness of reducing Adams's thought to a Mugwump's bitterness over his failure to get further in politics, and he has questioned whether Adams was all that keen on exercising conventional forms of political power. See Diggins, *The Promise of American Pragmatism: Modernism and the Crisis of Knowledge and Authority* (Chicago: University of Chicago Press, 1994), 23–24. Fair enough: one can make too much of Adams as a "displaced patrician." Yet at one period in his life Adams *did* seek power to implement a program of reform, and he *was* disappointed by his failure to get very far with it. Gore Vidal went so far as to say "there is little doubt that Henry inherited the family passion to be first in the nation," but found that a "plutocratic-democracy was not apt to take well to one with such an 'education'" as his. See Vidal, "The Four Generations of the Adams Family," in Vidal, *United States: Essays 1952–1992* (New York: Random House, 1993), 661. The author's own sense is that Adams liked power, but that the Athenian in him resisted specializing in it.

p. 85   *"I detest it"*: Samuels, *Henry Adams*, 296. "Bombard New York," Adams said in another letter. "I know no place that would be more improved by it. The chief population is Jew, and the rest is German Jew." See *The Letters of Henry Adams 1892–1899*, ed. J. C. Levenson, et al. (Cambridge, Mass.: Belknap Press, 1982), IV, 326.

p. 85   *"the Jew banker"*: Adams, *Education*, 285.

p. 85   *"old Ciceronian idea of government"*: Ibid., 32.

p. 85   *strives always to be original*: A certain degree of stupidity is essential to life; there is nothing more tedious than an irritable seeking after profundity.

p. 85   *"the old gentry"*: Hofstadter, *The Age of Reform*, 137.

p. 85   *"world was dead"*: Adams, *Education*, 238. Adams was hardly the only WASP to find the old Anglo pedigrees fainéant and enervated, or to envy the more recent immigrants their vitality. The novelist Henry Harland thought the WASP bloodstock so unpromising, as material for saleable fiction, that he adopted a pseudonym, Sidney Luska, and in this ethnic drag composed lurid novels in which he attempted to bring alive, for his readers, the more enticing life of Jewish New York in the fin de siècle. On Harland, see Loren Glass, "Choosing the Past: Agency and Ethnicity in Sidney Luska/Henry Harland's *As It Was Written*," *Journal x*, Autumn 2000–Spring 2001.

p. 86   *"disappointed and ineffectual"*: Edward Chalfant, *Improvement of the World: A Biography of Henry Adams, His Last Life 1891–1918* (Hamden, Conn.: Archon, 2001), 285.

p. 86   *"accursed Judaism"*: Anthony Julius, *T. S. Eliot, Anti-Semitism, and Literary Form* (Cambridge, U.K.: Cambridge University Press, 1996), 14.

p. 86   *"tongue-tied, stolid"*: For the quotations in this paragraph, see Santayana's *The Last Puritan*.

p. 87   *their weakness*: On Adams's anti-Semitism as a byproduct of his political impotence, see E. Digby Baltzell: "as Tocqueville clearly saw, privilege without power breeds resentment and the need for caste superiority." Baltzell, *Protestant Establishment*, 93.

p. 87   *"was not in politics"*: See James's novel *Pandora*.

p. 87   *Mr. Dixwell's School*: Epes Sargent Dixwell (1807–1899) graduated from Harvard College in 1827. He was called to the Bar in 1833 and in 1836 became headmaster of the Boston Latin School. In 1851 he resigned as headmaster of the Latin School and established his own school, "The Private Latin School," in which Henry Adams was educated. In retirement Dixwell amused his leisure by translating English verses into Latin, a selection of which he published in a volume aptly called *Otia Senectutis* (Cambridge, U.K.: University Press, 1885). See "American Academy of Arts and Sciences—Report of the Council" (May 9, 1900), in *Proceedings of the American Academy of Arts and Sciences, from May, 1899, to May, 1900* (Boston: John Wilson, 1900), XXXV, 625–628.

p. 88   *"oriented in one direction"*: Adams, *Education*, 298.

p. 88   *"as a horse goes back to its stables"*: Ibid., 317.

p. 88   *"of a sea-green translucency"*: *The Letters of Henry Adams 1868–1885*, ed. Levenson, et al., II, 603.

p. 88   "slaughter-house": *Letters of Henry Adams 1892–1918*, ed. Ford, 365.

p. 88   *felt the Madonna*: When he wrote to Lizzie Cameron about the Virgin Mother and Child forming "all the interest and power religion ever had," he added, "There you are again! you see how the thought always turns back to you." Samuels, *Henry Adams*, 270. It was, after all, not childless Clo but mama Lizzie who inspired Adams's pilgrimage to the Madonna of Chartres.

p. 88   *"collecting spires"*: Brooks, *New England: Indian Summer 1865–1915*, 483.

p. 89   *"those of their cooks"*: Adams, *Education*, 348.

p. 89   *"hugged his antiquated dislike"*: Adams, *Education*, 343–344.

p. 89   *"We are Love!"*: "Adams had gone straight to the Virgin at Chartres, and asked her to show him God, face to face, as she did for St. Bernard. She replied, kindly as ever, as though she were still the young mother of to-day, with a sort of patient pity for masculine dullness: 'My dear outcast, what is it you seek? This is the Church of Christ! If you seek him through me, you are welcome, sinner or saint; but he and I are one. We are Love!'" Adams, *Education*, 428.

p. 89   *"never knew* ennui": "When it was bored, somebody got killed." *The Letters of Henry Adams 1892–1918*, ed. Ford, 298.

p. 89   *"All the steam in the world"*: Adams, *Education*, 388.

p. 89   *"antimodern vitalist"*: T. J. Jackson Lears, *No Place of Grace: Antimodernism and the Transformation of American Culture 1880–1920* (Chicago: University of Chicago Press, 1994), xi, xv, 58.

p. 90   *amid the chaos of life*: Dante, in Canto XXXIII of the *Paradiso*, professed to have seen, in his ultimate apprehension, Love "gathering up the scattered pages of the universe and binding them together, as though in one book."

p. 90   *any mortal use*: Alfred Kazin pointed out that *Mont-Saint-Michel and Chartres* did bear fruit in, "of all places," the Upper West Side of Manhattan, "just before the Hispanic *barrio* is replaced by Columbia University." The WASP architect Ralph Adams Cram had been deeply influenced by the book, and he tried to give its ideals expression in the Cathedral of St. John the Divine in Morningside Heights, where a young worm cast out of his own Chartres tried and failed to recapture its poetry one Sunday morning in August or September 1984. See Kazin, "Religion as Culture: Henry Adams's *Mont-Saint-Michel and Chartres*," in *Henry Adams and His World*, ed. Contosta and Muccigrosso, 48.

p. 90   *"long-established ghost"*: *The Letters of Henry Adams 1906–1918*, ed. J. C. Levenson, et al. (Cambridge, Mass.: Belknap Press, 1988), VI, 371.

10. A CONSTANCY IN THE STARS: THE HARVARDS OF GEORGE SANTAYANA

p. 91   *wizard's mantle*: McCormick, *George Santayana*, 99.

p. 91   *steam yacht*: Sagamore: For Warwick Potter's voyage with Edgar Scott on the *Sagamore*, see Janny Scott, *The Beneficiary: Fortune, Misfortune, and the Story of My Father* (New York: Penguin, 2020), 70–73.

p. 92   *"full of laughter"*: For Santayana's account of Warwick Potter, see Santayana, *Middle Span*, 109–110.

p. 92   *"To W.P."*: George Santayana, *Poems* (New York: Scribner's, 1928), 60–63.

p. 92   *"my last real friend"*: George Santayana, *My Host the World* (London: Cresset Press, 1953), 10.

p. 92   *"philosophic metanoia"*: Ibid., 9–11, 15–16.

p. 92   *Possession*: "Possession," Nietzsche says, "usually diminishes the possession."

p. 92   *"disillusioned spirit"*: *Little Essays Drawn from the Writings of George Santayana*, ed. Logan Pearsall Smith (New York: Scribner's, 1921), 92.

p. 92   *"possess things and persons in idea"*: Santayana, *My Host the World*, 17.

p. 92   *"joy in youth"*: Santayana, "To W. P."

p. 93   *"a tiger well fed"*: Santayana, *Middle Span*, 44.

p. 93   *"muddy paths"*: Ibid.

p. 93   *"most often Keats"*: Ibid., 102.

p. 93   *"an exact but familiar"*: Santayana, *Persons and Places*, 202.

p. 94   *"more multifarious and more chaotic"*: Santayana, *Middle Span*, 159.

p. 94   *"fine domed forehead"*: McCormick, *George Santayana*, 99.

p. 94   *"Just why Santayana was in Cambridge"*: Walter Lippmann, "Education and the White-Collar Class," *Vanity Fair*, May 1923.

p. 94   *"invention and industry"*: George Santayana, "The Genteel Tradition in American Philosophy," in Santayana, *Winds of Doctrine: Studies in Contemporary Opinion* (New York: Scribner's, 1914), 188.

p. 94   *"an oppidum"*: Santayana, *Persons and Places*, 98.

p. 94   *"austere inspiration"*: Ibid., 97.

p. 95   *"spiritual penury"*: Ibid.

p. 95   *"exile and a foreigner"*: Ibid., 180.

p. 95   *"scene was filled with arts and virtues"*: Santayana, *Character and Opinion in the United States*, 120.

p. 95   *"solitary gaunt idealist"*: Ibid., 170.

p. 95   *"exceptionally cultivated"*: Santayana, *Middle Span*, 103.

p. 95   *"in spite of flashes of gun-powder"*: *The Letters of George Santayana*, ed. William G. Holzberger (Cambridge, Mass.: M.I.T. Press, 2002), II, 26.

p. 95   *"visibly killed by the lack of air to breathe"*: *The Letters of George Santayana*, ed. William G. Holzberger (Cambridge, Mass.: M.I.T. Press, 2003), V, 306.

p. 96   *"I was, of course, like my father"*: For this account of Learned Hand and his relations with Santayana, Gunther, *Learned Hand: The Man and the Judge*, 3–71.

p. 96   "the *undergraduate citadel*": Alsop, *I've Seen the Best of It*, 63.

p. 96   *"eagerly embraced the post"*: Amory, *Proper Bostonians*, 301.

p. 97   *Santayana's Harvard protégés*: McCormick, *George Santayana*, 99.

p. 97   *"piqué vest, spats, and suede"*: Ronald Steel, *Walter Lippmann and the American Century* (Boston: Little, Brown, 1980), 19.

p. 97   *"Leonardo's Mona Lisa"*: Ibid.

p. 97   *"pure intuition of essence"*: Santayana, "A Brief History of My Opinions," in *The Philosophy of George Santayana*, ed. Irwin Edman (New York: Scribner's, 1953), 19.

p. 97   *"something confused, hideous, and useless"*: Santayana, *Persons and Places*, 119.

p. 97   *"madly filling the universe"*: George Santayana, "Ultimate Religion," in Santayana, *Obiter Scripta: Lectures, Essays and Reviews*, ed. Justus Buchler and Benjamin Schwartz (New York: Scribner's, 1982), 282.

p. 97   *"He feared me"*: Santayana, *Middle Span*, 149.

p. 97   *"constancy in the stars"*: Santayana, *Dominations and Powers*, 34.

p. 97   *"charity will always judge a soul"*: Santayana, *Persons and Places*, 95.

p. 97   *"with his pearl gray beard and pearl gray tie"*: Lippmann, "Education and the White-Collar Class," *Vanity Fair*, May 1923.

p. 97   *"Nature is well-ordered enough"*: George Santayana, *Dominations and Powers: Reflections on Liberty, Society, and Government* (New York: Scribner's, 1951), 34.

p. 97   *"Why shouldn't things be largely absurd, futile, and transitory?"*: *Letters of George Santayana*, ed. Holzberger, II, 319.

11. TEDDY

p. 98   *"like a woman's in many ways"*: Hovey, *John Jay Chapman*, 51.

p. 99   *"My line of politics is war—war—war"*: The account of Chapman in this chapter is drawn principally from Howe, *John Jay Chapman*, and Hovey, *John Jay Chapman*.

p. 99   *"found him wonderfully calm"*: Ashburn, *Peabody of Groton*, 104.

p. 99   *"Get action"*: Oceans of ink have been spilt over Teddy, but Richard Hofstadter's essay in *The American Political Tradition* remains perhaps the most incisive account of the man's *thought*. In addition to Hofstadter's essay, the author has in this chapter drawn on the standard biographies of Theodore.

p. 99   *with a nod to Horace*: For Horace's *atra cura*, see *Odes* 3.1.40.

p. 100   *half a dozen bottles*: Paul Grondahl, *I Rose Like a Rocket: The Political Education of Theodore Roosevelt* (Lincoln: University of Nebraska Press, 2007), 206.

p. 101   "On sourit": Sylvia Jukes Morris, *Edith Kermit Roosevelt: Portrait of a First Lady* (New York: Modern Library, 2001), 490.

p. 102   *leader of men*: Henry James spoke of the "limitations by which men of genius . . . purchase their ascendancy . . . over mankind."

p. 102   *"pure government"*: Edmund Morris, *The Rise of Theodore Roosevelt* (New York: Ballantine, 1980), 152.

p. 102   *Elizabeth Astor Winthrop Chanler*: The author is indebted, for this account of the second Mrs. John Jay Chapman, to Donna M. Lucey, *Sargent's Women: Four Lives Behind the Canvas* (New York: Norton, 2018), and Margaret Chanler, *Family Vista: The Memoirs of Margaret Chanler Aldrich* (New York: William-Frederick Press, 1958).

p. 103   *"country needs a war"*: *Selections from the Correspondence of Theodore Roosevelt and Henry Cabot Lodge 1884–1918* (New York: Scribner's, 1925), 205.

p. 103   *"the wolf begins to rise in his heart"*: Peter Gay, *The Cultivation of Hatred* (New York: Norton, 1993), 122.

p. 103 *"the great day in my life"*: James M. Merrill, *The U.S.A.: A Short History of the American Republic* (Philadelphia: Lippincott, 1975), 165.

p. 104 *"simply poisonous"*: *Selections from the Correspondence of Theodore Roosevelt and Henry Cabot Lodge 1884–1918* (New York: Scribner's, 1925), 175.

p. 105 *"the lunatic fringe in all reform movements"*: Theodore Roosevelt, *An Autobiography*, 211.

12. VIDA SCUDDER EMULATES ST. FRANCIS

p. 106 *"We were well-to-do"*: Except where otherwise noted, the account of Vida Scudder in this chapter is drawn from Scudder's memoir *On Journey* (New York: E.P. Dutton, 1937).

p. 107 *"a sentimental old lay preacher"*: *The Letters of T.S. Eliot 1930–1931*, ed. Valerie Eliot and John Haffenden (New Haven, Conn.: Yale University Press, 2015), 153.

p. 108 *"interior & spiritual history of New England"*: *Emerson in His Journals*, 253.

p. 110 *"most sacred hope"*: Henry James, *The Bostonians* (New York: Modern Library, 1956), 13.

p. 110 *"immense desire"*: Ibid., 35.

p. 110 *France, Germany, and Scandinavia*: W.D.P. Bliss, *What Is Christian Socialism?* (Boston: Society of Christian Socialists, *circa* 1890), 8–11.

p. 110 *Russian Empire*: WASPs like Edmund Wilson and George Kennan felt a deep sympathy for the cultivated elites of ancien régime Russia, in whose culture they saw a mirror of their own. Encountering Tolstoy's last private secretary at Yasnaya Polyana, the hereditary estate of the Tolstoys, Kennan was gratified to hear "the authentic accent—rich, polished, elegant and musical—of the educated circles of those times. So, I thought to myself, must Tolstoi himself have spoken."

p. 110 *"to the people"*: James H. Billington, *The Icon and the Axe: An Interpretive History of Russian Culture* (New York: Vintage, 1970), 391, 394. In addition to an imperfectly realized dream of Christian charity, there are other points of resemblance between Mugwump WASPs and the gentlefolk of prerevolutionary Russia. Like their WASP counterparts, the inhabitants of the country houses depicted by Turgenev and Chekhov are well-bred and liberally educated, but a little worn-out and sad, nervously or dilettantishly shrinking from practical life, yet taking a high-minded interest in reform. And like the WASPs, they feel themselves, in spite of their enormous advantages in life, less secure in their privilege than their forebears were. Yet both groups, with all their grievances, were wary of radical change, and both were apprehensive when their children sought to go further, when the young *Narodniki* went "to the people," to live and work among them, and when idealistic young WASPs devoted themselves, as Eleanor Roosevelt did, to the urban slums or, as Edmund Wilson did, to radical politics. Yet the differences between the two elites are as notable. American Yankee civilization was materially prosperous in a way Russia's never was, and by a sad but inexorable law the comparatively healthy is less interesting than the colorfully sick. The Astors and Whitneys and Roosevelts on their country estates were mock landed gentry: the estates of their Russian counterparts were the real thing, founded on the blood and sweat of a peasantry that had fewer opportunities for advancement than did working-class Americans. The Russian landowners had a guilty conscience about the plight of their moujiks, but for all their anguish, none of them, not even Tolstoy, made much progress in improving their lot. Yet as Dostoevsky never tired of observing, suffering is the manure which fertilizes the spirit. Henry Adams, momentarily forsaking his blasé ironies to pray to the Virgin Mary, is, beside Dostoevsky, a tourist posing for the camera at Chartres; and although the stunted WASPs in the novels of Henry James and Edith Wharton seek the flower of life, what a pale and attenuated thing is life, as painted in those books, in comparison to *War and Peace* or *The Brothers Karamazov*.

p. 110 *"mad summer"*: Billington, *The Icon and the Axe*, 394–395.

p. 111 *"redeem their own sin"*: Orlando Figes, *Natasha's Dance: A Cultural History of Russia* (New York: Metropolitan, 2002), 220–221.

p. 111 *"sense of sin"*: See Beatrice Webb, *My Apprenticeship*, 2 vols. (Harmondsworth, U.K.: Pelican, 1938), I, 204–205.

p. 111 *"never questioned the right"*: Arthur V. Woodworth, *Christian Socialism and the Church of England* (Boston: Woodworth, 1902), 57. "Christian Socialism as Maurice conceived it," Jeremy Morris writes, "had little to do with theoretical socialism, with Marx and the redistribution of property." Maurice was "of a piece with many Liberal churchmen and politicians of his day" in being "socially conservative" and "suspicious of democracy." He "wanted to bring Christ to the poor as well as the rich, to Christianize the 'unchristian Socialists' and socialize the 'unsocial Christians.'" See *To Build Christ's Kingdom: F. D. Maurice and His Writings*, ed. Jeremy Morris (Norwich, U.K.: Canterbury Press, 2007), 15.

p. 111   *"delight in the vast Russian experiment"*: Scudder believed that the "fresh start" the Bolsheviks "have made is a relief to the Living God . . . I suspect that God patiently awaits to reveal Himself anew in Russia at the right moment." Scudder, *On Journey*, 334–335. But at the same time she believed, as Richard H. Schmidt has written, that the "Soviet system failed to realize its goals" precisely because it "lacked a Christian foundation" and "sought social reform without inward transformation." Richard H. Schmidt, *Glorious Companions: Five Centuries of Anglican Spirituality* (Grand Rapids, Mich.: Eerdmans, 2002), 223. Scudder recoiled, she said, from Russia's policies of coercion and violence, but she went on to imply that the "open violence" practiced by the Soviet regime was less "pernicious" than the "covert coercion" of capitalism. *On Journey*, 336–337.

p. 112   *"vast industrial energies"*: Vida Scudder, *The Witness of Denial* (New York: E.P. Dutton, 1895), 14.

p. 113   *"hell with the lid lifted"*: The words have been attributed to Charles Dickens, but the author has been unable to trace the original reference.

p. 114   *"strange hunger for fellowship"*: Scudder, *On Journey*, 140.

p. 114   *"displeased"*: James, *The Bostonians*, 23.

p. 114   *"pharisaical self-congratulation"*: *Glitter Around and Darkness Within: The Diary of Beatrice Webb 1872–1892*, ed. Norman and Jeanne Mackenzie (Cambridge, Mass.: Belknap Press, 1982), 85.

p. 115   *"I had a most wonderful morning"*: W. A. Swanberg, *Whitney Father, Whitney Heiress* (New York: Scribner's, 1980), 250.

p. 115   *"to work, and help"*: Ibid.

p. 115   *unconscious desire to lord it over others*: Thus George Moore (the novelist and memoirist, not to be confused with the bore from Trinity College, Cambridge) says, "be sure that when any man is more stupidly vain and outrageously egotistic than his fellows, he will hide his hideousness in humanitarianism."

13. THE VISIONARY NEURASTHENICS

p. 116   *"as he sat with his silver locks"*: For Alice James's breakdown in 1868, see Jean Strouse, *Alice James: A Biography* (Boston: Houghton Mifflin, 1980), 117–131.

p. 117   *"intense horror of life"*: Henry James to William James, July 31, 1891, in Henry James, *Letters*, ed. Leon Edel (Cambridge, Mass.: Belknap Press, 1980), III (1883–1895), 150.

p. 117   *"a clear, strong intelligence, housed in pain"*: Strouse, *Alice James*, 316.

p. 117   *Hume*: For Hume's "philosophical melancholy," see Hume, *A Treatise of Human Nature*, ed. L. A. Selby-Bigge (Oxford, U.K.: Clarendon, 1888), 268ff.

p. 118   *"ashamed of resting"*: Friedrich Nietzsche, *The Gay Science*, trans. Walter Kaufmann (New York: Vintage, 1974), 259.

p. 118   *"The man who lies ill in bed"*: Friedrich Nietzsche, *Human, All Too Human: A Book for Free Spirits*, trans. R. J. Hollingdale (Cambridge, U.K.: University of Cambridge Press, 1986), 133–34.

p. 119   *"fell behind his brothers"*: Adams, *Education*, 6.

p. 120   *"the air and movement of hysteria"*: Adams, *Education*, 499–500.

p. 120   *"vast and uniform"*: Thus Adams concluded his history of the United States during the presidencies of Jefferson and Madison. See Adams, *History of the United States During the Administrations of James Madison* (New York: Library of America, 1986), 1342, 1345.

p. 120   *"Never in his life"*: Adams, *Education*, 64.

p. 120   *"damned telephone book"*: Amory, *Proper Bostonians*, 13.

p. 121   *overstimulated*: In this reading of American history, Adams's own ancestors played a part in *inventing* the plutocrats: men who, for all their faults, enlarged the sphere of prosperity. The difficulty was that the creators of the Republic failed to supply anything that might have balanced or humanized the potent but crude energies their system would release, or so Adams came to believe.

p. 121 *"what might truly be called"*: See chapter five of *The Autobiography of John Stuart Mill*, "A Crisis in My Mental History."

p. 122 *"industrial operations depending on coal"*: Matthew Arnold, *Culture and Anarchy: An Essay in Political and Social Criticism* (London: Smith, Elder, 1869), 18.

p. 122 *"incomplete and mutilated men"*: Ibid., xvi.

p. 122 *"stunted"*: Ibid., 13.

p. 122 *cultural regeneration*: T. J. Jackson Lears has described the *Education* as among the "most sophisticated" manifestations of the "antimodern impulse toward regeneration . . ." See Lears, *No Place of Grace*, 286.

p. 123 *"classic and promiscuous turmoil"*: Adams, *Life of George Cabot Lodge*, 7–8.

p. 123 *acceleration*: The idea of the acceleration of modern life was a commonplace of nineteenth-century thought: it was the "wild pulsation" of Tennyson's "Locksley Hall," the "detestable quickening of the time" lamented by Ruskin in *Præterita*.

14. BILLY WAG'S *PAIDEIA*

p. 124 *"to see what he'd do"*: Ashburn, *Peabody of Groton*, 158–159.

p. 125 *"Amory, it's an impossible situation"*: Ibid., 159–160.

p. 125 *"family aspect"*: The quarrel between the Rector and Mr. Gardner concerning how best to maintain the family aspect of the school is documented in Beran, "A Glorious and Most Intensely Interesting Life," *Groton School Quarterly*, May 1984, 17–21.

p. 125 *subversive*: There would be sporadic intervals of hut-building at Groton after 1888, but the masters kept a close eye on the business.

p. 126 *"flavor"*: Gardner's desire to maintain the unique "personality" of Groton is evident on nearly every page of his *Groton Myths and Memories*.

p. 126 *"the excellent Percy"*: Richards, "My First Year at Groton," in *Views from the Circle*, 62.

p. 126 *offending whom"*: Ashburn, *Peabody of Groton*, 156.

p. 126 *"a spirit of mischief"*: Ashburn, *Peabody of Groton*, 154.

p. 126 *"emphasize the unity as well as the comprehensiveness"*: Peter W. Williams, *Religion, Art, and Money: Episcopalians and American Culture from the Civil War to the Great Depression* (Chapel Hill: University of North Carolina Press, 2016), 165.

p. 127 *"resident aesthete"*: This is Douglass Shand-Tucci's characterization of Gardner in his book *The Crimson Letter: Harvard, Homosexuality, and the Shaping of American Culture* (New York: St. Martin's Press, 2003).

p. 127 *"in his canoe"*: Arnold Whitridge, "Groton 1904–1905," in *Views from the Circle*, 148.

p. 127 *"with well-developed bodies"*: E. M. Forster, "Notes on the English Character," in Forster, *Abinger Harvest* (San Diego: Harcourt Brace, 1936), 5.

p. 127 *odd and gifted boys*: "If a boy was oversensitive or spastic or hysterical the school was, certainly during some periods, a cruel place." George W. Martin, "Preface to a Schoolmaster's Biography," in *Views from the Circle*, 142.

p. 127 *"He never hurried"*: Ibid., 133.

p. 127 *"usual allowance for a healthy-spirited boy"*: George Biddle, "As I Remember Groton School," in *Views from the Circle*, 116–117.

p. 128 *"he loved them all"*: Hinchman, "My Groton Years," in *Views from the Circle*, 159.

p. 128 *"The way he walked"*: Martin, "Preface to a Schoolmaster's Biography," in *Views from the Circle*, 137.

p. 128 *"was to stifle the creative impulse"*: Biddle, "As I Remember Groton School," in *Views from the Circle*, 122.

p. 128 *"fairy"*: Isaacson and Thomas, *Wise Men*, 54.

p. 128 *"Oddity"*: Oliver La Farge, *Raw Material: The Autobiographical Examination of an Artist's Journey into Maturity* (Santa Fe, N.M.: Sunstone Press, 2009), 12.

p. 128 *"At Groton I didn't happen to feel like conforming"*: Isaacson and Thomas, *Wise Men*, 55.

p. 128 *"the only recipe for success"*: Evan Thomas, *The Very Best Men: Four Who Dared: The Early Years of the C.I.A.* (New York: Simon & Schuster, 1995), 367.

p. 128 *"gorgeous scarlet"*: Douglass Shand-Tucci, *Boston Bohemia 1881–1900: Ralph Adams Cram: Life and Architecture* (Amherst: University of Massachusetts Press, 1995), 232.

p. 129 *"has a limitless power of converting the human soul"*: Werner Jaeger, *Paideia: The Ideals of Greek Culture: Archaic Greece, The Mind of Athens*, 2nd ed, 3 vols. (Oxford, U.K.: Oxford University Press, 1965), I, 36. The methods described by Jaeger were those that prevailed at Groton, as they did in many schools that carried on educational practices modeled on or descended from those of the old Greeks.

p. 129 *the Greeks did not distinguish between the two*: "In Greek culture," Werner Jaeger wrote in *Paideia*, "poetry and music, 'blest pair of sirens,' were inseparable. The same Greek word, music, designates them both." Jaeger, *Paideia: The Ideals of Greek Culture: In Search of the Divine Centre*, trans. Gilbert Highet, 2nd ed., 3 vols. (Oxford, U.K.: Oxford University Press, 1965), II, 224.

p. 129 *music and poetry*: Confucius would seem to have been no less conscious of the educative power of music than the Greeks: "As soon as he crossed the border from Loo, we are told he discovered from the gait and manners of a boy, whom he saw carrying a pitcher, the influence of the sage's music, and told the driver of his carriage to hurry on to the capital. Arrived there, he heard the strain, and was so ravished with it, that for three months he did not know the taste of flesh. 'I did not think,' he said, 'that music could have been made so excellent as this.'" James Legge, *The Life and Teachings of Confucius* (London: Trübner, 1887) 67.

p. 129 *the most important element in education*: The Greeks advanced the *theory* that music and poetry educate the mind: but the practice is found in nearly every culture, though it dies away as particular cultures outgrow their infancy and youth. "As civilization advances," Macaulay says, "poetry almost necessarily declines." Or rather: as poetry declines, civilization becomes more technically adept, and less imaginatively exuberant.

p. 129 *"furthest into the depths of the soul"*: Jaeger, *Paideia: The Ideals of Greek Culture: In Search of the Divine Centre*, II, 229.

p. 129 *"a shimmering fantasy"*: Richard Jenkyns, *The Victorians and Ancient Greece* (Cambridge, Mass.: Harvard University Press,1980), 13.

p. 130 *"set the works of good poets before the children"*: Plato, *Protagoras*, 326a. Plato puts these words into the mouth of Protagoras. "Poetry and music," Werner Jaeger writes, "had always been the foundation of the education of the mind" in Greece: a system of *paideia* which Plato, in the *Republic*, sought not to do away with but to reform. He "preserves poetry, as the best method of education, and as an expression of higher truth, but therefore he must relentlessly change or suppress anything in it which is incompatible with the standards of philosophy." See Jaeger, *Paideia: The Ideals of Greek Culture: In Search of the Divine Centre*, II, 213, 215.

p. 130 *"in the broadest and deepest sense the educator"*: Jaeger, *Paideia: The Ideals of Greek Culture: Archaic Greece, The Mind of Athens*, I, 35.

p. 130 *Athens*: Gardner spoke of the "beloved citadel" of Athena's Athens, and there is little doubt that Athens was never far from his mind at Groton. See William Amory Gardner, *In Greece with the Classics* (Boston: Little, Brown, 1908), 2.

p. 130 *"I remember one December"*: Recollection of a Groton graduate. By the fourth form the grammarian was reading, in Latin, nothing but Virgil, and in English, only Shakespeare leavened with Keats and Blake. It seeped into the ingenuous brain, so much so that the averted eyes of Dido in hell (*illa solo fixos oculos aversa tenebat*) became interchangeable with those of the Ophelia whom you saw each morning in chapel. [The grammarian, like many who have been indoctrinated in the scholarch's cult, exaggerates the salve of classic poetry even as he overlooks its reactionary and exclusive properties, once candidly confessed by Thomas Gaisford, quondam dean of Christ Church, Oxford. See Goldwin Smith, *Reminiscences* (New York: Macmillan, 1910), 50. The inquirer concedes what the grammarian will never admit, that wherever you are life is mostly *just* tolerable, just this side of actual discomfort, or overt boredom, and full of an untidiness like that at the back of desk drawers or under kitchen sinks. In even the sunniest of daylights, you do not escape the shadow, and neither Sophocles nor Shelley, let alone Virgil, will save you.] [The grammarian painfully rips up—*infandum dolorem*—these memories and fatuities from the psychic subsoil and exposes them to the gaze of such unsympathetic eyes as those of the inquirer because he would describe, as honestly as he can, the growth (or decay) of his mind when he was an innocent rat in more than one WASP educational laboratory.]

p. 130 *"old Greek" ideal*: Dean Acheson, Prize Day Address at Groton, June 1966.

p. 131 *"Aeschylus or Homer doubled back"*: Ellery Sedgwick, "Three Men of Groton," in *Views from the Circle*, 15.

p. 131 *"a play-house in a barn"*: Wordsworth, "Five Elegies," in *William Wordsworth: The Major Works*, ed. Stephen Gill (Oxford, U.K.: Oxford University Press, 1984), 145.

p. 131 *"That he was teaching a dead language"*: Whitridge, "Groton 1904–1905," in *Views from the Circle*, 148. *A Greek lesson*: Ashburn, *Peabody of Groton*, 158.

p. 131 *"tempest and dark hour are upon him"*: Ibid., 160.

15. HENRY STIMSON SEES THE STARS

p. 132 *The family of Henry Stimson*: Except where otherwise noted, the account of Henry Stimson in this chapter is drawn from Henry L. Stimson and McGeorge Bundy, *On Active Service in Peace and War* (New York: Harper, 1948) and Godfrey Hodgson, *The Colonel: The Life and Wars of Henry Stimson 1867–1950* (Boston: Northeastern University Press, 1992).

p. 133 *"Deformity and Odiousness of VICE"*: *Catalogue of Phillips Academy* (Andover: Andover Press, 1900), 9. See also *The High-Status Track: Studies of Elite Schools and Stratification*, ed. Paul William Kingston and Lionel S. Lewis (Albany: State University of New York Press, 1990), 4.

p. 133 *heresies of Harvard*: Harvard, Emerson said, had forsaken the "old religion" that once "dwelt like a Sabbath peace in the country population of New England," teaching "privation, self-denial, and sorrow," and absorbing the people in the "Spirit's holy errand." "I value Andover, Yale, and Princeton as altars of this same old fire, though I fear they have done burning cedar and sandalwood there also, and have learned to use chips and pine." Emerson had himself by this time largely forsaken both the old Calvinist religion of New England as well as its Unitarian successor.

p. 134 *"a most living"*: Santayana, *Middle Span*, 175. Santayana said that William Lyon Phelps, his host at Yale, "thought he had converted me to muscular Christianity; and in fact he had converted me to something Christian, namely, to charity even towards muscular Americanism." Santayana associated muscular Christianity far more with Yale than he did with Groton, whose graduates seemed to him a trifle effeminate. One sympathizes with Endicott Peabody: taken to task by modern scholars for having made a fetish of muscular toughness, he yet produced graduates who were criticized by contemporaries like Santayana for being so well-bred as to be ladylike.

p. 134 *"notoriously profitable"*: Baltzell, *Philadelphia Gentlemen*, 125.

p. 136 *"men do not"*: Lewis Namier, *The Structure of Politics at the Accession of George III* (New York: Palgrave Macmillan, 1957), 4.

p. 137 *"laborious study"*: Oliver Wendell Holmes, "The Profession of the Law," in Holmes, *Collected Legal Papers* (New York: Harcourt, Brace, 1921), 29.

16. PAX AMERICANA

p. 139 *"plump, pink"*: Geoffrey C. Ward, *Before the Trumpet: Young Franklin Roosevelt 1882–1905* (New York: Harper & Row, 1985), 110.

p. 140 *Miss Clay*: She was not, the reader will be happy to learn, dismissed, and she remained a part of the Roosevelt household until her death.

p. 140 *Bad Nauheim*: The atmosphere of the place is evoked by Ford Madox Ford in his novel *The Good Soldier*.

p. 140 *"especial treasure"*: Ward, *Before the Trumpet*, 172.

p. 141 *"Dear Mommerr & Popperr"*: *F.D.R.: His Personal Letters: Early Years*, ed. Elliott Roosevelt (New York: Duell, Sloan and Pearce, 1947), 35.

p. 141 *"subtle, almost masonic marks of distinction"*: Biddle, "As I Remember Groton School," in *Views from the Circle*, 113.

p. 141 *"I can learn better & quicker"*: Ward, *Before the Trumpet*, 189.

p. 142 *"gray-eyed, cool, self-possessed, intelligent"*: Biddle, "As I Remember Groton School," in *Views from the Circle*, 119.

p. 142 *flexibility:* Geoffrey Ward shows Franklin to have been an inveterate teller of tall tales. His lack of candor and his "deviousness" infuriated Henry Stimson. See Hodgson, *The Colonel*, 230–231. Franklin, indeed, was constantly "making stuff up," and framing stories that cast his deeds in a flattering light. It was an essential part of his fanatical optimism. When the facts were depressing or even merely boring, he altered them. Yet in Franklin's defense, it may be observed that, so far as our working memory of our own pasts goes, we all resemble George IV rather more than we would care to admit. In his table-talk Samuel Rogers told how the King used to boast, in the presence of the Duke of Wellington, that he had fought at Waterloo. When the King saw doubtful looks in the faces of those around him, he would appeal to the Duke to confirm his memory on the point, and the Duke would blandly reply, "I have heard your Majesty say so." We all have our inward Wellingtons, too courteous to disabuse us of our mnemonic romances.

p. 142 *"One looks almost in vain"*: Ashburn, *Peabody of Groton*, 112–114.

p. 142 *"I have been so selfish and so sinful"*: Ibid., 106.

p. 142 *"My religious feeling"*: Ibid., 105–106.

p. 143 *"Sweldom"*: Ibid., 108.

p. 143 *"a first-rate man"*: Ibid., 209.

p. 143 *"the leading headmaster"*: Karabel, *The Chosen*, 37.

p. 143 *"brought up in the most select and superior way"*: Santayana, *Persons and Places*, 182–183.

p. 143 *"My Child, Virginia, is a Boy"*: Edith Barnard Delano, "The Hundred Legged Table," *New England Magazine*, July 1909.

p. 144 *"death of McKinley and the advent of Roosevelt"*: Adams, *Education*, 413.

p. 144 *"of Teddy's luck"*: Taliaferro, *All the Great Prizes*, 409.

p. 144 *"lead of American energies"*: Adams, *Education*, 330.

p. 144 *"Power when wielded by abnormal energy"*: Ibid., 417.

p. 144 *"We waited twenty minutes"*: *The Letters of Henry Adams 1892–1918*, ed. Ford, 365–366.

p. 144 *"less of his old freshness"*: Ibid., 66.

p. 145 *an island floating in waters off the much larger Eurasian continent*: WASP leaders beginning with Theodore Roosevelt were influenced, directly and indirectly, by a "geopolitical" approach to diplomacy that owed a good deal both to Alfred Thayer Mahan and to Halford Mackinder. See John Lamberton Harper, *American Visions of Europe: Franklin D. Roosevelt, George F. Kennan, and Dean G. Acheson* (Cambridge, U.K.: Cambridge University Press, 1986), 38–40, 50, and Alexandros Petersen, *The World Island: Eurasian Geopolitics and the Fate of the West* (Santa Barbara, Calif.: Prager, 2011), 12. According to the geopoliticists, the United States is "an island off the shores of Eurasia," and as such it is in its interest "to resist the domination of Europe or Asia by any one power and, even more, the control of *both* continents by the *same* power." See Henry Kissinger, *Diplomacy* (New York: Simon & Schuster, 1994), 50–51. America, Kissinger notes, has "concluded twice in this [the twentieth] century that the domination of Eurasia by a hegemonic power threatens its vital interests." At the same time, Kissinger concedes that a purely geopolitical foreign policy does not "reflect" America's "national genius": its most "realistic" diplomacy must have an idealistic appeal if it is to command support at home. See Kissinger, "Expand NATO Now," *Washington Post*, December 19, 1994. See also Gerry Kearns, *Geopolitics and Empire: The Legacy of Halford Mackinder* (Oxford, U.K.: Oxford University Press, 2009) 8–9; Paul Kennedy, *The Rise and Fall of the Great Powers* (New York: Random House, 1987), 364; and Richard Szafranski, "Peer Competitors, the R.M.A., and New Concepts," *Naval War College Review*, Spring 1996, 114. Kearns observes that the language George Kennan used in "articulating the containment policy for the Cold War . . . could not be closer to Mackinder's." Gerry Kearns, *Geopolitics and Empire*, 25; compare Petersen, *World Island*, 36ff. The tension, in the WASP approach to foreign policy, between the realism of Theodore Roosevelt and the idealism of Woodrow Wilson is discussed above in chapters 22, "The New Patricians in War," 23, "The New Patricians in Peace," and 33, "Centurions of an American Century."

p. 145 *"I incline to let England sink"*: Samuels, *Henry Adams*, 345. Somewhat inconsistently with this "insular policy," Adams advocated an "Atlantic combine" in which the United States, Great Britain, France, and Russia would cooperate to constrain Germany: a geopolitical alliance which became operational in the First and Second World Wars. See Adams, *Education*, 439; Samuels, *Henry Adams*, 341; and Harper, *American Visions of Europe*, 186.

p. 145 *Edith Roosevelt left Washington*: Accounts of Ted's illness and his parents' visit to Groton in February 1902 appeared in numerous contemporary newspapers.

p. 146 *domesticated*: Lionel Trilling described how Dr. Arnold of Rugby sought "to channel bullying strength into a feudal protective nobility," with each sixth former "both police and magistrate, accountable for the discipline of the whole school." Lionel Trilling, *Matthew Arnold* (New York: Harcourt Brace Jovanovich, 1979), 66. Peabody had evidently taken note. "The Groton Boy and the Groton code cracked down on bullies swiftly, effectively; I've seen it happen," Oliver La Farge wrote. "But they gave extra impetus to the mass-bullying which exists in most places where boys are confined together in numbers." *Raw Material*, 12.

p. 146 *humped*: "The most notorious scene of horror was Eton's Long Chamber, where a horde of unsupervised boys buggered each other in the beds, while packs of rats romped under them and dead ones rotted under the floorboards. One man claimed he would rather murder his son than have him see what he had seen in the Long Chamber." Eve Auchincloss, "The Making of an Englishman," *Washington Post*, October 29, 1978. Before going up to Eton, Cyril Connolly and his school chums at St. Wulfric's were warned that they "must report any boy at once who tried to get into our bed . . ." Cyril Connolly, *Enemies of Promise*, 179.

p. 146 *"after a rather vehement debate"*: For Ted's pumping, see Biddle, "As I Remember Groton School," in *Views from the Circle*, 115–116.

p. 146 *"in which all the boys were bareheaded"*: *Buffalo Times*, February 7, 1902.

p. 147 *Cotty had tried to persuade him*: Ashburn, *Peabody of Groton*, 66.

p. 147 *"killing stories"*: *F.D.R.: His Personal Letters: Early Years*, ed. Elliott Roosevelt, 110.

p. 147 *"not to take champagne or butlers"*: Martin, "Preface to a Schoolmaster's Biography," in *Views from the Circle*, 142.

p. 147 *"Mrs. Peabody scrambled the eggs"*: Sedgwick, "Three Men of Groton," in *Views from the Circle*, 21.

p. 147 *"Pray do not think me grown timid"*: *The Letters of Theodore Roosevelt: The Square Deal 1901–1903*, ed. Elting E. Morison (Cambridge, Mass.: Harvard University Press, 1951) III, 215.

p. 147 *"burst into my room"*: William Lawrence, *Memories of a Happy Life* (Boston: Houghton Mifflin, 1926), 222.

p. 147 *"formation of a responsible elite"*: Hofstadter, *Age of Reform*, 163.

p. 148 *"If some Groton boys do not enter political life"*: Ashburn, *Peabody of Groton*, 113.

p. 148 *playing fields of Eton*: Perhaps the Duke never said or believed this. But it is one of those sayings that are too good to let go of.

17. THE GREAT WORLD AND J. P. MORGAN

p. 150 *"Mr. Rainsford, will you be our rector?"*: W. S. Rainsford, *The Story of a Varied Life: An Autobiography* (Garden City, N.Y.: Doubleday, Page, 1922), 200–201.

p. 150 *"The rector wants to democratize the church"*: Ibid., 281.

p. 150 *"I will never sit in this vestry again"*: Ibid., 283.

p. 150 *"pray for me, pray for me"*: Elizabeth Moulton, *St. George's Church, New York* (New York: St. George's Church, 1964), 80.

p. 151 *"incarnation of the will to power"*: J. W. Burrow, *The Crisis of Reason: European Thought 1848–1918* (New Haven, Conn.: Yale University Press, 2000) 118.

p. 151 *"metal-hard natures"*: Oswald Spengler, *The Decline of the West*, trans. Charles Francis Atkinson, abridged by Helmut Werner, ed. and abridged by Arthur Helps (Oxford, U.K.: Oxford University Press, 1991), 29.

p. 151 *"poignant"*: Holmes, *Collected Legal Papers*, 280.

p. 151 *"appalling excrescences"*: So Joseph Duveen, Bernard Berenson's collaborator, characterized the nose. See Dominic Hobson, *The Pride of Lucifer: Morgan Grenfell 1838–1988: The Unauthorized Biography of a Merchant Bank* (London: Hamish Hamilton, 1990), 35.

p. 151   *"too terrible to look at"*: Jean Strouse, *Morgan: American Financier* (New York: Random House, 2014), 492.

p. 151   *"perfect insensibility"*: Virginia Woolf, *Roger Fry: A Biography* (New York: Harcourt, Brace, 1940), 141.

p. 151   *"I wish the Vanderbilts didn't retard culture so very thoroughly"*: Louis Auchincloss, *The Vanderbilt Era: Profiles of a Gilded Age* (New York: Collier, 1990), 153.

p. 152   *"pawnbroker's shop for Croesuses"*: Strouse, *Morgan*, 504.

p. 152   *"sharpened appetite of the collector"*: Henry James, *The Golden Bowl*, 2 vols. (London: Macmillan, 1923), I, 125.

p. 152   *"This bronze Bust is in your library"*: Strouse, *Morgan*, 486.

p. 152   *"Morganatic harmony"*: A theme developed by Jean Strouse in her biography of Morgan.

p. 152   *"send your man to my man and they can fix it up"*: Geoffrey C. Ward, *The Roosevelts: An Intimate History* (New York: Knopf, 2014), 81.

p. 152   *"tremendous whack"*: Strouse, *Morgan*, 440.

p. 152   *"Bosh: I know Jack Morgan"*: *George Santayana's Marginalia: A Critical Selection*, ed. John McCormick (Cambridge, Mass.: M.I.T. Press, 2011), II, 260.

p. 153   *"big rival operator"*: James Ford Rhodes, *History of the United States*, 9 vols. (New York: Macmillan, 1928), IX, 223.

p. 153   *WASP big tent*: E. Digby Baltzell maintains that the "formation of the United States Steel Company (1901), the founding of Groton School (1884), the opening of the new 'millionaires' country club' at Tuxedo Park, New York (1885), the rule of Mrs. Ascot and Ward McAllister (1880s and 1890s), the Bradley-Martin ball (at the cost of $369,200 in 1897), and the first issue of the *Social Register* (1888)," represented a deliberate effort, on the part of WASPs, to nationalize America's elites. Old blood and new fortunes would combine to perpetuate the power of a "national upper class." Baltzell, *Philadelphia Gentlemen*, 21.

p. 153   *wherever-people-are-rich-together places*: Mount Desert (pronounced by WASPs as though it were spelled "dessert") was another of these places, though Bar Harbor tended to be "fast," while Northeast Harbor aspired (in theory) to the older ideal of plain living and high thinking. On a summer day on the island *circa* 1910 one might encounter such old WASPs as Cotty Peabody, Bishop Lawrence, Dr. Drury of St. Paul's School, and Harvard's President Eliot, as well as plutocrats newly initiated, among them the Rockefellers.

p. 153   *"little white hand"*: Henry James, *The American Scene* (New York: Harper, 1907), 203.

p. 153   *"vulgarest society in the world"*: Tyler Dennett, *John Hay: From Poetry to Politics* (New York: Dodd, Mead, 1933), 164.

p. 153   *"Newport cads"*: Edward Wagenknecht, *The Seven Worlds of Theodore Roosevelt* (Guilford, Conn.: Globe Pequot, 2009), 138.

p. 153   *"the chink of money"*: Henry James, *The Ivory Tower* (New York: Scribner's, 1917), 23.

p. 153   *"prohibited degrees of witlessness"*: James, *American Scene*, 217.

p. 154   *"money power"*: Adams, *Life of George Cabot Lodge*, 48.

p. 154   *"gold-fever"*: Wharton, *Backward Glance*, 56.

p. 154   *"famous Newbold Madeira"*: Ibid., 58.

p. 154   *"I have known"*: Charles Francis Adams, *An Autobiography* (New York: Russell and Russell, 1968), 190.

p. 155   *"Episcopalianization"*: Baltzell, *Philadelphia Gentlemen*, 391.

p. 155   *"cold roast"*: Amory, *Proper Bostonians*, 13.

p. 156   *"a scandal and a pollution"*: Ronald Syme, *The Roman Revolution* (Oxford, U.K.: Oxford University Press, 1989), 11.

p. 156   *"absolutely unmixed race"*: On Elizabeth Chanler Chapman's belief that the Brahmins were "as *bona fide* an aristocracy as exists anywhere in the world," as see Lucey, *Sargent's Women*.

p. 156   *"cramped horizontal gridiron of a town"*: Wharton, *Backward Glance*, 55.

p. 156   *"vast despair"*: Ron Chernow, *The House of Morgan: An American Banking Dynasty and the Rise of Modern Finance* (New York: Grove, 2010) (ebook available online).

p. 156   *anthracite coal strike*: Hofstadter, *Age of Reform*, 236.

p. 156   *"A man I do not trust"*: Strouse, *Morgan*, 13.

p. 157 *"to protect it by as many police"*: Hofstadter, *The American Political Tradition*, 282.

p. 157 *"apex as well as the type"*: Howe, *John Jay Chapman*, 227.

p. 157 *"genuine lover of the beautiful"*: Santayana, *Dominations and Powers*, 277–278.

p. 157 *"astonished by the luxury"*: Woolf, *Roger Fry*, 130. Beatrice Webb, who saw the life of the tycoons through her father's business dealings with them, came away with a similar impression. "The presidents of American railways, international financiers, company promoters and contractors, were forceful men, frequently of magnetic personality and witty conversation; but the common ideal which bound them in a close fraternity was a stimulating mixture of personal power and personal luxury; their common recreation was high living. Uniquely typical was the life on board a president's car on an American railway: the elaborate accommodation and fittings; the French chef; the over-abundant food; the extravagantly choice wines and liqueurs; above all, the consciousness of personal prestige and power; the precedence of the president's car over all other traffic; the obsequious attentions of ubiquitous officials; the contemptuous bargaining with political 'bosses' for land concessions and for the passage of bills through legislatures— altogether a low moral temperature." Beatrice Webb, *My Apprenticeship*, I, 24.

18. MANDARINISM

p. 158 *Learned Hand*: Except where otherwise noted, the account of Learned Hand in this chapter is drawn from Gunther's *Learned Hand: The Man and the Judge*.

p. 160 *"a kissing"*: Santayana, *The Life of Reason*, in *The Philosophy of George Santayana*, ed. Irwin Edman, 115.

p. 161 *high WASPs*: In concentrating on a few dozen notable WASPs, the author is conscious that he has failed to give an accurate account of the class as a whole, to do justice to the stockbrokers. A not easily avoided shortcoming: the stockbrokers left fewer records, and those records are, for the most part, dull. You find a comparable negligence in even the greatest histories. Pericles looms larger in Thucydides's history than do ordinary Athenians; you learn a good deal more, in Gibbon, about the emperors than the *proletarii*. The larger difficulty lies in defining the *limits* of particular groups, in fixing the boundaries of Terminus. In the course of this book the author distinguishes between WASPs and Brahmins, and between high WASPs and lesser WASPs. But while these categories are, the author believes, real, they are in their nature generalizations; you cannot draw definite lines between them.

p. 162 *Dorothy Whitney*: Except where otherwise noted, the account of Dorothy Whitney that follows is drawn from Swanberg's *Whitney Father, Whitney Heiress*; Michael Straight's *After Long Silence* (New York: Norton, 1984); and Herbert Croly's *Willard Straight* (New York: Macmillan, 1924).

p. 163 *"Wonderful ride"*: Swanberg, *Whitney Father, Whitney Heiress*, 236.

p. 163 *"a bullet wound in his right temple"*: Louise Pecquet du Bellet, *Some Prominent Virginia Families*; 4 vols. (Lynchburg: J. P. Bell, 1907), II, 90–91; *Philadelphia Inquirer*, May 8, 1906, 7.

p. 164 *"unusual frankness and charm of manner"*: Croly, *Willard Straight*, 135.

p. 165 *"magic of China"*: Ibid., 358.

19. FROM THEODORE AT ARMAGEDDON TO THE *NEW REPUBLIC* ON WEST TWENTY-FIRST STREET

p. 168 *"Work—fight—breed"*: Philip W. Kennedy, "The Racial Overtones of Imperialism as a Campaign Issue, 1900," in *Race and U.S. Foreign Policy in the Ages of Territorial and Market Expansion 1840–1900*, ed. Michael L. Krenn (New York: Routledge, 2013), 203; Thomas G. Dyer, *Theodore Roosevelt and the Idea of Race* (Baton Rouge: Louisiana State University Press, 1980), 148; Theodore Roosevelt, *American Ideals and Other Essays, Social and Political*; 2 vols. (New York: Scribner's, 1906) II, 156.

p. 168 *disposable*: "When men fear work or fear righteous war, when women fear motherhood, they tremble on the brink of doom; and well it is that they should vanish from the earth . . ." *The Real Roosevelt: His Forceful and Fearless Utterances on Various Subjects*, ed. Alan Warner (New York: Putnam's, 1910), 158.

p. 168 *boyishness undiminished*: William James thought Roosevelt in middle age less a boy than a teenager, "still mentally in the Sturm and Drang period of early adolescence . . ." William James, "Governor Roosevelt's Oration," *The Conservative*, May 18, 1899, 8.

p. 168 *"It has not the excuse of champagne"*: *Letters of Henry Adams 1892–1918*, ed. Ford, 419.

p. 171 *"hunted me up"*: Croly, *Willard Straight*, 472.

p. 172 *"Why don't you get out a weekly"*: David W. Levy, *Herbert Croly of the* New Republic: *The Life and Thought of an American Progressive* (Princeton, N.J.: Princeton University Press, 1985), 188–189.

p. 172 *a good WASP club*: See Steel, *Walter Lippmann and the American Century,* 61–62.

p. 172 *Young Walter*: The account of Walter Lippmann that follows is drawn primarily from Steel, *Walter Lippmann and the American Century.*

p. 173 *"I suppose it is humanistic . . ."*: Ibid., 62.

20. FRANKLIN AND ELEANOR

p. 176 *"slightly unnatural sunniness"*: Edward Gale Agran, *Herbert Hoover and the Commodification of Middle-Class America* (Lanham, Md.: Lexington, 2016), 214.

p. 176 *"utterly frivolous life"*: Harold Ivan Smith, *Eleanor: A Spiritual Biography* (Louisville, Ky.: Westminster John Knox Press, 2017), 25.

p. 176 *"Eleanor, I hardly know what's to happen to you"*: Alonzo Hamby, *Man of Destiny: F.D.R. and the Making of the American Century* (New York: Basic, 2015), 27.

p. 176 *"flagrant man swine"*: The author here follows Edmund Morris, who argues that Elliott figured in his brother's eyes as a human pig. See Morris, *The Rise of Theodore Roosevelt*, 430. But the author adopts Morris's position with some misgiving. Roosevelt uses the phrase "flagrant man swine" in his *Autobiography* to describe the sexual predator who "hunts down poor or silly or unprotected girls." See Theodore Roosevelt, *An Autobiography*, 204. If Elliott did, indeed, seduce "a servant girl named Katy Mann," he would certainly belong to his brother's category of predator. But whether Theodore himself actually saw his brother in that light may be doubted: for Roosevelt the public moralist and Roosevelt the private man were not invariably the same person. Morris himself is dead and can no longer shed light on the matter.

p. 176 *"dreadful flashes of his old sweetness"*: Morris, *Edith Kermit Roosevelt: Portrait of a First Lady*, 143.

p. 176 *"of past beauty and present attractiveness"*: Webb, *My Apprenticeship*, II, note 114.

p. 177 *"dignity of manner"*: Beatrice Webb, *Our Partnership*, ed. Barbara Drake and Margaret Cole (London: Longman's, Green, 1948), 302–303.

p. 177 *"a Promethean fire which warmed and coloured"*: Dorothy Strachey, *Olivia* (New York: Penguin, 2020), 24.

p. 177 *"had an eagle eye"*: For Marie Souvestre and Eleanor Roosevelt's schooldays at Allenswood, see Blanche Wiesen Cook, *Eleanor Roosevelt: Volume One: 1884–1933* (New York: Penguin, 1993), 102–124.

p. 177 *"narrowness of vision"*: Webb, *Our Partnership*, 303.

p. 179 *"a popular debutante"*: Cook, *Eleanor Roosevelt: 1884–1933*, 131.

p. 179 *"she was really rather attractive"*: Michael Teague, *Mrs. L.: Conversations with Alice Roosevelt Longworth* (Garden City, N.Y.: Doubleday, 1981), 154.

p. 180 *"a charming man"*: Cook, *Eleanor Roosevelt: 1884–1933*, 152.

p. 180 *"Feather Duster"*: Alsop, *F.D.R.: A Centenary Remembrance*, 36. Gore Vidal said that Alice Roosevelt Longworth habitually referred to her cousin in this way: "*We* were the President Roosevelt family. But then along came the Feather Duster." Vidal, *United States: Essays*, 724 (emphasis in original).

p. 180 *united the two severed Roosevelt lines*: In 1904 a Hyde Park Roosevelt, Helen, the daughter of Franklin's half-brother James "Rosy" Roosevelt, married an Oyster Bay Roosevelt, Theodore Douglas Robinson, the son of Theodore Roosevelt's sister (and Joe Alsop's grandmother) Corinne Roosevelt Robinson.

p. 180 *"man sent from God to help the world in its dire need"*: Geoffrey C. Ward, *A First-Class Temperament: The Emergence of Franklin Roosevelt 1905–1928* (New York: Vintage, 2014), 90.

p. 181 *Pragmatism was in fashion*: See Louis Menand, *The Metaphysical Club: A Study of Ideas in America* (New York: Farrar, Straus and Giroux, 2001) for a comprehensive treatment of the subject.

p. 181 *"It seems quite necessary for a Groton boy to have him"*: Joseph P. Lash, *Eleanor and Franklin* (ebook available online).

p. 181 *"drunk, loud, and silly"*: Cook, *Eleanor Roosevelt: 1884–1933*, 304.

p. 182   *"deserved a good time"*: Joseph P. Lash, *Love, Eleanor: Eleanor Roosevelt and Her Friends* (Garden City, N.Y.: Doubleday, 1982), 69.

p. 182   *"I have lived in this house many years"*: Ward, *First-Class Temperament*, 214.

p. 183   *"that is a very terrible thing to say to a young man"*: Vidal, *United States: Essays*, 662.

p. 183   *"very interesting but sad"*: Cook, *Eleanor Roosevelt: 1884–1933*, 207.

p. 183   *"steady remodeling"*: Adams, *Education*, 240.

21. THE WASPS THROW OFF VICTORIANISM

p. 184   *"awfully bad psychologically"*. The account of Alice Roosevelt Longworth that follows is drawn primarily from Cordery, *Alice: Alice Roosevelt Longworth*.

p. 185   *kissed by a boy*: F. Scott Fitzgerald, *This Side of Paradise* (New York, Scribner's, 1920), 65.

p. 186   *"greedy for sensation"*: Alice Roosevelt Longworth, *Crowded Hours: Reminiscences of Alice Roosevelt Longworth* (New York: Scribner's, 1933), 41.

p. 186   *Gertrude Vanderbilt*: The account of Gertrude Vanderbilt that follows is drawn primarily from Auchincloss, *The Vanderbilt Era*; Bernard Harper Friedman and Flora Miller Irving, *Gertrude Vanderbilt Whitney: A Biography* (Garden City, N.Y.: Doubleday, 1978); Flora Miller Biddle, *The Whitney Women and the Museum They Made: A Family Memoir* (New York: Simon & Schuster, 2017); and Clarice Stasz, *The Vanderbilt Women: Dynasty of Wealth, Glamour, and Tragedy* (New York: St. Martin's, 1991).

p. 186   *"Alas, when a girl is twenty she is on the road to being an old maid"*: Friedman and Irving, *Gertrude Vanderbilt Whitney*, 74.

p. 187   *"It never has made any difference to him"*: Avis Berman, *Rebels on Eighth Street: Juliana Force and the Whitney Museum of American Art* (New York: Atheneum, 1990), 62.

p. 187   *"Bomb"*: Stasz, *The Vanderbilt Women* (ebook available online), 263.

p. 187   *"Fatty"*: Ibid., 253.

p. 187   *"sympathetic and strong and magnetic"*: Ibid., 254.

p. 187   *"great passion of selfishness"*: Ibid.

p. 188   *"sapped and all her fine possibilities destroyed"*: Ibid., 261.

p. 188   *"his beautiful bare body"*: Friedman and Irving, *Gertrude Vanderbilt Whitney*, 233.
         "she has the true vocation": Stasz, *The Vanderbilt Women*, 288.

p. 188   *"attic kept warm by an iron stove"*: Edmund Wilson, *The American Earthquake: A Documentary of the Twenties and Thirties* (New York: Farrar, Straus and Giroux, 1979), 101.

p. 189   *"pianists, painters"*: Lois Palken Rudnick, *Mabel Dodge Luhan: New Woman, New Worlds* (Albuquerque: University of New Mexico Press, 1984), 95.

p. 189   *"Cubist balls"*: C. L. Edson, *The Gentle Art of Columning* (New York: Brentano's, 1920), 92.

p. 189   *"to get a cheap eyeful of Greenwich Village beauty"*: Ibid., 93.

p. 189   *"who had never been in touch before"*: Hofstadter, *Anti-intellectualism in American Life*, 205.

p. 189   *"quarrels, difficulties, entanglements, abrupt and violent detachments"*: Steel, *Walter Lippmann and the American Century*, 50.

p. 190   *"be as real as mud"*: Robert Hughes, *American Visions: The Epic History of Art in America* (New York: Knopf, 1997), 325.

p. 190   *"very few people that one could marry"*: Edmund Wilson, *A Prelude* (New York: Farrar Straus and Giroux, 1967), 31.

p. 191   *State Department*: Hugh R. Wilson (Hill School, Yale), a WASP diplomat and anti-Semite, described the State Department as "a pretty good club." Martin Weil, *A Pretty Good Club: The Founding Fathers of the U.S. Foreign Service* (New York: Norton, 1978), 47.

p. 191   *"We can't make cocktails"*: Hector MacQuarrie, *Over Here: Impressions of America by a British Officer* (Philadelphia: J.P. Lippincott, 1918), 40.

p. 192   *"The hand that mixes the Georgetown martini"*: C. David Heymann, *The Georgetown Ladies' Social Club: Power, Passion, and Politics in the Nation's Capital* (New York: Atria, 2003), 316.

p. 193 *"My brother had a ravenous appetite and bolted his food"*: For Halla's death, see Stein, *Edie*, 34–35.

p. 193 *"changed singularly little"*: Biddle, "As I Remember Groton School," in *Views from the Circle*, 127.

p. 193 *"something phony"*: George W. Martin, "Preface to a Schoolmaster's Biography," in *Views from the Circle*, 136.

p. 193 *"never bear to see the school or a boy anything but shipshape"*: Ashburn, *Peabody of Groton*, 95.

p. 194 *cocktails and spirits*: "Our drinking habits in America are of the worst possible nature. We drink a lot of hard liquor and that between meals. I wish very much that we could establish the fashion of drinking at meals only and then taking either wine or beer." Ibid., 198.

p. 194 *"contents of your letter from Bermuda"*: Ibid., 125.

p. 194 *whole business shallow*: Peabody had a point. Lucretius says that the fruits of Venus are sweetest when served without the garnish of love. This may be true, but the liberated WASPs discovered, to their chagrin, that if love is dispensable, guilt and shame are necessary seasonings: as they receded, so did the erotic imagination that they fed.

p. 195 *"punch Cotty Peabody's head"*: Hinchman, "My Groton Years," in *Views from the Circle*, 169.

p. 195 *"As long as I live"*: Karabel, *The Chosen*, 567.

22. THE NEW PATRICIANS IN WAR

p. 196 *"It was a perfect summer day"*: Wharton, *Backward Glance*, 336.

p. 197 *"Paris looked grubby"*: *The Letters of Henry Adams 1906–1918*, ed. J. C. Levenson et al. (Cambridge, Mass.: Belknap Press, 1988), VI, 654.

p. 197 *"I rather like November in Washington"*: Ibid., VI, 652.

p. 197 *"quick dash"*: Wharton, *Backward Glance*, 337.

p. 198 *"saturated with pure light"*: Wharton describes the outbreak of the war in *A Backward Glance*, 337–338.

p. 198 *"Everything blackened over"*: Henry James, *Letters*, ed. Leon Edel (Cambridge, Mass.: Belknap Press, 1984), IV (1895–1916), 569.

p. 198 *"crash of our civilization"*: Hazel Hutchinson, "'The Crash of Civilisation': James and the Idea of France, 1914–15," in *Henry James's Europe: Heritage and Transfer*, ed. Dennis Tredy, Annick Duperray, and Adrian Harding (Cambridge, U.K.: OpenBook, 2011), 61.

p. 198 *"comparatively parvenu"*: T. S. Eliot, "A Sceptical Patrician," *The Athenæum*, May 23, 1919, 362; Eric W. Sigg, *The American T. S. Eliot: A Study of the Early Writings* (Cambridge, U.K.: Cambridge University Press, 2009), 150.

p. 198 *"portentous"*: Edel, *Henry James: A Life*, 569.

p. 199 *"practiced black magic"*: Ford Madox Ford, *Thus to Revisit: Some Reminiscences* (New York: E.P. Dutton, 1921), 48.

p. 199 *aloofness*: Edel, *Henry James: A Life*, 569.

p. 199 *"well-meaning old trunk"*: Susan E. Gunter and Steven H. Jove, "Dearly Beloved Friends: Henry James's Letters to Younger Men," in *Henry James and Homo-Erotic Desire*, ed. John R. Bradley (New York: St. Martin's, 1999), 132.

p. 199 *"dramatized his own experience"*: For Wilson on James, see Wilson, "The Ambiguity of Henry James," in Wilson, *Triple Thinkers*, 150.

p. 199 *"native of the James family"*: Millicent Bell, *Edith Wharton & Henry James: The Story of Their Friendship* (New York: George Braziller, 1965), 46.

p. 199 *"actively gay"*: Fred Kaplan, "Henry James's Love Life," *Slate*, January 18, 1997.

p. 200 *"There is NO 'fascination' whatever"*: Henry James, *Letters*, ed. Leon Edel (Cambridge, Mass.: Belknap Press, 1984), IV (1895–1916), 339.

p. 200 *"However British you may be"*: Wilson, "The Ambiguity of Henry James," in Wilson, *Triple Thinkers*, 121.

p. 200 *"the sole, the exquisite England"*: Henry James, *Within the Rim: And Other Essays 1914–15* (London: Collins, 1918), 18.

p. 200 *"innocent little girl"*: Wilson, "The Ambiguity of Henry James," in Wilson, *Triple Thinkers*, 128.

p. 200 *"swathed in relative clauses as an invalid in shawls"*: West, *Henry James*, 41.

p. 200 *"just to please Brother"*: Robert D. Richardson, *William James: In the Maelstrom of American Modernism: A Biography* (Boston: Mariner, 2007), 464.

p. 200 *"I once gave* The Turn of the Screw": Wilson, "The Ambiguity of Henry James," in Wilson, *Triple Thinkers*, 127.

p. 201 *"Very sorry"*: Wharton, *Backward Glance*, 339.

p. 201 *"like an octogenarian rat"*: *The Letters of Henry Adams 1906–1918*, ed. J. C. Levenson, VI, 655.

p. 201 *"crumbling of worlds"*: Ibid., VI, 658.

p. 201 *"a religion of high explosives"*: Ibid., VI, 692.

p. 201 *"quite as Anti-Prussian"*: Samuels, *Bernard Berenson: The Making of a Legend*, 187.

p. 201 *"more changed and gone"*: James, *Letters*, IV (1895–1916), 722.

p. 202 *"To the honour of the British race"*: Wharton, *Backward Glance*, 342.

p. 202 *"just-send-a-cheque"*: It was Harry's refrain. See Stasz, *The Vanderbilt Women*, 254.

p. 202 *"is fighting then"*: Gertrude Vanderbilt Whitney's Juilly Hospital Journals 1914, Archives of American Art, Smithsonian.

p. 202 *"deadly cold winter trenches"*: Ibid.

p. 202 *"face of the world is black"*: Ibid.

p. 203 *"one of the best organized"*: Richard Derby, *"Wade In, Sanitary!": The Story of a Division Surgeon in France* (New York: G.P. Putnam's Sons, 1919), 51.

p. 203 *sought to remodel aspiration:* When America entered the war in 1917, fewer than seven hundred boys had graduated from Groton, and some seventy men had taught or were teaching there. According to Frank Ashburn, who wrote the first history of the school, 440 of these men served in the United States Armed Forces during the war (388 commissioned officers and 52 enlisted men), while 35 served in Allied units or in organizations such as the Red Cross: more than sixty percent of the total number of alumni and faculty. Six were killed in action, 36 were wounded, and 18 died in war service. Ashburn, *Fifty Years On*, 151–164.

p. 203 *Lord Kitchener:* "He startled his colleagues at the first cabinet which he attended by announcing that the war would last three years, not three months, and that Great Britain would have to put an army of millions into the field." He "expected the French army to be defeated," but he did not, however, foresee trench warfare. A.J.P. Taylor, *English History 1914–1945* (Oxford, U.K.: Oxford University Press, 2001), 20.

p. 204 *before his family could object:* *New York Times*, January 16, 1916; *Princeton Union*, January 20, 1916.

p. 204 *"to shake hands and thank them for a wonderful game"*: For Hobey Baker, see Nelson W. Aldrich Jr., *Old Money: The Mythology of Wealth in America* (New York: Allworth Press, 1996), 101–103, 173.

p. 204 *"growth of that dreadful military spirit"*: Lionel Arthur Tollemache, *Talks with Mr. Gladstone* (New York: Longman's, Green, 1898), 205.

p. 205 *"quite so great as the supreme triumphs of war"*: Gore Vidal, citing these words, once asked Alice Roosevelt Longworth "why her father was such a war-lover." "Oh, well," she replied, "that's the way they all sounded in those days." Vidal, *United States: Essays 1952–1992*, 733–734.

p. 205 *"true and adorable"*: Oliver Wendell Holmes Jr., "The Soldier's Faith," in Holmes, *An Address by Oliver Wendell Holmes Delivered on Memorial Day, May 30, 1895, at a Meeting Called by the Graduating Class of Harvard University* (Boston: Little, Brown, 1895), 6.

p. 205 *"natural instinct for self-assertion"*: Jaeger, *Paideia: The Ideals of Greek Culture: Archaic Greece, The Mind of Athens*, I, 13.

p. 206 *"Do you not believe"*: Theodore Roosevelt to Hugo Münsterberg, October 3, 1914, Theodore Roosevelt Papers, Library of Congress Manuscript Division.

p. 206 *"Thanks to the width of the ocean"*: Kissinger, *Diplomacy*, 43.

p. 206 *"I take you to my sister"*: Robert Graves, *Goodbye to All That* (London: Cassell, 1958), 80.

p. 206 *"You're wasting yourselves, lads"*: Ibid., 85.

p. 206 *"Jock Miller"*: Ibid.

p. 207 *"dropping like flies"*: "The Battle of Loos—1915," *The Guards Magazine: Journal of the Household Division*, Autumn 2015.

p. 207 *"After the first day or two the bodies swelled and stank"*: Graves, *Goodbye to All That*, 144.

p. 208	*"looking on while England and France"*: *Quentin Roosevelt: A Sketch with Letters*, ed. Kermit Roosevelt (New York: Scribner's, 1922), 31.

p. 208	*"was a message of death"*: Joseph Patrick Tumulty, *Woodrow Wilson as I Know Him* (Garden City, N.Y.: Doubleday, 1921), 256.

p. 208	*"there can be no assured security"*: "The War Message Delivered by President Woodrow Wilson," *New York Times Current History: The European War April–June 1917* (New York: New York Times Company, 1917), 196.

p. 208	*"great state papers"*: Joseph Bucklin Bishop, *Theodore Roosevelt and His Time*, 2 vols. (Charles Scribner's Sons, 1920), II, 423.

p. 209	*"Did you make that point quite clear"*: Edward J. Renehan Jr., *The Lion's Pride: Theodore Roosevelt and His Family in Peace and War* (Oxford, U.K.: Oxford University Press, 1999), 129; Joseph E. Persico, *Franklin and Lucy: President Roosevelt, Mrs. Rutherfurd, and the Other Remarkable Women in His Life* (New York: Random House, 2008) 4 (emphasis added).

p. 209	*"it's absolute worship on my part"*: Edmund Morris, *Colonel Roosevelt* (New York: Random House, 2011), 498.

p. 209	*"the hideous side of war"*: Stimson and Bundy, *On Active Service in Peace and War*, 98.

p. 210	*"Too much food and good wine"*: Swanberg, *Whitney Father, Whitney Heiress*, 376.

p. 210	*"Nick and I are both members of the Porc"*: Amory, *Proper Bostonians*, 304.

p. 211	*"a corker"*: Swanberg, *Whitney Father, Whitney Heiress*, 382.

p. 211	*"Hotspur Hal"*: Ibid., 387.

p. 211	*"Everybody with their tails up"*: Ibid., 423.

p. 211	*"watch sagamore hill in event of"*: Morris, *Colonel Roosevelt*, 528.

p. 211	*"No, it is true"*: Ibid., 530.

p. 211	*"dared the Great Adventure of Death"*: *The Americanism of Theodore Roosevelt: Selections from His Writings and Speeches*, ed. Hermann Hagedorn (Boston: Houghton Mifflin, 1923), 91.

p. 211	*"Poor Quenty-Quee"*: Peter Collier with David Horowitz, *The Roosevelts: An American Saga* (New York: Simon & Schuster, 1994), 239.

p. 212	*"would prefer short intense pleasures"*: See Werner Jaeger's discussion of this passage in Jaeger, *Paideia: The Ideals of Greek Culture: Archaic Greece, The Mind of Athens*, I, 12–14.

23. THE NEW PATRICIANS IN PEACE

p. 214	*"utterly irresponsible"*: Swanberg, *Whitney Father, Whitney Heiress*, 380.

p. 214	*"Vice is rampant"*: Margaret Macmillan, *Paris 1919: Six Months that Changed the World* (New York: Random House, 2003), 146.

p. 214	*"My dear Miss Maxwell"*: Elsa Maxwell, *I Married the World* (London: Quality Book Club, 1955), 109.

p. 214	*"dawn of a new era"*: Swanberg, *Whitney Father, Whitney Heiress*, 433.

p. 214	*"I am afraid it is a sort of diplomatic liaison job"*: Ibid.

p. 215	*"having such a wonderful time"*: Ibid., 429.

p. 215	*"even though you didn't get all the fighting you wanted"*: Ibid., 428.

p. 215	*"has been holding Marshal Foch's hand so successfully"*: Ibid., 438.

p. 215	*"tremendous world game"*: Ibid., 428.

p. 216	*"that he had various niches"*: Croly, *Willard Straight*, 532.

p. 216	*"Czechs and Jugoslavs"*: Swanberg, *Whitney Father, Whitney Heiress*, 433.

p. 216	*Larue*: For Straight's social life in Paris, see Swanberg, *Whitney Father, Whitney Heiress*, especially 433–442.

p. 216	*"whale of a job"*: Swanberg, *Whitney Father, Whitney Heiress*, 441.

p. 217	*Clemenceau*: Ibid., 439–40.

p. 217	*"people could be brought together"*: Ibid., 440.

p. 217	*"PLEASE HAVE HERBERT CROLY"*: For the last illness and death of Willard Straight, see Swanberg, *Whitney Father, Whitney Heiress*, 441–446.

p. 218 *"give to the whole world a new message"*: Harold Nicolson, *Peacemaking 1919* (London: Methuen, 1964), 52.

p. 218 *the old Calvinist modes lingered*: There was, of course, a residual puritanism in the WASPs themselves, but it was deeper down.

p. 218 *"were essentially theological not intellectual"*: John Maynard Keynes, *The Economic Consequences of the Peace* (New York: Harcourt Brace, 1920), 42.

p. 219 *Clemenceau was appalled*: Clemenceau adhered to the concepts of national interest and the balance of power: "There is an old system of alliances called the Balance of Power—this system of alliances, which I do not renounce, will be my guiding thought at the Peace Conference." Lloyd E. Ambrosius, *Woodrow Wilson and the American Diplomatic Tradition. The Treaty Fight in Perspective* (Cambridge, U.K.: Cambridge University Press, 1990), 54.

p. 219 *"Fourteen?"*: Clemenceau's words have been handed down in various versions. Following the precedent established by Thucydides, the author has set down what the Tiger *ought* to have said.

p. 219 *"visionary"*: *Roosevelt in* the Kansas City Star: *War-Time Editorials by Theodore Roosevelt* (Boston: Houghton Mifflin, 1921), 279.

p. 219 *"mean anything or nothing"*: Ibid., 229.

p. 219 *"You helped write these points"*: Steel, *Walter Lippmann and the American Century,* 149.

p. 219 *"the agilities of the council chamber"*: Keynes, *Economic Consequences of the Peace,* 43.

p. 220 *"slowness amongst the Europeans"*: Ibid.

p. 220 *Frank Polk*: Polk came to Paris after Lansing resigned as secretary of state in February 1920.

p. 220 *"ugly mood"*: Richard Striner, *Woodrow Wilson and World War I: A Burden Too Great to Bear* (Lanham, Md.: Rowman & Littlefield, 2014), 267.

p. 220 *"chart marking out the course"*: Robert Lansing, *The Peace Negotiations: A Personal Narrative* (Boston: Houghton Mifflin, 1921), 200.

p. 221 *"dark rather long-haired man"*: Samuels, *Bernard Berenson: The Making of a Legend,* 233. It was at a party given by another of Mrs. Wharton's friends, Princess Soutzo, that Proust met the diplomat Harold Nicolson, whom he found "exquisite, exceptionally intelligent," and about whose work in connection with the Peace Conference he was intensely curious. Proust might have found Nicolson still more interesting could he have known that Nicolson's wife, Lady Nicolson (Vita Sackville-West), would one day be portrayed as Orlando, the androgynous figure in Virginia Woolf's novel. Proust's hostess, Princess Soutzo, was herself an exotic figure. Hélène Chrissoveloni was born in 1879 in Moldovia, the daughter of a Greek banker; in 1903 she married Prince Dimitri Soutzo, a member of the Greek Phanariote family who was then serving as a military attaché in the Romanian diplomatic service.

p. 221 *"Have you any idea"*: Cohen, *Bernard Berenson: A Life in the Picture Trade,* 244.

p. 221 *"one of the most charming of the everybodies"*: Samuels, *Bernard Berenson: The Making of a Legend,* 252.

p. 221 *"a very average man"*: Ibid., 253.

p. 221 *"a radiant youngster of thirty-seven"*: Ibid.

p. 221 *"intrigue and bluster"*: Steel, *Walter Lippmann and the American Century,* 152–153.

p. 221 *"no attention was being paid"*: Ibid., 178.

p. 222 *"is full beyond belief"*: Ward, *First-Class Temperament,* 423.

p. 222 *"visual values"*: Samuels, *Bernard Berenson: The Making of a Legend,* 235.

p. 222 *"thoroughly inconsequential"*: Waldo H. Heinrichs Jr., *American Ambassador: Joseph C. Grew and the Development of the United States Diplomatic Tradition* (Oxford, U.K.: Oxford University Press, 1986), 5.

p. 223 *"a terribly nice fellow"*: Ibid., 37.

p. 223 *"backbone of diplomacy"*: Ibid., 46.

p. 223 *"dullness and dreariness"*: George F. Kennan, *Memoirs 1925–1950* (Boston: Little, Brown, 1967), 79.

p. 223 *"Every Groton fellow I know"*: Will Brownell and Richard N. Billings, *So Close to Greatness: A Biography of William C. Bullitt* (New York: Macmillan, 1987), 294.

p. 223 *"great spiritual awakening"*: Howard Jablon, *Crossroads of Decision: The State Department and Foreign Policy 1933–1937* (Lexington: University Press of Kentucky, 1983), 21.

p. 224 *Woodrow Wilson rejected a rapprochement*: Bullitt returned from Moscow "with Soviet proposals which were not ideal but which did offer the most favorable opportunity yet extended, or ever to be extended, to the Western powers for extracting themselves with some measure of good grace from the profitless involvements of the military intervention in Russia and for the creation of an acceptable relationship to the Soviet regime. He had been shabbily treated—disowned, in fact—on his return, by Wilson and Lloyd George." Kennan, *Memoirs 1925–1950*, 79–80.

p. 224 *limousines painted olive-drab*: John Dos Passos, *Three Soldiers* (Claremont, Calif.: Cayote Canyon, 2007), 225.

p. 225 *The treaty*: On the Treaty of Versailles, see Kissinger, *Diplomacy*, 218–265.

p. 225 *a defensive alliance in the east with Russia*: Moscow sought a military alliance with Paris in the middle thirties to counter German strength, but the French were suspicious. A Franco-Soviet Mutual Assistance Treaty was concluded in 1935, but it was largely hollow: the French thought that a stronger alliance would provoke Hitler. By the end of the decade both Paris and London, terrified by a now resurgent Germany, sought to come to terms with Moscow, but by then it was too late: Stalin spurned the democracies and thought he had a better deal in a nonaggression pact with Hitler.

p. 225 *"took a flight beyond the azure main"*: David Lloyd George, *Memoirs of the Peace Conference* (New Haven, Conn.: Yale University Press, 1939), I, 141–142.

p. 226 *looked to the League to correct the imperfections of the Treaty*: Wilson, John Maynard Keynes wrote, believed that the Covenant of the League of Nations in the Versailles Treaty outweighed "much evil in the rest of the Treaty," and that with the League as an accomplished fact, the world could look to it "for the gradual evolution of a more tolerable life for Europe." Keynes, *Economic Consequences of the Peace*, 256.

p. 226 *"the old Polish system"*: Santayana, *Dominations and Powers*, 456.

p. 226 *"collective action"*: *Events Leading Up to World War II*, ed. Library of Congress (Washington: U.S. Government Printing Office, 1944), 97.

p. 226 *"unwieldy polyglot debating society"*: Keynes, *Economic Consequences of the Peace*, 259.

p. 226 *"It is not a sufficient explanation"*: Nicholson, *Peacemaking 1919*, 73.

p. 226 *"conceited"*: Ibid., 52.

p. 226 *"obsessed by the conviction that the League Covenant"*: Ibid., 53.

p. 227 *"with one side of his face drooping"*: For Wilson's collapse and his subsequent invalidism, see A. Scott Berg, *Wilson* (New York: G.P. Putnam's Sons, 2013), 635ff.

p. 227 *"directed against specific threats"*: On the distinction between traditional alliances and collective security, see Kissinger, *Diplomacy*, 247.

p. 228 *"We live by poetry, not by prose"*: *The Papers of Woodrow Wilson*, ed. Arthur S. Link (Princeton, N.J.: Princeton University Press, 1966), XV, 229.

24. LOST IN THE JAZZ AGE

p. 229 *"an elderly literary gentleman"*: Morris, *Colonel Roosevelt*, 543.

p. 230 *"Theodore darling!"*: Joseph Lawrence Gardner, *Departing Glory: Theodore Roosevelt as Ex-President* (New York: Scribner, 1973), 399.

p. 230 *"But there was one President who was lovable"*: Steel, *Walter Lippmann and the American Century*, 597.

p. 230 *"You must write your mother"*: Louis Auchincloss, "Never Leave Me, Never Leave Me," *American Heritage*, February 1970; Auchincloss, *A Writer's Capital* (Boston: Houghton Mifflin, 1979), 146.

p. 231 *"It's the only way to taste good champagne"*: Auchincloss, "Never Leave Me," *American Heritage*, February 1970.

p. 231 *"I do nothing but talk about the Council of Trent"*: *The Letters of Henry Adams 1906–1918*, ed. J. C. Levenson et al. (Cambridge, Mass.: Belknap Press, 1988), VI, 771.

p. 231 *"posing to himself as the old cardinal"*: *The Pollock–Holmes Letters*, ed. Mark DeWolfe Howe (Cambridge, U.K.: Cambridge University Press, 1943) II, 18.

p. 231 *"waiting to drop into some new bit of darkness"*: *The Letters of Henry Adams 1906–1918*, Levenson, VI, 792.

p. 231 *"was kindly, courteous, and sarcastic to the last"*: Samuels, *Henry Adams*, 461.

p. 231   *"for what the final void will show"*: Henry Adams, "Prayer to the Virgin of Chartres," in *Letters to a Niece and Prayer to the Virgin of Chartres*, ed. Mabel La Farge (Boston: Houghton Mifflin, 1920), 131.

p. 231   *One piece of advice*: Miss Tone might have retorted that Uncle Henry had written a whole book about himself, an act which, it could be argued, was itself an instance of tasteless self-indulgence. But as faults of manner, the cases are different. One can easily shut another's book if one finds it tedious: there is no *polite* way of shutting another's mouth.

p. 232   *"cankered"*: Daniel Aaron, *American Notes: Selected Essays* (Boston: Northeastern University Press, 1994), 158.

p. 232   *"force of the female energy"*: Adams, *Education*, 388.

p. 232   *"unusually bright and cheerful"*. Samuels, *Henry Adams*, 161.

p. 232   *"creature of divine power"*: Howe, *John Jay Chapman*, 154.

p. 232   *"they are King's children in disguise"*: Wilson, "John Jay Chapman," in Wilson, *Triple Thinkers*, 148.

p. 233   *"look beyond the piece-work"*: Ibid., 127.

p. 233   *"I would rather it had been you"*: Howe, *John Jay Chapman*, 155.

p. 233   *"melon-seeds or cockroaches"*: Ibid., 157.

p. 233   *"If some one comes to dine"*: Ibid., 186.

p. 233   *"so glad to have this social set torn to pieces"*: Ibid., 186. The set included the Delano family. Warren Delano III, Sara Delano Roosevelt's older brother and Franklin Delano Roosevelt's uncle, lived at Steen Valetje in Barrytown on the Hudson. In August 1920 he was killed when his horse-drawn buggy was struck by a train near the Barrytown depot. His body was carried into the depot, where his friend and neighbor Elizabeth Chanler Chapman stood by the window to deflect the gazes of the curious.

p. 233   *"is probably* not *so malicious"*: Ibid., 371 (emphasis in original).

p. 233   *"For God's sake"*: Ashraf H. A. Rushdy, *The End of American Lynching* (New Brunswick, N.J.: Rutgers University Press, 2012), 23.

p. 233   *"I was greatly moved"*: Chapman, *Memories and Milestones*, 225.

p. 234   *"was to be done more by sack-cloth and ashes"*: Howe, *John Jay Chapman*, 168.

p. 234   *"Hurrah-for-us Americanism"*: Ibid., 224.

p. 234   *"We are met to commemorate"*: For Chapman's address at Coatesville, see Chapman, *Memories and Milestones*, 225–232.

p. 234   *"a younger brother of Shakespeare"*: Wilson, "John Jay Chapman," in Wilson, *Triple Thinkers*, 141.

p. 234   *"aloofness"*: John Jay Chapman, *Emerson and Other Essays* (London: David Nutt, 1898), 77. In Emerson, Chapman said, the "lower register of sensations and emotions which domesticate a man into fellowship with common life was weak." Chapman, *Emerson and Other Essays*, 76.

p. 234   *"anæmic incompleteness"*: Chapman, *Emerson and Other Essays*, 72.

p. 234   *"I prize my friends"*: Emerson, "Friendship," in *Select Writings of Ralph Waldo Emerson* (London: Walter Scott, 1888), 146.

p. 234   *"Good fences"*: And yet we find Emerson himself lamenting "how unfavorable" his "daily habits and solitude" were for friendship, and observing that if only he "could get over the fences," he might find a companion in Elliot Cabot. *The Heart of Emerson's Journals*, ed. Bliss Perry (New York: Dover, 1995), 321.

p. 234   *"If an inhabitant of another planet"*: Chapman, *Emerson and Other Essays*, 83.

p. 235   *abetted all that was least healthy*: Santayana described how Emerson's doctrines, which were intended to foster the "seminal bent" of each American soul—its "individual originality"—were "overwhelmed by the major current," and to such an extent that Emerson himself was hailed as the prophet of a way of being at odds with the soul-culture he sought to inculcate: a utilitarian individualism that had little in common with his own neo-Platonic solipsism. See Santayana, *Dominations and Powers*, 357.

p. 235   *"beautiful and complete"*: Howe, *John Jay Chapman*, 229. But if the old places were so beguiling, why did so many of the inhabitants flee them to come to America? In part because of the decay of their civic culture, the result of new technologies: see chapter 27 above, "Young Men Who Would Return to the Provinces." But this is not the whole explanation. The old places, if they were, on the whole, artistically and spiritually richer than most American places, were materially poorer. First eat, then spiritualize, or aestheticize.

In America one *ate* better. The high WASPs would have liked to go beyond this, to leaven America's practical life, its feats of comfortable utility, with the spirit of Aristotle's aristocrat, who strives to realize the highest *areté* in order that he might "take possession of the beautiful." See Jaeger, *Paideia: The Ideals of Greek Culture: Archaic Greece, The Mind of Athens*, I, 12. One is oppressed by the thought that the two ways of being are, perhaps, irreconcilable: it may be that it is the very coarseness, the very painfulness of life that stimulates the passion for beauty, while a surfeit of material abundance dulls the keenness of that longing. The rose blooms more fragrantly where it has been fertilized by the dunghill: there is a symbiotic relation between the chamber pot and the Shakespearian sonnet, between the sores of the leper and the Song of Solomon, between the open latrine and the Dantean *canto*. With the advent of flush toilets and antibiotics, poetry is doomed.

p. 235 *"the horizons of his old Harvard circle"*: Wilson, "John Jay Chapman," in Wilson, *Triple Thinkers*, 162.

p. 235 *"By the worst piece of luck"*: Stasz, *The Vanderbilt Women*.

p. 235 *"unstable, temperamental"*: Biddle, *The Whitney Women*.

p. 236 *"beautiful idiot"*: Morris, *Edith Kermit Roosevelt: Portrait of a First Lady*, 233.

p. 236 *"I'm stupid"*: Collier and Horowitz, *The Roosevelts*, 142 (note).

p. 236 *Rector's study drunk*: Monica Rico, *Nature's Noblemen: Transatlantic Masculinities and the Nineteenth-Century American West* (New Haven, Conn.: Yale University Press, 2013) (ebook available online); see also Kathleen Dalton, *Theodore Roosevelt: A Strenuous Life* (New York: Vintage, 2004), 326.

p. 237 *"came close to disliking simple human goodness"*: Alsop, *"I've Seen the Best of It,"* 91.

p. 237 *"basic unhappiness"*: Ibid., 93.

p. 237 *"I am quite certain"*: Ibid., 92.

p. 237 *first-hand reporting*: Adams pictured himself as a "spider, and squatting in silence in the middle of this Washington web . . . I have now a little the sense of being a sort of ugly, bloated, purplish-blue, and highly venomous hairy tarantula which catches and devours Presidents, senators, diplomats, congressmen and cabinet-officers . . ." O'Toole, *Five of Hearts*, 310.

p. 238 *"agonies of hell"*: Geoffrey Wolff, *Black Sun: The Brief Transit and Violent Eclipse of Harry Crosby* (New York: New York Review Books, 2003), 48.

p. 238 *"sexless"*: Wolff, *Black Sun*, 265.

p. 238 *"most vivid"*: Katinka Matson, *Short Lives: Portraits in Creativity and Self-Destruction* (New York: Morrow, 1980), 94.

p. 238 *Clytoris*: Tish Wrigley, "The Extraordinary Life of Caresse Crosby, Inventor of the Bra," *AnOther*, March 15, 2018; Jennifer Wright, "The Teen Who Invented Bras," *Racked*, February 26, 2016. Caresse *did* name her whippet bitch Clytoris. See Wolff, *Black Sun*, 261.

p. 238 *"Most people die of a sort of creeping common sense"*: Anne Conover, *Caresse Crosby: From Black Sun to Roccasinibalda* (Santa Barbara, Calif.: Capra, 1989) (ebook available online).

p. 239 "PLEASE SELL $10,000 WORTH OF STOCK": Wolff, *Black Sun*, 4.

p. 239 *"a New Copulation"*: *American Writers in Paris 1920–1939*, ed. Karen Lane Rood (Detroit: Gale, 1980), 95.

p. 239 *"the rod of the Sun"*: Wolff, *Black Sun*, 275.

p. 239 *"sun worshiper in love with death"*: Noël Riley Fitch, *Sylvia Beach and the Lost Generation: A History of Literary Paris in the Twenties and Thirties* (New York: Norton, 1983), 235.

p. 239 *"Demiurgos of everything sensible"*: Proclus, *Commentary on the Timaeus*, quoted in *The Platonist*, April 1888, 172 (note).

p. 239 *"Princess of the Sun"*: Malcolm Cowley, *Exile's Return: A Narrative of Ideas* (New York: Norton, 1984), 268.

p. 240 *"One is not in love"*: Linda Hamalian, *The Cramoisy Queen: A Life of Caresse Crosby* (Carbondale: Southern Illinois University Press, 2005), 73.

p. 240 *"the Sun-Death together"*: Conover, *Caresse Crosby*; compare Hugh D. Ford, *Published in Paris: American and British Writers, Printers, and Publishers in Paris 1920–1939* (New York: Macmillan, 1975), 208.

p. 240 *"alive with Wall Street Journals"*: Harry Crosby, "Scorn," in *The Morada*, Autumn 1929, 16.

p. 240 *.25 caliber Belgian automatic*: Wolff, *Black Sun*, 9.

25. IN THE SECRET PARTS OF FORTUNE

p. 241 *stained yellow*: Conversation with D.V.D. Brown at Groton, *circa* 2019.

p. 241 *two Groton boys found him:* Kent Sanger and Acosta "Corky" Nichols discussed Mr. Gardner on a Saturday afternoon in May 1980. (It was the fiftieth anniversary of their form's graduation.) A second-former at the time, the author had become acquainted with the two men in the late 1970s; in 1978 Nichols sent the author a copy of his history of the school, *Forty Years More*, which the author read and later discussed with Nichols during a visit, in October 1978, to Nichols's house in Oyster Bay, where he lived after retiring from the faculty of Groton in 1974. At the time the author could make little of the talk of Plato, who was hardly more than a name to him; but in subsequent years another Groton master, L. Hugh Sackett, gave him a better understanding of Mr. Gardner's teaching. Hugh's colleague Melvyn Mansur had known Mr. Gardner as a student at Groton, and Mansur himself had been the colleague of Frederick De Veau, who had been both a student and a colleague of Mr. Gardner. Few teachers can have embodied the educational ideals of the Greeks as beautifully as Hugh Sackett, who came to Groton from Oxford in 1955. In the classroom with Homer and Catullus, there was business to be done, though Hugh was forbearing in reproof: outside the classroom, his gift for friendship and his gentleness of manner made for an atmosphere of playfulness, and the little communities that formed about him, both at Groton and in Crete, had always a happy ludic quality about them. As much as Mr. Gardner, Hugh knew that all the serious business of a school is compromised if the place is a lousy playground.

p. 242 *"fanatical, wild devotion"*: Ashburn, *Peabody of Groton*, 156.

p. 242 *"I love the School just as much as ever"*: Ibid., 164.

p. 242 *metallic*: See Sedgwick, "Three Men of Groton," in *Views from the Circle*, 24.

p. 242 *"passing the door"*: Gardner expressed his dissatisfactions with the enlarged school in *Groton Myths and Memories*, 100–101.

p. 242 *"codes and systems"*: Ashburn, *Peabody of Groton*, 164.

p. 242 *"God's plaything"*: Plato, *Laws*, 803c.

p. 242 *google*: It consisted of raspberry syrup and water, and was served with cake.

p. 242 *"strung together by our choirmasters"*: Plato, *Laws*, 654a. See also Marcus Folch, *The City and the Stage: Performance, Genre, and Gender in Plato's Laws* (Oxford, U.K.: Oxford University Press, 2015). In Plato's Magnesia, Folch writes, "the city for which the *Laws* provides a code, every dimension of the citizen's life receives musical inflection, and many of the genres purged from the earlier dialogue [the *Republic*] become central to a life of virtue. For Plato in the *Laws*, what it means to be a citizen of the ideal city is shaped by and takes place within the performance of poetry, music, song, and dance. The *Laws*, in short, represents Plato's systematic rethinking of the nature of aesthetics and mimetic art, of the part played by poetry, music, song, and dance in the making of citizens, and of how the individual and collective life of the polis is constituted in performance; and it presents the reader a renegotiation of the relationship between poetry and philosophy, in which both are cast as collaborators in the fashioning of an ideal city and a virtuous life. The result is a profound reconceptualization of what performance is and can do in the city and the soul, a rehabilitation of Athenian choral and poetic art, and a vision of a philosophically inspired performance culture in which poetry, music, song, and dance occupy a seminal position in the ideal political community." Folch, *The City and the Stage*, 1–2.

p. 243 *"gods or sons of gods"*: Ibid., 739d. This is the author's own idiosyncratic reading of the *Laws*: what the dialogue means to *him*. It might, and might perhaps justly, be laughed out of scholarly court.

p. 243 *looked to music and poetry*: Plato did not, of course, mean *any* music: he distinguished between better and worse kinds of music.

p. 243 *Mr. Gardner, the aging Plato*: Author's conversation with Rogers V. Scudder, Groton School, *circa* 1983. Mr. Scudder, a Groton master, had little sympathy for Plato, and he lamented the fact that Groton was, as he maintained, so Platonic in character. This Platonism, he said, often turned its best students into insufferable prigs: where success in later life was concerned, he would always put his money, he said, on the rascals. There was some truth in this; with a few exceptions, none of Groton's more notable graduates served as senior prefect of the school. On the other hand, F.D.R. was not in the least a rascal or a rebel during his schooldays.

p. 243   *"result of a thousand little manners and customs"*: Gardner, *Groton Myths and Memories*, vi.

p. 243   *"mythology"*: Ibid. Americans, Wallace Stevens says, "never lived in a time/When mythology was possible."
Mr. Gardner would have begged to differ.

p. 243   *"stiffening of joints"*: Ibid., 101.

p. 243   *Palestrina*: Ashburn, *Fifty Years On*, 123 (note 1).

p. 244   *spiritually antiseptic*: There is almost nothing in, in these American academic spaces, of what Dante called the
dolce lira, the sweet lyre: the method of creating order that gave the fair sheepfold of Florence such beauty as it
possessed. It is true that, when the grammarian himself reached the English Cambridge in the last Michaelmas
Term of the 1980s, he was oppressed, at first, by a hyperborean gloom of rain and damp, the pale face of a
consumptive climate. Yet he soon felt the cloistered appeal of the place, that of an aristocracy of intellect allied
to one of worldly splendor, of external graces united to the higher dignities of mind—such a culture as had
gone into the making of Bacon and Newton, Macaulay and Tennyson and Gray. Wherever he turned he felt
the luxurious thickness, a sumptuousness of which the great confections of sculpted sugar he saw through
the bars of a kitchen window were as curiously evocative as the rich paneling he dimly perceived through the
bow-window of a master's lodge and the clipped luxuriance of the lawns and flower beds of the "Backs" that
flowed down to the placid river. The lyre had performed its office well. [The inquirer must again interrupt the
specious commentary of the grammarian, who labors under the misimpression that human beings possesses
souls which have an ideal end and purpose, such as may be more easily discovered and perfected in pretty
places with pretty music. "It may be difficult," says a noted writer, "for many of us to abandon the belief that
there is an instinct toward perfection at work in human beings." But this belief is, the writer observes, merely a
"benevolent illusion," for in reality the "development of human beings requires . . . no different explanation from
that of animals."] [Much later, when the grammarian read Johan Huizinga and Werner Jaeger, Henry James
and Henry Adams, he began to comprehend the nature of the education he had received. He had not previously
known that he was a guinea pig in a perfectionist experiment. But he remains a guinea pig grateful for the
"benevolent illusions" that were foisted upon him. See the note immediately below.]

p. 244   *WASP experiment in education*: This book is, in effect, an effort, to reconstruct that effort to educate the
mind. *Die WASPs als Erzieher*, it might have been called: *The WASPs as Educators* ; and indeed the author
was, from the age of thirteen to the age of thirty, a rat in more than one WASP laboratory.

p. 244   *"war issues"*: John J. Coss, "The Columbia College Course on Contemporary Civilization," *The Historical
Outlook*, June 1922; Eric Adler, *The Battle of the Classics: How a Nineteenth-Century Debate Can Save the
Humanities Today* (Oxford, U.K.: Oxford University Press, 2020), 83; Louis Menand, *The Marketplace of
Ideas: Reform and Resistance in the American University* (New York: Norton, 2010), 32–33.

p. 245   *liberating*: On the other hand, Professor Dan-el Padilla Peralta of Princeton argues that the study of
classic texts is a deeply and perhaps irredeemably racist enterprise, "so entangled with white supremacy as
to be inseparable from it." See Rachel Poser, "He Wants to Save Classics from Whiteness. Can the Field
Survive?" *New York Times*, February 2, 2021.

p. 245   *Columbia's Core*: See Lionel Trilling, "Some Notes for an Autobiographical Lecture," in Trilling, *The Last
Decade: Essays and Reviews 1965–1975* (New York: Harcourt Brace Jovanovich, 1981), 226–241, especially
231–234; Menand, *The Marketplace of Ideas*, 32–37. Erskine's General Honors course was discontinued in
1929, but it was revived in 1932 by Jacques Barzun as the Colloquium in Important Books. In 1934 Barzun
asked Lionel Trilling to teach the course with him, a partnership that led to lively sessions on Wednesday
evenings that were long celebrated in Columbia lore. In 1937 what had been an honors course with
limited enrollment was made available to all students as Humanities A (Great Books) and Humanities
B (great works of art and music). In 1947 the courses were made obligatory for all students. For many
years Humanities A, which came to be called Literature Humanities or Lit Hum, and Contemporary
Civilization or CC, have been the heart of the Core Curriculum. CC was not, like Lit Hum, originally a
Great Books class, but it became one, with an emphasis on classic works of moral and political thought,
beginning with Plato's *Republic*. In both courses the books were (perhaps still are) discussed in small
classes of some twenty students: there was a minimum of lecturing.

p. 245   *"had been the pupil of George Edward Woodberry"*: See Trilling's essay "Some Notes for an Autobiographical Lecture," in Trilling, *Last Decade,* 233, and Michael Kimmage, *The Conservative Turn: Lionel Trilling, Whittaker Chambers, and the Lessons of Anti-Communism* (Cambridge, Mass.: Harvard University Press, 2009), 24–25. For Woodberry's background, see John Erskine, *The Memory of Certain Persons* (Philadelphia, Lippincott, 1947), 88.

p. 245   *"in good agora form"*: Alfred Zimmern, *The Greek Commonwealth: Politics and Economics in Fifth-Century Athens* (Oxford, U.K.: Clarendon Press, 1924), 65.

p. 245   *"mingled with delightful loafing"*: Jacob Burckhardt, *History of Greek Culture,* trans. Palmer Hilty (Mineola, N.Y.: Dover, 2002), 10; Richard Franklin Sigurdson, *Jacob Burckhardt's Social and Political Thought* (Toronto: University of Toronto Press, 2004), 180.

p. 245   *office in Fayerweather*: John Erskine, *Memory of Certain Persons,* 89.

p. 245   *"He was the first teacher"*: Ibid., 93–94.

p. 246   *"the local attachments, the historical particularities"*: Ira Katznelson, "Evil and Politics," *Daedalus,* Winter 2002, 9–10.

p. 247   *Karl Marx had a half-baked notion*: Marx and Engels "had always before them—something which the later Marxists have sometimes quite lost sight of—the ideal man of the Renaissance of the type of Leonardo or Machiavelli, who had a head for both the sciences and the arts, who was both thinker and man of action. It was, in fact, one of their chief objections to the stratified industrial society that it specialized people in occupations in such a way as to make it impossible for them to develop more than a single aptitude; and it was one of their great arguments for communism that it would produce 'complete' men again. They themselves had shied desperately away from the pundits of idealist Germany, whom they regarded as just as fatally deformed through a specialization in intellectual activity as the proletarian who worked in the factory through his concentration on mechanical operations; and they desired themselves, insofar as it was possible, to lead the lives of 'complete' men." Edmund Wilson, *To the Finland Station: A Study in the Writing and Acting of History (with a New Introduction)* (London: Macmillan, 1972), 254.

p. 247   *eutrapelia*: In addition to the Funeral Oration in Thucydides and *A Lexicon Abridged from Liddell and Scott's Greek-English Lexicon* (Oxford, U.K.: Clarendon, 1953), 286, 712, see Matthew Arnold, "A Speech at Eton," in *The Works of Matthew Arnold,* 15 vols. (London: Macmillan, 1904), XL (*Irish Essays and Others*), 180–183. *Eutrapelos,* which for Pericles (as filtered by Thucydides) connoted a happy and gracious flexibility in action—that of the Athenian who was brought up to undertake the most "varied forms of activity" with "grace and *eutrapelos*"—came in the generation of Plato and Aristotle to stand more particularly for a suppleness in conversation, a gift for urbane and pleasant talk. One feels in the decline of the word the decline of the polis.

p. 247   *it supplied a poetry*: "And Julian inviolably preserved for Athens that tender regard which seldom fails to arise in a liberal mind from the recollection of the place where it discovered and exercised its growing powers." Gibbon, *The History of the Decline and Fall of the Roman Empire,* chapter XIX. The grammarian, having been installed in a stifling room on Morningside Heights in the late summer of 1984, felt himself a Roman from the Mediterranean, bred up on olives and Falernian, marched posthaste to the northern frontier, there to serve in some godforsakenhole, dark and gray as dead men's souls. The Circle was not Florence or even Oxford, but it was for one poor worm the center of his universe. Morningside Heights, when it was reached in those hot days of August, could only seem an outer circle of hell. There was no Bach in the morning, no ceremonious ritual, no compact wheel around which a community could form and revolve, only anonymous crowds in a concrete emptiness, in the shadow of buildings which, though done up in a travesty of Italy in the Cinquecento, were as remote from the piazze of Tuscany or Umbria as a satyr from Hyperion. The grammarian would have howled as one of his predecessors on those summits had done, if it would have served any purpose. Instead he fell into pits still lower, plunged into the decadence downtown, the cesspools of Limelight and the Palladium, hot anarchy and misrule. What saved and perhaps ruined him were the books . . . [The inquirer, as he and the grammarian make their way through the dusty pages of this book, observes that Columbia's Core Curriculum was never meant to encourage, in its scholars, the grammarian's style of romantic self-indulgence. It was intended to prepare young people for the active work of life, that they might live what George Eliot called "greatly effective" lives in the larger world, the world of politics and law, of science and useful scholarship, of all those benevolent pursuits that point the way toward an ever richer and more equitable tomorrow. He well remembers how, having closed his books of an evening, he would stand in the empty reception room at the top of the tallest building on the campus and look out to lights of the great city to the south, with all their beckoning promise, a sight and emotion the grammarian would seem to have forgotten.] [If only the inquirer did not insist on papering over his own uncertainties, mysteries, doubts, his readers might have a better sense of the truth or falsity of his inquiries. An inquirer ought to *confess* his dividedness and document his ambivalences. The inquirer knows very well that so sensitive a spirit as Macaulay could never have wholly believed his Whig Interpretation of History. "What a notable green-grocer was spoiled to make Macaulay!" Emerson exclaimed: but Macaulay *imposed* this green-grocer philistinism on himself only after an inward struggle. The grammarian hesitates to find fault with such a masterpiece as the *History of England*: but it would have been a greater book had its author confessed the different angels of his comfort and despair. Where Macaulay failed, the inquirer (who would have the whip hand in this lesser narrative) is unlikely to succeed.]

p. 247 *"I voted for your father"*: Ward, *A First-Class Temperament*, 531.

p. 248 *"figure of an idealized college football player"*: Ibid., 534.

p. 248 *"worshippers at his shrine"*: Ibid., 547.

p. 248 *"better looking than he used to be"*: Ibid., 509.

p. 248 *"not at ease with people not of his own class"*: Vidal, *United States: Essays*, 1269.

p. 248 *"I'm sure he didn't start out"*: Ward, *A First-Class Temperament*, 509.

p. 248 *"that lad's got a 'million vote smile.'"*: Robert Dallek, *Franklin D. Roosevelt: A Political Life* (New York: Penguin, 2017), 73.

p. 248 *"a progressive Democrat"*: Ward, *A First-Class Temperament*, 530.

p. 248 *"just a playboy"*: Ibid., 556.

p. 249 *"greatest disappointment"*: Lash, *Love, Eleanor*, 73.

p. 249 *Van Lear Black*: Ward, *A First-Class Temperament*, 560–563.

p. 249 *"dens where perverted practices are carried on"*: Ibid., 440.

p. 249 *"working that"*: Romans 1:27.

p. 249 *"clean the place up"*: Ward, *A First-Class Temperament*, 439.

p. 250 *"deplorable, disgraceful and unnatural"*: *Report of the Committee on Naval Affairs United States Senate . . . Relative to Alleged Immoral Conditions and Practices at the Naval Training Station, Newport, R.I.* (Washington: Government Printing Office, 1921), 29.

p. 250 *"most derelict in the performance of his duty"*: Ibid., 31.

p. 250 *"beastly acts"*: Ibid., 28.

p. 250 *"unprintable"*: Jonathan Alter, *The Defining Moment: F.D.R.'s First Hundred Days and the Triumph of Hope* (New York: Simon & Schuster, 2007), 49.

p. 250 *"too tired"*: Ward, *A First-Class Temperament*, 584.

p. 250 *"it refused to work"*: Jean Edward Smith, *F.D.R.* (New York: Random House, 2008), 189; Frank Freidel, *Franklin D. Roosevelt: The Ordeal* (Boston: Little Brown, 1952), 98.

26. THE WASTE LAND

p. 252 *"Mr. Apollinax"*: Except where otherwise noted, the author has relied, in quoting Eliot's poetry, on T. S. Eliot, *Collected Poems 1909–1962* (San Diego: Harcourt Brace Jovanovich, 1971).

p. 252 *Professor and Mrs. Channing-Cheetah*: Professor Channing-Cheetah was inspired by William Henry Schofield, a professor of comparative literature at Harvard. See *The Letters of T. S. Eliot 1898–1922*, ed. Valerie Eliot (San Diego: Harcourt Brace, 1988), 483 (note 1).

p. 253 *faith that has failed*: Eliot rejected the *eutrapelian* humanism of Arnold as an unsatisfactory attempt to "set up Culture in place of Religion." Arnoldian Culture (literature, poetry, great books) is meant to develop "all sides of our humanity," but Eliot believed that it could at most produce a tepid, priggish pseudo-religion, one that would inevitably degenerate into mere aestheticism, the prettiness of Walter Pater. The only hope for a soul seeking regeneration was to receive the inspiration of divine truth as revealed by some form of orthodox Christianity. There was, for Eliot, no middle ground between Christ (and him crucified) and Mammonism. See Eliot, "Arnold and Pater," in Eliot, *Selected Essays: New Edition* (San Diego: Harcourt Brace, 1978), 382–393.

p. 253 *"peculiar detachment and remoteness"*: T. S. Eliot, *On Poetry and Poets* (New York: Farrar, Straus and Giroux, 2009), 282.

p. 253 *transplanted New Englander*: This was Henry Adams's characterization of William Maxwell Evarts and William Tecumseh Sherman. Adams, *Education*, 245. Edmund Wilson said that "Middle Westerners . . . whose family roots are in the East" often develop "a special kind of snobbery more self-conscious than the Eastern kind. T. S. Eliot was something of a case and point." Wilson, *A Prelude*, 47. Eliot himself did *not* think of himself as Westerner: "I speak as a New Englander . . ." T. S. Eliot, *After Strange Gods: A Primer of Modern Heresy* (London: Faber and Faber, 1935), 16.

p. 254 *the salt was on the briar rose*: See Eliot's poem "The Dry Salvages."

p. 254 *"My idea"*: T. S. Eliot to Richard Aldington, November 6, 1921, in *Letters of T. S. Eliot 1898–1922*, 486.

p. 254 *neurasthenic*: "At present I am feeling tired and depressed," Eliot wrote to Richard Aldington on September 16, 1921: "I don't like to make your cottage a home for neurasthenics like [Frederic] Manning and myself . . ." *Letters of T. S. Eliot 1898–1922*, 469.

p. 255 *unable to get on with her sexually*: Lyndall Gordon, *Eliot's Early Years* (New York: Farrar, Straus and Giroux, 1977), 74–76.

p. 255 *"disreputable suburbs"*: Ibid., 71.

p. 255 *"form of* acedia": Eliot, "Baudelaire," in Eliot, *Selected Essays*, 375.

p. 255 *"hatred of life"*: Eliot, "Cyril Tourneur," Ibid., 166.

p. 255 *"some horror beyond words"*: Ibid.

p. 255 *"reconciled among the stars"*: See Eliot's poem "Burnt Norton."

p. 255 *cheek by jowl*: This was the method of poetic construction that underlay, for example, "The Love Song of J. Alfred Prufrock," in which visions of Lazarus come from the dead and the head of the prophet on a platter are mingled with "the cups, the marmalade, the tea" of the WASP tea-table, and in which the music of the mermaids accompanies the decision to wear the bottoms of one's flannel trousers rolled.

p. 255 *"The form in which I began to write"*: T. S. Eliot, Introduction to *Selected Poems of Ezra Pound* (London: Faber, 1928), viii.

p. 256 *"Tom has had rather a serious breakdown"*: *Letters of T. S. Eliot 1898–1922*, 478.

p. 256 *"Complimenti, you bitch"*: *Letters of T. S. Eliot 1898–1922*, 498–499.

p. 256 *"beautiful but ineffectual conscience"*: T. S. Eliot, "A Sceptical Patrician," *The Athenæum*, May 23, 1919, 362.

p. 256 *"want to do something great"*: Ibid., 361.

p. 257 *"is tongued with fire beyond the language of the living"*: See Eliot's poem "Little Gidding."

p. 257 *"that genuine poetry can communicate before it is understood"*: Eliot, "Dante," in Eliot, *Selected Essays*, 200 (emphasis added).

p. 257 *"direct shock of poetic intensity"*: Ibid.

p. 257 *"I was passionately fond of certain French poetry"*: Ibid., 199.

p. 258 *"disillusionment of a generation"*: When "I wrote a poem called *The Waste Land* some of the more approving critics said that I had expressed the 'disillusionment of a generation,' which is nonsense. I may have expressed for them their own illusion of being disillusioned, but that did not form part of my intention." Eliot, "Thoughts After Lambeth," in Eliot, *Selected Essays*, 324.

p. 258 *"a helpless and unspeakable wreck of drugs"*: Gordon, *Eliot's Early Years*, 124.

p. 258 *"the broken city"*: Choruses from "The Rock," IV.

p. 258 *"unsatisfactory"*: *Letters of T. S. Eliot 1898–1922*, 469–470.

p. 258 *"amalgamating disparate experience"*: Eliot, "The Metaphysical Poets," in Eliot, *Selected Essays*, 247.

p. 258 *old civic centers*: T. J. Jackson Lears has shown how Eliot sought, much as Henry Adams did, a "restored sacred center" to counterbalance "modern spiritual chaos." See Lears, *No Place of Grace*, 296.

p. 259 *Religious poetry*: Eliot, who was not consistent in his definitions, once wrote that when "we are considering poetry, we must consider it primarily as poetry and not as another thing." Poetry is not, he said, "the inculcation of morals or the direction of politics; and no more is it religion or an equivalent of religion, except by some monstrous abuse of words." But he clearly thought that religion was, among other things, a divinely inspired poetry: otherwise he could not have described the sacrifice of the Mass as a form of dramatic poetry, "the perfect and ideal drama," so ideal, indeed, that the believer will not be conscious of it *as* drama. She will "only be aware of the Mass as art, in so far as it is badly done and interferes with" her devotion, for a devout person, in assisting at Mass, is not in the frame of mind of a person attending a drama . . ." See Eliot, "A Dialogue on Dramatic Poetry," in Eliot, *Selected Essays*, 35–36.

p. 259 *"Hinduism"*: Sonia Chumber, "The Voices of the Bhagavad Gita and Upanishad in T. S. Eliot's *The Waste Land*," *International Journal of Language and Literature*, September 2014.

p. 259 *"to spend a day nobly"*: *Emerson in His Journals*, 223.

p. 259 *the infrastructure of daily life*: Of course we have only to press a button, today, for the poetry of whatever music we like to intervene in our lives. As I write these words I am listening to the Benedictus in Bach's Mass in B Minor. But this sort of experience of music has no place in the *infrastructure* of our common life, as we each day experience it. One listens to the music privately or, perhaps, with a small group of fellow listeners, or one hears it performed in a venue set apart from ordinary life, in a concert hall or a stadium.

p. 259 *"the perfect and ideal drama"*: Eliot, "A Dialogue on Dramatic Poetry," in Eliot, *Selected Essays*, 36.

p. 259 *"one of the highest forms of dancing"*: *T. S. Eliot: The Critical Heritage*, ed. Michael Grant, 2 vols. (Abingdon, U.K.: Routledge, 1997) II, 710.

p. 259 *"foreign races"*: T. S. Eliot, *After Strange Gods*, 16.

p. 259 *"free-thinking Jews"*: Ibid., 20. The anti-Semitism that disfigures *After Strange Gods* differs in certain respects from that of the WASPs with whom Eliot broke. He did not express it, as Henry Adams did, in shrieks and bleatings, but in apparently cool and emotionless prose and in intricately composed poetry. There was, to be sure, an element of blood-pride in his condescension to Jews, as there was also in Adams's, but he had little interest in using prejudice, as WASPs did, to promote a patrician class within a democracy, for he had largely left both WASPs and democracy behind. Nor was his anti-Semitism a way, as Adams's was, of relieving feelings of personal impotence. Eliot never sought political power as Adams did, and in his chosen line, poetry and criticism, he was, by the time he came to write *After Strange Gods*, a man of fame and influence, a sort of literary pope. He himself, in extenuation of his language, might have pointed to his belief, expressed in *After Strange Gods*, that a "diabolic influence" was undermining "tradition and orthodoxy" in the modern world. He illustrated this thesis by pointing to the way in which such *goy* artists as George Eliot and Thomas Hardy flaunted their "individualistic morals" and "unregenerate" personalities in their writings. They represented, Eliot contended, one of "the most fruitful operations of the Evil Spirit to-day," an "intrusion of the *diabolic* influence into modern literature" and modern life. He thought D. H. Lawrence a still more insidious case. The "dæmonic powers," he wrote, found in Lawrence "an instrument of far greater range" than they did in Hardy. With his "very much greater genius," his "profound intuition," and his "sexual morbidity," Lawrence was, Eliot contended, a genuine prophet, but one whose prophecy was "spiritually sick." Yet the devil did not, in Eliot's account, speak through *goy* littérateurs alone: he also numbered "free-thinking Jews" among the diabolic clerisy. Like Lawrence and Hardy, they, too, were vessels in which "a positive power for evil" could be seen "working through human agency"—were, in fact, under the direction of Satan himself. But the idea of the "possessed" intellectual, if it partly explains Eliot's animus against Jews, cannot be the whole explanation; and I am not sure whether even Anthony Julius, in his book on Eliot's anti-Semitism, pierces the deeper mystery of that dark and obscure soul. It is possible that Eliot actually believed, as he claimed to, that Lawrence and Hardy were agents of the devil, but it is not they, after all, who squat on the windowsill of the decayed house in "Gerontion," or who are below the rats underneath the piles of Venice in "Burbank."

For Eliot has persuaded himself that, not the *goy* heretic, but the "jew is underneath the lot"—is the
ultimate heresiarch, the chief subverter of the moral order.

p. 259 *"blood kinship"*: Ibid., 18.

p. 259 *"jokey"*: Lyndall Gordon, *T. S. Eliot: An Imperfect Life* (New York: Norton, 2000), 494.

p. 260 *"Manners is an obsolete word these days"*: Gordon, *T. S. Eliot: An Imperfect Life*, 44.

p. 260 *masked detachment*: The author here follows Lyndall Gordon once again.

p. 260 *"the music of some inspired Orpheus"*: See Carlyle's *Sartor Resartus*.

p. 260 *dialogue not only with Henry Adams*: In "Gerontion" Eliot alludes to Henry Adams and the *Education*.
Anthony Julius describes the poem as growing out of a dialogue between Eliot and Blake, yet his
explication gives one every reason to think that Eliot was talking to Adams as well. See Julius, *T. S. Eliot,
Anti-Semitism, and Literary Form*, 59.

p. 260 *"richest and noblest expression"*: Henry James, *A Small Boy and Others* (New York: Charles Scribner's Sons,
1913), 347.

p. 260 *no religious test*: Eliot seemed to believe that there can be no culture of any worthwhile kind without
religion. See Julius, *T. S. Eliot, Anti-Semitism, and Literary Form*, 164. And yet in his 1921 essay *"Ulysses,
Order, and Myth,"* Eliot suggested that a poetry not conventionally religious *can* create order in life, and
that an artist can counteract chaos through the use of myth. The myths Eliot had in mind were those
that Joyce derived from the *Odyssey* and those that Frazer restated in *The Golden Bough*: myths that were
largely or wholly pagan, and therefore did not for Eliot embody religious truth. Yet these myths were
nevertheless, he maintained, "a way of controlling, of ordering, of giving a shape and a significance to the
immense panorama of futility and anarchy which is contemporary history." Which suggests that art *can*
be experienced by its beholder as creating form and unity in life, though the beholder does not believe the
myth that animates the art to be divinely true. Such an art might therefore perform a *liturgical* function in
life, imposing order on chaos, though it does not perform a conventionally *religious* one, by facilitating the
worship of divinity.

27. YOUNG MEN WHO WOULD RETURN TO THE PROVINCES

p. 261 *In the late summer of 1927*: Except where otherwise noted, this account of Edmund Wilson's dinner with
himself is drawn from Wilson, "A Preface to Persius: Maudlin Mediations in a Speakeasy," (October 19,
1927), in Wilson, *Shores of Light*, 267–273.

p. 262 *"more or less in the eighteenth century"*: These were Wilson's words at sixty. See Wilson, "The Author at
Sixty," in Wilson, *A Piece of My Mind*, 211. But his "A Preface to Persius" shows that he was already partial
to the eighteenth century when he was not much more than thirty.

p. 262 *"republican tradition"*: Wilson, "An Appeal to Progressives" (January 14, 1931), in Wilson, *Shores of Light*, 528.

p. 262 *"social ideal which had survived from the founding of the Republic"*: Wilson, "A Vortex in the Nineties: Stephen
Crane" (January 2, 1924), in Wilson, *Shores of Light*, 110.

p. 263 *"who had been educated for the old America"*: Wilson, "A Vortex in the Nineties: Stephen Crane," in Wilson,
Shores of Light, 111.

p. 263 *"the slave of Business at one extreme or drink himself to death at the other . . ."*: Ibid.

p. 263 *"neurotic eclipses"*: Wilson, "The Author at Sixty," in Wilson, *A Piece of My Mind*, 214.

p. 263 *"a corporation lawyer whose principal function"*: Wilson, "A Vortex in the Nineties: Stephen Crane," in
Wilson, *Shores of Light*, 110–111.

p. 264 *"benignant incandescence"*: For Wilson's tribute to his old teacher, see "'Mr. Rolfe,'" in Wilson, *Triple
Thinkers*, 5.

p. 264 *"of that good eighteenth-century Princeton"*: Wilson, "Christian Gauss," in Wilson, *Shores of Light*, 110–111.

p. 265 *"appalled by the slackness of the training"*: Wilson, "'Mr. Rolfe,'" in Wilson, *Triple Thinkers*, 253.

p. 265 *The older sister of his Hill roommate Larry Noyes*: Wilson wrote that the older sister of his Hill roommate
Laurence Gilman "Larry" Noyes (1893–1954) married Robert deForest, Henry deForest's older brother.
Wilson, *Prelude*, 46. But Wilson's memory betrayed him: it was Henry deForest who, in 1898, married

Larry's older sister Julia Gilman Noyes. Henry deForest's older brother Robert Weeks deForest married Emily Johnston.

p. 265 *"perfect: house and grounds"*: Wilson, *Prelude*, 46.

p. 265 *"such families constituted a genuine 'Establishment.'"*: Ibid.

p. 265 *"on the whole the most brilliant young man"*: *The Letters of Theodore Roosevelt: The Days of Armageddon 1909–1919*, ed. Elting E. Morison (Cambridge, Mass.: Harvard University Press, 1954), IV, 872.

p. 265 *"Really, nothing more correct"*: Edmund Wilson to Stanley Dell, February 19, 1921, in Wilson, *Letters on Literature and Politics 1912–1972*, ed. Elena Wilson (New York: Farrar, Straus and Giroux, 1977) (ebook available online).

p. 265 *"attractive and even inspiring"*: See Wilson's essay on Roosevelt, "The Pre-Presidential T.R.," in the *New Yorker*, October 20, 1951, reprinted in Wilson, *Eight Essays* (Garden City, N.Y.: Anchor, 1954), and Wilson, *The Bit Between My Teeth: A Literary Chronicle of 1950–1965* (New York: Farrar, Straus and Giroux, 1965).

p. 266 *He would rise at five*: Except where otherwise noted, the account of Walter Lippmann that follows is drawn from Steel, *Walter Lippmann and the American Century*.

p. 266 *"vacancy"*: Walter Lippmann, *A Preface to Morals* (London: George Allen and Unwin, 1929), 3.

p. 266 *"My own mind has been getting steadily anti-democratic"*: Gunther, *Learned Hand: The Man and the Judge*, 382.

p. 266 *"bewildered herd"*: Walter Lippmann, *The Phantom Public* (New York: Harcourt, Brace, 1925), 155.

p. 266 *"dominant white Protestant culture"*: Steel, *Walter Lippmann and the American Century*, 193.

p. 266 *"specialized class"*: Walter Lippmann, *Public Opinion* (New York: Harcourt, Brace, 1922), 310.

p. 266 *"insiders"*: A recurring term in Lippmann, *Phantom Public*.

p. 266 *"new order of samurai"*: Steel, *Walter Lippmann and the American Century*, 214–215.

p. 266 *"modern man's discontent"*: Lippmann, *Preface to Morals*, 4.

p. 266 *"dissolution of ancient habits"*: Ibid., 67.

p. 267 *"religion of the spirit"*: Ibid., 326ff.

p. 267 *"infinite in extent and variety"*: Santayana, *Dominations and Powers*, 13. Nature, Santayana says, "breeds spirit as naturally as the lark sings": but only by a "proper hygiene" can it be "freed ideally." Santayana, *Soliloquies in England*, in *The Philosophy of George Santayana*, ed. Irwin Edman, 357–358.

p. 267 *"continual sense of the ultimate in the immediate"*: George Santayana, *Platonism and the Spiritual Life* (New York: Charles Scribner's Sons, 1937), 83.

p. 267 *"crop out marvelously in the sinner"*: Ibid., 84.

p. 267 *"play-life"*: Santayana, *The Realm of Essence*, in *The Philosophy of George Santayana*, ed. Irwin Edman, 466.

p. 267 *"established morality and religion"*: Santayana, *Platonism and the Spiritual Life*, 83–84.

p. 267 *"connections and education"*: Santayana, *Middle Span*, 20.

p. 267 *"ultimate reaches of contemplation"*: George Santayana, "Enduring the Truth," *Saturday Review*, December 7, 1929.

p. 268 *no chant:* That by now threadbare formula, Max Weber's "disenchantment of the world," is rarely read down to its roots, as the withdrawal, from everyday life, not merely of incantation (*incantare*, to consecrate with spells) but of song itself (*cantare*, to sing, to chant). An old Greek philosopher come to life would instantly perceive the connection between our disenchanted condition and the disappearance of poetry as a principle of order in the regulation of everyday life.

p. 268 *"certain unreality"*: Edmund Wilson, "Walter Lippmann's *A Preface to Morals*," in *From the Uncollected Edmund Wilson*, ed. Janet Groth and David Castronovo (Athens: Ohio University Press, 1995), 113.

p. 268 *"intensification of the poetic view of life"*: Van Wyck Brooks, "Our Awakeners," *The Seven Arts*, June 1917; Van Wyck Brooks, *Letters and Leadership* (New York: B.W. Huebsch, 1918), 103.

p. 268 *"old as nothing else anywhere in the world is old"*: Brooks, *Letters and Leadership*, 7.

p. 268 *"sadness and wreckage"*: William Wasserstrom, *Van Wyck Brooks* (Minneapolis: University of Minnesota Press, 1968), 13.

p. 268 *"bred in a richly poetic, a richly creative soil"*: Brooks, *Letters and Leadership*, 111.

p. 268   *"not a decorative adjustment"*: Rebecca West, *Black Lamb and Gray Falcon: A Journey through Yugoslavia* (New York: Penguin, 1994), 55.

p. 269   *"contract cancer and die in agony"*: James Hoopes, *Van Wyck Brooks: In Search of American Culture* (Amherst: University of Massachusetts Press, 1977), 234.

p. 269   *"rejected the American tradition in toto"*: Brooks, *New England: Indian Summer 1865–1915*, 523 (note).

p. 269   *"We had coffee"*: Ernest Hemingway, *The Sun Also Rises* (New York: Charles Scribner's Sons, 1926, 1970), 96.

p. 270   *myopic*: Keith Ferrell, *Ernest Hemingway: The Search for Courage* (Lanham, Md.: M. Evans, 2014), 28.

p. 270   *"snobbish, difficultly written shit"*: Eric Haralson, *Henry James and Queer Modernity* (Cambridge, U.K.: University of Cambridge Press, 2003), 173.

p. 270   *"The only [other] person I have ever known"*: Peter L. Hays, *The Critical Reception of Ernest Hemingway's* The Sun Also Rises (Rochester, N.Y.: Camden House, 2011), 1.

p. 270   *"Well, here comes James Joyce"*: Brenda Maddox, *Nora: The Real Life of Molly Bloom* (Boston: Mariner, 2000), 222.

p. 270   *"Jim could do with a spot of that lion hunting"*: Richard Ellmann, *James Joyce: New and Revised Edition* (Oxford, U.K.: Oxford University Press, 1983), 695 (note).

p. 270   *"Most people don't think of Hemingway as a poet"*: *Letters of Wallace Stevens*, ed. Holly Stevens (Berkeley: University of California Press, 1996), 411–412.

p. 271   *"ground to a fine powder"*: *Joseph Conrad: Centennial Essays*, ed. Ludwik Krzyżanowski (Folcroft, Penn.: Folcroft Library Editions, 1974), 16.

p. 271   in our time: A second book, *In Our Time*, was published in 1925 and interwove with the vignettes of *in our time* stories of an American boy growing up.

p. 271   *"We have lived very quietly, working hard"*: *Ernest Hemingway: Selected Letters 1917–1961*, ed. Carlos Baker (New York: Scribner, 2003), 128.

p. 272   *"alcoholic nymphomaniac"*: Lesley M. M. Blume, *Everybody Behaves Badly: The True Story Behind Hemingway's Masterpiece* The Sun Also Rises (Boston: Mariner, 2017) (ebook available online); Kendall Taylor, *Sometimes Madness is Wisdom: Zelda and Scott Fitzgerald: A Marriage* (New York: Ballantine, 2003), 157.

p. 272   *"how much human shit there is"*: James D. Brasch, *That Other Hemingway: The Master Inventor* (Victoria, B.C.: Trafford, 2009), 99. (Hemingway was reading Santayana's memoirs at the time and was put off by Santayana's homage to Ávila.)

p. 272   *sacramentalism of life*: The phrase is borrowed from Jane Harrison, the scholar of the ritual Mediterranean. See Harrison, *Prolegomena to the Study of Greek Religion* (Cambridge, U.K.: Cambridge University Press, 1922), 452.

p. 272   *"The festival requires style"*: Johan Huizinga, *The Waning of the Middle Ages* (Garden City, N.Y.: Anchor, 1954), 251. Robert Burton, the anatomist of melancholy, spoke of a pageantry of "dainty cheer, exquisite music, and facete jesters," for although the old forms had, Huizinga believed, "the dignity of a ritual," they often exhibited, too, a "naïve and popular sensuousness." Mythological figures (Andromeda, the Syrens, the goddesses judged by Paris) were often "represented nude by living women." Burton, *The Anatomy of Melancholy* (London: William Tegg, 1849), 372; Huizinga, *Waning of the Middle Ages*, 9, 315–316.

p. 273   *"is the only art in which the artist is in danger of death"*: Ernest Hemingway, *Death in the Afternoon* (New York: Scribner, 1999), 77.

p. 274   *stock characters of the commedia dell'arte*: See Martin Green and John Swan, *The Triumph of Pierrot: The Commedia dell'Arte and the Modern Imagination* (New York: Macmillan, 1986).

p. 275   *center of a world*: Spengler said that in the premodern world not a hamlet was "too small to be unimportant," while today a handful of world-cities "have absorbed into themselves the whole content of History." In these metropolises the "broad life of regions is collecting while the rest dries up."

28. FEAR ITSELF

p. 277   *"not a question of just resisting evil"*: Endicott Peabody, "A Groton Sermon," in *Views from the Circle*, 33.

p. 277   *"what the hero of Matthew's Arnold's poem, 'Rugby Chapel,' does"*: Peabody, "A Groton Sermon," in *Views from the Circle*, 32–33.

p. 277   *"shattered and spared for a purpose beyond his knowledge"*: Freidel, *Franklin D. Roosevelt: The Ordeal*, 100
(citing a May 1953 interview with Frances Perkins). In the same year T. S. Eliot, in the midst of his own
breakdown, found consolation in the belief that the revelations of illness may be a mark of divine election:
"It was not until Eliot heard 'What the Thunder Said,' during his illness in December 1921, that he was
able to conceive, once more, of a special destiny, and so complete his long unfinished poem." Gordon, *T. S.
Eliot: An Imperfect Life*, 150.

p. 278   *"quiet room"*: See Woolf's *A Room of One's Own*.

p. 278   *"I do not consider personal relations"*: Ashburn, *Peabody of Groton*, 346.

p. 278   *"Roosevelt, wake up!"*: Ward, *Before the Trumpet*, 207.

p. 278   *"My little man"*: Ibid., 124.

p. 278   *"amiable boy scout"*: Steel, *Walter Lippmann and the American Century*, 291.

p. 278   *"pleasant man"*: Ibid., 290.

p. 279   *"the dome of the Capitol looks like gray polished granite"*: For Wilson's account of the inauguration, see Wilson,
American Earthquake, 478–483.

p. 279   *Frank Polk*: Franklin Roosevelt once contemplated practicing law with Polk. After leaving the State
Department, Polk joined the New York firm now known as Davis Polk & Wardwell. His daughter Alice
would marry Winthrop Rutherfurd's son Winthrop Jr.: their son, Lewis Polk Rutherfurd, would marry
Janet Jennings Auchincloss, the daughter of Hugh D. Auchincloss Jr. and Janet Lee Bouvier, and the half-
sister of Mrs. John F. Kennedy.

p. 279   *"started like a horse in fear of a hornet"*: Persico, *Franklin and Lucy*, 139.

p. 280   *"I experimented with gold"*: *Franklin D. Roosevelt: A Profile*, ed. William E. Leuchtenburg (New York: Hill
and Wang, 1967), 97.

p. 280   *"literate, economically speaking"*: Frances Perkins, *The Roosevelt I Knew* (New York: Viking, 1946), 226.

p. 280   *"It is common sense"*: Hofstadter, *American Political Tradition*, 410.

p. 280   *"utterly failed to stabilize industrial prices"*: Alan Brinkley, *Liberalism and Its Discontents* (Cambridge, Mass.:
Harvard University Press, 1998), 32.

p. 280   *"this magnificent man"*: Collier and Horowitz, *The Roosevelts*, 314–315.

p. 281   *"hanging in the air, like a goose about to be plucked"*: Ward, *First-Class Temperament*, 783–784 (note). There
are various versions of the story; in one, the white-bearded poet Edwin Markham, whose poem "The Man
with the Hoe" long appealed to sentimental reformers, stumbled into James Roosevelt, who then collided
with his father.

p. 281   *"dipped in phosphorous"*: Alter, *Defining Moment*, 376.

p. 281   *"There is a sort of angelic"*: Hovey, *John Jay Chapman*, 330.

p. 281   *"This delightful, youthful-looking man"*: Morgan, *F.D.R.: A Biography* (New York: Simon & Schuster, 1985), 382.

p. 281   *"His face would smile and light up"*: Perkins, *The Roosevelt I Knew*, 72.

p. 282   *"odd Eastern accent"*: Saul Bellow, *There Is Simply Too Much to Think About: Collected Nonfiction*, ed. Benjamin
Taylor (New York: Penguin, 2016), 329.

p. 282   *"President of all the people"*: Edmund Wilson, *Upstate: Records and Recollections of Northern New York* (New
York: Farrar, Straus and Giroux, 1971), 12.

p. 282   *"easy greeting which milord"*: Dean Acheson, *Morning and Noon: A Memoir* (Boston: Houghton Mifflin,
1965) 165; Robert Beisner, *Dean Acheson: A Life in the Cold War* (Oxford, U.K.: Oxford University Press,
2006), 15.

p. 282   *"clap her hand over"*: Acheson, *Morning and Noon*, 164.

p. 283   *"couldn't have missed it"*: Ward, *First-Class Temperament*, 527–528. Ward gives the year of the wedding as 1937.

p. 283   *"No, not Dickie Whitney!"*: Ted Morgan, *F.D.R.*, 491.

p. 283   *gold Porcellian pig*: Amory, *Proper Bostonians*, 305; "Broker Whitney Starts His Stretch at Sing Sing as
Convict No. 94,835," *Life*, April 25, 1938, 18–19.

p. 283   *"did wrong"*: Malcolm MacKay, *Impeccable Connections: The Rise and Fall of Richard Whitney* (New York:
Brick Tower Press, 2013) (ebook available online).

p. 283   *"knowledge of economic principles"*: Ashburn, *Peabody of Groton*, 347.

p. 283   *John Frederick Denison Maurice:* "The Reverend Malcolm Strachan, who knew the Rector's intimate
spiritual life in later years and who had unusual opportunity to know of his reading and thinking, feels
that John Frederick Denison Maurice [together with Frederick W. Robertson] had great influence on the
Rector and that in Maurice's sermons and writings is found possibly the best of all reflections on Peabody's
religious thought. Mrs. Peabody implied to Strachan that she also felt this." Ashburn, *Peabody of Groton*,
179 (note).

p. 284   *"I do most heartily rejoice"*: Ashburn, *Peabody of Groton*, 347.

p. 284   *might not have wanted to see his head on a pike:* The author has, for better or worse, passed much of his life
in what was once prime WASP commuting country, in Fairfield County, Connecticut, and Westchester
County, New York. The story is told of a commuter in the thirties who at the railway station each morning
purchased a copy of the newspaper and glanced at the front page before casting it aside. He had been doing
this for some time when the vendor was finally moved to ask him why he bothered to buy the paper only
to throw it away. "I'm looking for an obituary," came the reply. "But mister, the obituaries are in the back."
"The son of a bitch I'm looking for is going to be page one!"

p. 284   *"I believe Franklin Roosevelt to be a gallant and courageous gentleman"*: Biddle, "As I Remember Groton
School," in *Views from the Circle*, 127.

p. 284   *inducted into the Conversazione Society*: Straight, *After Long Silence*, 92–93.

p. 284   *Greek city-state*: Except where otherwise noted, the account of Michael Straight that follows is drawn from
Straight, *After Long Silence*, 33, and Roland Perry, *Last of the Cold War Spies: The Life of Michael Straight*
(Cambridge, Mass.: Da Capo, 2005).

p. 284   *Pot and Kettle*: Baltzell, *Philadelphia Gentlemen*, 222.

p. 285   *"the greatest man alive"*: Hesketh Pearson, *George Bernard Shaw: His Life and Personality* (New York:
Atheneum, 1963), 458.

p. 285   *"combination of playboy and Sir Galahad"*: Andrew Sinclair, *The Red and the Blue: Intelligence, Treason and the
Universities* (London: Weidenfeld and Nicolson, 1986), 37.

p. 285   *poetry and common sense*: Strachey, *Eminent Victorians*, 16.

p. 286   *"highly complex organic unities"*: G. E. Moore, *Principia Ethica* (Mineola, N.Y.: Dover, 2004), 189.
According to Moore, "personal affections and aesthetic enjoyments include *all* the greatest, and *by far*
the greatest, goods we can imagine . . ." (emphasis in original). If Keynes subscribed to Moore's theory
of community devoted to beauty and friendship, he also used Moore's philosophy to justify an amoral
Cyrenaicism which, according to some, was alien to Moore's own intention. On the other hand, Beatrice
Webb never saw in the *Principia Ethica* anything other than "a metaphysical justification for doing what
you like and what other people disapprove of.'" See Gertrude Himmelfarb, *Marriage and Morals Among the
Victorians and Other Essays* (New York: Vintage, 1987), 36 (note).

p. 286   *"higher sodomy"*: Zachary D. Carter, *The Price of Peace: Money, Democracy, and the Life of John Maynard
Keynes* (New York: Random House, 2020), 29.

p. 286   *controlled by Moscow*: Straight, *After Long Silence*, 60.

p. 286   *communist cell in Trinity*: Ibid.

p. 286   *"gentle, graceful"*: Benjamin C. Bradlee, *A Good Life: Newspapering and Other Adventures* (New York: Simon
& Schuster, 1995), 302.

p. 287   *"like a millionaire pretending to be a proletarian"*: Perry, *Last of the Cold War Spies*, 44.

p. 287   *elegant cadaver*: Meeting Blunt in 1964, Michael Straight found him looking "pale and skeletal, as he
always had." Straight, *After Long Silence*, 320.

p. 287   *"coquettishly chaste"*: Barrie Penrose and Simon Freeman, *Conspiracy of Silence: The Secret Life of Anthony
Blunt* (New York: Vintage, 1988), 158.

p. 287   *"slightly camp"*: Miranda Carter, *Anthony Blunt: His Lives* (New York: Farrar, Straus and Giroux, 2001),
118.

p. 288   *"intoxicated by Marxism"*: Ibid., 112.

p. 288 *"If you want to know about dialectical materialism"*: Ibid., 123.

p. 288 *"Cambridge was still full of Peter Pans"*: Gregory Woods, *Homintern: How Gay Culture Liberated the Modern World* (New Haven, Conn.: Yale University Press, 2017), 177.

p. 288 *"You are a bourgeois by education"*: John Costello and Oleg Tsarev, *Deadly Illusions: The K.G.B. Orlov Dossier—Stalin's Master Spy* (New York: Crown, 1993), 136.

p. 288 *"must have been one of the very few people"*: Andrew Lownie, *Stalin's Englishman: Guy Burgess, the Cold War, and the Cambridge Spy Ring* (New York: St. Martin's, 2015), 55.

p. 288 *"pederasts"*: Nigel West and Oleg Tsarev, *The Crown Jewels: The British Secrets at the Heart of the KGB Archives* (New Haven, Conn.: Yale University Press, 1999), 128.

p. 289 *"For food she had to go to the police station"*: Wilson, *American Earthquake,* 281–291.

p. 289 *"hunger and cold and fatigue and hopelessness"*: Ibid., 421–431.

p. 289 *"little flat yellow houses on stilts that look like chicken-houses"*: Ibid., 310–327.

p. 289 *"hope and exaltation"*: Wilson, *Axel's Castle,* 298.

p. 289 *"first splendor of the New Deal"*: Wilson, *American Earthquake,* 564–565.

p. 289 *"The 'gradualism' of the New Deal"*: Scudder, *On Journey,* 334.

p. 290 *"fundamental 'breakthrough'"*: Wilson, *To the Finland Station,* v.

p. 290 *"which will be homogenous and cooperative"*: Edmund Wilson, "Marxism at the End of the Thirties" (February-March 1941), in Wilson, *Shores of Light,* 743.

p. 290 *"first really human society"*: Wilson, *To the Finland Station,* v.

p. 290 *"presented in intelligible human terms"*: Edmund Wilson, *The Thirties,* ed. Leon Edel (New York: Washington Square Press, 1980), 299. He pondered "the possibilities of a narrative that would quite get away from the pedantic frame of theory." Hallelujah.

p. 290 *"freewheeling leftism"*: See Leon Edel's commentary in Wilson's journey to the Soviet Union in Wilson, *The Thirties,* 521.

p. 290 *"worked hard to see what he wanted to see"*: The account of Wilson and the Soviet Union that follows is drawn primarily from Wilson, *The Thirties,* ed. Edel, 519–590; Edmund Wilson, *Travels in Two Democracies* (New York: Harcourt, Brace, 1936); and Edmund Wilson, "Leonid Leonov" (December 9, 1944), in Wilson, *Classics and Commercials: A Literary Chronicle of the Forties* (New York: Farrar, Straus and Giroux, 1950), 250–256.

p. 290 *"people who don't work"*: Yet Wilson knew of the Soviet prison camps. See Wilson, *Travels in Two Democracies,* 247.

p. 290 *"spied upon every moment"*: Edmund Wilson, "Comrade Prince: A Memoir of D. S. Mirsky," in *From the Uncollected Edmund Wilson,* 272.

p. 291 *D. S. Mirsky*: The account of Mirsky and his relations with Wilson that follows is drawn primarily from Wilson, "Comrade Prince," in *From the Uncollected Edmund Wilson,* ed. Groth and Castronovo, 256–279, and G. S. Smith, *D. S. Mirsky: A Russian-English Life 1890–1939* (Oxford, U.K.: Oxford University Press, 2000).

p. 292 *"no worse"*: Wilson, *Travels in Two Democracies,* 242. Wilson did, however, concede that "the penalties— death and deportation—are greater" in the Soviet Union. One would say so!

p. 292 "moral top of the world": Wilson, *Travels in Two Democracies,* 321.

p. 292 *"Political tyranny"*: Roosevelt delivered his acceptance speech at Philadelphia on July 27, 1936.

p. 292 *"until I reached the line about 'economic royalists'"*: Ward, *First-Class Temperament,* 784 (note).

p. 293 *"millions who never had a chance"*: The address was delivered at Madison Square Garden on October 31, 1936.

p. 293 *"good democratic antidote"*: Perkins, *The Roosevelt I Knew,* 308.

p. 293 *"drunk with power"*: Steel, *Walter Lippmann and the American Century,* 319.

p. 294 *effort to forestall inflation*: Douglas Irwin, "What Caused the Recession of 1937–38?" *VoxEU & CEPR,* September 11, 2011.

p. 294 *government mandarinism*: Henry Adams warned that plutocrats might "ultimately succeed in directing government itself," a fear Roosevelt echoed when he said that private power in the United States threatened to become "stronger than the democratic state itself." The New Deal, F.D.R. believed, met the problem Adams described by altering the balance of power between private capital and the national government. At the same time, he was convinced that the New Deal was doing something to meliorate the wretched poverty in which many Americans lived: its laws were turning the idea of a welfare state Theodore Roosevelt sketched at Osawatomie into a reality. See Henry Adams, "The New York Gold Conspiracy," in Adams and Adams, *Chapters of Erie*, 134. Adams himself saw how delicate the question of balance was. Even as he warned of the dictatorship of tycoons, he pointed to the dangers of a federal superstate. "The national government," he wrote, "in order to deal with the corporations, must assume powers refused to it by its fundamental law [the Constitution], and even then is always exposed to the chance of forming an absolute central government which sooner or later is likely to fall into the very hands it is struggling to escape, and thus destroy the limits of its power only in order to make corruption omnipotent. Nor is this danger confined to America alone. The corporation is in its nature a threat against the popular institutions which are spreading so rapidly over the whole world. Wherever there is a popular and limited government this difficulty will be found in its path, and unless some satisfactory solution of the problem can be reached, popular institutions may yet find their very existence endangered."

p. 294 *"public wealth"*: "Without fully realizing it, he [Roosevelt] was embracing the essence of what would soon be known as Keynesian economics." Alan Brinkley, "The New Deal and the Idea of the State," in *The Rise and Fall of the New Deal Order 1930–1980,* ed. Steve Fraser and Gary Gerstle (Princeton, N.J.: Princeton University Press, 1989), 97.

p. 294 *retreat*: On the New Deal's "retreat from reform," see Alan Brinkley, *The End of Reform: New Deal Liberalism in Recession and War* (New York: Vintage, 1996).

p. 294 *"doing America over"*: Collier and Horowitz, *The Roosevelts*, 346.

p. 294 *"sad man because he couldn't get it all at once"*: Jason R. Jividen, *Claiming Lincoln: Progressivism, Equality, and the Battle for Lincoln's Legacy in Presidential Rhetoric* (DeKalb: Northern Illinois University Press, 2011), 106.

29. THE TERRORS OF THE EARTH

p. 296 *Blacks*: Roosevelt's recalcitrance where the rights of people of color were concerned, which grew out of his need to accommodate segregationist senators in order to advance his legislative agenda, is a subject beyond the scope of this book. For a useful introduction to the political calculus involved, see Louis Menand, "How the Deal Went Down," *New Yorker*, March 4, 2013.

p. 296 *"a certain lack of humor on her part"*: Dallek, *Franklin D. Roosevelt*, 233.

p. 296 *"phone calls and letters distracted and upset him"*: Blanche Wiesen Cook, *Eleanor Roosevelt: The War Years and After 1939–1962* (New York: Penguin, 2017), 528.

p. 296 *"'Sis, you handle these tomorrow morning.'"*: Ibid., 503.

p. 296 *"as a positive force in world affairs"*: Joseph P. Lash, *Eleanor Roosevelt: A Friend's Memoir* (Garden City, N.Y.: Doubleday, 1964), 47.

p. 296 *"democratic socialist"*: Cook, *Eleanor Roosevelt: The War Years and After*, 1.

p. 297 *tea with Franklin and Eleanor*: Straight, *After Long Silence*, 110; John Earl Haynes, Harvey Klehr, and Alexander Vassiliev, *Spies: The Rise and Fall of the KGB in America* (New Haven, Conn.: Yale University Press, 2009), 246.

p. 298 *he called George:* Such was Straight's recollection in *After Long Silence*. In fact Deutsch may have used the codename Stephan. See Allen Weinstein and Alexander Vassiliev, *The Haunted Wood: Soviet Espionage in America—The Stalin Era* (New York: Random House, 1990), 75.

p. 298 *his mother's apartment in Manhattan*: In his memoir *After Long Silence*, Straight describes his first encounter with Akhmerov as having taken place in Washington. But Straight's F.B.I. file and records in the Soviet archives point to New York. See Haynes, Klehr, and Vassiliev, *Spies*, 247. Straight, in *After Long Silence,* maintains that he first met Akhmerov *after* he had begun working in the State Department; documents in Soviet archives suggest that, on the contrary, he went to work there "at the request of the local *rezident*," Akhmerov. See West and Tsarev, *The Crown Jewels*, 133–134. The account of Straight's recruitment by the NKVD and his first encounter with Akhmerov is derived mainly from *After Long Silence*; for a slightly different account based on Soviet archives, see Weinstein and Vassiliev, *Haunted Wood*, 72–76.

p. 298 *"I would be a Communist"*: Straight, *After Long Silence*, 124.

p. 299 *"great drift"*: Whittaker Chambers, *Witness* (New York: Random House, 252), 269.

p. 299 *"students for Eastern Colleges"*: Advertisement in *National Popular Review*, March 1894. The account of Whittaker Chambers that follows is drawn primarily from Chambers, *Witness*; Sam Tanenhaus, *Whittaker Chambers: A Biography* (New York: Random House, 1997); and Lionel Trilling, Introduction to Trilling, *The Middle of the Journey* (New York: Harcourt Brace Jovanovich, 1975), vii–xxv.

p. 299 *"buried herself"*: Chambers, *Witness*, 102.

p. 299 *"desperate monologues"*: Ibid., 119.

p. 299 *"The voices around me"*: Ibid., 97.

p. 300 *"never quite able to shake off its rigors"*: Ibid., 109–110.

p. 300 *"I am an outcast"*: Ibid., 148.

p. 300 *"the logic of all totalitarian organization"*: Ibid., 107.

p. 301 *"one or two days on that beautiful but expensive campus"*: Ibid., 164.

p. 301 *"was simply brilliant"*: Tanenhaus, *Whittaker Chambers*, 40.

p. 301 *The course made a deep impression on him*: Chambers "clearly assimilated" the spirit of the General Honors course and its faith that "great works of art and thought have a decisive part in shaping the life of a polity." Kimmage, *Conservative Turn*, 25.

p. 301 *"in a world that is dying"*: See Chambers, *Witness*, 193, 195, 769.

p. 301 *"meaningless"*: Ibid., 183. Richard Chambers committed suicide in September 1926, more than a year after Whittaker Chambers became a communist.

p. 301 *"ascetism (or puritanism)"*: Ibid., 283.

p. 301 *"was the first person I ever knew"*: See Trilling, Introduction to Trilling, *Middle of the Journey*, vii–xxv.

p. 302 *"tragic comedian"*: Ibid., xxii.

p. 302 *"filled with the politeness of centuries of humanistic culture"*: Ibid., 239.

p. 302 *"impassioned longing to believe"*: Ibid., xix–xx.

p. 302 *"into crypts of Communism"*: Chambers, *Witness*, 271.

p. 302 *"May I speak to the President?"*: Joseph Alsop and Robert Kintner, *American White Paper: The Story of American Diplomacy and the Second World War* (London: Michael Joseph, 1940), 11–12; Grace Tully, *F.D.R., My Boss* (Chicago: People's Book Club, 1949) 235; Joseph E. Persico, *Roosevelt's Secret War: F.D.R. and World War II Espionage* (New York: Random House, 2001), 15.

p. 303 *lit a cigarette*: Steven M. Gillon, *Pearl Harbor: F.D.R. Leads the Nation into War* (New York: Basic Books, 2012) (ebook available online).

p. 303 *noted the date and time*: "Bedside Note of President Franklin D. Roosevelt Regarding the Invasion of Poland by Germany, 09/01/1939," National Archives and Records Administration, File Unit: PSF: Diplomatic Correspondence—Poland, 1933—1945; Collection F.D.R.-F.D.R.PSF: President's Secretary's File (Franklin D. Roosevelt Administration), 1933—1945; Franklin D. Roosevelt Library (NLF.D.R.).

p. 303 *"when something is happening every minute"*: Richard M. Ketchum, *The Borrowed Years 1938–1941: America on the Way to War* (New York: Anchor, 1991), 545.

p. 303 *relaxed among the pillows*: Ibid., 203.

p. 304 *"to do something" about Hitler*: Hofstadter, *American Political Tradition*, 447.

p. 304 *"About three years ago"*: Morgan, *F.D.R.*, 504.

p. 304 *"delusion that we of the United States can safely permit the United States to become a lone island"*: Franklin Roosevelt, Address at the University of Virginia, June 10, 1940, in *Senate Documents, 77th Congress, 2d Session—Miscellaneous* (Washington: Government Printing Office, 1942), 62–65.

30. JOY LANE

p. 305 *"such a host of impassioned friends"*: Howe, *John Jay Chapman*, 35.

p. 306 *"the only real pageant"*: Ibid., 440.

p. 306 *"His tiny shrunken body looked as Gandhi looks"*: Sedgwick, "Three Men of Groton," in *Views from the Circle*, 17–18.

p. 306 *"Franklin I am very fond of"*: Ashburn, *Peabody of Groton*, 346.

p. 306 *"rejoiced"*: Ibid., 348.

p. 306 *"Our love and prayers"*: Ibid., 353.

p. 306 *"I can't understand this thing about Frank"*: Ward, *Before the Trumpet*, 208.

p. 307 *"Franklin, dear boy"*: Acosta Nichols, *Forty Years More: A History of Groton School 1934–1974* (Groton, Mass.: Trustees of Groton School, 1976), 10.

p. 307 *"shouting Father's name"*: Ward, *Before the Trumpet*, 209.

p. 307 *"unquestionably"*: Ibid., 207.

p. 307 *"Intelligent and expert persons"*: Martin, "Preface to a Schoolmaster's Biography," in *Views from the Circle*, 131.

p. 307 *"a great deal of talk about self-expression and creativity"*: Ashburn, *Peabody of Groton*, 238.

p. 307 *"graces human and divine"*: "England's Lane," Hymn 296, in *The Hymnal of the Protestant Episcopal Church in the United States of America 1940* (New York: Church Pension Fund, 1961).

p. 308 *wait on table, make his bed, or clean his cubicle*: Nichols, *Forty Years More*, 5.

p. 308 *"Groton a splendid place"*: Howe, *John Jay Chapman*, 257.

p. 308 *"a set of social technologies"*: James Hankins, *Virtue Politics: Soulcraft and Statecraft in Renaissance Italy* (Cambridge, Mass.: Harvard University Press, 2019), 2–3; see also Werner Jaeger's *Paideia* volumes. Peabody was, to say the least, very far from being an aesthete, but under his leadership Groton developed an arts program rather impressive for the time, with a studio in what is now the Gammons Recital Hall. In addition to drawing and painting, sculpture, too, was taught. The story is told that Peabody, seeking a sculptor to instruct the boys, interviewed an artist who was reputed to be an atheist. "Do you believe in God?" Peabody asked the applicant. "No." "Would you feel the need to tell that to the boys?" "No." The man was hired. The story is repeated, the author seems to recall, in a book by Edward Pulling, perhaps his memoir *The Early Years of Millbrook School*. Pulling taught at Groton before founding Millbrook.

p. 308 *"God's mercy that all of us didn't go into it"*: Sedgwick, "Three Men of Groton," in *Views from the Circle*, 25.

p. 308 *"Grotonian consciences never twinged properly"*: Heinrichs, *American Ambassador*, 5.

p. 308 *"Groton ethic"*: "Galbraith has called this [emphasis on conscientious public service], in tribute to the most prestigious of American private schools, 'the Groton ethic.'" Godfrey Hodgson, *America in Our Time: From World War II to Nixon—What Happened and Why* (Princeton, N.J.: Princeton University Press, 2005), 118.

p. 308 *"More than forty years ago"*: Ashburn, *Peabody of Groton*, 352.

p. 309 *his last Prize Day*: Ibid., 400–406

p. 309 *"Church School"*: Ibid., 402.

p. 309 *"to see the new house"*: Ibid., 356.

p. 309 *Malcolm Strachan*: Strachan, Auchincloss wrote in his memoir *A Writer's Capital*, looked up to the Rector as an exemplary Christian who had a much profounder insight into his faith than was generally credited: "The only times that I ever heard [Strachan] speak with grating harshness about other human beings were when he spoke of persons who had hurt the Rector. When Peabody died, very suddenly at the wheel of his car which he had just parked by the side of the road, Malcolm bought the automobile from the estate and preserved it almost as a relic. He and I over the years discussed a novel that he was vaguely planning to write about the Rector or about a headmaster like the Rector, and his school and his theology. He believed that the Rector's theology was subtler and more complicated than any of us supposed. . ."

p. 309 *Peabody showed Strachan a side of himself*: Auchincloss, in *A Writer's Capital*, said that Strachan's "close relationship with the Rector, which provided the source of inspiration for my novel, *The Rector of Justin*, developed after I graduated from Groton [in 1935]. While I was still at school, Malcolm was too young and too new; Peabody too old and formidable. But the Rector cared for faith more than for anything else, and the younger man's passionate interest in the ministry ultimately drew them together. After Malcolm had been ordained and had returned to Groton as an assistant chaplain as well as a faculty member, he became the spiritual intimate of Peabody's last years. I suspect that the Rector found much relief and comfort in this friendship with a devoted disciple who still did not treat him as a legend. He was able to tell Malcolm things that he could tell nobody else: things about his disappointments, for example. Nobody else could believe that his had not been the happiest and most successful of lives. But the Rector, although a great headmaster, was basically a humble man. He knew in his heart that half the Groton family only paid lip service to his ideals. He knew Mammon dominated his graduates and that he had failed to persuade his boys to receive Christ. Yet he was surrounded by what I can only call a conspiracy of applause—applause by men who wanted him to believe that he had succeeded because believing in nothing themselves but their own boyhood faith in him, they could not face a world which had disillusioned the Rector . . . Malcom's love and compassion made the frame for a clear window into truth."

p. 309 *confessing his doubts*: See Auchincloss, *Writer's Capital*, and Auchincloss, *Rector of Justin*. Auchincloss never intended Francis Prescott to be a portrait of Peabody, but he was candid enough in admitting how much his novel owed both to Groton and to Strachan's understanding of Peabody, the outgrowth of the conversations in Joy Lane. It should be added that Auchincloss did *not* admire Peabody in the way Strachan did. Strachan, Auchincloss wrote, "loved the Rector and, quite seriously, regarded him as a saint." Auchincloss, *Writer's Capital*, 60. Auchincloss, for his part, endorsed Stewart Alsop's characterization of his old headmaster: "The Rector was a great man. He was also a bit of a shit." Auchincloss's feelings about Groton itself were as mixed. He found the school "brutal," but rated the quality of its education high. "Groton in my day was good for its time. I had close friends there. Among the twenty-seven boys in my form, you could not find a better group. We had diplomats, an assistant Secretary of State, eminent doctors and lawyers, even a Benedictine monk. There was not a failure among them. Not one." The school, he believed, "is even more successful today. There is a large waiting list. I sent two sons there." On Auchincloss, Groton, Peabody, and Strachan, see Gelderman, *Louis Auchincloss*, 52–54, and Christopher C. Dahl, *Louis Auchincloss* (New York: Ungar, 1986), 4.

p. 309 *and lamenting his mistakes*: Frank Ashburn visited Peabody in Joy Lane in the spring of 1943. "I ventured a few words of admiration," Ashburn wrote, "for what he had accomplished. He waved it aside, simply and decisively. . . . 'The things for which people are kind enough to give me credit were largely not my doing and they were very little and for them I have to thank my wife, my friends, the trustees, the masters, and the boys. They forget the failures and the mistakes.'" Ashburn, *Peabody of Groton*, 418–419.

p. 309 *"I shall be recompensed in part"*: Ibid., 354.

p. 310 *"my idea of it"*: Auchincloss, *Writer's Capital*, 60.

p. 310 *"I wish Pierre Jay were not quite so profane"*: Ashburn, *Peabody of Groton*, 128.

p. 311 *"street cads of London curse"*: Letter from Kent Sanger to the author, *circa* 1983. It is a testament both to how greatly times have changed and how rarefied was the atmosphere in which certain WASPs once moved that a grown man, not actually retired to a monastery, should have passed so many years without hearing any of the familiar Saxon words spoken until that fatal day on the golf course! (The golf course itself no longer exists.)

p. 311 *"snobbishness and materialism"*: Auchincloss, *Rector of Justin*, 324.

p. 311 *"no life whatever"*: The words from Emerson's journals essentially reproduce what Prescott found missing in his characteristic graduate.

p. 311 *"the greatest prep school in the nation"*: David Halberstam, *The Best and the Brightest* (New York: Random House, 1972), 51.

p. 312 *"covert teaching"*: Halberstam, *Best and the Brightest*, 51.

p. 312 cui servire: David Evett, "Luther, Cranmer, Service, and Shakespeare," in *Centered on the Word: Literature, Scripture, and the Tudor-Stuart Middle Way*, ed. Daniel W. Doerksen and Christopher Hodgkins (Newark, Del.: University of Delaware Press, 2004), 88; John Field, *University and Other Sermons* (London: Longman, 1853), 175; Ioannis Laurentii Berti, *Opus de Theologicis Disciplinis*, II (Venice: Recurti, 1750), 106.

p. 312 *Sacramentary of Gregory the Great*: William Palmer, *Origines Liturgicæ, or, Antiquities of the English Ritual, and a Dissertation on Primitive Liturgies*, 2 vols. (Oxford: Oxford University Press, 1836), II, 39. est regnare: Depending on the context, *regnare*, in Latin, may mean "to reign, to rule, to have royal power, to be king," or it may mean, as it at times does in Cicero and Virgil, "to have mastery," "to prevail." Earlier Christians (among them Peabody) who had a good deal of Latin would have had little difficulty in understanding *cui servire est regnare* to mean "through Whose service one obtains mastery (or prevails) [over oneself]." On *regnare*, see J. E. Riddle, *A Complete Latin-English Dictionary* (London: Longman, 1844), 577; Charlton Lewis, *An Elementary Latin Dictionary* (New York: American Book Company, 1915), 714.

p. 313 "*Compared to Groton*": Arthur M. Schlesinger Jr., *A Life in the Twentieth Century: Innocent Beginnings 1917–1950* (Boston: Houghton Mifflin, 2000), 91.

p. 313 *failure to make Christ really live for his boys*: Auchincloss, *Writer's Capital*, 59.

p. 313 "*a minor, but mean way*": Ashburn, *Peabody of Groton*, 336.

p. 313 "*grieved the Rector and Mrs. Peabody deeply*": Ibid., 336–337.

p. 314 "*It is because I care so terribly*": See chapter eight above, "A Glorious and Most Intensely Interesting Life."

p. 314 "*You know he would be an awful bully*": Richard Bissell, *You Can Always Tell a Harvard Man* (Lake Oswego, Ore.: eNet Press, 2012), 164.

p. 314 "*that's it, my boys*": Ashburn, *Peabody of Groton*, 419.

p. 315 *last of the Rector's boys still active in the world*: The account of John Goodenough that follows is drawn from John B. Goodenough, *Witness to Grace* (Frederick, Md.: PublishAmerica, 2008) (ebook available online).

31. THE DEATH OF MEN

p. 319 "*You are leaving Andover*": "Stimson Hails Boys Facing Issues as They Enter World's 'Dark Hour,'" *New York Times*, June 15, 1940; David Chase, "Speaking at Andover, Speaking to the World," *Andover: The Magazine of Phillips Academy*, Spring 2010; Richard Ben Cramer, *Being Poppy: A Portrait of George Herbert Walker Bush* (New York: Simon & Schuster, 2013), 22–23; Jon Meacham, *Destiny and Power: The American Odyssey of George Herbert Walker Bush* (New York: Random House, 2016), 33–40; Claude Moore Fuess, *Independent Schoolmaster* (Boston: Little Brown, 1952), 248.

p. 319 *Stimson went to New Haven*: For Stimson's travels in June 1940, see Hodgson, *The Colonel*, 213–214.

p. 319 "*defeatist arguments*": Stimson and Bundy, *On Active Service in Peace and War*, 319.

p. 319 *He was in his office*: Ibid., 323. Jonathan W. Jordan says that Stimson took the call in the Pierre. Jonathan W. Jordan, *American Warlords: How Roosevelt's High Command Led America to Victory in World War II* (New York: Random House, 2016), 38.

p. 319 *almost seventy-three*: Roosevelt had discreetly made inquiries into the state of Stimson's health and had been assured that he was sufficiently well to undertake high office. He may well have been in better health than Franklin himself at the time.

p. 319 *his wife and his professional associates*: Stimson and Bundy, *On Active Service in Peace and War*, 323–324. Stimson was of counsel in the Winthrop, Stimson firm in 1940 and was no longer a partner or "member of the firm." In his appearance before the Senate Committee on Military Affairs in July 1940 he described the position of counsel to the senators: "That is a euphemistic term for a gentleman who sits in an office without sharing the profits." Stimson and Bundy, *On Active Service in Peace and War*, 327.

p. 320 "*Have you heard the news?*": Ibid., 390–392.

p. 320 "*first feeling*": Ibid., 393.

p. 320 *smaller than Portugal's*: Hodgson, *The Colonel*, 227.

p. 320 *ride with Mrs. Stimson*: Ibid., 241. Hodgson also describes Stimson's recreative journeys to South Carolina, the Adirondacks, and Highhold.

p. 322 "*generous attempts by the President*": Acheson, *Present at the Creation: My Years in the State Department* (New York: Norton, 1969), 3.

p. 322 *Grau San Martin-Batista dictatorship*: Ibid., 11.

p. 322 "*Pardon me*": Ibid., 12.

p. 322 *"frosty patrician who drank too much"*: Peter Rand, *Conspiracy of One: Tyler Kent's Secret Plot against F.D.R.,*
        Churchill, and the Allied War Effort (Guilford, Conn.: Lyons Press, 2013), 81. Yet Schlesinger was "greatly
        impressed" by Welles's intelligence, candor, lucidity of mind, distinction of manner . . . He seemed not at
        all a cold and unfeeling man as advertised." Schlesinger, *Life in the Twentieth Century,* 91.

p. 322 *chronicler of the WASPs*: Auchincloss himself rejected the term WASP. There was, he said, so much
        "nonsense written about WASPs today. I am tired of the whole subject. I never heard the term WASP
        when I was growing up. We just thought of them as people. I find that word annoying. I don't know where
        it came from. I prefer the term Protestant if you must use one."

p. 323 *propositioned several Pullman porters*: See Welles, *Sumner Welles*; Gregory Wallance, *America's Soul in*
        Balance: The Holocaust, F.D.R.'s State Department, and the Moral Disgrace of an American Aristocracy (Austin,
        Tx: Greenleaf, 2012); Persico, *Roosevelt's Secret War*; Lillian Faderman, *The Gay Revolution: The Story of the*
        Struggle (New York: Simon & Schuster, 2016).

p. 323 *He told future Vice President Alben Barkley*: Persico, *Roosevelt's Secret War,* 255.

p. 323 *"You should have told me!"*: Al Cimino, *Roosevelt and Churchill: A Friendship That Saved the World* (New York:
        Chartwell Books, 2018), 15; Doris Kearns Goodwin, *No Ordinary Time: Franklin & Eleanor Roosevelt: The*
        Home Front in World War II (New York: Simon & Schuster, 1994), 300.

p. 323 *"my wolves—my beloved pack of wolves"*: Merriman Smith, "Thank You, Mr. President," *Life,* August 19, 1946.

p. 323 *"No lover"*: Martin Gilbert, *Winston S. Churchill: Never Despair 1945–1965* (London: Heinemann, 1966), 415.

p. 323 *"fun to be in the same decade"*: Robert H. Pilpel, *Churchill in America, 1895–1961: An Affectionate Portrait*
        (New York: Harcourt Brace Jovanovich, 1976), 161.

p. 323 *"was like opening your first bottle of champagne"*: *America in Quotations,* ed. Bahman Dehgan (Jefferson, N.C.:
        McFarland, 2003), 182.

p. 324 *"more of the panther than of the woman"*: William Manchester, *The Last Lion: Winston Spencer Churchill:*
        Visions of Glory 1874–1932 (New York: Bantam, 2013), 116.

p. 324 *"It was astonishing to me"*: Pilpel, *Churchill in America,* 156.

p. 324 *"must have a tumbler of sherry"*: Cita Stelzer, *Dinner with Churchill: Policy-Making at the Dinner Table* (New
        York: Pegasus, 2013) (ebook available online); Goodwin, *No Ordinary Time,* 302.

p. 324 *"a charming country gentleman"*: Martin Gilbert, *Winston S. Churchill: Road to Victory 1941–1945* (Toronto:
        Stoddart, 1986), 564.

p. 324 *"topsy-turvy, upside-side down"*: Richard W. Steele, *The First Offensive 1942: Roosevelt, Marshall and the*
        Making of American Strategy (Bloomington: Indiana University Press, 1973), 38.

p. 324 *"Conferences with the President are difficult matters"*: Blaine T. Browne, *Mighty Endeavor: The American*
        Nation and World War II (Lanham, Md.: Rowman & Littlefield, 2019), 74.

p. 324 *"Mr. President, I don't like you to dissemble with me"*: Hodgson, *The Colonel,* 231.

p. 325 *"calculating the future"*: Erwin C. Hargrove, *The President as Leader: Appealing to the Better Angels of Our*
        Nature (Lawrence: University Press of Kansas, 1998), 81.

p. 325 *"a superb war President"*: Stimson and Bundy, *On Active Service in Peace and War,* 666.

p. 325 *"had more serenity than any man I have ever seen"*: Arthur M. Schlesinger Jr., *The Age of Roosevelt: The Crisis of*
        the Old Order 1919–1933 (Boston: Houghton Mifflin, 1957), 407.

p. 325 *"There's something he's got"*: Morgan, *F.D.R.,* 552.

p. 325 *"Captain Naar here"*: Timothy M. Gay, *Savage Will: The Daring Escape of Americans Trapped Behind Nazi*
        Lines (New York: Penguin, 2017), 3–4.

p. 326 *law-abiding opponents*: Ibid., 523.

p. 326 *"After some delay"*: Winston S. Churchill, *The Grand Alliance* (Boston: Houghton Mifflin, 1950), 697.

p. 326 *"liked and understood each other"*: Curt Gentry, *J. Edgar Hoover: The Man and the Secrets* (New York: Norton,
        2001), 223.

p. 326 *"to smack too much of the Gestapo methods"*: Ibid., 299.

p. 327 *"By God, Edgar, that's the first time"*: William E. Leuchtenburg, *In the Shadow of F.D.R.: From Harry*
        Truman to George W. Bush (Ithaca, N.Y.: Cornell University Press, 2001), 171.

p. 327   *"loved reading his secret documents"*: Cook, *Eleanor Roosevelt: The War Years and After*, 467.

p. 327   *"Do you realize"*: Gilbert, *Winston S. Churchill: Road to Victory*, 794.

p. 327   *took up his prayer book*: Mark Tooley, "F.D.R.'s June 6 D-Day Prayer, War, Churches, & Drones," *Juicy Ecumenism*, June 6, 2013.

p. 327   *stained Arabia's waters red*: Dante, *Inferno*, X, 85–86.

p. 327   *anxious over the succession:* Morgan, *F.D.R.*, 725–727.

p. 328   *"he got more cream in the saucer"*: Michael Dobbs, *Six Months in 1945: F.D.R., Stalin, Churchill, Truman—From World War to Cold War* (New York: Knopf, 2012), 5.

p. 328   *"physical capacity"*: Joseph Lelyveld, *His Final Battle: The Last Months of Franklin Roosevelt* (New York: Knopf, 2016) (ebook available online).

p. 328   *"Have you noticed that the President"*: Robert H. Ferrell, *The Dying President: Franklin D. Roosevelt 1944–1945* (Columbia: University of Missouri Press, 1998), 28.

p. 328   *"was absolutely terrific"*: Steven Lomazow and Eric Fettmann, *F.D.R.'s Deadly Secret* (New York: PublicAffairs, 2009), 151.

p. 328   *"shocked and horrified"*: Lelyveld, *His Final Battle*. Roosevelt suffered from "fainting spells" before 1944, but the episodes described toward the end of his life seem to have been more frequent and, to those who knew him, more worrisome.

p. 329   *Tory radical*: On the WASP statesman as Tory radical, see Lipset, *Political Man*, 299–301.

p. 329   *"a man with both feet firmly planted—in the air"*: "A radical is a man with both feet firmly planted—in the air. A conservative is a man with two perfectly good legs, who, however, has never learned to walk forward. A reactionary is a somnambulist walking backwards. A liberal is a man who uses his legs and hands at the behest of his head." "Radio Address by Hon. Franklin D. Roosevelt," *Congressional Record*, November 1, 1939 to November 3, 1939, Appendix, 560–561.

p. 330   *"Mama, will you please get off the line"*: Goodwin, *No Ordinary Time*, 273.

p. 330   *"himself off from the world"*: Ibid., 272.

p. 330   *"Franklin Roosevelt is a very religious man"*: Ashburn, *Peabody of Groton*, 421.

p. 330   *"shaken"*: Karabel, *The Chosen*, 37.

p. 330   *"I have leaned on the Rector"*: Ibid.

p. 330   *"my old schoolmaster, Dr. Peabody"*: *Inaugural Addresses of the Presidents of the United States* (Washington: United States Government Printing Office, 1989), 283.

p. 331   *"I can't stand this unless you get me a stiff drink"*: James Roosevelt, "F.D.R.'s Lonely Last Days," *The Saturday Evening Post*, November 7, 1959.

p. 331   *"To a doctor's eye"*: Lord Moran [Charles McMoran Wilson, 1st Baron Moran], *Churchill: Taken from the Diaries of Lord Moran: The Struggle for Survival 1940–1965* (Boston: Houghton Mifflin, 1966), 242.

p. 331   *"the most cruel and unscrupulous"*: Wilson, *To the Finland Station*, v.

p. 331   *"doesn't want anything but security for his country"*: William C. Bullitt, "How We Won the War and Lost the Peace," *Life*, August 30, 1948.

p. 331   *"a Caucasian bandit"*: Ibid.

p. 331   *"play my hunch"*: Ibid.

p. 331   *"There I sat"*: Sir Alexander Cadogan, *The Diaries of Sir Alexander Cadogan O.M. 1938–1945*, ed. David Dilks (New York: G. P. Putnam's Sons, 1972), 582.

p. 331   *"Germany is finished"*: James C. Humes, *Churchill: The Prophetic Statesman* (Washington: Regnery, 2012), 157 (emphasis added).

p. 331   *"I love that man"*: Moran, *Churchill: Taken from the Diaries of Lord Moran, 1940–1965*, 243.

p. 331   *"particularly distinguished himself"*: Milovan Djilas, *Conversations with Stalin*, trans. Michael B. Petrovich (San Diego: Harcourt Brace, *circa* 1963) (ebook available online).

p. 332   *"heart-to-heart talk"*: Moran, *Churchill: Taken from the Diaries of Lord Moran, 1940–1965*, 144.

p. 332   *"the way in which a Christian gentleman should behave"*: Kissinger, *Diplomacy*, 417.

p. 332 *the inhabitant of a small island floating off Eurasia*: "For three centuries, British leaders . . . operated from the assumption that, if Europe's resources were marshaled by a single dominant power, that country would then have the resources to challenge Great Britain's command of the seas, and thus threaten its independence." Kissinger, *Diplomacy*, 50.

p. 333 *"worst looking man I ever saw who was still alive"*: David Michaelis, *Eleanor* (New York: Simon & Schuster, 2020), 228.

p. 333 *"He sits a little straighter in his chair"*: *Closest Companion: The Unknown Story of the Intimate Friendship between Franklin Roosevelt and Margaret Suckley*, ed. Geoffrey C. Ward (New York: Simon & Schuster, 2009), 412 (emphasis in original).

p. 333 *"Have a cig?"*: Merriman Smith, "Thank You, Mr. President," *Life*, August 19, 1946.

p. 333 *"It was an intense thing"*: Ibid.

p. 334 *"expression of joy on F.D.R.'s face"*: Nigel Hamilton, *War and Peace: F.D.R.'s Final Odyssey, D–Day to Yalta 1943–1945* (Boston: Houghton Mifflin, 2019), 495.

p. 334 *"Heigh-O, Silver"*: Smith, "Thank You, Mr. President."

p. 334 *"aged terrifically"*: Susan Butler, *Roosevelt and Stalin: Portrait of a Partnership* (New York: Knopf, 2015 (ebook available online).

p. 334 "so many *problems & difficulties*": Resa Willis, *F.D.R. and Lucy: Lovers and Friends* (New York: Routledge, 2004), 5–6 (emphasis in original).

p. 334 *"a jolly fellow"*: Ibid., 6.

p. 334 *"The last I remember"*: Ibid., 7.

p. 334 *"Have you dropped your cigarette?"*: Persico, *Roosevelt's Secret War*, 434.

p. 334 FLASH WASHN—FDR DEAD: Bernard Asbell, *When F.D.R. Died* (New York: Holt, Rinehart and Winston, 1961), 79; *Franklin D. Roosevelt: His Life and Times: An Encyclopedic View*, ed. Otis L. Graham Jr., Meghan Robinson Wander (Boston: G.K. Hall, 1985), 91.

p. 335 *"this artist, this seducer"*: Harper, *American Visions of Europe*, 114.

p. 335 *"a very superficial man, ignorant, dilettantish"*: Lelyveld, *His Final Battle*.

p. 335 *"was really incapable of a personal friendship"*: Kenneth S. Davis, *F.D.R.: Into the Storm 1937–1940: A History* (New York: Random House, 1993), 290.

p. 335 *"When you are in the center of world affairs"*: Goodwin, *No Ordinary Time*, 108.

p. 335 *"perhaps the most gifted political and strategic genius"*: Hodgson, *The Colonel*, 308.

32. *POUR LE MÉRITE*

p. 336 *anti-Semitic clichés*: The anti-Semitism of the WASPs found very little justification in Dante, who in his treatment of usury in Canto 17 of the *Inferno* refused to indulge the anti-Semitic prejudices of his age. "Rather than scapegoat the marginal," Teodolinda Barolini writes, "Dante focuses instead on his society's most normative members: on the great Christian families whom he indicts through the heraldic crests that blazon the moneybags worn around their necks." Barolini finds in the *Commedia* not hostility to the stranger but rather various "forms of sympathy toward the other," from the "profound psychological identification that causes Dante to faint after meeting Francesca, to his assertive dignifying of the Ethiopian and his ability actively to imagine the salvation of sodomites and pagans, to his demonstrable lack of interest in stereotyping ethnic groups different from his own, such as the Jews." See Teodolinda Barolini, "Usury and the Absence of Jews," Commentary on *Inferno* 17 (available online), and Barolini, "Dante's Sympathy for the Other, or the Non-Stereotyping Imagination: Sexual and Racialized Others in the *Commedia*," in *Critica del testo*, ed. Roberto Antonelli, Annalisa Landolfi, and Arianna Punzi (Rome: Viella, 2011), 177–206.

p. 336 *"three anemic Gentiles"*: Gunther, *Learned Hand: The Man and the Judge*, 246.

p. 337 *"Jew party"*: Smith, *Eleanor: A Spiritual Biography*, 112.

p. 337 *"The summer hotel that is ruined"*: Karabel, *The Chosen*, 88.

p. 337 *"several of the members of the club would not go"*: Baltzell, *Protestant Establishment*, 196.

p. 337 *"The Puritanism of New England"*: Wilson, *A Piece of My Mind*, 90.

p. 338 *"is a Protestant country"*: Carol Felsenthal, *Princess Alice: The Life and Times of Alice Roosevelt Longworth* (New York: St. Martin's, 1988), 199.

p. 338 *"although I loathe anti-Semitism"*: Kenneth L. Marcus, *The Definition of Anti-Semitism* (Oxford, U.K.: Oxford University Press, 2015), 36.

p. 338 *"for some time been surreptitiously at work"*: Richard H. Rovere, "The American Establishment," *Esquire*, May 1, 1962. See also Rovere, "The American Establishment," *The Wilson Quarterly*, Summer 1979; Rovere, *The American Establishment and Other Reports, Opinions, and Speculations* (Westport, Conn.: Greenwood Press, 1980).

p. 339 *"moral attitudes of dominant and privileged groups"*: Reinhold Niebuhr, *Moral Man and Immoral Society: A Study in Ethics and Politics* (New York: Scribner's, 1932), 117.

p. 340 *"tuition was an insurmountable obstacle"*: Ashburn, *Fifty Years On*, 46.

p. 340 *"its own flesh and blood"*: Ibid., 48.

p. 340 *Henry Chauncey*: The crucial book here is Nicholas Lemann, *The Big Test: The Secret History of the American Meritocracy* (New York: Farrar, Straus and Giroux, 2000).

p. 341 *"meritocratic children"*: Daniel Markovits, "How Life Became an Endless, Terrible Competition," *The Atlantic*, September 2019.

p. 342 *"She began to go on and on about polio"*: Marie Brenner, "Scenes from a Marriage," *Vanity Fair*, February 1988.

p. 342 *a guest of the Binghams*: Mel Gussow, "At Home With: Mary Bingham," *New York Times*, December 22, 1994.

p. 342 *"Darky servants came"*: Ward, *First-Class Temperament*, 448.

p. 342 *"Amid a world of people"*: Ibid., 447.

p. 342 *"I came across two mentions of 'darky.'"*: Blanche Wiesen Cook, *Eleanor Roosevelt, Vol. 2: The Defining Years 1933–1938* (New York: Penguin, 2000), 439.

p. 343 *"incubating the music"*: Cheryl A. Kirk-Duggan, "African American Hymnody," in *Encyclopedia of Women and Religion in North America*, ed. Rosemary Skinner Keller, Rosemary Radford Ruether, and Marie Cantlon (Bloomington: Indiana University Press, 2006), 988.

p. 343 *"supporting the darkies"*: *Letters of Henry Adams 1892–1899*, IV, 155; Michael O'Brien, *Henry Adams & the Southern Question* (Athens: University of Georgia Press, 2005), 118. See also Charles Vandersee, "Henry Adams and the Invisible Negro," *South Atlantic Quarterly*, Winter 1967.

p. 343 *an antislavery family*: For Henry Adams and race, see the excellent account in David S. Brown, *The Last American Aristocrat* (New York: Scribner, 2020), 95–99.

p. 343 *"cross the color-line"*: *The Letters of Henry Adams 1906–1918*, ed. J. C. Levenson et al. (Cambridge, Mass.: Belknap Press, 1988), VI, 284.

p. 344 *"as if we were a Black* tabula rasa*"*: Ernest J. Wilson III, "The Reform of Tradition, the Tradition of Reform," in *Blacks at Harvard*, ed. Werner Sollors, Caldwell Titcomb, and Thomas A. Underwood (New York: New York University Press, 1993), 429.

p. 344 *"simple unity"*: Du Bois, *Souls of Black Folk*, 81.

33. CENTURIONS OF AN AMERICAN CENTURY

p. 346 douleurs: Kennan, *Memoirs 1925–1950*, 292.

p. 346 *"Long live great Stalin"*: J. Stalin, *Speeches Delivered at Meetings of Voters of the Stalin Electoral District, Moscow, December 11, 1937 and February 9, 1946* (Moscow: Foreign Language Publishing House, 1950), 9ff.

p. 347 *"brush the question off"*: Kennan, *Memoirs 1925–1950*, 293.

p. 347 *"outrageous encumberment"*: Ibid., 294.

p. 347 *"capitalist encirclement"*: For the Long Telegram, see Kennan, *Memoirs 1925–1950*, 547–559.

p. 347 *"the silence is impressive"*: Santayana, *Dominations and Powers*, 457.

p. 348 *"contain"*: Barton Gellman, *Contending with Kennan: Toward a Philosophy of American Power* (Westport, Conn.: Praeger, 1984), 134.

p. 349 *"The life of this elder Kennan"*: The account of George Kennan that follows is drawn primarily from Kennan, *Memoirs 1925–1950*, and John Lewis Gaddis, *George F. Kennan: An American Life* (New York: Penguin, 2011); except where otherwise noted, the quoted words pertaining to Kennan are drawn from those works.

p. 351 *paradise regained*: The Greek *paradeisos* and the Avestan *pairidaeza* signify a garden enclosed: the sort of ideal space high WASPs sought.

p. 351 *"They would all argue at the top of their lungs"*: Isaacson and Thomas, *Wise Men*, 431.

p. 351 *"Get out of my house!"*: Ibid.

p. 351 *"I was staggered"*: Arthur M. Schlesinger, Jr., *A Life in the Twentieth Century: Innocent Beginnings 1917–1950* (Boston: Houghton Mifflin, 2000), 473.

p. 352 *a shapely blonde*: It was said that her figure, in its prime, might (to borrow the image of Casanova) have tempted the chisel of Praxiteles. The grammarian has so far refrained from speculating on the influence of WASP beauty on the fortunes of the WASPs as a class. It is true that many of the most notable specimens were sadly shaped. Henry Adams was little more than a dwarf, &c., &c. Yet they were, on the whole, a rather good-looking group: "In what perfection they produce them!" to adapt the words of the narrator in James's *The Wings of the Dove*.

p. 352 *great center and gathering-place*: See C. A. Sainte-Beuve, *Portraits of the Eighteenth Century, Historic and Literary*, trans. Katharine P. Wormeley, 2 vols. (New York: G. P. Putnam's, 1905), I, 388.

p. 352 *boxer shorts*: Joan Mellen, *Hellman and Hammett: The Legendary Passion of Lillian Hellman and Dashiell Hammett* (New York: Harper Perennial, 1997), 372.

p. 354 *"I shall testify"*: The account of Whittaker Chambers that follows is drawn primarily from Chambers, *Witness*, and Tanenhaus, *Whittaker Chambers*.

p. 356 *"freedom is threatened by tyranny, Christianity by paganism"*: Ashburn, *Peabody of Groton*, 403.

p. 356 *"mortal incompleteness"*: Chambers, *Witness*, 489.

p. 356 *"At least four classics of European autobiography"*: John V. Fleming, *The Anti-Communist Manifestos: Four Books that Shaped the Cold War* (New York: Norton, 2009), 270.

p. 356 *"very emblem of a liberally educated mind"*: Ibid., 272.

p. 357 *"never more beastly"*: Chambers, *Witness*, 13.

p. 357 *"It is a witness against the world"*: For Chambers's account of the Pipe Creek farm, see Chambers, *Witness*, 517–525.

p. 357 *the different backgrounds*: Humane education at its lowest ebb had little purpose *other* than to preserve distinctions of class: thus Thomas Gaisford, dean of Christ Church, Oxford, is said to have declared that it is worth your while to study Greek literature because it "elevates" you "above the vulgar herd" and "enables you to look down with contempt on those who are less learned than yourself." See Goldwyn Smith, *Reminiscences*, 50. Smith remarks of Gaisford that his friends, by way of apology for his disagreeable personality, "could only say that his heart was good; which, as an autopsy was not possible, could give little satisfaction to those who suffered from his rudeness."

p. 358 *"Danubian Hun"*: *The Letters of Henry Adams 1906–1918*, VI, 710.

p. 358 *I was in prison*: Digby Baltzell believed that Endicott Peabody "would have been proud of the fact that" Dean Acheson "stood up for his Christian convictions as to the duties of friendship in regard to Alger Hiss." Batzell, *Protestant Establishment*, 306.

p. 358 *"powers within the Government"*: Chambers, *Witness*, 741–742.

p. 359 *"Groton vocabulary of the Hiss-Acheson group"*: Hofstadter, *Anti-intellectualism in American Life*, 12.

p. 359 *"crackpotism"*: Tanenhaus, *Whittaker Chambers*, 487.

p. 359 *"should sooner live"*: Keyes, *Quote Verifier*, 82–83.

34. BURNT OFFERINGS: THE EMBER DAYS OF THE WASPS

p. 360 *"I can't relax"*: Paula Span, "Peter Duchin's Key Role," *Washington Post*, January 17, 1989.

p. 361 *Portsmouth Priory*: It is now called Portsmouth Abbey.

p. 361 *"The next regular step was Harvard College"*: Adams, *Education*, 54.

p. 361 *"clerk of the world"*: Halberstam, *Best and the Brightest*, 59.

p. 361 *"feeling for history and how it works"*: Alsop, C-SPAN interview with Brian Lamb, 1980s.

p. 361 *"We got on the subject of family backgrounds"*: Benjamin C. Bradlee, *Conversations with Kennedy* (New York: Norton, 1984), 190.

p. 362 "That *took them three hundred years"*: Wilson, *The Sixties*, 76–77 (emphasis added).

p. 362 *"Lay it on old Torb good"*: Bradlee, *Conversations with Kennedy*, 237–239.

p. 362 "he was unable to do work of any kind": *Gore Vidal: A Critical Companion*, ed. Susan Baker and Curtis S. Gibson (Westport, Conn.: Greenwood, 1997), 3 (emphasis in original).

p. 363 *"I wouldn't have put it past her"*: Apple Parish Bartlett and Susan Bartlett Crater, *Sister: The Life of Legendary Interior Decorator Mrs. Henry Parish II* (New York: St. Martin's, 2000), 78.

p. 363 *"treasure dug up"*: For this and the quotations that follow, see James's *The Ambassadors*.

p. 364 *"power corrupts, poetry cleanses"*: John F. Kennedy, "Remarks at Amherst College," October 26, 1963, in *Public Papers of the Presidents of the United States: John F. Kennedy . . . January 1 to November 22, 1963* (Washington: United States Government Printing Office, 1964), 817.

p. 365 *"This is a most Presidential country"*: Steel, *Walter Lippmann and the American Century*, 525.

p. 365 *"physically in love with him"*: Wilson, *The Sixties*, 166.

p. 365 *"cheerful, corpulent, chuckling gentleman"*: *The Collected Essays of Elizabeth Hardwick* (New York: New York Review of Books, 2017), 481.

p. 365 *"It's strange"*: Wilson, *The Sixties*, 864–865.

p. 366 *"full of tacky-looking people"*: Ibid., 201.

p. 366 *"My reaction to all things that I disapprove and dislike"*: Wilson, *Upstate*, 380.

p. 366 *"anarchy and what seems to me stupidity"*: Ibid., 386.

p. 366 *"of the many cars"*: Ibid., 377.

p. 366 *"ambitious of meeting, outside the fields of technology"*: Ibid., 380.

p. 366 *"freshly shaved, with a cherubic glow on his Roman features"*: For Wilson's daily routine, see Leon Edel's essay "Edmund Wilson in Middle Age," in Wilson, *The Forties: From Notebooks and Diaries of the Period*, ed. Leon Edel (New York: Farrar, Straus and Giroux, 1984), xiii–xxvi.

p. 367 *"I sit here in this old house alone"*: Wilson, *Upstate*, 3.

p. 367 *"changed very much less"*: Ibid., 4.

p. 367 *"The day was marred at the end"*: For these and similar lamentations, see Wilson's diaries from the 1950s and '60s.

p. 367 *"read Macaulay and somewhat regained my equanimity"*: Wilson, *The Sixties*, 790–791.

p. 367 *"Though he was dying"*: Ibid., 818.

p. 367 *"violently insane"*: Wilson, "Comrade Prince," in *From the Uncollected Edmund Wilson*, ed. Groth and Castronovo, 256–279.

p. 367 *"I came to feel an* absolute hatred of the Soviet system": Wilson, *The Sixties*, 358 (emphasis in original).

p. 368 *"the Agora, the Theatre, the Crowns of Laurel"*: See Cavafy's *Poems*.

p. 368 *"crowned with all the snows"*: George Santayana, *Dialogues in Limbo* (New York: Charles Scribner's Sons, 1925), 36.

p. 368 *"sacred awe"*: For Wilson's visit to Santayana in Rome, see Wilson, *The Forties*, 56–67.

p. 368 *"Your name, the aspect of your book"*: McCormick, *George Santayana*, 454.

p. 368 *"my* new *young friend"*: Vidal, *Palimpsest*, 159 (emphasis in original).

p. 368 *"that belonged at all to my moral and poetical world"*: McCormick, *George Santayana*, 454.

p. 369 *"anthropological centre"*: Santayana, *My Host the World*, 123.

p. 369 discontented man in Lucretius's poem: *De rerum natura*, 3.1053ff.

p. 369 *"enough, and too much, with myself"*: Santayana, *Middle Span*, 35.

p. 369 *"felt like Phaedo with Socrates"*: *"my* new *young friend"*: Vidal, *Palimpsest*, 159.

p. 370 *"My old age judges more charitably"*: Santayana, *Middle Span*, 111.

p. 370 *eternal*: See Santayana's extraordinary account of "ideal immortality" in *The Life of Reason*, excerpted in *The Philosophy of George Santayana*, ed. Irwin Edman, 201–211.

p. 370 *"unannounced, took the painting off the wall"*: Lucey, *Sargent's Women* (ebook available online).

p. 371 *"Chanler was one person who could be rough"*: Christopher T. Rand, *Silver Diaspora: A Journey up from Hudson Aristocracy* (Bloomington, Ind.: iUniverse, 2013) (ebook available online).

p. 371 *"cupolaed castles on their towering dark-wooded hills"*: Wilson, "John Jay Chapman," in Wilson, *Triple Thinkers*, 149.

p. 371 *"most eccentric man in America"*: Robert H. Boyle, "Step in and Enjoy the Turmoil," *Sports Illustrated*, June 13, 1977.

p. 371 *"He ran a gambling den there"*: Ibid.

p. 372 *"Close the blinds at night"*: Ibid.

p. 372 *"Kingston Attacked by Giant Mall"*: Daniel Middleton, "The Chanler Chapman Show," AboutTown (undated article available online).

p. 372 *"Isn't it remarkable, Chanler"*: Boyle, "Step in and Enjoy the Turmoil," *Sports Illustrated*, June 13, 1977.

p. 372 *"Ricky would give you the shirt off his back"*: Ibid.

p. 372 *"his own psychiatrist in the house"*: Ibid.

p. 372 *"Jesus Christ, maybe I should have gone Chinese the third time around"*: Ibid.

p. 372 *"absurd seeker of high qualities"*: See Bellow's novel, *Henderson the Rain King*. Bellow makes Henderson the sole survivor among his father's children; Chanler Chapman was *not* the sole survivor among John Jay Chapman's children. His half-brother, Conrad, outlived him to die in 1989 at the age of ninety-two.

p. 373 *"It's such an unattractive death"*: Cook, *Eleanor Roosevelt: The War Years and After*, 399.

p. 373 *"on the verge of a breakthrough"*: Collier and Horowitz, *The Roosevelts*, 454.

p. 373 *"Mummy looked at me very seriously"*: Curtis Roosevelt, *Too Close to the Sun: Growing Up in the Shadow of My Grandparents, Franklin and Eleanor* (New York: PublicAffairs, 2008), 212.

p. 373 *"She hated my father"*: Thurston Clarke, *Ask Not: The Inauguration of John F. Kennedy and the Speech that Changed America* (New York: Henry Holt, 2005), 184.

p. 374 *"coasted instead of working at his job"*: James Roosevelt with Bill Libby, *My Parents: A Differing View* (Chicago: Playboy Press, 1976), 314.

p. 374 *"was defeated because they put a very good Jew"*: Collier and Horowitz, *The Roosevelts*, 461 (emphasis in original).

p. 374 *"the only sister-in-law I haven't had"*: Collier and Horowitz, *The Roosevelts*, 466.

p. 374 *"some name like Vanderweevil"*: For Wilson's account of his evening in the Dakota, see Wilson, *The Sixties*, 437–441.

p. 375 *"profound dejection"*: Schlesinger, *A Life in the Twentieth Century*, 413–415.

p. 376 *"We're convinced that you're the best man for the job"*: Straight, *After Long Silence*, 310–311.

p. 376 *"The F.B.I. check"*: Ibid, 311.

p. 376 *"ablest group of British agents"*: Christopher Andrew, *Defend the Realm: The Authorized History of MI5* (New York: Knopf, 2009), 420.

p. 377 *"About Kennedy"*: George H. Douglas, *Edmund Wilson's America* (Lexington: University Press of Kentucky, 1983), 167.

p. 377 *"a rather queer portrait of Lincoln"*: For Wilson's account of the Malraux dinner, see Wilson, *The Sixties*, 74–80.

p. 378 *"talking so loudly that any real conversation was impossible"*: For Wilson's visit to Europe and his reaction to the death of Kennedy, see Ibid., 255–337.

p. 379 *"male widows"*: Alsop, *"I've Seen the Best of It,"* 464.

p. 379 *"I've never felt about another man in my life"*: Joseph W. Alsop Oral History Interview, June 18, 1964, John F. Kennedy Presidential Library.

p. 380 *Kennan made so bold*: This précis of Kennan's theory of an elite in a democracy is drawn principally from Kennan's two volumes of memoirs, from Gaddis's life of Kennan, from Kennan's *Around the Cragged Hill:*

A Personal and Political Philosophy (New York: Norton, 1993), and from Kennan's *American Diplomacy* (Chicago: University of Chicago Press, 1984).

p. 380 *"The trouble with this country"*: Isaacson and Thomas, *Wise Men*, 171–173.

p. 380 *Alsop among the farmers* (footnote): Bradlee, *A Good Life: Newspapering and Other Adventures*, 196–197.

p. 380 *John Lobb*: Yoder, *Joe Alsop's Cold War*, 29.

p. 381 *perils of elitism*: This account of Hand's skepticism concerning the virtues of elites is drawn principally from Gunther, *Learned Hand: The Man and the Judge.*

p. 382 *transplanted into new realms*: See Erwin Chemerinsky, *Constitutional Law: Principles and Policies* (New York: Wolters Kluwer, 2019), 594; Melvin I. Urofsky, *The Warren Court: Justices, Rulings, and Legacy* (Santa Barbara, Calif.: A.B.C. Clio, 2001), 11; Calvin R. Massey and Brannon P. Denning, *American Constitutional Law: Powers and Liberties* (New York: Wolters Kluwer, 2019), 481.

p. 383 *ennobling the citizenry*: See Adams, *History of the United States During the Administrations of James Madison,* 1345.

p. 383 *"there are mediocre men everywhere"*: Isaacson and Thomas, *Wise Men*, 718.

p. 383 *"are made in the image of the masses"*: Beisner, *Dean Acheson: A Life in the Cold War,* 638.

p. 383 *"a puff of smoke"*: Wilson, *Upstate,* 251.

p. 385 *"boldest lyric inspiration"*: See Emerson's essay "Prudence."

p. 385 *"a nest of singing birds"*: See Boswell's life of Johnson.

p. 385 *"by monotony, by sameness"*: Gerald Brenan, *The Spanish Labyrinth: An Account of the Social and Political Background of the Spanish Civil War* (Cambridge, U.K.: University of Cambridge Press, 2014), xvii.

p. 385 *"His city was the only city"*: Alfred Zimmern, *The Greek Commonwealth,* 67.

p. 386 *"enveloped in an atmosphere of mythology"*: Ernest Renan, *Recollections of My Youth* (London: Chapman and Hall, 1897), 7.

p. 386 *so vicious is Fama*: See Virgil, *Aeneid,* IV, 773ff.

p. 387 *"altars to the Naiads, or Faunus"*: See Ovid's *Metamorphoses.*

p. 388 *"Your grandfather"*: The grammarian is not a tape recorder, still less a filing cabinet; he must rely on naked memory for the substance of the conversations he has heard. Yet he believes that he has a good memory for what interests him, and he is confident that he has faithfully reproduced the spirit of such dialogue as he relates.

p. 389 *the pastoral one of helping young souls to ripen*: The school, in the late 1970s and early 1980s, retained all the pastoral care and inspired teaching of the old Groton, but the institutionalized bullying, the pressure to conform, and the hysterical athleticism of the earlier school had been done away with; Hofstadter's "little Greek democracy" had been purged of the spirit of Draco. There was, too, the presence of girls to counterbalance the savagery of adolescent boys, making for a more civilized campus than Franklin Roosevelt and Dean Acheson could have known, or even than Bill Patten knew in the 1960s, when the culture of hazing still lingered. See Patten, *My Three Fathers,* 214.

p. 389 *in their prime*: "'What were the main influences of your school days, Sister Helena? Were they literary or political or personal? Was it Calvinism?' Sandy said: 'There was a Miss Jean Brodie in her prime.'" Muriel Spark, *The Prime of Miss Jean Brodie* (New York: Plume, 1984; orig. 1962), 186–187.

p. 389 *the whole of an emotional weight*: The inquirer oversimplifies. In fact you got along with your parents better, during your boarding school years, than you did when you lived with them mostly at home precisely because adult authority was more widely diffused at school, and not concentrated in the mom-and-dad domestic pressure-cooker. Much like the children of Margaret Mead's Samoans, you had an extended parent-family: so many step-parents (Hugh Sackett, Bill Polk, Bob Gula, Doug Brown, Jake Congleton, Jack Smith, Michael Tronic, Michael Gerard, Jon Choate, Warren and Micheline Meyers, Charley and Ann Alexander, John and Joan Holden, etc.) who cared about you, and from whom you could learn, but in a relationship more relaxed than that of the conventional parent-child one. This made up for your remoteness, during six or seven months of the year, from the family dog.

p. 389 *"The ancients"*: Santayana, *The Life of Reason,* excerpted in *Philosophy of Santayana,* ed. Edman, 120.

p. 389 *could live by friendship*: Reading the letters of Henry Adams, Lionel Trilling wondered whether Adams was not "the last man, or perhaps the last American, to have had actual friendships." Trilling, "Adams at Ease," in Trilling, *A Gathering of Fugitives* (New York: Harcourt Brace, 1956), 129.

p. 390 *"Mr. Crocker is not a bad Headmaster"*: Robert A. Moss, *A Memoir of Jack Crocker* (Groton, Mass.: Groton School, 2014), 70.

p. 390 *first boy of color*: Groton "was the first of the St. Grottlesex schools to accept Negro students." So advanced was the school, the Proper Philadelphian Baltzell added, that its "faculty now includes a Jew." Baltzell, *Protestant Establishment*, 306.

p. 390 *Endicott Peabody had himself contemplated such a step*: Ashburn, *Peabody of Groton*, 408.

p. 391 *"My dear sir"*: Nichols, *Forty Years More*, 59 (note) (emphasis in original).

p. 391 *"the fruit of anguish"*: Moss, *A Memoir of Jack Crocker*, 192.

p. 391 *Bill Polk*: He is Frank Polk's grandson.

p. 391 *"Groton, again and again"*: Harrison Salisbury, *Without Fear or Favor: The New York Times and Its Times* (New York: Times Books, 1980), 565.

p. 394 *literary celebrity in the city*: See, for example, Jared Paul Stern, "Author Intrusions," *Manhattan File*, September 1995, 64–69.

p. 395 *a Greek rather than an Anglican poetry*: The grammarian, sifting the shards of shattered memory, finds himself perplexed by the revolution that took place in his mind in Crete in those historic summers of 1989 and 1990, when so many Bastilles were stormed, and so many garrisons hoisted the white flag and surrendered at discretion. The domed and icon-laden church, the odor of roasting lamb and Levantine cigarettes, the bare geometrical hills that framed the olive plain, the warm under-scent of goat: these might have converted Alaric to the agora. They had their effect even on a prospective American law student. The Cretan June would have shocked Schopenhauer out of his pessimism, but drunk though the grammarian was with sweetness and light, he knew that the enthrallments of the place had sources other than an ideal climate. Naturally he was too indolent to pursue the thought; in the shadow of the ancient plane tree he could but lift his glass of raki and accept the fact of the miracle. [The inquirer observes that the grammarian was on vacation.]

p. 395 *"There is no place for the Artist"*: Evelyn Waugh, "An Englishman's Home," in Waugh, *Work Suspended and Other Stories* (Harmondsworth, U.K.: Penguin, 1982), 53.

p. 396 *a few famous*: The metropolitan system of virtuosi has, through its promotion of genius and rare ability, the advantage of suppressing mediocrity: but it has the disadvantage of increasing misery, by leaving the mediocre unsatisfied. A just punishment, perhaps, for the vanity of dullness. The old agora system was more forgiving, for although it crowned the citizen of genius with ivy or laurel, it did not disdain the citizen of humbler talent, without whom the festivals would never have gotten off the ground. Just as the modern welfare state recognizes the claims of the economically less gifted, so the old agora culture afforded scope for the artistically less talented. Our modern morality recoils from the idea that only the economically fittest should survive: why should it not do the same in the case of the creatively crippled, the musically lame, the poetically inept?

p. 397 *"You will be dead soon"*: For this and other quotations from *Pure Slaughter Value*, see Robert Bingham, *Pure Slaughter Value* (New York: Doubleday, 1997).

p. 398 *"Mao got down into his crouch"*: For this and other quotations from *Lightning on the Sun*, see Robert Bingham, *Lightning on the Sun* (New York: Doubleday, 2000).

p. 398 *embalms the still living flesh*: The lute of Orpheus is strung with poets' sinews.

p. 400 *"I was a mess"*: The monologue reproduced here is a mélange of Rob's conversation and letters he wrote to the author. It is not a verbatim transcription; the author was not wearing a wire; and his memory may have betrayed him here and there. But if he cannot vouch for every single word, he is confident that the passage reflects the spirit of his exchanges with Rob.

p. 400 *have gotten in fights*: He was a most complex character, brutal one moment, tender the next. He would kick you, and a short time later do his utmost to help you. The author remembers how, not long after he had been kicked on Nantucket, his considerable debts at the Yale bookstore were paid. The point of Jane Austen's Lady Catherine de Bourgh and George Eliot's Henleigh Grandcourt is that, if they are gentle in name, they are not so in spirit: they have fallen below the acceptable standard of patrician breeding. The Swedish baron Axel Heyst, in Joseph Conrad's *Victory*, would pronounce them recalcitrant scholars of the art of nobility. When Sir Willoughby Patterne, in George Meredith's *The Egoist*, is "not at home" to his cousin Lieutenant Patterne because the latter has not "the stamp of the gentleman," it is understood that it is Sir Willoughby himself who has grievously offended against the faith and morals of his caste. Unlike Sir Willoughby, Rob, under so much surface roughness, was deeply gentle.

35. THE *EUTRAPELIAN* IMAGINATION, OR WASP NEURASTHENIA—AND OURS

p. 403 *got to early*: Even earlier, indeed, than Columbia. When Trilling was six years old his mother told him that he would one day take a doctorate at Oxford, and to this end she supervised his early reading. The doctorate, when it came, would come from Columbia rather than Oxford, but otherwise Trilling remained faithful to the Hannibalic vow his mother extracted from him. For "it was finally neither money nor social status which was most important to her," Diana Trilling wrote, "but something else, something she called 'culture.'" Her son was from childhood consecrated to that Arnoldian vocation.

p. 403 *"a fundamental criticism of American democratic education"*: Lionel Trilling, "The Van Amringe and Keppel Eras," in *A History of Columbia College on Morningside* (New York: Columbia University Press, 1954), 44.

p. 403 *history of Columbia College*: Ibid., 14–47.

p. 403 *"Renaissance ideal of the whole man"*: Ibid., 19.

p. 403 *"that humanistic studies were of the first importance"*: Ibid.

p. 404 *"the Columbia College* mystique": Trilling, "Some Notes for an Autobiographical Lecture," in Trilling, *The Last Decade*, 232.

p. 404 eutrapelian *miracle:* Trilling was committed to the humane model of education, but he was not optimistic about its future: general education in the humanities "is now, I need scarcely remark, in eclipse. Even in Columbia College it is in process of being attenuated and I believe that it will soon be wholly rejected." Ibid., 233. See also Trilling, "The Uncertain Future of the Humanistic Educational Ideal" in Trilling, *Last Decade*, 160–176.

p. 404 *"humanistic versatility"*: Trilling, "The Van Amringe and Keppel Eras," in *A History of Columbia College on Morningside*, 25.

p. 404 *believed that citizens "who were in any degree responsible"*: Trilling, "Some Notes for an Autobiographical Lecture," in Trilling, *The Last Decade*, 234.

p. 405 *"first essential imagination"*: The preface to *The Liberal Imagination* has often been read as referring principally to the imagination in its relation to modern political liberalism. It does, of course, refer to that, but it also refers to the imagination of the liberally educated mind. For after all Anglo-American political liberalism, with its origins in Locke, Madison, the British Whigs, Gladstone, Morley, Bagehot, the American Progressive Reformers, the British Fabians, was always a rather prosaic business, a technics of political economy and the reformed statute book: a (quite valuable) program of rights and liberties, but one that was often remote from the higher culture of the mind. It embodied a much narrower idea of the good life than you find in, say, in the classical Greeks. What concerned Trilling as much or more than the narrowing of *political* liberalism was the narrowing of the liberally educated mind, its loss of *eutrapelian* suppleness.

p. 405 *"variousness"*: See Trilling's *The Liberal Imagination*.

p. 405 *"cared for and cherished"*: *Heart of Emerson's Journals*, ed. Perry, 314.

p. 405 *"quite vanish"*: See Trilling's essay on *The Princess Casamassima* in *The Liberal Imagination*.

p. 405 *"literarism"*: Steven Pinker, "The Trouble with Harvard," *New Republic*, September 4, 2014. Pinker associates this "literarism" with a "bohemian authenticity" which he contrasts unfavorably with "worldly success and analytical brainpower." Pinker was criticizing an essay in which William Deresiewicz defended the traditional liberal arts approach to education in which "the humanities are still accorded pride of place" and an "allegiance to real educational values" is maintained. See Deresiewicz, "Don't Send Your Kid to the Ivy League," *New Republic*, July 21, 2014.

p. 406 *fitness, proportion, balance, and harmony*: A theme developed by Werner Jaeger in his *Paideia* books. "The old *paideia*," Jaeger wrote, "tried to educate not specialists, but universally capable citizens." Poetry was essential to the enterprise because "harmony and rhythm can have an *ethos*, a moral character. . . . Anyone who is properly educated in music takes it into his soul while he is still young and his spiritual growth is unconscious; and he develops an unerring accuracy in enjoying what is beautiful and hating what is ugly . . ." Jaeger, *Paideia: The Ideals of Greek Culture: In Search of the Divine Centre*, II, 223, 227, 229.

p. 406 *since Goethe's service*: An exaggeration, but not much of one. There was Senghor of Senegal.

p. 406 *"true human perfection"*: See the preface to Arnold's *Culture and Anarchy* (emphasis in original).

p. 406 *"astonishing array of genius"*: J. H. Plumb, *The Italian Renaissance* (New York: Harper & Row, 1965), 61.

p. 407 *"tragic and latently insane"*: Henry James to William James, March 24, 1894, in Henry James, *Letters*, ed. Leon Edel (Cambridge, Mass.: Belknap Press, 1980), III (1883–1895), 470 (emphasis in original).

p. 407 *"sex was strength"*: Adams, *Education*, 384.

p. 407 *modern masters*: The French critic Sainte-Beuve was among the first to recognize Sade as "one of the greatest inspirers of the modern." Robespierre's part in the tragedy was of course self-evident.

p. 408 *worships at a single shrine*: Thus Messalina, the consort of Claudius, as (perhaps fancifully) depicted by Juvenal: "Then look at those who rival the Gods, and hear what Claudius endured. As soon as his wife perceived that her husband was asleep, this august harlot was shameless enough to prefer a common mat to the imperial couch. Assuming a night-cowl, and attended by a single maid, she issued forth; then, having concealed her raven locks under a yellow peruque, she took her place in a brothel reeking with long-used coverlets. Entering an empty cell reserved for herself, she there took her stand, under the feigned name of Lycisca, her nipples bare and gilded, and exposed to view the womb that bore thee, O nobly-born Britannicus! Here she graciously received all comers, asking from each his fee; and when at length the keeper dismissed his girls, she remained to the very last before closing her cell, and with passion still raging hot within her went sorrowfully away. Then exhausted by men but unsatisfied, with soiled cheeks, and begrimed with the smoke of lamps, she took back to the imperial pillow all the odours of the stews." The actual poetry is a bit stronger than the foregoing prose recapitulation suggests: "*Adhuc ardens, rigidae tentigine vulvae,/Et lassata viris, nondum satiate . . .*" (Hot for hardness, her love-place blighted,/Tired of men, yet her lust unrequited . . .) Juvenal, portraying the Rome of Claudius, depicts Messalina as a part-person, a fragment rather than a whole. The theme of fractured Eros was further developed, in the age of Marcus Aurelius, by the grammarian Athenaeus of Naucratis, who in his *Deipnosophistae* depicts second-century courtesans as "fragmented" beings unable to integrate Eros in a larger cultural framework as the hetaerae of classical Athens are said to have done. See Laura McClure, *Courtesans at the Table: Gender and Greek Literary Culture in Athenaeus* (London: Routledge, 2013), 5.

p. 409 *"small, beautifully dressed"*: The account of Bernard Berenson that follows is drawn principally from Kenneth Clark's memoir *Another Part of the Wood*.

p. 409 *"a whole, a unity of manifold, internally connected powers"*: Goethe, "Der Sammler und die Seinigen," in *Goethe's Werke* (Stuttgart: J.G. Cotta, 1830), XXXVIII, 103.

p. 410 *"the noblest models for mankind to attain"*: Berenson, *Aesthetics and History*, 131.

p. 410 *"clearest and most convincing visions"*: Berenson, *Aesthetics and History*, 132.

p. 410 *of our own*: The author here follows Santayana, who says something similar.

p. 410 *"his vigour and many-sidedness"*: McCormick, *George Santayana*, 240.

p. 411 *abhorrence of the poetically archaic*: Yet as poetic mysticism has receded as an element in everyday life, a substitute has been found for it in the higher reaches of learning and art, one that takes the form of a delight in riddles, puzzles, and recherché jokes. Literary scholars are drawn to the verbal bafflements of Henry James and James Joyce, and to their less readable epigoni; in poetry Wallace Stevens and John Ashbery beguile the bored professors; philosophers wallow in the obscurities of Heidegger or lose themselves in the cryptic labyrinths of David Lewis. It is true that the growth of this technical esoterism owes something to the economy of an ever-expanding academia, where initial preferment depends on the scholar's composition of an unreadable dissertation. (See Kingsley Amis, *Lucky Jim*.) Novelists with less lucrative copyrights than Amis's have been known, on occasion, to pique themselves on the number of doctoral dissertations their literary cryptograms have inspired. But cap-and-gowned specialists lost in the wandering mazes of an often pointless scholasticism seem, too, to be indulging the guilty pleasures of mysticism, a natural enough pastime which, however, is rigorously suppressed wherever a merely cosmetic rationality prevails: it must find as it were unnatural outlets. Thus the poetry of our academical mystagogues is perversely concentrated in the obscurest recesses of their ivory towers. As a result it is incapable of nourishing the imaginations of the larger world beyond, which is just as famished.

p. 412   *so much nervous dread*: Paging Rousseau: A study conducted by McGill University and the Institute of Environmental Sciences and Technologies at the Universitat Autònoma de Barcelona investigated feelings of well-being in contemporary premodern communities in Bangladesh and the Solomon Islands, communities of the kind, we are told, "not usually included in global happiness surveys." The study "found that the majority of people reported remarkably high levels of happiness. This was especially true in the communities with the lowest levels of monetization, where citizens reported a degree of happiness comparable to that found in Scandinavian countries which typically rate highest in the world." According to Chris Barrington-Leigh, a professor in McGill's Bieler School of Environment, the study suggests that "important supports for happiness are not in principle related to economic output. When people are comfortable, safe, and free to enjoy life within a strong community, they are happy—regardless of whether or not they are making any money." See "Happiness Really Does Come for Free," McGill Newsroom, February 8, 2021.

p. 412   *"city had the air and movement of hysteria"*: Adams, *Education*, 499.

p. 413   *"the pleasures of imagination"*: Tocqueville, *Democracy in America*, trans. Henry Reeve, ed. Phillips Bradley, 2 vols. (New York: Vintage, 1945), II, 36–37.

p. 413   *"makes every man forget"*: Ibid., 106.

p. 414   *empty noise*: "To the deep quiet and majestic thoughts/Of loneliness succeeded empty noise/And superficial pastimes . . . ." Wordsworth, *The Prelude*, III, 210ff.

p. 414   *"neurosis in the air"*: See Waugh's *Brideshead Revisited: The Sacred and Profane Memories of Captain Charles Ryder*.

p. 414   *cathartic benefits*: Nietzsche, for all his exaltation of Zarathustra on his mountaintop, was drawn to the poetry of the agora, its power of "discharging the emotions, of purifying the soul, of easing the *ferocia animi*—precisely by means of rhythm. When the proper tension and harmony of the soul had been lost, one had to dance, following the singer's beat: that was the prescription of this therapy. That is how Terpander put an end to a riot, how Empedocles soothed a raging maniac . . ." Plutarch similarly speaks of "those strokes of the harp, which the Pythagoreans made use of before they went to sleep, to allay the distempered and irrational part of the soul." See Nietzsche, *The Gay Science*, trans. Walter Kaufmann (New York: Vintage, 1974), 139, and Plutarch, "Of Isis and Osiris," in *Plutarch's Lives and Writings*, ed. A. H. Clough and William W. Goodwin, 5 vols. (Boston: Little, Brown, 1909), IV, 138.

p. 415   *state of the atmosphere*: The author borrows the image from Newman's *Apologia pro vita sua*.

p. 415   *prison-house of perpendicularity*: Henry James had a profound aversion to these quadrilateral cages: he knew how delightful it is to be caught up in the Sphinx's riddle of winding streets and passageways of an old city. It is a disorientation that leaves you in an agreeable state of suspense, like that which you feel when the lights are dimmed in the theatre before the curtain goes up. Just as a woman does not reveal her private beauty all at once to a lover, so an old town conceals behind so many veils its innermost treasures. But in time you *do* reach the central place. [What the grammarian likes best is a hermaphroditic city, such as Paris. The boulevards are, perhaps, a little too faithfully expressive of Baron Haussmann's passion for the rigid geometries of Apollo, yet their masculine *virtù* is everywhere counterbalanced by the soft, placental warmth of the back streets, where you are always coming upon charming little irregular spaces, femininely bright with young mothers, old shop ladies, eternities of gossip.]

p. 416   *no catalogue raisonné*: The Greek agora itself is less well understood than one would have thought. See
          Christopher P. Dickenson, *On the Agora: The Evolution of a Public Space in Hellenistic and Roman Greece*
          (Leiden, Netherlands: Brill, 2017), 6.

p. 416   *tells us almost nothing*: This was Alfred Kazin's complaint about *Mont-Saint-Michel and Chartres*: "No
          tiresome wars of tribute, no looting crusaders, no murders in the cathedral and disease raging outside it.
          Nothing but the glorious achievers of Chartres, Rheims, Amiens, Coutances . . ." See Kazin, "Religion as
          Culture: Henry Adams's *Mont-Saint-Michel and Chartres*," in *Henry Adams and His World*, ed. Contosta
          and Muccigrosso, 54.

p. 417   *"penetrated and enriched the recesses of the whole being"*: R. P. Blackmur, *Henry Adams*, ed. Veronica A.
          Makowsky (New York: Harcourt Brace Jovanovich, 1980), 27.

p. 417   *"a more or less effaced or affected echo"*: Henry Adams, *Mont-Sant-Michel and Chartres* (Boston: Houghton
          Mifflin, 1913), 331.

p. 417   *adapting at least some of the older techniques to a changed world*: Gerald Brenan noted how in the middle of the
          nineteenth century Catalonia sought to revive her ancient culture. "In the fifties there were competitions
          between Catalan poets, and medieval festivals such as the *Jocs Florals* [flower-games] were revived." But
          this was easier to do in Spain than it would be in, say, the United States precisely because Spain was
          comparatively unmodern. It remained, Brenan said, "the land of *patria chica* [the small homeland]. Every
          village, every town, is the centre of an intense social and political life," for Spaniards "have gone on living
          the intense life of the Greek city-state or Arab tribe or medieval commune." Brenan, *The Spanish Labyrinth*,
          xix–xxii, 43.

p. 417   *the* eutrapelian *imagination*: Yet in fallen moments and insipid hours, the grammarian has himself
          doubted the reality of *eutrapelia*. However deep the impressions which the market centers of Provence
          or Umbria, Croatia or Crete, made upon his neurasthenic imagination, they were always a little eroded
          by the time he got back to his agoraless American life. To go down lower Fifth Avenue at seven o'clock
          on a November evening, amid anonymous crowds engrossed in solipsistic technologies, was to feel one's
          dream die within one, like a fading narcotic. (The "crowded, stinking, smoky, golden city, with its iron
          money-getting and beastly, under-bred snobs . . .") Of course he knew that this despair in the face of the
          blasted heath of a New York November must be sharply discounted, that it was not he but they who were
          wrong. It is not easy to be a voice weeping in Ramah . . . [How ingenuously the grammarian quaffs his
          soma, imagining himself an Avatar of Vishnu, a Zoroaster in Balkh, a Hidden Imam before the gates
          of Constantinople, as though his whole existence were not so much liberally educated *folie de grandeur*.]
          [The inquirer professes himself a "man of realities," a "man of facts and calculations." But King Oedipus
          may have an eye too many . . . The inquirer resembles nothing so much as Francia of Paraguay, that
          adept of "the *Encyclopédie* and gospel according to Volney, Jean-Jacques and Company," the "tawny-
          visaged, lean, inexorable Dr. Francia," who with "a kind of aptitude for madness" would "interrogate
          nature" and dissolve, in his new conquering empire of light, all that shadow in which we are sacredly
          enveloped. Drink deep, my friend, in your Café Procope . . .]

36. RECESSIONAL: THE WASP AND GOD

p. 419   *Adams himself*: See Susan Hanssen's monograph, "'Shall We Go to Rome?'—The Last Days of Henry
          Adams" (available online).

p. 419   *"a principle of order in the human soul"*: T. S. Eliot, "Virgil and the Christian World," in Eliot, *On Poetry and
          Poets*, 131.

p. 419   *"wanted to begin going to church regularly"*: Alsop, *"I've Seen the Best of It,"* 52.

p. 419   *"Is there a God?"*: Patten, *My Three Fathers*, 300–301.

p. 420   *"I mean that religion is the inevitable reaction"*: Daniel Cory, *Santayana: The Later Years: A Portrait with
          Letters* (New York: George Braziller, 1963), 232.

p. 421   *"He believes that he communicates with God"*: Milton Hindus, *Essays: Personal and Impersonal* (Los Angeles:
          Black Sparrow Press, 1988), 92.

37. WHEN WE ARE GONE

p. 423 *reduced under Nero*: Tacitus, *Annals*, XIV.14.3.

p. 423 *"under our democratic stimulants"*: Henry Adams, *History of the United States During the Administrations of Thomas Jefferson* (New York: Library of America, 1986), 122.

p. 423 *"highest individual development"*: See Burckhardt's *Civilization of the Renaissance in Italy* (New York: Penguin Classics, 1990).

p. 424 *the road to Olympia's pillars*: The inquirer notes the tendency of the grammarian to become absorbed in a private dream, a fantasy with which to accuse an unsympathetic reality, the witches' brew of life, its backdoor plumbing, etc. There is in such a temperament a tendency to prefer words to things, to pursue some receding, impossible Jerusalem in the pale alphas and omegas of literary composition, fretting over words as a Taoist priest worries his joss sticks. The inquirer finds this additional pathos in the grammarian, that he almost certainly suffers from agoraphobia. [A curious way to dismiss the studies of one who has spent a quarter of a century and more in the WASP jungle, living among the natives, pursuing them into the recesses of their tribal seminaries, law firms, banks, and trusts, their Nantucket Islands and Mecox Bays, Myopia Hunt and Racquet and Tennis Clubs, Society Libraries and Colony Clubs. Margaret Mead (nine months in Samoa) and Claude Lévi-Strauss (scarcely more in the Brazilian rain forest) were anthropological tyros in comparison . . .]

p. 425 *castles*: "Castles," Emerson says, "are proud things, but 'tis safest to be outside of them." With flashing eyes the grammarian's friend exhibited the treasures of his palace. It was a *Spoils of Poynton* sort of place, and in a shuttered drawing room he fingered a crayon sketch. "Matisse," he nodded knowingly, with such an inflection as a salesman might give to the words "genuine leather." One drank more than one full beaker of the blushful Hippocrene that day, and rejoiced in the friendship the nectar sealed and sanctified. In the interval between lunch and the denting of the pillow on that brackish bay in Paumanok, one squandered quantities of Mouton, Lafite, and Chambertin. The unction of the grape anointed the dark places of the grammarian's spirit, but as the hours flew on into their higher madness, he was too dull-witted to see that the Bacchic revel was by anticipation a wake. A friend in a castle is a friend lost. When Fortune has exalted one's pal to so remote a constellation, the friendship must perish. Unlike the wine-god, it can never know another spring. A more delicate nose would have detected the charnel odor, and sought the fresher air of an agora.

p. 425 *"steady contemplation of all things in their order and worth"*: George Santayana, *Three Philosophical Poets: Lucretius, Dante, and Goethe* (Cambridge, Mass.: Harvard University Press, 1922), 11.

p. 426 *"we have not seen it in the past"*: Lionel Trilling, "The Princess Casamassima," in Trilling, *The Liberal Imagination*, 84. Veiled and muted though it was, Trilling's critique of what he called a "vulgar and facile progressivism" did not go unchallenged. Philip Rahv, the editor of *Partisan Review*, scented heresy, and he commissioned the poet Delmore Schwartz to write a counter-sally exposing Trilling as a betrayer of the dream of the progressive apocalypts. Festering with resentment against a man who had supposedly sabotaged his appointment to the Columbia faculty, Schwartz seized on certain questionable paragraphs in the essay, "Manners, Morals, and the Novel" in which Trilling seemed to adopt the high Jamesian position that a complexity of manners, a thickness of institutional tradition, even a judicious gradation of rank and privilege, could in fact nourish the artist. In his piece—it was published in the January-February 1953 number of *Partisan Review* as "The Duchess' Red Shoes"—Schwartz accused Trilling of heterodoxy and suggested that he was, in spirit if not in fact, an aristocrat, a reactionary prince, as little a good progressive as Proust's Duc de Guermantes himself.

p. 426 *"For some time I had been increasingly aware"*: Lionel Trilling, "Two Notes on David Riesman," in Trilling, *A Gathering of Fugitives*, 96.

p. 427 *"In the final state"*: Mark Lilla, *The Reckless Mind: Intellectuals in Politics* (New York: New York Review of Books, 2006), 135.

p. 427 *"Everybody wants the same, everybody is the same"*: See Nietzsche's *Also sprach Zarathustra*.

p. 427 *"universal hygienic hypnotisation"*: Santayana developed the theme at length in the third book of his *Dominations and Powers*, chapters 15, "Restricted Democracy," and 16, "The American 'Melting-Pot,'"

359–362. The philosopher Alain Locke similarly argued that the United States, "for all its boasted absorption of types, absorbs them only to remake them or re-cast them into a national mold." Menand, *Metaphysical Club*, 397.

p. 427   *three categories*: Riesman was or pretended to be more sympathetic to the "other-directed" personality than most of his readers have been. Yet even he admitted that he "found it almost impossible" to compare "inner-direction" and "outer-direction" without "making inner-direction seem the more attractive of the two." "It is still inner-direction," Lionel Trilling said, "that must seem the more fully human, even in its excess." Trilling, "Two Notes on David Riesman," in Trilling, *A Gathering of Fugitives*, 97. The author suspects that most readers of *The Lonely Crowd* flatter themselves, as they make their way through the book, that they are rather inner- than outer-directed, with the possible exception of those who conceive themselves to be civic-directed.

p. 427   *Riesman entirely overlooked*: Although those in "the upper socioeconomic levels in the western democracies" are, according to Riesman, "strongly permeated by other-direction," he made an exception for what he called the "aristocracy" in those societies. But it is not clear just what he meant by aristocracy, or whether he would have considered the civic humanist ideals of America's WASPs to be an aristocratic phenomenon. See Riesman, *The Lonely Crowd: A Study of the American Character* (New Haven, Conn.: Yale University Press, 1950), 301. The reference to aristocracy was dropped in later editions of *The Lonely Crowd*: see page 294 of the Anchor edition.

p. 429   *"him back forever upon himself alone"*: Tocqueville, *Democracy in America*, II, 106.

p. 429   *every passing fad*: How quaint today seems Michael Oakeshott's encomium of the humane education by which the young learner is "moved by intimations of what he has never yet dreamed," and is "invited to pursue satisfactions he has never yet imagined or wished for," in "sheltered places where excellences may be heard because the din of local partialities is no more than a distant rumble." Michael Oakeshott, *The Voice of Liberal Learning: Michael Oakeshott on Education*, ed. Timothy Fuller (New Haven, Conn.: Yale University Press, 1989), 24. Columbia's Core Curriculum was intended to give students a perspective on the partialities of their times, to see the preoccupations of their age in the light of a larger human experience. See Wm. Theodore de Bary, *Confucian Tradition and Global Education* (New York: Columbia University Press, 2007), 28–29.

p. 429   *"anything to do with 'today.'"*: See Nietzsche's *On the Genealogy of Morals*.

p. 429   *Diotima*: See Plato's *Symposium*.

p. 429   *"full human flourishing"*: Danielle Allen, *Education and Equality* (Chicago: University of Chicago Press, 2016), 11.

p. 429   *Humanities 10*: Craig Lambert, "Louis Menand," *Humanities*, Fall 2016.

p. 430   *"poetry intervening in life"*: Santayana, *My Host the World*, 5.

p. 432   *"five times as much respect"*: Walter Bagehot, *The English Constitution*, in *The Works of Walter Bagehot*, ed. Forrest Morgan, 5 vols. (Hartford, Conn.: Travelers, 1889), IV, 124.

p. 434   *Heraclitus*: See Kenneth Dorter, "The Problem of Evil in Heraclitus," in *Early Greek Philosophy: The Presocratics and the Emergence of Reason*, ed. Joe McCoy (Washington: Catholic University of America Press, 2013), 40–41.

p. 434   *community, which becomes an ever less helpful word*: Rousseau interpreted the Greek polis in a way that turned community into communitarianism, a thing that is less likely, perhaps, to lead to the Athens of Aeschylus than to the Cuba of Castro. When the windows in his chamber are open toward Jerusalem, the grammarian would be the anatomist of the old common spaces and the elucidator of the poetry that made them *places*. A grammarian without an agora . . . He is like Giotto's Joachim, expelled from the temple and cast out of the circle of light, adrift in the ultramarine void. He is like a pale, deracinated Gaucho homesick for the pampas, the stimulus of *mate*, the odor of cattle, reduced to twanging, "in a plaintive manner, rough love-melodies on a kind of guitar . . ." He is like Aristotle on Chalcis, conscious of "an almost terrifying gulf" between himself and an alien environment, forced, for the first time in his life, to be "solitary and isolated," and seeking solace in myths. In *myths*, mind you: all that poetry which philosophers pretend to find irrational until they have need of it themselves. See Werner Jaeger, *Aristotle: Fundamentals of the History of His Development*, trans. Richard Robinson, 2nd ed. (Oxford, U.K.: Oxford University Press, 1962), 321. [The grammarian is a sentimentalist who labors under the misimpression that the hallucinogenic playfulness of childhood can be maintained in adulthood. But shades of the prison-house will close, however the grammarian may deny it. "The truly strong, green, fruitful, creative imagination," Leopardi says, "belongs to children only." It is true that Plato, in the *Laws*, suggests that a modest imbibulation of wine may sufficiently counterfeit youthful playfulness to make the aging citizen jolly enough to sing in the choirs. "As a man gets into years, the reluctance to sing grows upon him. He feels less pleasure in the act, and, if it is forced on him, the older and more sober-minded he grows, the more bashful he feels about it. . . ." Such a citizen may therefore seek the benedictions of Dionysus "in that sacrament and pastime of advancing years—I mean the wine cup— which the god bestowed on us for a comfortable medicine against the dryness of old age, that we might renew our youth . . ." See Plato, *Laws*, 665d–666b. But mark, this is the *simulation* of youthful playfulness, not its restoration. If the grammarian misses, in the scenes of adult life, the glow of romance in which he passed his younger and more imaginative years, it is not because society is in conspiracy against poetry, but because he himself has grown old.]

p. 434 *the artistry that commands the heart*: Our American situation is in many ways the obverse of that of the agora-centered, plasquagórazza communities of the past. Athens in its classical period had, partly on account of its smallish size, a healthy artistic culture (*eutrapelian*, civic) and an unhealthy politics (vulnerable to the passion of internal faction). The American founders, in their effort to create a stable free state, solved the political problem that bedeviled the faction-ridden city-states of the past by reconciling order and liberty in a larger national state: "Extend the sphere," Madison says in *Federalist* No. 10, "and you take in a greater variety of parties and interests; you make it less probable that a majority of the whole will have a common motive to invade the rights of other citizens; or if such a common motive exists, it will be more difficult for all who feel it to discover their own strength, and to act in unison with each other." But if the founders' extension of the sphere solved the *political* problem of the free state, it exacerbated the *cultural* one by failing to provide an adequate infrastructure of common life, of civic poetry: their system had no *eutrapelian* means of putting the different energies in the individual citizen's soul to constructive uses. The founders' sacrifice of culture on the altar of politics was arguably justified at the time. An arrangement that made possible a high degree of order and liberty was preferable to one which, however culturally potent it might have been, was perpetually unstable and never securely free. Athens and Florence each had a superior culture: yet (among a multitude of other sins) they condemned Socrates to death and Dante to exile. We Americans, on the contrary, rarely die for our opinions, though (such are our cultural arrangements) we do spend a lot of money on antidepressants. The difficulty is that the new social technologies have undermined the founders' arrangements, and billions of dollars' worth of Prozac have failed to shore up the psychologically inadequate foundations of the regime. Discontented citizens today, stewing in passions unmediated by culture, no longer suffer in politically harmless ways, in spite of so many infusions of Zoloft: in our sickness we have (to use Madison's words) discovered our own strength. We now merge our individual distresses (by means of social technology) in factional units which, having been formed in uncivil spaces without the mediation of face-to-face encounters, are sufficiently virulent to undermine both order *and* liberty. Political success finds itself at the mercy of the culture failure.

p. 434 *"Improvised Europeans, we were"*: Chalfant, *Improvement of the World*, 249.

p. 434 *"is the final perfection"*: T. S. Eliot, "In Memory of Henry James," *Egoist*, January 1918.

p. 435 *"deep spiritual meaning"*: Ernest Robert Curtius, *European Literature and the Latin Middle Ages*, trans. Willard R. Trask (Princeton, N.J.: Princeton University Press, 2013), 587.

p. 435 *"on a thread of poetry and play"*: Plato, *Laws*, 654a.

p. 436 *a deeper reasonableness*: The tug of Plato's golden cord, the connective art of Dante's *amor* (binding together the scattered pages of existence), the song of Shakespeare's swan that dies in a music Hamlet in Act V will associate with "a divinity that shapes our ends, rough hew them how we will": they are the attempts of poets and mystics to express a sanity beyond words, and a rebuke to more superficial knowers who,

Heraclitus says, think they understand a great deal, but know "not even day from night: they are one." Not all high WAPs consciously sought this deeper reasonableness: but you have only to look on their works to see the unconscious attraction.

p. 436 *"decline of a class"*: Michael Knox Beran, "Louis S. Auchincloss '35, P'76, P'82," *Groton School Quarterly*, Fall 2010.

p. 436 *"I used to say to my father"*: Vivian Yee, "Author Louis Auchincloss '39 Dies at 92," *Yale Daily News*, January 27, 2010.

POSTSCRIPT: ORPHEUS'S HEAD

p. 438 *humane culture*: To be sure, many liberally educated Englishmen suspected this sort of culture. Upon being told by a German that there was "no word in English equivalent to *'gelehrt'* (cultivated)," the utilitarian philosopher Henry Sidgwick replied, "Oh yes there is, we call it a prig." And as we have seen (see the relevant note above), T. S. Eliot, the adoptive Englishman, rejected Matthew Arnold's ideal of *eutrapelian* culture as an unconvincing substitute for religion.

p. 439 *speak to the heart*: It is because they *do* speak to the heart that places formed in the old artistry become dream-encrusted, and appear so regularly in the (imaginatively distorted) dreams of those who have known them.

p. 439 *banished*: See Plato, *Laws*, 656e–657b. The best music, Plato believes, "must enchant the souls of our children." Such poetry "will effectually charm the young into virtue." *Laws*, 664b, 671a.

p. 441 *divinely lodged there*: The poetic faculty of perceiving rhythm and harmony is, Plato believed, innate in human beings, a gift of the gods. *Laws*, 654a. See also Glenn R. Morrow, *Plato's Cretan City: An Historical Interpretation of the* Laws (Princeton, N.J.: Princeton University Press, 1993), 305. There are buried within each of us treasures that outshine "the wealth of Ormus and of Ind," only they are not easy of access: they lie forgotten as last night's dream until some chance word recalls it to life. It is genius that supplies the chance word. Those freaks of nature, the great poets and music-makers, have a readier access to the inward splendors than do the rest of us: and it is their music that awakens in us what would otherwise remain asleep. Thus there are places in the depths of one's own *logos* that one should never have found had one not encountered, say, the *Inferno* or *The Tempest* or Mozart's *Requiem*. "Every man," says Saint-Beuve, "contains a dead poet in his soul." But it often takes a living one to awaken him. Or so the high WASPs believed: it is the theory on which their schools are founded.

p. 441 *"No heart is dark when that moon shines"*: Compare Laurence Sterne in *A Sentimental Journey*: "I had an affair with the moon, in which there was neither sin nor shame." As such it must have been a tepid conjunction. Miguel Coronados speaks more candidly of the illumination he received when those divine hetaerae, Aspasia and Egeria, cast off the last of their veils in the moonlight.

p. 441 *underworld of dreams*: "The sleeping," Heraclitus says, "are coworkers and fabricators of the things that happen in the world." The sun was hot on the plateau, and there were goats, hundreds of them, braying peevishly in the light. The first you met were shy and leapt into brushy growths of thyme and arbutus. But as you grew tired, they grow bold, and pressed you closely. Their eyes seem almost those of men, transfigured by some variation of Circean art into mere brutishness. It was as though someone had thrown a switch and the vestibule that connects the sleeping and the waking states, ordinarily so dimly lit, was illuminated by a thousand chandeliers. It was as though some master philologist, some Bentley or Porson, was continuously annotating your thoughts by comparing them to the more genuine text of your night visions, leading you to stores of perception which, overlooked by your conscious intelligence, lay neglected in the *archivum secretum* of your brain. Eventually you descended to the olive plain and returned to the village: but something had happened. The match was struck, and so many splinters of insight, kindled into flame, illuminated the dark side of your memory's moon. [The neurasthenic sufferer is apt to confuse such altered physical states with revelation: an upheaving of so much psychological detritus that were better left in its mental grave. If only the soul of the neurotic had a Judas hole, through which it could glimpse its craziness unawares . . .] ["Sir, there is more knowledge of the heart in one letter of Richardson's, than in all *Tom Jones*."]

p. 441 *veil upon veil*: But if, after stripping the Mysterious Female of her last veil, you do not find what you sought, the deeper reasonableness may be only a deeper dullness, or even a deeper horror. The possibility is explored by Coronados in his *Sade y Robespierre: su historia de amor* (Ascasubi: Utyches, 1935). [Could the revelation be true, though the sibyl herself were cracked? The grammarian's skepticism was heightened by his sense that there were strangenesses in her story of which she herself seemed unaware. "I can assure you that it is real," she said when he confessed to her his doubts. The room smelt like a trunk of winter clothes opened on a summer's day; she reached, from habit, for a cigarette, then remembered that she had been forbidden to smoke. "I know what you are thinking, that it is a dream out of the ivory gate—a delusion. You think you should be a realist, a philistine like King Cyrus. I fell into that error once, and it ruined my life." (For the philistinism of Cyrus, see Herodotus, *Histories*, I, 153.)]

p. 441 *preferred the lyrical wisdom of Dante*: See Lears, *No Place of Grace*, 283.

p. 441 "Credo quia absurdum": The actual words used by Tertullian are: *credibile est, quia ineptum est . . . certum est, quia impossibile*—it is credible because it is ridiculous . . . it is certain because it is impossible. According to Eric Osborn, *credo quia absurdum* both "misquotes and misrepresents Tertullian's logic and exegesis." See Osborn, *Tertullian, First Theologian of the West* (Cambridge, U.K.: Cambridge University Press, 1997), 28, 52–55. Yet the formula *credo quia absurdum* deeply influenced Kierkegaard and became, Pierre Bühler writes, "a central aspect of his understanding of Christianity." See *A Companion to Kierkegaard*, ed. Jon Stewart (Chichester, U.K.: Wiley Blackwell, 2015), 283.

p. 441 *Hamann*: Language, the means by which we attempt to discern and describe the rational and the reasonable, is itself, Hamann believed, imbrued in mysticism, a congeries of myth and symbol: it is, in other words, poetry, even when it pretends to be prose. See Isaiah Berlin, *The Magus of the North*, ed. Henry Hardy (New York: Farrar, Straus and Giroux, 1993), 74ff. Berlin thought that Hamann's "irrationalism," as he called it, was "often ill-judged," yet it led, he believed, to "inspired insights" into all those "aspects of human life" which the empirical and scientific approach, with its monopoly of the rational, has overlooked. See Berlin, *Magus of the North*, 23–24, 122, 128. One might of course argue that Hamann's was merely an effort to "turn down the lights so as to give miracle a chance," to borrow the words Wendell Holmes applied to William James and his philosophy. The difficulty is that, however high we turn up the lights, a good deal of shadow remains.

p. 442 *spiritually overdressed*: Katágaios, "The Youth of Osiris."

p. 442 *When a cat torments a rodent*: "Evolutionary ethics are fraudulent," Noel Annan has written. "Ethics tell us what we ought to do, they deal with the problem of obligations; evolutionary ethics tell us nothing about obligation." See Michael Knox Beran, *Pathology of the Elites* (Chicago: Ivan R. Dee, 2010), 135.

p. 443 *human difference*: It is much the same with Eros, else Poussin and Jefferson should not have marveled, as they did at Nîmes, that biological passion could be so transfigured as to produce the Maison Carrée.

p. 443 *they could not say*: In their defense, they were not metaphysicians. We could "brush aside much tedious metaphysic," Katágaios says, "if only we could see once more that poetry *can* be truth . . ."

p. 443 *"I am furious"*: Peter Gay, *The Party of Humanity: Essays in the French Enlightenment* (New York: Norton, 1971), 126.

p. 443 *the Abbé Le Camus*: Pierre Adolphe Chéruel, *Histoire de France sous le ministère de Mazarin 1651–1661* (Paris: Hachette, 1882) III, 238–239; H. Noel Williams, *Five Fair Sisters: An Italian Episode at the Court of Louis XIV* (New York: G. P. Putnam's Sons, 1906), 104–106.

p. 443 *mystery*: "Do not always be fighting the mystery," says Katágaios. "Be nourished by it."

p. 444 *some perhaps obscure but worthwhile truth of our being*: The soul-shallow methods of modern utilitarian philosophy cannot reach such truths, and so could not satisfy a man like Coleridge who, John Stuart Mill said, "saw so much farther into the complexities of the human intellect and feelings—he considered the long or extensive prevalence of any opinion as a presumption that it was not altogether a fallacy; that, to its first authors at least, it was the result of a struggle to express in words something which had a reality to them, though perhaps not to many of those who have since received the doctrine by mere tradition. The long duration of a belief, he thought, is at least proof of an adaptation in it to some portion or other of the human mind; and if, on digging down to the root, we do not find, as is generally the case, some truth, we shall find some natural want or requirement of human nature which the doctrine in question is fitted to satisfy . . ." *Mill on Bentham and Coleridge*, ed. F. R. Leavis (London: Chatto & Windus, 1959), 99. The high WASPs had a good deal of Coleridge in them.

p. 444 *poetry*: Poetry, Aristotle says, "is a more philosophical and a higher thing than history: for poetry tends to express the universal, history the particular." This is true. Yet it is also true that every work of history is the creation of a particular soul, and that every soul is composed of innumerable poetries. History, Charles Whibley believed, is "an interpretation of the past as seen through another's temperament." It would be truer to say that it is a vision of the past as filtered through another's poetries. Thucydides went so far to say that, where memory and records failed him, he supplied out of his imagination the words spoken by his historical actors, making them "say what was in my opinion demanded of them by the various occasions" on which they spoke. At all events we would have a better sense of the truth of particular inquiries if the inquirers acquainted their readers with the nature of those imaginations which have illuminated or, as the case may be, distorted the past which they would bring to light.

p. 445 *golden cord*: The cord by which the human plaything is drawn toward a humane and civic forum. See Plato, *Laws*, 644e–645a, 803c–804b, and the works of Bléterie, Katágaios, Coronados, and such other poets who, with a tap of the magician's rod, have been summoned from an auteurial Acheron. *Flectere si nequeo superos Acheronta movebo . . .* Near the river at Groton, in a meadow edged with conifers, stands an old stone *exedra*, or semi-circular seat flanked by sculpted hounds. How oddly the WASPs combined their high Grecian aspirations with the coarser recreations of the English squires, the pleasures of the chase. (Hugh Sackett thought the enchanted grove would make an ideal place for reading plays.) For there was, undoubtedly, something ridiculous in the characters that are the subject of this book, figures who, in their white flannel trousers and silly rowing blazers, felt, however improbably, the pull of that golden cord. In their longing for mother-goddesses and vegetation princes, for a delicate Hyacinth or a virginal Mary, the preppy comedians really did seek a flowering in the dead places in their souls and their cities. "I grew up in the arms of the gods," says Hölderlin, and the child of the divine embrace eventually found his Patmos: but with a few exceptions, such as the radiant Franklin, our poor WASPs were so many Lambert Strethers and J. Alfred Prufrocks, fated to yearn for nightingale ecstasies that mostly eluded them.

Illa cantat: nos tacemus.

Quando ver venit meum?

She sings; we silent be.

When does the spring-tide come for me?

Index